CHIANS

AU

NORTH CAROLINA

TH CAROLINA

ATLANTIC OCEAN

N

| 0 | 100 Kilometers |
| 0 | 100 Miles |

EVERGLADES

Aquatic Fauna in Peril

The Southeastern Perspective

Aquatic Fauna in Peril

The Southeastern Perspective

Edited By

George W. Benz
and
David E. Collins

Southeast Aquatic Research Institute
Special Publication 1

Lenz Design & Communications · Decatur, Georgia · 1997

Cambarus fasciatus Hobbs, a threatened crayfish native to the Southeast. (photograph courtesy of Raymond W. Bouchard)

We need another and a wiser and perhaps a more mystical concept of animals. Remote from universal nature, and living by complicated artifice, man in civilization surveys the creature through the glass of his knowledge and sees thereby a feather magnified and the whole image in distortion. We patronize them for their incompleteness, for their tragic fate of having taken form so far below ourselves. And therein we err, and greatly err. For the animal shall not be measured by man. In a world older and more complete than ours they move finished and complete, gifted with extensions of the senses we have lost or never attained, living by voices we shall never hear. They are not brethren, they are not underlings; they are other nations, caught with ourselves in the splendour and travail of the earth.

— Henry Beston, *The Outermost House*, 1928.

Benz, G. W., and D. E. Collins (editors). 1997. *Aquatic Fauna in Peril: The Southeastern Perspective*. Special Publication 1, Southeast Aquatic Research Institute, Lenz Design & Communications, Decatur, Georgia.

To purchase this book, address orders to:
Tennessee Aquarium Gift Shop
P.O. Box 11048
Chattanooga, Tennessee 37401, USA
Telephone (423) 785-4199 (24 hours) or (800) 262-0695 (ext. 4199) (Daytime).

Cover design, book design, layout, graphics, indexing, editing, and publishing services by Lenz Design & Communications, Inc., 119 E. Court Square, Suite 201, Decatur, Georgia 30030.

Cover photography by Richard T. Bryant.

Chapter heading illustrations by Tom Tarpley.

Library of Congress Cataloging in Publication Data:
　　Aquatic fauna in peril : the southeastern perspective / edited by
　　George W. Benz & David E. Collins.
　　　　　　　p. cm. -- (Southeast Aquatic Research Institute special
　　publication ; 1)
　　　　Updated versions of papers presented at a conference held in
　　Chattanooga, Tenn., Mar. 31-Apr. 1, 1994.
　　　　Includes bibliographical references and index.
　　　　ISBN 0-9654841-0-6 (hardcover)
　　　　1. Freshwater animals--Southern States--Congresses. 2. Endangered
　　species--Southern States--Congresses. 3. Endangered ecosystems-
　　-Southern States--Congresses. 4. Nature conservation--Southern
　　States--Congresses. I. Benz, George W. (George William), 1954-
　　II. Collins, David E. (David Ellsworth), 1950-　　. III. Series.
　　QL141.A68 1997
　　333.95´4811´0975--dc21

Table of Contents

Preface

Soon it will be spring, and in a handful of southeastern rivers a freshwater mussel known as the orange-nacre mucket will once again fish for a home for its young. As if driven by some insane inspiration, this unpretentious looking invertebrate will package its young in a self-made fishing lure which looks like two minnows swimming side-by-side. The likeness is truly amazing. When conditions are just right, the mussel's maternal instinct will instigate it to produce a long, clear, gelatinous line which it will attach to the lure. As the line is produced, the lure is payed-out into the stream, taking with it the lot of a future generation. Waving in the shallows of a clear stream, the line is nearly invisible, yet the lure is quite the opposite. Under direct force of the passing water, and being further influenced by its invisible tether, the lure looks like and acts like two lovesick minnows — minnows who seem oblivious to their surroundings while carrying out a dramatic courtship dance. As the fishing continues the lure is noticed by a passing bass. Its reaction is startlingly quick. In a blink of an eye it charges and engulfs the lure. The force of being sucked in ruptures the lure and out spill the tiny mussels. At this point in their lives, each mussel is like a miniature mousetrap. As some of them contact the gills of the bass they snap shut, clamping onto their would be killer. Here they will live for a while, deriving some unknown need without which they cannot continue to develop. Eventually they will mature enough to drop off of the bass, and they will disappear into the stream's bottom to slowly grow into adults.

Few know the wonderful story of the orange-nacre mucket. In fact, it was only recently discovered. The life history of this remarkable mussel hints at some possible reasons for its apparent scarcity. For example, could it be that the high levels of siltation which today so commonly cloud streams throughout much of the Southeast are detrimental to the fishing action of this species? If this is proved correct, then ultimately it will be through an understanding of the life history requirements of this species that the critical information needed to help ensure its survival will be identified.

Without life history information, few plants or animals are colorful enough or oddly shaped enough to interest most people. It is the action of life, the interactions and peculiarities, which excites. Unfortunately, we know little about the lives of some of the most commonplace plants and animals. So little in fact, that with very minor training most

Aquatic Fauna in Peril: The Southeastern Perspective, edited by George W. Benz, and David E. Collins. 1997. Special Publication 1, Southeast Aquatic Research Institute, Lenz Design & Communications, Decatur, GA, 554 p.

anyone can make detailed contributions to the understanding of our natural heritage. But beyond the nature specials aired on television, is such information important? Absolutely. For one, life history information can sometimes be applied as in the foregoing example to help conserve and restore some natural resources. Secondly, the desire to properly manage nature stems from an appreciation of the organisms which compose it. Beyond the relative handful of plants and animals which we have domesticated or have otherwise knowingly come to rely upon, the greatest abundance of living things can best be appreciated if the roles they play in nature are understood. For it is through this understanding that we are amazed and humbled by the great mysteries of life, and by the great capacities of species to mingle together in the grandest of networks. Only through such understanding will we realize why our natural heritage is so special and important. And only through such understanding will we build the resolve to preserve nature so that future generations may inherit its marvels.

Of course, education is crucial to cultivate the appreciation required to preserve the rich biological potential which can help ensure that new, yet currently unidentified opportunities will become realities over the years ahead. With this in mind, we are sorry to report that our children often go hungry regarding their appetite for information about the natural world in which they are immersed. Nowadays, most children will probably learn more about lions on the African plains, white sharks off the coast of Australia, or giant tortoises on the Galapagos Islands in one evening of public broadcasting than they will learn throughout their entire childhood about the individual plants and animals that live in their own backyards. This is unfortunate, for children have a natural curiosity about nature. Broadcasting depicting exotic animals and the plight of the rainforest will no doubt interest and benefit children. However, without bridges linking such programming to objects closer to home, children become stranded without mechanisms for firsthand experience. Seldom are such bridges built, as the system of higher education which produces our elementary and secondary school teachers is woefully inadequate at arming these vitally important professionals with the information to inspire wonder and to dispel the myths which ultimately conspire to drive children indoors and away from their world. By the time many children reach college age, most have been indoctrinated into a lifestyle of seclusion from nature, a lifestyle through which urban and suburban dwellers come to view cattlefields and cornfields as the great outdoors, and one in which we constantly devise new ways to vicariously experience the natural world.

It is amazing, therefore, that by college age some students are still interested in learning about nature, and overall this is powerful testimony of the allure of plants and animals. Unfortunately, most university life science curricula require so much minutia to be crammed into students' heads that personal exigencies linked to a genuine curiosity about nature and the need to participate in the excitement of scientific discovery are soon betrayed. Many students become disillusioned. Sometimes they feel they can salvage their creativity and curiosity by transferring into other disciplines. Often they choose those which also use the concepts of discovery and prediction, and often the curricula associated with these "foster" disciplines are better at facilitating student contribution — a form of self-reward which goes a long way toward creating successful professionals. Without mechanisms for interested students to experience firsthand the thrill of science, it is no wonder that science continues to loose some of its brightest young minds.

The loss of bright, young, energetic science students has direct bearing on our ability to correct and avoid environmental problems such as the imperilment of native plants and animals. Most obviously, science helps to level the playing field regarding the management of natural resources. Just as an accountant and a financial forecaster can be vitally important in predicting the potential ramifications of a corporation's financial actions, scientists can do likewise regarding manipulations of natural resources.

However, there is a less apparent and yet potentially more important reason why the loss of students from scientific disciplines along with the aforementioned general dissociation from nature collude to undermine the responsible stewardship of natural resources. The problem here is one associated with identity, empathy, and science literacy, and to illustrate the dilemma we will advance the following analogy. Many of us enjoy and support professional sports, yet few of us have been professional athletes. Much of our vicarious enjoyment of and support for professional sports was probably nurtured early in our lives through programs which allow youngsters to play various games as if they were in the big leagues. The excitement associated with these experiences is not trivial, and it no doubt has deposited an indelible mark in the minds of many. A great urgency exists to create similar connections with science, and in particular the biological disciplines, to expand upon opportunities for non-scientists to really participate in science. This is especially true regarding experiences for high school and undergraduate students. Ultimately it will only be through the widespread understanding of science that the important work of scientists will be financially endorsed.

The chapters contained in this volume are updated versions of most of the presentations given at a conference of the same name held in Chattanooga, Tennessee on March 31 and April 1 in 1994. The conference was both organized and sponsored by the Tennessee Aquarium. The overall goal of the conference was to examine the historical and current state of affairs regarding imperiled aquatic animals in the southeastern United States. The importance of holding such a conference becomes obvious when one considers that the Southeast contains the highest level of species richness in North America, that aquatic organisms are well represented in this fauna, and that many of the Southeast's aquatic habitats are under increasing pressures which have resulted in and continue to result in deleterious effects on wildlife. While other conferences addressing these matters from the perspective of individual groups of plants and animals had been convened, we felt it would be beneficial to bring together a wider group of specialists to frame the history of this dilemma and chart some possible solutions from more of an ecosystem perspective.

Presentations on the first day of the conference focused on historical perspectives of major groups of aquatic animals and ecosystems. Those of the second day concentrated on the management history of many of these same groups, and in doing so presenters (authors) often developed recommendations and advanced philosophies concerning future conservation and restoration efforts. Presenters were given some latitude regarding the geographic boundaries of their respective tasks. However, unless otherwise stated, the "Southeast" was defined as a region composed of the states of Alabama, Arkansas, Florida, Georgia, Kentucky, Louisiana, Mississippi, North Carolina, South Carolina, and Tennessee. Presenters were also given leeway concerning the measurement of imperilment and the status of imperilment of animals under their consideration, and were similarly given the flexibility to assign "aquatic status" to animals which are obligatorily or strongly facultatively tied to aquatic environments through non-physiological and sometimes unappar-

Table 1. Where did they come from? Numbers of paid registrants, and their general affiliations, who attended *Aquatic Fauna In Peril: The Southeastern Perspective* on March 31 and April 1, 1994 in Chattanooga, Tennessee.

Affiliation	Number
Colleges and Universities[1]	77
Federal Agencies	57
State Agencies	53
Private Companies[2]	44
Aquariums, Zoos, Nature Centers[3]	6
Communications Media	5
Total	242

[1] includes 60 faculty members and 17 students.

[2] includes for-profit and not-for-profit companies/institutions; does not include aquariums, zoos, nature centers or communications media.

[3] does not include attendance of 36 Tennessee Aquarium staff members and volunteers.

ent or seldom considered mechanisms. Together, these factors might seem to overly swell the ranks of imperiled southeastern aquatic animals, but we think not. As many human water-use issues have recently illustrated, a species doesn't have to continually swim, dive, or float to be intimately dependent on aquatic environments. In fact, if we look at the distribution and nature of human populations, we might even consider ourselves to be facultatively semi-aquatic.

In fleshing out the conference program, the organizers sought the participation of authoritative professionals. In some instances this task was relatively simple, while in other situations the dearth of information and professional activity regarding some important groups of aquatic animals became painfully apparent. Along with time constraints, this unfortunately resulted in some groups of animals, as well as representatives from four other living Kingdoms, from being discussed. For this we apologize. Furthermore, even though they outnumber the sum of all fishes, amphibians, reptiles, birds, and mammals by orders of magnitude, invertebrates were only represented by several ambassador groups such as some insects, crustaceans, and mollusks.

Ultimately the conference schedule gelled into a cohesive program with an impressive roster of presenters consisting of many fine field biologists representing a wide array of state and federal agencies, universities and colleges, and private for-profit and not-for-profit institutions. Interest in the conference was considerable, and the event attracted 242 paid registrants (see Table 1) and 282 total attendants. The regional focus of the conference did not deter the attendance of people from as far away as Arizona, Colorado, Massachusetts, and Missouri, and in all, registrants represented a total of 22 states and the District of Columbia. We hope that these statistics and this volume will build the confidence of other institutions to carry out similar regional conferences.

The success of the conference generated considerable interest regarding the publication of a quasi proceedings. Not only was there support for this from many of the attendees seeking additional information, but the potential ability of such a volume to extend the temporal and spatial reach of the conference seemed significant and worthwhile. Thus plans for this volume were born.

Toward best fulfilling their chapter obligations, authors typically had to rely on some information gleaned from personal communications as well as some contained in what is commonly referred to as "gray" literature. Many scientific journals and books shy away from the latter. We, however, consider the matters associated with imperilment to be urgent; too urgent to wait for the process of peer review to legitimize well-studied natural phenomena. This situation is further exacerbated by the fact that in many agencies, heavy workloads do not facilitate the formal publication of important research results, and it is information contained in "gray" literature which has formed much of the working foundation associated with actual management decisions. Because of this, we maintain that this literature needs to be properly recognized and that the value of many intra- and interagency reports should not be underestimated regarding their importance to conservation and restoration initiatives. We are especially proud, therefore, that this volume exposes a portion of the wealth contained in unpublished yet otherwise accessible literature.

We hope that this volume will interest you — for the fate of many of the animals discussed throughout its pages ultimately relies on us. We hope that this volume will perturb you — for it chronicles an unfortunate odyssey which has resulted in the imperilment of much of our natural heritage. Finally, we hope this volume will instill the kind of desire that encourages change — for the loss of our priceless aquatic resources need not continue.

George W. Benz
Southeast Aquatic Research Institute and Tennessee Aquarium
and
David E. Collins
Tennessee Aquarium

Chattanooga, Tennessee
February 1997

General Acknowledgements

We thank the many people, agencies, and institutions that facilitated the successful conference which served to germinate this volume. Special thanks are extended to the entire Tennessee Aquarium staff for organizing and hosting this conference. In large part, the success of this event was due to the efforts of Janet Allen, Jackson Andrews, Jim Hekkers, Sandy Skorput, and Sandra White, who skillfully formulated the conference preparations. Bruz Clark (The Lyndhurst Foundation), David Etnier (The University of Tennessee at Knoxville), Robert Hatcher (Tennessee Wildlife Resources Agency), John Jenkinson (Tennessee Valley Authority), and Gary Litchford (The University of Tennessee at Chattanooga) were both helpful and kind in serving as outside consultants to the aforementioned committee. Janet Allen was indispensable both before and after the conference, recognizing and tying together many loose ends such that the overall conference process was so well-coordinated that it gave us confidence. Many others at the Tennessee Aquarium, including Charlie Arant, Sally Boals, Peter Burman, William Flynn, Barbara Hailey, Jim Hill, John Kelley, Cheryl Key, Joe Kilgore, Carson Malone, Gene Pinder, Cathy Parker, Judy Powell, Allen Roberts, Neil Robinson, Todd Stailey, Gordon Stalans, Cindy Todd, and Jeff Worley, as well as Aquarium receptionists, membership staff, and volunteer docents played important conference and/or publication roles. We thank the staff at the Chattanooga Choo Choo Holiday Inn for working well with the Aquarium's staff to provide a supportive conference venue. Of course the success of the program itself was ensured by the fine group of presentation authors that flattered us with their willingness to participate. In addition to these knowledgeable professionals, we also thank the many people who pointed the way to these experts. No doubt we have unintentionally overlooked mentioning some that were important to this event or to this publication, and we sincerely apologize for this.

We also thank the authors and official reviewers who unselfishly took time from their busy professional and personal schedules to prepare and refine the chapters contained herein. The names and addresses of these fine people are presented toward the end of this volume. Mark Schorr (University of Tennessee at Chattanooga) and Paul Johnson (Southeast Aquatic Research Institute) read several chapters and a portion of the index (respectively) and provided comments which were useful to us. A very talented Aquarium research intern named Tom Tarpley is thanked for his wonderful illustrations which adorn the chapter headings, and a determined and persistent young biologist named Heather Grant is thanked for ungripingly donating her time to check literature references. Janice Gay Williams (Tennessee Aquarium) is thanked for her assistance in preparing portions of the volume draft and also for her help with many logistical tasks which were critical in getting this volume published. The production of this volume was greatly facilitated by computer technology which we know little about, and a bright young Aquarium research intern named Aaron Fitzsimmons allowed us to be productive without having to battle any of those "how to" manuals which are usually indecipherable by those such as ourselves who are now firmly established in mid-life. Hilary Vinson, Donna Stanek, and Richard Biggins (all U.S. Fish and Wildlife Service), Raymond Bouchard (The Academy of Natural Sciences of Philadelphia), Alan Buchanan (Missouri Department of Conservation),

George Folkerts (Auburn University), Marvin Cook (Wilderness Graphics, Inc.), Debbie Petticord and Max McKenzie (both Chattanooga Magazine), Ray Andersen, and Richard Bryant are all thanked for facilitating or providing pictures or artwork for use in the volume. The critical suggestions of all of the above and others was extremely helpful as our expertise in some topic areas is clearly limited. We hope we have done the authors right in getting their ideas into print, and we accept responsibility for any errors which we have introduced or which have otherwise evaded our notice.

John Brown (formerly U.S. Fish and Wildlife Service) was kind in facilitating a contract that bolstered our conviction that this volume would be useful to biologists and resource managers. The Tennessee Aquarium's commitment to this volume in the form of publication funding, as well as our duty assignment as volume editors of course was critical.

Lastly, we thank Richard Lenz, John Lenz, Pam Holliday, and others at Lenz Design & Communications for efficiently doing a fine job publishing this volume, as well as for their leadership in supporting publications which promote the conservation of our precious natural heritage.

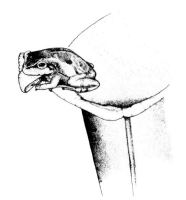

CHAPTER 1

State and Fate of the World's Aquatic Fauna

George W. Folkerts

Although a keynote speaker may have a function in a symposium in setting the tone, raising audience interest level, and other such things, I doubt that the written versions of such presentations have as important a role in the proceedings. I, therefore, intend to be brief, and I have not cited literature sources for a number of examples presented. Much of this information has been obtained through conversations, correspondence, and in other less formal ways.

In this volume, I see my duties as:

1) reminding the reader of the general state of the world's freshwater aquatic habitats,
2) briefly noting the condition of freshwater habitats in our own area, i.e., the southeastern United States, and
3) preaching softly and briefly about our duties, our outlook, and a few goals.

Most of us who work in aquatic habitats realize that they are being degraded. In some cases we may have no quantitative data to document our feelings. Nevertheless, we know beyond doubt that things are going wrong. It is this widespread conviction that is the most compelling reason for concern about these places. The fact that those who know aquatic habitats and their constituent species are worried, is strong evidence that degradation is occurring.

Although most experts are convinced that deterioration of aquatic habitats is occurring, few realize how extensive this deterioration is, fewer realize the extent to which aquatic habitats have been destroyed in the past two decades, and fewer still are cognizant of how rapidly the rate of degradation is likely to increase in the future. Most aquatic biologists have never worked in a system that has not been significantly disturbed. Hence, although we may be concerned because of our impressions about habitat degradation, we may not

Aquatic Fauna in Peril: The Southeastern Perspective, edited by George W. Benz, and David E. Collins. 1997. Special Publication 1, Southeast Aquatic Research Institute, Lenz Design and Communications, Decatur, GA, 554 p.

be as concerned as conditions warrant because our experience has never included familiarity with truly pristine habitats. In the fall of 1993, I was fortunate enough to spend a small amount of time in Four Holes Swamp in South Carolina, a relatively large area of aquatic and wetland habitat preserved and cared for by the National Audubon Society. The fact about the site that struck me most was the apparent superabundance of many elements of the aquatic fauna, including aquatic insects, fishes, and brown water snakes, *Nerodia taxispilota*. I can only attribute this superabundance to the very small amounts of disturbance in the Four Holes Swamp watershed and to the nearly complete lack of anthropogenic disturbance at the sites I visited. I feel that most of my impressions about how abundant aquatic animals "ought to be" have been jaundiced by the fact that almost all of my experiences have been in habitats that were altered, even though I may have thought of some of them as relatively undisturbed. I have had experiences similar to those at Four Holes Swamp at other sites where little unnatural disturbance had occurred.

Even though knowledge of the world's freshwater fauna has advanced significantly in the past few decades, much of the information that is needed to understand, conserve, and protect it is still absent. In many parts of the world, especially in the tropics and Asia, little reliable information can be obtained except perhaps on some elements of the charismatic megafauna such as porpoises, otters, and crocodilians. For most groups of aquatic invertebrates, the information available amounts to little more than a smattering. In some areas, the fauna is so incompletely known that even characterizing it before it disappears seems hopeless. Thus, the information aggregated here is, at best, an approximation of reality.

It is far beyond the scope of this paper to discuss the status of any significant fraction of the world's aquatic habitats or fauna. My concept of freshwater habitats in the following discussion is broad, perhaps including sites and habitat types which many would rather refer to as wetlands. Fresh water comprises less than 0.5 percent of the water on Earth. This fact alone makes the habitats we are concerned with very precious.

Throughout much of human history, human population levels have had only localized and ephemeral effects on the world's biota. Although the Pleistocene overkill, resulting from early man's development of hafted weapons and from his ability to use fire to drive game, decimated some components of the terrestrial megafauna, the freshwater fauna was little affected as far as we know. Most of the early anthropogenic extinctions of aquatic organisms, such as that of Steller's sea cow and the great auk, were of marine species rather than freshwater forms. Decimation of the freshwater biota of the planet has, therefore, been a relatively recent phenomenon in human history.

The recent rapid destruction of freshwater habitats and concomitant massive decimation of the fauna is difficult to grasp. Much of the deterioration has been associated with increased human population levels. At the beginning of this century, Earth supported about 1.5 billion people. The bulk of the human population occupied coastal areas, and few drainage systems or aquatic-wetland complexes of continental interiors suffered from perturbation by the presence of large human populations. During this century humans have come to occupy continental interiors in large numbers, partly as a result of population pressure and partly as a result of development and redistribution schemes promulgated by various countries, such as the development of the Brasilia area in Brazil. Penetration of interiors and population growth away from the coast was coincident with the development of technologies which could be used to drastically alter freshwater systems physically (damming, canalization, diversions, etc.), and with the development of a host of artificial chemicals which have potential for interference with the function of aquatic systems in many ways. As a result, lentic habitats away from coasts and the upstream reaches of many drainages are now being degraded. It is likely that this trend will continue and intensify greatly in the near future.

FACTORS DAMAGING WORLD AQUATIC HABITATS

It is not possible to assemble a complete list of causes for the degradation of freshwater systems throughout the world. Nevertheless, a host of general factors are known. In what follows, I merely touch upon factors that serve to exemplify the types of degradation that exist. I have adopted a rather staccato style of presentation in order to mention briefly a wide variety of topics. Most of the factors mentioned are degrading aquatic habitats in many areas, often throughout the world. The subheadings that follow are used for convenience and are meant to be representative, rather than exhaustive.

Global Problems

Aquatic organisms are not normally considered to be prone to damage by ultraviolet radiation. However, many amphibians lay eggs in masses at the water surface and thus may expose an exceptionally vulnerable part of their life history to potential damage. Kerr and McElroy (1993) found a 35 percent increase in ultraviolet radiation in the winter and a seven percent increase in the summer at Toronto, Canada. Because the decrease in the ozone shielding effect occurs first near Earth's poles, boreal amphibians would be expected to be the first to show the effects of increased UV radiation. Blaustein et al. (1994) found that two anurans, the cascades frog, *Rana cascadae*, and the boreal toad, *Bufo boreas*, showed low levels of the egg enzyme (photolyase) that is involved in repair of damage caused by UV radiation. This finding suggested that ultraviolet damage to these eggs could not be effectively corrected. These two northern species have shown precipitous population declines in the last two decades. The extent to which increased levels of ultraviolet radiation are harming or will harm other aquatic species cannot be reliably estimated at this time.

Global warming resulting from increases in the levels of greenhouse gases will affect all life on Earth. World temperatures were up markedly in 1994 (Kerr, 1995; MacCracken, 1995). Although it is difficult to predict the precise nature of the climatic changes, it seems likely that, in aquatic habitats, elements of the fauna that cannot tolerate changes in thermal regimes will be among the first to be affected. Of major concern, but seldom mentioned, is the possible mass invasion of temperate aquatic systems by tropical species. There have been essentially no studies specifically directed toward an understanding of the problems of global warming in aquatic habitats.

Acidification of freshwater ecosystems has been documented for so many areas of the world that it must be considered a global problem (Fleischer et al., 1993). Long distance movement of sulfur oxides and other acidifying air pollutants means that few parts of the planet escape some perturbation from this source, although most of the conspicuous damage has been near the industrialized areas of Europe and North America. In Sweden, up to 1992, about 6,000 lakes had been limed in attempts to reverse the effects of acidification and preserve fish populations. Russia's Lake Baikal, the oldest, deepest, and faunistically most unique lake in the world is being acidified by pollutants from industry in Irkutsk (Williams and Conroy, 1993). Its 1,800 endemic species have little formal protection of any kind.

Changes in Water Quality

Changes in water quality include chemical pollution from a variety of sources and changes in thermal regimes. The examples mentioned below are intended to represent the great variety of problems that are occurring in the world's freshwater habitats. Although water quality changes are degrading aquatic habitats throughout the world, much of the damage is attributable to western countries where the driving technology was developed, where the perturbing materials are manufactured, and where the distributors are located. "Midnight shipments," via which industries from First World countries illegally dump hazardous wastes in Third World countries are now common.

Molasses seeping from a sugar mill in 1992 caused massive fish kills along a 160 km (about 100 miles) stretch of rivers in northern Thailand. Fish stocks were devastated in three tributaries of the Mekong, the Mool, the Nam Pong, and the Chee rivers. A dam under construction on the Mool will prevent recolonization of the river from downstream areas. The Mekong drainage has 141 species of fishes.

It is important to remember that many chemicals banned in the United States are still used in other parts of the world and that the U.S. exports many banned chemicals to other countries. Fish eagle (*Haliaetus vocifer*) eggs in Zimbabwe showed a 60 percent increase in DDT and metabolites in nine years from 1980 to 1989 (Douthwaite, 1992).

In many cases we do not know the precise causes of decline in animal populations. According to Sweden's salmon research institute, the disease M74, apparently caused by a damaging combination of pollutants (perhaps PCBs and related chemicals) could wipe out the Baltic salmon population within a few generations (MacKenzie, 1993). No definite causes have been found for the recent bald eagle deaths in Sauk and Columbia counties, Wisconsin and at DeGray Lake in Arkansas (K. Miller, National Wildlife Health Service, pers. comm.).

Although problems should have been obvious for a quarter of a century (Bitman and Cecil, 1970), concern about risks from exposure to endocrine disrupting chemicals in both animals and humans has only received wide attention recently (Colborn et al., 1993). The potential problems are extensive, including feminization of males (Peterson et al., 1992), masculinization of females (Bortone and Davis, 1994), disruption of reproductive cycles, alteration of sexual behavior, interference with pheromone communications, and others. In the United States, the Environmental Protection Agency has demonstrated that dioxin and related chemicals pose a major threat to both wildlife species and humans. It is becoming clear that many artificial chlorinated compounds have the potential to disrupt the physiology of animals. In the United States, chlorination of sewage alone could wreak drastic havoc in aquatic systems in the near future.

Rapid increases in the rate at which metals are released into the environment accompany economic development and increased use of western technology. Ecological "hot spots," where contamination by trace metals exceeds rural levels by five to ten fold and exceeds the levels in pristine areas by more than 100 fold, are invariably associated with urban sites (Nriagu, 1990). As urbanization sweeps the earth, the likelihood of contamination of aquatic sites will increase greatly. The atmosphere is becoming a major medium through which trace metals are transported to remote aquatic habitats. Atmospheric fallout alone delivers 100,000 metric tons of lead to world aquatic systems per year (Nriagu and Pacyna, 1988).

Controls on pollution invariably fail to keep up with development. As the former Soviet Union frantically tries to revamp its industrial structure, horrifying pollution episodes, common before glasnost, have become more common. Recently, an oil spill in the Komi republic, as revealed by satellite photos, may have released eight times the amount lost during the Exxon Valdez disaster. Russian officials denied this.

Failure to devise methods to control nonpoint-source pollution and the near impossibility of monitoring nonpoint sources necessitate that the flow of pollutants be halted earlier in the chain of events that leads to the degradation of habitats. This means that changes in agricultural and industrial methodologies are needed. Ultimately, we need to change the way in which we view natural habitats and in our understanding of the purpose of nature.

Physical Alteration of Aquatic Habitats

Drainage schemes in Iraq are destroying the vast Mesopotamian marshes. The projects, initiated by the Iraqi government, have resulted in the diversion of virtually the entire Euphrates River into the so-called "Third River." Along with canalization and drainage work on the Tigris River, the projects prevented water from reaching two-thirds of the delta marshes in 1993. A study by the University of Exeter indicated that this is an ecological catastrophe of a scale not seen in recent times. Conditions are worsened by the huge Ataturk Dam upstream on the Euphrates River in Turkey. These factors not only threaten this region's freshwater and marine systems, they are also destroying the way of life of the Madan people, the so-called "Marsh Arabs." In a deliberate campaign of genocide, Sadaam Hussein has ordered that the marshes be burned. Large fires in the marshes are clearly visible on satellite photos.

The following examples are included to make it clear that in many parts of the world, the era of dams is still in its infancy. Many developing countries see damming as a way out of some of their economic problems. In many cases, diplomatic nudges and technical assistance come from the United States or other western countries.

Japan has completed plans to dam its last wild river, the free-flowing Nagara near Nagoya. The Ministry of Construction claims that the dam is necessary to prevent flooding and that it will have "no serious effect on natural ecology" (see Cross, 1992). Spanish environmental groups are campaigning to prevent the construction of the Vidrieros Dam on the River Carrion in northern Castilla y Leon. Environmental groups in Czeckoslovakia, Austria, and Hungary have asked that an international park be created along the Danube between Vienna and Gyor, Hungary. It is hoped that such a park will prevent the construction of dams planned at Hainburg, Gabcikovo, and Nagymaros. In India, more than 100 opponents to the dams in the Narmada Valley were held in jail without charge, under miserable conditions. A fifteen-year-old tribal youth was killed by police gunfire. In India, as in many other parts of the world, the local citizenry has little say about environmental alterations that may be detrimental. Four protesters were killed by Indonesian security forces when they opened fire on a peaceful demonstration against the Nipah irrigation dam on the island of Madura. The recent execution of eight anti-government rebels in Nigeria was largely a result of their protests about destruction of their land by international oil interests.

Perhaps the most harmful dam project currently going forward is the Three Gorges Dam on the Changjiang (Yangtze) River in China. When finished, it will be the world's biggest dam, creating a lake nearly 645 km (about 400 miles) long and displacing over 1.5 million people. It threatens many of the unique components of the Changjiang fauna including the baiji or Chinese river dolphin (*Lipotes vexillifer*) and the Chinese sturgeon (*Acipenser sinensis*). Two U.S. agencies, the Bureau of Reclamation and the Corps of Engineers, are providing assistance in design and construction of the dam. In a bold critique of Chinese government policy, Dai Qing (Qing, 1994) argued convincingly against the dam from almost every possible angle. She was imprisoned for ten months without trial and her book on the subject was banned in China.

Lest the impression be left that only large dams harm aquatic faunas, Winston et. al. (1991) documented the upstream disappearance of four species of cyprinids after creation of a small dam on the North Fork of the Red River in Oklahoma. This example also emphasizes that dams can cause upstream as well as downstream effects.

Mr. W. Pircher, the president of the International Commission on Large Dams contended recently that free-flowing rivers and associated conditions are not suited for humans and that "engineered infrastructure" must be made the basis for our survival.

The damages wreaked by dams on aquatic systems of the world need not be enumerated in detail here. They are a well-known and well-studied narrative of environmental degradation, including the impending loss of Pacific salmon stocks, the destruction of the Mediterranean sardine fishery, the loss of Grand Canyon habitats, the destruction of coastal barrier islands, the loss of fertile bottomlands throughout the world, and much more.

Loss of Watershed Integrity

Many of the problems facing aquatic habitats are caused by changes in terrestrial habitats. Most of these terrestrial alterations cause aquatic perturbations because they alter normal watershed functions, changing sediment and nutrient levels, water chemistry, flow rates, or water temperatures.

Chief among the current reasons for loss of watershed functions are forest practices that bare the soil, remove woody and herbaceous undergrowth, add herbicides to systems, replace native communities with monocultures, and modify land contours.

Per capita paper consumption in the world is growing at an alarming rate. The pulp and paper portion of the wood products industry is not only involved in clearcutting and conversions to tree farm conditions, but pulp mills release a number of extremely harmful chemicals into the rivers along which they are located.

In Papua New Guinea, the major threat to flowing water habitats is the predicted destruction of all accessible rain forests in the next ten years. Tim Neville, forestry minister in the country, has attempted to halt the threat. He has escaped two assassination attempts by person or persons unknown within the last year.

New threats to forest-associated waters include the aquatic habitats in the forests of Siberia, which now face destruction as Russia attempts to increase its timber exports. Japanese, Korean, and U.S. companies are involved in logging huge areas in Siberia. Economic problems associated with the demise of communism will make many countries in Europe and Asia susceptible to new forms of unscrupulous exploitation by western companies.

It is likely that forestry practices combined with other factors have destroyed the majority of small headwater streams in many areas of the world. These tiny streams have been largely ignored by biologists. They are so fragile that a single event that significantly perturbs the drainage can destroy them, essentially forever. In 1958, I witnessed the destruction of approximately 0.5 km (about 0.3 mile) of stream habitat in Lane County, Oregon through the simple act of careless culvert placement under a road associated with a selection logging operation. Most of the aquatic insects, and tailed frogs (*Ascaphus truei*) had not yet recolonized the site in 1973. Sediment from the road was still present. Corn and Bury (1989) found that logging extirpated amphibian species from a number of sites in western Oregon.

Fuelwood cutting has also sometimes damaged watersheds and the associated aquatic fauna beyond any hope of recovery. In some portions of Africa and Asia, the expanding treeless areas around human settlements can be seen in satellite photos. Reforestation of logged sites with tree species not characteristic of the sites is occurring on all continents. The eventual changes in soil structure, litter fauna, nutrient runoff, and other factors will certainly affect aquatic habitats. Few studies have addressed these problems.

Introduction of Exotic Species

Although many of the problems resulting from the introduction of non-native species into aquatic systems have been highly publicized, comparatively little effort has been made to understand or solve these problems. If governmental agencies in developed countries can be accused of criminal neglect of a major environmental problem, it is in their failure to address problems of exotic species introduction and control. In the United States, no agency has taken a strong lead or shouldered major responsibility for control of exotic species, even though some of the legal framework to do so evidently exists (Stanley et al., 1991).

Many of the introductions of damaging exotics have been associated with the pet trade, with fisheries "improvement," or have occurred accidentally as water containing exotics was transported. However, the recent unauthorized introduction of lake trout (*Salvelinus namaycush*) into Yellowstone Lake in Yellowstone National Park points out that vandalism can also represent a significant threat. If the lake trout cannot be removed, extinction of the native cutthroat trout (*Oncorhynchus clarki*) in the lake is almost certain.

The fish fauna of Lake Victoria in east Africa was originally one of the most unique in the world, including an autochthonous species flock of more than 200 species of haplochromine cichlids. Sometime about 1963, the Nile perch, *Lates niloticus*, a large predaceous cichlid, was introduced into the lake. Currently it comprises 80 percent of all fishes in the lake and has caused the extinction of the majority of the lake's native endemic fishes. The change in the fish fauna has also detrimentally affected the native peoples around the lake who depended on the haplochromines for food and for sale in east African markets. The small haplochromines could be sun dried, but Nile perch are so large that they must be fire dried. Cutting of woody vegetation around the lake to use in drying fires has resulted in essentially denuding a large area and has totally disrupted proper functioning of the region's ecosystem. The end product of this process may be the collapse of the local indigenous cultures.

Similar tragedies are occurring throughout the world. The introduction of *Cichla ocellata*, a highly predaceous fish, to Lake Gatun in Panama has greatly reduced fish diversity in the lake. The associated decimation of populations of small fishes that feed on mosquito larvae has been held responsible for a resurgence of human malaria in the area. The unique cyprinids of Lake Lanao in the Philippines are being wiped out by introduced species including largemouth bass (*Micropterus salmoides*), walking catfish (*Clarias batrachus*), and an introduced goby (*Glossogobius* sp.). In Lake Titicaca in the central Andes, the introductions of rainbow trout (*Oncorhynchus mykiss*) and the pejerry (*Basilichthys bonairiensis*) are destroying the native cyprinodonts of the genus *Orestias*. The Lake Titicaca endemics have also been detrimentally affected by the introduced parasitic ciliophoran, ich, *Ichthyophthirius multifiliis* (see Wurtsbaugh and Tapia, 1988).

Exotic species do not have to be from different continental faunas in order to be damaging. The introduction of the flathead catfish (*Pylodictis olivaris*) from its native range in the Gulf drainages of North America to drainages of the Atlantic Slope has decimated the ichthyofauna of some Atlantic drainages.

Ichthyologists and fisheries biologists sometimes downplay the results of fish introductions if the introduced types have not drastically affected local fish faunas. Affects on the amphibians, aquatic insects, crustaceans, mollusks, and other elements of the aquatic fauna are often overlooked. Bradford (1989) found evidence to indicate that fish introductions to high lakes in the Sierras eliminated some native frog species. To contend that some fish introductions have been harmless or beneficial appears to be naive.

In the Philippines, the introduction of the exotic apple snail, *Ampullaria canaliculata*, has resulted in an ecological nightmare of major proportions (Anderson, 1993). Not only has it nearly driven the native snail, *A. luzonica*, to extinction, but it also feeds on rice. The snail turned out not to be exportable as food because of health regulations in First World markets. Additionally, molluscides used in control attempts had serious affects on human health, including blindness and death, and undoubtedly decimated the native aquatic biota further. The subsequent introduction of large flocks of ducks in attempts to control the snail will probably have further detrimental ramifications.

In the Rhine River in Europe, the introduced amphipod *Corophium curvispinum*, a tube building species, now exists in concentrations as great as 100,000 per m² (109,361 per square yard). Native substrate dwellers and filter feeders are threatened by its presence. Oddly, the amphipod has also decimated populations of the introduced zebra mussel in the Rhine, causing wildlife biologists to become concerned about some waterfowl species that had come to depend on the zebra mussel for food (Van Den Brink et al., 1991).

The North American Great Lakes now contain a fauna that includes at least 4,500 non-indigenous species (Mills et al., 1994). The rate of damaging introductions to the area has seemingly not slowed, zebra mussels (*Dreissena polymorpha*), quagga mussels (*Dreissena bugensis*), spiny water fleas (*Bythotrephes cederstroemii*), Eurasian ruffes (*Gymnocephalus cernuus*), and gobies of the genera *Neogobius* and *Proterorhinus* having become established in the 1980s.

Although our perspective commonly causes us to think that damaging introductions are introductions from elsewhere that wreak havoc on the North American fauna, North American species are causing problems in many other parts of the world. The red-eared slider, *Trachemys scripta elegans*, seems to be outcompeting the European pond turtle, *Emys orbicularis* in parts of France. A North American turbellarian, *Phagocata woodworthi*, is decimating the triclad fauna of Loch Ness in Scotland. It is thought to have been introduced as cysts on the air tanks of divers looking for the Loch Ness Monster.

Introduced aquatic plants can often be as harmful to freshwater systems as introduced animals. Unintentional introduction of plants is difficult to control and monitor because seeds and other propagules are often hard to detect and can survive for long periods during transport. Water hyacinth (*Eichornia crassipes*), the most troublesome of the world's aquatic weeds, now causes problems in 60 countries. Recently it spread into Lake Victoria in Africa. Its presence bodes ill for the lake's already taxed endemic fish population.

In the southeastern United States, Eurasian water milfoil (*Myriophyllum spicatum*) has rapidly invaded both reservoirs and natural waters in the past two decades. It displaces native plants, reduces the food available to waterfowl, impedes navigation, and alters substrates available for aquatic invertebrates. There is some indication that white amur (*Ctenopharyngodon idella*), a fish introduced to control the plant, preferentially feed on native aquatic plant species, thus aggravating the problem.

Other Problems

Rather than create a number of additional categories, I use this catchall heading to mention a spectrum of problems not mentioned above. These are presented merely to apprise the reader of the great diversity of troubles that exist.

Perhaps not really an additional problem but rather a problem resulting from the synergy of many degrading factors is decline of populations as a result of hormonal stress. Although the study of this phenomenon is still in its infancy, Larson and Fivizzani (1994) have documented, in *Ambystoma tigrinum* larvae, elevated corticosterone levels that were positively associated with the amount of agricultural land in the vicinity of the pond used by the larvae. The assumption is that alterations associated with agriculture stress species more than do conditions present in less altered habitats.

Recreational rafting along the Maligne River in Jasper National Park in Canada has caused damage to the population of harlequin ducks (*Histrionicus histrionicus*) on the river. In the five-year period 1986 to 1991, raft trips increased from six to 1,700 per year.

In early 1992, Croatian fisherman crossed the border into Hungary and shot 2,000 cormorants, *Phalacrocorax carbo*, in a nature reserve on the Drava River near the Croatian town of Donji Mihojlac. This was two-thirds of the cormorant population in the reserve.

A study by the U.S. Fish and Wildlife Service indicated that lead weights from fishing tackle may be responsible for 30 percent of all loon deaths. In the survey, 60 percent of the loons autopsied had lead weights in their digestive systems (Pokras, 1993).

The giant grebe (*Podilymbus gigas*) of Lake Atitlan in the Guatemala highlands is threatened by guerrilla warfare, by condominium development, and by reed cutting by natives who use the reeds in a cottage industry making chair seats and mats. Increased native populations spell more damage to reed beds in which the grebe nests.

Fishing by use of explosives is common in many tropical aquatic systems although illegal in most developed countries. In some areas the aquatic fauna has been locally pauperized. The Irrawady River dolphin, *Orcaella brevirostris*, has been significantly harmed by this practice.

What should our viewpoint be on the introduction of genetically altered animals and plants into freshwater habitats? Genetically altered salmon with abnormally high growth rates have been produced for use in commercial fish farms (Devlin et al., 1994). Although the assurance has been given that transgenic salmon will be sterilized to make sure that they do not breed with wild salmon, it would seem to require omnipotence to control the spread of all genetically altered types. Tiedje et al. (1989) presented some viewpoints on genetically altered types and noted possible problems.

FUTURE OF THE WORLD'S FRESHWATER FAUNA

Conservation efforts in most parts of the world have been largely focused on terrestrial habitats (Ryman et al., 1994). This seemingly has resulted simply from the fact that man is a terrestrial species. As a consequence, not only have aquatic sites sometimes received less protection, but they have also received less attention by biologists. In addition, it is often more difficult to protect aquatic habitats because entire watersheds must usually be protected in order to safeguard aquatic species.

Many Third World countries see exploitation of their natural resources as a panacea for their real or perceived economic or environmental problems. In 1992, President Nujoma of Namibia declared that protected animals in Etosha National Park must be utilized to provide food for the populace during the drought.

In many areas of the world, decline in conditions of freshwater habitats has created additional unforeseen problems whose solutions are problematical. For instance, muskrat predation has been implicated in the further decline of endangered freshwater mussel populations on the North Fork of the Holston River in southwestern Virginia (Neves and Coom, 1989). Should the muskrat, a native animal, be controlled, as has been suggested? Do we set a dangerous precedent by controlling one native animal to promote the welfare of another? Perhaps muskrats are anthropogenically overabundant, like white-tailed deer (*Odocoileus virginianus*) and raccoons (*Procyon lotor*) are in many areas of the region? Should we introduce predators to control the muskrats? Is concentrating on proximate causes reducing the attention given to and efforts made to address the ultimate reasons for the decline of populations of aquatic species? Answers may exist to these questions, but I am not aware of any carefully reasoned ones.

Polhemus (1993) noted that populations of the threatened aquatic bug, the Ash Meadows naucorid (*Ambrysus amargosus*), were harmed as a result of modifications of the habitat designed to provide a refugium for the endangered Devils Hole pupfish (*Cyprinodon diabolis*). Plans to "fatally remove" sea lions (*Eumetopias jubatus*) which are preying on wild steelhead trout (*Oncorhynchus mykiss*) at Ballard Locks on the Cedar River in Washington have caused an uproar in the Pacific Northwest. Conflicts related to possibly benefiting one declining species at the expense of another will become more common as conditions in aquatic systems continue to deteriorate.

Small gains have often been made. I will mention only a few examples. Kenya's president has decreed that the Tana River Delta is to become a protected area. This Ramsar site was proposed for development. Beavers (*Castor fiber*) have been successfully reintroduced into the Vistula River Basin in Poland. A recent census revealed 130 lodges. An endangered anabantid fish, *Sandelia bainsii*, is now protected in a reserve on the Blaauwkrantz River in South Africa. It occurs in only four river systems and is threatened by water withdrawal, pollution, sedimentation, and the presence of the introduced aquatic fern, *Azolla filliculoides*. Duck numbers in the prairie pothole region of North America were up in 1994, largely as a result of programs now considered for cancellation or major emendation. River otters once again inhabit Great Smoky Mountains National Park after an absence of 50 years.

However, with rose tinted glasses laid aside, the future of the planet's freshwater systems seems rather bleak. It is clear that human population growth alone, even without commensurate increases in technology or affluence, will significantly degrade freshwater systems within the next few decades. By 2050, there will be 10 billion people on Earth. It is unlikely that per capita effects on freshwater habitats at that time will be less than they are presently. To put this in a clearer perspective, if the size of the human population is related to the rate of destruction and degradation of aquatic habitats, there will be three times the damage in the year 2025 as in the year 1965. The results of such an increase are obvious.

STATE OF AQUATIC HABITATS IN SOUTHEASTERN NORTH AMERICA

The southeastern portion of North America once harbored one of the most diverse temperate aquatic faunas in the world, with species richness in many groups being exceeded only by some areas in southeastern Asia. As examples only, there are about 200 fish species endemic to the Southeast, approximately 250 species of freshwater mussels native to the area, and more than 30 of the world's 257 turtle species. This rich fauna is still poorly known, especially for invertebrate groups. It is certain that some species disappeared before their discovery.

In 1970, the human population of the southeastern United States (i.e., Alabama, Arkansas, Georgia, Florida, Kentucky, Louisiana, Mississippi, North Carolina, South Carolina, Tennessee) was approximately 35 million. In the year 2000 it will be 62 million, having nearly doubled in thirty years. Per capita pressures on natural systems are unlikely to decrease significantly in the next few decades. If by some near miracle, per capita effects were cut in half by the year 2030, resultant benefits to aquatic systems would be negated by population growth.

In many ways, the southeastern United States has been treated as a Third World country by the rest of the nation, or, perhaps more accurately, by industrial interests throughout the world. Industrial sitings in the region have often been based on the same criteria used to site plants in Latin American countries, i.e., lower salaries can be paid, tax rates on industries are lower, and perhaps most importantly, pollution laws and other measures to preserve environmental integrity are poorly enforced and easily circumvented by using political pressure.

One of the greatest known extinction episodes in the first half of the twentieth century took place in the Southeast — the virtual disappearance of the Coosa River molluscan fauna. Dams on the Coosa River destroyed the shoals on which the snails and mussels depended. Although accurate information will never be available, perhaps 40 snail species and a number of mussel species disappeared (Stansbery, 1976; Stein, 1976; Bogan and Pierson, 1993; Hartfield, 1993). Today, most of the remnants of this once diverse fauna teeter on the brink of extinction.

Proof of the Third World status of the Southeast lies in the fact that the damming era is not yet over in the area, as it essentially is in the rest of the nation. Plans to dam many of the remaining free-flowing rivers or reaches are in various stages of development even though not highly publicized.

Although alarm about the rate of destruction of tropical forests is certainly justified, the rate of forest destruction in the southeastern United States exceeds that of any tropical area of comparable size. Since the late 1960s, the practices of clearcutting and pine monoculture have altered fully one-third of all of the forested areas on the Coastal Plain of the Southeast and have affected virtually every aquatic habitat in the area. We tend to think that the rate of damage must be decreasing, but, as an example, in the period 1980 to 1990 the rate of logging doubled in the areas surrounding Great Smoky Mountain National Park.

Herbicides used to kill hardwoods and control the growth of herbaceous plants will cause further harm to associated watersheds. Not only do these chemicals destroy plants which help to retain nutrients on site, but some have been shown to be toxic to algae (Austin et al., 1991) and thus are bound to interfere with processes in aquatic habitats. There have been no thorough tests of how herbicides applied to forests will affect aquatic systems.

Although surface waters of the Southeast have been thought of as being less susceptible to acidification than those in more northerly areas, atmospheric deposition of sulfur oxides has been cited as at least a partial cause of stream acidification in the Great Smoky Mountains (Cook et al., 1994). Acid mine runoff has already destroyed stream biotas in many areas.

The rate of introduction of damaging exotics is increasing in the Southeast. The fish fauna of southern Florida has been permanently altered by tropical types. The zebra mussel has entered the Tennessee River drainage. Little effort is being made to keep it from invading the unique Gulf and Atlantic drainages. Biofouling, competition with native mussels, and alteration of substrate associated with its encroachment will change southeastern aquatic habitats in unpredictable ways.

River beds in the southeastern United States are lined with an array of toxic chemicals deposited over the last half century. Even if we stop all pollution immediately, these chemicals will cause effects for at least the next century. The stretch of the Mississippi River between Baton Rouge and New Orleans is often given the appellation "cancer alley." Not only do the banks support a large number of industries that release dangerous materials into the water, but the lower Mississippi lies downstream from sites as far away and as widely separated as New Mexico, Alberta, Minnesota, New York, and North Carolina. Thus, the Southeast receives contaminants from most of the continent.

Preservation of wild and scenic segments of flowing water habitats and setting aside tracts containing important lentic sites is necessary and laudable. However, it is clear that isolated preserves are not a long-term answer to the maintenance of aquatic biodiversity. Habitat fragmentation has already affected numerous freshwater species in the region (e.g., the flattened musk turtle; see Dodd, 1990).

DUTIES OF BIOLOGISTS

There are biologists who profess to believe that a dispassionate and detached view of nature is necessary to perform unbiased scientific work. They are wrong. In most cases those who attempt such a view dehumanize their relationship with what they study to the extent that their talents cannot be effectively used or focused. Second, they often function as parasites on those in the scientific community who are willing to spend portions of their careers attempting to conserve, preserve, and protect the natural systems so vital to their work and absolutely vital to the future well-being of our species. Third, those who claim that resource custodianship is outside the realm of their proper endeavors sometimes fear that their funding, derived from sources committed to environmental destruction, may be lost. All in all there is little justification, ethically, practically, or scientifically for scientists to ignore the fate of the life forms that they study.

Those who are most aware of the declining health of natural systems must be the ones to sound the alarm. They must be willing to take a stand. Some biologists are reluctant to vigorously defend sound practices in the treatment of the earth because they feel that their jobs, funding, and perhaps even their lives may be threatened, as indeed they may. Even so, if those who understand freshwater systems best, and are most aware of their inestimable value to mankind are not to be advocates, then there will be little effective advocacy.

Biologists, as a group, have been rather sluggish and timid in active protection of freshwater resources. Somehow there has been the feeling that compromise, half-hearted defense, and carefully not treading on the toes of the agents of destruction were appropriate postures. Evidence for the continuation of this trend is present in recent works on aquatic systems, some of which have apologist overtones. Many papers considering degradation of habitats include tacit support for the folklore inherent in currently fashionable themes such as "sustainable growth," "managed development," and "economic realities." Such positions, if continued, will soon result in the loss of all of our natural systems and their diverse faunas. Supposed economic realities are created by those in power to insure their continued power and economic gain. Considering these artifices to be reality is not compatible with the health of the planet's life support systems.

Perhaps the most obvious failure on our part is our failure to educate the public about the significance of nature to our future well-being. Although some surveys show that a majority of the American public supports environmental concerns, few understand natural systems well enough to know when to be concerned. In most cases, the majority of the educated public still believes that jobs are more important than protection of natural systems. When the representative governing body of a nation can consider weakening, destroying, and making a sham of major pieces of legislation designed to make the world a more livable place for all life, it is clear that the educational process has malfunctioned badly.

Zero future alteration and rapid return of natural systems to functioning states is the only realistic goal. When this is mentioned, many carp by contending that man must alter the earth in order to live. This is undoubtedly true. The question is, does the alteration inevitably have to be destructive? Rather than continue to work toward goals which will only slow the degradation for short periods, let us admit that the only way to maintain the earth in a state that will continue to support both a diverse biota and a human population is to quickly reverse many of the trends of the past half century.

What should some of our goals be in the southeastern United States? Perhaps we could set as one goal, the removal of all dams from rivers and large streams by the year 2050. Considerable planning would be necessary. Reservoir waters would have to be released gradually over a period of years. Sediment in reservoirs would have to be removed and partially returned to the land. Downstream developments and cities in floodplains would have to be flood-proofed or moved. A new "science" would have to emerge, combining biology, hydrology, geology, engineering, agriculture, sociology, and many other disciplines. This proposal clearly presents many difficulties. Perhaps, 2050 is unrealistically soon, but putting off goals may make their achievement impossible. If we let these challenges thwart our efforts to repair potentially mortal wounds to natural systems, then we have accepted the demise of nature as inevitable. Coupled with energy conservation, development of solar energy, and use of more efficient means of materials transport than barging, removal of dams should be good for human and non-human biota.

Protection of watersheds and ensuring the quality, quantity, and periodicity of the run-off is absolutely vital. Current common forest practices such as large tract clearcutting, monoculture, and the use of heavy machinery on forest lands are incompatible with both natural systems and the welfare of the citizenry. They must be abandoned immediately.

We came to the symposium in Chattanooga to consider the fate of our region's freshwater fauna. If all we do is consider, then the gathering will have been meaningless. We must be strong advocates of proper treatment of the world. We must be much less willing to compromise with the forces of ruin. If we do not take the lead and take it immediately, it is absolutely certain that the freshwater biota will be pauperized to a functionless level within the lifetimes of many of us. In some cultures, water and the life associated with it are sacred. In western culture, aquatic habitats have been viewed as enemies, to be controlled, defeated, and destroyed. If we cannot successfully change this viewpoint, we will have little left to study or enjoy.

ACKNOWLEDGEMENTS

The author gratefully acknowledges assistance and advice received from George Benz, Dave Collins, Dave Etnier, Debbie Rymal Folkerts, Bud Freeman, Paul Hartfield, and Bill Redmond. Partial support for the generation of this paper was supplied by the Alabama Agricultural Experiment Station.

REFERENCES

Anderson, B. 1993. The Philippine snail disaster. *The Ecologist* **23**:70-72.

Austin, A. P., G. E. Harris, and W. P. Lucey. 1991. Impact of an organophosphate herbicide (GlyphosateR) on periphyton communities developed in experimental streams. *Bulletin of Environmental Contamination and Toxicology* 47:29-35.

Bitman, J., and H. C. Cecil. 1970. Estrogenic activity of DDT analogs and polychlorinated biphenyls. *Journal of Agricultural Food Chemistry* 1:1108-1112.

Blaustein, A. R., P. D. Hoffman, D. Grant Hokit, J. M. Kiesacker, S. C. Walls, and J. B. Hays. 1994. UV repair and resistance to solar UV-B in amphibian eggs: A link to population declines. *Proceedings of the National Academy of Science USA* 91:1791-1795.

Bogan, A. E., and J. M. Pierson. 1993. Survey of the aquatic gastropods of the Coosa River basin, Alabama: 1992. Unpublished Report submitted to the Alabama Natural Heritage Program, Montgomery, AL, 20 p. + appendices.

Bortone, S. A., and W. P. Davis. 1994. Fish intersexuality as indicator of environmental stress. *BioScience* 44:165-172.

Bradford, D. F. 1989. Allotopic distribution of native frogs and introduced fishes in high Sierra Nevada lakes of California: Implication of the negative effect of fish introduction. *Copeia* 1989:775-778.

Colborn, T., F. S. vom Sall, and A. M. Soto. 1993. Developmental effects of endocrine disrupting chemicals in humans and wildlife. *Environmental Health Perspectives* 101:378-384.

Cook, R. B., J. W. Elwood, R. R. Turner, M. A. Bogle, P. J. Mulholand, and A. V. Palumbo. 1994. Acid-base chemistry of high-elevation streams in the Great Smoky Mountains. *Water, Air, and Soil Pollution* 72:331-356.

Corn, P. S., and R. B. Bury. 1989. Logging in western Oregon: Responses of headwater habitats and stream amphibians. *Forest Ecology and Management* 29:39-57.

Cross, M. 1992. Japanese river scheme survives barrage of criticism. *New Scientist* 134:8.

Devlin, R. H., T. Y. Yesaki, and C. A. Biagi. 1994. Extraordinary salmon growth. *Nature* 371:209-210.

Dodd, C. K., Jr. 1990. Effects of habitat fragmentation on a stream-dwelling species, the flattened musk turtle *Sternotherus depressus*. *Biological Conservation* 54:33-45.

Douthwaite, R. J. 1992. Effects of DDT on the Fish Eagle, *Haliaetus vocifer*, population of Lake Kariba in Zimbabwe. *IBIS* 134:250-258.

Fleischer, S., G. Andersson, and Y. Brodin. 1993. Acid water research in Sweden - knowledge for tomorrow? *Ambio* 22:258-263.

Hartfield, P. 1993. Status review of aquatic snails in the Coosa River, Alabama. Unpublished Report, U.S. Fish and Wildlife Service, Jackson, MS, 17 p.

Kerr, R. A. 1995. Studies say — tentatively — that greenhouse warming is here. *Science* 268:1567-1568.

Kerr, J. B., and C. T. McElroy. 1993. Evidence for large upward trends of ultraviolet-B radiation linked to ozone depletion. *Science* 262:1032-1034.

Larson, D. L., and A. J. Fivizzani. 1994. Hormonal response to acute stress as a biomarker for chronic stress in larval *Ambystoma tigrinum*. *Froglog* 11:2-3.

MacCracken, M. C. 1995. The evidence mounts up. *Nature* 376:645-646.

MacKenzie, D. 1993. Disease could wipe out Baltic salmon. *New Scientist* 140:8.

Mills, E. L., J. H. Leach, J. T. Carlton, and Carol J. Secor. 1994. Exotic species and the integrity of the Great Lakes. *BioScience* 44:666-676.

Neves, R. J., and M. C. Coom. 1989. Muskrat predation on endangered freshwater mussels in Virginia. *Journal of Wildlife Management* 53:934-941.

Nriagu, J. O. 1990. Global metal pollution: Poisoning the biosphere? *Environment* 32:7-11, 28-29.

Nriagu, J. O., and J. N. Pacyna. 1988. Quantitative assessment of worldwide contamination of air, water, and soils with trace metals. *Nature* 333:134-139.

Peterson, R. E., R. W. Moore, T. A. Mabry, D. L. Bjerke, and R. W. Goy. 1992. Male reproductive system ontogen: Effects of perinatal exposure to 2,3,7,8-tetrachloro-dibenzo-*p*-dioxin. In *Advances in Modern Environmental Toxicology: The Human/ Wildlife Connection*. T. Colborn, and C. Clement (eds.). Princeton Scientific, Princeton, NJ, p. 175-193.

Pokras, M. A. 1993. Get the lead out. *Wildlife Conservation* 96:15.

Polhemus, D. A. 1993. Conservation of aquatic insects: Worldwide crisis or localized threats? *American Zoologist* 33:588-598.

Qing, D. 1994. *Yangtze! Yangtze! Debate over the Three Gorges Project*. Earthscan Publications, Seattle. [translation of the 1989 Chinese version].

Ryman, N., F. Utter, and L. Laikre. 1994. Protection of aquatic biodiversity. In *The State of the World's Fisheries Resources*. C. W. Voigtlander (ed.). Proceedings of the World Fisheries Congress Plenary Session. Oxford and IBH, New Delhi, p. 87-109.

Stanley, J. G., R. A. Peoples, Jr., and J. A. McCann. 1991. U.S. federal policies, legislation, and responsibilities related to importation of exotic fishes and other aquatic organisms. *Canadian Journal of Fisheries and Aquatic Science* 48 (Supplement 1):162-166.

Stansbery, D. 1976. Naiad mollusks. In *Endangered and Threatened Species of Alabama.* H. Boschung (ed.). Bulletin No. 2, Alabama Museum of Natural History, Tuscaloosa, AL, p. 46-52.

Stein, C. 1976. Gastropods. In *Endangered and Threatened Species of Alabama.* H. Boschung (ed.). Bulletin No. 2, Alabama Museum of Natural History, Tuscaloosa, AL, p. 21-41.

Tiedje, J. M., R. K. Colwell, Y. L. Grossman, R. E. Hodson, R. E. Lenski, R. N. Mack, and P. J. Regal. 1989. The planned introduction of genetically engineered organisms: Ecological considerations and recommendations. *Ecology* 70:298-315.

Van Den Brink, F. W. B., G. Van Der Valde, and A. Bij De Vaate. 1991. Amphipod invasion on the Rhine. *Nature* 352:576.

Williams, D. S., and A. D. Conroy. 1993. Safeguarding the world's largest lake. *Water Environment and Technology* 5:31-32.

Winston, M. R., C. M. Taylor, and J. Pigg. 1991. Upstream extirpation of four minnow species due to damming of a prairie stream. *Transactions of the American Fisheries Society* 120:98-105.

Wurtsbaugh, W. A., and R. A. Tapia. 1988. Mass mortality of fishes in Lake Titicaca (Peru-Bolivia) associated with the protozoan parasite, *Ichthyophthirius multifiliis. Transactions of the American Fisheries Society* 117:213-217.

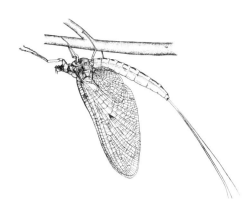

CHAPTER 2

Southern Appalachian and Other Southeastern Streams at Risk: Implications for Mayflies, Dragonflies and Damselflies, Stoneflies, and Caddisflies

John C. Morse, Bill P. Stark, W. Patrick McCafferty, and Kenneth J. Tennessen

The regional focus of this paper is the southern Appalachian Mountains. The aquatic insect fauna of the southern Appalachians is especially distinctive and generally appears to be most threatened among aquatic insects. The Piedmont, Sandhills, Coastal Plain, and Interior Highland regions of the Southeast also are interesting, with several endemic species of freshwater insects known in these other areas.

The taxonomic focus of this paper is the four orders of aquatic insects containing the

Aquatic Fauna in Peril: The Southeastern Perspective, edited by George W. Benz, and David E. Collins. 1997. Special Publication 1, Southeast Aquatic Research Institute, Lenz Design and Communications, Decatur, GA, 554 p.

mayflies, dragonflies and damselflies, stoneflies, and caddisflies. There are many other orders of insects with freshwater representatives, including a few that are exclusively aquatic. However, the mayflies, stoneflies, and caddisflies (Ephemeroptera, Plecoptera, and Trichoptera, or EPT) have generally long been considered especially sensitive to pollution and disturbance and thus are now used in most developed countries to help indicate the presence of pollution. These three orders of insects are also of special interest to those involved with sport fishing because they often serve as the primary food for many species of game fish. An ability to fabricate or "tie" imitations of these insects and to cast them in such a way as to emulate natural insect behavior is considered the mark of an excellent trout angler. Unlike the secretive adults of the EPT orders, however, the adults of dragon-flies and damselflies, or the Odonata, are large and colorful insects that have attracted popular attention. Consequently, we probably know more about the biology and distribu-tion of Odonata species than of those of the three EPT orders. Collectively these four orders, whose approximately 3,000 North American species constitute about 26 percent of the aquatic insect species on the continent (Table 1), are in many ways representative of the situation in the remaining groups of aquatic insects.

The objectives of this chapter are to consider:

1) the southeastern and southern Appalachian insect fauna of mayflies, dragonflies and damselflies, stoneflies, and caddisflies;

2) the structural features that account for these species' uniqueness in the southern Appalachians;

3) the historical changes that humans and other forces have made in the streams and rivers of the region; and

4) the impacts of these environmental changes on the region's aquatic insect fauna, again paying particular attention to species of Ephemeroptera, Odonata, Plecoptera, and Trichoptera.

THE FAUNA

Collectively there are about 11,053 species of aquatic insects in America north of Mexico. Of these, 611 species are mayflies, about 500 species are dragonflies and damselflies, 595 are stoneflies, and 1,369 are caddisflies (Table 1). About 40 percent of the North Ameri-can aquatic insect fauna is represented in the Southeast, a region occupying only about six percent of the continental area north of Mexico.

The mayflies, or Ephemeroptera, are represented in the Southeast by 238 species, be-longing to 63 genera in 16 families, constituting 39 percent of the continental mayfly fauna. Eighty-eight mayfly species (14 percent of the Nearctic species) are endemic to the Southeast. The larvae of these insects occur in a wide range of habitats, including both lentic and lotic environments, with most species intolerant of organic pollution, toxicants, and siltation. Highest mayfly diversity is found in rocky bottomed headwater streams (second to third order). Mayflies spend most of their lives as larvae, emerging as alate forms (subimagoes and adults) at particular times of the year and particular times of day or night, living for only a few hours to a few days during which they mate and lay eggs. Larvae of most species feed by collecting, scraping or brushing detritus and algae from rocks and other substrates, often filtering it through the fine hairs associated with their

Table 1. Approximate numbers of known aquatic insect species of the world, North America north of Mexico, and the United States of America.

Taxon	World[1]	North America	Southeastern United States
Ephemeroptera — mayflies	2,000	611	238
Odonata — dragon/damselflies	4,870	500	241
Plecoptera — stoneflies	2,000	595	189
Trichoptera — caddisflies	10,000	1,369	544
All Other Aquatic Insects[1]	45,000	8,000	3,000
Total Species[1]	63,870	11,053	4,212

[1] Approximate number of species reported.

mouthparts. Mayflies require space among the stream-bottom rocks for feeding and for harborage. Some of the larger species burrow in silt, clay, or sand.

The dragonflies and damselflies, or Odonata, are represented in the Southeast by 241 species, belonging to 48 genera in ten families, constituting 48 percent of the continental dragonfly and damselfly fauna. Forty-two Odonata species (17 percent of the Nearctic species) are endemic to the Southeast. The larvae of these insects also occur in a wide variety of mostly lentic habitats, either burrowing just under the surface of the sediments, sprawling in sediment or detritus, or climbing vascular plants. They are all predators that have a uniquely elaborated lower lip that is elbowed beneath the head when at rest and capable of capturing prey when extended at very high speed. Larvae are so intimately associated with stream and pond bottoms that disturbance of the substrate or increase of fine silt seriously impacts the ability of these insects to survive. Adults typically fly during the daylight hours and hunt by sight, contributing to their familiarity among casual naturalists.

The stoneflies, or Plecoptera, are represented in the Southeast by 189 species, belonging to 40 genera in nine families, constituting 32 percent of the continental stonefly fauna. Forty-four species (7.4 percent of the Nearctic species) are endemic to the Southeast. Stonefly larvae occur mostly in streams, with highest diversity in rocky headwater streams of second to third order, mostly either scurrying about among the rocks looking for prey or in accumulations of dead leaves and sticks where they shred these materials for food. They usually emerge into adulthood after crawling from the water at the shore or on a rock or log protruding from the water. The adults are secretive, poor flyers, and seldom seen in large numbers except near their stream habitats, with much of their adult activity occurring after dark. Like those of mayflies, stonefly adults also do not live long before mating, laying eggs, and dying, occasionally feeding on epiphytic algae or young leaves and buds of riparian vegetation. Plecoptera are especially sensitive to sedimentation and organic pollution, quickly disappearing from streams where these problems exist.

The caddisflies, or Trichoptera, are represented in the Southeast by 544 species, belonging to 78 genera in 22 families, constituting 40 percent of the continental caddisfly fauna. One hundred sixty-eight species (12 percent of the Nearctic species) are endemic to the Southeast. Caddisfly larvae occur in a wide range of habitats, with highest diversity in

rocky headwater streams of second to fourth order. They exhibit the widest range of behaviors of the insect groups discussed here and can be found burrowing in sediments,
sprawling or clinging on substrates, or swimming in quieter waters. Some species are free-
living, others build silken retreats which may have special nets to filter fine food particles
from the flowing water, and others construct cases in which they live and which they drag
over the bottom as they move. Caddisflies feed by shredding dead leaves, collecting detritus and algae and microcrustaceans from the bottom, filtering food items from the water
column, scraping algae from stable solid substrates, piercing individual cells of filamen-
tous algae, and preying on other insects. To facilitate pupation, larvae either construct a
pupation chamber or attach the larval case to something stable and seal it. After a few
weeks, they swim to the surface of the water to emerge as adults. Adults live for several
days to several weeks, imbibing liquids for sustenance, mating and eventually laying their
eggs above, on, or in the water. Caddisflies have a wider range of pollution tolerances than
some of the other aquatic insect groups, with some being very pollution sensitive and
others being able to withstand modest environmental insults. Like the other insect orders
discussed here, caddisflies are generally very dependent on an unsilted stream bottom
because they require spaces among rocks for shelter and stable surfaces for grazing and
attaching their retreats and filter nets.

STRUCTURAL FEATURES

The southern Appalachian Mountains apparently have held a special fascination for
people in North America for thousands of years. The relatively mild climate of these
mountains, their rich plant and animal life, and their abundant water have encouraged
settlement by Native Americans and the descendants of European colonists. The rugged
terrain and dense vegetation historically discouraged travel, large-scale agriculture, and
heavy industrialization. In recent years, however, the spectacular vistas have attracted tourists
and encouraged development aimed at the vacation and retirement markets.

For purposes of this chapter, we define the Southeast as the states of Alabama, Arkansas,
Florida, Georgia, Louisiana, Mississippi, North Carolina, South Carolina, and Tennessee.
We recognize the southern Appalachian Mountains as the region covered by the Blue
Ridge and the Ridge and Valley physiographic provinces from Maryland and West Virginia southward into Georgia and Alabama. The Appalachian Mountains are bordered on
the northwest by the Allegheny and Cumberland Plateau region. They are bordered on
the southeast by the wide Piedmont region, from which the Mountains are separated by
the Blue Ridge Escarpment, sometimes dropping 300 m (984 feet) or more on an average 45
degree angle. Streams crossing the Blue Ridge Escarpment often produce spectacular water-
falls. Elevations in the Blue Ridge region generally range between 600-1,000 m (1,969-3,281
feet); those in the Ridge and Valley region are generally between 300-900 m (984-2,953 feet)
(Isphording and Fitzpatrick, 1992).

Streams of the southern Appalachians are unique for several reasons. These mountains
were never glaciated. Therefore, the saprolitic ultisol and inceptisol soils are generally
residual and not sedimentary; that is, they weathered chemically in place. Soils at the
lower elevations frequently are deep and highly structured vertically, with a conspicuous
sandy or loamy horizon above a loamy or clayey horizon. Soils at higher elevations have

undergone less alteration of the parent rock. These are young soils lacking much clay accumulation (Isphording and Fitzpatrick, 1992). The fact that the southern Appalachians were not glaciated also means that many species, including aquatic insects, evolved in place; while others moved south with the glaciers and were left as isolated populations with high speciation potential when the ice receded (Ross and Ricker, 1971).

The southern Appalachian Mountains have relatively mild winters and summers. This warmer climate means that there is greater biological activity than is found at higher latitudes. Therefore, at both high and low elevations, although the vegetation is dense, the surface organic layer is shallow because of rapid decay on the generally humid, warm, temperate forest floor. Concurrently, a much smaller portion of the southeastern caddisfly fauna, for example, consists of shredding detritivores, such as Limnephilidae, than is found in other parts of the continent (Hamilton and Morse, 1990). During the Pleistocene Epoch, the climate was cooler and drier, probably resulting in fewer streams with less flow. Such conditions would have created isolated aquatic insect populations and thus facilitated higher rates of species diversification.

Shade associated with vegetation is seasonal throughout the southern Appalachians, and this limits autochthonous primary production in headwater streams during April through October. Thus, most of the nutrient energy for the heterotrophic fauna enters the headwater streams as allochthonous leaf and wood debris (Hornick et al., 1981; Webster et al., 1983), averaging about 400 g dry mass per m² per year (1.3 ounces dry mass per square foot per year) in the southern Appalachians (Bray and Gorham, 1964).

Precipitation is relatively high in the southern Appalachians, averaging 100-200 cm per year (40-80 inches per year; Wallace et al., 1992). Consequently, most southern Appalachian streams are permanent, with small seeps and springs occurring frequently. Because infiltration through the topsoil exceeds rainfall in undisturbed forests of the southern Appalachians, there is little overland flow and consequently little movement of sediments. When topsoils are removed or compacted (crushing their macropores), surface runoff increases and sediment is transported to streams, especially in mountainous areas with greater topographic relief.

Streams of the southern Appalachians have high natural structural complexity, with rocks, some sand, large woody debris, and leaf packs providing cover and protection from predators and scouring; attachment surfaces for periphyton, sprawlers, and clingers; means for entrainment of organic and inorganic matter; complicated flow patterns; and sediment heterogeneity.

These streams also have high physicochemical variability, especially in mid-order reaches (third to fifth order streams). This variability is the result of two general features: (a) distinctive seasons that affect temperature, flow regimes, and sunlight penetration, and (b) irregularities of flow caused by heavy storms at all times of year that affect temperature, current velocity, and nutrient pulses. Thus, abiotic factors may control the freshwater communities here more than biotic factors such as competition and predation (Allan, 1983; Peckarsky, 1983).

Together, the aforementioned major factors, and probably others, have resulted in some of the highest aquatic insect species diversity and one of the highest concentrations of endemic species on the continent, especially for Ephemeroptera, Plecoptera, and Trichoptera (Holt et al., 1969). For example, 72, 89, and 73 percent of the species of mayflies, stoneflies, and caddisflies, respectively, in the two Carolinas occur in the southern Appalachian Mountains (Table 2), with 31, 36, and 38 percent of them occurring there exclusively (Brigham et al., 1982). Usually dwelling in more slowly moving water, dragonflies and damselflies have

Table 2. Number and percent (in parentheses) of species of mayflies (Ephemeroptera), dragonflies and damselflies (Odonata), stoneflies (Plectoptera), and caddisflies (Trichoptera) in the mountains and other physiographic regions of North and South Carolina (Brigham et al., 1982).

Taxon	Mountains Only	Mountains & Other Areas	Total In Mountains	Non-mountainous Areas Only	Total in NC & SC
Ephemeroptera	54 (31)	70 (41)	124 (72)	49 (28)	173 (100)
Odonata	26 (14)	92 (51)	118 (65)	63 (35)	181 (100)
Plecoptera	42 (36)	63 (53)	105 (89)	13 (11)	118 (100)
Trichoptera	104 (38)	96 (35)	200 (73)	74 (27)	274 (100)
TOTAL	226 (30)	321 (43)	547 (73)	199 (27)	746 (100)

relatively fewer endemic species in these mountains (14 percent, Table 2). Among all 1,653 caddisfly species known in North America (including Greenland and Mexico; Morse, 1993), 104 (six percent) are endemic to the Eastern Highlands, defined as the Cumberland Plateau, Appalachian plateaus, Appalachian Mountains, and Piedmont (Hamilton and Morse, 1990), and 63 species (four percent) are endemic to the southern Appalachian Mountains.

HUMAN IMPACTS

What are the historical factors that have influenced the southern Appalachian streams and their faunas? Their aboriginal inhabitants, primarily Cherokee Indians, used fire extensively as an aid in hunting, for clearing cropland, and for maintaining habitats for berries, deer, and turkey (Hughes, 1983). Beaver built millions of dams on small order streams which slowed flow rates, opened canopies, and provided habitat for many species of freshwater plants and animals. Beaver were essentially eliminated from the southern Appalachians by the late 1700s (Hackney and Adams, 1992). Early European settlers practiced slash-and-burn agriculture and traveled on dirt roads that forded the many streams in the region, causing unknown amounts of sedimentation. They also built mill ponds, drained swamps, and snagged and dredged streams to make them navigable.

The United States Army Corps of Engineers, the Tennessee Valley Authority, and electrical power companies have built many reservoirs throughout the Southeast, especially during the past 50 years. Most southeastern reservoirs have been built in the upland regions, including many in the southern Appalachian Mountains (Soballe et al., 1992). Other lentic habitats have been created on private lands as generally small ponds, mostly for controlling erosion, irrigating crops, watering cattle, fishing, and swimming; their significance lies in their sheer number (Menzel and Cooper, 1992). Thus, many streams in the southern

Appalachians now have small ponds in their headwaters and huge reservoirs in their lower reaches. Of course, these structures affect flow rates, oxygen levels, and temperatures; they accelerate phytoplankton and macrophyte production rates and obstruct movements of fish. Because the Southeast had few natural lakes, many of the species inhabiting these recently constructed reservoirs, at least among caddisflies, tend to be generalists that apparently have invaded them from slowing moving streams (Hudson et al., 1981). At the same time, those collector-filterer species that can tolerate highly variable flow and temperature regimes and that thrive especially on planktonic organisms have proliferated below the dams.

Although the cutting of trees in the southern Appalachians has continued for a long time, large-scale removal of wood began in the late 1800s, after most of the primary forests of the Northeast and Midwest had been removed. Deforestation continued for about 45 years, resulting in severe erosion and sedimentation (Trimble, 1975; Meade, 1976). Beginning in 1925, professional foresters of the U.S. Forest Service began providing protection from fire and heavy cutting. Initially, they favored selection management, maintaining uneven-aged forests. However, this type of management was difficult because the small canopy openings did not permit regeneration of desirable species, and the frequent re-entry into the forests to cut selected trees caused continual sources of sedimentation in the streams. Clearcutting became standard practice on national forest lands by about 1965 and continues to the present.

Another major alteration of the flora was the loss of the co-dominant tree species in the southern Appalachians during the first half of this century. Most mature specimens of the American chestnut (*Castanea dentata* [Marshall]) were killed by the chestnut blight fungus (*Cryphonectria parasitica* [Murrill and Barr]), introduced from Asia in 1904. The chestnuts were replaced mostly by various species of oaks. Because of differences in processing rates of dead leaves among these tree species and resulting differences in insect growth rates, adult body mass, and fecundity, some evidence suggests that insect faunas in headwater streams in the southern Appalachians may have experienced subtle changes (Smock and MacGregor, 1988). Shredding detritivore species among the stoneflies and caddisflies and some other insect groups probably were especially affected.

Changes brought about by these activities, especially the heavy cutting adjacent to the streams that was common logging practice at the turn of the century, have reduced the amount of large woody debris currently in southern Appalachian streams. Because new stands regenerated in the cutover riparian zones, the sources of large woody debris (i.e., large, old trees) declined and will remain low for decades (Hedman, 1992; Hedman and Van Lear, 1994; Hedman et al., 1996). Opening of the canopies has allowed the increase of *Rhododendron* understory, which now outcompetes shoots of other species and which provides poor quality allochthonous input for macroinvertebrate shredders (D. H. Van Lear, Clemson University, pers. comm.).

With this historical background, what are the forces presently influencing the quality of stream habitats in the southern Appalachian Mountains? Streams in the otherwise well-protected Great Smoky Mountains National Park are threatened by acid precipitation. Both acid precipitation and outbreaks of forest pests (mostly foreign invaders) weaken and kill trees and other vegetation in the stream riparian zones (C. R. Parker, U.S. Department of the Interior, National Park Service, pers. comm.), reducing allochthonous nutrient inputs.

Agriculture in the region is often the primary nonpoint-source of sedimentation, pesticides, and excess nutrients. Sedimentation apparently causes most of the damage in stream systems, and effective erosion control practices can help prevent it (Lenat, 1984).

Trout farms are a serious concern. Because of their need for large amounts of cold water, they are usually built on outstanding resource waterways, often in a succession of private farms, each contributing a heavy load of organic nutrients.

Residential development, especially for tourism and retirement, is another major problem for stream biotas. Residential developments are generally in "the nicest places" (e.g., beside streams) and are generally associated with golf courses kept "pretty" with pesticides and fertilizers. Housing starts in the southern Appalachian Mountains of Georgia, North Carolina, South Carolina, and Tennessee declined somewhat in the late 1980s, probably because of downturns in the economy, from a high of 9,500 in 1984 to a low of 5,600 in 1990. With economic improvements we are likely to see a significant rise in housing starts, and with them associated declines in stream water quality.

Sedimentation problems associated with forestry operations are diminishing in the southern Appalachians. Clearcuts average only about ten ha (25 acres) in Appalachian national forests, covering much smaller tracts than in the Pacific Northwest for example. Cleared areas are occasionally burned of slash and replanted, and the roads and staging areas are seeded with grasses and legumes. The use of 30-160 m (98-525 foot) buffer strips (depending on the slope of the land) and other Best Management Practices, especially on logging roads and skid trails (which ordinarily provide about 90 percent of the forestry-associated sediment in streams), has significantly reduced the sediment input in national forest lands. However, much forest land is in private ownership, and in South Carolina, for example, landowners are accepting the South Carolina Forestry Commission (SCFC) Best Management Practices, albeit more slowly than such practices have been instituted on national forest lands (85 percent compliance in South Carolina in 1992) (D.H. Van Lear, Clemson University and T.O. Adams, SCFC, both pers. comm.).

Industrial effluent provides point sources of pollution that can harm streams. Reducing or stopping these problems is often complicated by legal, political, and economic circumstances, with regulators, private citizens, lawmakers, employers, and employees often at odds. The wheels are turning very slowly to rectify existing legal uncertainties associated with industrial effluent. For example, progress is being made to reduce damage caused by Champion Paper Company effluent into the Pigeon River in western North Carolina (D. R. Lenat, North Carolina Division of Environmental Management, pers. comm.).

IMPACTS ON MAYFLIES, DRAGONFLIES AND DAMSELFLIES, STONEFLIES, AND CADDISFLIES

What have been the impacts of human activity on the aquatic insects of the southern Appalachians? For the most part we do not know. As we indicated above, the most serious sedimentation problems in the region apparently occurred with deforestation during the early part of this century, before much was known about the biota of these streams. Apart from a few descriptions by Nathan Banks (stoneflies and caddisflies, mostly during 1905-1914; e.g., Banks 1905, 1914) and Traver (mayflies during 1932-1937; e.g., Needham et al., 1935; Traver, 1937), extensive studies of the aquatic insects of the region were undertaken by staff of the Illinois Natural History Survey in the 1930s, examining the region's mayflies (Burks, 1953), stoneflies (Frison, 1937, 1942), and caddisflies (e.g., Ross, 1938). However, faunistic and ecological knowledge was gathered in such a sporadic manner in those early years that few general statements can be made about modern changes in the stream biota. The work by Brigham et al. (1982) provided keys for all the southeastern genera and many of the southeastern species of aquatic insects and oligochaetes, along with discussions of their habits and life histories.

We consider 19 species of mayflies, seven species of dragonflies, 17 species of stoneflies, and 38 species of caddisflies to be probably rare and vulnerable to extirpation at present in the southern Appalachian Mountains (Tables 3-6). Because of taxonomic problems and the fact that some habitats, such as small streams and seeps, have been poorly explored, the included species should be understood as probable examples of the many rare and vulnerable species in the southern Appalachians rather than as members of definitive lists. The United States Fish and Wildlife Service (1994) cited one of these mayfly species, all seven of these dragonfly species, and ten of these caddisfly species in their Category 2 (now Federal Species of Concern), for which further information is needed in order to justify listing them as endangered or threatened. Whether these particular 81 species have always been rare or whether there were at one time other species that were then rare and now extinct cannot be determined. Some of these species have not been collected since the 1930s and 40s and may now be extirpated, such as the caddisfly *Agapetus vireo* Ross, and the stoneflies *Acroneuria arida* (Hagen) and *Amphinemura mockfordi* (Ricker). Furthermore, one dragonfly, *Ophiogomphus edmundo* Needham, is known only from two males collected in the late 1800s at some unknown location in North Carolina, and the distinctive mayfly *Isonychia diversa* Traver is known from only a single male taken in Knoxville, Tennessee, in 1916.

Many of these rare species are known from only one or a few locations with pea-size gravel or in springbrooks and seepage areas. Of course, species requiring pea-gravel are susceptible to sedimentation problems. For example, one of us (BPS) has observed the disappearance of the stoneflies *Malirekus hastatus* (Banks), *Yugus bulbosus* (Frison), and *Remenus bilobatus* (Needham and Claassen) from Scaly Creek, near the Scaly Mountain community in Macon County, North Carolina, where development of summer homes has greatly increased stream run-off and turbidity. In other locations, rock outcrop inhabitants such as the caddisfly *Pseudogoera singularis* Carpenter and *Heterocloeon* sp. mayflies have been observed (by JCM) as having disappeared as a result of clearcutting to the stream banks. Another riffle-dwelling mayfly species, *Serratella spiculosa* Berner and Allen, is listed by the U.S. Fish and Wildlife Service (1994) as not having been reported in 30 years. Drought, acid precipitation, or development may impair or eliminate the small "island" populations of the spring-habitat species such as *Ceratopsyche etnieri* (Schuster and Talak) and *Hydroptila decia* Etnier and Way. These two caddisfly species are among those listed in the United States Fish and Wildlife Service's (1994) Category 2. The stoneflies *Beloneuria georgiana* (Banks), *Megaleuctra williamsae* Hanson, and *Oconoperla innubila* (Needham and Claassen) are also vulnerable spring-inhabiting species. The stonefly *Zapada chila* (Ricker) may also be threatened by acid precipitation because its habitat is only at high elevations in the Appalachians.

RARE SPECIES ELSEWHERE IN THE SOUTHEAST

The freshwater habitats of the southeastern Piedmont, Coastal Plain, and Interior High-

Table 3. Rare and vulnerable Ephemeroptera of the southern Appalachian Mountains.

Family: Species	Species Notes
Baetidae:	
Barbaetis benfieldi Kennedy	— medium to large streams with pea-gravel and clean water.
Callibaetis pretiosus Banks	— rare in scattered southern localities, including mountain stream pools.
Heterocloeon petersi (Müller-Liebenau)	— only known from a few well-oxygenated southern Appalachian streams.
Procloeon quaesitum (McDunnough)	— mountain streams with pea-gravel substrate.
P. rivulare (Traver)	— requires very high water quality.
Ephemerellidae:	
Drunella longicornis Traver	— widespread, clean-water, riffle species.
D. waya Traver	— somewhat rare species on sand-gravel substrates with moderate current.
Ephemerella berneri Allen & Edmunds	— rare southeastern species with little known of its ecological requirements.
E. floripara McCafferty	— rare species in headwater streams 200-800 m elevation with mixture of stones and sand or bedrock and sand substrate and with moderate to somewhat stronger currents.
Serratella carolina Berner & Allen	— rare, southeastern riffle species.
S. spiculosa Berner & Allen	— "spiculose serratellan mayfly," rare, southeastern riffle species; Category 2 of U.S. Fish and Wildlife Service (1994), not reported since 1963.
Ephemeridae:	
Litobrancha recurvata (Morgan)	— mainly a northeastern species, somewhat rare in Southeast, requiring small, clean, cold-water streams with silt/marl substrate.
Heptageniidae:	
Iron subpallidus Traver, *Rhithrogena amica* Traver, *R. exelis* Traver, *R. fuscifrons* Traver, *R. rubicunda* Traver	— all relatively rare in streams with moderate to fast current and mixed substrate, feed on periphyton that require some open canopy; some may be synonyms of other species.
Stenonema carlsoni Lewis	— known only from streams with very high water quality.
Isonychiidae:	
Isonychia georgiae McDunnough	— rare in moderately large streams with a variety of stream conditions.

lands also are home to aquatic insects in peril. We recognize 11 species of mayflies, 17 species of dragonflies and damselflies, 17 species of stoneflies, and 28 species of caddisflies as being very rare, known from only one or a very few locations, and thus quite susceptible to extirpation (Tables 7-10).

Table 4. Rare and vulnerable Odonata of the southern Appalachian Mountains.

Family: Species	Species Notes
Gomphidae:	
Gomphus (*Stenogomphurus*) *consanguis* (Selys)	— "Cherokee clubtail," known from only 6 or 7 localities in very small populations in AL, GA, NC, TN, and VA; Category 2 of U.S. Fish and Wildlife Service (1994).
Gomphus (*Gomphus*) *parvidens* Currie	— known from only 8 or 9 localities in AL, GA, MD, NC, and VA; subspecies *G. p. carolinus* Carle, "sandhills clubtail," is known from about 7 localities in southeastern Piedmont and Sandhills in small populations and is in Category 2 of U.S. Fish and Wildlife Service (1994).
Gomphus (*Gomphurus*) *septima* Westfall	— "Septima's clubtail," known from only 4 or 5 localities; AL population has not been seen since about 1940; unpublished TN record is based on 1 male; there are only 1 or 2 well-established populations in NC; Category 2 of U.S. Fish and Wildlife Service (1994).
Ophiogomphus edmundo Needham	— "Edmund's snaketail," known from 2 males collected in late 1800s in NC; Category 2 of U.S. Fish and Wildlife Service (1994).
O. incurvatus alleghaniensis Carle	— "Alleghany snaketail," some questions exist regarding taxonomic status of this animal, some believing that it is a distinct species; few known populations are small, except for 1 healthy population in Smoky Mountains; adult stage is difficult to find; Category 2 of U.S. Fish and Wildlife Service (1994).
Stylurus townesi Gloyd	— "bronze clubtail," known from 4 localities; TN record is based on 1 male; the only large population is in northwestern FL; Category 2 of U.S. Fish and Wildlife Service (1994).
Macromiidae:	
Macromia margarita Westfall	— "Margarita river skimmer," known from only 6 or 7 localities, all known populations small; Category 2 of U.S. Fish and Wildlife Service (1994).

Table 5. Rare and vulnerable Plecoptera of the southern Appalachian Mountains.

Family: Species	Species Notes
Capniidae:	
Allocapnia brooksi Ross	— known from 2 streams in Hawkins and Sevier counties, TN.
A. fumosa Ross	— known from five streams at high elevations in Haywood County, NC; Sevier County, TN; and near Mt. Rogers, VA.
Leuctridae:	
Megaleuctra williamsae Hanson	— known from scattered localities around Great Smoky Mountains National Park, TN; and 1 locality each in NC, SC, and VA.
Nemouridae:	
Amphinemura mockfordi (Ricker)	— known from 2 localities at Monteagle, TN; last seen in 1938.
Zapada chila (Ricker)	— known from only a short stretch of 1 stream near Newfound Gap, TN.
Taeniopterygidae:	
Strophopteryx inaya Ricker & Ross	— known from 2 localities, 1 each in Jackson and McDowell counties, NC.
Taeniopteryx nelsoni Kondratieff & Kirchner	— known only from Mount Rogers area of VA.
Chloroperlidae:	
Sweltsa urticae (Ricker)	— until recently known from 1 locality in Great Smoky Mountains National Park and reported from VA without specific locality; Kondratieff (Colorado State University, pers. comm.) reports the species is quite common in spring seeps in Haywood and Macon counties, NC.
Peltoperlidae:	
Tallaperla elisa Stark	— known from 1 locality in Great Smoky Mountains National Park.
Perlidae:	
Acroneuria petersi Stark & Gaufin	— known from 1 locality in GA and 1 in Great Smoky Mountains National Park, TN.
A. arida (Hagen)	— reported from GA, NC, NJ, PA, and TN, but there are no recent GA, NC, or TN records; most records are from 1930s.
Beloneuria georgiana (Banks)	— fairly common in a restricted area of NC and GA, but at low densities; probably a top carnivore in small spring seepage areas.
B. stewarti Stark & Szczytko	— fairly common in low elevation seeps of GA, NC, SC, and TN, but at low densities.

Table 5. Continued.

Family: Species	Species Notes
Perlodidae:	
Diploperla morgani Kondratieff & Voshell	— known from several localities in southwestern VA and adjacent areas of WV and NC.
Isoperla bellona Banks	— known from Black Mountain, NC, and from GA, no recent sightings.
I. distincta Nelson	— known from 2 localities in TN and 1 in NC.
Oconoperla innubila (Needham & Claassen)	— known from 8 scattered spring seepage areas in NC, SC, and TN.

CONSTRAINTS ON KNOWLEDGE OF AQUATIC INSECT SYSTEMATICS AND BIOLOGY

Although we do not know the specific habitat requirements of most of these species, the probability that they are very limited in distribution suggests that some features of their environments are holding their populations in check, whether these features are anthropogenic or natural. Obviously, we do not know very much about the biology of rare aquatic insects in the Southeast, although there can be little doubt that many are in peril. Perhaps as much or more for the insects as for any other taxonomic group reported on in this volume, knowledge of the very existence of these tiny, cryptic, yet fascinating creatures, let alone their distribution, ecology, life history, and habitat requirements is sorely lacking. We are still finding new species every year in the Southeast, and commonly adding range extensions to species that have already been described. Part of the difficulty, of course, is their small size and cryptic habits. Insects change form dramatically during their development, and their species can be identified usually only in the adult form that lives for just a few hours to a few days each year. Furthermore, the taxonomy of aquatic insects usually relies heavily on characteristics possessed only by males of each species. Rearing and associating the females and the immature stages with their respective males is a very time-consuming task that is naturally lagging far behind the study of the systematics of the males. But it is those very studies that are needed in order to allow ecologists to investigate life histories and habitat requirements.

On top of all of the above, the incredible diversity of the entomofauna, representing about 85 percent of the plant and animal species of the world, makes for a very huge task for the practicing insect systematists, of whom there are fewer each year to provide scientific support for the growing interest in biodiversity protection. Unlike the situation associated with various macrobiota, most species of insects can be identified by only a handful of people in the world, each of whom are experts regarding only specific taxa. It is difficult for these experts to carry this workload alone. They need the support and encouragement of a much larger group of interested persons such as natural historians, conservationists, scientists, and other concerned citizens, all of whom depend on systematics research conclusions. Systematists need the political and financial support of the wider constituency to maintain collections of living and preserved biodiversity in research museums and at other

Table 6. Rare and vulnerable Trichoptera of the southern Appalachian Mountains.

Family: Species	Species Notes
Brachycentridae: *Brachycentrus etowahensis* Wallace	— reported from 4 medium sized rivers with scattered, sparse riverweed, *Podostemum ceratophyllum* Michaux in GA and TN.
Glossosomatidae: *Agapetus jocassee* Morse	— reported from only 2 adjacent headwater streams in NC and SC; Category 2 of U.S. Fish and Wildlife Service (1994).
A. vireo Ross	— known from only 2 small streams in TN and 1 in GA; not seen since 1955.
Protoptila cahabensis Harris	— "Cahaba saddle-case caddisfly," known only from upper reaches of Cahaba River, AL; Category 2 of U.S. Fish and Wildlife Service (1994).
Helicopsychidae: *Helicopsyche paralimnella* Hamilton	— known only from 2 adjacent, medium sized rivers in NC and SC; Category 2 of U.S. Fish and Wildlife Service (1994).
Hydropsychidae: *Ceratopsyche etnieri* (Schuster & Talak)	— "Buffalo Springs caddisfly," known only from a fairly constant temperature springbrook, about 1000 m below its spring source in Grainger County, TN, and from a stream in Smyth County, VA (B. C. Kondratieff, Colorado State University, pers. comm.); Category 2 of U.S. Fish and Wildlife Service (1994).
Cheumatopsyche bibbensis Gordon et al.	— known only from Cahaba River, AL.
C. cahaba Gordon et al.	— known only from headwaters of Cahaba River, AL.
Homoplectra flinti Weaver	— reported previously from only 2 intermittent spring seeps about 30 km apart above 1,200 m in NC, and from a stream in White County, TN; Kondratieff (loc. cit.) has collected adults from seeps in Jackson County, NC.
Oropsyche howellae Ross	— reported previously from only 2 localities in neighboring Jackson and Macon counties, NC; Kondratieff (loc. cit.) has collected adults from Haywood County, NC.
Hydroptilidae: *Hydroptila anisoforficata* Parker & Voshell	— reported from only 2 localities in VA.
H. cheaha Harris	— known from only Dry Creek, a small stream in Talladega County, AL.

Table 6. Continued.

Family: Species	Species Notes
H. decia Etnier & Way	— "Knoxville hydroptilan micro caddisfly," reported from only 2 small, clear, springfed streams with lush growths of watercress, *Nasturtium officianale*, in eastern TN; Category 2 of U.S. Fish and Wildlife Service (1994).
H. englishi Hamilton	— known from only 1 medium sized stream at NC/SC border; Category 2 of U.S. Fish and Wildlife Service (1994).
H. lagoi Harris	— known from 2 streams in Tuscaloosa County, AL; especially abundant in Big Sandy Creek just below a large spring; Category 2 of U.S. Fish and Wildlife Service (1994).
H. micropotamis Harris	— restricted to Little River, DeKalb County, northeastern AL.
H. setigera Harris	— known from only 1 specimen from a headwater stream in Calhoun County, AL.
H. talladega Harris	— known from 3 adjacent small and medium sized streams at NC/SC border and 2 small headwater streams in northeastern AL.
Stactobiella cahaba Harris	— known only from Schultz Creek, a tributary of Cahaba River, Bibb County, central AL; Category 2 of U.S. Fish and Wildlife Service (1994).
Lepidostomatidae: *Lepidostoma etnieri* Weaver	— known from 1 specimen found at a stream in Knoxville, TN; Category 2 of U.S. Fish and Wildlife Service (1994).
L. flinti Wallace & Sherberger	— reported from a few high altitude spring locations in NC and SC.
L. glenni Wallace & Sherberger	— reported from only 2 small spring-fed streams in Union County, GA.
L. lobatum Wallace & Sherberger	— reported from 3 small spring-fed streams in Macon County, NC, and Union County, GA.
L. mitchelli Flint & Wiggins	— known from springs at 3 locations in NC above 1,350 m elevation.
Leptoceridae: *Ceraclea alabamae* Harris	— restricted to Little River and its tributaries, De Kalb County, northeastern AL.
Limnephilidae: *Manophylax altus* (Huryn & Wallace)	— larvae and pupae found only on vertical rock faces over which flows a minimal film of water (madicolous or hygropetric habitat) for at least part of the year on Mt. Mitchell (1,800 m elevation), NC, and possibly near Cranberry Glades (823 m elevation), WV.

Table 6. Continued.

Family: Species	Species Notes
Philopotamidae:	
Dolophilodes sisko (Ross)	— reported specifically for a small stream in Macon County, NC; 2 other published reports for NC and SC do not provide specific locations.
Wormaldia mohri (Ross)	— known from only a few specimens captured at Smokemont, NC, and Little Pigeon River, Gatlinburg, TN, Great Smoky Mountains National Park, in 1940 and 1944.
W. oconee Morse	— known from only 2 adjacent streams in Oconee County, SC, near NC border; Category 2 of U.S. Fish and Wildlife Service (1994).
Rhyacophilidae:	
Rhyacophila accola Flint	— previously reported from only Smokemont Campground, Great Smoky Mountains National Park, NC; Kondratieff (loc. cit.) has found it outside the Park in a small stream in Haywood County, NC, and by springs in Shining Rock Wilderness Area, NC.
R. amicis Ross	— reported as rare from 3 locations in Henderson, Swain, and Transylvania counties, NC.
R. montana Carpenter	— originally seen at Newfound Gap, TN, and Bryson City, NC, in 1930, recently rediscovered in several other locations by C. R. Parker (National Biological Service, pers. comm.) in small, cold, high elevation seeps with *Theliopsyche* spp. (Lepidostomatidae).
R. mycta Ross	— reported previously from only 3 locations above 1,300 m in NC; recently seen by Parker (loc. cit) from 2 locations, one in Smoky Mountains and one in the Blue Ridge.
Uenoidae:	
Neophylax auris Vineyard & Wiggins	— reported from 3 locations in Clairborne, Blount, and Anderson counties, TN in springs and small streams.
N. etnieri Vineyard & Wiggins	— found in small, cool streams and spring runs in Clairborne and Knox counties, TN.
N. mitchelli Carpenter	— seen in a few mountain stream locations in NC and SC; recent larval collections by Parker (loc. cit.) suggest that this species may be more common.
N. stolus Ross	— known from only 2 locations along Middle Fork South Branch Potomac River in adjoining counties of VA and WV.
N. toshioi Vineyard & Wiggins	— reported from only Reed Creek, Wythe County, VA, a broad, shallow, warm stream with a bed of rocks and fine sediments; larvae on large rocks.

Table 7. Rare and vulnerable Ephemeroptera of the southeastern Piedmont, Coastal Plain, and Interior Highlands.

Family: Species	Species Notes
Acanthametropodidae: *Acanthametropus pecatonica* (Burks)	— "Pecatonica River mayfly," Coastal Plains province in central and eastern GA and southwestern SC; a fast swimming predator restricted to shifting sand substrates; Category 2 of U.S. Fish and Wildlife Service (1994).
Baetidae: *Apobaetis etowah* (Traver)	— Valley and Ridge province in extreme northwestern GA; unknown as larvae.
Baetis ochris Burks	— Ozark and Ouachita mountains of AR; fairly common in Midwest, but known from only a couple of adults in Southeast; unknown as larvae.
Behningiidae: *Dolania americana* Edmunds & Traver	— "American sandburrowing mayfly," rare, localized in Coastal Plain streams with clean, shifting sand; Category 2 of U.S. Fish and Wildlife Service (1994).
Heptageniidae: *Anepeorus simplex* (Walsh)	— Coastal Plains province in central GA; generally from larger sandy rivers at considerable depths where little else is known to live.
Stenonema sinclairi Lewis	— Appalachian Plateaus province in southeast central TN; restricted to very clean, small, soft-water streams with mixed substrate on sandstone bedrock.
Leptophlebiidae: *Paraleptophlebia georgiana* Traver	— Valley and Ridge province in north central GA; larva unknown.
P. jeanae Berner	— East Gulf Coastal Plains province in central AL; larva unknown.
Ephemerellidae: *Dannella provonshai* McCafferty	— Ozark Mountains of western AR; known only from type locality; larvae occur in a clean, medium sized stream in moderate erosional currents among filamentous algal growth.
Serratella frisoni McDunnough	— "Frison's serratellan mayfly," limited in Southeast to Interim Low Plateaus province in northwestern AL; somewhat common in Midwest, but its ecology is unknown; Category 2 of U.S. Fish & Wildlife Service (1994).

Table 7. Continued.

Family: Species	Species Notes
Tricorythidae:	
Leptohyphes robacki Allen	— Coastal Plains province in eastern GA and southwestern SC from the Savannah River, but no other data are available.
Tricorythodes texanus Traver	— East Gulf Coastal Plains province in south-central MS; larvae unknown.

institutions such as large zoos and aquariums. Support is also needed for the research by which these scientists make biodiversity known to all of us. Working together we should be able to slow the demise of the many species great and small that still share with us our southeastern waters.

Table 8. Rare and vulnerable Odonata of the southeastern Piedmont and Coastal Plain.

Family: Species	Species Notes
Gomphidae:	
Arigomphus maxwelli Ferguson	— known from AL, AR, IL, LA, MS, TN, TX.
Dromogomphus armatus Selys	— known from AL, FL, GA, SC.
Gomphus diminutus Needham	— known from NC, SC.
G. hodgesi Needham	— known from AL, FL, LA, MS.
G. sandrius Tennessen	— "Tennessee clubtail," known from Bedford, Marshall, and Maury counties, TN; Category 2 of U.S. Fish and Wildlife Service (1994).
G. modestus Needham	— known from AL, AR, LA, MS, TX.
Ophiogomphus australis Carle	— known from LA, MS.
O. acuminatus Carle	— known from AL, TN.
O. howei Bromley	— "midget snaketail," known from KY, MA, ME, MN, NC, NY, PA, TN, VA, WI; Category 2 of U.S. Fish and Wildlife Service (1994).
O. westfalli Cooke & Daigle	— "Ozark snaketail," known from AR, MO; Category 2 of U.S. Fish and Wildlife Service (1994).
Progomphus bellei Knopf & Tennessen	— "variegated clubtail," known from AL, FL, NC; Category 2 of U.S. Fish and Wildlife Service (1994).
Stylurus notatus Rambur	— not reported from Southeast in past 80 years, but recently recorded in Midwest.
S. potulentus (Needham)	— known from FL, MS.
Cordulegastridae:	
Cordulegaster sayi Selys	— known from FL, GA.
Corduliidae:	
Somatochlora georgiana Walker	— known from AL, FL, MS, NC.
S. ozarkensis Bird	— known from AR.
Libellulidae:	
Libellula jesseana Williamson	— known from FL; a lentic species.
Coenagrionidae:	
Nehalennia pallidula Calvert	— known from southern tip of FL; a lentic species.
Lestidae:	
Lestes spumarius Hagen	— known from southern tip of FL; a lentic species.

Table 9. Rare and vulnerable Plecoptera of the southeastern Piedmont and Coastal Plain.

Family: Species	Species Notes
Capniidae:	
Allocapnia perplexa Ross & Ricker	— known from 5 specimens and 1 locality in Trousdale County, TN.
A. polemistis Ross & Ricker	— known from 4 localities in northwestern AL.
A. tennessa Ross & Yamamoto	— known from 4 localities along the eastern edge of Cumberland Plateau in TN.
Leuctridae:	
Leuctra alabama James	— known from 1 locality in Jackson County, AL.
L. alta James	— known from 2 localities in Calhoun and Tuscaloosa counties, AL.
L. cottaquilla James	— known from 1 locality each in AL, FL, and MS.
L. crossi James	— known from 1 locality in Calhoun County, AL.
L. szczytkoi Stark & Stewart	— known from 1 locality in LA.
Taeniopterygidae:	
Taeniopteryx robinae Kondratieff & Kirchner	— known from 1 stream in Barnwell County, SC.
Chloroperlidae:	
Alloperla furcula Surdick	— known from 3 localities in South AL and the Savannah River Site, SC.
A. natchez Surdick & Stark	— known from several sites in southwestern MS.
Perlidae:	
Beloneuria jamesae Stark & Szczytko	— known from 2 sites near Cheaha Mountain, AL.
Neoperla harrisi Stark & Lentz	— known from 3 localities in northwestern AL.
Perlesta lagoi Stark	— known from 4 locations in MS.
Perlodidae:	
Hydroperla phormidia Ray & Stark	— known from 3 streams in northwestern FL and from Savannah River of GA/SC.

Table 10. Rare and vulnerable Trichoptera of the southeastern Piedmont and Coastal Plain.

Family: Species	Species Notes
Dipseudopsidae:	
Phylocentropus harrisi Schuster & Hamilton	— recorded from only 2 small Coastal Plain streams in Southern Pine Hills of AL.
Glossosomatidae:	
Agapetus alabamensis Harris	— known from only 2 small intermittent streams of Cumberland Plateau in AL.
A. diacanthus Edwards	— reported once from Cumberland Plateau of TN, its specific habitat is unknown.
A. spinosus Etnier & Way	— known from only 5 locations on Cumberland Plateau in AL and TN from both large and small streams.
Protoptila georgiana Denning	— reported from AL, GA, and VA; this rarely encountered Piedmont species is known from large, fast-flowing streams.
Lepidostomatidae:	
Lepidostoma compressum Etnier & Way	— known from only 3 specimens taken at University of Tennessee Cumberland Plateau Research and Education Center.
L. weaveri Harris	— reported from 2 small, spring-fed, intermittent streams at southern edge of Cumberland Plateau in AL.
Theliopsyche tallapoosa Harris	— only 3 specimens collected once beside a swift, rocky bottomed Piedmont stream 6 m wide in AL; Category 2 of U.S. Fish and Wildlife Service (1994).
Hydropsychidae:	
Cheumatopsyche kinlockensis Gordon et al.	— known only from type locality, a small stream on Cumberland Plateau in Bankhead National Forest, AL.
C. richardsoni Gordon	— known only from Upper Three Runs Creek, Savannah River Site, downstream of southern Aiken, SC; presently one of the most common species in this vulnerable stream.
Hydropsyche alabama Lago & Harris	— only known from Cowarts Creek, a small, sand bottomed stream of Coastal Plain southern AL.
H. catawba Ross	— rarely collected species of Piedmont region from Savannah River basin to VA in small to medium-sized streams.
H. patera Schuster & Etnier	— known only from type locality, Harpath River in Nashville Basin, central TN.
H. rotosa Ross	— rare in AL, TN, and VA in upland streams.
Hydroptilidae:	
Hydroptila coweetensis Huryn	— reported from 3 small tributaries in higher elevations of AL and NC.

Table 10. Continued.

Family: Species	Species Notes
H. fuscina Harris	— restricted in distribution to 3 known streams of Cumberland Plateau and Highland Rim in AL.
H. metteei Harris	— known from 2 small streams in Coastal Plain of southern AL.
H. scheiringi Harris	— reported from 3 steams in Southern Pine Hills region of Coastal Plain in southern AL.
H. wetumpka Harris	— known only from a small, rocky Piedmont stream in AL.
Neotrichia sepulga Harris	— known only from a small tributary of Sepulga River in Coastal Plain of AL.
Ochrotrichia elongiralla Harris	— recorded only from type locality, a small, gravel bottomed stream in upper Cumberland Plateau in AL; Category 2 of U.S. Fish and Wildlife Service (1994).
O. weoka Harris	— reported only from type locality, a small, rocky Piedmont stream in AL.
Polycentropodidae: *Polycentropus carlsoni* Morse	— "Carlson's *Polycentropus* caddisfly," Category 2 of U.S. Fish and Wildlife Service (1994); known from only 2 nearby first order stream localities in Upper Piedmont of SC and from 2 nearby first order streams in the Upper Piedmont of AL.
P. rickeri Yamamoto	— known from 3 records from small upland streams in AL, TN, and VA.
Rhyacophilidae: *Rhyacophila alabama* Harris	— single known population occurs in a small, intermittent tributary in Paint Rock River system of northern AL.
R. carolae Harris	— known from only 2 specimens collected from a tributary of Bee Branch in Bankhead National Forest of AL.
Sericostomatidae: *Agarodes alabamensis* Harris	— known from only 2 specimens collected at type locality, a small, sandy-bottomed stream in Lime Hills of AL Coastal Plain; Category 2 of U.S. Fish and Wildlife Service (1994).
Uenoidae: *Neophylax securis* Vineyard & Wiggins	— reported from 3 widely separated, small, headwater streams on Cumberland Plateau of AL and TN.

ACKNOWLEDGEMENTS

This text is moderately revised from a paper by Morse et al. (1993). This revised version is published here with the permission of John Wiley and Sons, Ltd., and we thank them. We are grateful to Mrs. A. H. Hyder (Clemson University) for data on housing permits in the southern Appalachian Mountains. Dr. C. R. Parker (U.S. Department of Interior, National Park Service) and Dr. B. C. Kondratieff (Colorado State University) provided new collection records of several rare species. Dr. Parker, Dr. D. H. Van Lear (Clemson University), Dr. T. O. Adams (South Carolina Forestry Commission), and Mr. D. R. Lenat (North Carolina Division of Environmental Management) kindly reviewed the earlier manuscript and provided many useful insights. Mr. J. Sistare graciously assisted the senior author in reaching the venue for the symposium in Chattanooga wherein this paper was presented.

This chapter is Technical Contribution No. 4057 of the South Carolina Agricultural Experiment Station, Clemson University.

REFERENCES

Allan, J. D. 1983. Predator-prey relationships in streams. In *Stream Ecology.* J. R. Barnes, and G. W. Minshall (eds.). Plenum Press, New York, NY, p. 191-229.

Banks, N. 1905. Descriptions of new species of Nearctic neuropteroid insects from the Black Mountains, N.C. *Bulletin of the American Museum of Natural History* 21:215-218.

Banks, N. 1914. American Trichoptera — notes and descriptions. *Canadian Entomologist* 46:149-156, 201-205, 252-258, 261-268, plates 9, 10, 15, 20.

Bray, J. R., and E. Gorham. 1964. Litter production in forests of the world. *Advances in Ecological Research* 2:101-157.

Brigham, A. R., W. U. Brigham, and A. Gnilka (eds.). 1982. *Aquatic Insects and Oligochaetes of North and South Carolina.* Midwest Aquatic Enterprises, Mahomet, IL.

Burks, B. D. 1953. The mayflies or Ephemeroptera of Illinois. *Illinois Natural History Survey Bulletin* 26(1):1-216.

Frison, T. H. 1937. Studies of Nearctic aquatic insects: Descriptions of Plecoptera. *Illinois Natural History Survey Bulletin* 21:78-99.

Frison, T. H. 1942. Studies of North American Plecoptera, with special reference to the fauna of Illinois. *Illinois Natural History Survey Bulletin* 22:235-355.

Hackney, C. T., and S. M. Adams. 1992. Aquatic communities of the southeastern United States: Past, present, and future. In *Biodiversity of the Southeastern United States: Aquatic Communities.* C. T. Hackney, S. M. Adams, and W. H. Martin (eds.). John Wiley and Sons, Inc., New York, NY, p. 747-760.

Hamilton, S. W., and J. C. Morse. 1990. Southeastern caddisfly fauna: Origins and affinities. *Florida Entomologist* 73(4):587-600.

Hedman, C. W. 1992. Southern Appalachian Riparian Zones: Their Vegetative Composition and Contributions of Large Woody Debris to Streams. Ph.D. dissertation, Clemson University, Clemson, SC.

Hedman, C. W., and D. H. Van Lear. 1994. Large woody debris loading patterns in southern Appalachian streams. In *Riparian Ecosystems in the Humid U.S: Functions, Values, and Management.* R. Lowrance (ed.). National Association of Conservation Districts, Washington, D.C., p. 240-244.

Hedman, C. W., D. H. Van Lear, and W. T. Swank. 1996. In-stream large woody debris loading and riparian forest seral stage associations in the southern Appalachian Mountains. *Canadian Journal of Forest Research* 26:1218-1227.

Holt, P. C., R. L. Hoffman, and C. W. Hart, Jr. (eds.). 1969. *The Distributional History of the Biota of the Southern Appalachians, I: Invertebrates.* Research Division Monographs 1, Virginia Polytechnic Institute and State University, Blacksburg, VA.

Hornick, L. E., J. R. Webster, and E. F. Benfield. 1981. Periphyton production in an Appalachian Mountain trout stream. *American Midland Naturalist* 106:22-36.

Hudson, P. L., J. C. Morse, and J. R. Voshell, Jr. 1981. Larva and pupa of *Cernotina spicata. Annals of the Entomological Society of America* 74:516-519.

Hughes, J. D. 1983. *American Indian Ecology.* Texas Western Press, University of Texas, El Paso, TX.

Isphording, W. C., and J. F. Fitzpatrick, Jr. 1992. Geologic and evolutionary history of drainage systems in the southeastern United States. In *Biodiversity of the Southeastern United States: Aquatic Communities.* C. T. Hackney, S. M. Adams, and W. H. Martin (eds.). John Wiley and Sons, Inc., New York, NY, p. 19-56.

Lenat, D. R. 1984. Agriculture and stream water quality: A biological evaluation of erosion control practices. *Environmental Management* **8**:333-344.

Meade, R. H. 1976. Sediment problems in the Savannah River basin. In *The Future of the Savannah River.* B. L. Dillman, and J. M. Stepp (eds.). Clemson University Water Resources Research Institute, Clemson, SC, p. 105-129.

Menzel, R. G., and C. M. Cooper. 1992. Small impoundments and ponds. In *Biodiversity of the Southeastern United States: Aquatic Communities.* C. T. Hackney, S. M. Adams, and W. H. Martin (eds.). John Wiley and Sons, Inc., New York, NY, p. 389-420.

Morse, J. C. 1993. A checklist of the Trichoptera of North America, including Greenland and Mexico. *Transactions of the American Entomological Society* **119**(1):47-93.

Morse, J. C., B. P. Stark, and W. P. McCafferty. 1993. Southern Appalachian streams at risk: Implications for mayflies, stoneflies, caddisflies, and other aquatic biota. *Aquatic Conservation: Marine and Freshwater Ecosystems* **3**:293-303.

Needham, J. G., J. R. Traver, and Y. C. Hsu. 1935. *The Biology of Mayflies, with a Systematic Account of North American Species.* Comstock, Ithaca, NY, p. 615.

Peckarsky, B. L. 1983. Biotic interaction or abiotic limitations? A model of lotic community structure. In *Dynamics of Lotic Ecosystems.* T. D. Fontaine, and S. M. Bartell (eds.). Ann Arbor Science, Ann Arbor, MI, p. 303-324.

Ross, H. H. 1938. Descriptions of Nearctic caddis flies. *Illinois Natural History Survey Bulletin* **21**:(4):101-183.

Ross, H. H., and W. E. Ricker. 1971. The classification, evolution, and dispersal of the winter stonefly genus *Allocapnia. Biological Monographs of the University of Illinois* **45**:1-166.

Smock, L. A., and C. M. MacGregor. 1988. Impact of the American chestnut blight on aquatic shredding macroinvertebrates. *Journal of the North American Benthological Society* **7**:212-221.

Soballe, D. M., B. L. Kimmel, R. H. Kennedy, and R. F. Gaugush. 1992. Reservoirs. In *Biodiversity of the Southeastern United States: Aquatic Communities.* C. T. Hackney, S. M. Adams, and W. H. Martin (eds.). John Wiley and Sons, Inc., New York, NY, p. 421-474.

Traver, J. R. 1937. Notes on mayflies of the southeastern states (Ephemeroptera). *Journal of the Elisha Mitchell Scientific Society* **53**:27-86.

Trimble, S. W. 1975. A volumetric estimate of man-induced soil erosion on the southern Piedmont Plateau. In *Agricultural Research Service, Present and Prospective Technology for Predicting Sediment Yields and Sources.* ARS-S-40, Agricultural Research Service, Southern Region, U.S. Department of Agriculture, Washington, D.C., p. 142-154.

U. S. Fish and Wildlife Service. 1994. Endangered and threatened wildlife and plants; animal candidate review for listing as endangered or threatened species: proposed rule. Federal Register, part IV U.S. Department of the Interior 50 CFR part 17, 59(219):58982-59028.

Wallace, J. B., J. R. Webster, and R. L. Lowe. 1992. High gradient streams of the Appalachians. In *Biodiversity of the Southeastern United States: Aquatic Communities.* C. T. Hackney, S. M. Adams, and W. H. Martin (eds.). John Wiley and Sons, Inc., New York, NY, p. 133-191.

Webster, J. R., M. E. Gurtz, J. J. Hains, J. L. Meyer, W. T. Swank, J. B. Waide, and J. B. Wallace. 1983. Stability of stream ecosystems. In *Stream Ecology.* J. R. Barnes, and G. W. Minshall (eds.). Plenum Press, New York, NY, p. 355-395.

CHAPTER 3

Status of Aquatic Mollusks in the Southeastern United States: A Downward Spiral of Diversity

Richard J. Neves, Arthur E. Bogan, James D. Williams,
Steven A. Ahlstedt, and Paul W. Hartfield

Aquatic mollusks in the southeastern United States reside in a wide variety of permanent and seasonal aquatic habitats, and the diversity of bivalves and gastropods in the Southeast is globally unparalleled. Aquatic mollusks are distributed throughout the many tributaries of major rivers in the Interior Basin that drain various physiographic provinces along the South Atlantic and Gulf Coasts. Rivers of the southern Interior Basin, and of the Coastal Plain, originate in or traverse through several physiographic provinces: Appalachian Highlands, Ridge and Valley, Blue Ridge, Piedmont Plateau, Cumberland Plateau, and Coastal Plain. Regional and historical differences in physiography, geology, water chemistry, and other stream characteristics have resulted in distinct faunal assemblages and considerable endemism within river basins. Heard (1970) attributed striking differences in the southeastern freshwater molluscan fauna to assemblages adapted to specific lotic conditions (small streams vs. large rivers) and to locales

Aquatic Fauna in Peril: The Southeastern Perspective, edited by George W. Benz, and David E. Collins. 1997. Special Publication 1, Southeast Aquatic Research Institute, Lenz Design and Communications, Decatur, GA, 554 p.

with differences in specific environmental conditions (substratum, food availability, etc.). Riverine ecosystems may account for the highest diversity of freshwater mollusks because they are more permanent in an evolutionary time scale than lakes or other freshwater environments. They also contain a greater heterogeneity of physico-chemical characteristics and biological niches for aquatic organisms to adapt to and evolve with — from small headwater streams with swift current and allochthonous energy contributions to large coastal plain rivers with slow flow and autochthonous production.

A plethora of natural and anthropogenic factors have influenced the current distribution of freshwater mollusk species. However, differentiating between these factors is difficult without sufficient historic surveys and collection records to support conclusions. Extensive biological inventories were never conducted in most Southeast aquatic ecosystems. Therefore, the degree of aquatic faunal losses is unknown (Schindler, 1989). Because freshwater mollusks have never been a faunal group of great interest to federal and state natural resource agencies, much historic knowledge is derived from the collections and writings of early naturalists who traveled the eastern United States, in search of new animals and environments. Unfortunately, the early taxonomy and systematics of freshwater mollusks were based principally on shell characteristics that vary within and between rivers. As a result, an abundance of nominal species was described in the 19th century (Rafinesque, 1820, 1831; Lea, 1834-1874). Only in the 20th century has a concerted effort been made to evaluate early descriptions, identify synonymies, and compile a more accurate list of resident mollusk species in the rivers of the United States. For purposes of this chapter, we adopt the nomenclature of Turgeon et al. (1988).

Species richness of freshwater mollusks in the United States consists of more than 850 species in three taxonomic groups (Table 1). Snails are the most diverse taxon, accounting for 60 percent of all mollusk species. When this species richness is assessed from a regional perspective, it is readily apparent that the "rain forest" of mollusk diversity is in the southeastern United States. Based on Turgeon et al. (1988) and taxonomic keys and distribution records, we calculate that 91 percent of the mussels, 53 percent of the fingernail clams, and 61 percent of the snails in the United States occur in one or more states of the Southeast (Table 1). It is important to acknowledge that new species of freshwater mollusks continue to be described (Thompson and Hershler, 1991; Bogan and Hoeh, 1994), because sampling in localized habitats and new genetic techniques provide more decisive data and tools to help indicate the phylogenies and origins of mollusks in the Southeast. These tallies of species richness, especially for the mussels and snails, will undoubtedly increase.

Much knowledge of affinities among mollusk assemblages in rivers is derived from studies of freshwater mussels (Unionoidea). Unionids offer three advantages for zoogeographic study: they are relatively sedentary, reasonable numbers of species are readily distinguishable, and generic affinities have been fairly well defined (Burch, 1973). The dispersal ability of mussels is restricted principally to the glochidial stage and the mobility of their host fish species. Freshwater fishes are generally confined to specific river drainages and can migrate between adjacent river basins only after physiographic changes to the landscape, such as stream captures or base leveling during glacial events. For these reasons, mussel distributions seem to be excellent indicators of physiographic change between adjacent river systems through geologic time. Molluscan faunal zones have been defined by their distinctive mussel and snail assemblages — sharing various numbers of species with

TABLE 1. Species richness of freshwater mollusks in the southeastern United States.

Taxonomic Group	Number of U.S. Species	Number of Species in Southeast [1]
Mussels	297	269 (91)
Fingernail Clams	38	20 (53)
Snails	516	313 (61)

[1] Percent of U.S. species in parentheses.

other rivers according to drainage modification, isolation, confluence, stream capture, and other phenomena from regional or global events such as glaciation and sea level changes. The direct and indirect effects of these events on local biota and ecology have shaped distinctive communities with traceable phylogenies. For example, mussels have provided convincing evidence of major stream confluences (van der Schalie, 1945). Historic connections between the Apalachicola and Savannah rivers are suggested by their mollusk assemblages. Suffice it to say that lengthy discussions of zoogeography and zonation of aquatic fauna in the Southeast have been made possible by the distribution patterns of mollusks (van der Schalie and van der Schalie, 1950; Johnson, 1970, 1980; Hocutt and Wiley, 1986).

Because few extensive or intensive historic surveys were conducted on southeastern freshwater mollusk taxa, except for perhaps freshwater mussels, it is not possible to document the many changes in diversity, abundance, and distribution that have occurred in the last 100 years. Therefore, we are unable to describe the extent of decline of many mollusk groups throughout the Southeast. Our approach here is to select river systems with historic and recent collection records to serve as case studies for mollusks, principally freshwater mussels and river snails. These are the most diverse families of mollusks in the Southeast, and they are suitable indicators of change to their communities and environments. Other families of bivalves (fingernail clams: Sphaeriidae) and gastropods (e.g., freshwater limpets: Ancylidae) have been too poorly surveyed or sampled to provide an assessment of species stability or decline. Hopefully the results of this paper will stimulate interest in determining the status of other families and genera of mollusks in this region. There is still much to be done in the taxonomy, biology, and ecology of freshwater mollusks so that appropriate conservation efforts can be directed to those taxa or habitats in need of protection or recovery.

FRESHWATER BIVALVES

Freshwater mussels of the families Unionidae and Margaritiferidae are the best studied group of freshwater mollusks in the United States, with adequate historic and recent collection records to document changes in distribution and abundance of many species. Of the 297 species and subspecies currently recognized (Turgeon et al., 1988), 269 species had historic ranges that overlapped the political boundaries of one or more states of the Southeast. Species richness varies among southeastern states, ranging from an historic high of 175 species in Alabama to 33 species in South Carolina (Figure 1). These totals were compiled principally during the early 20th century and have changed drastically during the last 70 years.

Figure 1. Number of freshwater mussel species in the eleven southeastern states.

The Endangered Species Act of 1973 and subsequent amendments provided the legal means for recognition of rare mollusks that deserve federal protection. In June 1976, 23 species of freshwater mussels were designated as endangered. Because of internal priorities in the U.S. Fish and Wildlife Service and because of the overwhelming number of vertebrate and invertebrate species deserving of consideration under the Act, no additional species of mussels were listed until 1988 (Figure 2). Since then, a profound increase in listings has reflected the recognition of serious declines in freshwater bivalves by field biologists of the U.S. Fish and Wildlife Service, particularly in the Southeast. As of January 1995, 56 mussel species are federally listed as endangered or threatened in the United

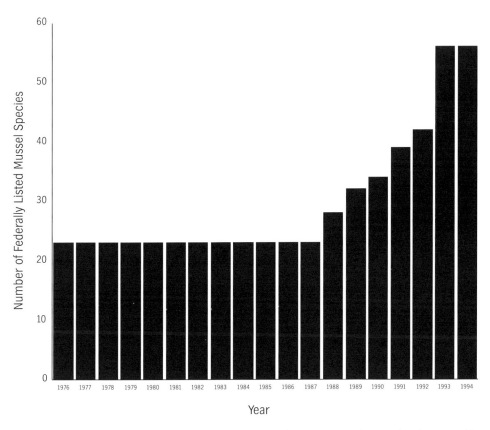

Figure 2. Chronology of the listing of freshwater mussel species as endangered or threatened in the United States.

States. Except for the Curtis pearlymussel (*Epioblasma florentina curtisi*) in Missouri and the white catspaw (*E. obliquata perobliqua*) in Indiana, Michigan, and Ohio, the 53 other listed species were known historically from one or more states in the Southeast (Table 2). In addition to these protected species, federal biologists identified 51 candidate species of mussels awaiting evaluation for possible listing (Table 3), all of which occur in southeastern states. Thus, more than 34 percent of all mussel species nationwide are in varying degrees of rarity, and 98 percent of these rare species occur in the Southeast.

A recent status review of the mussel fauna in the entire United States revealed significant nationwide declines (Williams et al., 1993). Many mussel species are more depleted than federal lists indicate. In the southeastern states, between 34 percent and 71 percent of the species or populations of species are imperiled, defined here to include endangered, threatened, or of special concern species (Table 4). In spite of the large differences in diversity of mussels among states, the decline of species is ubiquitous in coastal and in Interior Basin rivers. States in the Tennessee River Basin such as Alabama, Tennessee, and Virginia have the highest percentages of imperiled species, whereas coastal states with lower species richness have lower percentages of imperiled species. Best available data indicate that mussel species in the Tennessee River Basin, which includes portions of seven states in the South-

TABLE 2. Species of freshwater mussels and snails federally designated as endangered or threatened in the southeastern United States in 1994.

Scientific Name	Common Name	Historic Range	Status
Mussels:			
Alasmidonta heterodon (Lea, 1829)	dwarf wedgemussel	CT, DC, DE, MA, MD, NC, NH, PA, VT, VA	E
Arkansia wheeleri (Ortmann and Walker, 1912)	Ouachita rock pocketbook	AR, OK	E
Cyprogenia stegaria (Rafinesque, 1820)	fanshell	AL, IL, IN, KY, OH, PA, TN, VA, WV	E
Dromus dromas (Lea, 1834)	dromedary pearlymussel	AL, KY, TN, VA	E
Elliptio steinstansana (Johnson and Clarke, 1983)	Tar spinymussel	NC	E
Epioblasma florentina florentina (Lea, 1857)	yellow blossom	AL, TN	E
E. f. walkeri (Wilson and Clark, 1914)	tan riffleshell	KY, TN, VA	E
E. metastriata (Conrad, 1840)	upland combshell	AL, GA, TN	E
E. obliquata obliquata (Rafinesque, 1820)	catspaw	AL, IL, IN, KY, OH, TN	E
E. othcaloogensis (Lea, 1857)	southern acornshell	AL, GA, TN	E
E. penita (Conrad, 1834)	southern combshell	AL, MS	E
E. torulosa gubernaculum (Reeve, 1865)	green blossom	TN, VA	E
E. t. rangiana (Lea, 1839)	northern riffleshell	IL, IN, KY, MI, OH, PA, WV	E
E. t. torulosa (Rafinesque, 1820)	tubercled blossom	IL, IN, KY, TN, WV	E
E. turgidula (Lea,1858)	turgid blossom	AL, TN	E
Fusconaia cor (Conrad, 1834)	shiny pigtoe	AL, TN, VA	E
F. cuneolus (Lea, 1840)	fine-rayed pigtoe	AL, TN, VA	E
Hemistena lata (Rafinesque, 1820)	cracking pearlymussel	AL, IL, IN, KY, OH, TN, VA	E
Lampsilis abrupta (Say, 1831)	pink mucket	AL, IL, IN, KY, MO, OH, PA, TN, VA, WV	E
L. altilis (Conrad, 1834)	fine-lined pocketbook	AL, GA	E
L. perovalis (Conrad, 1834)	orange-nacre mucket	AL, MS	E
L. powelli (Lea, 1852)	Arkansas fatmucket	AR	T
L. streckeri (Frierson, 1927)	speckled pocketbook	AR	T
L. virescens (Lea, 1858)	Alabama lampmussel	AL, TN	E
Lasmigona decorata (Lea, 1852)	Carolina heelsplitter	NC, SC	E
Lemiox rimosus (Rafinesque, 1820)	birdwing pearlymussel	AL, TN, VA	E
Margaritifera hembeli (Conrad, 1838)	Louisiana pearlshell	LA	T
Medionidus acutissimus (Lea, 1831)	Alabama moccasinshell	AL, GA, MS	T
M. parvulus (Lea, 1860)	Coosa moccasinshell	AL, GA, TN	E

TABLE 2. Continued.

Scientific Name	Common Name	Historic Range	Status
Obovaria retusa (Lamarck, 1819)	ring pink	AL, IL, IN, KY, OH, PA, TN, WV	E
Pegias fabula (Lea, 1838)	little-wing pearlymussel	AL, KY, NC, TN, VA	E
Plethobasus cicatricosus (Say, 1829)	white wartyback	AL, IN, TN	E
P. cooperianus (Lea, 1834)	orange-foot pimpleback	AL, IN, IA, KY, OH, PA, TN	E
Pleurobema clava (Lamarck, 1819)	clubshell	AL, IL, IN, KY, MI, OH, PA, TN, WV	E
P. collina (Conrad, 1837)	James spinymussel	VA, WV	E
P. curtum (Lea, 1859)	black clubshell	AL, MS	E
P. decisum (Lea, 1831)	southern clubshell	AL, GA, MS, TN	E
P. furvum (Conrad, 1834)	dark pigtoe	AL	E
P. georgianum (Lea, 1841)	southern pigtoe	AL, GA, TN	E
P. gibberum (Lea, 1838)	Cumberland pigtoe	TN	E
P. marshalli (Frierson, 1927)	flat pigtoe	AL, MS	E
P. perovatum (Conrad, 1834)	ovate clubshell	AL, GA, MS, TN	E
P. plenum (Lea, 1840)	rough pigtoe	AL, IN, KY, TN, VA	E
P. taitianum (Lea, 1834)	heavy pigtoe	AL, MS	E
Potamilus capax (Green, 1832)	fat pocketbook	AR, IN, MO, OH	E
P. inflatus (Lea, 1831)	inflated heelsplitter	AL, LA, MS	T
Ptychobranchus greeni (Conrad, 1834)	triangular kidneyshell	AL, GA, TN	E
Quadrula fragosa (Conrad, 1835)	winged mapleleaf	IA, IL, IN, KY, MN, MO, NE, OH, OK, TN, WV	E
Q. intermedia (Conrad, 1836)	Cumberland monkeyface	AL, TN, VA	E
Q. sparsa (Lea, 1841)	Appalachian monkeyface	AL, TN, VA	E
Q. stapes (Lea, 1831)	stirrupshell	AL, MS	E
Toxolasma cylindrellus (Lea, 1868)	pale lilliput	AL, TN	E
Villosa trabalis (Conrad, 1834)	Cumberland bean	KY, TN	E
Snails:			
Tulotoma magnifica (Conrad, 1834)	tulotoma snail	AL	E
Athearnia anthonyi (Redfield, 1854)	Anthony's riversnail	AL, TN	E
Pyrgulopsis ogmorphaphe (Thompson, 1977)	royal marstonia	TN	E

TABLE 3. Species of freshwater mussels on the federal candidate list in the southeastern United States in 1994.[1]

Scientific Name	Common Name	State(s) of Occurrence
Alasmidonta arcula (Lea, 1838)	Altamaha arc-mussel	GA
A. atropurpurea (Rafinesque, 1831)	Cumberland elktoe	KY, TN
A. raveneliana (Lea, 1834)	Appalachian elktoe	NC
A. varicosa (Lamarck, 1819)	brook floater	GA, NC, SC, VA
A. wrightiana (Walker, 1901)	Florida arc-mussel	FL
Amblema neislerii (Lea, 1858)	fat three-ridge	FL, GA
Anodontoides denigrata (Lea, 1852)	Cumberland papershell	KY, TN
Cumberlandia monodonta (Say, 1829)	spectaclecase	AL, AR, KY, TN, VA
Cyprogenia aberti (Conrad, 1850)	western fanshell	AR
Elliptio sp.	Waccamaw lance	NC
E. chipolaensis Walker, 1905	Chipola slabshell	AL, FL
E. judithae Clarke, 1986	Neuse slabshell	NC
E. lanceolata (Lea, 1828)	yellow lance	NC, VA
E. marsupiobesa Fuller, 1972	Cape Fear spike	NC
E. monroensis (Lea, 1843)	St. Johns elephantear	FL
E. nigella (Lea, 1852)	winged spike	AL, GA
E. shepardiana (Lea, 1834)	Altamaha lance	GA
E. spinosa (Lea, 1836)	Altamaha spinymussel	GA
E. waccamawensis (Lea, 1863)	Waccamaw spike	NC
E. waltoni (Wright, 1888)	Florida lance	FL
Elliptoideus sloatianus (Lea, 1840)	purple bankclimber	AL, GA, FL
Epioblasma brevidens (Lea, 1831)	Cumberlandian combshell	AL, KY, TN, VA
E. capsaeformis (Lea, 1834)	oyster mussel	AL, KY, TN, VA
E. triquetra (Rafinesque, 1820)	snuffbox mussel	AL, KY, MS, TN, VA
Fusconaia escambia Clench and Turner, 1956	narrow pigtoe	AL, FL
F. masoni (Conrad, 1834)	Atlantic pigtoe	GA, NC, SC, VA
Lampsilis australis Simpson, 1900	southern sandshell	AL, FL
L. binominata Simpson, 1900	lined pocketbook	AL, GA
L. cariosa (Say, 1817)	yellow lampmussel	GA, NC, SC, VA
L. fullerkati Johnson, 1984	Waccamaw fatmucket	NC
L. rafinesqueana Frierson, 1927	Neosho mucket	AR
L. subangulata (Lea, 1840)	shiny-rayed pocketbook	AL, FL, GA
Lasmigona sp.	Barrens heelsplitter	KY
L. holstonia (Lea, 1838)	Tennessee heelsplitter	AL, GA, KY, TN, VA
L. subviridis (Conrad, 1835)	green floater	NC, SC, VA
Leptodea leptodon (Rafinesque, 1820)	scaleshell	AR, KY
Lexingtonia dolabelloides (Lea, 1840)	slabside pearlymussel	AL, TN, VA
Margaritifera marrianae Johnson, 1983	Alabama pearlshell	AL
Medionidus penicillatus (Lea, 1857)	Gulf moccasinshell	AL, FL, GA
M. simpsonianus Walker, 1905	Ochlocknee moccasinshell	FL
M. walkeri (Wright, 1897)	Suwanee moccasinshell	FL
Obovaria rotulata (Wright, 1899)	round ebonyshell	AL, FL
Pleurobema oviforme (Conrad, 1894)	Tennessee clubshell	KY, TN, VA
P. pyriforme (Lea, 1857)	oval pigtoe	AL, FL, GA
P. rubellum (Conrad, 1834)	Warrior pigtoe	AL
P. rubrum (Rafinesque, 1820)	pink pigtoe	AL, KY, MS, TN, VA
P. strodeanum (Wright, 1898)	fuzzy pigtoe	AL, FL
P. verum (Lea, 1860)	true pigtoe	AL

TABLE 3. Continued.

Scientific Name	Common Name	State(s) of Occurrence
Potamilus amphichaenus (Frierson, 1898)	Texas heelsplitter	LA
Ptychobranchus jonesi (van der Schalie, 1934)	southern kidneyshell	AL, FL
P. occidentalis (Conrad, 1836)	Ouachita kidneyshell	AR
Quadrula cylindrica cylindrica (Say, 1817)	rabbitsfoot	AL, AR, KY, TN
Q. c. strigillata (Wright, 1898)	rough rabbitsfoot	KY, TN, VA
Quincuncina burkei Walker, 1922	tapered pigtoe	AL, FL
Simpsonaias ambigua (Say, 1825)	salamander mussel	AR, KY, TN
Toxolasma lividus (Rafinesque, 1831)	purple lilliput	KY, TN
T. pullus (Conrad, 1838)	Savannah lilliput	GA, NC, SC
Villosa choctawensis Athearn, 1964	Choctaw bean	AL, FL
V. fabalis (Lea, 1831)	rayed bean	AL, TN, VA
V. ortmanni (Walker, 1925)	Kentucky creekshell	KY
V. perpurpurea (Lea, 1861)	purple bean	TN, VA

[1] Information from U.S. Federal Register 59(219):59008-59010; November 15, 1994.

east, are in the most severe decline. Many of the extinct species occurred in the Tennessee and Cumberland rivers and in their major tributaries in Alabama, Tennessee, and Kentucky (Table 5). All 36 species that are presumed extinct occurred in the Southeast, and nearly 40 percent (14) of these were *Pleurobema* spp. endemic to the Mobile River Basin. As a group, the riffleshells (*Epioblasma* spp.) have suffered the highest level of extinctions, presumably because of their occurrence in the shoals of mid-size and large rivers that were destroyed by dams and dredging and their intolerance of degraded water quality (Ahlstedt, 1991a). This group of species is seemingly sensitive to physical or chemical changes in habitat suitability, and they are the first to disappear from rivers under anthropogenic disturbance.

A recent assessment of the aquatic mollusks in North Carolina typifies the extent of decline in some populations (Scientific Council on Freshwater and Terrestrial Mollusks, 1990). Thirty-three (53 percent) of the freshwater mussels in the state are threatened with extinction, and another 42 species of mollusks are too poorly known to define their statuses. The collapse of mussel populations in North Carolina is severe: 62 of 147 populations are reported to be in poor or very poor condition, and only 19 populations are in very good condition (Rader, 1994). According to Alderman et al. (1992), only 51 of the 147 mussel populations are likely to maintain viable populations over the next 30 years in North Carolina. Causes for these declines include waste discharges, nonpoint-source pollution (especially sediment), reduced instream flow, and competition from exotic species.

The current status and prognosis for the Southeast region's mussel fauna is grim. Of the 269 species in the Southeast, 13 percent are presumed extinct, 28 percent are endangered, 14 percent are threatened, 18 percent are of special concern, and only 25 percent are considered stable at this time.

Exploitation of the mussels by humans for food, tools, and ornaments and the deposition of shells in midden piles have provided an excellent archaeological record of species composition during the past 10,000 years. The presence of mussels at archaeological sites

Table 4. Status of freshwater mussels in the southeastern United States in 1994.

State	Number of Species	Number Extinct	Number Endangered	Number Threatened	Number Special Concern	Total Number Imperiled (Percent)
AL	175	28	51	20	37	136 (78)
TN	132	17	41	10	29	93 (70)
KY	102	12	22	7	19	60 (58)
GA	98	8	23	14	34	72 (73)
MS	84	0	9	10	21	40 (48)
VA	80	2	21	9	25	57 (71)
AR	70	1	6	9	13	29 (41)
LA	64	0	2	7	13	22 (34)
FL	51	1	5	10	13	29 (57)
NC	49	1	6	6	16	29 (59)
SC	33	1	2	5	10	18 (55)

has been invaluable in reconstructing prehistoric faunal assemblages and ecological conditions in early times (Bogan, 1990). For example, as judged by the species in shell middens, at least 91 species of mussels occurred in the mainstem Tennessee River during pre-colonial times. That original diversity profoundly changed in this century from human perturbations to the mainstem river. A plethora of dams and degradation of water quality produced irreconcilable changes to the river and its fauna. Results of surveys during the last ten years indicated that only 49 mussel species remain, of which 28 are reproducing and 21 likely are not (Figure 3). Most species with healthy populations were able to tolerate impounded waters and have increased in abundance above pre-impoundment population levels.

FINGERNAIL CLAMS

The fingernail clams (Sphaeriidae) are small bivalves that live in lotic, lentic, and ephemeral habitats throughout the United States. Of the 38 recognized species (Burch, 1975), about 20 species have ranges that extend into the southeastern states (Table 6). Members of this family are highly adaptable and exhibit an array of species-specific phenotypes to accommodate a variety of abiotic and biotic factors found in aquatic habitats. Some species inhabit stress-prone habitats such as ephemeral ponds and small streams, whereas others seemingly do well in profundal zones of lakes and reservoirs subject to hypoxia.

Fingernail clams, the smallest of freshwater bivalves, release the largest young. A combination of r-selected traits (short life span, early maturity, small size) and k-selected traits (ovoviviparity, low fecundity, large young) seemingly promotes fitness and survival of species that are subjected to periodic stress. Several species prefer coldwater habitats and are restricted to northern climates, whereas species in the Southeast are eurythermal and widespread. Therefore, except for three species of fingernail clams considered to be rare in the Pacific Northwest, none are imperiled in the Southeast. Comprehensive distributional or status reviews of sphaeriids in the United States have not been conducted principally because of the small size, difficulty of identification, and low physical and ecological profile of these clams. More extensive and intensive sampling of permanent and vernal habitats is needed before the occurrence, diversity, and

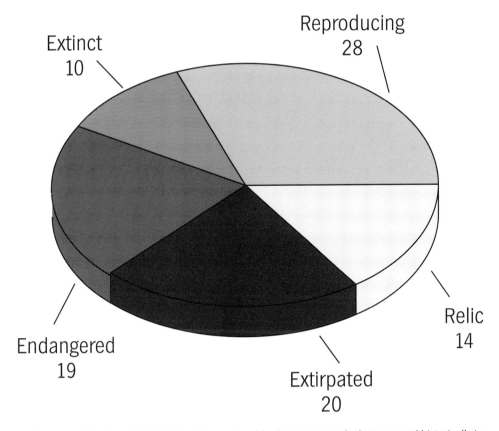

Figure 3. Status (as of 1994) of the 91 species of freshwater mussels that occurred historically in the Tennessee River.

stability of fingernail clam species in the Southeast can be described.

FRESHWATER GASTROPODS

The freshwater gastropod fauna of North America is classified within 14 families and is represented by 516 species (Table 1). Diversity in the southeastern United States consists of 313 species or 61 percent of the native North American freshwater gastropod fauna. Freshwater gastropod diversity was greatest in the Mobile River Basin (118 species), and in the Tennessee River Basin (96 species; Table 7). The Coosa River drainage of the Mobile River Basin was home to four endemic genera (Hydrobiidae: *Clappia*; Pleuroceridae: *Gyrotoma*; Planorbidae: *Amphigyra*, *Neoplanorbis*). During the past 160 years, the aquatic gastropod fauna of the southeastern United States has been extensively described by Lea (1834-1874) and Goodrich (e.g., Goodrich, 1922, 1924, 1936, 1944a, 1944b), and summarized by Tryon (1873) and Burch (1989). The Hydrobiidae and the Pleuroceridae reached their greatest species richness in rivers of the Southeast. In spite of this great diversity, the ecology and life history of these animals are poorly understood. The freshwater periwinkles (Pleuroceridae) are relatively large snails that live on rocks, cobbles, and

Table 5. Species of freshwater mussels in the United States presumed to be extinct.

Scientific Name	Common Name [1]	State(s) of Occurrence
Alasmidonta maccordi Athearn, 1964	Coosa elktoe	AL
A. robusta Clarke, 1981	Carolina elktoe	NC, SC
A. wrightiana (Walker, 1901)	Ochlocknee arc-mussel	FL
Elliptio nigella (Lea, 1852)	winged spike	AL, GA
Epioblasma arcaeformis (Lea, 1831)	sugar spoon	AL, KY, TN
E. biemarginata (Lea, 1857)	angled riffleshell	AL, KY, TN
E. flexuosa (Rafinesque, 1820)	leafshell	AL, KY, TN
E. f. florentina (Lea, 1857)	yellow blossom	AL, KY, TN
E. haysiana (Lea, 1833)	acornshell	AL, KY, TN, VA
E. lenior (Lea, 1843)	narrow catspaw	AL, TN
E. lewisii (Walker, 1910)	forkshell	AL, KY, TN
E. obliquata obliquata (Rafinesque, 1820)	catspaw	AL, KY, TN
E. personata (Say, 1829)	round combshell	KY
E. propinqua (Lea, 1857)	Tennessee riffleshell	AL, KY, TN
E. sampsonii (Lea, 1861)	wabash riffleshell	KY
E. stewardsoni (Lea, 1852)	Cumberland leafshell	AL, KY, TN
E. torulosa gubernaculum (Reeve, 1865)	green blossom	TN, VA
E. t. torulosa (Rafinesque, 1820)	tubercled blossom	AL, KY, TN
E. turgidula (Lea, 1858)	turgid blossom	AL, AR, TN
Lampsilis binominata Simpson, 1900		AL, GA
Medionidus macglameriae van der Schalie, 1939	Tombigbee moccasinshell	AL
Pleurobema aldrichianum Goodrich, 1831		AL, GA
P. altum (Conrad, 1854)	highnut	AL
P. avellanum Simpson, 1900	hazel pigtoe	AL
P. chattanoogaense (Lea, 1858)	painted clubshell	AL, GA, TN
P. flavidulum (Lea, 1831)	yellow pigtoe	AL
P. hagleri Frierson, 1906		AL
P. hanleyanum (Lea, 1852)	Georgia pigtoe	AL, GA, TN
P. hartmanianum (Lea, 1860)		AL, GA
P. johannis (Lea, 1859)	Alabama pigtoe	AL
P. murrayense (Lea, 1868)	Coosa pigtoe	AL, GA, TN
P. nucleopsis (Conrad, 1849)	longnut	AL, GA
P. rubellum (Conrad, 1834)	Warrior pigtoe	AL
P. troschelianum (Lea, 1852)	Alabama clubshell	AL
P. verum (Lea, 1860)	true pigtoe	AL
Quadrula tuberosa (Lea, 1840)	rough rockshell	TN, VA

[1] Not all species have common names.

bedrock in riffles and shoals and are readily identified by shell characters. Conversely, the hydrobes (Hydrobiidae) are small (<8mm, = less than 0.3 inches) snails that reside in an array of freshwater habitats, from small seeps to large rivers, and typically require anatomical dissection for species identification.

Attention to the status of aquatic mollusk populations was uncommon. Ortmann (1909, 1918) recognized the effects of pollution, acid mine drainage, and dams on the native aquatic fauna. However, that attention was not focused on the decline and disappearance

Table 6. Fingernail clams occurring in the southeastern United States.

Scientific Name	Common Name
Sphaerium fabale (Prime, 1852)	river fingernail clam
S. occidentale (Lewis, 1856)	Herrington fingernail clam
S. striatinum (Lamarck, 1818)	striated fingernail clam
S. simile (Say, 1817)	grooved fingernail clam
Musculium lacustre (Müller, 1774)	lake fingernail clam
M. partumeium (Say, 1822)	swamp fingernail clam
M. securis (Prime, 1852)	pond fingernail clam
M. transversum (Say, 1829)	long fingernail clam
Eupera cubensis (Prime, 1865)	mottled fingernail clam
Pisidium dubium (Say, 1817)	greater eastern peaclam
P. adamsi Stimpson, 1851	Adam peaclam
P. casertanum (Poli, 1791)	ubiquitous peaclam
P. compressum Prime, 1852	ridged-back peaclam
P. equilaterale Prime, 1852	round peaclam
P. fallax Sterki, 1895	river peaclam
P. nitidum Jenyns, 1832	shiny peaclam
P. variable Prime, 1852	triangular peaclam
P. walkeri Sterki, 1895	Walker peaclam
P. punctatum Sterki, 1895	perforated peaclam
P. punctiferum (Guppy, 1867)	striate peaclam

of the aquatic gastropod fauna of the Southeast until the publications of Athearn (1970), Stansbery (1971), Stein (1976) and more recently Bogan and Parmalee (1983), Palmer (1986), and Ahlstedt (1991b). Even now, the life history and ecology of most snail species is poorly understood, and the status of southeastern drainage faunas is virtually unknown. Based primarily on the papers cited above, Turgeon et al. (1988) assembled a list of 23 aquatic gastropods presumed to be extinct in the United States, all of which were endemic to the Mobile River Basin. With 118 species, this basin contained the most diverse aquatic gastropod fauna in the Southeast, and perhaps in the world (Table 7).

Freshwater gastropods also have been neglected, relative to freshwater bivalves, as candidates for federal protection; only three freshwater gastropods are listed as endangered in the Southeast: *Tulotoma magnifica*, *Athearnia anthonyi*, and *Pyrgulopsis ogmorphaphe*. The tulotoma snail, which is endemic to the Mobile Basin, was presumed extinct until Hershler et al. (1990) discovered several extant populations. As of November 1994, roughly 210 species of 11 families of freshwater gastropods are on the federal list of candidate species. Of these candidate species, 144 (69 percent) occur in the Southeast (Table 8). Taxa from the Southeast account for most of the freshwater prosobranchs and about half of the freshwater pulmonate taxa on the candidate list. Two families (Hydrobiidae, Pleuroceridae) have the greatest number of candidate gastropod taxa.

Of the aquatic gastropod fauna of four major river basins in the Southeast, the Mobile River Basin had the greatest original diversity but also suffered the greatest destruction and impairment of this fauna. This basin has one endangered species, 70 candidate taxa, and 26 presumed extinct taxa (Table 9). The Mobile fauna has suffered from the effects of

Table 7. Summary of the freshwater gastropod fauna in four major river systems in the southeastern United States.

Taxon	Cumberland River Basin	Tennessee River Basin	Mobile River Basin	Apalachicola River Basin
Family:				
Neritidae	0	0	1	1
Valvatidae	1	1	1	1
Pilidae	0	0	0	1
Viviparidae	1	4	4	3
Hydrobiidae	2	20	18	5
Pomatiopsidae	2	3	1	1
Pleuroceridae	14	50	76	11
Lymnaeidae	2	2	2	2
Physidae	5	5	2	2
Planorbidae	5	6	9	5
Ancylidae	3	7	4	4
Total Species	35	96	118	36
Endangered Species	0	0	1	0
Candidate Species	8	35	70	3
Extinct Species	0?	0?	26	0?

damming of the major rivers, sedimentation from poor forestry and farming practices, pollution from industry, and the degradation of water quality as water passes through numerous water treatment facilities. The loss of species richness of the various drainages of the Mobile River Basin ranges from 33 to 84 percent (Table 9). In 1990, the U. S. Fish and Wildlife Service encouraged and supported studies to determine the range distribution and status of this remarkable fauna. Based on results of recent aquatic gastropod surveys by Bogan and Pierson (1993a, 1993b) and U.S. Fish and Wildlife Service personnel, we present a list of freshwater gastropods presumed to be extinct (Table 10). Losses in the Coosa River Basin are most severe. Four genera, with 13 species endemic to the Coosa River drainage, are presumed extinct (*Clappia, Gyrotoma, Amphigyra,* and *Neoplanorbis*). Most taxa resided in the main channel of the Coosa River. For example, the extinction of *Gyrotoma* probably occurred in the mid-1960s with the filling of Logan Martin Reservoir. The last living specimens were collected as the backwaters of the reservoir flooded the rocky shoals occupied by these species (H. Athearn, private museum, Cleveland, Tennessee, pers. comm.). When the series of dams on the Coosa River raised the water over the free-flowing shoals and covered them with silt, most of the fauna probably became extinct.

The aquatic gastropod fauna of the southeastern United States is continuing to decline. Dams on the major rivers of the Southeast eliminated these animals from much of their former range such that only relict populations survive immediately below some of the dams. The fragmented ranges and the isolated populations result in species becoming susceptible to extirpation and extinction.

Table 8. Species of freshwater gastropods on the federal candidate list in the southeastern United States, in 1994. [1]

Taxon	Common Name [2]	State(s) of Occurrence
Prosobranchia (135 Species):		
Viviparidae (2 species):		
Campeloma decampi (Binney, 1865)	slender campeloma	AL
Lioplax cyclostomaformis (Lea, 1841)	cylindrical lioplax	AL, GA, LA
Hydrobiidae (50 species):		
Antrorbis breweri Herschler and Thompson, 1990		AL
Aphaostracon asthenes Thompson, 1968	Blue Spring hydrobe	FL
A. monas (Pilsbry, 1899)	Wekiwa hydrobe	FL
A. pycnum Thompson, 1968	dense hydrobe	FL
A. xynoelictus Thompson, 1968	Fenney Spring hydrobe	FL
Cincinnatia helicogyra Thomspon, 1968	Crystal siltsnail	FL
C. mica Thompson, 1968	Ichetucknee siltsnail	FL
C. monroensis (Dall, 1885)	Enterprise siltsnail	FL
C. parva Thompson, 1968	pygmy siltsnail	FL
C. ponderosa Thompson, 1968	ponderous siltsnail	FL
C. vanhyningi (Vanatta, 1934)	Seminole siltsnail	FL
C. wekiwae Thompson, 1968	Wekiwa siltsnail	FL
Clappia cahabensis Clench, 1965	Cahaba pebblesnail	AL
C. umbilicata (Walker, 1904)	umbilicate pebblesnail	AL
Lepyrium showalteri (Lea 1861)	flat pebblesnail	AL
Pyrgulopsis sp.	Briley Creek pyrg	AL
Pyrgulopsis sp.	Spring Creek pyrg	AL
Pyrgulopsis sp.	Flint River pyrg	AL
P. agarhecta Thompson, 1969	Ocmulgee marstonia	GA
P. castor (Thompson, 1977)	beaver pond marstonia	GA
P. olivacea (Pilsbry, 1895)	olive marstonia	AL
P. ogmoraphe (Thompson, 1977)	royal marstonia	TN
P. ozarkensis Hinkley, 1915	Ozark pyrg	AR
P. pachyta (Thompson, 1977)	armored marstonia	AL
Somatogyrus amnicoloides Walker, 1915	Ouachita pebblesnail	AR
S. aureus Tryon, 1865	golden pebblesnail	AL
S. biangulatus Walker, 1906	anglar pebblesnail	AL
S. constrictus Walker, 1904	knotty pebblesnail	AL
S. coosaensis Walker, 1904	Coosa pebblesnail	AL
S. crassilabris Walker, 1915	thick-lipped pebblesnail	AR
S. crassus Walker, 1904	stocky pebblesnail	AL
S. currierianus (Lea, 1863)	Tennessee pebblesnail	AL
S. decipiens Walker, 1909	hidden pebblesnail	AL
S. excavatus Walker, 1906	ovate pebblesnail	AL
S. hendersoni Walker, 1909	fluted pebblesnail	AL
S. hinkleyi Walker, 1904	granite pebblesnail	AL
S. humerosus Walker, 1906	atlas pebblesnail	AL
S. nanus Walker, 1904	dwarf pebblesnail	AL
S. obtusus Walker, 1904	moon pebblesnail	AL
S. parvulus Tryon, 1865	sparrow pebblesnail	TN

Table 8. Continued.

Taxon	Common Name [2]	State(s) of Occurrence
S. pilsbryanus Walker, 1904	Tallapoosa pebblesnail	AL
S. pygmaeus Walker, 1909	pygmy pebblesnail	AL
S. quadratus Walker, 1906	quadrate pebblesnail	AL
S. sargenti Pilsbry, 1895	mud pebblesnail	AL
S. strengi Pilsbry and Walker, 1906	rolling pebblesnail	AL
S. tenax Thompson, 1969	Savannah pebblesnail	GA
S. tennesseensis Walker, 1906	opaque pebblesnail	AL, TN
S. virginicus Walker, 1904	panhandle pebblesnail	NC, VA
S. wheeleri Walker, 1915	channeled pebblesnail	AR
Stiobia nana Thompson, 1978	sculpin snail	AL
Pleuroceridae (83 species):		
Athearnia anthonyi (Redfield, 1854)	Anthony's riversnail	AL, GA, TN
Elimia acuta (Lea, 1831)	acute elimia	AL, TN
E. alabamensis (Lea, 1861)	mud elimia	FL
E. albanyensis (Lea, 1864)	black-crest elimia	FL
E. ampla (Anthony, 1854)	ample elimia	AL
E. annettae Goodrich, 1941	Lily Shoals elimia	AL
E. aterina (Lea, 1863)	coal elimia	TN
E. bellula (Lea, 1861)	walnut elimia	AL
E. boykiniana (Lea, 1840)	flaxen elimia	AL
E. brevis (Reeve, 1860)	short-spire elimia	AL
E. cahawbensis (Lea, 1861)	Cahaba elimia	AL
E. capillaris (Lea, 1861)	spindle elimia	AL
E. crenatella (Lca, 1860)	lacy elimia	AL
E. fascinans (Lea, 1861)	banded elimia	AL
E. fusiformis (Lea, 1861)	fusiform elimia	AL
E. gerhardti (Lea, 1862)	coldwater elimia	AL
E. hartmaniana (Lea, 1861)	high-spired elimia	AL
E. haysiana (Lea, 1843)	silt elimia	AL
E. hydei (Conrad, 1834)	gladiator elimia	AL
E. impressa (Lea, 1841)	constricted elimia	AL
E. interrupta (Haldeman, 1840)	knotty elimia	NC, TN
E. interveniens (Lea, 1862)	slowwater elimia	AL
E. jonesi (Goodrich, 1936)	hearty elimia	AL
E. laeta (Jay, 1839)	ribbed elimia	AL
E. nassula (Conrad, 1834)	round-ribbed elimia	AL
E. olivula (Conrad, 1834)	caper elimia	AL
E. perstriata (Lea, 1852)	engraved elimia	AL
E. pilsbryi (Goodrich, 1927)	rough-lined elimia	AL
E. porrecta (Lea, 1863)	nymph elimia	AL
E. pupaeformis (Lea, 1864)	pupa elimia	AL
E. pybasi (Lea, 1862)	spring elimia	AL
E. pygmaea (Smith, 1936)	pygmy elimia	AL
E. showalteri (Lea, 1860)	compact elimia	AL
E. strigosa (Lea, 1841)	brook elimia	TN
E. teres (Lea, 1841)	elegant elimia	TN
E. troostiana (Lea, 1838)	mossy elimia	TN
E. vanuxemiana (Lea, 1843)	cobble elimia	AL

Table 8. Continued.

Taxon	Common Name [2]	State(s) of Occurrence
E. varians (Lea, 1861)	puzzle elimia	AL
E. variata (Lea, 1861)	squat elimia	AL
Gyrotoma excisa (Lea, 1843)	excised slitshell	AL
G. lewisii (Lea, 1869)	striate slitshell	AL
G. pagoda (Lea, 1845)	pagoda slitshell	AL
G. pumila (Lea, 1860)	ribbed slitshell	AL
G. pyramidata Shuttleworth, 1845	pyramid slitshell	AL
G. walkeri (Smith, 1924)	round slitshell	AL
Io fluvialis (Say, 1825)	spiny riversnail	AL, TN, VA
Leptoxis ampla (Anthony, 1855)	round rocksnail	AL
L. clipeata (Smith, 1922)	agate rocksnail	AL
L. compacta (Anthony, 1854)	oblong rocksnail	AL
L. crassa (Halkeman, 1841)	boulder snail	AL, GA, TN
L. formani (Lea, 1843)	interrupted rocksnail	AL
L. formosa (Lea, 1860)	maiden rocksnail	AL
L. ligata (Anthony, 1860)	rotund rocksnail	AL
L. lirata (Smith, 1922)	lyrate rocksnail	AL
L. melanoidus (Conrad, 1834)	black mudalia	AL
L. minor (Hinkley, 1912)	knob mudalia	AL
L. occultata (Smith, 1922)	bigmouth rocksnail	AL
L. picta (Conrad, 1834)	spotted rocksnail	AL
L. plicata (Conrad, 1834)	plicate rocksnail	AL
L. praerosa (Say, 1821)	onyx rocksnail	AL, TN, VA
L. showalterii (Lea, 1860)	Coosa rocksnail	AL
L. taeniata (Conrad,1834)	painted rocksnail	AL
L. virgata (Lea,1841)	smooth rocksnail	AL, TN, NC
L. vittata (Lea, 1860)	stripped rocksnail	AL
Lithasia armigera (Say, 1821)	armored rocksnail	AL, IN, KY, TN
L. curta (Lea, 1868)	knobby rocksnail	AL
L. duttoniana (Lea, 1841)	helmet rocksnail	TN
L. geniculata Haldeman, 1840	ornate rocksnail	AL, KY, TN
L. jayana (Lea,1841)	rugose rocksnail	TN
L. lima (Conrad, 1834)	warty rocksnail	AL, TN
L. salebrosa (Conrad, 1834)	muddy rocksnail	AL, TN
L. verrucosa (Rafinesque, 1820)	varicose rocksnail	AL, KY, TN
Pleurocera alveare (Conrad, 1834)	rugged hornsnail	AL, AR, KY, TN
P. annulifera (Conrad, 1834)	ringed hornsnail	AL
P. brumbyi (Lea, 1852)	spiral hornsnail	AL
P. corpulenta (Anthony, 1854)	corpulent hornsnail	AL, TN
P. curta (Haldeman, 1841)	shortspire hornsnail	AL, TN
P. foremani (Lea, 1843)	rough hornsnail	AL, GA
P. postelli (Lea, 1862)	broken hornsnail	AL
P. pyrenella (Conrad, 1834)	skirted hornsnail	AL, GA
P. showalteri (Lea, 1862)	upland hornsnail	AL, GA
P. viridulum (Anthony, 1854)		GA
P. walkeri (Goodrich, 1928)	telescope hornsnail	AL, TN

Pulmonata (9 Species):
Basommatophora

Table 8. Continued.

Taxon	Common Name [2]	State(s) of Occurrence [1]
Ancylidae (3 species):		
Ferissia mcneili Walker, 1925	hood ancylid	AL, FL
Rhodacmea elatior (Anthony, 1855)	domed ancylid	AL
R. filosa (Conrad, 1834)	wicker ancylid	AL
Planorbidae (6 species):		
Amphigyra alabamensis Pilsbry, 1906	shoal sprite	AL
Neoplanorbis carinatus (Walker, 1908)		AL
N. smithi Walker, 1908		AL
N. tantillus Walker, 1906		AL
N. umbilicatus Walker, 1908		AL
Planorbella magnifica (Pilsbry, 1903)	magnificent rams-horn	NC
Total Aquatic Gastropods: 144 species		

[1] Information from U.S.Federal Register 59(219):59000-59008; November 15, 1994.

[2] Not all species have common names.

CAUSES OF DECLINES

The extinction, extirpation, or decline of most freshwater mollusks can be attributed to biological attributes and ecological requirements that make species particularly vulnerable to anthropogenic effects. Freshwater mussels have an unusual reproductive cycle; the larval stage (glochidium) is an obligate parasite on the gills or fins of host fishes. Host specificity is the rule rather than the exception in most freshwater mussels (Hoggarth, 1992). Gravid female mussels release tens of thousands to several million glochidia, depending on the species and the size of the female (Surber, 1912; Coker et al., 1921; Yeager and Neves, 1986; Hove and Neves, 1994). Although the number of larvae produced is high, few glochidia contact and attach to the appropriate host fishes during this r-selected stage in the life cycle. Thus, the timely presence and abundance of appropriate fishes to complete the reproductive cycle is critical to the continued existence of freshwater mussel species. Because less than 20 percent of mussel species in the Southeast have known host fishes, this potential reproductive bottleneck cannot be evaluated until hosts are identified for the imperiled mussels. Any factor that alters the natural assemblage of fishes can threaten the viability or composition of the associated mussel assemblage.

Habitat loss and degradation affects mollusks directly by reducing population sizes and inhibiting long-term reproductive success. The degrees of rarity of nearly all species stem from anthropogenic losses and alterations of habitats. Because these perturbations to the biology and ecology of mollusks are documented, we provide a summary of those factors most lethal to the continued existence of mollusk populations. The dynamic changes in mollusk assemblages in rivers and reservoirs is evidenced by declining diversity, changes in species composition, and lowered abundance of some species resulting from acute and chronic alteration and degradation of habitat suitability for native species. It is these insidious factors that perpetuate the downward spiral of distribution and diversity of our native mollusks.

Table 9. Summary of the aquatic gastropod fauna in the Mobile River Basin. [1]

Taxon	Alabama River	Tombigbee River Drainage	Black Warrior River Drainage	Cahaba River Drainage	Coosa River Drainage	Talapoosa River Drainage	Mobile River Basin Total
Gastropod Families:							
Neritidae	1	0	0	0	0	0	1
Valvatidae	U	U	U	U	U	U	1
Viviparidae	5	2	0	2	3	1	4
Hydrobiidae	1	U	1	3	12	2	18
Pomatiopsidae	U	U	U	U	U	U	1
Pleuroceridae	7	2	11	22	55	1	76
Lymnaeidae	2	2	2	2	2	2	2
Physidae	2	2	2	2	2	2	2
Planorbidae	U	0	0	0	6	0	9
Ancylidae	1	U	1	1	2	0	4
Approximate total of historic gastropod species diversity	19	8	17	36	82	8	118
Approximate number of collections	150	50	100	160	324	16	800
Number of species found in recent surveys	3	3	7	24	30	4	80
Federally listed endangered species	1	0	0	0	1	0	1
Federal candidate species	4	1	6	16	43	2	70
Number species presumed extinct	U	0	2	4	26	U	38
Percent decline in fauna	84	62	58	33	63	50	32

[1] Data from Bogan et al. (1995). U = unknown or uncertain information.

Table 10. List of the freshwater gastropod species presumed extinct in the Mobile River Basin.[1]

Taxon	Common Name[2]
Hydrobiidae:	
Clappia cahabensis Clench, 1965	Cahaba pebblesnail
C. umbilicata (Walker, 1904)	umbilicate pebblesnail
Pleuroceridae:	
Elimia brevis (Reeve, 1860)	short-spire elimia
E. clausa (Lea, 1861)	closed elimia
E. fusiformis (Lea, 1861)	fusiform elimia
E. gibbera (Goodrich, 1922)	
E. hartmaniana (Lea, 1861)	high-spired elimia
E. impressa (Lea, 1841)	constricted elimia
E. jonesi (Goodrich, 1936)	hearty elimia
E. lachryma (Reeve, 1861)	
E. laeta (Jay, 1839)	ribbed elimia
E. macglameriana (Goodrich, 1936)	
E. pilsbryi (Goodrich, 1927)	rough-lined elimia
E. pupaeformis (Lea, 1864)	pupa elimia
E. pygmaea (Smith, 1936)	pygmy elmia
E. vanuxemiana (Lea, 1843)	cobble elimia
Gyrotoma excisa (Lea, 1843)	excised slitshell
G. lewisii (Lea, 1869)	striate slitshell
G. pagoda (Lea, 1845)	pagoda slitshell
G. pumila (Lea, 1860)	ribbed slitshell
G. pyramidata (Shuttleworth, 1845)	pyramid slitshell
G. walkeri (Smith, 1924)	round slitshell
Leptoxis clipeata (Smith, 1922)	agate rocksnail
L. compacta (Anthony, 1854)	oblong rocksnail
L. foremani (Lea, 1843)	interrupted rocksnail
L. formosa (Lea, 1860)	maiden rocksnail
L. ligata (Anthony, 1860)	rotund rocksnail
L. lirata (Smith, 1922)	lirate rocksnail
L. melanoidus (Conrad, 1834)	black mudalia
L. occultata (Smith, 1922)	bigmouth rocksnail
L. showalterii (Lea, 1860)	Coosa rocksnail
L. torrefacta (Goodrich, 1922)	
L. vittata (Lea, 1860)	striped rocksnail
Planorbidae:	
Amphigyra alabamensis Pilsbry, 1906	shoal sprite
Neoplanorbis carinatus Walker, 1908	
N. smithi Walker, 1908	
N. tantillus Pilsbry, 1906	
N. umbilicatus Walker, 1908	

[1] Data from Bogan et al. (1995).

[2] Not all species have common names.

Dams and Reservoirs

The effects of dams and resultant impoundments are detrimental to riverine fishes and freshwater mollusks. Changes in mussel faunas are perhaps best documented in the Tennessee River, impounded by a series of 36 multi-purpose dams on the mainstem and on major tributaries. Reductions in the diversity and abundance of mussels are principally attributed to habitat shifts caused by impoundment. Upstream of dams, the change from lotic to lentic waters, increased depths and sedimentation, decreased dissolved oxygen, and the drastic alteration in resident fish populations inevitably can jeopardize the survival of some mussels and their reproductive success. The loss of benthic host fishes and the spatial separation of remaining pelagic and littoral fishes from residual mussel populations preclude the sympatric requirement for glochidial infestations. Downstream of dams, fluctuations in flow regime, scouring, seasonal dissolved oxygen sags, reduced water temperatures, and changes in fish assemblages also can jeopardize the survival and reproductive success of many mollusk species. This tailwater effect may extend for many kilometers downstream and result in the gradual attrition of environmentally sensitive mollusks. Because mussels are thought to be the longest-lived freshwater invertebrates, with a longevity of more than 100 years for some species, population declines due to poor reproductive success may continue for decades. Thus, the extirpation of species is a prolonged event, lagging decades behind the factors directly responsible for attrition of the fauna.

Effects of impoundments on the mussel fauna of coastal rivers are similar to those reported for the Tennessee River. In the Tombigbee River, a large Coastal Plain river in western Alabama and northeastern Mississippi, Williams et al. (1992) reported a loss of about 70 percent of the preimpoundment fauna. A preimpoundment mussel survey of the Black Warrior River is incomplete, but it appears that the loss in species richness is similar to that reported in the Tombigbee River. Most of the species of mussels that survive in Coastal Plain impoundments are the same as those that survive impoundments in upland areas such as the Tennessee River.

Mussel surveys before and after reservoir construction on several rivers in the Southeast attest to the drastic changes in mussel fauna caused by habitat shifts. In the Tennessee River, the Pickwick Dam inundated perhaps the most diverse assemblage of mussels in the world, about 70 species in 31 genera. The disappearance of nearly half of the species seems directly attributed to destruction of riverine habitat. Other species suffered a similar but prolonged fate for lack of reproductive success. At Muscle Shoals, Ortmann (1925) reported 69 mussel species before the Wilson Dam was constructed. Mussel diversity in this river reach declined to 44 species in 1968 (Isom, 1969), and to fewer than 30 species now. From the mouth of the Tennessee River upstream to Fort Loudoun Dam (963 km, = 598 miles), only tailwaters and overbanks in the lower river remain as suitable habitat for riverine species. There is little or no reproduction of mussels in the Tennessee River upstream of Fort Loudoun Dam, perhaps because the upper river lacks the necessary flow conditions for reproduction by riverine species. The loss of riverine species was accompanied by the invasion of mud-tolerant species into the reservoirs through either stocking of fishes with incidental infestations, natural fish movements upstream, or the seeding of reservoirs with commercially important species by entrepreneurial mussel harvesters. Irrespective of the path of entry, the reservoir-tolerant species (e.g., *Anodonta* spp., *Potamilus* spp., etc.) greatly increased in abundance and now dominate the mussel fauna in many reservoirs (Ahlstedt and McDonough, 1993). The loss of reservoir-intolerant species meant an end to the indigenous and endemic fauna, and set the stage for invasive non-native species to proliferate in artificial but suitable environments.

The historic species composition of the Tennessee River indicates that at least 49 species of mussels or their host fishes are intolerant of reservoir conditions or the subsequent physico-chemical changes in the river (Figure 3). Conversely, about 28 species of native and non-native mussels increased in abundance to occupy primarily the overbank areas where conditions were best suited to successful reproduction and juvenile survival in the soft sediments. As judged by the longevity of some species, the mussel assemblage continues to approach a climax community, with some semblance of long-term stability.

Impoundments have had similar detrimental effects on freshwater gastropods, although poorly documented. In the Mobile River Basin, 38 species of snails are presumed extinct, primarily as a result of impoundment (Table 10).

Commercial Harvest of Mussels

Although freshwater mussels have been commercially harvested since the late 1800s, there is no evidence of permanent damage to populations or species due to this industry. From the beginning of harvesting to provide shells for a burgeoning pearl button industry and now for the cultured pearl trade, the dozen or so commercial species have persevered the waxing and waning of harvest effort by musselers. The most sought after commercial species such as the ebonyshell (*Fusconaia ebena*), the threeridge (*Amblema plicata*), the washboard (*Megalonaias nervosa*), and others are widespread and abundant. Harvests in the Mississippi and Tennessee river systems were most intense, and some river reaches were exploited to economic overharvest before being allowed to slowly recover (Claassen, 1994). Similar problems occurred in Gulf Coast rivers, but the fishery was less intense because of low-quality shell and smaller mussel populations. Reduced catch per unit effort and the law of diminishing returns functioned to prevent biological overharvest of healthy mussel beds. These populations and their essential host fishes remained in sufficient abundance to begin the gradual recovery from economic overharvest. As a result of this early onslaught and the realization that mussels were a renewable but exhaustible resource, state fish and wildlife agencies began to actively manage this fishery in the 1960s through restrictions on species, size, gear, location, and time of year. Most states that allow commercial harvest now have regulations to manage the fishery and personnel to monitor and enforce these regulations.

Concurrent with commercial exploitation of mussel populations in the Mississippi Basin during the early 1900s, a profusion of dams and reservoirs constructed by the Tennessee Valley Authority, U.S. Army Corps of Engineers, and public utilities created lentic habitats preferred by several commercial species (Ahlstedt and McDonough, 1993). The natural invasion or human transfer and proliferation of desirable species to these new impoundments supplemented the availability of commercially exploitable populations. This cornucopia of economically valuable species, however, came at the expense of native biodiversity.

Water Quality of Rivers

The condition of streams and rivers in the United States has been monitored by the United States Environmental Protection Agency (EPA) for roughly 20 years. Prior to this national monitoring of river basins, assessments of ecological health were limited to rivers of high priority in a state or to interjurisdictional rivers. The most recent biennial assess-ment by EPA was of the quality of about 18 percent of all United States river miles (U.S. Environmental Protection Agency, 1994). Of the roughly 643,000 miles (1,028,800 km) of assessed rivers, 56 percent fully supported their designated uses of fishable and swim-mable (Figure 4). The remaining 44 percent of river miles were threatened (6.7 percent), only partially supported (25.7 percent), or did not support (13.2 percent) designated uses. In the southeastern states, the degree of impairment of public waters varied tremendously (Table 11). Although reported values represent a limited sample of waters per state, the general impression is that many of the monitored rivers in the Southeast have impaired water quality. Pollutants that contribute to the impairment of water quality in rivers are principally sedimentation (45 percent) and excess nutrients (37 percent) (Figure 5). Other causes of impairment originate from point- and nonpoint-sources of discharge.

The most widely reported source of pollution to rivers is agriculture (Figure 5). Tradi-tional farming practices, feed-lot operations, and associated poor land-use practices con-tribute many pollutants. Agriculture affects 72 percent of impaired river kilometers in the United States, yet it has been largely neglected in legislative efforts to curb pollution to public waterways. Although the U.S. Congress explicitly referenced land-use requirements in the Water Pollution Control Act of 1972 to control nonpoint-source pollution (Selzer, 1994), the legislation has been largely ineffective on agriculture. Some areas in the South-east, such as southwestern Georgia, have experienced severe losses of topsoil and nutrient additions to local streams due to agriculture. Most major forests in this region were cut by the late 1920s, and intensive agriculture ensued. The Flint River watershed in the center of this agricultural belt has been greatly affected by this landscape transition. Soil erosion and runoff of fertilizer and pesticides into groundwater and surface water have had a profound effect on water quality in the river and on the indigenous biota (Patrick, 1992). Nationwide decreases in lead and fecal coliform bacteria in streams have been countered by increases in nitrate, chloride, arsenic, and cadmium concentrations (Smith et al., 1987). These water quality changes are seemingly the result of improved sewage treatment and unleaded gas consumption, and increased use of fertilizers and highway salt. The increased use of fertilizer and subsequent eutrophication is thought to have been a dominant influ-ence in water quality changes during the 1980s. Fuller (1974) provided an excellent but somewhat outdated review of the effects of pollutants on freshwater bivalves.

National statistics on water quality problems adequately reflect the situation in the South-east, as judged by technical documents such as 305b reports submitted to the EPA in alternate years by states. Although too voluminous to present in this assessment of fresh-water mollusks, trends in water quality in Tennessee, a centrally located and significant state for mollusk diversity, provide a suitable southeastern perspective (Tennessee Depart-ment of Environment and Conservation, 1990). Most stream kilometers and lake hectares are clean enough to fully support designated uses. Degradation to streams from agricul-tural crops is most intense in western Tennessee, whereas runoff from animal holding lots is troublesome throughout the state. Mining effects are most severe in the Cumberland Plateau region of eastern Tennessee. As a result of point-source control of pollutants after enactment of the Tennessee Water Control Act of 1972, water quality improved drasti-cally. Statewide, 83 percent of streams have stable water quality, four percent have im-proved quality, and 13 percent are continuing to degrade. The cause for most degradation

Table 11. An assessment of water quality in rivers of the southeastern United States in 1992.[1]

State	River Kilometers Assessed[2]	Kilometers of Impaired Water (Percent)
Alabama	19,667	5,507 (28)
Arkansas	11,939	6,089 (51)
Florida	12,693	4,569 (36)
Georgia	6,486	4,605 (71)
Kentucky	15,579	5,141 (33)
Louisiana	14,542	10,761 (74)
Mississippi	57,366	53,924 (94)
North Carolina	56,096	35,340 (63)
South Carolina	6,326	1,771 (28)
Tennessee	17,317	9,178 (53)
Virginia	28,733	5,747 (20)

[1] Data from U.S. Environmental Protection Agency (1994).

[2] One kilometer equals 0.62 miles.

of water quality is attributed to nonpoint effects. Hence, national legislation such as the Clean Water Act of 1977 has drastically and significantly improved the regulation of point-source discharges. One of the goals of this act was the maintenance and restoration of the chemical, physical, and biological integrity of the nation's waters. Progress toward this goal is well under way. Still lacking are the legislative means to significantly reduce nonpoint runoff from agricultural and urban areas. Support within each of the states for mandatory Best Management Practices (BMPs) would go a long way toward curbing the dominant nonpoint problems that continue to degrade water quality and jeopardize all aquatic biodiversity in southeastern streams.

Voluminous research and management experience have clearly documented the interdependence of terrestrial and aquatic ecosystems for the overall health of biota (Pajak et al., 1994). However the implementation of this knowledge through effective and comprehensive policy change has been egregiously slow. A quantum leap in progress occurred with passage of the Farm Bill (Food Security Act of 1985) and its subsequent reauthorization in 1990. Through its Conservation Reserve Program (CRP), more than 14.6 million hectares (= 36 million acres) of marginal farmland have been retired from production (Agricultural Stabilization and Conservation Service, 1993). The estimated reduction in soil erosion and nonpoint-source pollution exceeds 694 million tons of soil per year, with fish and wildlife habitat improved in a few southeastern states. Managing for clean water, fish and wildlife habitats, and other nontraditional products may be the most beneficial use for inherently marginal agricultural land, riparian zones, and other ecologically sensitive areas in watersheds. The maintenance of buffer strips along streams and rivers is particularly crucial to the welfare of freshwater mollusks. Forested buffer strips (30-50 m wide, = 100-164 feet wide) and grass buffer strips (4.6-27 m wide, = 15-89 feet wide) can reduce nitrate and phosphorus concentrations in surface runoff by 79-98 percent and 54-84 percent, respectively (Osborne and Kovacic, 1993). Similarly, 95 percent of soil lost through cropland runoff can be retained with a 9 m wide (30 feet) vegetation strip (Schultz and

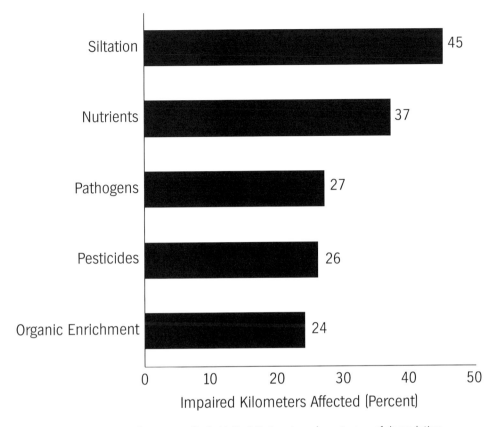

Figure 4. Impairment of water quality in United States rivers by category of degradation.

Cruse, 1992). However, because less than one percent of CRP land occurs in close proximity to water resources, the benefits of this program to aquatic ecosystems have been more trickle down than overflow economics. Until aquatic biologists participate directly in agricultural programs designed to produce and conserve resources of societal benefit, the degradation of public waters through runoff from private property will continue to jeopardize the existence of silt-intolerant species and their communities.

Declines in mollusk populations from water pollution were chronicled in the 19th and early 20th centuries (Lewis, 1868; Ortmann, 1909; Baker, 1928), when the problems from industrial effluent became widespread. Mollusks can avoid or tolerate short-term exposures to toxic chemicals by valve or operculum closure, but most cannot tolerate chronic exposures to contaminated water. Havlik and Marking (1987) summarized the few available data on body burdens and toxicity levels of various contaminants. Because many adult mollusks can avoid exposure, they are not suitable bioassay organisms for standard toxicity tests. However, pulmonate snails and the early life stages of freshwater mussels are more readily suited to toxicity testing, especially because early life stages tend to be more sensitive than adults. The recent use of glochidia and juvenile mussels in bioassays may foster standardized techniques and acceptance of these and other mollusks (e.g., *Corbicula fluminea*) for toxicity testing (Johnson, 1990; Keller and Zam, 1991; Goudreau

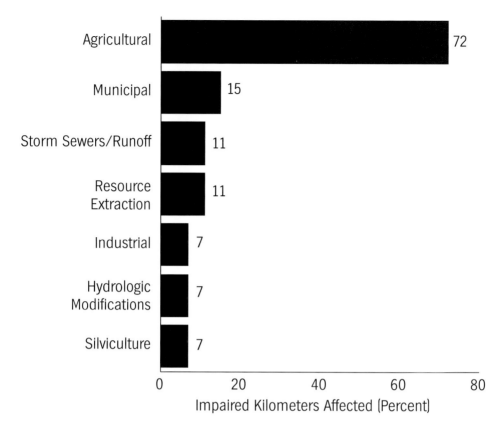

Figure 5. Impairment of water quality in United States rivers by various sources of anthropogenic degradation.

et al., 1993; Jacobson et al., 1993). Determination of sensitivities of mussels to particular contaminants, relative to the standard aquatic bioassay organisms such as the zooplankter *Ceriodaphnia dubia* and fathead minnow *Pimephales promelas*, also would help establish general and site-specific criteria for water quality in rivers where no suitable surrogates are available. The identification of appropriate surrogate species is important for routine use in standard bioassays to establish environmentally safe criteria for contaminants or whole effluents discharged into waterways containing biologically significant mollusk populations. As judged by the decline and degree of rarity of mollusks in southeastern rivers, criteria to protect this faunal group are urgently needed.

Sediment and contaminants in nonpoint-source runoff are insidious factors in aquatic ecosystem degradation. Sediment degrades water quality and substratum suitability for mollusks by clogging gills, reducing feeding efficiency, and eventually covering algae scraped from rocks by snails or smothering mussels after sufficient accumulation (Ellis, 1936; Marking and Bills, 1979; Kat, 1982; Willis et al., 1994). Field and laboratory studies implicated silt and sedimentation from agriculture, mining, and other land-use practices in the decline of mollusks in streams (Ellis, 1931; Coon et al., 1977; Wilber, 1983; Aldridge et al., 1987). The subtleties of these effects usually are not documented because erosional silt enters waterways during storm events and from construction sites lacking suitable Best Management Practices. However, these periodic additions of sediment have profound effects on long-term sustainability of mollusk populations. For example, depleted snail populations in pools of the upper Powell River, Virginia, were found on the surface of cobbles and boulders in spring but on the underside of rocks in summer. Presumably, the accumulation of silt from abandoned mined lands on cobbles and boulders in summer inhibits the growth of algae and discourages the attachment and grazing by snails. Thus, seasonal pulses of erosional silt are precluding the establishment of healthy populations of resident gastropods in riffle and run habitats.

Mining Effects on Mollusks

The southern Appalachians are characterized by high topographic relief with steep slopes and high gradient streams. Coal mining in this region includes contour strip mining, mountain-top removal, and limited deep and longwall mining operations. Surface mining has degraded many streams that drain the Appalachian coal fields in southwestern Virginia, eastern Tennessee, eastern Kentucky, and northern Alabama (Barnhisel and Massey, 1969; Curry and Fowler, 1978). Because coal deposits are numerous in the Cumberland Plateau region (an area noted for its diversity and endemism of aquatic fauna), many species of mollusks have been extirpated from headwater streams where mining has been most intense. The market price of coal does not portray the array of external costs to society and to ecosystems associated with mining (Herlihy et al., 1990; Cullen, 1993). Surface mining strips away the overburden and exposes underlying coal seams; the result is typically dysfunction of vegetation, increased sedimentation, and mine drainage. The formation of sulfuric acid from exposure of iron pyrite acts as a solvent for metallic minerals bound in rock strata. Subsequent runoff may contain high levels of heavy metals, determined by local geology, that have toxic effects on aquatic fauna (Stiefel and Busch, 1983; Caruccio et al., 1988). Ahmad (1973) estimated that nearly 29,000 km (18,020 miles) of streams in Appalachia have been destroyed for decades to come from mining activities.

Erosion from mined slopes and haul roads has increased sedimentation and turbidity in streams. Branson and Batch (1972) recorded a 90 percent reduction in benthos in two Kentucky streams that receive low-level mine drainage and a high level of siltation and turbidity from spoil banks. From comparisons of flora and fauna in streams of mined and undisturbed watersheds, overwhelming evidence has been presented of the large declines in biological diversity and abundance of organisms (Vaughan, 1979; Matter and Ney, 1981).

Historic and recent accounts of surface mining effects on aquatic mollusks are replete in the scientific literature. Neel and Allen (1964) attributed the decline of riffleshells (*Epioblasma* spp.) in the Cumberland River system to increased coal mining, particularly in the Big South Fork watershed. Starnes and Starnes (1980) indicated coal mining as the cause for the disappearance of the little-wing pearlymussel (*Pegias fabula*) and for the rapid decline of other mollusks in the Big South Fork. Stansbery (1969) attributed declines in diversity and density of mussels below the Cumberland Falls to acid mine drainage from upstream mines. Branson et al. (1984) reported the extirpation of mollusks from two streams in Kentucky affected by surface mining. Williams (1969) observed deposited coal waste on the periostracum of mussels in Kentucky but could not determine whether such debris was detrimental to mussels. In Virginia, aquatic mollusks were eliminated in the North Anna River below an acid mine drainage outfall (Simmons, 1972). In the upper Powell River, Virginia, freshwater mussels and gastropods were eliminated for about 24 river km (about 15 miles). Ortmann (1918) collected mussels as far upstream as Powell River Mile (PRM) 178.2, but subsequent surveys recorded sites above PRM 140 to be seriously degraded by coal waste and sediment disposition, and no mussels were found upstream of PRM 165 (Ahlstedt and Brown, 1979; Neves et al., 1980; Dennis, 1981; Wolcott and Neves, 1994).

Although the Surface Mine Control and Reclamation Act of 1977 (SMCRA) has done much to reduce severe degradation caused by erosion and acid mine drainage (Doll, 1988), increased demand for coal in the 1980s expanded mining in existing coal fields and in previously undisturbed areas. Documentation of declines in freshwater mollusks in the Southeast continue to appear in the literature and are attributed principally to sedimentation from active mines. Houp (1993) reported excessive sand deposits from coal mining in the North Fork of the Red River, Kentucky, and described how chronic sedimentation can gradually alter species composition of mussels through habitat degradation, shell erosion, and reproductive failure. Anderson (1989) evaluated the mussel assemblages in four streams of the Cumberland River drainage where coal mining began in the 1980s. In situ toxicity tests indicated lethal conditions in stream segments below mined areas regardless of pH conditions. He concluded that surface mining regulations are inadequate to protect mussels in this drainage. Thus, although environmental safeguards are much improved, negative effects of coal mining continue to jeopardize mollusks in headwater streams.

One effect of coal mining that has not been addressed in previous reports is the treatment and disposal of hydraulic oils by longwall mining operations. Hydraulic oil emulsions in the hydraulic jacks and other underground equipment are acutely toxic to aquatic life. These oils contain a variety of additives, including biocides, to prolong their use and purity in hydraulic systems. Depending on the oil product, LC50 values on standard bioassay organisms demonstrated toxicity levels ranging from parts per million (mg/L) to parts per billion (μg/L) (Biological Monitoring, Inc., 1991, 1993). Results of these studies also indicate that available treatment technologies can profoundly reduce the concentration of emulsion present and resulting effluent toxicity. Contaminated minewater treatment and effluent monitoring by fluorometry should be mandatory requirements imposed by federal and state regulatory agencies responsible for discharges from longwall mining operations.

Other types of mining activities also affect aquatic mollusks. Ortmann (1924) suggested that phosphate and iron mines in the Duck River watershed, Tennessee, caused a precipitous decline in mussel populations. Reduced growth rates have been reported in mussel populations in the Tennessee River downstream of sand and gravel mining operations (Yokley, 1976). Hartfield (1993) has reported mussel extirpations associated with offsite impacts of instream and floodplain sand and gravel mines. In western North Carolina, the mining of industrial minerals (kaolin, mica, feldspar) caused significant water quality problems in receiving streams (Tennessee Valley Authority, 1971; U.S. Environmental Protection Agency, 1977; Duda and Penrose, 1980). The North Toe River has been categorized as a biological desert (Tennessee Valley Authority, 1971) with such severe sedimentation that the Davy Crockett Reservoir, more than 200 river km (124 miles) downstream of the mines, is now filled with sediment and is inoperable for power generation.

Channel Degradation

Dredging and channelization contribute to stream channel instability as running water seeks its base level of gravitational flow. The destructive effects of channelization and extensive dredging include accelerated erosion, substratum instability, and the loss of habitat heterogeneity for fishes and benthic invertebrates. Maintenance dredging for navigation and gravel dredging in large rivers has been a perpetual problem for sedentary mollusks that are displaced and killed in dredge spoils. According to reports of commercial mussel harvesters, dredging causes some of the most serious effects on mussel beds in the Mississippi, Ohio, Tennessee, and other rivers that sustain commercial harvest. Except for consideration given to federally listed endangered species, dredging projects have little regard for resident aquatic fauna, destroying faunal habitat and promoting community instability.

Although the volume of literature demonstrating negative on-site and off-site environmental and economic consequences of dredging for navigation and flood control is substantial (Smith and Patrick, 1991), these activities continue in the Southeast. For example, a channel maintenance project ostensibly for flood control is currently planned for the Big Sunflower River, which drains the western portion of the Yazoo River Basin, located in Mississippi. The Yazoo River Basin historically supported a diverse and dense assemblage of freshwater mussels in every major tributary. The Big Sunflower River is unusual in this portion of the Mississippi River alluvial plain, in that much of the mainstem river has not been subjected to dredging and continues to support a fairly diverse and dense mussel assemblage. Miller et al. (1992) and Miller and Payne (1994) have reported 32 species of mussels from the river, and densities exceeding 100 mussels per m^2 (about nine per square foot) at many locations. The channel maintenance project includes dredging much of the mainstem river where mussels are found. This project likely will have little long-term benefit towards flood control, but will undoubtedly destabilize the river bottom, destroy mussel beds, and jeopardize the ecology of this river.

Endangered mussels of big rivers such as the white wartyback (*Plethobasus cicatricosus*), orange-foot pimpleback (*P. cooperianus*), pink mucket (*Lampsilis abrupta*), and ring pink (*Obovaria retusa*) have been under siege for decades by navigational dredging mostly by the U.S. Army Corps of Engineers. Even the presence of federally endangered species does not prevent the modification of habitats where these animals reside. For example, the navigation channel below Pickwick Dam on the Tennessee River was slated for dredging, even though this river reach is a state-designated mussel sanctuary with federally endangered species present. After consultation with the U.S. Fish and Wildlife Service, the project was approved contingent on 1992-1994 sampling efforts to collect and translocate rare mussels from the affected zone. Tennessee Valley Authority divers nearly completed their transect sampling to remove mussels in 1994 before the dredging began. Although many animals were collected and saved from destruction, there is something inherently troublesome with human biases in the sacrifice of habitats for some species (e.g., invertebrates) but not for others. For purposes of analogy, if this project was to remove vegetation from the right-of-way for an existing powerline, where red-cockaded woodpeckers had taken up residence, would the nesting trees and surrounding woodlands be removed? Aren't the trees used by woodpeckers analogous to the substratum occupied by aquatic mollusks? The legislative goal of equal treatment under the law continues to elude the non-charismatic creatures of America's heritage.

A more insidious result of channel degradation is head cutting, the effect of base level-ing of the modified channel on upstream reaches. Hartfield (1993) noted two primary sources of headcuts: channelization for flood control or navigation and gravel mining. Changes in stream channel, slope, discharge, and other physical factors are typically ac-companied by erosional processes that adjust and maintain channel equilibrium (Smith and Patrick, 1991). The longitudinal profile or change in elevation over distance of a stream is typically concave, and has a decreasing slope from the upstream (eroding) reaches to the lower (depositional) reaches. This profile is modified by local topography and stream-bed features, where an abrupt change in slope (knickpoint) can occur. Because of increases in transport capacity through downstream dredging, degradation through erosion will progress upstream until some knickpoint is reached. Water movements and erosion are typically pronounced at this location and eventually lead to failure of the overlying mate-rial and upstream migration of the knickpoint (Gordon et al., 1992). Thus modifications to the downstream channel can have repercussions far upstream, particularly in coastal plain streams with easily erodible substrata.

Hartfield (1993) described the following characteristics of recently headcut streams: extensive bank erosion; wide, degraded channels; extensive bank sloughing; unconsoli-dated and shifting sediment; perched tributaries at low flow; and the absence of character-istic mature trees of stable riparian zones. Freshwater mussels are particularly susceptible to headcuts because they are immobile and highly subject to channel instability. Hartfield (1993) reported headcut effects on mussels and snails to include federally endangered species in several rivers in Mississippi and Louisiana. Although the full extent of faunal losses is unknown, effects on rare species and their habitats are inevitable. The threatened inflated heelsplitter (*Potamilus inflatus*) is jeopardized by gravel mining in the Amite River, Mississippi. The black clubshell (*Pleurobema curtum*), heavy pigtoe (*P. taitianum*), and southern combshell (*Epioblasma penita*) are threatened with extinction; and the southern clubshell (*P. decisum*), ovate clubshell (*P. perovatum*), orange-nacre mucket (*Lampsilis perovalis*), and Alabama moccasinshell (*Medionidus acutissimus*) are in danger of extirpa-tion from remaining habitats in the Tombigbee River drainage due to habitat degradation. The Big Black rocksnail (*Lithasia hubrichti*) is on the verge of extinction because of chan-nel degradation in the Big Black River, Mississippi.

Nonindigenous Species

The introduction or translocation of non-native freshwater mollusks into the southeast-ern United States has been adversarial to native assemblages. The Asian clam (*Corbicula fluminea*) invaded the Gulf Coast and Interior Basin rivers in the 1960s and spread rap-idly throughout every major drainage in the southern United States. Its prolific reproduc-tive ability and ecological role as a filter-feeder are traits conducive to competitive interac-tions with native mussels. Although debatable evidence has been presented to document competitive exclusion between these bivalve taxa (Sickel, 1986), substratum space and food utilization are requisite resources that could be limiting in rivers with high densities of Asian clams. Juvenile freshwater mussels may become victims of stress from the highly mobile and abundant young Asian clams. After tens of millions of years of evolutionary speciation and adaptation to river systems in the Southeast, it is possible that native mol-lusks have filled all suitable niches in the benthos. Effects of competitive interaction are difficult to document and research is required to identify factors allowing coexistence or causing exclusion among mollusk species.

Several species of exotic snails have infiltrated aquatic habitats in the Southeast (Table 12), but there has not been the proliferation or degree of invasion that occurred with the Asian clam. Most of these exotic snails have specific habitat requirements, such that their distribution and competitive interaction has been limited. At this time, there is little evidence to suggest past or future significant changes to diversity of native gastropods because of these nonindigenous species.

Of greatest concern now and in the future is the massive invasion of the exotic zebra mussel (*Dreissena polymorpha*) and its sister species the quagga mussel (*Dreissena bugensis*) into North America (Rosenberg and Ludyanskiy, 1994). The zebra mussel presumably was transported to the Great Lakes in 1986 in ballast water derived from a European port. It ravaged native mussel populations in Lake St. Clair and Lake Erie (Schloesser and Kovalak, 1991; Hunter and Bailey, 1992), entered the Illinois River from Lake Michigan, and rapidly spread like a plague throughout the entire Mississippi River Basin (Ludyanskiy et al., 1993). In only nine years since its introduction into U.S. waterways, the zebra mussel now infests rivers, reservoirs, and lakes in 19 states.

The fate of native mussels in the Illinois River will be the test case for what can be anticipated in many southeastern rivers due to zebra mussels, and the status of native unionids and snails in this river is foreboding to other rivers (Blodgett et al., 1994; Tucker, 1994). From 1989-90 canals linking Lake Michigan and the Illinois River became infested, and zebra mussels were first collected at multiple sites in the river's mainstem in 1991. In 1992, they spread throughout the entire river, achieving densities of nearly 1,600 per m^2 (149 per square foot). By 1993, maximum densities approached 61,000 per m^2 (5,667 per square foot), and a gradient of increasing numbers was progressing downstream. Zebra mussels were attached to all solid substrates, including native unionid mussels and gastropods. From 4 percent to 100 percent of unionids had zebra mussels attached, up to about 1,500 per native mussel. Mortalities of unionids from attachments were apparent in 1993, caused ostensibly by the occlusion of unionid valves preventing normal respiration and feeding activity. As judged by the well-documented effects in this river, many native mussel species may soon be extirpated from the Illinois River and from other rivers in the Mississippi Basin with suitable environmental conditions for this prolific and deadly pest.

The transport of this zebra mussel into the Tennessee River up to the head of commercial navigation (Knoxville, Tennessee) was complete by 1993. Commercial barge traffic was obviously the major vector of transport to large rivers, but pleasure craft will probably continue to spread the zebra mussel into smaller rivers and reservoirs. It is almost inevitable that zebra mussel-infested waters will occur in nearly all southeastern states, and that some level of effect will occur to native mollusks. The zebra mussel will probably be the final nail in the coffin of several federally protected mussels that succumb to infestations in large rivers. Other commercial and rare mussels may require endangered species status if the zebra mussel infestations extirpate river and reservoir populations and drastically reduce the ranges of one-time widespread big-river species. The urgency of protection and conservation of native mussels cannot be overemphasized. Natural resource agencies in the Southeast must be proactive in efforts to prevent the wholesale extinction of mussels in

Table 12. Species of introduced freshwater mollusks in the United States.

Taxon	Common Names
Bivavia:	
Sphaeriidae:	
Pisidium amnicum (Müller, 1774)	greater European peaclam
P. henslowanum (Sheppard, 1825)	Henslow peaclam
P. supinum (Schmidt, 1850)	humpback peaclam
Sphaerium corneum (Linnaeus, 1758)	European fingernailclam
Corbiculidae:	
Corbicula fluminea (Müller, 1774)	Asian clam
Dreissenidae:	
Dreissena polymorpha (Pallas, 1977)	zebra mussel
D. bugensis (Andrusov, 1897)	quagga mussel
Gastropoda:	
Viviparidae:	
Cipangopaludina chinensis malleata (Reeve, 1863)	Chinese mysterysnail
C. japonica (von Martens, 1861)	Japanese mysterysnail
Pilidae:	
Marisa cornuarietis (Linnaeus, 1758)	giant rams-horn
Thiaridae:	
Melanoides tuberculatus (Müller, 1774)	red-rim melania
M. turriculus (Lea, 1850)	fawn melania
Tarebia granifera (Lamarck, 1822)	quilted melania
Lymnaeidae:	
Radix auricularia (Linnaeus, 1758)	big-ear radix
Physidae:	
Physa skinneri (Taylor, 1954)	glass physa
Planorbidae:	
Biomphalaria glabrata (Say, 1818)	bloodfluke planorb
Drepanotrema aeruginosum (Morelet, 1851)	rusty rams-horn
D. cimex (Moricand, 1839)	ridged rams-horn
D. kermatoides (d'Orbigny, 1835)	crested rams-horn

the direct path of the zebra mussel invasion.

The United States has had only piecemeal legislation to regulate the intentional importation of fish and wildlife species. The Lacey Act was the primary law for excluding harmful imports that posed a threat "to humans, aquaculture, horticulture, forestry, or to wildlife or the wildlife resources of the United States." However black-listed species under this legislation included very few species of finfish or shellfish. The Nonindigenous Aquatic Nuisance Prevention and Control Act of 1990 was the first legislation authorizing the U.S. Fish and Wildlife Service and the National Oceanic and Atmospheric Administration to issue regulations preventing the unintentional introductions of aquatic nuisance species such as the zebra mussel (Office of Technology Assessment, 1993). Regulations under this act will hopefully prevent the incidental importation of other aquatic mollusks harmful to native species. However, there is negligible federal involvement in the interstate transfers of nonindigenous fish and wildlife. Although states assume primary responsibility for interstate trafficking of nonindigenous species, most have insufficient standards of review and enforcement. Taken together, regulations at the federal and state levels are inadequate to exclude or regulate the import or transfer of harmful mollusks among states. It is essential therefore that new national legislation be prepared to increase the rigors of protocol for importation and release of nonindigenous animals and to establish state roles and responsibilities for transfers of such species. To prevent the intentional introduction of undesirable non-native aquatic species, the Lacey Act should be strengthened.

THE FATE OF SOUTHEASTERN RIVERS

Rivers of global significance in the Southeast have been permanently altered to provide human benefits measured in mere seconds of evolutionary time. The direct exploitation of rivers, which accelerated rapidly in the 1930s for water supply, flood control, hydropower, and navigation, has nearly ended. However, what remains are disjunct river reaches in most states with faunas isolated either by dams, pollution blocks, or other barriers preventing holistic recovery. The Federal Energy Regulatory Commission (FERC) has regulatory authority for relicensing hydropower dams, as well as authority to require the eventual decommissioning of old dams that have outlived their utility. For functional dams, conservation improvements to include fish passage, epilimnetic discharges, and minimum stream flows for fauna and for recreation are highly desirable. Too many dams in the Southeast continue to impede the migrations of fish and recovery of mollusks and other taxa in tailwater areas. Of the original 5.2 million km (3.2 million miles) of rivers in the United States, only 42 high-quality free-flowing rivers greater than 200 km (greater than 124 miles) remain (Benke, 1990). Very few of these rivers occur in the Southeast, and few federal or state programs are being actively pursued to protect these rivers. The federal government owns roughly 30 percent of the land in the United States, which is managed by the U.S. Forest Service, National Park Service, and Bureau of Land Management. Most of this land and inclusive watersheds occur in the western United States or in high-gradient areas (national parks and forests) in the East. Protection of the most biologically significant watersheds is unavailable through federal ownership.

The Wild and Scenic Rivers Act of 1968 provided a means to identify and conserve river reaches and to prohibit federal assistance on water projects that would adversely affect the naturalness of rivers. The legislation, however, did not protect rivers from private development beyond a narrow corridor (Goldfarb, 1988). As of December 1994, 17,175 km (10,672 miles) of river reaches were designated as wild and scenic under the Act (American Rivers, 1994). Of the 150 designated river reaches, only 17 are in the Southeast (Table 13). Arkansas dominates this region with 336 (45 percent) stream km (208.7 miles) under legislative protection, whereas Virginia and Tennessee have no stream reaches in the system. Most designated reaches are in national forests and do not include rivers and watersheds with high molluscan diversity in most urgent need of protection. The bulk of protection has seemingly been directed at streams that already receive federal, state or local protection under other means; i.e., streams of least resistance. American Rivers, the largest national river conservation organization, identified 25 rivers in 1993 considered to be the most endangered and threatened in the United States (American Rivers, 1993). On that list were the Everglades in Florida, St. Marys River in Virginia,

Table 13. Components of the National Wild and Scenic Rivers System in the southeastern United States in 1994.

River	State	Administrating Agency	Total River Kilometers (Miles)
Sipsey Fork of the West Fork	AL	U.S. Forest Service	98.2 (61.0)
Big Piney	AR	U.S. Forest Service	72.3 (44.9)
Buffalo River	AR	U.S. Forest Service	25.3 (15.7)
Cossatot River	AR	U.S. Forest Service Corps of Engineers State of AR	49.3 (30.6)
Hurricane Creek	AR	U.S. Forest Service	24.8 (15.4)
Little Missouri River	AR	U.S. Forest Service	25.1 (15.6)
Mulberry River	AR	U.S. Forest Service	89.6 (55.7)
North Sylamore Creek	AR	U.S. Forest Service	23.2 (14.4)
Richland Creek	AR	U.S. Forest Service	26.4 (16.4)
Loxahatchee River	FL	State of FL	12.0 (7.5)
Red River	KY	U.S. Forest Service	31.0 (19.3)
New River	NC	State of NC	42.4 (26.3)
Chattooga River	NC, SC, GA	U.S. Forest Service	91.0 (56.5)
Saline Bayou	LA	U.S. Forest Service	30.4 (18.9)
Black Creek	MS	U.S. Forest Service	33.6 (20.9)
Horsepasture River	NC	U.S. Forest Service	6.7 (4.2)
Obed River	TN	National Park Service	72.3 (44.9)
Total			753.6 (468.3)

Tennessee River in Kentucky, and White River in Arkansas. The Everglades, threatened by water diversion and pollution with agricultural and animal wastes, is home to a diversity of gastropods. The Tennessee and White rivers also have rich molluscan faunas. The Tennessee River, below the Kentucky Dam to its confluence with the Ohio River, is home to threatened and endangered mussels and is a state-designated mussel sanctuary. Hazardous wastes and toxic chemicals emanating from companies in Calvert City, Kentucky have placed the river fauna at risk. The White River is threatened by animal waste effluent, by effluent of wastewater treatment plants from the upper Missouri portion of the basin, and by resultant dissolved oxygen deprivation in the lower river. These organic wastes threaten finfish and shellfish in the reservoirs and free-flowing streams in the White River basin.

With such an underfunded effort by regulatory agencies to maintain the biological diversity and integrity of rivers in this region, it is little wonder that the extirpation and extinction of mollusks is occurring at an accelerated pace. The vanguards of river protection have become the national conservation groups such as American Rivers, Izaac Walton League, The Nature Conservancy, and Sierra Club, as well as local organizations such as the Cahaba River Society and others in the Southeast. Citizens organized into local groups under titles such as river keepers, stream and lake watch groups, and friends of various rivers have become the watch dogs of water quality. These groups are making considerable contributions to conservation and protection of water resources and should be encouraged to become more active and vocal in issues that threaten the integrity of aquatic habitats. The designations of outstanding resource waters in states have come most often by local organizations and grass roots support at the county and state level. The shakers and movers of aquatic habitat conservation are those individuals with a long-term vision and vested interest in their living space and quality of life. The 21st century will owe these visionaries a debt of gratitude for their perseverance to sustain islands of aquatic life amid clonal landscapes that have lost their biological exuberance.

CONCLUSION

The accelerating rate of decline of aquatic mollusks and other faunal groups in aquatic ecosystems of the Southeast is a national tragedy. Federal laws such as the Endangered Species Act, National Environmental Policy Act, Clean Water Act and others have decelerated but not prevented the degradation of habitats and the loss of biological integrity that we chronicle for posterity. Short-sighted and economically suspect projects damaging to mollusk populations, such as the proposed dredging of the Big Sunflower River, Mississippi, continue to appear. Even administrators acknowledge the recurrence of pork barrel projects, initiated to please wealthy constituents of local and national politicians at the expense of federal taxpayers (Bean, 1994). Riverine ecosystems are capital assets that will sustain local communities and economies as long as they are renewable, to provide long-term benefits to generations of residents. Sustainable development must include the wealth and health of the local environment; otherwise, people and businesses will seek greener pastures.

The piecemeal approach to conservation, focused on particular species and habitats, has not been effective. However, there is promise in new initiatives being proposed by federal agencies to address habitat and biodiversity issues on a watershed or ecosystem level. Water quality is inextricably linked to landscape ecology and land-use patterns in the watershed. The new vision of the U.S. Fish and Wildlife Service and National Biological Service is to conserve the nation's native animal and plant diversity through the perpetuation of dynamic and healthy ecosystems. Ecosystem management will promote the sustainability of ecological functions in watersheds of the Southeast. Thus an ecosystem approach to fish and wildlife conservation will enable natural resource agencies to conserve and restore the structure, function, and natural assemblage of biota in ecosystems, while accommodating sustainable economic development. The long-term viability of healthy ecosystems mandates compatibility between the needs of humans and those of our fellow creatures. As with most aquatic organisms, mollusks living invisibly beneath the water surface do not stir human emotions of endearment or physical affection. The bias towards terrestrial life and its conservation is an ecological malediction (Ryman et al., 1994). In spite of this inherent prejudice, the ecological and technological knowledge of scientists, engineers, and environmental specialists is of sufficient acuity to conserve aquatic species and resolve concerns for competing demands for water, environmentally safe effluent, restoration of damaged habitats, and maintenance of biological diversity and integrity. Implementing a program of ecosystem conservation requires the cooperation of all agencies that share responsibilities for public waters and the biota therein, as well as individuals who reside along waterways that are easily jeopardized.

Riparian landowners are the keystone players in aquatic ecosystem management. Without their interest, concern, and willingness to do what is best for the long-term sustainability of their properties and adjacent streams, holistic management will fail. Therefore, public education and awareness is crucial to establish the network of partnerships necessary to implement conservation in a country that has condoned economic development at any cost. News media lament the destruction of biodiversity in tropical rain forests while neglecting the comparably significant biological diversity in our southeastern rivers. Should we not tend to the needs of our own globally significant aquatic diversity before chastising other nations for their short-sighted mismanagement? We should educate as practitioners, rather than as pedagogues. One of the most respected aquatic malacologists of the early 20th century provided prophetic insight to what was and is a lasting legacy (Ortmann, 1909; page 91): "The destruction of our freshwater fauna forms a chapter of the book on the destruction of our natural resources, a record which is not at all to the credit of the nation."

REFERENCES

Agricultural Stabilization and Conservation Service. 1993. Conservation Reserve Program: Summary report. Agricultural Stabilization and Conservation Service, U.S. Department of Agriculture, Washington, D.C., 15 p.

Ahlstedt, S. A. 1991a. Twentieth century changes in the freshwater mussel fauna of the Clinch River (Tennessee and Virginia). *Walkerana* **5**:73-122.

Ahlstedt, S. A. 1991b. Reintroduction of the spiny river snail *Io fluvialis* (Say, 1825) (Gastropoda: Pleuroceridae) into the North Fork Holston River, southwest Virginia and northeast Tennessee. *American Malacological Bulletin* **8**:139-142.

Ahlstedt, S. A., and S. R. Brown. 1979. The naiad fauna of the Powell River in Virginia and Tennessee. *Bulletin of the American Malacological Union* **1979**:40-43.

Ahlstedt, S. A., and T. A. McDonough. 1993. Quantitative evaluation of commercial mussel populations in the Tennessee River portion of Wheeler Reservoir, Alabama. In *Conservation and Management of Freshwater Mussels.* K. S. Cummings, A. C. Buchanan, and L. M. Koch (eds.). Proceedings of a UMRCC symposium, St. Louis, MO. Upper Mississippi River Conservation Committee, Rock Island, IL, p. 38-49.

Ahmad, M. U. 1973. Strip mining and water pollution. *Groundwater* **11**:37-41.

Alderman, J. M., W. F. Adams, S. Hall, and C. McGrath. 1992. Status of North Carolina's state listed freshwater mussels. North Carolina Wildlife Resources Commission, Raleigh, NC, 7 p.

Aldridge, D. W., B. S. Payne, and A. C. Miller. 1987. The effects of intermittent exposure to suspended solids and turbulence on three species of freshwater mussels. *Environmental Pollution* **45**:17-20.

American Rivers. 1993. The most endangered rivers of 1993. *American Rivers* **21**(2):7.

American Rivers. 1994. The National Wild and Scenic Rivers System: 25th anniversary offers opportunity to reflect on progress. *American Rivers* **21**(4):10-11.

Anderson, R. M. 1989. The effect of coal surface mining on endangered freshwater mussels (Mollusca: Unionidae) in the Cumberland River drainage. M.S. Thesis, Tennessee Technological University, Cookeville, TN.

Athearn, H. 1970. Discussion of Dr. Heard's paper in American Malacological Union Symposium on Rare and Endangered Mollusks. *Malacologia* **10**:28-31.

Baker, F. C. 1928. Freshwater Mollusca of Wisconsin Part II. Pelecypoda. *Bulletin of the Wisconsin Geological and Natural History Survey* **70**:1-495.

Barnhisel, R. I., and H. F. Massey. 1969. Chemical, mineralogical, and physical properties of eastern Kentucky, acid-forming coal spoil materials. *Soil Science* 108:367-372.

Bean, M. J. 1994. Conserving endangered species by accident: The Duck River experience. In *The Big Kill: Declining Biodiversity in America's Lakes and Rivers.* D. S. Wilcove, and M. J. Bean (eds.). Environmental Defense Fund, Washington, D.C., p. 111-122.

Benke, A. C. 1990. A perspective on America's vanishing streams. *Journal of the North American Benthological Society* 9:77-88.

Biological Monitoring, Inc. 1991. Environmental risk assessment of the mining emulsion Texaco LWM-18. Final Report, Westmoreland Coal Company, Big Stone Gap, VA, 14 p.

Biological Monitoring, Inc. 1993. Environmental toxicity and treatment studies for Westmoreland Coal Holton Mine and Texaco LWM-18 emulsion. Final Report, Westmoreland Coal Company, Big Stone Gap, VA, 38 p.

Blodgett, K. D., S. D. Whitney, and R. E. Sparks. 1994. Zebra mussels in the Illinois River and implications for native mollusks in the Mississippi Basin. *River Almanac* 1994(September):3.

Bogan, A. E. 1990. Stability of recent unionid (Mollusca: Bivalvia) communities over the past 6000 years. In *Paleocommunity Temporal Dynamics: The Long-term Development of Multispecies Assemblies.* W. Miller III (ed.). Special Publication Number 5, Paleontological Society, Columbus, OH, p. 112-136.

Bogan, A. E., and W. R. Hoeh. 1994. *Utterbackia peninsularis*, a newly recognized freshwater mussel (Bivalvia: Unionidae: Anodontinae) from peninsular Florida, USA. *Walkerana* 7:275-287.

Bogan, A. E., and P. W. Parmalee. 1983. *Tennessee's Rare Wildlife, Volume II: The Mollusks.* Tennessee Wildlife Resources Agency, Nashville, TN.

Bogan, A. E., and J. M. Pierson. 1993a. Survey of the aquatic gastropods of the Coosa River Basin, Alabama: 1992. Final Report submitted to the Alabama Natural Heritage Program, Montgomery, AL, 14 p.

Bogan, A. E., and J. M. Pierson. 1993b. Survey of the aquatic gastropods of the Cahaba River Basin, Alabama: 1992. Final Report submitted to the Alabama Natural Heritage Program, Montgomery, AL, 20 p.

Bogan, A. E., J. M. Pierson, and P. Hartfield. 1995. Decline in the freshwater gastropod fauna in the Mobile Bay Basin. In *Our Living Resources: A Report to the Nation on the Distribution, Abundance, and Health of U.S. Plants, Animals, and Ecosystems.* E. T. LaRoe (ed.). National Biological Service, U.S. Department of the Interior, Washington, D.C., p. 249-252.

Branson, B. A., and D. L. Batch. 1972. Effects of strip mining on small-stream fishes in east-central Kentucky. *Proceedings of the Biological Society of Washington* 84:507-518.

Branson, B. A., D. L. Batch, and W. R. Curtis. 1984. Small-stream recovery following surface mining in east-central Kentucky. *Transactions of the Kentucky Academy of Science* 45:55-72.

Burch, J. B. 1973. Freshwater unionacean clams (Mollusca: Pelecypoda) of North America. Biota of Freshwater Ecosystems Identification Manual Number 11, Environmental Protection Agency, Washington, D.C., 176 p.

Burch, J. B. 1975. *Freshwater Sphaeriacean Clams (Mollusca: Pelecypoda) of North America.* Malacological Publication, Hamburg, MI.

Burch, J. B. 1989. *North American Freshwater Snails.* Malacological Publications, Hamburg, MI.

Caruccio, F. T., L. R. Hossner, and G. Geidel. 1988. Pyritic materials: Acid drainage, soil acidity, and liming. In *Reclamation of Surface-mined Lands. Volume I.* L. R. Hossner (ed.). CRC Press, Boca Raton, FL, p. 159-190.

Claassen, C. 1994. Washboards, pigtoes, and muckets: Historic musseling in the Mississippi watershed. *Historical Archaeology* 28:1-145.

Coker, R. E., A. F. Shira, H. W. Clark, and A. D. Howard. 1921. Natural history and propagation of fresh-water mussels. *Bulletin of the U.S. Bureau of Fisheries* 37:75-181.

Coon, T. G., J. W. Eckblad, and P. M. Trygstad. 1977. Relative abundance and growth of mussels (Mollusca: Eulamellibranchia) in pools 8, 9, and 10 of the Mississippi River. *Freshwater Biology* 7:279-285.

Cullen, R. 1993. The true cost of coal. *Atlantic Monthly* 272:38-52.

Curry, J. A., and D. K. Fowler. 1978. Coal strip mining in Appalachia-fish and wildlife considerations. In *Surface Mining and Fish/Wildlife Needs in the Eastern United States: Proceedings of a Symposium.* D. E. Samuel, J. R. Stauffer, C. H. Hocutt, and W. T. Mason, Jr. (eds.). FWS/OBS-78/81, U.S. Fish and Wildlife Service, Washington, D.C., p. 23-28.

Dennis, S. D. 1981. Mussel fauna of the Powell River, Tennessee and Virginia. *Sterkiana* 71:1-7.

Doll, E. C. 1988. Relation of public policy to reclamation goals and responsibilities. In *Reclamation of Surface-mined Lands. Volume I.* L. R. Hossner (ed.). CRC Press, Boca Raton, FL, p. 41-54.

Duda, A. M., and D. L. Penrose. 1980. Impacts of mining activities on water quality in western North Carolina. *Water Resources Bulletin* 16:1034-1040.

Ellis, M. M. 1931. Some factors affecting the replacement of the commercial fresh-water mussels. Circular Number 7, U.S. Bureau of Fisheries, Washington, D.C., 10 p.

Ellis, M. M. 1936. Erosion silt as a factor in aquatic environments. *Ecology* 17:29-42.

Fuller, S. L. H. 1974. Clams and mussels (Mollusca: Bivalvia). In *Pollution Ecology of Freshwater Invertebrates.* C. W. Hart, and S. L. H. Fuller (eds.). Academic Press, New York, NY, p. 215-273.

Goldfarb. W. 1988. *Water Law. Second Edition.* Lewis Publishers, Inc., Chelsea, MI.

Goodrich, C. 1922. The Anculosae of the Alabama River drainage. *Miscellaneous Publications (University of Michigan, Museum of Zoology)* 7:1-57.

Goodrich, C. 1924. The genus *Gyrotoma. Miscellaneous Publications (University of Michigan, Museum of Zoology)* 12:1-29.

Goodrich, C. 1936. *Goniobasis* of the Coosa River, Alabama. *Miscellaneous Publications (University of Michigan, Museum of Zoology)* 31:1-60.

Goodrich, C. 1944a. Certain operculates of the Coosa River. *The Nautilus* 58:1-10.

Goodrich, C. 1944b. Pulmonates of the Coosa River. *The Nautilus* 58:11-15.

Gordon, N. D., T. A. McMahon, and B. L. Finlason. 1992. *Stream Hydrology: An Introduction for Ecologists.* John Wiley and Sons, New York, NY.

Goudreau, S. E., R. J. Neves, and R. J. Sheehan. 1993. Effects of wastewater treatment plant effluents on freshwater mollusks in the upper Clinch River, Virginia, USA. *Hydrobiologia* 252:211-230.

Hartfield, P. 1993. Headcuts and their effects on freshwater mussels. In *Conservation and Management of Freshwater Mussels*. K. S. Cummings, A. C. Buchanan, and L. M. Koch (eds.). Proceedings of a UMRCC Symposium, St. Louis, MO. Upper Mississippi River Conservation Committee, Rock Island, IL, p. 131-141.

Havlik, M. E., and L. F. Marking. 1987. Effects of contaminants on naiad mollusks (Unionidae). Resource Publication 164, U.S. Fish and Wildlife Service, Washington, D.C., 20 p.

Heard, W. H. 1970. Eastern freshwater mollusks (II). The South Atlantic and Gulf drainages. *Malacologia* 10:23-31.

Herlihy, A. T., P. R. Kaufman, and M. E. Mitch. 1990. Regional estimates of acid mine drainage impact on streams in the mid-Atlantic and southeastern United States. *Water, Air, and Soil Pollution* 50:91-107.

Hershler, R., J. M. Pierson, and R. S. Krotzer. 1990. Rediscovery of *Tulotoma magnifica* (Conrad) (Gastropoda: Viviparidae). *Proceedings of the Biological Society of Washington* 103:815-824.

Hocutt, C. H., and E. O. Wiley. 1986. *The Zoogeography of North American Freshwater Fishes*. John Wiley and Sons, New York, NY.

Hoggarth, M. A. 1992. An examination of the glochidia-host relationships reported in the literature for North American species of Unionacea (Mollusca: Bivalvia). *Malacology Data Net* 3:1-20.

Houp, R. E. 1993. Observations on long-term effects of sedimentation on freshwater mussels (Mollusca: Unionidae) in the North Fork of Red River, Kentucky. *Transactions of the Kentucky Academy of Science* 54:93-97.

Hove, M. C., and R. J. Neves. 1994. Life history of the endangered James spinymussel *Pleurobema collina* (Conrad, 1837) (Mollusca: Unionidae). *American Malacological Bulletin* 11:1-12.

Hunter, R. D., and J. F. Bailey. 1992. *Dreissena polymorpha* (zebra mussel): Colonization of soft substrata and some effects on unionid bivalves. *The Nautilus* 106:60-67.

Isom, B. G. 1969. The mussel resource of the Tennessee River. *Malacologia* 7:397-425.

Jacobson, P. J., J. L. Farris, D. S. Cherry, and R. J. Neves. 1993. Juvenile freshwater mussel (Bivalvia: Unionidae) responses to acute toxicity testing with copper. *Environmental Toxicology and Chemistry* 12:879-883.

Johnson, I. C. 1990. Proposed guide for conducting acute toxicity tests with early-life stages of freshwater mussels. Contract Number 68-024278, Final Report, U.S. Environmental Protection Agency, Washington, D.C., 64 p.

Johnson, R. I. 1970. The systematics and zoogeography of the Unionidae (Mollusca: Bivalvia) of the southern Atlantic Slope region. *Bulletin of the Museum of Comparative Zoology* (*Harvard*) 140:263-450.

Johnson, R. I. 1980. Zoogeography of North American Unionacea (Mollusca: Bivalvia) north of the maximum Pleistocene glaciation. *Bulletin of the Museum of Comparative Zoology* (*Harvard*) 149:77-189.

Kat, P. W. 1982. Effects of population density and substratum type on growth and migration of *Elliptio complanata* (Bivalvia: Unionidae). *Malacological Review* **15**:199-127.

Keller, A. E., and S. G. Zam. 1991. The acute toxicity of selected metals to the freshwater mussel, *Anodonta imbecillis*. *Environmental Toxicology and Chemistry* **10**:539-546.

Lea, I. 1834-1874. *Observations on the Genus Unio. Volumes 1-13.* Printed for the author, Philadelphia, PA.

Lewis, J. 1868. Remarks on mollusks of the Valley of the Mohawk. *American Journal of Conchology* 4:241-245.

Ludyanskiy, M. L., D. McDonald, and D. MacNeill. 1993. Impact of the zebra mussel, a bivalve invader. *BioScience* **43**:533-544.

Marking, L. L., and T. D. Bills. 1979. Acute effects of silt and sand sedimentation on freshwater mussels. J. L. Rasmussen (ed.). *Proceedings of the UMRCC Symposium on Upper Mississippi River Bivalve Mollusks*, Rock Island, IL, p. 204-211.

Matter, W. J., and J. J. Ney. 1981. The impact of surface mine reclamation on headwater streams in southwest Virginia. *Hydrobiologia* **28**:63-71.

Miller, A. C., and B. S. Payne. 1994. An analysis of freshwater mussels (Unionidae) in the Big Sunflower River, Mississippi, 1993 studies for the Big Sunflower River Maintenance Project, Mississippi. Final Report, U.S. Army Corps of Engineers, Vicksburg, MS, 106 p.

Miller, A. C., B. S. Payne, and P. D. Hartfield. 1992. Characterization of a dense mussel bed in the Big Sunflower River, Mississippi. *Journal of the Mississippi Academy of Sciences* 37:8-11.

Neel, J. K., and W. R. Allen. 1964. The mussel fauna of the upper Cumberland Basin before its impoundment. *Malacologia* 1:427-459.

Neves, R. J., G. B. Pardue, E. F. Benfield, and S. D. Dennis. 1980. An evaluation of endangered mollusks in Virginia. Project E-F-1, Final Report, Virginia Commission of Game and Inland Fisheries, Richmond, VA, 140 p.

Office of Technology Assessment. 1993. Harmful non-indigenous species in the United States. OTA-F-565, U.S. Congress, Washington, D.C., 391 p.

Ortmann, A. E. 1909. The destruction of the fresh-water fauna in western Pennsylvania. *Proceedings of the American Philosophical Society* **48**:90-110.

Ortmann, A. E. 1918. The nayades (freshwater mussels) of the Upper Tennessee drainage with notes on synonymy and distribution. *Proceedings of the American Philosophical Society* 57:521-626.

Ortmann, A. E. 1924. The naiad-fauna of Duck River in Tennessee. *American Midland Naturalist* 9:18-62.

Ortmann, A. E. 1925. The naiad fauna of the Tennessee River system below Walden Gorge. *American Midland Naturalist* 9:321-371.

Osbourne, L. L., and D. E. Kovacic. 1993. Riparian vegetated buffer strips in water-quality restoration and stream management. *Freshwater Biology* 29:243-258.

Palmer, S. 1986. Some extinct molluscs of the U.S.A. *Atala* 13:1-7.

Pajak, P., R. E. Wehnes, L. Gates, G. Siegwarth, J. Lyons, J. M. Pitlo, R. S. Holland, D. P. Rosebloom, and L. Zuckerman. 1994. Agricultural land use and reauthorization of the 1990 Farm Bill. *Fisheries* **19**(12):22-27.

Patrick, R. 1992. *Surface Water Quality: Have the Laws Been Successful?* Princeton University Press, Princeton, NJ.

Rader, D. 1994. Programs to protect aquatic biodiversity in North Carolina. In *The Big Kill: Declining Biodiversity in America's Lakes and Rivers.* D. S. Wilcove, and M. J. Bean (eds.). Environmental Defense Fund, Washington, D.C., p. 81-100.

Rafinesque, C. S. 1820. Monographie des coquilles bivalves et fluviatiles de la Riviere Ohio. *Annales Generales des Sciences Physiques, Bruxelles* 5(13):287-322.

Rafinesque, C. S. 1831. Continuation of a monograph of the bivalve shells of the river Ohio, and other rivers of the western states. Privately printed, Philadelphia, PA, 8 p.

Rosenberg, G., and M. L. Ludyanskiy. 1994. A nomenclatural review of *Dreissena* (Bivalvia: Dreissenidae), with identification of the quagga mussel as *Dreissena bugensis. Canadian Journal of Fisheries and Aquatic Sciences* 51:1474-1484.

Ryman, N., F. Utter, and L. Laikre. 1994. Protection of aquatic biodiversity. In *The State of the World's Fishery Resources: Proceedings of the World Fisheries Congress Plenary Sessions.* C. W. Voigtlander (ed.). International Science Publishers, Lebanon, NH, p. 92-115.

Schindler, D. W. 1989. Biotic impoverishment at home and abroad. *BioScience* 39:426.

Schloesser, D. W., and W. P. Kovalak. 1991. Infestation of unionoids by *Dreissena polymorpha* in a power plant canal in Lake Erie. *Journal of Shellfish Research* 10:355-359.

Schultz, J., and R. Cruse. 1992. Effectiveness of vegetated buffer strips. Final Report, Leopold Center for Sustainable Agriculture, Ames, IA.

Scientific Council on Freshwater and Terrestrial Mollusks. 1990. A report on the conservation status of North Carolina's freshwater and terrestrial molluscan fauna. The Scientific Council on Freshwater and Terrestrial Mollusks, Raleigh, NC, 246 p.

Selzer, L. 1994. Water: Our next crisis. In *Proceedings of the Fifth National Conference: Water: Our Next Crisis?* S. Durdu, and R. Patrick (eds.). Academy of Natural Sciences, Philadelphia, PA, p. 153-163.

Sickel, J. B. 1986. *Corbicula* population mortalities: Factors influencing population control. *American Malacological Bulletin, Special Edition Number* 2:89-94.

Simmons, G. M., Jr. 1972. A preliminary report on the use of sequential comparison index to evaluate acid mine drainage on macrobenthos in pre-impoundment basin. *Transactions of the American Fisheries Society* 101:701-713.

Smith, L. M., and D. M. Patrick. 1991. Erosion, sedimentation, and fluvial systems. *In The Heritage of Engineering Geology: The First Hundred Years. Volume 3.* G. A. Kiersch (ed.). Geological Society of America, Boulder, CO, p. 169-181.

Smith, R. A., R. B. Alexander, and M. G. Wolman. 1987. Water-quality trends in the nation's waters. *Science* 235:1607-1615.

Stansbery, D. H. 1969. Changes in the naiad fauna of the Cumberland River at Cumberland Falls in eastern Kentucky. *Annual Report of the American Malacological Union* 1969:16-17.

Stansbery, D.H. 1971. Rare and endangered mollusks in eastern United States. In *Proceedings of a Symposium on Rare and Endangered Mollusks (Naiads) of the U.S. Bureau of Sport Fisheries and Wildlife.* S. E. Jorgenson, and R. E. Sharp (eds.). U.S. Fish Wildlife Service, U.S. Department of the Interior, Washington, D.C., p. 5-18.

Starnes, L. B., and W. C. Starnes. 1980. Discovery of a new population of *Pegias fabula* (Lea) (Unionidae). *The Nautilus* 94:5-6.

Stein, C.B. 1976. Gastropods. In *Endangered and Threatened Species of Alabama.* H. Boschung (ed.). *Bulletin of the Alabama Museum of Natural History* 2:21-41.

Stiefel, R. C., and L. L. Busch. 1983. Surface water quality monitoring, coal mining and water quality. In *Surface Mining Environmental Monitoring and Reclamation Handbook*. L. A. Sendlein, H. Yazicigil, and C. L. Carlson (eds.). Elsevier Science Publishing Co., New York, NY, p. 187-212.

Surber, T. 1912. Identification of the glochidia of freshwater mussels. Document Number 771, U.S. Bureau of Fisheries, Washington, D.C., p. 1-10.

Tennessee Department of Environment and Conservation. 1990. The status of water quality in Tennessee. Division of Water Pollution Control, Nashville, TN, 129 p.

Tennessee Valley Authority. 1971. Water quality management plan for the French Broad River basin-Nolichucky sub-basin. Tennessee Valley Authority, Chattanooga, TN, 66 p.

Thompson, F. G., and R. Hershler. 1991. Two new hydrobiid snails (Amnicolinae) from Florida and Georgia, with a discussion of the biogeography of freshwater gastropods of south Georgia streams. *Malacological Review* 24:55-72.

Tryon, G.W. 1873. Land and fresh-water shells of North America. Part IV. Strepomatidae (American Melanians). *Smithsonian Miscellaneous Collections* 253:1-435.

Tucker, J. K. 1994. Windrow formation of two snails (families Viviparidae and Pleuroceridae) colonized by the exotic zebra mussel, *Dreissena polymorpha*. *Journal of Freshwater Ecology* 9:85-86.

Turgeon, D. D., A. E. Bogan, E. V. Coan, W. K. Emerson, W. G. Lyons, W. L. Pratt, E. F. E. Roper, A. Scheltema, F. G. Thompson, and J. D. Williams. 1988. *Common and Scientific Names of Aquatic Invertebrates from the United States and Canada: Mollusks*. Special Publication 16, American Fisheries Society, Bethesda, MD.

U.S. Environmental Protection Agency. 1977. North Toe River study. Surveillance and Analysis Division, U.S. Environmental Protection Agency, Athens, GA, 49 p.

U.S. Environmental Protection Agency. 1994. The quality of our nation's water: 1992. EPA 841-R-94-001, U.S. Environmental Protection Agency, Washington, D.C., 328 p.

van der Schalie, H. 1945. The value of mussel distribution in tracing stream confluence. *Papers of the Michigan Academy of Science, Arts and Letters* 30:355-373.

van der Schalie, H., and A. van der Schalie. 1950. The mussels of the Mississippi River. *American Midland Naturalist* 44:448-466.

Vaughan, G. L. 1979. Effects of stripmining on fish and diatoms in streams of the New River drainage basin. *Journal of the Tennessee Academy of Science* 54:110-114.

Wilber, C. G. 1983. *Turbidity in the Aquatic Environment: An Environmental Factor in Fresh and Oceanic Waters*. C. C. Thomas, Springfield, IL.

Williams, J. C. 1969. Mussel fishery investigation: Tennessee, Ohio and Green Rivers. Final Report, Department of Fish and Wildlife Resources and Murray State University Biological Station, Murray, KY, 107 p.

Williams, J. D., S. L. H. Fuller, and R. Grace. 1992. Effects of impoundments on freshwater mussels (Mollusca: Bivalvia: Unionidae) in the main channel of the Black Warrior and Tombigbee rivers in western Alabama. *Bulletin of the Alabama Museum of Natural History* 13:1-10.

Williams, J. D., M. L. Warren, Jr., K. S. Cummings, J. L. Harris, and R. J. Neves. 1993. Conservation status of freshwater mussels of the United States and Canada. *Fisheries* 18(9):6-22.

Willis, R., M. Wilson, T. Hibner, and A. Robison. 1994. An investigation of sediment toxicity in the Horse Lick Creek System (Upper Cumberland River Drainage). Final Report, U.S. Fish and Wildlife Service, Cookeville, TN, 9 p.

Wolcott, L. T., and R. J. Neves. 1994. Survey of the freshwater mussel fauna of the Powell River, Virginia. *Banisteria* 3:1-14.

Yeager, B. L., and R. J. Neves. 1986. Reproductive cycle and fish hosts of the rabbit's foot mussel, *Quadrula cylindrica strigillata* (Mollusca: Unionidae) in the Upper Tennessee River drainage. *American Midland Naturalist* 116:329-340.

Yokley, P. 1976. The effect of gravel dredging on mussel production. *Bulletin of the American Malacological Union* 1976:20-22.

CHAPTER 4

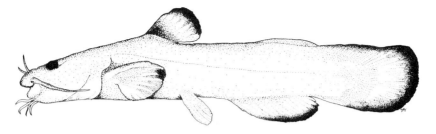

Jeopardized Southeastern Freshwater Fishes: A Search for Causes

David A. Etnier

E tnier and Starnes (1991) analyzed the approximately 300 taxa of native Tennessee fishes in an attempt to detect patterns associated with jeopardization or imperilment. Their analysis indicated that two habitat types (medium-sized rivers and springs) and two families (Ictaluridae and Percidae) contained disproportionately large numbers of jeopardized taxa. At the other extreme, no jeopardized Tennessee fish taxa were characteristic of quiet water (lentic) habitats, and none were centrarchids. In the following admittedly very subjective analysis I attempt to expand coverage to include all native freshwater fishes in a broadly defined southeastern United States, and to include reasons for imperilment.

ANALYSIS METHODS

For the purposes of this analysis, the southeastern United States includes the Ohio and Susquehanna rivers and their tributaries, south through peninsular Florida and to the Gulf of Mexico, and west to the west bank of the Mississippi River. Diadromous fishes (those that migrate to or from the sea to spawn) are included, but euryhaline species such as *Cyprinodon variegatus* (sheepshead minnow) and marine fishes such as *Trinectes maculatus* (hogchoker) are not. Nomenclature is essentially that used by Robins et al. (1991) except that *Hybopsis* is retained as a valid genus in Cyprinidae as has been done by Jenkins and Burkhead (1993; page 345) and Etnier and Starnes (1993; page 174). I have assigned preferred habitat (big river, medium river, creeks, headwaters [streams of first or second

Aquatic Fauna in Peril: The Southeastern Perspective, edited by George W. Benz, and David E. Collins. 1997. Special Publication 1, Southeast Aquatic Research Institute, Lenz Design & Communications, Decatur, GA, 554 p.

order], springs, caves, lentic, or diadromous) based on available published information, input from colleagues, and personal experience. In many cases where an obvious choice of preferred habitat was not possible, two habitats are listed (see Appendix 1), but the first of the two listed habitats is the one utilized in the analysis. This occurred most commonly within the continuum of lotic habitats. If, for instance, a species occurred commonly in both creeks and medium rivers, the habitat listed first and the one used for the analysis was the one where I perceived the majority of the populations to occur. Jeopardized taxa are those protected under the U.S. Endangered Species Act plus those that I feel (again with input from colleagues) warrant protected status because of rapidly decreasing size of range or naturally very small and localized range. Reasons for jeopardized status are based on knowledge of the species' biology, former range, and potentially disruptive anthropogenic activities within that range. For each of the 91 jeopardized species selected for analysis, one or two primary causes were identified as most likely responsible for their jeopardized status. For each identified cause, a score of one was recorded for each species for which it was the only cause identified, and a score of one-half for each species for which it was one of two causes identified. Total scores per cause were divided by 91 to obtain their percentage contribution to jeopardized status of southeastern fishes. While there is a large subjective element associated with assigning habitat preference, determining jeopardized status, and reason(s) for imperilment, I feel that Appendix 1 is sufficiently similar to the data set that would be generated by a consensus of southeastern ichthyologists, such that no major differences in interpretation would occur.

RESULTS AND DISCUSSION

The southeastern region treated contains 490 species of native freshwater fishes. Twelve of these species are currently under study, and are believed to consist of two or more species or subspecies in the Southeast. I consider 91 of these 490 species (19 percent) to be jeopardized. An additional 11 species have been considered by others to be deserving of protected status throughout their range. Two species on the list (*Lagochila lacera*, harelip sucker; *Fundulus albolineatus*, whiteline topminnow) are conceded to be extinct, and two additional species (*Noturus trautmani*, Scioto madtom; *Etheostoma sellare*, Maryland darter) are regarded as probably extinct (Etnier, 1994). Few if any southeastern ichthyologists consider the Alabama sturgeon (*Scaphirhynchus suttkusi*) to be extinct, in spite of the U.S. Fish and Wildlife Service's recent refusal to list the species because it was presumed to be extinct (U.S. Federal Register, 1994).

Since Tennessee's fish fauna contains approximately three-fifths of the native freshwater fish fauna of southeastern United States, it is hardly surprising that medium-sized rivers and springs, identified as jeopardized habitats in Tennessee by Etnier and Starnes (1991), again appear to be the habitats that contain a disproportionately large number of jeopardized fishes (Table 1). Creeks are preferred habitats for 51 percent of our southeastern fishes, but contain only 35 percent of the jeopardized species of the region. Lentic habitats contain 14 percent of southeastern fishes, but only three percent of the region's jeopardized species. Big river, headwater, cave, and diadromous habitats have jeopardized taxa proportional to total taxa that occur in each habitat (Table 1).

Medium-sized rivers are uncommon relative to creeks, heavily impounded, and have

Table 1. Total and jeopardized amounts of native southeastern freshwater fishes listed according to major habitat preference. [1]

Habitat	Number of Species	Percent of Total	Number Jeopardized	Percent of Total Jeopardized	Percent Jeopardized
Big River	45	9	6	7	13
Medium River	90	18	36	40	40
Creek	248	51	32	35	13
Headwaters	16	3	4	4	25
Springs	10	2	7	9	70
Caves	3	1	1	1	33
Lentic	70	14	3	3	4
Diadromous	8	2	2	2	25
Total	490		91		19

[1] Values derived from information contained in Appendix 1.

fish communities dominated by species dependent on coarse, silt-free substrates for feeding, reproduction, or both. Springs are noted for high endemism, may be drastically altered due to human demands on the high quality water they contain, and many have been inundated by reservoirs. Creeks (stream orders 3 and 4) continue to be "abundant," many are relatively unperturbed, and they are occupied by fishes that are likely to be equally adept at utilizing headwater streams as temporary refugia and using medium rivers as dispersal routes. Big rivers, such as the Alabama, lower Cumberland, Cape Fear, Mississippi, Ohio, Pee Dee, Roanoke, Santee, Savannah, and Tennessee, are certainly less "common" than medium-sized rivers, but their fish communities are dominated by species tolerant of the fine-grained depositional substrates that predominate in these habitats. Impoundments result in less drastic changes in these big-river habitats, and may actually convert medium-sized river habitats into ones ecologically more similar to those of big rivers. Three of six jeopardized big-river fishes are sturgeons. Lentic habitats, except for oxbows and temporary floodplain ponds along big rivers, have surely increased in abundance in the Southeast coincident with construction of farm ponds and reservoirs. The alligator gar (*Atractosteus spatula*) is treated herein as a big-river species, but its jeopardized status is likely due at least in part to a loss of floodplain waters adjacent to big rivers. As appears to be the case for big rivers, the number of jeopardized diadromous fishes and fish species in headwater streams and caves is approximately proportional to the number of taxa with a preference for these habitats (Table 1).

When analyzed by family (Table 2), the results are again virtually identical to those reported by Etnier and Starnes (1991). Catfishes (Ictaluridae) and percids (Percidae) have 26 percent and 31 percent of their species jeopardized, respectively — well above the overall 19 percent of southeastern fish species that are jeopardized. Sturgeons (Acipenseridae), with five out of six taxa jeopardized, were apparently capable of coping nicely with changes that occurred since the late Cretaceous (about 70 million years), until the past half century of dam construction and utilization of big rivers as silt and waste

Table 2. Numbers and percents of native southeastern jeopardized fishes by family. [1]

Family	Number of Species	Number Jeopardized	Percent Jeopardized
Acipenseridae	6	5	83
Cyprinidae	155	18	12
Catostomidae	35	5	14
Ictaluridae	31	8	26
Fundulidae	20	3	15
Centrarchidae	28	0	0
Percidae	149	46	31
Other Families	66	6	9
Total	490	91	

[1] Values derived from information contained in Appendix 1.

conduits jeopardized nearly the entire family. At the other extreme, the large and primarily lentic family Centrarchidae (sunfishes) contains no jeopardized taxa.

Catfishes (31 species) and percids (150 species) are well-represented in the Southeast, and contain 46 of 91 (51 percent) jeopardized southeastern fish species, but only 37 percent of southeastern native freshwater fishes. If these two families, or percids alone, have a disproportionately high number of taxa with a medium-sized river or spring habitat preference, the conclusion that we have been particularly abusive to spring and medium-river habitats may be unjustified, and an artifact of habitat preference of jeopardized families. Should this be the case, there must be something about the biology of catfishes and/or percids that results in their being susceptible to jeopardization. Nine of 31 catfishes (29 percent) and 36 of 149 percids (24 percent) are associated with medium-river habitats (data from Appendix 1). Both percentages are well above the overall mean of only 18 percent of all southeastern fishes with a medium-river habitat preference. On the other hand, 17 of 36 percids (47 percent) and four of nine catfishes (44 percent) with medium-river habitats are jeopardized. These figures are well above the overall 31 percent of percid and 26 percent of catfish species jeopardized in the Southeast. This indicates that there is both a familial and a preferred habitat aspect to imperilment, and the combined effect of these two variables has resulted in the large number of catfishes and percids that are jeopardized. All jeopardized catfish are madtoms, and all jeopardized percids are darters. Specialized reproductive behavior (both families), high endemism (darters), and high sensitivity to olfactory pollution (madtoms) have been suggested as contributing to the high percentages of jeopardized taxa in these groups (Etnier and Starnes, 1991).

Since only ten species have a habitat preference for springs, and these ten represent six different families, the conclusion that spring habitats have been jeopardized is inescapable. Only three percids were classified as spring inhabitants; all three are jeopardized.

As mentioned above, five of six southeastern sturgeon species are jeopardized. All are either anadromous or have big-river habitats. Impoundments have certainly been the major cause for their plight, either by blocking migratory routes (anadromous species), by blanketing spawning areas with silt in combination with the aforementioned factor (*Acipenser fulvescens*, *Scaphirhynchus suttkusi*), or by drastically altering flow regimes (*Scaphirhynchus albus*).

Factors contributing to the jeopardized status of southeastern native freshwater fishes are indicated in Appendix 1 and are summarized in Table 3. Based on these data, the combination of nonpoint-source pollution (primarily siltation) and alteration of flow regimes (primarily impoundment) are anthropogenic factors responsible for 72 percent of fish imperilment problems in the Southeast. A non-anthropogenic factor that contributes 23 percent to causes of jeopardization is high endemism (small native range). Point-source pollution and introduction of exotic fish species (less than two percent for each) have been far less influential. It should be noted that a similar analysis in western North America, especially the Southwest, likely would result differently and indicate exotic species introductions to rival alteration of flow regimes and exceed siltation in importance in contributing to jeopardized status of native fishes of that area. As an ichthyologist, fisherman, and former mentor of many students now associated with the aquarium hobby, it is reassuring for me to find that activities of people of these persuasions apparently have not resulted in jeopardizing native southeastern fish species.

Table 3. Percent contribution of various factors toward jeopardizing native southeastern freshwater fishes. [1]

Factor	Percent Contribution
Nonpoint-source pollution	40
Alteration of water flow	32
Small native range	23
Introduction of exotics	2
Point-source pollution	2
Overzealous collectors	0
Unknown	1

[1] Values derived from information contained in Appendix 1.

ACKNOWLEDGEMENTS

The author wishes to thank the two anonymous reviewers of this paper, whose considerable efforts resulted in significant improvements.

REFERENCES

Etnier, D. A. 1994. Our southeastern fishes — what have we lost and what are we likely to lose. *Proceedings of the Southeastern Fishes Council* **29**:5-9.

Etnier, D. A., and W. C. Starnes. 1991. An analysis of Tennessee's jeopardized fish taxa. *Journal of the Tennessee Academy of Science* **66**:129-133.

Etnier, D. A., and W. C. Starnes. 1993. *The Fishes of Tennessee.* University of Tennessee Press, Knoxville, TN.

Jenkins, R. E., and N. M. Burkhead. 1993. *Freshwater Fishes of Virginia.* American Fisheries Society, Bethesda, MD.

Robins, C. R., R. M. Bailey, C. E. Bond, J. R. Brooker, E. A. Lachner, R. N. Lea, and W. B. Scott. 1991. *A List of the Common and Scientific Names of Fishes from the United States and Canada.* Special Publication 20, American Fisheries Society, Bethesda, MD.

U.S. Federal Register. 1994. Endangered and threatened wildlife and plants; withdrawal of proposed rule for endangered status and critical habitat for the Alabama sturgeon. *U.S. Federal Register* **59**(240):64794-64809.

Appendix 1. Jeopardized southeastern fishes, their preferred habitat, and reason for jeopardized status. Preferred habitats were determined subjectively by the author with input from colleagues. Jeopardized fishes (and associated data) are listed in boldface, reason for jeopardized status was determined subjectively by the author with input from colleagues. Additional species whose status has been considered as jeopardized by other workers are indicated with a question mark in the status column, but were not treated as jeopardized in this analysis. Preferred habitats are as follows: BR = big river, MR = medium river, CR = creeks, HW = headwaters (orders 1 and 2), SP = springs, CA = caves, LE = lentic, DI = diadromous. MR/CR = medium river is my best guess, but some uncertainty is involved (treated as MR in analysis). Under the "Reason for Status" column: NPSP = nonpoint-source pollution, PSP = point-source pollution, Altered Flow = altered flow regimes such as impoundment or rechanneling, Small Range = taxa under no current threat but with a range so small that a single accident could result in federal threatened or endangered status, Exotics = taxa jeopardized due to introduced fish species. Area covered in this analysis includes: Ohio River and all of its tributaries, the Susquehanna River drainage, and south from there to the Gulf of Mexico, then west to the west bank of the Mississippi River. Marine and euryhaline fishes, such as *Trinectes maculatus* and *Cyprinodon variegatus*, respectively, are not included. Species preceded with an asterisk are currently considered to be complexes of two to several species or subspecies. [1]

Taxon	Preferred Habitat	Reason for Status
Petromyzontidae		
Ichthyomyzon bdellium	MR	
I. castaneus	MR	
I. fossor	CR	
I. gagei	CR	
I. greeleyi	CR	
I. unicuspis	MR	
Lampetra aepyptera	CR	
L. appendix	CR	
Acipenseridae		
Acipenser brevirostrum	**DI**	**Altered Flow**
A. fulvescens	**BR**	**Altered Flow**
A. oxyrhynchus	**DI**	**Altered Flow**
Scaphirhynchus albus	**BR**	**Altered Flow**
S. platorynchus	BR	
S. suttkusi	**BR**	**Altered Flow**
Polyodontidae		
Polyodon spathula	BR	
Lepisosteidae		
Atractosteus spatula	**BR/LE**	**Altered Flow**
Lepisosteus oculatus	LE	
L. osseus	BR	
L. platostomus	BR	
L. platyrhyncus	LE	
Amiidae		
Amia calva	LE	
Hiodontidae		
Hiodon alosoides	BR	
H. tergisus	MR/BR	
Anguillidae		
Anguilla rostrata	DI	
Clupeidae		
Alosa aestivalis	DI	
A. alabamae	**BR**	**Altered Flow**

Appendix 1. Continued.

Taxon	Preferred Habitat	Reason for Status
A. chrysochloris	BR	
A. mediocris	DI	
A. pseudoharengus	DI	
A. sapidissima	DI	
Dorosoma cepedianum	MR/BR	
D. petenense	LE/BR	
Cyprinidae		
*Campostoma anomalum	CR	
C. oligolepis	CR	
C. pauciradii	CR	
Clinostomus elongatus	CR	
C. funduloides	CR	
Clinostomus sp., smoky dace	CR	
Cyprinella analostana	CR	
C. caerulea	**MR/CR**	NPSP
C. callisema	**MR**	NPSP
C. callistia	CR	
C. callitaenia	**MR**	NPSP
C. camura	CR	
C. chloristia	CR	
C. galactura	CR	
C. gibbsi	CR	
C. labrosa	CR	
C. leedsi	MR	
C. lutrensis	CR	
C. monacha	**MR**	Altered Flow, NPSP
C. nivea	CR/MR	
C. pyrrhomelas	CR	
C. spiloptera	CR	
C. trichroistia	CR	
C. venusta	CR	
C. whipplei	MR	
C. xaenura	**CR/MR**	NPSP
C. zanema	CR	
Cyprinella sp. cf. zanema	CR	
Ericymba buccata	CR	
Erimystax cahni	**MR**	Altered Flow, NPSP
E. dissimilis	MR	
E. insignis	CR	
E. x-punctatus	MR	
Exoglossum laurae	CR	
E. maxillingua	CR	
Hemitremia flammea	SP	?
Hybognathus argyritis	BR	
H. hayi	LE	
H. nuchalis	BR	
H. placitus	BR	
H. regius	BR	
Hybopsis amblops	CR	

Appendix 1. Continued.

Taxon	Preferred Habitat	Reason for Status
H. amnis	MR	
H. hypsinotus	CR	
H. lineapunctata	CR	
H. rubrifrons	CR	
H. winchelli	CR/MR	
Hybopsis sp. cf. *winchelli*	CR	
Luxilus albeolus	CR	
L. cerasinus	CR	
L. chrysocephalus	CR	
L. coccogenis	CR	
L. cornutus	CR	
L. zonistius	CR	
*Lythrurus ardens	CR	
L. atrapiculus	CR	
L. bellus	CR	
L. fumeus	CR	
L. lirus	CR	
L. roseipinnis	CR	
L. umbratilis	CR	
Macrhybopsis aestivalis (Mississippi River)	BR	
Macrhybopsis sp. cf. *aestivalis* (Tennessee River)	MR	Altered Flow
***Macrhybopsis* sp. cf *aestivalis* (Mobile River)**	**MR**	**Altered Flow, NPSP**
M. gelida	BR	?
M. meeki	BR	?
M. storeriana	BR	
Margariscus margarita	LE	
Nocomis biguttatus	CR	
N. effusus	CR	
N. leptocephalus	CR	
N. micropogon	CR	
N. platyrhynchus	CR	
N. raneyi	CR	
Notemigonus crysoleucas	LE	
Notropis alborus	CR	
N. altipinnis	CR	
N. albizonatus	**MR**	**NPSP, Altered Flow**
N. ammophilus	CR	
N. amoenus	CR	
N. ariommus	MR	?
N. asperifrons	CR	
N. atherinoides	BR	
N. baileyi	CR	
N. bifrenatus	**CR**	**?**
N. blennius	BR	
N. boops	CR	
N. buchanani	BR	
N. cahabae	**MR**	**NPSP**

Appendix 1. Continued.

Taxon	Preferred Habitat	Reason for Status
N. candidus	BR	
N. chalybaeus	CR	
N. chiliticus	CR	
N. chlorocephalus	CR	
N. chrosomus	HW/CR	
N. cummingsae	CR	
N. dorsalis	CR	
N. edwardraneyi	BR	
N. euryzonus	CR	
N. harperi	SP	
N. heterolepis	LE/CR	
N. hudsonius	CR/LE	
N. hypselopterus	CR	
N. hypsilepis	CR	
*N. leuciodus	CR	
N. longirostris	CR	
N. lutipinnis	CR	
N. maculatus	LE	
N. mekistocholas	**CR/MR**	**NPSP**
N. melanostomus	**LE**	**?**
N. petersoni	CR	
N. photogenis	MR	
N. potteri	BR	
N. procne	CR	
N. rafinesquei	CR	
*N. rubellus	CR/MR	
N. rubricroceus	CR	
N. rupestris	**CR**	**Small Range**
N. sabinae	CR	
N. scabriceps	CR	
N. scepticus	CR	
N. semperasper	CR/MR	
Notropis sp., sawfin shiner	MR	
N. shumardi	BR	
N. signipinnis	HW/CR	
N. spectrunculus	CR	
N. stilbius	CR	
N. stramineus	CR	
N. telescopus	CR	
N. texanus	CR	
N. uranoscopus	CR/MR	
N. volucellus	CR/MR	
N. welaka	LE/CR	
N. wickliffi	BR	
N. xaenocephalus	CR	
Opsopoeodus emiliae	LE	
Phenacobius catostomus	CR/MR	
P. crassilabrum	CR	
P. mirabilis	CR	

Appendix 1. Continued.

Taxon	Preferred Habitat	Reason for Status
P. teretulus	CR/MR	
P. uranops	MR	
Phoxinus cumberlandensis	**HW**	NPSP
P. erythrogaster	HW	
P. oreas	CR	
P. tennesseensis	**HW**	NPSP
Phoxinus* sp. cf. *erythrogaster	**HW**	Small Range
Pimephales notatus	CR	
P. promelas	LE	
P. vigilax	BR	
Platygobio gracilis	BR/MR	
Rhinichthys atratulus	HW	
R. cataractae	CR	
Semotilus atromaculatus	HW	
S. corporalis	CR	
S. lumbee	**HW**	Small Range
S. thoreauianus	HW	
Catostomidae		
Carpiodes carpio	BR	
C. cyprinus	BR	
C. velifer	MR	
Catostomus commersoni	HW	
Cycleptus elongatus	**BR/MR**	Altered Flow
Erimyzon oblongus	CR	
E. succeta	LE	
E. tenuis	CR	
Hypentelium etowanum	CR	
H. nigricans	CR	
H. roanokense	CR	
Ictiobus bubalus	BR/MR	
I. cyprinellus	BR	
I. niger	BR	
Lagochila lacera	**MR**	NPSP, Altered Flow
Minytrema melanops	MR	
Moxostoma anisurum	MR	
M. ariommum	CR	
M. atripinne	**CR**	Small Range
M. carinatum	MR	
M. cervinum	CR	
M. duquesnei	CR	
M. erythrurum	CR	
Moxostoma sp. cf. *poecilurum*	CR/MR	
M. hamiltoni	CR	
M. lachneri	CR	
M. macrolepidotum	MR	
M. pappilosum	CR/MR	
M. poecilurum	CR	
M. rhothoecum	CR	
M. robustum	**MR**	Exotics, Altered Flow

Appendix 1. Continued.

Taxon	Preferred Habitat	Reason for Status
M. rupiscartes	CR	
M. valenciennesi	MR/CR	
Moxostoma sp., brassy jumprock	CR	
Moxostoma sp., sicklefin redhorse	**MR/CR**	**Altered Flow**
Ictaluridae		
Ameiurus brunneus	CR	
A. catus	MR	
A. melas	LE	
A. natalis	LE	
A. nebulosus	LE	
A. platycephalus	CR	
A. serracanthus	MR	
Ictalurus furcatus	BR	
I. punctatus	MR/BR	
Noturus baileyi	**CR**	**Small Range, PSP**
*N. elegans	CR	
N. eleutherus	MR	
N. exilis	CR	
N. flavipinnis	**CR**	**NPSP**
*N. flavus	MR/CR	
N. funebris	CR	
N. furiosus	**MR**	**NPSP**
N. gilberti	**CR/MR**	**NPSP**
N. gyrinus	LE	
N. hildebrandi	CR	
N. insignis	CR	
N. leptacanthus	CR	
N. miurus	CR	
N. munitus	**MR**	**Altered Flow, NPSP**
N. nocturnus	CR	
N. phaeus	CR	
N. stanauli	**MR**	**Altered Flow, NPSP**
N. stigmosus	**MR**	**NPSP**
N. trautmani	**CR/MR**	**Small Range, NPSP**
Noturus sp., broadtail madtom	LE	
Pylodictis olivaris	BR	
Esocidae		
Esox americanus	LE	
E. lucius	LE	
E. masquinongy (southeastern races)	MR	?
E. niger	LE	
Umbridae		
Umbra limi	LE	
U. pygmaea	LE	
Salmonidae		
Salvelinus fontinalis (Southeast)	HW	?
Percopsidae		
Percopsis omiscomaycus	MR	

Appendix 1. Continued.

Taxon	Preferred Habitat	Reason for Status
Aphredoderidae		
Aphredoderus sayanus	LE	
Amblyopsidae		
Amblyopsis spelaea	CA	?
Chologaster cornuta	LE	
Forbesichthys agassizi	SP	
Speoplatyrhinus poulsoni	**CA**	**Small Range**
Typhlichthys subterraneus	CA	
Gadidae		
Lota lota	MR	
Cyprinodontidae		
Jordanella floridae	LE	
Fundulidae		
Fundulus albolineatus	**SP**	**Small Range, PSP**
F. auroguttatus	LE	
F. bifax	CR	
F. catenatus	CR	
F. chrysotus	LE	
F. diaphanus	LE	
F. dispar	LE	
F. escambiae	LE	
F. euryzonus	CR	
F. julisia	**SP**	**NPSP**
F. lineolatus	LE	
F. notatus	CR	
F. notti	LE	
F. olivaceus	CR	
F. rathbuni	CR	
F. seminolis	CR	
F. stellifer	CR	
F. waccamensis	**LE**	**Small Range, NPSP**
Leptolucania ommata	LE	
Lucania goodei	LE	
Poeciliidae		
Gambusia affinis	LE	
G. holbrooki	LE	
Heterandria formosa	LE	
Atherinidae		
Labidesthes sicculus	MR	
Menidia beryllina	BR	
M. extensa	**LE**	**Small Range, NPSP**
Gasterosteidae		
Culaea inconstans	LE	
Cottidae		
Cottus baileyi	CR	
*C. bairdi	CR	
C. carolinae	CR	
C. cognatus	CR	
C. pygmaeus	**SP**	**Small Range**

Appendix 1. Continued.

Taxon	Preferred Habitat	Reason for Status
Cottus sp., broadband sculpin	MR/CR	
Moronidae		
Morone americanus	LE/MR	
M. chrysops	BR	
M. mississippiensis	LE/BR	
M. saxatilis	DI	
Elassomatidae		
Elassoma alabamae	**SP**	**Altered Flow, NPSP**
E. boehlkei	LE	?
E. evergladei	LE	
E. okatie	LE	?
E. okefenokee	LE	
E. zonatum	LE	
Centrarchidae		
Acantharchus pomotis	LE	
Ambloplites ariommus	MR	
A. cavifrons	MR	?
A. rupestris	MR	
Centrarchus macropterus	LE	
Enneacanthus chaetodon	LE	
E. gloriosus	LE	
E. obesus	LE	
Lepomis auritus	CR	
L. cyanellus	CR	
L. gibbosus	LE	
L. gulosus	MR	
L. humilis	LE	
L. macrochirus	LE	
L. marginatus	LE	
L. megalotis	CR	
L. microlophus	LE	
L. miniatus	LE	
L. punctatus	LE	
L. symmetricus	LE	
Micropterus sp., shoal bass	MR	
M. coosae	CR	
M. dolomieu	MR	
M. notius	MR	
M. punctulatus	MR	
M. salmoides	LE	
Pomoxis annularis	LE	
P. nigromaculatus	LE	
Percidae		
Ammocrypta beani	CR/MR	
A. bifascia	MR/CR	
A. clara	MR	
A. meridiana	MR/CR	
A. pellucida	MR/CR	
A. vivax	CR/MR	

Appendix 1. Continued.

Taxon	Preferred Habitat	Reason for Status
Crystallaria asprella	**MR**	**Altered Flow**
Etheostoma acuticeps	**MR**	**Altered Flow, NPSP**
Etheostoma (Doration) sp. (Caney Fork)	CR/MR	Small Range, NPSP
E. aquali	**MR**	**Small Range, NPSP**
E. asprigene	BR	
E. baileyi	CR	
E. barbouri	CR	
E. barrenense	CR	
*E. bellator	CR	
E. bellum	CR	
*E. blennioides	CR	
E. blennius	CR	
E. boschungi	**CR**	**Altered Flow, NPSP**
*E. brevirostrum	**CR**	**Altered Flow, NPSP**
E. caeruleum	CR	
E. camurum	MR/CR	
E. chermocki	**CR**	**Small Range**
E. chienense	**CR**	**Small Range, NPSP**
E. chlorobranchium	CR	
E. chlorosomum	MR/BR	
E. chuckwachatte	**CR**	**NPSP, Small Range**
E. cinereum	**MR**	**NPSP, Altered Flow**
E. collis	CR	
E. colorosum	CR	
E. coosae	CR	
E. corona	**CR**	**Small Range, NPSP**
E. crossopterum	CR	
E. davisoni	CR	
E. ditrema	**SP**	**NPSP, Altered Flow**
E. douglasi	**CR**	**NPSP**
E. duryi	CR	
E. edwini	CR	
E. etnieri	CR	
E. etowahae	**CR**	**NPSP**
E. exile	LE	
E. flabellare	CR	
E. flavum	CR	
E. forbesi	**CR**	**Small Range, NPSP**
E. fricksium	CR	
E. fusiforme	LE	
E. gracile	CR	
E. histrio	BR/MR	
E. hopkinsi	CR	
E. inscriptum	CR	
E. jessiae	CR	
E. jordani	CR/MR	
E. kanawhae	CR	
E. kennicotti	CR	

Appendix 1. Continued.

Taxon	Preferred Habitat	Reason for Status
E. lachneri	CR	
E. longimanum	CR	
E. luteovinctum	CR	
E. lynceum	CR	
E. maculatum	MR	Altered Flow
E. mariae	CR	Small Range
E. microlepidum	MR	Altered Flow
E. microperca	CR	
E. neopterum	CR	Small Range
E. nigripinne	CR	
E. nigrum	CR	
E. nuchale	SP	NPSP, Altered Flow
E. obeyense	CR	
E. okaloosae	CR	Exotics, Small Range
E. olivaceum	CR	Small Range
E. olmstedi	CR	
E. oophylax	CR	
E. osburni	CR	NPSP
E. parvipinne	HW	
Etheostoma percnurum	MR	NPSP, Altered Flow
E. podostemone	CR	
E. proeliare	LE	
E. pseudovulatum	CR	Small Range
E. pyrrhogaster	CR	NPSP, Altered Flow
E. rafinesquei	CR	
E. ramseyi	CR	
E. raneyi	CR	NPSP
E. rubrum	CR/MR	Small Range, NPSP
E. rufilineatum	CR	
E. rupestre	CR/MR	
E. sagitta	HW	?
E. sanguifluum	MR	
E. scotti	CR	NPSP
E. sellare	CR/MR	Exotics, Small Range
E. serrifer	LE	
E. simoterum	CR	
E. smithi	CR	
*E. spectabile	HW	
E. squamiceps	CR	
*E. stigmaeum	CR	
E. striatulum	CR	NPSP, Small Range
E. swaini	CR	
E. swannanoa	CR	
E. tallapoosae	CR	
E. thalassinum	CR	
E. tippecanoe	MR	Altered Flow, NPSP
E. trisella	CR	Altered Flow
E. tuscumbia	SP	Altered Flow, PSP
E. variatum	CR	

Appendix 1. Continued.

Taxon	Preferred Habitat	Reason for Status
E. virgatum	CR	
E. vitreum	CR	
E. vulneratum	MR	
E. wapiti	**MR**	Altered Flow
E. whipplei	HW	
E. zonale	CR	
E. zonifer	CR	
*E. zonistium	CR	
Perca flavescens	LE	
Percina antesella	**MR**	Altered Flow, NPSP
P. aurantiaca	MR	
P. aurolineata	**MR**	NPSP, Altered Flow
P. aurora	**MR**	Altered Flow, NPSP
P. austroperca	CR	
P. brevicauda	**MR**	Altered Flow, NPSP
P. burtoni	**MR**	Altered Flow, NPSP
P. caprodes	CR/MR	
P. copelandi	MR	
P. crassa	CR	
P. evides	MR/CR	
Percina (*Alvordius*) sp., bridled darter	**MR/CR**	NPSP, Small Range
P. gymnocephala	CR	
P. jenkinsi	**MR**	Small Range
P. lenticula	**MR**	Altered Flow, NPSP
P. macrocephala	**MR**	NPSP, Altered Flow
P. maculata	CR	
P. nigrofasciata	CR/MR	
P. notogramma	CR	
P. oxyrhynchus	MR	
P. palmaris	MR/CR	
P. peltata	CR	
P. phoxocephala	MR	
P. rex	**MR**	NPSP, Small Range
P. roanoka	CR	
P. sciera	CR	
P. shumardi	BR	
P. squamata	MR	
P. stictogaster	CR/MR	?
P. tanasi	**MR**	Altered Flow
P. uranidea	MR	
P. vigil	CR	
Percina (Hadropterus) sp. (Chattahoochee River)	CR/MR	
Percina (Percina) sp. (Coosa River, etc)	CR/MR	
Percina (Percina) sp. (Gulf Coast)	CR	
Stizostedion canadense	BR	
S. vitreum	BR	

Appendix 1. Continued.

Taxon	Preferred Habitat	Reason for Status
Sciaenidae		
Aplodinotus grunniens	BR	

[1] DATA SUMMARY: 490 taxa, 91 jeopardized taxa. Habitat summary (number of total taxa:number of jeopardized taxa): Big River = 45:6, Medium River = 90:36, Creeks = 248:32, Headwaters = 16:4, Springs = 10:7, Caves = 3:1, Lentic = 70:3, Diadromous = 8:2. Family summary (number of total taxa:numbers of jeopardized taxa): Acipenseridae = 6:5, Cyprinidae = 155:18, Catostomidae = 35:5, Ictaluridae = 31:8, Fundulidae = 20:3, Centrarchidae = 28:0, Percidae = 150:46.

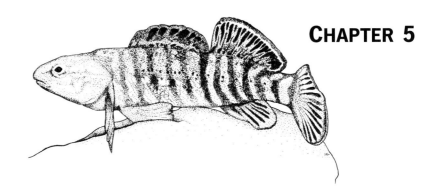

CHAPTER 5

Decline of a Diverse Fish Fauna: Patterns of Imperilment and Protection in the Southeastern United States

Melvin L. Warren, Jr., Paul L. Angermeier,

Brooks M. Burr, and Wendell R. Haag

The southeastern United States harbors the richest freshwater fish fauna on the North American continent north of Mexico (Burr and Mayden, 1992), but portents of decline of this great fauna are increasingly acknowledged (e.g., Burr and Warren, 1986; Mount, 1986; Burkhead and Jenkins, 1991; Etnier and Starnes, 1991; Ross and Brenneman, 1991; Gilbert, 1992; Warren and Burr, 1994; Angermeier, 1995; Menhinick, in press). Southeastern fishes (493 species) comprise about 47 percent of the North American fish fauna (1,061 species) and 62 percent of the fauna in the United States (790 species) (Page and Burr, 1991; Burr and Mayden, 1992). Within the United States, imperilment of southeastern fishes is second only to that of western fishes (Williams et al., 1989; Minckley and Deacon, 1991; Warren and Burr, 1994). Unlike the southeastern fish fauna, the western fish fauna of North America is relatively depauperate, and the proportion of the western fish fauna that is extinct or threatened with extinction

Aquatic Fauna in Peril: The Southeastern Perspective, edited by George W. Benz, and David E. Collins. 1997. Special Publication 1, Southeast Aquatic Research Institute, Lenz Design & Communications, Decatur, GA, 554 p.

is high (Miller et al., 1989; Moyle and Williams, 1990; Warren and Burr, 1994). In response to wholesale losses of native fishes, comprehensive programs in the west are underway or planned to conserve and recover fish diversity (e.g., Minckley and Deacon, 1991; Moyle and Yoshiyama, 1994), but success of these reactive approaches are as yet unknown. Increasing recognition of the decline of fishes and aquatic habitats in the Southeast, both harbingers of the western situation (Minckley and Deacon, 1991), should be the clarion call for proactive efforts toward conservation of the richest fish fauna in the United States.

Known extinctions of southeastern fishes are limited to two species, the harelip sucker (*Moxostoma lacerum*) and whiteline topminnow (*Fundulus albolineatus*) (Miller et al., 1989), but reduction in range, extreme isolation of extant populations, and extirpation of fishes from entire drainages are common (e.g., Etnier et al., 1979; Burr and Page, 1986; Starnes and Etnier, 1986; Jenkins and Burkhead, 1994; Warren et al., 1994). Fish extinction or local extirpation is nearly always attributable to multiple human impacts, and cumulative effects from complex aquatic degradation may obscure association of geographic, population, or ecological characteristics with extinction or extirpation patterns (Miller et al., 1989; Moyle and Leidy, 1992; Frissel, 1993; Angermeier, 1995).

Successful management for maintenance of fish diversity in the Southeast is, as in the West, a battle against extinction (Minckley and Deacon, 1991) and ultimately, a battle for ecological integrity at landscape scales (Angermeier and Karr, 1994). Studies of fishes (Sheldon, 1987; Etnier and Starnes, 1991; Nagel, 1991; Angermeier, 1995), island birds (Terborgh and Winter, 1980; Karr, 1990), and meta-population dynamics (Hanski, 1982) relate the process of extinction to factors that decrease habitat area and increase insularization (Angermeier, 1995). However, loss of diversity via extinction is not usually observable nor cataclysmic. Rather, the process is incremental with total extinction preceded by local or regional extirpations that usually reflect a population's sensitivity to decreasing habitat area and increasing isolation (Angermeier, 1995). Recent state and regional analyses of extirpation patterns (Sheldon, 1987; Etnier and Starnes, 1991; Nagel, 1991; Moyle and Leidy, 1992; Frissel, 1993) indicate that landscape-scale phenomena such as decreasing habitat area and increasing habitat fragmentation are associated strongly with regional loss of fish diversity. Theoretical considerations suggest that local extinction is accelerated when landscapes are insularized if meta-population dynamics are important (Hanski, 1982). Meta-population concepts have been applied only recently to stream fish conservation issues (Schlosser and Angermeier, 1995). Understanding (and ultimately preventing) anthropogenic extinction is likely to require greater focus on landscape-level patterns and processes than in traditional conservation approaches.

The Clean Water Act of 1972, as amended, is a potentially powerful statutory vanguard for proactive management for ecological integrity of aquatic systems (Blockstein, 1992; Angermeier and Karr, 1994), but the last line of defense against extinction of fishes in the United States is the Endangered Species Act of 1973, as amended. To effectively implement existing laws, two primary types of information are needed in the conservation arsenal (Warren and Angermeier, in press): accounting and ecological information. Accounting information (e.g., the presence or absence of taxa or communities) comes from inventories of sites, watersheds, or ecoregions. These data are necessary to integrate levels and geographic distributions of fish diversity across multiple spatial scales and to identify fishes and fish communities that are unique, rare, or imperiled. Ecological information, such as habitat needs or evolutionary history, helps elucidate factors involved in the generation and maintenance of fish diversity, may help predict potential losses of fish diversity, enhances successful recovery of diminished fish diversity, and identifies taxa or communities that are sensitive indicators of ecological integrity. The availability and synthesis of these two types of information are requisite to elucidating landscape-level patterns and developing effective management for native fishes.

Basic accounting information is available for southeastern fishes but has not been generally synthesized or analyzed for conservation assessment or planning (Etnier and Starnes, 1991; Angermeier, 1995; Warren and Angermeier, in press). Although ecological information also is available, the quality of that information varies widely for different fishes. As such, we rely here primarily on accounting information to discern patterns of imperilment at landscape scales. To date, there has been little effort to examine large-scale patterns of diversity and imperilment of southeastern fishes with the objectives of discovering general principles underlying imperilment that may be useful in proactive management or conservation triage (Frissel, 1993; Angermeier, 1995).

We provide here a beginning toward the large-scale synthesis of accounting and to a limited extent ecological information for fishes of the southeastern United States. In doing so, we present an up-to-date, comprehensive inventory of fishes of the Southeast and use geographical displays of fish and stream diversity and imperilment to convey the richness, spatial extent, and variation in these characteristics. For individual fishes and fish families, we ask two questions: is range size associated with imperilment, and is imperilment a function of familial membership? For major river drainages of the Southeast, we pose three questions: is fish imperilment associated with drainage area, native fish taxa richness, endemism, or stream-type diversity; which of these variables are the best predictors of imperilment; and what are the implications of the identified predictors?

Our specific objectives are to provide an updated distributional checklist of all southeastern freshwater fishes; summarize geographical patterns of fish imperilment, fish diversity, and stream diversity by state and major rivers in the southeastern United States; and examine relationships of numbers of imperiled taxa to native fish taxa richness, geographic range, drainage area, and stream-type diversity. We believe the maps and accompanying analyses are useful initial steps in prioritizing and coordinating conservation actions for fishes and other aquatic resources in the Southeast and in highlighting the urgent need for holistic approaches to aquatic conservation.

METHODS

Geographic Units

Our study area, referenced as the Southeast or southeastern United States, includes Alabama, Florida, Georgia, Kentucky, Louisiana, Mississippi, North Carolina, South Carolina, Tennessee, Virginia, and West Virginia (Figure 1). We followed Warren and Burr (1994) for the number of native fishes in each state. Although these totals may not exactly match those of others, they do illustrate patterns in fish diversity and levels of imperilment among southeastern states (Warren and Burr, 1994).

Within the 11-state study area, we recognized 33 drainage units (DU1-DU33) grouped

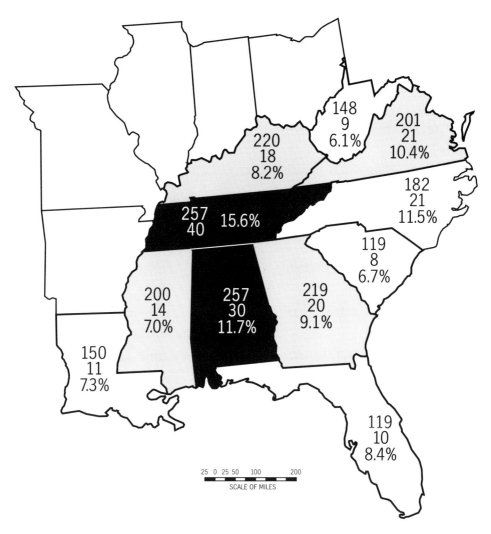

Figure 1. Total number of native fish taxa (upper value), number of imperiled fish taxa (middle value), and percent of total native fish fauna that is imperiled (lower or right value) for eleven southeastern states (modified from Warren and Burr, 1994). Imperiled fish taxa are those included in American Fisheries Society conservation status categories (see Williams et al., 1989). Dark to light shading indicates highest to lowest levels of native taxa richness.

into 11 regions (A-K) (Table 1; Figure 2). We delimited drainage units and regions based upon fish faunal similarity analyses (Burr and Warren, 1986; Hocutt et al., 1986; Swift et al., 1986; Warren et al., 1991), vicariance biogeography analyses (Mayden, 1988), drainage propinquity and interconnectivity, and debauchment into a common lake, sound, or bay (e.g., Chesapeake Bay, DU1-DU2; Albemarle and Pamlico sounds, DU3-DU4; Lake Pontchartrain, DU21).

As a measure of stream-type diversity, we calculated the number of hydrologic-physiographic types for each drainage unit and state in the study area. Each "stream type" is a unique combination of three attributes: drainage unit, stream size, and physiography.

Table 1. Hierarchical list of regions (A-H) and drainage units (1-33) for the southeastern United States.

A. Western Chesapeake Bay Region
    1) Potomac-Rappahannock-York River Drainages
    2) James River Drainage
B. Albemarle-Pamlico Sounds Region
    3) Roanoke River Drainage (including Chowan River)
    4) Tar-Neuse River Drainages
C. Long-Onslow Bays/Cooper-Santee Region
    5) Cape Fear River Drainage (including coastal drainages from Cape Lookout to mouth of Cape Fear River)
    6) Peedee River Drainage (from mouth of Cape Fear River to and including Peedee River)
    7) Santee-Cooper River Drainages (from mouth of Peedee River to mouth of Cooper River)
D. Edisto-Savannah-Altamaha Region (mouth of Cooper River to and including Altamaha River)
    8) Edisto-Combahee River Drainages (from mouth of Cooper River including Combahee and Coosahatchie systems to mouth of Savannah River)
    9) Savannah River Drainage
    10) Ogeechee-Altamaha River Drainages (from mouth of Savannah River to and including Altamaha River)
E. Peninsular Florida Region
    11) Satilla-St. Marys-St. Johns River Drainages (from mouth of Altamaha River to and including St. Johns River)
    12) Everglades-Tampa Bay-Waccasassa River Drainages (northwest to and including Waccasassa River)
    13) Suwannee-Aucilla-Ochlockonee River Drainages (from mouth of Waccasassa River to Apalachicola Bay)
F. Apalachicola-Florida Panhandle Region
    14) Apalachicola Basin (including Chipola, Chattahoochee, and Apalachicola rivers)
    15) St. Andrew-Choctawhatchee-Pensacola Bay Drainages
G. Mobile Bay Basin Region
    16) Coosa-Tallapoosa River Systems
    17) Lower Alabama-Cahaba River Systems (including Mobile Bay)
    18) Tombigbee-Black Warrior River Systems
H. Pascagoula-Pearl-Pontchartrain Region
    19) Pascagoula-Biloxi-Bay St. Louis Drainages (from Mobile Bay including Escatawpa and Bay St. Louis systems to mouth of Pearl River)
    20) Pearl River Drainage
    21) Lake Pontchartrain Drainage (from mouth of Pearl River)

Table 1. Continued.

I. Yazoo-Black-Mississippi Minor Tributary Region
      22) Minor Mississippi Tributaries South (eastern tributaries from mouth of North River to mouth of Black River)
      23) Black-Yazoo River Systems
      24) Minor Mississippi Tributaries North (from mouth of Yazoo River to and including Mayfield Creek)
      25) Mississippi River Mainstem
J. Tennessee-Cumberland Region
      26) Lower Tennessee River System (from mouth Sequatchie River downstream)
      27) Upper Tennessee River System (from and including Sequatchie River upstream)
      28) Cumberland River System
K. Southeastern Ohio River Region
      29) Green-Tradewater River Systems (from Mayfield Creek to mouth of Green River)
      30) Kentucky-Salt River Systems (from mouth of Green River to mouth of Licking River)
      31) Licking-Big Sandy River Systems (from and including mouth of Licking River to mouth Guyandotte River)
      32) Kanawha-New-Guyandotte River Systems (from and including Guyandotte to Kanawha-New)
      33) Ohio River Mainstem

Drainage units are defined in Table 1. Using a $1:10^6$-scale map (Fenneman and Johnson, 1964), we recognized three stream sizes: ≤ fourth order, fifth through seventh order, and ≥ eighth order. We used six physiographies (Fenneman and Johnson, 1964): Coastal Plain, Piedmont, Blue Ridge, Ridge and Valley, Appalachian Plateau, and Interior Low Plateaus. We took drainage-unit areas (n = 30) from stream gauging station compendia (Anderson, 1950; Hains, 1968) and Burr and Warren (1986), Swift et al. (1986), and Jenkins and Burkhead (1994). We did not estimate areas for DU12, DU25, or DU33.

Faunal Status

We obtained presence or absence and native versus non-indigenous status of fishes within a particular drainage unit (Appendix 1) from Lee et al. (1980), Hocutt et al. (1986), Starnes and Etnier (1986), and Swift et al. (1986). We updated this information from distribution maps in Burr and Warren (1986), Page and Burr (1991), Ross and Brenneman (1991), Etnier and Starnes (1993), and Jenkins and Burkhead (1994). We obtained distribution information concerning species described subsequent to the previously cited works, those resurrected from synonymy, and subspecies elevated to species from the following sources: Bauer et al. (1995, *Etheostoma scotti*); Boschung et al. (1992, *Etheostoma chermocki*); Burr and Page (1993, *Percina stictogaster*); Gilbert et al. (1992, *Fundulus auroguttatus* and *F. rubrifrons*); Mayden (1993, *Elassoma alabamae*); Page et al.

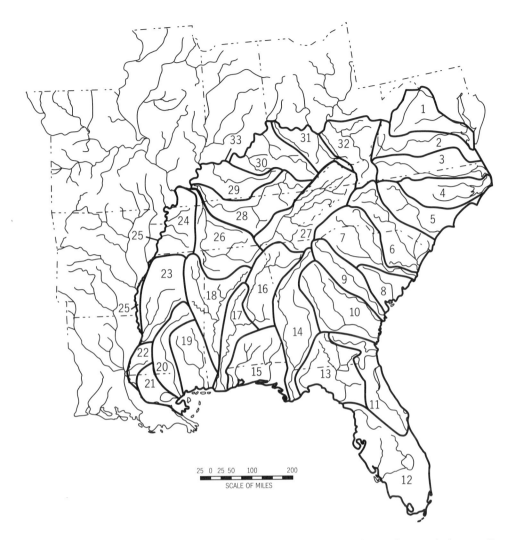

Figure 2. Drainage units within the southeastern United States. Numbers reference drainage unit names and delimitations set forth in Table 1.

(1992, *Etheostoma chienense*, *E. pseudovulatum*, *E. oophylax*, *E. corona*, and *E. forbesi*); Suttkus (1991, *Notropis rafinesquei*); Suttkus and Etnier (1991, *Etheostoma tallapoosae* and *E. brevirostrum*); Suttkus and Bailey (1993, *Etheostoma colorosum* and *E. bellator*); Suttkus et al. (1994a, *Etheostoma raneyi*, *E. lachneri*, and *E. ramseyi*); Suttkus et al. (1994b, *Percina aurora* and *P. brevicauda*); Thompson (1995, *Percina austroperca*); Warren (1992, *Lepomis miniatus*); Warren et al. (1994, *Notropis albizonatus*); Williams and Clemmer (1991, *Scaphirhynchus suttkusi*); and Wood and Mayden (1993, *Etheostoma douglasi*, *E. chuckwachatte*, and *E. etowahae*). For native fishes, we followed the familial arrangement, common names, and nomenclature of Mayden et al. (1992), and for exotic species, Page and Burr (1991). In the checklist (Appendix 1), we arranged genera and species alphabetically within families.

"Unique taxa" and "range extent" are indices of endemicity and cosmopolitanism, respectively, across the Southeast, as judged from known historical distributions of extant native fishes. Unique taxa are those restricted to one drainage unit. Most of these are endemic to one drainage unit in the Southeast, but a few are peripheral and occur outside the area. Range extent is the number of drainage units in which a particular taxon occurs or historically occurred.

We took the conservation status of fishes from lists published by the American Fisheries Society (AFS) (Deacon et al., 1979; Williams et al., 1989) and U.S. Fish and Wildlife Service (1994a, 1994b) (Appendix 1). Reference to "imperilment" or "imperiled" includes those taxa with any one of three AFS conservation status categories as recognized by Williams et al. (1989). We used this definition of imperilment for statistical analyses because of the time lag between recognition of a species as being imperiled and actual protection under the Endangered Species Act of 1973, as amended (Reffalt, 1991; Warren and Burr, 1994). The AFS categories included endangered (AFS-E), threatened (AFS-T), and of special concern (AFS-SC). We also used two combinations of these, AFS-ET and AFS-ETSC, in analyses to distinguish among: 1) the most critically imperiled fishes and 2) all fishes with a conservation status, respectively. Reference to "federal status categories" included endangered (E), threatened (T), proposed endangered (PE), proposed threatened (PT), candidate 1 (C1), and candidate 2 (C2) as listed in U.S. Fish and Wildlife Service (1994a, 1994b). "Protected federal categories" included only the first four of these (Littell, 1992).

We calculated "percentage imperilment" as the number of imperiled fishes in a drainage unit divided by the total number of native fish taxa in that unit × 100. We estimated percentage increase in imperilment as the total number of imperiled fish taxa in a drainage unit minus the total number of taxa recognized in Deacon et al. (1979) divided by the native fish taxa richness in the unit × 100. As ostensible temporal rates, we recognize these estimates do not account for the discovery of new or better distribution information for fishes nor the discovery of previously unrecognized taxa. As such, the assumption of a linear increase in imperilment over the ten-year interval may be invalid. The Deacon et al. (1979) and Williams et al. (1989) papers remained, however, the only temporal benchmarks available from which estimates could be made.

Statistical Analyses

We calculated familial imperilment, expressed in percent, as the number of imperiled taxa (AFS-ETSC) in a family divided by the number of native taxa represented in that family in the Southeast. We tested independence of total imperiled taxa in a family and familial taxa richness for the six most taxa-rich families using the likelihood ratio test (LI) (StatXact-Turbo, Mehta and Patel, 1992; G-test equivalent, Sokal and Rohlf, 1981). To help insure that no variables with potentially useful associative or predictive value were overlooked, we conducted all hypothesis testing at $p < 0.10$ (see Angermeier, 1995 and papers cited therein).

We assessed the relationship between range extent and imperilment across fish taxa using the Kruskal-Wallis test, analysis of variance with a priori orthogonal contrasts of means, and logistic regression (SAS Institute, Inc., 1994). For the Kruskal-Wallis test and analysis of variance, class variables were AFS-E, AFS-T, AFS-SC, and no status; the response variable was range extent. For logistic regression, imperilment (AFS-ETSC) and no status were the response variables, and range extent, the independent variable. We evaluated goodness of fit of the logistic model following Hosmer and Lemeshow (1989).

We tested total native taxa richness, imperilment (AFS-ET and AFS-ETSC), unique taxa, and stream-type diversity across the 33 drainage units for the departure of spatial distribution from random using the Index of Dispersion (I_D) where: $I_D = s^2(n - 1)/\bar{x}$ and s^2 is the variance; n, the sample size; and $\bar{x}$ is the mean (Southwood, 1978). The index is distributed approximately as χ^2 and approaches zero for samples from a random spatial distribution (i.e., Poisson distribution). Conversely, a large I_D implies spatial aggregation or clumping.

Across drainage units, we examined relationships of imperilment (AFS-ET and AFS-ETSC) to drainage-unit area, unique taxa, stream-type diversity, and total native taxa richness using correlation and multiple regression analyses in SAS Institute, Inc. (1994). We used both nonparametric and parametric correlation coefficients (Kendall's tau-b and Pearson's, respectively). We used Type II sums of squares to assess relative predictive capabilities of several independent variables for imperilment (Angermeier and Schlosser, 1989). After examination of scatterplots, we log-transformed drainage-unit area, imperilment, and native taxa richness as $\log_{10}(x)$ or $\log_{10}(x + 1)$ to minimize effects of non-linearity (Sokal and Rohlf, 1981).

RESULTS

We compiled a comprehensive list of 530 freshwater fish taxa for the southeastern United States (Appendix 1). This inventory included 496 extant native taxa (493 species) and 34 nonindigenous, established fishes. Interdrainage transfers of indigenous fishes by humans also are common in the Southeast. At least 62 indigenous southeastern fish species, 13 percent of the fauna, have been introduced to drainages in the Southeast to which they are not native.

Eighty-four fish taxa in the Southeast are recognized as imperiled (Table 2). Fifty taxa (ten percent of the fauna) are placed in AFS-E and AFS-T categories and 34 (seven percent) are recognized as AFS-SC. Thirty-two fishes (six percent of the fauna) are in protected federal categories and an additional 52 (11 percent) are candidate species. Although total numbers recognized in federal status categories versus AFS status categories are equal, the AFS assessment differs notably in the number of fish species considered threatened. By either source about 17 percent of the southeastern fish fauna is considered in need of conservation actions.

Patterns of Diversity and Imperilment Among States

The southeastern states have a high diversity of fishes, moderate to high imperilment, and a wide range of stream-type diversity. Six southeastern states have native freshwater fish faunas of 200 or more taxa (Figure 1). Tennessee and Alabama are centers of diversity; each harbors at least 257 native fish taxa. Kentucky and Georgia follow with 220 and 219 fishes, respectively. No southeastern state has fewer than 119 fish taxa.

Nine of the 11 southeastern states support ten or more imperiled fishes (Figure 1). Alabama and Tennessee have the highest number of imperiled fishes (30 and 40 taxa, respectively) followed by Georgia, Kentucky, North Carolina, and Virginia (18-21 fishes). Percentage imperilment is highest in Tennessee (15.6 percent), is greater than ten percent in Alabama, North Carolina, and Virginia, and is lowest in West Virginia (6.1 percent).

The Southeast lies within several major physiographic regions and is drained by numerous large rivers. These factors are reflected in the tally by state for stream-type diversity. Stream-type diversity ranges from seven stream types in Louisiana to 42 in Virginia. Geor-

Table 2. Federal and American Fisheries Society (AFS) conservation status category totals for fishes of the southeastern United States.

Status Categories	Federal	AFS
Endangered	18	14
Proposed Endangered	1	-
Threatened	13	36
Proposed Threatened	-	-
Subtotal	32	50
Candidate	52	-
Special Concern	-	34
Total	84	84

gia, Alabama, and North Carolina also show high stream-type diversity (≥ 34; Figure 3).

Patterns of Imperilment Among Fish Families

Imperilment is not distributed evenly among fish families in the Southeast. Of 30 families of native fishes, 12 have one or more imperiled members (Table 3). Among these 12 families, percent imperilment is variable, ranging from seven percent regarding the sunfishes (Centrarchidae) to 86 percent regarding the sturgeons (Acipenseridae). High percent imperilment also occurs in the pygmy sunfishes (Elassomatidae) and cavefishes (Amblyopsidae), with 50 percent and 40 percent (respectively) of family members imperiled.

Among the six most taxa-rich families, imperilment status (AFS-ETSC versus no status) and family membership are associated (LI = 30.41, $p < 0.0001$, 5 df) (Table 4). The perches and darters (Percidae, primarily the genera *Ammocrypta*, *Etheostoma*, and *Percina*) and bullhead catfishes (Ictaluridae, mostly madtoms of the genus *Noturus*) have more imperiled members than expected based on their representation in the fauna; the suckers (Catostomidae) are imperiled in approximate proportion to faunal representation; and the minnows (Cyprinidae), topminnows (Fundulidae), and sunfishes (Centrarchidae) have fewer imperiled taxa than expected (Table 4).

Imperilment and Range Extent

Imperilment is related negatively to range extent for native fishes in the Southeast. Both the Kruskal-Wallis test and analysis of variance showed significant differences in range extent among status categories ($\chi^2 = 9.08$, $p < 0.0282$; F = 3.674, $p < 0.0122$, respectively). Orthogonal contrasts of the means indicated range extent of imperiled taxa is significantly lower than non-imperiled taxa (F = 10.63, $p < 0.0012$)(Table 5). Contrasts did not reveal significant differences in range extent among imperiled taxa (AFS-SC versus AFS-ET, F = 1.17, $p < 0.28$; AFS-E versus AFS-T, F = 0.47, $p < 0.47$), but mean range extent was distributed along an increasing gradient from AFS-E to AFS-SC (Table 5).

Probability of imperilment increased with decreasing range extent. Logistic regression, modeling the probability of imperilment on range extent, yielded a significant model with a good fit (a = -1.16, Wald's $\chi^2 = 9.07$, $p < 0.0026$; b = -0.06, Wald's $\chi^2 = 50.15$, $p < 0.0001$; Hosmer and Lemeshow $\chi^2 = 4.97$, $p = 0.3855$). Calculations from estimates of

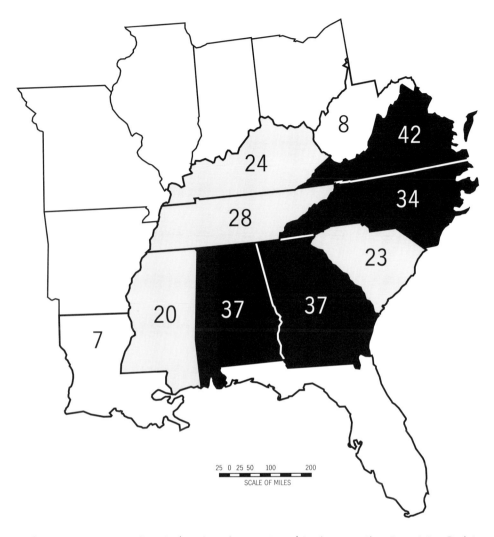

Figure 3. Stream-type diversity (number of stream types) in eleven southeastern states. Dark to light shading indicates highest to lowest levels of diversity.

model parameters (following Rita and Ranta, 1993) indicated probability of imperilment increases from > 0.1 to > 0.2 as range extent decreases from < 16.2 to < 3.5 drainage units.

Geographic Patterns Among Drainage Units

FISH TAXA RICHNESS

Fish diversity among the 33 drainage units was less variable than any other attribute examined and was not distributed randomly (Table 6). Drainage units with the highest fish species richness (>150 taxa) formed a geographically contiguous core of diversity (Figure 4; Appendix 1) that included the Lower Tennessee River System (DU26), Cumberland River System (DU28), and Green-Tradewater River Systems (DU29). A rough

Table 3. Familial imperilment (i.e., number of imperiled taxa in family; percent of family taxa that are imperiled reported in parentheses), familial taxa richness, and percent familial representation for native fishes of the southeastern United States. Imperiled taxa are those recognized by the American Fisheries Society (see Williams et al., 1989).

Family	Familial Imperilment	Familial Taxa Richness	Familial Percent of Native Fishes
Acipenseridae	6 (86)	7	1
Amblyopsidae	2 (40)	5	1
Amiidae	0	1	<1
Anguillidae	0	1	<1
Aphredoderidae	0	1	<1
Atherinidae	0	3	<1
Catostomidae	6 (18)	34	7
Centrarchidae	2 (7)	28	6
Clupeidae	0	8	2
Cottidae	1 (14)	7	1
Cyprinidae	16 (11)	151	31
Cyprinodontidae	0	2	<1
Elassomatidae	3 (50)	6	1
Esocidae	0	3	<1
Fundulidae	2 (9)	22	4
Gasterosteidae	0	1	<1
Hiodontidae	0	2	<1
Ictaluridae	7 (21)	33	7
Lepisosteidae	0	5	1
Lotidae	0	1	<1
Moronidae	0	4	<1
Percidae	36(24)	152	31
Percopsidae	0	1	<1
Petromyzontidae	0	8	2
Poeciliidae	0	4	<1
Polyodontidae	1(100)	1	<1
Rivulidae	1(100)	1	<1
Salmonidae	0	1	<1
Sciaenidae	0	1	<1
Umbridae	0	2	<1

semicircle of secondary richness (125 to 147 fishes) is formed to the south (Mobile Basin Region, DU16-DU18), east (Upper Tennessee River System, DU27), and west (Minor Mississippi Tributaries North, DU24) of the richest units.

UNIQUE TAXA

Among all 33 drainage units, 128 fishes (26 percent of the native fauna) are unique to a given, single unit. Numbers of unique taxa across drainage units were highly variable spatially and were not distributed randomly (Table 6). A primary center of unique taxa (> 10 unique taxa) was located in the Coosa-Tallapoosa River Systems (DU16) and the Tennessee-Cumberland Region (DU26-28) (Figure 5). A secondary tier of unique taxa (five

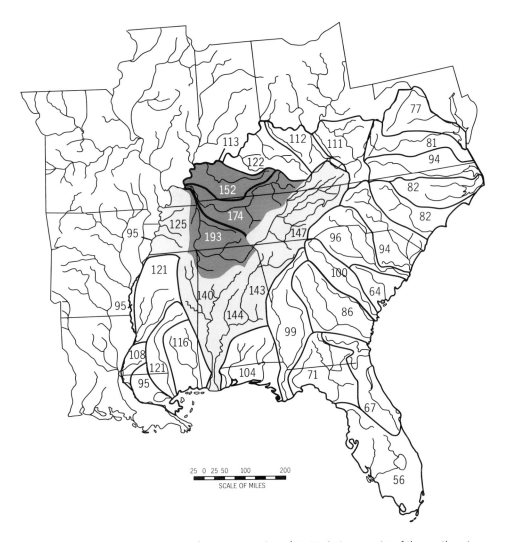

Figure 4. Native fish taxa richness (i.e., number of taxa) in 33 drainage units of the southeastern United States. Dark to light shading indicates highest to lowest levels of richness.

to seven unique taxa) occurred peripheral to the primary center and included the Tombigbee-Black Warrior River Systems (DU18) and Apalachicola-Florida Panhandle Region (DU14-DU15) to the southwest and east, respectively; the Green-Tradewater River Systems (DU29) to the northwest; and the Roanoke River Drainage (DU3) and Kanawha-New-Guyandotte River Systems (DU32) to the northeast.

LEVELS OF IMPERILMENT

Imperilment was highly variable among drainage units and neither AFS-ET nor AFS-ETSC status combinations were distributed randomly (Table 6). Highest imperilment overlayed the core of drainage units with high numbers of unique taxa and, in part, units of highest taxa richness (Figure 6). The drainage units with highest numbers of unique

Table 4. Imperilment for the six most diverse fish families in the southeastern United States. Expected values reflect a 17 percent overall imperilment of the southeastern fish fauna. A likelihood ratio test indicated association between status (imperiled vs nonimperiled) and family membership (LI = 30.41, p ‹ 0.0001, 5 df).

Family	Imperilment	
	Observed[1]	Expected
Percidae (perches and darters)	36 (24)	26
Ictaluridae (bullhead catfishes)	7 (21)	6
Catostomidae (suckers)	6 (18)	6
Cyprinidae (minnows and carps)	16 (11)	26
Fundulidae (topminnows)	2 (9)	4
Centrarchidae (sunfishes)	2 (7)	5

[1] Percent reported in parentheses.

taxa (Tennessee-Cumberland Region, DU26-DU28; Coosa-Tallapoosa River Systems, DU16) also had the highest percentages of imperiled fishes (16 to 19 taxa, 9.2 to 12.6 percent, respectively)(Figure 6). The Lower Alabama-Cahaba River Systems (DU17) and the Kanawha-New-Guyandotte River Systems (DU32) formed a secondary tier of imperilment. Imperilment was lowest along drainages of the Atlantic and easternmost Gulf slopes but ranged as high as seven taxa and seven percent of drainage-unit taxa richness.

INCREASES IN IMPERILMENT

For all drainage units combined, imperiled species increased from 14.4 to 17.4 percent of total native fishes from 1979 to 1989 (Deacon et al., 1979; Williams et al., 1989). Percentage increases in imperilment among drainage units are uneven for the ten-year period, but no unit showed decreases (Figure 7). The largest increases (greater than three percent) occurred in two geographically contiguous drainage units, the Coosa-Tallapoosa (DU16) and the Upper Tennessee (DU27) river systems, both with the highest numbers of imperiled fishes (Figures 6 and 7), and a geographically disjunct unit, the Mississippi River Mainstem (DU25). Eleven other units showed increases from one to two percent: Roanoke River Drainage (DU3); Edisto-Savannah-Altamaha Region (DU8-DU10); Everglades-Tampa Bay-Waccasassa River Drainages (DU12); the remainder of the Mobile Bay Basin Region (DU17, DU18); Lower Tennessee River System (DU26); and units in the Southeastern Ohio River Region (DU31-DU33). With the exceptions previously noted, most streams on the Atlantic and Gulf slopes, the Mississippi Embayment, and the Southeastern Ohio River Region showed low (less than one percent) or no percentage increases in imperilment.

STREAM-TYPE DIVERSITY

Stream-type diversity among drainage units was variable over the study area and was not characterized by abrupt geographic breaks or discontinuities (Figure 8). The departure of the distribution of stream-type diversity from random was weaker than for native taxa richness, imperilment, or unique taxa (Table 6). High stream-type diversity occurred in drainage units that arise in uplands and continue through and/or across lowlands; low

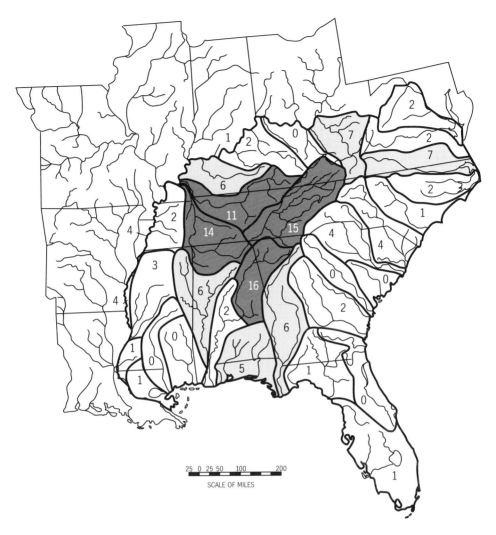

Figure 5. Numbers of unique fish taxa in 33 drainage units of the southeastern United States. Dark to light shading indicates highest to lowest levels of unique taxa.

diversity occurred in units primarily restricted to lowlands (Figure 8). Drainage units with the highest stream-type diversity (nine to ten) included: James River Drainage (DU2); Roanoke River Drainage (DU3); Coosa-Tallapoosa River Systems (DU16); Potomac-Rappahannock-York River Drainages (DU1); and the Lower Tennessee River System (DU26). Low stream-type diversity (≥ three) occurred in a geographically and faunistically eclectic group of drainage units, but with few exceptions these units have relatively small drainage areas and/or are predominated by lowlands. These units included the Green-Tradewater River Systems (DU29) and Ohio River Mainstem (DU33); Yazoo-Black-Mississippi Minor Tributaries Region (DU22-DU24); Pascagoula-Pearl-Pontchartrain Region (DU19-DU21); St. Andrew-Choctawhatchee-Pensacola Bay Drainages (DU15); Peninsular Florida Region (DU11-DU13); and the Edisto-Combahee River Drainages (DU8).

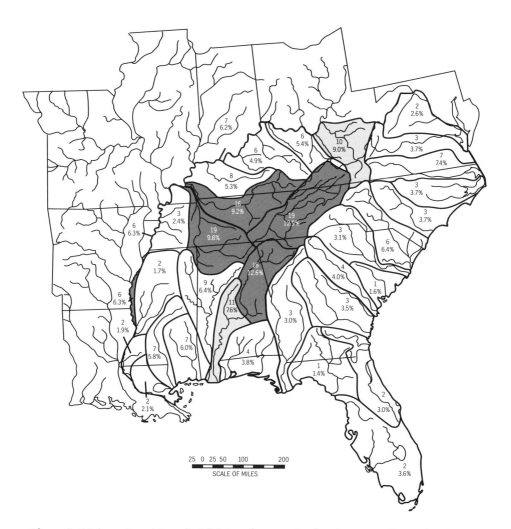

Figure 6. Total number of imperiled fish taxa (upper values) and percent of imperiled fish taxa (lower values) in 33 drainage units of the southeastern United States. Imperiled fishes are those included in American Fisheries Society conservation status categories (see Williams et al., 1989). Dark to light shading indicates highest to lowest levels of imperilment.

Correlation and Prediction of Imperilment

Variables with potential to predict imperilment of fishes in the drainage units included native fish taxa richness, stream-type diversity, drainage-unit area, and unique taxa (Table 7). Native fish taxa richness and unique taxa were correlated significantly with imperilment (AFS-ET and AFS-ETSC). Drainage-unit area and stream-type diversity showed weaker correlations with imperilment.

Because of the tendency for "predictor" variables to be intercorrelated (e.g., stream-type diversity and drainage-unit area; native taxa richness and unique taxa), we used two multiple regression models (Angermeier and Schlosser, 1989) to assess the relative usefulness of native fish taxa richness, stream-type diversity, drainage-unit area, and unique taxa in

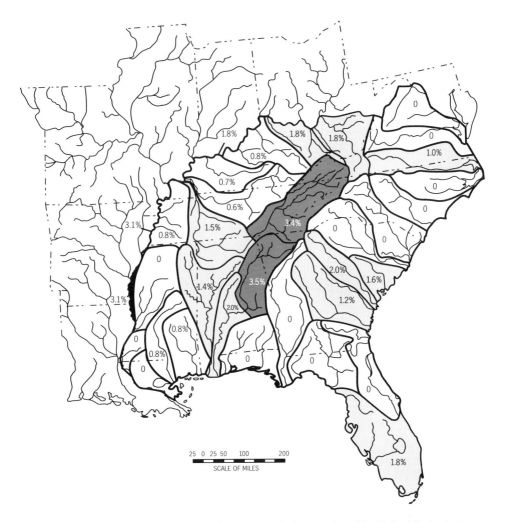

Figure 7. Percent increase in fish imperilment in 33 drainage units of the United States between 1979 and 1989 (see Deacon et al., 1979; Williams et al., 1989). Dark to light shading indicates highest to lowest increases in imperilment.

predicting imperilment (AFS-ET and AFS-ETSC) (Table 8). The first models regressed imperilment on all four variables. Drainage-unit area and unique taxa did not contribute a significant proportion of the sums of squares (Type II SS) for imperilment, and their removal from the models reduced R^2 values by < 1.5 percent for both AFS-ET and AFS-ETSC status combinations. The second model included only native taxa richness and stream-type diversity as independent variables. Both variables contributed a significant proportion of the sums of squares for imperilment and were useful predictors for fish imperilment in drainages of the Southeast. In addition, we regressed imperilment on drainage-unit area only, and although the models were significant, R^2 values were < 0.15 for both status combinations.

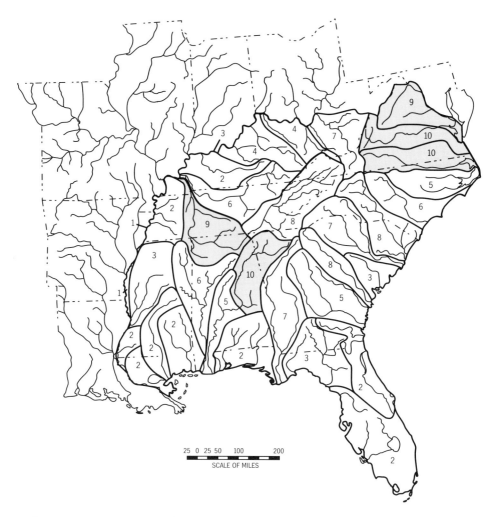

Figure 8. Stream-type diversity (number of stream types) of 33 drainage units in the southeastern United States. Dark to light shading indicates highest to lowest levels of stream-type diversity.

DISCUSSION

Patterns and Management Among States

Alabama, Georgia, North Carolina, Tennessee, and Virginia face some of the greatest and most immediate challenges of all southeastern states in future management of native fishes. Each of these states ranks within the top three for two or more of the attributes of fish taxa richness, imperilment, and stream-type diversity (Figures 1 and 3). Nevertheless, we emphasize that all southeastern states support relatively rich fish faunas. The average taxa richness of 188 fishes among southeastern states equals or surpasses that of all other of the lower 48 states except Arkansas and Missouri (Warren and Burr, 1994). Likewise, even states that do not show high values for fish taxa richness, imperilment, or stream-

Table 5. Means and variation in range extent of native fishes grouped by status categories across 33 drainage units in the southeastern United States. Tabled entries include mean, two standard errors of the mean (2×SE), and coefficient of variation (CV).

Status	Mean	2 × SE	CV
AFS-E (n = 14)	3.3[1]	1.34	80
AFS-T (n = 36)	4.9[1]	1.86	114
AFS-SC (n = 34)	5.9[1]	2.04	103
AFS-ETSC (n = 84)	5.0[1]	1.16	108
No Status (n = 409)	7.7	0.76	99

[1] Values not significantly different in orthogonal contrasts.

type diversity face critical problems in conservation of native fishes. In Florida (and other Atlantic states), for example, spawning runs are severely curtailed for several anadromous species as a result of dams on large coastal tributaries (Gilbert, 1992). In Mississippi, flood control projects and short interval (about 15 years) channel maintenance operations threaten riverine fishes in the Yazoo River basin despite growing recognition of the socio-economic and cultural value of this resource (Jackson et al., 1993).

We explicitly recognize that states are artificial geographic entities but acknowledge that their jurisdictional and civic importance cannot be ignored in any pragmatic approach to aquatic conservation in spite of our scientific tendency (and necessity) to do so. Through statutory obligation, many state-bound, natural-resource decision makers simply do not divide the land-scape among natural units, like drainages or watersheds, but see and manage only within political boundaries. Even so, states are capable of recognizing problems and offering solutions for recovery and management of fishes. For example, most southeastern states now have heri-tage-based programs charged with inventorying and monitoring (i.e., accounting informa-tion) imperiled fishes (e.g., Eager and Hatcher, 1980; Mount, 1986; Warren et al., 1986; Terwilliger, 1991; Gilbert, 1992; Menhinick, in press). State agencies also are making efforts to maintain fish diversity rather than targeting specific species (e.g., Holman et al., 1993; Toth and Aumen, 1994). Obversely, many state-based programs for nongame fishes are left to lan-guish on "soft" money (Williams, 1986; Pister, 1992), are underemphasized (Cain, 1993; Angermeier and Karr, 1994), and lack the force of institutional will or statutory authority, short of federal mandate, to effect change (Johnson, 1987; Pister, 1991).

Notwithstanding parochial sovereignty and nongame fish program development in states, conflicts in use of streams among and within southeastern states are common (e.g., Voigtlander and Poppe, 1989; Neves and Angermeier, 1990; Anderson et al., 1991; Jack-son et al., 1993; Saylor et al., 1993; Crawford, 1994). Of the 33 drainage units recog-nized here, 21 cross state boundaries (Figure 2). Obviously both federal-state and inter-state cooperation toward long-term management of these drainages is appropriate and critical. Historical cooperation was limited to ostensible "improvement" of waterways for flood control and navigation, generally imposed through federal water projects, with in-calculable losses to aquatic habitat (e.g., Hunt, 1988; Neves and Angermeier, 1990). Re-cent cooperation goes little beyond attempts to resolve acute and immediate water re-source conflicts (e.g., Saylor et al., 1993) or occurs through federal abandonment of contin-

Table 6. Means and measures of spatial variation for fish taxa richness, unique taxa, imperilment, and stream-type diversity for 33 drainage units of the southeastern United States. Table entries each include mean, two standard errors of the mean ($2 \times SE$), minimum (Min.) and maximum (Max.) values, coefficient of variation (CV), Index of Dispersion (I_D), and the significance level (p-value) for departure from a random spatial distribution.

Variable	Mean	$2 \times SE$	Min.	Max.	CV	I_D	p-value
Fish Taxa Richness	108.6	10.97	56	193	29	292	$p \ll 0.01$
Unique Taxa	3.9	1.44	0	16	107	142	$p \ll 0.01$
Imperilment							
AFS-ET	3.2	0.59	0	14	104	113	$p \ll 0.01$
AFS-ETSC	6.2	0.39	1	19	83	138	$p \ll 0.01$
Stream Types	5	1	1	10	57	53	$p < 0.05$

ued waterway "improvement" (e.g., Jackson and Jackson, 1989; Hupp, 1992). For example, the Tennessee River drainage includes portions of seven states, most of which are centers of fish imperilment and diversity. However, no comprehensive, coordinated management plan exists for the Tennessee, and the priority for sustainable management of this resource is low (Voigtlander and Poppe, 1989). Federal-state and intra- and interstate coordination is confounded within southeastern states primarily because jurisdiction over water, waterways, and the aquatic fauna is fragmented among agencies with different and often contradictory regulatory mandates (e.g., providing drinking water versus recreational fishing versus waste disposal).

Familial Imperilment

If imperilment were the result of random sampling among families, familial imperilment would be proportional to familial representation in the total native fish fauna; however, this is not the case (Tables 3 and 4). Imperilment is disproportionately bestowed on both diverse and depauperate fish families. Fish families with disproportionately high levels of imperilment are characteristically dependent on vegetated, isolated wetland habitats; hypogean habitats; or benthic habitats (Tables 3 and 4). Three relatively depauperate fish families, the pygmy sunfishes (Elassomatidae), cavefishes (Amblyopsidae), and sturgeons (Acipenseridae), and two diverse families, darters and perches (Percidae) and bullhead catfishes (Ictaluridae) are exemplars. Imperiled members of the pygmy sunfishes primarily inhabit vegetated, often spring-fed, permanent wetlands (Rohde and Arndt, 1987; Mayden, 1993). These habitats, particularly those with springs, are among the most jeopardized in the Southeast (Etnier and Starnes, 1991; Cubbage and Flather, 1993; Mayden, 1993; Dickson and Warren, 1994). Likewise, the cavefishes depend on the integrity of a food base originating from surface waters and, ultimately, must live in a habitat that often serves as a sump for a variety of anthropogenic pollutants. Subterranean habitats and their dramatically evolved fishes are under threat worldwide (Groombridge, 1992). High imperilment also is concentrated among the sturgeons, darters and perches, and bullhead catfishes, all of which have a benthic life style. For some sturgeons, vulnerability to imperilment is associated with dams blocking migratory spawning runs, but most members of these families are dependent on the ecological integrity of the benthic environment and often require specific substrate sizes and configurations for spawning, feeding,

Table 7. Results of correlation analyses (Pearson's correlation coefficient and Kendall's tau-b coefficient) of fish imperilment and drainage-unit area, native fish taxa richness, unique taxa, and stream-type diversity in 33 drainage units of the southeastern United States. AFS-ET and AFS-ETSC refer to combinations of American Fisheries Society conservation status categories (see Williams et al., 1989).

Status Category	Drainage-unit Area[1]	Fish Taxa Richness	Unique Taxa	Stream-type Diversity
AFS-ET				
Pearson's	0.374	0.753	0.800	0.401
	(p < 0.0415)	(p < 0.0001)	(p < 0.0001)	(p < 0.0206)
Kendall's	0.214	0.589	0.363	0.177
	(p < 0.1140)	(p < 0.0001)	(p < 0.0072)	(p < 0.1890)
AFS-ETSC				
Pearson's	0.448	0.828	0.854	0.425
	(p < 0.0130)	(p < 0.0001)	(p < 0.0001)	(p < 0.0137)
Kendall's	0.249	0.636	0.473	0.247
	(p < 0.0630)	(p < 0.0001)	(p < 0.0004)	(p < 0.0629)

[1] n = 30.

and cover (Page and Swofford, 1984; Etnier and Starnes, 1993; Kessler and Thorp, 1993).

High levels of imperilment in fishes with multiple niche axes converging on benthic resources is not unexpected. Degradation of streams is often first manifested in benthic habitats and communities (Reice and Wohlenberg, 1993). Streams entrain organic and inorganic material from the watershed, and this material is deposited, stored, and biologically recycled largely on or within the stream's substrate (Merritt et al., 1984). Being in intimate contact with these materials, benthic fishes (and their benthic food resources) are affected directly by sediment particles (Minshall, 1984; Berkman and Rabeni, 1987; Haro and Brusven, 1994) and by nutrients and toxins contained within sediments (Reice and Wohlenberg, 1993). We conclude that the disproportionately high imperilment of these benthic fish families is simply the initial, expected manifestation of long-term, complex, cumulative aquatic degradation.

Imperilment and Range Extent

Mean range extent was lower for imperiled than nonimperiled fishes (Table 5), and probability of imperilment increased with decreasing range extent. However, the explanatory power of these relationships is weak. Although significant statistically, conservation status accounted for only 2.2 percent of the variation in range extent in the analysis of variance model. Likewise, in the logistic regression model, the increase in probability of imperilment as range extent decreases was low, and misclassifications of imperiled and nonimperiled fishes was high.

Imperilment, a measure of extinction potential, and range extent, a categorical measure of area inhabited, might be expected to show stronger relationships than detected in these models. Restricted geographic range is often associated with fish vulnerability to extinction (Moyle and Williams, 1990; Etnier and Starnes, 1991; Angermeier, 1995). The weak

Table 8. Summary of multiple regression analyses of fish imperilment, drainage-unit area, native fish taxa richness, stream-type diversity (S-T), and unique taxa (UT) in 33 drainage units of the southeastern United States. Tabled entries include intercept, slope, and the proportion of variance (R^2) in imperilment accounted for by each model. AFS-ET and AFS-ETSC refer to combinations of American Fisheries Society conservation status categories [see Williams et al., 1989]. * = probability (parameter = 0) < 0.10; ** = probability (parameter = 0) < 0.05; *** = probability (parameter = 0) < 0.001.

Status Category	Model 1						Model 2			
	Intercept	Richness	S-T	UT	Area	R^2	Intercept	Richness	S-T	R^2
AFS-ET	-4.46**	1.99***	0.04*	-0.11	0.18	0.616	-3.43***	1.85***	0.03**	0.609
AFS-ETSC	-5.65***	2.51***	0.04**	-0.11	0.23	0.809	4.39***	2.38***	0.04***	0.800

explanatory power of the resultant models is less enigmatic considering:

1) the relatively large spatial scale of resolution of range extent, as defined here, and

2) a scenario of complex, widespread degradation of southeastern fish habitats (Angermeier, 1995).

Many nonimperiled fishes in the Southeast are restricted to one or few drainage units (i.e., limited in range extent) but occur widely and commonly within those units. In contrast, some imperiled fishes are known from a number of southeastern drainage units but inhabit very limited stream reaches within each unit. Populations of the latter are effectively subject to effects of reduced habitat area and insularization (Angermeier, 1995) regardless of overall range extent. In either case, our measure of range extent does not account well for the actual area occupied. If examined at finer spatial scales (e.g., kilometers of stream inhabited), geographic range might account for greater variance in imperilment, and limited range might show a higher increase in risk of imperilment. Even at smaller spatial scales and using only extirpated fishes, Angermeier (1995) also noted relatively weak statistical associations between extinction and limited physiographic range for fishes in Virginia.

Weak relationships between range extent and imperilment are expected if widespread, complex degradation of southeastern fish habitats is a strong determinant of imperilment (Angermeier, 1995). Complex degradation over a large geographic area involves numerous forms of insult to aquatic systems that affect various vulnerable fish taxa differentially depending on the intensities and combinations of exposures. Angermeier (1995) identified three uncontrolled factors interacting to randomize degradation "treatments" among species in ecosystems subject to anthropogenic impacts:

1) differential effects of various types of degradation among species;

2) differential occurrence of species among ecosystems; and

3) differential exposure of species to degradation among ecosystems. The expected pattern of imperilment in a complex degradation scenario would be statistically "noisy" (Angermeier, 1995). Dependence of models on only one deterministic variable, like range extent, may further decrease the signal to noise ratio. Perhaps most importantly, the results raise the premise of pervasive habitat degradation as a strong determinant of imperilment in southeastern fishes.

Geographic Patterns Among Drainage Units

Fish taxa richness, unique taxa, and stream-type diversity showed variable, but aggregated, distribution patterns that overlap considerably with one another and with the spatial distribution of imperilment in drainage units of the Southeast (Table 6; Figures 4-8). Statistical results generally supported association of these attributes and fish imperilment (Table 7). The Tennessee-Cumberland Region (DU26-DU28) and Mobile Bay Basin Region (DU16-DU18) consistently had one or more drainage units forming part of a core of high fish taxa richness, unique taxa, and imperilment (Figures 4-6). Drainage units adjacent to these core regions usually showed intermediate values (i.e., Southeastern Ohio River Region, DU29-DU33). Most drainage units of the Atlantic and Gulf slopes and Mississippi embayment showed low to intermediate values for fish taxa richness, unique taxa, and imperilment.

Drainage units congruent in levels of taxa richness, unique taxa, or stream-type diversity and imperilment often share common biogeographic histories. Although the relationships between imperilment and these other attributes were positive (Table 7), we discern a clear temporal distinction in the origin of imperilment and the other attributes. Patterns of fish taxa richness, unique taxa, and stream types in the Southeast all have a strong association with Earth history (Burr and Page, 1986; Hocutt et al., 1986; Starnes and Etnier, 1986; Swift et al., 1986; Mayden, 1988; Warren et al., 1991). In contrast, patterns of imperilment are primarily products of the past century that were only documented in the past 30 or so years (Deacon et al., 1979; Miller et al., 1989; Williams et al., 1989). For example, the highlands of the Tennessee-Cumberland, Southeastern Ohio River, and the Mobile Bay Basin regions were subjected to a series of complex, major geological vicariance events initiated in the pre-Pleistocene and as a result, were relatively isolated from much of the remaining diverse and widespread Central Highlands ichthyofauna (Mayden, 1988). Likewise, much of the ichthyofaunal composition and endemicity of the Atlantic and Gulf slope lowlands is associated with eustatic cycles, dating at least to the Miocene, superimposed on physiographic features and drainage trends (Swift et al., 1986). The implication of the association of imperilment with recent environmental degradation following millions of years of Earth history is clear. In a geological "blink of the eye" the fish fauna across the entire Southeast is being compromised.

The largest increases in imperilment of fishes overlapped with high fish taxa richness, unique taxa, and stream-type diversity, but substantial increases also occurred across a wide diversity of drainage units (e.g., Everglades-Tampa Bay-Waccasassa River Drainages, DU12, and Mississippi River Mainstem, DU25) (Figure 7). However, even at relatively low rates of increase, imperilment of the fauna can increase dramatically in brief time periods. A 0.2 percent annual increase in imperilment in a given drainage unit for 50 years yields a fauna with nearly ten percent of its members imperiled. We emphasize our estimates of increases in imperilment for southeastern drainages are uncertain and not amenable to tests for accuracy or precision, particularly for predictive purposes. We do not suggest by the hypothetical example that even low rates of imperilment or more correctly, its corollary, extinction, could be sustained over long periods (e.g., 100 years? 200 years?). The numbers of imperiled and ultimately, extinct fishes, necessarily reach an asymptote as the pool of vulnerable taxa is exhausted over time. Nevertheless, it is certain that integrity of the fish fauna will not be maintained even if low rates of increase are projected into the next century.

The mapped patterns of imperilment, increased imperilment, fish taxa richness, and unique taxa among southeastern drainage units provide a starting point for applying conservation triage and prioritizing proactive efforts to sustain overall fish and other aquatic diversity within a historical ecological context (Figures 3-7). Certain geographic aggregations of drainage units are in greater need of action than others in terms of sheer numbers of imperiled, unique, or native taxa, particularly the Tennessee-Cumberland and Mobile Bay Basin regions. We note, however, that every drainage unit in the Southeast shows some level of imperilment and many show high levels of increase in imperilment regardless of fish taxa richness or stream-type diversity. The management actions required to go beyond triage or simple prioritization and actually affect change must be grounded in a framework of interstate and federal cooperation that is, to date, unprecedented.

Predicting Imperilment Among Drainage Units

FISH TAXA RICHNESS AND STREAM-TYPE DIVERSITY

Drainage units with high fish taxa richness and stream-type diversity contained more imperiled species than units with low richness and stream-type diversity (Table 8). In the final regression models, however, fish taxa richness accounted for 85 percent of the Type II SS contributed by fish taxa richness and stream-type diversity. The predictive power of the regression models thus lies primarily in fish taxa richness; national patterns of animal endangerment are associated similarly (Flather et al., 1994). A log-log regression model of imperilment and fish taxa richness approximates a power function (Conner and McCoy, 1979), where: $I = k(R)^Z$ and I is imperilment, R is fish taxa richness, and k and Z are constants. Interpreted as such, the proportion of imperiled fishes in a drainage unit increases with increasing fish taxa richness. This does not imply direct causation or circularity (e.g., high taxa richness begats high imperilment). Rather, a hypothesis is supported that imperilment (as a measure of extinction vulnerability) is largely an epiphenomenon of sampling of the available pool of fish taxa in a drainage unit. Similar hypotheses are prescribed for analogous regression models (Connor and McCoy, 1979; Angermeier and Schlosser, 1989). Simply, drainage units with large fish faunas have more individual fish taxa vulnerable to extinction. This result is a direct expectation under a scenario of complex, pervasive degradation of aquatic habitats (Angermeier, 1995). We conclude that conditions favorable for extinction are pervasive across southeastern drainages but are most visibly manifested in the richest drainage units.

DRAINAGE-UNIT AREA

Imperilment is not predicted effectively by drainage-unit area despite correlation of drainage area and fish taxa richness in subsections of the Southeast (Swift et al., 1986; Sheldon, 1987; Warren and Angermeier, in press). Drainage unit area not only failed to add explanatory power to multiple regression models (Table 8), but it was not an effective substitute for total native taxa richness in predicting imperilment. As a single independent variable, drainage-unit area explained less than 15 percent of the variation in imperilment. From this, we infer two things:

1) particular drainage units or groups of drainage units by virtue of their shared Earth histories have produced more fish species than other similar-sized units, and

2) the general species-area relationship is not an effective model at this spatial scale for predicting imperilment. Our models for predicting fish imperilment showed stronger effects from historical ecology (i.e., production of species) than from components of equilibrium-based island-biogeographic theory (i.e., area). It is not clear such a pattern holds at smaller regional scales where effects of historical ecology may be minimized. Future analyses aimed at groups of drainage units with shared Earth histories may provide additional insight into relationships between fish imperilment and ecological or drainage-unit attributes (Gorman, 1992; Mayden, 1992).

UNIQUE TAXA

The relative lack of usefulness of unique taxa for predicting imperilment complements the weak associations between range extent and imperilment. In addition, we found no difference for the total native fish fauna in the proportion of unique taxa among imperiled and nonimperiled fishes (LI = 2.58, p < 0.1337). We do not suggest these results negate the intuitively appealing and empirically supported associations between restricted geographic range and imperilment in fishes (Etnier and Starnes, 1991; Moyle and Leidy, 1992; Angermeier, 1995) or other organisms (Flather et al., 1994). Instead, we invoke reasoning analogous to that forwarded for the models of range extent and imperilment. Vulnerability to extinction in southeastern fishes is not a simple function of endemicity (or "degree" of cosmopolitanism). Some unique taxa are widely distributed within a drainage unit; others are severely limited in distribution. Via the randomized "treatments" of pervasive, complex degradation, vulnerability to extinction may be allocated among fishes with diverse range sizes and ecological attributes (Angermeier, 1995). Weak associations of range size and imperilment in concert with the final multiple regression models support a scenario of pervasive, complex habitat degradation as a strong determinant of observed imperilment patterns in southeastern fishes.

IMPLICATIONS

Development of models associating vulnerability to the extinction process and ecological and zoogeographic characteristics of organisms and communities is a high priority for conservation biology (Soulé and Kohm, 1989). Aside from this effort, few related analyses are available for fishes in the Southeast (Sheldon, 1987; Nagel, 1991; Angermeier, 1995). Geographic and ecological range restrictions are primary among attributes associated with many southeastern imperiled, extirpated, and extinct fishes (Mayden, 1992; Etnier and Starnes, 1991; Angermeier, 1995). We find that several promising geographic and faunal attributes (i.e., drainage-unit area, range extent, and unique taxa) are not completely satisfactory in explaining individual fish imperilment nor levels of imperilment in drainage units, but this finding is not unprecedented (Moyle and Leidy, 1992; Frissel, 1993; Etnier and Starnes, 1991; Angermeier, 1995). We do not construe this as meaning no associations exist among imperilment and these geographic and faunal attributes but only that no strong associations exist (Angermeier, 1995).

The final models identifying taxa richness, and to a lesser degree, stream-type diversity as the best predictors of imperilment were more revealing and complementary to the relative ineffectiveness of other variables. The synthesis of these results implicates pervasive, complex degradation of fish habitats across southeastern drainages as the engine of imperilment. To this we add an important caveat taken from the familial analyses. Degradation appears most strongly manifested in imperilment of fishes associated with benthic habitats; a habitat predictably impacted first by cumulative, long-term abuse of aquatic systems. Decline of other benthic organisms, such as freshwater mussels, strongly supports this contention (Williams et al., 1993).

Society must recognize that all upstream activities, including those on the terrestrial component of the catchment, have cumulative downstream effects and address this reality in prioritization, resource allocation, and implementation of conservation management. The linear, unidirectional nature of rivers and streams is a singular attribute that dictates emphasis on whole-system approaches to management. The prevailing strategy of waiting for species to become imperiled before activating conservation programs is a major and costly shortcoming in conservation in the Southeast and elsewhere (Scott et al., 1988; Blockstein, 1992; Angermeier,

1995). The current situation for aquatic resource management among and within southeastern states is described succinctly by Noss and Cooperrider (1994; page 264): "Nowhere is the fragmentation of our thinking and institutions and the arrogance of our management more pronounced than in our stewardship of aquatic ecosystems."

We believe it should be quite clear that successful management for aquatic biological integrity must transcend political boundaries, jurisdictional subdivisions, and short-term economic policies and ultimately focus on the long-term interaction of humans and the environment within ecologically definable units (Karr, 1993; Angermeier and Karr, 1994; Maser and Sedell, 1994; Noss and Cooperrider, 1994). Society must move toward proactive management centered on maintaining ecological integrity of aquatic ecosystems and hence protecting existing diversity as a whole (Blockstein, 1992; Hughes and Noss, 1992; Allan and Flecker, 1993; Angermeier and Karr, 1994; Marcot et al., 1994).

The last line of defense against extinction of fishes in the Southeast and elsewhere in the United States is the Endangered Species Act of 1973, as amended. It should remain just that, the last line of defense. Clearly, this Act, the strongest environmental law on Earth, cannot begin to meet the herculean task of conserving the Southeast's imperiled fishes, and as a species-by-species safety net, it simply cannot and should not be expected to function alone in conservation of the great southeastern fish fauna. We need shifts in management approaches that avert continued endangerment of fishes. The foundation of such an approach should include a system-led (e.g., drainage unit) rather than species-led focus; explicit biological integrity goals in the context of preventing degradation of high-quality systems and restoring poor-quality systems; commitment to implementing effective land-water management practices rather than implementing bureaucracies; and recognition of land and water resources as integrated parts of the same system.

We present evidence from the fish fauna pointing to the widespread, pervasive decline of aquatic habitats across the Southeast. The associated problems, if there is a will to correct them (see Meyer, 1995), are simply beyond the statutory and fiscal abilities of any one piece of legislation or agency to correct. In short, we believe the need for transcendence, focus, and action is clear and urgent.

REFERENCES

Allan, J. D., and A. S. Flecker. 1993. Biodiversity conservation in running waters. *BioScience* **43**:32-43.

Anderson, I. E. 1950. Surface waters of Mississippi. *Mississippi State Geological Survey Bulletin* **68**:1-338.

Anderson, R. M., J. B. Layzer, and M. E. Gordon. 1991. Recent catastrophic decline of mussels (Bivalvia: Unionidae) in the Little South Fork Cumberland River, Kentucky. *Brimleyana* **17**:1-8.

Angermeier, P. L. 1995. Ecological attributes of extinction-prone species: Loss of freshwater fishes of Virginia. *Conservation Biology* **9**:143-158.

Angermeier, P. L., and J. R. Karr. 1994. Biological integrity versus biological diversity as policy directives. *BioScience* **44**:690-697.

Angermeier, P. L., and I. J. Schlosser. 1989. Species-area relationships for stream fishes. *Ecology* **70**:1450-1462.

Bauer, B. H., D. A. Etnier, and N. M. Burkhead. 1995. *Etheostoma (Ulocentra) scotti* (Osteichthyes: Percidae), a new darter from the Etowah River system in Georgia. *Bulletin of the Alabama Museum of Natural History* **17**:1-16.

Berkman, H. E., and C. F. Rabeni. 1987. Effect of siltation on stream fish communities. *Environmental Biology of Fishes* **18**:285-294.

Blockstein, D. E. 1992. An aquatic perspective on U.S. biodiversity policy. *Fisheries* **17**(3):26-30.

Boschung, H. T., R. L. Mayden, and J. R. Tomelleri. 1992. *Etheostoma chermocki* (Teleostei: Percidae) from the Black Warrior River drainage of Alabama. *Bulletin of the Alabama Museum of Natural History* **13**:11-20.

Burkhead, N. M., and R. E. Jenkins. 1991. Fishes. In *Virginia's Endangered Species*. K. Terwilliger (coord.). McDonald and Woodward Publishing Company, Blacksburg, VA, p. 321-409.

Burr, B. M., and R. L. Mayden. 1992. Phylogenetics and North American freshwater fishes. In *Systematics, Historical Ecology, and North American Freshwater Fishes*. R. L. Mayden (ed.). Stanford University Press, Stanford, CA, p. 18-75.

Burr, B. M., and L. M. Page. 1986. Zoogeography of fishes of the lower Ohio-upper Mississippi River basin. In *The Zoogeography of North American Freshwater Fishes*. C. H. Hocutt, and E. O. Wiley (eds.). John Wiley and Sons, Inc., New York, NY, p. 287-324.

Burr, B. M., and L. M. Page. 1993. A new species of *Percina (Odontopholis)* from Kentucky and Tennessee with comparisons to *Percina cymatotaenia* (Teleostei: Percidae). *Bulletin of the Alabama Museum of Natural History* **16**:15-28.

Burr, B. M., and M. L. Warren, Jr. 1986. *A Distributional Atlas of Kentucky Fishes*. Kentucky Nature Preserves Commission Scientific and Technical Series Number 4, Kentucky Nature Preserves Commission, Frankfort, KY.

Cain, T. 1993. Beyond dollars and sense: Debating the value of nongame fish. *Fisheries* **18**(7):20-21.

Conner, E. F., and E. D. McCoy. 1979. The statistics and biology of the species-area relationship. *American Naturalist* **113**:791-833.

Crawford, T. V. 1994. Integrated environmental management at the Savannah River site. In *Implementing Integrated Environmental Management*. J. Cairns, Jr., T. V. Crawford, and H. Salwasser (eds.). University Center for Environmental and Hazardous Materials Studies, Virginia Tech, Blacksburg, VA, p. 109-116.

Cubbage, F. W., and C. H. Flather. 1993. Forested wetland distribution: A detailed look at the south. *Journal of Forestry* **91**(5):35-40.

Deacon, J. E., G. Kobetich, J. D. Williams, and S. Contreras. 1979. Fishes of North America endangered, threatened, or of special concern: 1979. *Fisheries* **4**(2):30-44.

Dickson, J. G., and M. L. Warren, Jr. 1994. Wildlife and fish communities of eastern riparian forests. In *Functions, Values, and Management: Proceedings of Riparian Ecosystems in the Humid U.S.* National Association of Conservation Districts, Washington, D.C., p. 1-31.

Eager, D. C., and R. M. Hatcher (eds.). 1980. *Tennessee's Rare Wildlife. Volume 1: The Vertebrates*. Tennessee Wildlife Resources Agency and Tennessee Department of Conservation, Nashville, TN.

Etnier, D. A., and W. C. Starnes. 1991. An analysis of Tennessee's jeopardized fish taxa. *Journal of the Tennessee Academy of Science* **66**:129-133.

Etnier, D. A., and W. C. Starnes. 1993. *The Fishes of Tennessee.* University of Tennessee Press, Knoxville, TN.

Etnier, D. A., W. C. Starnes, and B. H. Bauer. 1979. Whatever happened to the silvery minnow (*Hybognathus nuchalis*) in the Tennessee River? *Proceedings of the Southeastern Fishes Council* 2:1-3.

Fenneman, N. M., and D. W. Johnson. 1964. Physical divisions of the United States. United States Geological Survey, Reston, VA, 1 p.

Flather, C. H., L. A. Joyce, and C. A. Bloomgarden. 1994. Species endangerment patterns in the United States. General Technical Report RM-GTR-241, Rocky Mountain Forest and Range Experiment Station, Forest Service, U.S. Department of Agriculture, Fort Collins, CO, 42 p.

Frissel, C. A. 1993. Topology of extinction and endangerment of native fishes in the Pacific Northwest and California (U.S.A.). *Conservation Biology* 7:342-354.

Gilbert, C. R. (ed.). 1992. *Rare and Endangered Biota of Florida. Volume II. Fishes.* University Press of Florida, Gainesville, FL.

Gilbert, C. R., R. C. Cashner, and E. O. Wiley. 1992. Taxonomic and nomenclatural status of the banded topminnow, *Fundulus cingulatus* (Cyprinodontiformes: Cyprinodontidae). *Copeia* 1992:747-759.

Gorman, O. T. 1992. Evolutionary ecology and historical ecology: Assembly, structure, and organization of stream fish communities. In *Systematics, Historical Ecology, and North American Freshwater Fishes.* R. L. Mayden (ed.). Stanford University Press, Stanford, CA, p. 659-688.

Groombridge, B. (ed.). 1992. *Global Biodiversity.* Chapman and Hall, London.

Hains, C. F. 1968. Flow characteristics of Alabama streams. Circular 32, Geological Survey of Alabama, University, AL, 382 p.

Hanski, I. 1982. Dynamics of regional distribution: The core and satellite species hypothesis. *Oikos* 38:210-221.

Haro, R. J., and M. A. Brusven. 1994. Effects of cobble embeddedness on the microdistribution of the sculpin *Cottus beldingi* and its stonefly prey. *Great Basin Naturalist* 54:64-70.

Hocutt, C. H., R. E. Jenkins, and J. R. Stauffer, Jr. 1986. Zoogeography of the fishes of the central Appalachians and central Atlantic Coastal Plain. In *The Zoogeography of North American Freshwater Fishes.* C. H. Hocutt, and E. O. Wiley (eds.). John Wiley and Sons, Inc., New York, NY, p. 161-211.

Holman, T., J. Skains, and D. Riecke. 1993. The Big Black River, Mississippi: A case history. *National Biological Survey, Biological Report* 19:266-281.

Hosmer, D. W., Jr., and S. Lemeshow. 1989. *Applied Logistic Regression.* John Wiley and Sons, Inc., New York, NY.

Hughes, R. M., and R. F. Noss. 1992. Biological diversity and biological integrity: Current concerns for lakes and streams. *Fisheries* 17(3):11-19.

Hupp, C. R. 1992. Riparian vegetation recovery patterns following stream channelization: A geomorphic perspective. *Ecology* 73:1209-1226.

Hunt, C. E. 1988. *Down by the River.* Island Press, Washington, D.C.

Jackson, D. C., and J. R. Jackson. 1989. A glimmer of hope for stream fisheries in Mississippi. *Fisheries* 14(3):4-9.

Jackson, D. C., N. J. Brown-Peterson, and T. D. Rhine. 1993. Perspectives for rivers and their fishery resources in the upper Yazoo River basin, Mississippi. *National Biological Survey, Biological Report* **19**:255-265.

Jenkins, R. E., and N. M. Burkhead. 1994. *Freshwater Fishes of Virginia.* American Fisheries Society, Bethesda, MD.

Johnson, J. E. 1987. *Protected Fishes of the United States and Canada.* American Fisheries Society, Bethesda, MD.

Karr, J. R. 1990. Avian survival rates and the extinction process on Barro Colorado Island, Panama. *Conservation Biology* **4**:391-397.

Karr, J. R. 1993. Measuring biological integrity: Lessons from streams. In *Ecological Integrity and the Management of Ecosystems.* S. Woodley, J. Kay, and G. Francis (eds.). St. Lucie Press, Delray Beach, FL, p. 83-104.

Kessler, R. K., and J. H. Thorp. 1993. Microhabitat segregation of the threatened spotted darter (*Etheostoma maculatum*) and closely related orangefin darter (*E. bellum*). *Canadian Journal of Fisheries and Aquatic Sciences* **50**:1084-1091.

Lee, D. S., C. R. Gilbert, C. H. Hocutt, R. E. Jenkins, D. E. McAllister, and J. R. Stauffer, Jr. 1980 et seq. *Atlas of North American Freshwater Fishes.* North Carolina State Museum of Natural History, Raleigh, NC.

Littell, R. 1992. *Endangered and Other Protected Species: Federal Law and Regulations.* Bureau of National Affairs, Inc., Washington, D.C.

Marcot, B. G., M. J. Wisdom, H. W. Li, and G. C. Castillo. 1994. Managing for featured, threatened, endangered, and sensitive species and unique habitats for ecosystem sustainability. General Technical Report PNW-GTR-329, Pacific Northwest Research Station, Forest Service, U.S. Department of Agriculture, Portland, OR, 39 p.

Maser, C., and J. R. Sedell. 1994. *From the Forest to the Sea: The Ecology of Wood in Streams.* St. Lucie Press, Delray Beach, FL.

Mayden, R. L. 1988. Vicariance biogeography, parsimony, and evolution in North American freshwater fishes. *Systematic Zoology* **37**:329-355.

Mayden, R. L. 1992. An emerging revolution in comparative biology and the evolution of North American freshwater fishes. In *Systematics, Historical Ecology, and North American Freshwater Fishes.* R. L. Mayden (ed.). Stanford University Press, Stanford, CA, p. 864-890.

Mayden, R. L. 1993. *Elassoma alabamae*, a new species of pygmy sunfish endemic to the Tennessee River drainage of Alabama (Teleostei: Elassomatidae). *Bulletin of the Alabama Museum of Natural History* **16**:1-14.

Mayden, R. L., B. M. Burr, L. M. Page, and R. R. Miller. 1992. The native freshwater fishes of North America. In *Systematics, Historical Ecology, and North American Freshwater Fishes.* R. L. Mayden (ed.). Stanford University Press, Stanford, CA, p. 827-863.

Mehta, C., and N. Patel. 1992. *StatXact-Turbo.* Cytel Software Corporation, Cambridge, MA.

Menhinick, E. F. (ed.). in press. Endangered, threatened, and rare fauna of North Carolina. Part III. A re-evaluation of the freshwater fishes. *Occasional Papers of the North Carolina Biological Survey.*

Merritt, R. W., K. W. Cummings, and T. M. Burton. 1984. The role of aquatic insects in the processing and cycling of nutrients. In *The Ecology of Aquatic Insects.* V. H. Resh, and D. M. Rosenberg (eds.). Praeger Scientific, New York, NY, p. 134-163.

Meyer, S. M. 1995. The role of scientists in the "New Politics." *The Chronicle of Higher Education* 26 May 1995, Section B, p. 1-2.

Miller, R. R., J. D. Williams, and J. E. Williams. 1989. Extinctions of North American fishes during the past century. *Fisheries* **14**(6):22-38.

Minckley, W. L., and J. E. Deacon (eds.). 1991. *Battle Against Extinction: Native Fish Management in the American West.* University of Arizona Press, Tucson, AZ.

Minshall, G. W. 1984. Aquatic insect-substratum relationships. In *The Ecology of Aquatic Insects.* V. H. Resh, and D. M. Rosenberg (eds.). Praeger Scientific, New York, NY, p. 358-400.

Mount, R. H. (ed.). 1986. *Vertebrate Animals of Alabama in Need of Special Attention.* Alabama Agricultural Experiment Station, Auburn University, AL.

Moyle, P. B., and R. A. Leidy. 1992. Loss of aquatic ecosystems: Evidence from the fish faunas. In *Conservation Biology: The Theory and Practice of Nature Conservation, Preservation, and Management.* P. L. Fiedler, and S. K. Jain (eds.). Chapman and Hall, New York, NY, p. 127-169.

Moyle, P. B., and J. E. Williams. 1990. Biodiversity loss in the temperate zone: Decline of the native fish fauna of California. *Conservation Biology* **4**:275-284.

Moyle, P. B., and R. M. Yoshiyama. 1994. Protection of aquatic biodiversity in California: A five-tiered approach. *Fisheries* **19**(2):6-18.

Nagel, J. W. 1991. Is the decline of brook trout in the southern Appalachians resulting from competitive exclusion and/or extinction due to habitat fragmentation? *Journal of the Tennessee Academy Science* **66**:141-143.

Neves, R. J., and P. L. Angermeier. 1990. Habitat alteration and its effects on native fishes in the upper Tennessee River system, east-central U.S.A. *Journal of Fish Biology* **37**(Supplement A):45-52.

Noss, R. F., and A. Y. Cooperrider. 1994. *Saving Nature's Legacy: Protecting and Restoring Biodiversity.* Island Press, Washington, D.C.

Page, L. M., and B. M. Burr. 1991. *A Field Guide to Freshwater Fishes.* Houghton Mifflin Company, Boston, MA.

Page, L. M., P. A. Ceas, D. L. Swofford, and D. G. Buth. 1992. Evolutionary relationships within the *Etheostoma squamiceps* complex (Percidae; subgenus *Catonotus*) with descriptions of five new species. *Copeia* 1992:615-646.

Page, L. M., and D. L. Swofford. 1984. Morphological correlates of ecological specialization in darters. *Environmental Biology of Fishes* **11**:139-159.

Pister, E. P. 1991. The Desert Fishes Council: Catalyst for change. In *Battle Against Extinction: Native Fish Management in the American West.* W. L. Minckley, and J. E. Deacon (eds.). University of Arizona Press, Tucson, AZ, p. 55-68.

Pister, E. P. 1992. Ethical considerations in conservation of biodiversity. *Transactions of the North American Wildlife and National Resources Conference* **57**:355-358.

Reffalt, W. 1991. The endangered species lists: Chronicles of extinction? In *Balancing on the Brink of Extinction.* K. A. Kohm (ed.). Island Press, Washington, D.C., p. 77-85.

Reice, S. R., and M. Wohlenberg. 1993. Monitoring freshwater benthic macroinvertebrates and benthic processes: Measures for assessment of ecosystem health. In *Freshwater Biomonitoring and Benthic Macroinvertebrates.* D. M. Rosenberg, and V. H. Resh (eds.). Chapman and Hall, New York, NY, p. 287-305.

Rita, H., and E. Ranta. 1993. On analyzing species incidence. *Annales Zoologici Fennici* **30**:173-176.

Rohde, F. C., and R. G. Arndt. 1987. Two new species of pygmy sunfishes (Elassomatidae, *Elassoma*) from the Carolinas. *Proceedings of the Academy of Natural Sciences, Philadelphia* **139**:65-85.

Ross, S. T., and W. M. Brenneman. 1991. *Distribution of Freshwater Fishes in Mississippi.* Freshwater Fisheries Report Number 108, Mississippi Department of Wildlife, Fisheries, and Parks, Jackson, MS.

SAS Institute, Inc. 1994. *SAS for Windows, Release 6.1.* SAS Institute, Inc., Cary, NC.

Saylor, C. F., A. D. McKinney, and W. H. Schacher. 1993. Case study of the Pigeon River in the Tennessee River drainage. *National Biological Survey, Biological Report* **19**:241-254.

Schlosser, I. J., and P. L. Angermeier. 1995. Spatial variation in demographic processes in lotic fishes: Conceptual models, empirical evidence, and implications for conservation. In *Evolution and the Aquatic Ecosystem: Defining Units in Population Conservation.* J. L. Nielsen (ed.). Symposium Number 17, American Fisheries Society, Bethesda, MD, p. 392-401.

Scott, J. M., F. Davis, F. Csuti, K. Smith, J. E. Estes, and S. Caicco. 1988. Beyond endangered species: An integrated conservation strategy for the preservation of biological diversity. *Endangered Species Update* **5**:43-48.

Sheldon, A. L. 1987. Rarity: Patterns and consequences for stream fishes. In *Community and Evolutionary Ecology of North American Stream Fishes.* W. J. Matthews, and D. C. Heins (eds.). University of Oklahoma Press, Norman, OK, p. 203-209.

Sokal, R. R., and F. J. Rohlf. 1981. *Biometry. 2nd Edition.* W. H. Freeman and Company, New York, NY.

Soulé, M. E., and K. A. Kohm. 1989. *Research Priorities for Conservation Biology.* Critical Issues Series Number 1, Island Press, Washington, D.C.

Southwood, T. R. E. 1978. *Ecological Methods. 2nd Edition.* Chapman and Hall, New York, NY.

Starnes, W. C., and D. A. Etnier. 1986. Drainage evolution and fish biogeography of the Tennessee and Cumberland rivers drainage realm. In *The Zoogeography of North American Freshwater Fishes.* C. H. Hocutt, and E. O. Wiley (eds.). John Wiley and Sons, Inc., New York, NY, p. 325-361.

Suttkus, R. D. 1991. *Notropis rafinesquei*, a new cyprinid fish from the Yazoo River system in Mississippi. *Bulletin of the Alabama Museum of Natural History* **10**:1-9.

Suttkus, R. D., and R. M. Bailey. 1993. *Etheostoma colorosum* and *E. bellator*, two new darters, subgenus *Ulocentra*, from southeastern United States. *Tulane Studies in Zoology and Botany* **29**:1-28.

Suttkus, R. D., R. M. Bailey, and H. L. Bart, Jr. 1994a. Three new species of *Etheostoma*, subgenus *Ulocentra*, from the Gulf Coastal Plain of southeastern United States. *Tulane Studies in Zoology and Botany* **29**:97-126.

Suttkus, R. D., and D. A. Etnier. 1991. *Etheostoma tallapoosae* and *E. brevirostrum*, two new darters, subgenus *Ulocentra*, from the Alabama River drainage. *Tulane Studies in Zoology Botany* **28**:1-24.

Suttkus, R. D., B. A. Thompson, and H. L. Bart, Jr. 1994b. Two new darters, *Percina* (*Cottogaster*), from the southeastern United States, with a review of the subgenus. *Occasional Papers of the Tulane University Museum of Natural History* **4**:1-46.

Swift, C. C., C. R. Gilbert, S. A. Bortone, G. H. Burgess, and R. W. Yerger. 1986. Zoogeography of the freshwater fishes of the southeastern United States: Savannah River to Lake Pontchartrain. In *The Zoogeography of North American Freshwater Fishes.* C. H. Hocutt, and E. O. Wiley (eds.). John Wiley and Sons, Inc., New York, NY, p. 213-265.

Terborgh, J. W., and B. Winter. 1980. Some causes of extinction. In *Conservation Biology: An Evolutionary-Ecological Perspective.* M. E. Soulé, and B. A. Wilcox (eds.). Sinauer, Sunderland, MA, p. 119-133.

Terwilliger, K. (coord.). 1991. *Virginia's Endangered Species.* McDonald and Woodward Publishing Company, Blacksburg, VA.

Thompson, B. A. 1995. *Percina austroperca*: A new species of logperch (Percidae, subgenus *Percina*) from the Choctawhatchee and Escambia rivers in Alabama and Florida. *Occasional Papers of the Museum of Natural Science, Louisiana State University* **69**:1-20.

Toth, L. A., and N. G. Aumen. 1994. Integration of multiple issues in environmental restoration and resource enhancement projects in southcentral Florida. In *Implementing Integrated Environmental Management.* J. Cairns, Jr., T. V. Crawford, and H. Salwasser (eds.). University Center for Environmental and Hazardous Materials Studies, Virginia Tech, Blacksburg, VA, p. 61-78.

U.S. Fish and Wildlife Service. 1994a. Endangered and threatened wildlife and plants; animal candidate review for listing as endangered or threatened species, proposed rule. *U.S. Federal Register* **59**:58982-59028.

U.S. Fish and Wildlife Service. 1994b. Endangered and threatened wildlife and plants. *U.S. Federal Register* **50** CFR (17.11 and 17.12):1-42.

Voigtlander, C. W., and W. L. Poppe. 1989. The Tennessee River. In *Proceedings of the International Large River Symposium (LARS).* D. P. Dodge (ed.). Special Publication 106, Canadian Fisheries and Aquatic Sciences, Toronto, Ottawa, Canada, p. 372-384.

Warren, M. L., Jr. 1992. Variation of the spotted sunfish, *Lepomis punctatus* complex (Centrarchidae): Meristics, morphometrics, pigmentation and species limits. *Bulletin of the Alabama Museum of Natural History* **12**:1-47.

Warren, M. L., Jr., and P. L. Angermeier. in press. Protocols for assessing aquatic biodiversity: GIS applications in Virginia. Proceedings of the United States Fish and Wildlife Service GIS Workshop for 1993, U.S. Fish and Wildlife Service, Lafayette, LA.

Warren, M. L., Jr., and B. M. Burr. 1994. Status of freshwater fishes of the United States: Overview of an imperiled fauna. *Fisheries* **19**(1):6-18.

Warren, M. L., Jr., B. M. Burr, D. A. Etnier, and W. C. Starnes. 1991. Fishes of Kentucky and Tennessee: A hierarchical classification of drainages. *Journal of the Tennessee Academy of Science* **66**:135-140.

Warren, M. L., Jr., B. M. Burr, and J. M. Grady. 1994. *Notropis albizonatus*, a new cyprinid endemic to the Tennessee and Cumberland River drainages, with a phylogeny of the *Notropis procne* species group. *Copeia* 1994:868-886.

Warren, M. L., Jr., W. H. Davis, R. R. Hannan, M. Evans, D. L. Batch, B. D. Anderson, B. Palmer-Ball, Jr., J. R. MacGregor, R. R. Cicerello, R. Athey, B. A. Branson, G. J. Fallo, B. M. Burr, M. E. Medley, and J. M. Baskin. 1986. Endangered, threatened, and rare plants and animals of Kentucky. *Transactions of the Kentucky Academy of Science* 47:83-98.

Williams, J. D., and G. H. Clemmer. 1991. *Scaphirhynchus suttkusi*, a new sturgeon (Pisces: Acipenseridae) from the Mobile Basin of Alabama and Mississippi. *Bulletin of the Alabama Museum of Natural History* 10:17-31.

Williams, J. D., M. L. Warren, Jr., K. S. Cummings, J. L. Harris, and R. J. Neves. 1993. Conservation status of freshwater mussels of the United States and Canada. *Fisheries* 18(9):6-23.

Williams, J. E., J. E. Johnson, D. A. Hendrickson, S. Contreras-Balderas, J. D. Williams, M. Navarro-Mendoza, D. E. McAllister, and J. E. Deacon. 1989. Fishes of North America endangered, threatened, or of special concern: 1989. *Fisheries* 14(6):2-20.

Williams, T. 1986. Who's managing the wildlife managers? *Orion Nature Quarterly* 5(4):16-23.

Wood, R. M., and R. L. Mayden. 1993. Systematics of the *Etheostoma jordani* species group (Teleostei: Percidae), with descriptions of three new species. *Bulletin of the Alabama Museum of Natural History* 16:31-46.

Appendix 1. Checklist of extant fishes (N = native, I = introduced), their conservation status, and distribution within 33 drainage units of the southeastern United States. Conservation status is listed for each species as recognized by the United States Fish and Wildlife Service (Federal, E = endangered, T = threatened, PE = proposed endangered, PT = proposed threatened, C1 = candidate 1, and C2 = candidate) and the American Fisheries Society (AFS, E = endangered, T = threatened, SC = special concern) (see Williams et al., 1989). Drainage units are cross-referenced by number to Table 1 and Figure 2.

TAXA	Federal E	T	PE	PT	C1	C2	AFS E	T	SC	1	2	3	4	5	6	7	8	9	10	11	12	13	14	15	16	17	18	19	20	21	22	23	24	25	26	27	28	29	30	31	32	33
PETROMYZONTIDAE - Lampreys																																										
Ichthyomyzon bdellium (Ohio lamprey)	–	–	–	–	–	–	–	–	–	–	–	–	–	–	–	–	–	–	–	–	–	–	–	–	N	N	–	–	–	–	–	–	–	–	N	N	N	N	N	N	N	N
I. castaneus (chestnut lamprey)	–	–	–	–	–	–	–	–	–	–	–	–	–	–	–	–	–	–	–	–	–	–	–	–	N	N	N	–	N	N	N	N	N	N	N	N	N	N	N	–	–	N
I. fossor (northern brook lamprey)	–	–	–	–	–	–	–	–	–	–	–	–	–	–	–	–	–	–	–	–	–	–	–	–	–	–	–	–	–	–	–	–	–	–	–	–	–	N	N	–	–	–
I. gagei (southern brook lamprey)	–	–	–	–	–	–	–	–	–	–	–	–	–	–	–	–	–	–	–	–	N	N	N	N	N	N	N	N	N	N	N	N	N	N	N	N	N	N	–	–	–	–
I. greeleyi (mountain brook lamprey)	–	–	–	–	–	–	–	–	–	–	–	–	–	–	–	–	–	–	–	–	–	–	–	–	–	–	–	–	–	–	–	–	–	–	–	N	N	N	–	–	–	–
I. unicuspis (silver lamprey)	–	–	–	–	–	–	–	–	–	–	–	–	–	–	–	–	–	–	–	–	–	–	–	–	N	N	N	–	–	N	N	–	N	N	–	N	N	N	N	N	N	N
Lampetra aepyptera (least brook lamprey)	–	–	–	–	–	–	–	–	–	N	N	–	N	–	–	–	–	–	–	–	–	–	–	–	N	N	N	–	N	N	N	–	N	–	N	–	N	N	N	N	N	N
L. appendix (American brook lamprey)	–	–	–	–	–	–	–	–	–	N	N	N	–	–	–	–	–	–	–	–	–	–	–	–	N	–	–	–	–	–	N	–	–	–	N	N	N	N	N	N	–	–
ACIPENSERIDAE - Sturgeons																																										
Acipenser brevirostrum (shortnose sturgeon)	X	–	–	–	–	–	–	X	–	N	–	N	–	–	–	–	–	N	N	N	N	–	–	–	–	–	–	–	–	–	–	–	–	–	–	N	N	–	–	–	–	–
A. fulvescens (lake sturgeon)	–	–	–	–	X	–	–	X	–	–	–	–	–	–	–	–	–	–	–	–	–	N	N	N	N	N	–	–	–	–	–	–	–	–	N	N	–	–	–	–	–	N
A. oxyrhynchus desotoi (Gulf sturgeon)	X	–	–	–	–	–	–	–	X	–	–	–	–	N	N	–	–	N	N	N	N	–	N	N	N	N	N	N	N	N	N	N	–	–	–	–	–	–	–	–	–	–
A. o. oxyrhynchus (Atlantic sturgeon)	–	–	–	–	–	–	–	–	X	N	N	N	N	–	–	–	–	N	N	–	–	–	–	–	–	–	–	–	–	–	–	–	–	–	–	N	N	–	–	–	–	–
Scaphirhynchus albus (pallid sturgeon)	X	–	–	–	–	–	X	–	–	–	–	–	–	–	–	–	–	–	–	–	–	N	–	–	–	–	–	–	–	–	–	N	–	N	–	–	–	–	N	–	–	N
S. platorynchus (shovelnose sturgeon)	–	–	–	–	–	–	–	–	–	–	–	–	–	–	–	–	–	–	–	–	–	–	–	–	–	–	–	–	–	N	N	N	N	–	N	N	–	–	–	–	–	–
S. suttkusi (Alabama sturgeon)	–	X	–	–	–	–	X	–	–	–	–	–	–	–	–	–	–	–	–	–	–	–	–	–	N	N	N	N	–	–	–	–	–	–	–	–	–	–	–	–	–	–
POLYODONTIDAE - Paddlefishes																																										
Polyodon spathula (paddlefish)	–	–	–	–	X	–	–	–	X	–	–	–	–	–	–	–	–	–	–	–	–	–	–	–	N	N	N	N	N	N	N	N	N	N	N	N	N	N	N	N	N	N
LEPISOSTEIDAE - Gars																																										
Atractosteus spatula (alligator gar)	–	–	–	–	–	–	–	–	–	–	–	–	–	–	–	–	–	–	–	–	–	–	–	N	N	–	N	N	N	N	N	N	N	N	–	N	–	N	–	–	–	N

Appendix 1. Continued.

TAXA	Federal						AFS			Drainage Units																															
	E	T	PE	PT	C1	C2	E	T	SC	1	2	3	4	5	6	7	8	9	10	11	12	13	14	15	16	17	18	19	20	21	22	23	24	25	26	27	28	29	30	31	32	33
Lepisosteus oculatus (spotted gar)	-	-	-	-	-	-	-	-	-	-	N	N	N	N	N	N	-	-	-	-	-	-	N	N	N	N	N	N	N	N	-	N	N	N	N	N	N	N	-	-	-	N
L. osseus (longnose gar)	-	-	-	-	-	-	-	-	-	N	N	N	N	N	N	N	N	N	N	N	N	N	N	N	N	N	N	N	N	N	N	N	N	N	N	N	N	N	N	N	N	N
L. platostomus (shortnose gar)	-	-	-	-	-	-	-	-	-	-	-	-	-	-	-	-	-	-	-	-	-	-	-	-	-	-	-	-	-	N	N	N	N	N	N	-	N	N	-	-	-	N
L. platyrhyncus (Florida gar)	-	-	-	-	-	-	-	-	-	-	-	-	-	-	-	-	-	N	N	N	N	N	-	-	-	-	-	-	-	-	-	-	-	-	-	-	-	-	-	-	-	-
AMIIDAE – Bowfins																																										
Amia calva (bowfin)	-	-	-	-	-	-	-	-	-	N	N	N	N	N	N	N	N	N	N	N	N	N	N	N	N	N	N	N	N	N	N	N	N	N	N	N	N	N	N	N	N	N
HIODONTIDAE – Mooneyes																																										
Hiodon alosoides (goldeye)	-	-	-	-	-	-	-	-	-	-	-	-	-	-	-	-	-	-	-	-	-	-	-	-	-	-	-	-	-	-	-	N	N	N	N	N	N	N	N	N	-	N
H. tergisus (mooneye)	-	-	-	-	-	-	-	-	-	-	-	-	-	-	-	-	-	-	-	-	-	-	-	-	N	N	N	N	N	N	N	-	N	N	N	N	N	N	N	N	-	N
ANGUILLIDAE – Freshwater Eels																																										
Anguilla rostrata (American eel)	-	-	-	-	-	-	-	-	-	N	N	N	N	N	N	N	N	N	N	N	N	N	N	N	N	N	N	N	N	N	N	N	N	N	N	N	N	N	N	N	N	N
CLUPEIDAE – Herrings and Shads																																										
Alosa aestivalis (blueback herring)	-	-	-	-	-	-	-	-	-	N	N	N	N	N	N	-	-	N	N	N	-	-	-	-	-	-	-	-	-	-	-	-	-	-	-	-	-	-	-	-	-	-
A. alabamae (Alabama shad)	-	-	-	-	-	-	-	-	-	-	-	-	-	-	-	-	-	-	-	N	-	N	-	-	-	-	-	-	-	-	-	-	-	-	-	-	-	-	-	-	-	-
A. chrysochloris (skipjack herring)	-	-	-	-	-	-	-	-	-	-	-	-	-	-	-	-	-	-	-	-	-	N	N	N	N	N	N	N	N	N	-	N	N	N	N	N	N	N	N	N	-	N
A. mediocris (hickory shad)	-	-	-	-	-	-	-	-	-	N	N	N	N	N	N	N	-	-	N	N	-	-	-	-	-	-	-	-	-	-	-	-	-	-	-	-	-	-	-	-	-	-
A. pseudoharengus (alewife)	-	-	-	-	-	-	-	-	-	N	N	N	N	N	N	N	-	-	N	N	N	-	-	-	-	-	-	-	-	-	-	-	-	-	-	I	I	-	-	-	-	I	-
A. sapidissima (American shad)	-	-	-	-	-	-	-	-	-	N	N	N	N	N	N	N	N	N	N	N	N	N	N	N	N	N	N	N	N	-	-	-	-	-	-	-	-	-	-	-	-	-
Dorosoma cepedianum (gizzard shad)	-	-	-	-	-	-	-	-	-	N	N	N	N	N	N	N	N	N	N	N	N	N	N	N	N	N	N	N	N	N	N	N	N	N	N	N	N	N	N	N	N	N
D. petenense (threadfin shad)	-	-	-	-	-	-	-	-	-	I	I	I	I	-	I	I	-	I	I	I	-	N	N	I	I	I	I	I	-	-	-	I	I	I	I	I	I	I	I	I	I	-

Appendix 1. Continued.

TAXA	Federal						AFS			Drainage Units																																
	E	T	PE	PT	C1	C2	E	T	SC	1	2	3	4	5	6	7	8	9	10	11	12	13	14	15	16	17	18	19	20	21	22	23	24	25	26	27	28	29	30	31	32	33
CYPRINIDAE – Minnows and Carps																																										
Campostoma anomalum (central stoneroller)	-	-	-	-	-	-	-	-	-	N	N	N	-	-	N	N	-	N	-	-	-	-	-	N	N	N	N	-	-	N	N	N	N	N	-	-	N	N	N	N	N	-
C. oligolepis (largescale stoneroller)	-	-	-	-	-	-	-	-	-	-	-	-	-	-	-	-	-	-	-	-	-	-	-	N	N	N	N	-	-	-	N	N	N	N	N	N	N	N	N	N	N	-
C. pauciradii (bluefin stoneroller)	-	-	-	-	-	-	-	-	-	-	-	-	-	-	-	-	-	-	-	-	-	-	-	-	-	-	-	-	-	-	-	-	N	-	-	-	-	-	-	-	-	-
Carassius auratus (goldfish)	-	-	-	-	-	-	-	-	-	I	-	-	-	I	I	I	-	N	-	-	-	-	-	-	-	-	-	-	-	-	I	I	I	-	I	I	I	I	I	I	I	I
Clinostomus elongatus (redside dace)	-	-	-	-	-	-	-	-	-	-	-	-	-	-	-	-	-	-	-	-	-	-	-	-	-	-	-	-	-	-	-	-	-	-	-	-	-	N	N	N	-	-
C. funduloides (rosyside dace)	-	-	-	-	-	-	-	-	-	N	N	N	N	N	N	N	-	N	-	-	-	-	-	-	-	-	-	-	-	-	N	N	N	-	N	N	N	-	-	N	N	-
C. funduloides ssp. (Little Tennessee dace)	-	-	-	-	-	-	-	-	-	-	-	-	-	-	-	-	-	-	-	-	-	-	-	N	-	-	-	-	-	-	-	-	-	-	-	-	-	-	-	-	-	-
Ctenopharyngodon idella (grass carp)	-	-	-	-	-	-	-	-	-	I	I	-	-	-	I	I	I	I	I	I	I	I	I	I	I	I	I	-	-	I	I	I	I	I	I	I	I	I	I	I	I	I
Cyprinella analostana (satinfin shiner)	-	-	-	-	-	-	-	-	-	N	N	N	N	N	N	-	-	-	-	-	-	-	-	-	-	-	-	-	-	-	-	-	-	-	-	-	-	-	-	-	-	-
C. caerulea (blue shiner)	X	-	-	-	-	-	-	-	X	-	-	-	-	-	-	-	-	-	-	-	-	-	-	-	N	N	N	-	-	-	-	-	-	-	-	-	-	-	-	-	-	-
C. callisema (Ocmulgee shiner)	-	-	-	-	X	-	-	-	-	-	-	-	-	-	-	-	-	-	-	-	-	-	-	-	-	-	-	-	-	-	-	-	-	-	-	-	-	-	-	-	-	-
C. callistia (Alabama shiner)	-	-	-	-	-	-	-	-	-	-	-	-	-	-	-	N	-	-	-	-	-	-	-	N	N	N	-	-	-	-	-	-	-	-	-	-	-	-	-	-	-	-
C. callitaenia (bluestripe shiner)	-	-	-	-	X	-	-	X	-	-	-	-	-	-	-	-	-	-	-	-	-	-	N	-	-	-	-	-	-	-	-	-	-	-	-	-	-	-	-	-	-	-
C. camura (bluntface shiner)	-	-	-	-	-	-	-	-	-	-	-	-	-	-	-	-	-	-	-	-	-	-	-	-	-	-	-	-	N	-	N	N	N	N	N	N	-	-	-	-	-	-
C. chloristia (greenfin shiner)	-	-	-	-	-	-	-	-	-	-	-	-	-	-	-	N	-	N	-	-	-	-	-	-	-	-	-	-	-	-	-	-	-	-	-	-	-	-	-	-	-	-
C. galactura (whitetail shiner)	-	-	-	-	-	-	-	-	-	-	-	-	-	-	-	-	-	-	-	-	-	N	-	N	N	N	-	-	-	-	-	-	-	N	N	N	-	-	-	-	-	-
C. gibbsi (Tallapoosa shiner)	-	-	-	-	-	-	-	-	-	-	-	-	-	-	-	N	-	-	-	-	-	-	-	-	-	-	-	-	-	-	-	-	-	-	-	-	-	-	-	-	-	-
C. leedsi (bannerfin shiner)	-	-	-	-	-	-	-	-	-	-	-	-	-	-	-	-	-	-	-	-	-	-	-	-	-	-	-	-	-	-	-	-	-	-	-	-	-	-	-	-	-	-
C. lutrensis (red shiner)	-	-	-	-	-	-	-	-	-	-	-	I	-	-	I	-	-	-	-	-	-	N	-	I	I	I	I	-	-	-	N	N	N	N	I	-	-	-	N	-	-	-
C. nivea (whitefin shiner)	-	-	-	-	-	-	-	-	-	-	-	-	N	N	N	N	-	N	-	-	-	-	-	-	-	-	-	-	-	-	-	-	-	-	-	-	-	-	-	-	-	-
C. pyrrhomelas (fieryblack shiner)	-	-	-	-	-	-	-	-	-	-	-	-	-	-	N	N	-	-	-	-	-	-	-	-	-	-	-	-	-	-	-	-	-	-	-	-	-	-	-	-	-	-
C. spiloptera (spotfin shiner)	-	-	-	-	-	-	-	-	-	N	-	I	-	-	-	-	-	-	-	-	-	-	-	-	-	-	-	-	-	-	-	-	-	-	-	-	-	N	N	N	N	N

Appendix 1. Continued.

TAXA	Federal					AFS			Drainage Units																																	
	E	PE	PT	C1	C2	E	T	SC	1	2	3	4	5	6	7	8	9	10	11	12	13	14	15	16	17	18	19	20	21	22	23	24	25	26	27	28	29	30	31	32	33
C. trichroistia (tricolor shiner)	–	–	–	–	–	–	–	–	–	–	–	–	–	–	–	–	–	–	–	–	–	–	–	–	–	–	–	–	–	–	–	–	–	–	–	–	–	–	–	–	–
C. venusta (blacktail shiner)	–	–	–	–	–	–	–	–	–	–	–	–	–	–	–	–	–	–	–	–	N	N	N	N	N	N	N	N	N	–	N	N	N	N	–	–	–	–	–	–	N
C. whipplei (steelcolor shiner)	–	–	–	–	–	–	–	–	–	–	–	–	–	–	–	–	–	–	–	–	N	–	N	N	–	N	–	–	–	–	–	N	N	N	N	N	N	N	N	N	N
C. xaenura (Altamaha shiner)	–	–	–	X	–	–	–	–	–	–	–	–	–	–	–	–	N	–	–	–	–	–	–	–	–	–	–	–	–	–	–	–	–	–	–	–	–	–	–	–	–
Cyprinus carpio (common carp)	–	–	–	–	–	–	–	–	I	I	–	I	I	I	I	–	–	–	–	–	I	I	I	I	I	I	–	I	I	I	I	I	I	I	I	I	I	I	I	I	I
Ericymba buccata (silverjaw minnow)	–	–	–	–	–	–	–	–	N	–	–	–	–	–	–	–	–	–	–	–	N	N	N	N	N	N	N	N	N	N	–	N	–	–	N	N	N	N	N	N	N
Erimonax monachus (spotfin chub)	X	–	–	–	–	X	–	–	–	–	–	–	–	–	–	–	–	–	–	–	–	–	–	–	–	–	–	–	–	–	–	–	N	N	N	N	N	N	–	–	–
Erimystax cahni (slender chub)	X	–	–	–	–	X	–	–	–	–	–	–	–	–	–	–	–	–	–	–	–	–	–	–	–	–	–	–	–	–	–	–	–	–	–	–	–	–	–	–	–
E. dissimilis (streamline chub)	–	–	–	–	–	–	–	–	–	–	–	–	–	–	–	–	–	–	–	–	–	–	–	–	–	–	–	–	–	–	N	–	–	N	N	N	N	N	N	N	N
E. insignis (blotched chub)	–	–	–	–	–	–	–	–	–	–	–	–	–	–	–	–	–	–	–	–	–	–	–	–	–	–	–	–	–	–	N	–	N	N	N	N	–	–	–	–	–
E. x-punctatus (gravel chub)	–	–	–	–	–	–	–	–	–	–	–	–	–	–	–	–	–	–	–	–	–	–	–	–	–	–	–	–	–	–	–	–	–	–	–	–	N	–	–	–	N
Exoglossum laurae (tonguetied minnow)	–	–	–	–	–	–	–	–	–	–	–	–	–	–	–	–	–	–	–	–	–	–	–	–	–	–	–	–	–	–	–	–	–	–	–	–	–	–	N	–	–
E. maxillingua (cutlips minnow)	–	–	–	–	–	–	–	–	N	N	N	N	–	–	–	–	–	–	–	–	–	–	–	–	–	–	–	–	–	–	–	–	–	–	–	–	–	–	I	–	–
Hemitremia flammea (flame chub)	–	–	–	X	–	–	–	X	–	–	–	–	–	–	–	–	–	–	–	–	–	–	–	N	–	–	–	–	–	–	N	N	N	N	N	N	–	–	–	–	–
Hybognathus hayi (cypress minnow)	–	–	–	–	–	–	–	–	–	–	–	–	–	–	–	–	–	–	–	–	–	–	N	–	–	–	N	N	N	N	N	N	N	N	N	N	–	N	–	–	N
H. nuchalis (Mississippi silvery minnow)	–	–	–	–	–	–	–	–	–	–	–	–	–	–	–	–	–	–	–	–	–	–	–	N	N	N	N	N	N	N	N	N	N	N	N	N	N	N	N	–	–
H. placitus (plains minnow)	–	–	–	X	–	–	–	–	–	–	–	–	–	–	–	–	–	–	–	–	–	–	–	–	–	N	–	–	–	–	N	–	N	N	–	–	–	–	–	–	–
H. regius (eastern silvery minnow)	–	–	–	–	–	–	–	–	N	N	N	N	N	N	N	–	N	–	–	–	–	–	–	–	–	–	–	–	–	–	–	–	–	–	–	–	–	–	–	–	–
Hybopsis alborus (whitemouth shiner)	–	–	–	–	–	–	–	–	–	–	N	–	N	N	N	–	–	–	–	–	–	–	–	–	–	–	–	–	–	–	–	–	–	–	–	–	–	–	–	–	–
H. amblops (bigeye chub)	–	–	–	–	–	–	–	–	–	–	–	–	–	–	–	–	–	–	–	–	–	–	–	–	–	–	–	–	–	–	–	–	–	–	–	–	–	–	N	N	N
H. ammophilus (orangefin shiner)	–	–	–	–	–	–	–	–	–	–	–	–	–	–	–	–	–	–	–	–	–	–	N	N	–	N	–	–	–	–	N	–	–	–	–	N	N	N	–	–	–
H. amnis (pallid shiner)	–	–	–	–	–	–	–	–	–	–	–	–	–	–	–	–	–	–	–	–	–	–	N	N	N	N	–	–	–	–	N	N	N	–	N	N	N	N	–	–	–

Appendix 1. Continued.

TAXA	Federal						AFS			Drainage Units																																
	E	T	PE	PT	C1	C2	E	T	SC	1	2	3	4	5	6	7	8	9	10	11	12	13	14	15	16	17	18	19	20	21	22	23	24	25	26	27	28	29	30	31	32	33
H. bifrenatus (bridle shiner)	-	-	-	-	-	-	-	-	-	N	N	N	N	-	-	-	-	-	-	-	-	-	-	-	-	-	-	-	-	-	-	-	-	-	-	-	-	-	-	-	-	-
H. labrosa (thicklip chub)	-	-	-	-	-	-	-	-	-	-	-	-	-	-	N	N	-	-	-	-	-	-	-	-	-	-	-	-	-	-	-	-	-	-	-	-	-	-	-	-	-	-
H. hypsinotus (highback chub)	-	-	-	-	-	-	-	-	-	-	-	-	-	-	N	N	-	-	-	-	-	-	-	-	-	-	-	-	-	-	-	-	-	-	-	-	-	-	-	-	-	-
H. lineapunctata (lined shiner)	-	-	-	-	-	-	-	-	-	-	-	-	-	-	-	-	-	-	-	-	-	-	-	-	N	-	-	-	-	-	-	-	-	-	-	-	-	-	-	-	-	-
H. longirostris (longnose shiner)	-	-	-	-	-	-	-	-	-	-	-	-	-	-	-	-	-	-	-	-	-	-	N	N	N	N	-	N	N	N	N	N	-	-	-	-	-	-	-	-	-	-
H. rubrifrons (rosyface chub)	-	-	-	-	-	-	-	-	-	-	-	-	-	-	-	N	-	N	N	-	-	-	-	-	-	-	-	-	-	N	N	N	-	-	-	-	-	-	-	-	-	-
H. sabinae (Sabine shiner)	-	-	-	-	-	-	-	-	-	-	-	-	-	-	-	-	-	N	N	-	-	-	-	-	-	-	-	-	-	-	-	N	-	-	-	-	-	-	-	-	-	-
H. winchelli (clear chub)	-	-	-	-	-	-	-	-	-	-	-	-	-	-	-	-	-	-	-	-	-	I	N	N	N	N	N	N	N	N	N	-	-	-	-	-	-	-	-	-	-	-
H. zanema (Santee chub)	-	-	-	-	-	-	-	-	-	-	-	-	-	N	N	N	-	-	-	-	-	-	-	-	-	-	-	-	-	-	-	-	-	-	-	-	-	-	-	-	-	-
Hypophthalmichthys molitrix (silver carp)	-	-	-	-	-	-	-	-	-	-	-	-	-	-	-	-	-	-	-	-	-	-	-	I	-	-	-	-	-	-	-	-	-	-	-	-	-	-	-	I	I	I
H. nobilis (bighead carp)	-	-	-	-	-	-	-	-	-	-	-	-	-	-	-	-	-	-	-	-	-	-	-	-	I	-	-	-	-	-	-	-	-	-	-	-	-	-	-	N	N	I
Luxilus albeolus (white shiner)	-	-	-	-	-	-	-	-	-	-	N	N	-	N	-	-	-	-	-	-	-	-	-	-	-	-	-	-	-	-	-	-	-	-	-	-	-	-	-	-	-	-
L. cerasinus (crescent shiner)	-	-	-	-	-	-	-	-	-	I	N	-	-	I	-	-	-	-	-	-	-	-	-	-	-	-	-	-	-	-	-	-	-	-	-	-	-	-	-	I	I	-
L. chrysocephalus (striped shiner)	-	-	-	-	-	-	-	-	-	-	-	-	-	-	-	-	-	-	-	-	-	-	N	N	N	N	N	N	N	N	N	N	N	N	N	N	N	N	N	N	N	N
L. coccogenis (warpaint shiner)	-	-	-	-	-	-	-	-	-	-	-	-	-	-	-	N	-	N	-	-	-	-	-	-	-	-	-	-	-	-	-	-	-	-	N	N	-	-	-	N	-	-
L. cornutus (common shiner)	-	-	-	-	-	-	-	-	-	N	N	-	-	-	-	-	-	-	N	N	-	-	N	N	N	-	-	-	-	-	-	-	-	-	-	-	-	-	-	-	N	-
L. zonistius (bandfin shiner)	-	-	-	-	-	-	-	-	-	-	-	-	-	-	-	-	-	-	-	-	-	-	-	-	N	-	-	-	-	-	-	-	-	-	-	-	-	-	-	-	-	-
Lythrurus ardens (rosefin shiner)	-	-	-	-	-	-	-	-	-	I	N	N	-	I	-	-	-	-	-	-	-	-	N	N	N	-	-	-	-	-	-	-	-	-	-	-	-	-	-	N	-	-
L. atrapiculus (blacktip shiner)	-	-	-	-	-	-	-	-	-	-	-	-	-	-	-	-	-	-	-	-	-	-	N	N	I	-	-	-	-	-	-	-	-	-	-	-	-	-	-	-	-	-
L. bellus (pretty shiner)	-	-	-	-	-	-	-	-	-	-	-	-	-	-	-	-	-	-	-	-	-	-	-	-	N	N	N	-	-	-	-	-	-	N	-	-	-	-	-	-	-	-
L. fasciolaris (scarletfin shiner)	-	-	-	-	-	-	-	-	-	-	-	-	-	-	-	-	-	-	-	-	-	-	-	-	-	-	-	-	-	-	-	-	-	N	N	N	N	N	N	N	N	-
L. fumeus (ribbon shiner)	-	-	-	-	-	-	-	-	-	-	-	-	-	-	-	-	-	-	-	-	-	-	-	-	-	-	-	-	-	N	N	N	N	N	N	-	N	N	-	-	-	-

Appendix 1. Continued.

TAXA	Federal						AFS			Drainage Units																																
	E	T	PE	PT	C1	C2	E	T	SC	1	2	3	4	5	6	7	8	9	10	11	12	13	14	15	16	17	18	19	20	21	22	23	24	25	26	27	28	29	30	31	32	33
L. lirus (mountain shiner)	-	-	-	-	-	-	-	-	-	-	-	-	-	-	-	-	-	-	-	-	-	-	-	-	-	-	-	-	-	-	-	-	-	-	N	N	-	-	-	-	-	-
L. matutinus (pinewoods shiner)	-	-	-	-	-	-	-	-	-	-	-	-	-	-	-	-	-	-	-	-	-	-	-	-	-	-	-	-	-	-	-	-	-	-	-	-	-	-	-	-	-	-
L. roseipinnis (cherryfin shiner)	-	-	-	-	-	-	-	-	-	-	-	-	N	-	-	-	-	-	-	-	-	-	-	-	-	-	-	-	-	N	N	N	-	-	-	-	-	-	-	-	-	-
L. umbratilis (redfin shiner)	-	-	-	-	-	-	-	-	-	-	-	-	-	-	-	-	-	-	-	-	-	-	-	-	-	-	-	-	-	-	-	N	N	-	N	-	N	N	N	N	N	-
Macrhybopsis aestivalis (speckled chub)	-	-	-	-	-	-	-	-	-	-	-	-	-	-	-	-	-	-	-	-	-	-	-	-	N	N	N	N	N	N	N	N	N	N	N	N	N	N	N	N	N	N
Macrhybopsis sp. (Florida chub)	-	-	-	-	-	-	-	-	-	-	-	-	-	-	-	-	-	-	-	-	-	-	-	N	-	-	-	-	-	-	-	-	-	-	-	-	-	-	-	-	-	-
M. gelida (sturgeon chub)	-	-	-	-	X	-	-	-	X	-	-	-	-	-	-	-	-	-	-	-	-	-	-	-	-	-	-	-	-	-	-	-	N	-	-	-	-	-	-	-	-	-
M. meeki (sicklefin chub)	-	-	-	-	X	-	-	X	-	-	-	-	-	-	I	-	-	-	-	-	-	-	-	-	-	-	-	-	-	-	-	-	N	-	-	-	-	-	-	-	-	N
M. storeriana (silver chub)	-	-	-	-	-	-	-	-	-	-	-	-	-	-	-	-	-	-	-	-	-	-	-	-	N	N	N	N	N	N	N	N	N	N	N	N	N	N	N	N	N	-
Margariscus margarita (pearl dace)	-	-	-	-	-	-	-	-	-	N	-	-	-	-	-	-	-	-	-	-	-	-	-	-	-	-	-	-	-	-	-	-	-	-	-	-	-	-	-	-	-	-
Nocomis biguttatus (hornyhead chub)	-	-	-	-	-	-	-	-	-	-	-	-	-	-	-	-	-	-	-	-	-	-	-	-	-	-	-	-	-	-	-	-	-	-	-	-	-	-	N	-	-	-
N. effusus (redtail chub)	-	-	-	-	-	-	-	-	-	-	-	-	-	-	-	-	-	-	-	-	-	-	-	-	-	-	-	-	-	-	-	-	-	-	N	-	N	N	-	-	-	-
N. leptocephalus (bluehead chub)	-	-	-	-	-	-	-	-	-	N	N	-	N	N	N	N	N	N	-	-	-	-	-	-	N	N	N	N	N	-	N	N	-	-	N	-	-	-	-	N	-	-
N. micropogon (river chub)	-	-	-	-	-	-	-	-	-	N	N	-	-	-	-	I	-	-	-	-	-	-	-	-	N	-	-	-	-	N	-	-	-	-	N	-	N	-	N	-	-	-
N. raneyi (bull chub)	-	-	-	-	-	-	-	-	-	-	-	-	N	-	-	-	-	-	-	-	-	-	-	-	-	-	-	-	-	-	-	-	N	-	N	-	N	-	-	-	-	-
Notemigonus crysoleucas (golden shiner)	X	-	-	-	-	-	-	-	-	N	N	-	N	N	N	N	N	N	N	N	N	N	N	-	N	N	N	N	N	N	N	N	N	N	N	N	N	N	N	N	N	N
Notropis albizonatus (palezone shiner)	-	-	-	-	-	-	-	X	-	-	-	-	-	-	-	-	-	-	-	-	-	-	-	-	-	-	-	-	-	-	-	-	-	-	N	N	N	-	-	-	-	-
N. altipinnis (highfin shiner)	-	-	-	-	-	-	-	-	-	-	-	-	-	-	-	-	-	-	-	-	-	-	-	-	-	-	-	-	-	-	-	-	-	-	N	N	-	-	-	-	-	-
N. amoenus (comely shiner)	-	-	-	-	-	-	-	-	-	N	N	N	N	N	I	-	-	-	-	-	-	-	-	-	-	-	-	-	-	-	-	-	-	-	-	-	-	-	-	-	-	-
N. ariommus (popeye shiner)	-	-	-	-	-	-	-	-	-	-	-	-	-	-	-	-	-	-	-	-	-	-	-	-	-	-	-	-	-	-	-	-	-	-	-	-	-	-	-	-	-	-
N. asperifrons (burrhead shiner)	-	-	-	-	-	-	-	-	-	-	-	-	-	-	-	-	-	-	-	-	-	-	-	-	-	-	-	-	-	-	-	-	-	-	-	-	-	-	-	N	-	-
N. atherinoides (emerald shiner)	-	-	-	-	-	-	-	-	-	-	-	-	-	-	-	-	-	-	-	-	-	-	-	-	N	N	N	N	N	N	N	N	N	N	N	N	N	N	N	N	N	N

Appendix 1. Continued.

TAXA	Federal E	T	PE	PT	C1	C2	AFS E	T	SC	1	2	3	4	5	6	7	8	9	10	11	12	13	14	15	16	17	18	19	20	21	22	23	24	25	26	27	28	29	30	31	32	33
N. baileyi (rough shiner)	-	-	-	-	-	-	-	-	-	-	-	-	-	-	-	-	-	-	-	-	-	-	-	I	N	N	N	N	N	-	-	-	-	-	-	N	-	-	-	-	-	-	-
N. biennius (river shiner)	-	-	-	-	-	-	-	-	-	-	-	-	-	-	-	-	-	-	-	-	-	N	N	N	-	-	-	-	-	-	N	N	N	N	N	N	-	N	N	N	N	N	N
N. boops (bigeye shiner)	-	-	-	-	-	-	-	-	-	-	-	-	-	-	N	-	-	-	-	-	-	-	-	-	-	-	-	-	-	-	-	-	-	-	-	N	-	N	N	N	N	-	-
N. buchanani (ghost shiner)	-	-	-	-	-	-	-	-	-	-	-	-	-	-	-	-	-	-	-	-	-	-	N	N	-	-	-	-	-	-	N	N	N	-	N	N	N	N	N	N	N	N	N
N. cahabae (Cahaba shiner)	X	-	-	-	-	-	X	-	-	-	-	-	-	-	-	-	-	-	-	-	-	-	-	-	N	-	-	-	-	-	-	-	-	-	-	-	-	-	-	-	-	-	-
N. candidus (silverside shiner)	-	-	-	-	-	-	-	-	-	-	-	-	-	-	-	-	-	-	N	-	-	-	-	-	-	N	N	-	-	-	-	-	-	-	-	-	-	-	-	-	-	-	-
N. chalybaeus (ironcolor shiner)	-	-	-	-	-	-	-	-	-	N	N	N	N	N	N	N	N	N	N	N	N	N	N	N	N	N	N	N	N	-	-	-	-	N	-	N	-	-	-	-	N	N	-
N. chiliticus (redlip shiner)	-	-	-	-	-	-	-	-	-	-	-	N	-	-	N	-	-	-	-	-	-	-	-	-	-	-	-	-	-	-	-	-	-	-	-	-	-	-	-	-	I	-	-
N. chlorocephalus (greenhead shiner)	-	-	-	-	-	-	-	-	-	-	-	-	-	-	-	N	N	-	-	-	-	-	-	-	-	-	-	-	-	-	-	-	-	-	-	-	-	-	-	-	-	-	-
N. chrosomus (rainbow shiner)	-	-	-	-	-	-	-	-	-	-	-	-	N	N	N	N	N	N	N	N	N	-	N	N	N	N	N	N	-	-	-	-	-	-	-	-	-	-	-	-	-	-	-
N. cummingsae (dusky shiner)	-	-	-	-	-	-	-	-	-	-	-	-	-	-	-	-	-	N	N	-	-	-	-	N	N	-	-	-	-	-	-	-	-	-	-	-	-	-	-	-	-	-	-
N. edwardraneyi (fluvial shiner)	-	-	-	-	-	-	-	-	-	-	-	-	-	-	-	-	-	-	-	-	-	N	N	N	-	N	N	N	-	-	-	-	-	-	-	-	-	-	-	-	-	-	-
N. harperi (redeye chub)	-	-	-	-	-	-	-	-	-	-	-	-	-	-	-	-	-	-	-	N	N	N	N	N	-	-	-	-	-	-	-	-	-	-	-	-	-	-	-	-	-	-	-
N. hudsonius (spottail shiner)	-	-	-	-	-	-	-	-	-	N	N	N	N	N	N	N	-	N	N	N	N	N	N	N	N	N	N	N	N	N	N	N	N	-	N	-	-	-	-	-	I	-	-
N. hypsilepis (highscale shiner)	-	-	-	X	-	-	-	-	-	-	-	-	-	-	-	-	-	-	N	-	-	N	-	-	-	-	-	-	-	-	-	-	-	-	-	-	-	-	-	-	-	-	-
N. leuciodus (Tennessee shiner)	-	-	-	-	-	-	-	-	-	-	-	-	-	-	-	-	-	N	N	-	-	N	-	-	-	-	-	-	-	-	-	-	-	-	-	N	N	N	N	-	I	-	-
N. ludibundus (sand shiner)	-	-	-	-	-	-	-	-	-	-	-	-	-	-	-	-	-	N	N	-	-	-	-	-	-	N	-	-	-	-	-	-	-	N	-	-	N	N	-	N	N	N	N
N. lutipinnis (yellowfin shiner)	-	-	-	-	-	-	-	-	-	-	-	-	-	-	-	N	N	N	N	N	N	N	N	N	-	-	-	-	-	-	-	-	-	-	-	-	-	-	-	-	-	-	-
N. maculatus (taillight shiner)	-	-	-	-	-	-	-	-	-	-	-	-	-	N	N	N	N	N	N	N	N	N	N	N	N	-	-	N	N	N	N	N	N	-	-	-	-	-	-	-	-	-	-
N. mekistocholas (Cape Fear shiner)	X	-	-	-	-	-	X	-	-	-	-	-	N	-	N	-	-	-	-	-	-	-	-	N	-	-	-	-	-	-	-	-	-	-	-	-	-	-	-	-	-	-	-
N. melanostomus (blackmouth shiner)	-	-	-	-	X	-	X	-	-	-	-	-	-	N	-	N	N	N	N	N	N	N	N	N	N	N	-	-	N	-	-	-	-	-	-	-	-	-	-	-	-	-	-
N. petersoni (coastal shiner)	-	-	-	-	-	-	-	-	-	-	-	-	-	N	N	N	N	N	N	N	N	N	N	N	-	-	-	-	-	-	-	-	-	-	-	-	-	-	-	-	-	-	-

Appendix 1. Continued.

TAXA	Federal						AFS			Drainage Units																															
	E	T	PE	PT	C1	C2	E	T	SC	1	2	3	4	5	6	7	8	9	10	11	12	13	14	15	16	17	18	19	20	21	22	23	24	25	26	27	28	29	30	31	32	33
N. photogenis (silver shiner)	-	-	-	-	-	-	-	-	-	-	-	-	-	-	-	-	-	-	-	-	-	-	-	-	-	-	-	-	-	-	-	-	-	-	N	N	N	N	N	N	N	N
N. potteri (chub shiner)	-	-	-	-	-	-	-	-	-	-	-	-	-	-	-	-	-	-	-	-	-	-	-	-	-	-	-	-	-	-	-	-	N	-	-	-	-	-	-	-	-	-
N. procne (swallowtail shiner)	-	-	-	-	-	-	-	-	-	N	-	N	N	N	N	N	-	-	-	-	-	-	-	-	-	-	-	-	-	-	-	-	-	-	-	-	-	-	-	-	I	-
N. rafinesquei (Yazoo shiner)	-	-	-	-	-	-	-	-	-	-	-	-	-	-	-	-	-	-	-	-	-	-	N	-	-	-	-	-	-	-	-	-	-	-	-	-	-	-	-	-	-	-
N. rubellus (rosyface shiner)	-	-	-	-	-	-	-	-	-	N	N	-	-	-	-	-	-	-	-	-	-	-	-	-	-	-	-	-	-	-	-	-	-	-	N	N	N	N	N	N	N	N
N. rubricroceus (saffron shiner)	-	-	-	-	-	-	-	-	-	-	-	-	-	-	-	-	N	-	-	-	-	-	-	-	-	-	-	-	-	-	-	-	-	-	-	N	-	-	-	I	-	-
N. rupestris (bedrock shiner)	-	-	-	-	-	-	-	-	-	-	-	-	-	-	-	-	-	-	-	-	-	-	-	-	-	-	-	-	-	-	-	-	-	-	N	-	-	-	-	-	-	-
N. scabriceps (New River shiner)	-	-	-	-	-	-	-	-	-	-	-	-	-	-	-	-	-	-	-	-	-	-	-	-	-	-	-	-	-	-	-	-	-	-	-	-	-	-	-	-	N	-
N. scepticus (sandbar shiner)	-	-	-	-	-	-	-	-	-	-	-	-	-	N	N	-	-	-	-	-	-	-	-	-	-	-	-	-	-	-	-	-	-	-	-	-	-	-	-	-	-	-
N. semperasper (roughhead shiner)	-	-	-	-	-	X	-	X	-	-	N	-	-	-	-	-	-	-	-	-	-	-	-	-	-	-	-	-	-	-	-	-	-	-	-	-	-	-	-	-	-	-
N. shumardi (silverband shiner)	-	-	-	-	-	-	-	-	-	-	-	-	-	-	-	N	-	-	-	-	-	-	-	-	-	-	-	-	-	N	N	N	N	N	-	-	-	-	-	-	-	N
N. spectrunculus (mirror shiner)	-	-	-	-	-	-	-	-	-	-	-	-	-	-	-	-	-	N	-	-	-	-	-	-	-	-	-	-	-	-	-	-	-	-	N	-	-	-	-	-	-	-
N. stilbius (silverstripe shiner)	-	-	-	-	-	-	-	-	-	-	-	-	-	-	-	-	-	-	-	-	-	-	-	-	-	N	N	N	-	-	-	-	-	-	-	-	-	-	-	-	-	-
N. telescopus (telescope shiner)	-	-	-	-	-	-	-	-	-	-	-	-	-	-	-	I	-	-	-	-	-	-	-	-	-	-	-	-	-	-	-	-	-	-	-	-	-	-	-	-	-	-
N. texanus (weed shiner)	-	-	-	-	-	-	-	-	-	-	-	-	-	-	-	-	-	-	-	-	-	N	N	N	N	N	N	N	N	N	N	N	N	N	N	N	N	N	-	-	-	-
N. uranoscopus (skygazer shiner)	-	-	-	-	-	-	-	-	-	-	-	-	-	-	-	-	N	N	N	N	N	N	N	N	N	N	N	-	-	-	-	-	-	-	-	-	-	-	-	-	-	-
N. volucellus (mimic shiner)	-	-	-	-	-	-	-	-	-	-	N	N	N	-	-	-	-	-	-	-	-	-	-	-	-	-	-	-	-	-	-	-	-	-	-	N	-	-	-	-	-	-
N. xaenocephalus (Coosa shiner)	-	-	-	-	-	-	-	-	-	-	-	-	-	-	-	-	-	-	-	-	-	-	-	N	N	N	-	-	-	-	-	-	-	-	-	-	-	-	-	-	-	-
Notropis sp. cf. N. spectrunculus (sawfin shiner)	-	-	-	-	-	-	-	-	-	-	-	-	-	-	-	-	-	-	-	-	-	-	-	-	-	-	-	-	-	-	-	-	-	-	-	N	N	-	-	-	-	-
Opsopoeodus emiliae (pugnose minnow)	-	-	-	-	-	-	-	-	-	-	-	-	-	-	-	-	N	N	N	N	N	N	N	N	N	N	N	N	N	N	N	N	N	N	N	N	N	N	N	N	N	N
Phenacobius catostomus (riffle minnow)	-	-	-	-	-	-	-	-	-	-	-	-	-	-	-	-	-	-	-	-	-	-	-	-	-	-	-	-	-	-	-	-	-	-	-	-	-	-	-	-	-	-
P. crassilabrum (fatlips minnow)	-	-	-	-	-	-	-	-	-	-	-	-	-	-	-	-	-	-	-	-	-	-	-	-	-	-	-	-	-	-	-	-	-	-	-	N	-	-	-	-	-	-

Appendix 1. Continued.

TAXA	Federal						AFS			Drainage Units																																
	E	T	PE	PT	C1	C2	E	T	SC	1	2	3	4	5	6	7	8	9	10	11	12	13	14	15	16	17	18	19	20	21	22	23	24	25	26	27	28	29	30	31	32	33
P. mirabilis (suckermouth minnow)	-	-	-	-	-	-	-	-	-	-	-	-	-	-	-	-	-	-	-	-	-	-	-	-	-	-	-	-	-	-	-	N	N	N	N	-	N	N	N	N	N	N
P. teretulus (Kanawha minnow)	-	-	-	-	-	X	-	-	X	-	-	-	-	-	-	-	-	-	-	-	-	-	-	-	-	-	-	-	-	-	-	-	-	-	-	-	-	-	-	-	N	-
P. uranops (stargazing minnow)	-	-	-	-	-	-	-	-	-	-	-	-	-	-	-	-	-	-	-	-	-	-	-	-	-	-	-	-	-	-	-	-	-	-	-	N	N	-	-	-	-	-
Phoxinus cumberlandensis (blackside dace)	X	-	-	-	-	-	X	-	-	-	-	-	-	-	-	-	-	-	-	-	-	-	-	-	-	-	-	-	-	-	-	-	-	-	-	N	-	-	-	-	-	-
P. erythrogaster (southern redbelly dace)	-	-	-	-	-	-	-	-	-	-	-	-	-	-	-	-	-	-	-	-	-	-	-	-	-	-	-	-	-	-	-	N	N	N	N	-	N	N	N	N	N	N
P. oreas (mountain redbelly dace)	-	-	-	-	-	-	-	-	-	N	N	-	N	N	I	-	-	-	-	-	-	-	-	-	-	-	-	-	-	-	-	-	-	-	I	-	-	-	-	-	-	-
P. tennesseensis (Tennessee dace)	-	-	-	-	-	-	-	-	X	-	-	-	-	-	-	-	-	-	-	-	-	-	-	-	-	-	-	-	-	-	-	-	-	-	N	-	-	-	-	-	-	-
Phoxinus sp. cf. *P. tennesseensis* (Waldens Ridge dace)	-	-	-	-	-	X	-	-	-	-	-	-	-	-	-	-	-	-	-	-	-	-	-	-	-	-	-	-	-	-	-	-	-	-	-	N	-	-	-	-	-	-
Pimephales notatus (bluntnose minnow)	-	-	-	-	-	-	-	-	-	I	I	I	-	-	-	-	-	-	-	-	-	-	-	N	N	N	N	-	N	N	N	N	N	N	N	N	N	N	N	N	N	N
P. promelas (fathead minnow)	-	-	-	-	-	-	-	-	-	I	-	-	-	I	-	-	-	-	-	-	-	-	-	-	-	-	I	I	-	N	N	N	N	N	N	N	N	N	N	N	N	N
P. vigilax (bullhead minnow)	-	-	-	-	-	-	-	-	-	-	-	-	-	-	-	-	-	-	-	-	-	-	-	N	N	N	N	N	N	N	N	-	N	N	N	N	N	N	N	N	N	N
Platygobio gracilis (flathead chub)	-	-	-	-	-	X	-	-	-	-	-	-	-	-	-	-	-	-	-	-	-	N	N	N	-	-	-	-	-	-	-	-	N	-	N	-	-	-	-	-	-	-
Pteronotropis euryzonus (broadstripe shiner)	-	-	-	-	-	X	-	-	-	-	-	-	-	-	-	-	N	-	-	-	N	N	N	N	N	N	-	-	-	-	-	-	-	-	-	-	-	-	-	-	-	-
P. hypselopterus (sailfin shiner)	-	-	-	-	-	-	-	-	-	-	-	-	-	-	N	N	N	N	N	-	N	N	N	N	N	N	N	N	N	-	-	-	-	-	-	-	-	-	-	-	-	-
P. signipinnis (flagfin shiner)	-	-	-	-	-	-	-	-	-	-	-	-	-	-	-	N	-	-	-	N	-	-	-	N	N	N	N	N	N	-	-	-	-	-	-	-	-	-	-	-	-	-
P. welaka (bluenose shiner)	-	-	-	-	-	-	-	-	-	-	-	-	-	-	N	N	-	-	-	-	-	-	-	N	N	N	N	N	-	-	-	-	-	-	-	-	-	-	-	-	-	-
Rhinichthys atratulus (blacknose dace)	-	-	-	-	-	-	-	-	-	N	N	N	N	-	N	N	-	N	-	N	-	N	N	N	N	N	N	N	N	N	-	N	N	N	N	N	N	N	N	N	N	-
R. cataractae (longnose dace)	-	-	-	-	-	-	-	-	-	N	N	I	-	-	N	-	-	N	-	-	-	-	-	-	-	-	-	-	-	-	-	-	-	N	-	N	-	-	-	-	-	-
Semotilus atromaculatus (creek chub)	-	-	-	-	-	-	-	-	-	N	N	N	N	N	N	N	N	N	N	-	N	N	N	N	N	N	N	N	N	N	N	N	N	N	-	N	N	N	N	N	N	N
S. corporalis (fallfish)	-	-	-	-	-	-	-	-	-	N	N	I	-	-	-	-	-	-	-	-	-	-	-	-	-	-	-	-	-	-	-	-	-	-	-	-	-	-	-	-	-	-
S. lumbee (sandhills chub)	-	-	-	-	-	-	-	-	X	-	-	-	-	-	-	-	-	-	-	-	-	-	-	-	-	-	-	-	-	-	-	-	-	-	-	-	-	-	-	-	-	-
S. thoreauianus (Dixie chub)	-	-	-	-	-	-	-	-	-	-	-	-	-	-	-	-	-	-	-	-	-	N	N	N	N	N	N	N	-	-	-	-	-	-	-	-	-	-	-	-	-	-

Appendix 1. Continued.

TAXA	Federal E	PE	PT	C1	C2	AFS E	T	SC	1	2	3	4	5	6	7	8	9	10	11	12	13	14	15	16	17	18	19	20	21	22	23	24	25	26	27	28	29	30	31	32	33
CATOSTOMIDAE – Suckers																																									
Carpiodes carpio (river carpsucker)	-	-	-	-	-	-	-	-	N	N	N	-	-	N	-	-	-	-	-	-	N	N	N	-	-	-	-	-	-	N	N	N	N	N	N	N	N	N	N	N	N
C. cyprinus (quillback)	-	-	-	-	-	-	-	-	N	N	N	-	-	N	N	-	N	-	-	-	-	N	N	-	-	-	N	N	N	N	N	N	N	N	N	N	N	N	N	N	N
C. velifer (highfin carpsucker)	-	-	-	-	-	-	-	-	-	-	-	-	N	-	N	-	N	-	-	-	-	-	N	N	-	N	N	N	-	N	-	N	-	N	N	N	N	N	N	-	N
Catostomus commersoni (white sucker)	-	-	-	-	-	-	-	-	N	N	N	N	N	N	N	-	N	-	-	-	-	-	-	-	-	-	-	-	-	-	N	N	N	-	N	N	N	N	N	N	N
Cycleptus elongatus (blue sucker)	-	-	-	-	X	-	-	X	-	-	-	-	-	-	-	-	-	-	-	-	-	-	-	-	-	-	-	N	-	-	N	N	N	N	N	N	N	N	N	N	N
Cycleptus sp. cf. C. elongatus (Gulf blue sucker)	-	-	-	-	-	-	-	-	-	-	-	-	-	-	-	-	-	-	-	-	-	-	-	N	N	N	N	N	-	N	N	N	N	-	N	-	-	-	-	-	-
Erimyzon oblongus (creek chubsucker)	-	-	-	-	-	-	-	-	N	N	N	N	N	N	N	N	N	-	N	N	-	-	N	N	N	N	N	N	N	N	N	N	N	N	N	N	N	N	-	-	-
E. sucetta (lake chubsucker)	-	-	-	-	-	-	-	-	-	-	N	N	N	N	N	N	N	N	N	-	N	N	N	N	N	N	N	N	N	N	N	N	-	N	-	N	-	N	-	-	N
E. tenuis (sharpfin chubsucker)	-	-	-	-	-	-	-	-	-	-	-	-	N	N	-	-	-	-	-	-	-	-	-	N	N	N	N	N	N	-	-	-	-	-	-	-	-	-	-	-	-
Ictiobus bubalus (smallmouth buffalo)	-	-	-	-	-	-	-	-	-	-	-	-	N	N	I	I	-	-	N	-	N	-	N	N	N	N	N	N	-	N	N	N	N	N	N	N	N	N	N	N	N
I. cyprinellus (bigmouth buffalo)	-	-	-	-	-	-	-	-	-	-	-	-	-	-	-	-	-	-	-	-	-	-	-	-	-	-	-	-	-	-	N	N	-	N	-	N	-	N	-	-	N
I. niger (black buffalo)	-	-	-	-	-	-	-	-	-	-	-	-	-	-	-	-	-	-	-	-	-	-	-	-	-	-	-	-	-	-	N	N	N	N	N	N	N	N	N	N	N
Hypentelium etowanum (Alabama hog sucker)	-	-	-	-	-	-	-	-	-	-	-	-	-	-	-	-	-	-	-	-	N	-	-	N	N	N	N	-	-	-	-	-	-	-	N	N	-	-	-	-	-
H. nigricans (northern hog sucker)	-	-	-	-	-	-	-	-	N	N	N	N	-	N	-	-	N	-	-	-	N	-	-	I	I	I	N	N	N	N	N	N	N	N	N	N	N	N	N	N	N
H. roanokense (Roanoke hog sucker)	-	-	-	-	-	-	-	-	-	-	N	N	-	-	-	-	-	-	-	-	-	-	-	-	-	-	-	-	-	-	-	-	-	-	N	-	-	-	-	-	-
Minytrema melanops (spotted sucker)	-	-	-	-	-	-	-	-	-	-	-	-	N	N	N	N	N	N	-	-	N	N	N	N	N	N	N	N	N	N	N	N	N	N	N	N	N	N	N	N	N
Moxostoma anisurum (silver redhorse)	-	-	-	-	-	-	-	-	-	-	N	N	N	N	N	-	N	-	-	-	-	-	-	-	-	-	N	N	-	-	-	-	-	-	N	N	N	N	N	N	N
M. carinatum (river redhorse)	-	-	-	-	-	-	-	-	-	-	-	-	-	-	-	-	-	-	-	-	-	-	N	N	N	N	N	N	N	-	-	-	N	-	N	N	-	N	-	N	N
M. duquesnei (black redhorse)	-	-	-	-	-	-	-	-	-	-	-	-	-	-	-	-	-	-	-	-	-	-	-	-	N	N	-	-	-	-	-	-	-	-	N	-	-	N	-	N	N
M. erythrurum (golden redhorse)	-	-	-	-	-	-	-	-	N	N	N	-	-	-	I	-	-	-	-	-	-	-	-	N	N	N	N	N	N	N	N	N	N	N	N	N	N	N	N	N	N
M. macrolepidotum (shorthead redhorse)	-	-	-	-	-	-	-	-	N	N	N	N	N	N	N	-	-	-	-	-	-	-	-	N	N	N	N	N	-	-	-	-	N	N	N	N	N	N	N	N	N

Appendix 1. Continued.

TAXA	Federal						AFS			Drainage Units																																
	E	T	PE	PT	C1	C2	E	T	SC	1	2	3	4	5	6	7	8	9	10	11	12	13	14	15	16	17	18	19	20	21	22	23	24	25	26	27	28	29	30	31	32	33
M. pappilosum (suckermouth redhorse)	-	-	-	-	-	-	-	-	-	-	-	N	N	N	N	N	-	-	-	-	-	-	-	-	-	-	-	-	-	-	-	-	-	-	-	-	-	-	-	-	-	-
M. poecilurum (blacktail redhorse)	-	-	-	-	-	-	-	-	-	-	-	-	-	-	-	-	-	-	-	-	-	-	-	-	-	-	-	-	-	-	-	-	-	-	-	-	-	-	-	-	-	-
M. robustum (robust redhorse)	-	-	-	-	X	-	-	X	-	-	-	-	-	-	-	N	-	-	-	-	-	-	-	-	-	-	-	-	-	-	-	-	-	-	-	-	-	-	-	-	-	N
M. valenciennesi (greater redhorse)	-	-	-	-	-	X	-	-	-	-	-	-	-	-	-	-	-	-	-	-	-	-	-	-	-	-	-	-	-	-	-	-	-	-	-	-	-	-	-	-	-	-
Moxostoma sp. cf. M. poecilurum (grayfin redhorse)	-	-	-	-	-	-	-	-	X	-	-	-	-	-	-	-	-	-	-	-	-	N	-	-	-	-	-	-	-	-	-	-	-	-	-	-	-	-	-	-	-	-
Scartomyzon ariommus (bigeye jumprock)	-	-	-	-	-	-	-	-	X	-	-	-	-	-	-	-	-	-	-	-	-	-	-	-	-	-	-	-	-	-	-	-	-	-	-	-	-	-	-	-	-	-
S. cervinus (black jumprock)	-	-	-	-	-	-	-	-	-	-	N	N	-	-	-	-	-	-	-	-	-	-	-	-	-	-	-	-	-	-	-	-	-	-	-	-	-	-	-	-	-	-
S. lachneri (greater jumprock)	-	-	-	-	-	-	-	-	-	-	-	-	-	-	-	-	-	-	-	-	-	-	-	N	-	-	-	-	-	-	-	-	-	-	-	-	-	-	-	-	-	-
S. rupiscartes (greater jumprock)	-	-	-	-	-	-	-	-	-	-	-	-	-	-	-	-	-	-	-	-	-	N	-	N	-	-	-	-	-	-	-	-	-	-	-	-	-	-	-	-	-	-
Scartomyzon sp. cf. S. lachneri (striped jumprock)	-	-	-	-	-	-	-	X	-	-	-	-	-	N	N	N	N	N	N	-	-	-	-	-	-	-	-	-	-	-	-	-	-	-	-	-	-	-	-	-	-	-
Thoburnia atripinnis (brassy jumprock)	-	-	-	-	-	-	-	X	-	-	-	-	-	-	N	N	-	N	N	-	-	-	-	-	-	-	-	-	-	-	-	-	-	-	-	-	-	-	-	-	-	-
T. hamiltoni (blackfin sucker)	-	-	-	-	-	-	-	X	-	N	N	-	-	-	-	-	-	-	-	-	-	-	-	-	-	-	-	-	-	-	-	-	-	-	-	-	-	N	-	-	-	-
T. rhothoeca (rustyside sucker)	-	-	-	-	-	-	-	X	-	N	N	N	-	-	-	-	-	-	-	-	-	-	-	-	-	-	-	-	-	-	-	-	-	-	-	-	-	-	-	-	N	-
(torrent sucker)	-	-	-	-	-	-	-	-	-	-	-	-	-	-	-	-	-	-	-	-	-	-	-	-	-	-	-	-	-	-	-	-	-	-	-	-	-	-	-	-	-	-
ICTALURIDAE – Bullhead Catfishes																																										
Ameiurus brunneus (snail bullhead)	-	-	-	-	-	-	-	-	-	-	-	-	N	N	N	N	N	N	N	N	N	N	N	-	N	N	N	N	N	N	N	N	N	N	N	N	N	N	N	-	-	-
A. catus (white catfish)	-	-	-	-	-	-	-	-	-	N	N	N	N	N	N	N	N	N	N	N	-	-	-	-	-	N	N	N	N	N	N	N	N	N	N	N	I	N	N	N	N	N	N
A. melas (black bullhead)	-	-	-	-	-	-	-	-	-	I	-	I	-	-	I	I	-	-	-	-	-	-	-	-	-	-	N	N	N	N	N	N	N	N	N	N	N	N	N	N	N	I	N
A. natalis (yellow bullhead)	-	-	-	-	-	-	-	-	-	N	N	N	N	N	N	N	N	N	N	N	N	N	N	N	N	N	N	N	N	N	N	N	N	N	N	N	N	N	N	N	N	N	N
A. nebulosus (brown bullhead)	-	-	-	-	-	-	-	-	-	N	N	N	N	N	N	N	N	N	N	N	N	-	-	N	N	N	N	N	-	-	N	N	N	N	N	N	N	N	N	N	N	N	N
A. platycephalus (flat bullhead)	-	-	-	-	-	-	-	-	-	-	-	-	-	-	-	-	-	-	-	-	-	-	N	N	-	N	N	N	-	-	-	-	N	N	-	I	I	-	-	-	-	-	-
A. serracanthus (spotted bullhead)	-	-	-	-	-	-	-	-	-	-	-	-	-	-	-	-	-	-	-	-	-	-	N	-	N	-	-	-	-	-	-	-	-	-	-	-	-	-	-	-	-	-	-
Ictalurus furcatus (blue catfish)	-	-	-	-	-	-	-	-	-	I	I	-	I	I	I	-	-	-	-	-	-	-	-	-	-	N	N	N	N	N	N	N	N	N	N	N	N	N	N	N	N	N	N

Appendix 1. Continued.

TAXA	Federal						AFS			Drainage Units																																
	E	T	PE	PT	C1	C2	E	T	SC	1	2	3	4	5	6	7	8	9	10	11	12	13	14	15	16	17	18	19	20	21	22	23	24	25	26	27	28	29	30	31	32	33
I. punctatus (channel catfish)	-	-	-	-	-	-	-	-	-	I	I	I	I	I	I	I	-	N	N	N	N	N	N	N	N	N	N	N	N	N	N	N	N	N	N	N	N	N	N	N	N	N
Noturus baileyi (smoky madtom)	X	-	-	-	-	-	X	-	-	-	-	-	-	-	-	-	-	-	-	-	-	-	-	-	-	-	-	-	-	-	-	-	-	-	-	-	-	-	-	-	-	-
N. elegans (elegant madtom)	-	-	-	-	-	-	-	-	-	-	-	-	-	-	-	-	-	-	-	-	-	-	-	-	-	-	-	-	-	-	-	-	-	-	-	-	-	-	-	-	-	-
N. eleutherus (mountain madtom)	-	-	-	-	-	-	-	-	-	-	-	-	-	-	-	-	-	-	-	-	-	-	-	-	-	-	-	-	-	-	N	N	N	N	N	N	N	N	N	N	N	N
N. exilis (slender madtom)	-	-	-	-	-	-	-	-	-	-	-	-	-	-	-	-	-	-	-	-	-	-	-	-	-	-	-	-	-	-	-	-	-	-	-	-	-	N	-	-	-	-
N. flavipinnis (yellowfin madtom)	-	X	-	-	-	-	-	X	-	-	-	-	-	-	-	-	-	-	-	-	-	-	-	-	-	-	-	-	-	-	-	-	-	-	-	-	-	-	-	-	-	-
N. flavus (stonecat)	-	-	-	-	-	-	-	-	-	-	-	-	-	-	-	-	-	-	-	-	-	-	-	N	N	N	N	N	N	N	N	N	N	N	N	N	N	N	N	N	N	N
N. funebris (black madtom)	-	-	-	-	-	-	-	-	-	-	-	-	N	-	-	-	-	-	-	-	-	-	-	-	-	-	-	-	-	-	-	-	-	N	-	-	-	-	-	-	-	-
N. furiosus (Carolina madtom)	-	-	-	-	-	-	-	-	X	-	-	-	-	-	-	-	-	-	-	-	-	-	-	-	-	-	-	-	-	-	-	-	-	-	-	-	-	-	-	-	-	-
N. gilberti (orangefin madtom)	-	-	-	-	X	-	-	X	-	-	N	N	-	-	-	-	-	-	-	-	-	-	-	-	-	-	-	-	-	-	-	-	-	-	-	-	-	-	-	-	-	-
N. gyrinus (tadpole madtom)	-	-	-	-	-	-	-	-	-	N	N	N	N	N	N	N	N	N	N	N	N	N	N	N	N	N	N	N	N	N	N	N	N	N	N	N	N	N	N	N	-	N
N. hildebrandi (least madtom)	-	-	-	-	-	-	-	-	-	-	-	-	-	-	-	-	-	-	-	-	-	-	-	-	-	N	N	N	-	N	N	N	N	-	-	-	-	-	-	-	-	-
N. insignis (margined madtom)	-	-	-	-	-	-	-	-	-	N	N	N	N	N	N	N	N	N	N	N	N	N	-	-	-	-	-	-	-	-	-	-	-	-	-	I	-	-	-	-	-	-
N. leptacanthus (speckled madtom)	-	-	-	-	-	-	-	-	-	-	-	-	-	-	-	N	-	N	N	-	-	-	-	-	-	-	-	-	N	N	-	-	-	-	-	-	-	-	-	N	-	-
N. miurus (brindled madtom)	-	-	-	-	-	-	-	-	-	-	-	-	-	-	-	-	-	-	-	-	-	-	-	-	-	-	-	-	N	N	N	N	N	N	-	-	-	-	-	-	-	-
N. munitus (frecklebelly madtom)	-	-	-	-	-	-	-	X	-	-	-	-	-	-	-	-	-	-	-	-	-	-	-	-	-	N	N	N	N	N	N	N	N	N	-	-	-	-	-	-	-	-
N. nocturnus (freckled madtom)	-	-	-	-	-	-	-	-	-	-	-	-	-	-	-	-	-	-	-	-	-	-	-	-	-	N	N	N	N	N	N	N	N	N	N	-	N	N	N	N	-	N
N. phaeus (brown madtom)	-	-	-	-	-	-	-	-	-	-	-	-	-	-	-	-	-	-	-	-	-	-	-	-	-	-	-	N	N	N	N	N	N	N	-	-	-	-	-	-	-	-
N. stanauli (pygmy madtom)	X	-	-	-	-	-	X	-	-	-	-	-	-	-	-	-	-	-	-	-	-	-	-	-	-	-	-	-	-	-	-	-	-	-	N	-	-	-	-	-	-	-
N. stigmosus (northern madtom)	-	-	-	-	-	-	-	-	-	-	-	-	-	-	-	-	-	-	-	-	-	-	-	-	-	-	-	-	-	-	-	N	N	N	N	-	N	N	N	N	-	-
Noturus sp. cf. N. leptacanthus (broadtail madtom)	-	-	-	-	-	-	-	-	X	-	-	-	N	N	-	-	-	-	-	-	-	-	-	-	-	-	-	-	-	-	-	-	-	-	-	-	-	-	-	-	-	-
Noturus sp. cf. N. elegans (Chucky madtom)	-	-	-	-	-	X	-	-	-	-	-	-	-	-	-	-	-	-	-	-	-	-	-	-	-	-	-	-	-	-	-	-	N	-	-	-	-	-	-	-	-	-

Appendix 1. Continued.

TAXA	Federal						AFS			Drainage Units																																
	E	T	PE	PT	C1	C2	E	T	SC	1	2	3	4	5	6	7	8	9	10	11	12	13	14	15	16	17	18	19	20	21	22	23	24	25	26	27	28	29	30	31	32	33
Noturus sp. cf. *N. elegans* (saddled madtom)	-	-	-	-	X	-	-	-	-	-	-	-	-	-	-	-	-	-	-	-	-	-	-	-	-	-	-	-	-	-	-	-	-	-	-	N	-	-	-	-	-	-	-
Noturus sp. cf. *N. insignis* (spotted madtom)	-	-	-	-	X	-	-	-	-	-	-	N	-	-	-	-	-	-	-	-	-	-	-	-	-	-	-	-	-	-	-	-	-	-	-	-	-	-	-	-	-	-	-
Pylodictis olivaris (flathead catfish)	-	-	-	-	-	-	-	-	-	-	-	-	-	I	I	I	-	-	-	-	-	-	-	-	-	N	N	N	N	N	N	N	N	N	N	N	N	N	N	N	N	N	N
CLARIIDAE – Labyrinth Catfishes																																											
Clarias batrachus (walking catfish)	-	-	-	-	-	-	-	-	-	-	-	-	-	-	-	-	-	-	-	-	-	I	-	-	-	-	-	-	-	-	-	-	-	-	-	-	-	-	-	-	-	-	-
LORICARIIDAE – Suckermouth Catfishes																																											
Hypostomus spp. (suckermouth catfishes)	-	-	-	-	-	-	-	-	-	-	-	-	-	-	-	-	-	-	-	-	I	-	-	-	-	-	-	-	-	-	-	-	-	-	-	-	-	-	-	-	-	-	-
Liposarcus multiradiatus (sailfin catfish)	-	-	-	-	-	-	-	-	-	-	-	-	-	-	-	-	-	-	-	-	-	I	-	-	-	-	-	-	-	-	-	-	-	-	-	-	-	-	-	-	-	-	-
L. disjunctivus (vermiculated sailfin catfish)	-	-	-	-	-	-	-	-	-	-	-	-	-	-	-	-	-	-	-	-	-	I	-	-	-	-	-	-	-	-	-	-	-	-	-	-	-	-	-	-	-	-	-
ESOCIDAE – Pikes																																											
Esox americanus (grass or redfin pickerel)	-	-	-	-	-	-	-	-	-	N	N	N	N	N	N	N	N	N	N	N	N	N	N	N	N	N	N	N	N	N	N	N	-	N	N	N	-	N	N	N	N	-	-
E. masquinongy (muskellunge)	-	-	-	-	-	-	-	-	-	-	I	I	I	-	-	-	-	-	-	-	-	-	-	-	-	-	-	-	-	-	-	-	-	-	-	-	N	N	N	N	N	-	-
E. lucius (northern pike)	-	-	-	-	-	-	-	-	-	I	I	I	-	-	-	-	-	-	-	-	-	-	-	-	-	-	-	-	-	-	-	-	-	-	-	-	-	-	-	-	-	-	-
E. niger (chain pickerel)	-	-	-	-	-	-	-	-	-	N	N	N	N	N	N	N	N	N	N	N	N	N	N	N	N	N	N	N	N	N	N	N	-	N	-	N	-	N	-	-	-	-	-
UMBRIDAE – Mudminnows																																											
Umbra limi (central mudminnow)	-	-	-	-	-	-	-	-	-	-	-	-	-	N	-	-	-	-	-	-	-	-	-	-	-	-	-	-	-	-	-	-	-	N	-	N	-	-	-	-	-	-	-
U. pygmaea (eastern mudminnow)	-	-	-	-	-	-	-	-	-	-	-	-	-	-	-	-	-	-	N	-	-	-	-	-	-	-	-	-	-	-	-	-	-	-	-	-	-	-	-	-	-	-	-
OSMERIDAE – Smelts																																											
Osmerus mordax (rainbow smelt)	-	-	-	-	-	-	-	-	-	-	-	-	-	-	-	-	-	-	-	-	-	-	-	-	-	-	-	I	-	-	-	-	-	-	-	-	-	-	-	-	-	-	-
SALMONIDAE – Trouts, Salmons and Whitefishes																																											
Oncorhynchus mykiss (rainbow trout)	-	-	-	-	-	-	-	-	-	I	I	I	-	I	I	I	-	-	-	-	-	-	-	-	-	-	-	-	-	-	-	-	-	-	I	I	I	I	I	I	I	I	-
Salmo trutta (brown trout)	-	-	-	-	-	-	-	-	-	I	I	I	-	I	I	I	-	-	-	-	-	-	-	-	-	-	-	-	-	-	-	-	-	-	-	I	I	I	I	I	I	I	-

Appendix 1. Continued.

TAXA	Federal E	T	PE	PT	C1	C2	AFS E	T	SC	1	2	3	4	5	6	7	8	9	10	11	12	13	14	15	16	17	18	19	20	21	22	23	24	25	26	27	28	29	30	31	32	33
Salvelinus fontinalis (brook trout)	-	-	-	-	-	-	-	-	-	N	N	N	N	-	I	N	-	N	-	-	-	N	-	-	I	-	-	-	-	-	-	-	-	-	-	N	I	-	I	-	N	-
PERCOPSIDAE – Trout-perches																																										
Percopsis omiscomaycus (trout-perch)	-	-	-	-	-	-	-	-	-	-	-	-	-	-	-	-	-	-	-	-	-	-	-	-	-	-	-	-	-	-	-	-	-	-	-	-	-	N	N	N	N	N	N
APHREDODERIDAE – Pirate Perches																																										
Aphredoderus sayanus (pirate perch)	-	-	-	-	-	-	-	-	-	N	N	N	N	N	N	N	N	N	N	N	N	N	N	N	N	N	N	N	N	N	N	N	N	N	N	N	-	N	N	N	-	-	N
AMBLYOPSIDAE – Cavefishes																																										
Amblyopsis spelaea (northern cavefish)	-	-	-	-	-	X	-	X	-	-	-	-	-	-	-	-	-	-	-	-	-	-	-	-	-	-	-	-	-	-	-	-	-	-	-	-	-	-	N	N	-	-	-
Chologaster cornuta (swampfish)	-	-	-	-	-	-	-	-	-	-	-	N	N	N	N	N	N	N	-	-	-	-	-	-	-	-	-	-	-	-	-	-	-	-	-	-	-	-	-	-	-	-	-
Forbesichthys agassizi (spring cavefish)	-	-	-	-	-	-	-	-	-	-	-	-	-	-	-	-	-	-	-	-	-	-	-	-	-	N	-	-	-	-	-	-	-	-	N	-	-	N	N	-	-	-	-
Speoplatyrhinus poulsoni (Alabama cavefish)	X	-	-	-	-	-	X	-	-	-	-	-	-	-	-	-	-	-	-	-	-	-	-	-	N	-	-	-	-	-	-	-	-	-	-	-	-	-	-	-	-	-	-
Typhlichthys subterraneus (southern cavefish)	-	-	-	-	-	-	-	-	-	-	-	-	-	-	-	N	-	-	-	-	-	-	-	-	N	-	N	-	N	-	-	N	-	-	-	-	-	-	-	-	-	-	-
LOTIDAE – Cuskfishes																																										
Lota lota (burbot)	-	-	-	-	-	-	-	-	-	-	-	-	-	-	-	-	-	-	-	-	-	-	-	-	-	-	-	-	-	-	-	-	-	-	-	-	-	-	-	-	-	-	N
ATHERINIDAE – Silversides																																										
Labidesthes sicculus (brook silverside)	-	-	-	-	-	-	-	-	-	N	N	N	N	N	N	N	N	N	N	N	N	N	N	N	N	N	N	N	N	N	N	N	N	N	N	N	N	N	N	N	N	N	-
Menidia beryllina (inland silverside)	-	-	-	-	-	-	-	-	-	-	-	-	-	-	-	-	-	N	-	N	-	N	N	N	N	N	N	-	-	-	-	-	-	-	-	-	-	-	-	-	-	-	-
M. extensa (Waccamaw silverside)	X	-	-	-	-	-	-	-	X	-	-	-	-	-	N	-	-	-	-	-	-	-	-	-	-	-	-	-	-	-	-	-	-	-	-	-	-	-	-	-	-	-	-
RIVULIDAE – Rivulines																																										
Rivulus marmoratus (rivulus)	-	-	-	-	-	-	-	-	X	-	-	-	-	-	N	-	-	-	-	-	-	-	-	-	-	-	-	-	-	-	-	-	-	-	-	-	-	-	-	-	-	-	-
FUNDULIDAE – Topminnows																																										
Fundulus auroguttatus (banded topminnow)	-	-	-	-	-	-	-	-	-	-	-	-	-	-	-	-	-	-	-	-	-	-	-	-	-	-	-	-	-	-	-	-	-	-	-	-	-	-	-	-	-	-	-
F. bifax (stippled studfish)	-	-	-	-	-	-	-	-	-	-	-	-	-	-	-	N	-	-	-	-	-	-	-	-	-	-	-	-	-	-	-	-	-	-	-	-	-	-	-	-	-	-	-

Appendix 1. Continued.

TAXA	Federal						AFS			Drainage Units																																
	E	T	PE	PT	C1	C2	E	T	SC	1	2	3	4	5	6	7	8	9	10	11	12	13	14	15	16	17	18	19	20	21	22	23	24	25	26	27	28	29	30	31	32	33
F. blairae (western starhead topminnow)	-	-	-	-	-	-	-	-	-	-	-	-	-	-	-	-	-	-	-	-	-	-	-	-	N	N	N	N	N	-	-	-	-	-	-	-	-	-	-	-	-	-
F. catenatus (northern studfish)	-	-	-	-	-	-	-	-	-	-	-	-	-	-	-	-	-	-	-	N	N	N	N	N	-	N	-	-	-	N	N	N	-	N	N	N	N	N	N	I	N	-
F. chrysotus (golden topminnow)	-	-	-	-	-	-	-	-	-	-	-	-	-	-	N	N	N	N	N	N	N	N	N	N	N	N	N	N	N	N	N	N	N	N	N	-	-	-	-	-	-	-
F. diaphanus (banded killifish)	-	-	-	-	-	-	-	-	-	N	N	N	N	-	-	-	-	-	-	-	-	-	-	-	-	-	-	-	-	-	-	N	N	N	-	-	-	-	-	-	-	-
F. dispar (northern starhead topminnow)	-	-	-	-	-	-	-	-	-	-	-	-	N	N	N	N	-	-	-	-	-	-	-	-	-	-	N	N	N	-	-	-	N	N	-	-	-	-	-	-	-	-
F. escambiae (eastern starhead topminnow)	-	-	-	-	-	-	-	-	-	-	-	-	-	-	-	-	-	-	-	-	-	N	N	-	N	-	-	-	-	-	-	-	-	-	-	-	-	-	-	-	-	-
F. euryzonus (broadstripe topminnow)	-	-	-	-	-	-	-	-	-	-	-	-	-	-	-	-	-	-	-	-	-	-	-	-	-	-	-	-	-	N	-	-	-	-	-	-	-	-	-	-	-	-
F. julisia (Barrens topminnow)	-	-	-	-	X	-	-	-	X	-	-	-	-	-	-	-	-	-	-	-	-	-	N	-	-	-	-	-	-	-	-	-	-	-	N	-	-	-	-	-	-	-
F. lineolatus (lined topminnow)	-	-	-	-	-	-	-	-	-	-	-	N	N	N	N	N	N	N	N	N	N	N	N	-	-	-	-	-	-	N	N	N	N	N	N	N	N	N	-	-	-	-
F. notti (southern starhead topminnow)	-	-	-	-	-	-	-	-	-	-	-	-	-	-	-	-	-	-	-	-	-	-	-	-	-	N	N	N	N	N	N	N	N	N	N	N	N	N	-	-	-	-
F. notatus (blackstripe topminnow)	-	-	-	-	-	-	-	-	-	-	-	-	-	-	-	-	-	-	-	N	N	N	-	-	-	-	-	N	N	N	N	N	N	N	N	N	N	N	N	N	N	N
F. olivaceus (blackspotted topminnow)	-	-	-	-	-	-	-	-	-	-	-	-	-	-	-	-	-	-	-	N	N	N	-	N	N	N	N	N	N	N	N	N	N	N	N	N	N	N	-	-	-	-
F. rathbuni (speckled killifish)	-	-	-	-	-	-	-	-	-	-	-	N	N	N	N	N	-	-	-	-	-	-	-	-	-	-	-	-	-	-	-	-	-	-	-	-	-	-	-	-	-	-
F. rubrifrons (redface topminnow)	-	-	-	-	-	-	-	-	-	-	-	-	-	-	-	-	-	-	-	N	N	-	-	-	-	-	-	-	-	N	-	-	-	-	-	-	-	-	-	-	-	-
F. seminolis (Seminole killifish)	-	-	-	-	-	-	-	-	-	-	-	-	-	-	-	-	-	-	-	N	N	-	-	-	-	-	-	-	-	N	-	-	-	-	-	-	-	-	-	-	-	-
F. stellifer (southern studfish)	-	-	-	-	-	-	-	-	-	-	-	-	-	-	-	-	N	-	-	-	-	-	-	N	-	N	-	-	-	N	-	-	-	-	-	-	-	-	-	-	-	-
F. waccamensis (Waccamaw killifish)	-	-	-	-	-	X	-	X	-	-	-	I	-	-	-	-	-	-	-	-	-	-	-	-	-	-	-	-	-	-	-	-	-	-	N	-	-	-	-	-	-	-
Leptolucania ommata (pygmy killifish)	-	-	-	-	-	-	-	-	-	-	-	-	-	-	-	-	-	N	N	N	N	N	N	N	N	-	-	N	-	-	-	-	-	-	-	-	-	-	-	-	-	-
Lucania goodei (bluefin killifish)	-	-	-	-	-	-	-	-	-	-	-	-	-	-	-	-	N	N	N	N	N	N	N	N	-	-	-	-	-	-	-	-	-	-	-	-	-	-	-	-	-	-
L. parva (rainwater killifish)	-	-	-	-	-	-	-	-	-	N	N	N	N	N	N	-	N	N	N	N	N	N	N	N	N	N	N	N	N	N	-	-	-	-	-	-	-	-	-	-	-	-
POECILIIDAE - Livebearers																																										
Belonesox belizanus (pike killifish)	-	-	-	-	-	-	-	-	-	-	-	-	-	-	-	-	-	-	-	-	I	-	-	-	-	-	-	-	-	-	-	-	-	-	-	-	-	-	-	-	-	-

Appendix 1. Continued.

Column groups: **Federal** (E, T, PE, PT, C1, C2); **AFS** (E, T, SC); **Drainage Units** (1–33). Federal and AFS columns are "-" for all taxa listed on this page.

TAXA	E	T	PE	PT	C1	C2	E	T	SC	1	2	3	4	5	6	7	8	9	10	11	12	13	14	15	16	17	18	19	20	21	22	23	24	25	26	27	28	29	30	31	32	33
Gambusia affinis (mosquitofish)	-	-	-	-	-	-	-	-	-	N	N	N	N	N	N	N	N	N	N	N	N	-	N	N	N	N	N	N	N	N	N	N	N	N	N	N	I	N	N	I	I	-	N
G. holbrooki (eastern mosquitofish)	-	-	-	-	-	-	-	-	-	-	-	-	-	-	-	-	-	-	-	-	-	-	-	-	-	-	-	-	-	-	-	-	-	-	-	-	-	-	-	-	-	-	N
Heterandia formosa (least killifish)	-	-	-	-	-	-	-	-	-	-	-	-	-	N	N	-	N	-	-	N	N	N	N	N	N	N	N	N	N	N	-	-	-	-	-	-	-	-	-	-	-	-	-
Poecilia latipinna (sailfin molly)	-	-	-	-	-	-	-	-	-	-	-	-	-	N	-	-	N	-	-	N	-	-	-	-	-	-	-	-	-	-	-	-	-	-	-	-	-	-	-	-	-	-	-
Xiphophorus helleri (green swordtail)	-	-	-	-	-	-	-	-	-	-	-	-	-	-	-	-	-	-	-	I	-	-	-	-	-	-	-	-	-	-	-	-	-	-	-	-	-	-	-	-	-	-	-
X. maculatus (southern platyfish)	-	-	-	-	-	-	-	-	-	-	-	-	-	-	-	-	-	-	-	-	-	I	-	-	-	-	-	-	-	-	-	-	-	-	-	-	-	-	-	-	-	-	-
X. variatus (variable platyfish)	-	-	-	-	-	-	-	-	-	-	-	-	-	-	-	-	-	-	-	I	-	I	-	-	-	-	-	-	-	-	-	-	-	-	-	-	-	-	-	-	-	-	-
CYPRINODONTIDAE – Pupfishes																																										
Cyprinodon variegatus (sheepshead minnow)	-	-	-	-	-	-	-	-	-	N	N	-	N	N	N	-	N	N	-	N	N	N	N	N	-	N	N	N	N	N	-	-	-	-	-	-	-	-	-	-	-	-	-
Jordanella floridae (flagfish)	-	-	-	-	-	-	-	-	-	-	-	-	-	-	-	-	-	-	-	N	N	N	-	-	-	-	-	-	-	-	-	-	-	-	-	-	-	-	-	-	-	-	-
GASTEROSTEIDAE – Sticklebacks																																										
Apeltes quadracus (fourspine stickleback)	-	-	-	-	-	-	-	-	-	N	N	-	N	-	-	-	-	-	-	-	-	-	-	-	-	-	-	-	-	-	-	-	-	-	-	I	-	-	-	-	-	-	-
Culaea inconstans (brook stickleback)	-	-	-	-	-	-	-	-	-	-	-	-	-	-	-	-	-	-	-	-	-	-	-	-	-	-	-	-	-	-	-	-	-	-	-	-	I	-	-	-	-	-	-
Gasterosteus aculeatus (threespine stickleback)	-	-	-	-	-	-	-	-	-	N	N	-	-	-	-	-	-	-	-	-	-	-	-	-	-	-	-	-	-	-	-	-	-	-	-	I	-	-	-	-	-	-	-
MORONIDAE – Temperate Basses																																										
Morone americanus (white perch)	-	-	-	-	-	-	-	-	-	N	N	N	N	N	N	N	N	N	N	-	-	-	-	-	-	-	-	-	-	-	-	-	-	-	I	-	-	-	-	-	-	-	-
M. chrysops (white bass)	-	-	-	-	-	-	-	-	-	-	-	-	-	-	I	-	-	-	-	-	-	-	-	I	-	-	-	-	-	-	-	-	-	-	-	-	-	-	-	-	-	-	-
M. mississippiensis (yellow bass)	-	-	-	-	-	-	-	-	-	-	-	-	-	-	-	-	N	N	-	-	-	-	-	-	-	-	-	N	N	N	-	-	-	-	N	N	-	N	-	N	-	N	-
M. saxatilis (striped bass)	-	-	-	-	-	-	-	-	-	N	N	-	N	N	N	N	N	N	N	N	N	N	N	N	N	N	N	N	N	N	N	-	I	I	I	I	I	I	I	I	I	-	I
CENTRARCHIDAE – Sunfishes																																										
Acantharchus pomotis (mud sunfish)	-	-	-	-	-	-	-	-	-	N	N	-	-	-	-	-	-	-	-	-	-	-	-	-	-	-	-	N	N	N	N	-	-	-	-	-	-	-	-	-	-	-	-
Ambloplites ariommus (shadow bass)	-	-	-	-	-	-	-	-	-	-	-	-	-	-	-	-	-	-	-	-	-	-	-	-	-	-	-	N	N	N	-	-	-	-	-	-	-	-	-	-	-	-	-

Appendix 1. Continued.

TAXA	Federal						AFS			Drainage Units																															
	E	T	PE	PT	C1	C2	E	T	SC	1	2	3	4	5	6	7	8	9	10	11	12	13	14	15	16	17	18	19	20	21	22	23	24	25	26	27	28	29	30	31	32	33
A. cavifrons (Roanoke bass)	-	-	-	-	-	-	-	-	X	-	-	N	N	N	-	-	-	-	-	-	-	-	-	-	-	-	-	-	-	-	-	-	-	-	-	-	-	-	-	-	-	-
A. rupestris (rock bass)	-	-	-	-	-	-	-	-	-	I	I	I	-	-	I	I	-	-	-	-	-	-	-	-	-	-	-	-	-	-	-	-	-	-	N	N	N	N	N	N	N	N
Centrarchus macropterus (flier)	-	-	-	-	-	-	-	-	-	N	N	N	N	N	N	N	N	N	N	N	N	N	N	N	N	N	N	N	N	N	N	N	N	N	N	N	N	N	N	N	-	N
Chaenobryttus gulosus (warmouth)	-	-	-	-	-	-	-	-	-	N	-	N	N	N	N	N	N	N	N	N	N	N	N	N	N	N	N	N	N	N	N	N	N	N	N	N	N	N	N	N	-	N
Enneacanthus chaetodon (blackbanded sunfish)	-	-	-	-	-	-	-	-	-	-	-	N	N	-	-	-	-	-	-	-	-	-	-	-	-	-	-	-	-	-	-	-	-	-	-	-	-	-	-	-	-	-
E. gloriosus (bluespotted sunfish)	-	-	-	-	-	-	-	-	-	N	N	N	N	N	N	N	N	N	N	N	N	N	N	N	N	N	N	N	N	N	N	I	N	N	N	N	N	N	-	-	-	-
E. obesus (banded sunfish)	-	-	-	-	-	-	-	-	-	N	N	N	N	N	N	N	N	N	N	N	N	N	N	N	N	-	-	-	-	-	-	-	-	-	-	-	-	-	-	-	-	-
Lepomis auritus (redbreast sunfish)	-	-	-	-	-	-	-	-	-	N	N	I	I	I	I	I	-	-	-	-	-	-	-	I	I	I	I	I	I	I	I	I	I	I	I	I	I	I	I	I	I	-
L. cyanellus (green sunfish)	-	-	-	-	-	-	-	-	-	I	I	I	I	I	I	I	-	-	-	-	-	-	I	N	N	N	N	N	N	N	N	N	N	N	N	N	N	N	N	N	N	N
L. gibbosus (pumpkinseed)	-	-	-	-	-	-	-	-	-	N	N	N	N	N	N	N	N	I	-	-	-	-	-	-	-	-	-	-	-	-	-	-	-	-	-	I	I	-	-	I	N	N
L. humilis (orangespotted sunfish)	-	-	-	-	-	-	-	-	-	-	-	-	-	-	-	-	-	-	-	-	-	-	I	I	-	N	N	N	N	N	N	N	N	N	-	-	I	-	N	N	-	N
L. macrochirus (bluegill)	-	-	-	-	-	-	-	-	-	I	I	I	I	N	N	N	N	N	N	N	N	N	N	N	N	N	N	N	N	N	N	N	N	N	N	N	N	N	N	N	N	N
L. marginatus (dollar sunfish)	-	-	-	-	-	-	-	-	-	-	-	-	N	N	N	N	N	-	-	-	-	-	-	N	N	N	N	N	N	N	N	N	N	N	N	-	N	N	-	N	N	N
L. megalotis (longear sunfish)	-	-	-	-	-	-	-	-	-	-	-	-	-	I	I	I	-	-	-	-	-	-	-	-	-	-	-	-	-	N	N	N	N	N	N	N	N	N	N	N	N	N
L. microlophus (redear sunfish)	-	-	-	-	-	-	-	-	-	I	I	I	I	I	I	I	-	N	N	N	N	N	N	N	N	N	N	N	N	N	N	N	N	N	N	N	N	N	I	I	-	N
L. miniatus (redspotted sunfish)	-	-	-	-	-	-	-	-	-	-	-	-	-	-	-	-	-	-	-	-	-	-	-	-	N	N	N	N	N	N	N	N	N	N	-	N	-	N	N	-	-	-
L. punctatus (spotted sunfish)	-	-	-	-	-	-	-	-	-	-	-	-	-	-	-	-	-	-	-	-	-	-	-	-	-	-	-	N	N	N	N	N	N	N	-	N	-	N	N	-	-	-
L. symmetricus (bantam sunfish)	-	-	-	-	-	-	-	-	-	-	-	-	-	-	-	-	-	-	-	-	-	-	-	N	-	-	N	N	N	N	N	N	N	N	-	-	-	-	-	-	-	-
Micropterus coosae (redeye bass)	-	-	-	-	-	-	-	-	-	-	-	-	-	I	-	-	-	-	N	-	-	-	N	-	N	N	N	-	-	-	-	-	-	-	-	-	I	I	-	-	-	-
M. dolomieu (smallmouth bass)	-	-	-	-	-	-	-	-	-	I	I	I	I	-	I	I	-	N	N	-	-	N	-	-	N	N	-	-	-	-	-	-	-	-	-	N	N	N	N	N	N	N
M. notius (Suwannee bass)	-	-	-	-	-	-	-	-	-	-	-	-	-	-	-	-	-	-	-	-	-	N	-	-	-	-	-	-	-	-	-	-	-	-	-	-	-	-	-	-	-	-
M. punctulatus (spotted bass)	-	-	-	-	-	-	-	-	-	I	I	I	-	I	I	I	-	-	N	-	-	-	I	N	N	N	N	N	N	N	N	N	N	-	N	N	N	N	N	N	N	N

Appendix 1. Continued.

TAXA	Federal E	T	PE	PT	C1	C2	AFS E	T	SC	1	2	3	4	5	6	7	8	9	10	11	12	13	14	15	16	17	18	19	20	21	22	23	24	25	26	27	28	29	30	31	32	33
M. salmoides (largemouth bass)	–	–	–	–	–	–	–	–	–	I	N	N	N	N	N	N	N	N	N	N	N	N	N	N	N	N	N	N	N	N	N	N	N	N	N	N	N	N	N	N	N	N
Micropterus sp. cf. *M. coosae* (shoal bass)	–	–	–	–	–	–	–	–	X	–	–	–	–	–	–	–	–	–	–	–	–	–	N	–	–	–	–	–	–	–	–	–	–	–	–	–	–	–	–	–	–	–	–
Pomoxis annularis (white crappie)	–	–	–	–	–	–	–	–	–	I	I	I	I	I	I	I	N	N	N	N	N	N	N	N	N	N	N	N	N	N	N	N	N	N	N	N	N	N	N	–	–	–	–
P. nigromaculatus (black crappie)	–	–	–	–	–	–	–	–	–	I	I	N	N	N	N	N	N	N	N	N	N	N	N	N	N	N	N	N	N	N	N	N	N	N	N	N	N	N	N	N	N	N	N
ELASSOMATIDAE – Pygmy Sunfishes																																											
Elassoma alabamae (spring pygmy sunfish)	–	–	–	–	X	–	–	X	–	–	–	–	–	–	–	–	–	–	–	–	–	–	–	–	–	–	–	–	–	–	–	–	N	–	–	–	–	–	–	–	–	–
E. boehlkei (Carolina pygmy sunfish)	–	–	–	–	–	X	–	–	X	–	–	–	–	–	N	N	–	–	–	–	–	–	–	–	–	–	–	–	–	–	–	–	–	–	–	–	–	–	–	–	–	–
E. evergladei (Everglades pygmy sunfish)	–	–	–	–	–	–	–	–	–	–	–	–	–	N	N	–	N	N	N	N	N	N	–	–	–	–	–	–	–	–	–	–	–	–	–	–	–	–	–	–	–	–
E. okatie (bluebarred pygmy sunfish)	–	–	–	–	–	–	–	–	X	–	–	–	–	–	–	–	–	N	–	–	–	–	–	–	–	–	–	–	–	–	–	–	–	–	–	–	–	–	–	–	–	–
E. okefenokee (Okefenokee pygmy sunfish)	–	–	–	–	–	–	–	–	–	–	–	–	–	–	–	–	N	–	–	–	–	–	–	–	–	–	–	–	–	–	–	–	–	N	–	–	–	–	–	–	–	–
E. zonatum (banded pygmy sunfish)	–	–	–	–	–	–	–	–	–	–	–	N	N	N	N	N	N	N	N	N	N	N	N	N	N	N	N	N	N	N	N	–	N	–	N	–	–	–	N	–	–	–
PERCIDAE – Perches and Darters																																											
Ammocrypta beanii (naked sand darter)	–	–	–	–	–	–	–	–	–	–	–	–	–	–	–	–	–	–	–	–	–	–	N	N	N	–	N	N	–	–	–	–	N	N	–	–	–	–	–	–	–	–
A. bifascia (Florida sand darter)	–	–	–	–	–	–	–	–	–	–	–	–	–	–	–	–	–	–	–	–	N	–	–	N	N	–	–	–	–	–	–	–	–	–	–	–	–	–	–	–	–	–
A. clara (western sand darter)	–	–	–	–	–	–	–	–	–	–	–	–	–	–	–	–	–	–	–	–	–	N	–	–	–	–	–	N	N	–	–	–	–	–	–	–	–	–	–	–	–	–
A. meridiana (southern sand darter)	–	–	–	–	–	–	–	–	–	–	–	–	–	–	–	–	–	–	–	–	–	–	N	N	N	–	–	–	–	–	–	–	–	–	–	–	–	–	–	–	–	–
A. pellucida (eastern sand darter)	–	–	–	–	X	–	–	X	–	–	–	–	–	–	–	–	–	–	–	–	–	–	–	–	–	–	–	–	–	–	–	–	–	–	–	–	–	–	–	–	–	–
A. vivax (scaly sand darter)	–	–	–	–	–	–	–	–	–	–	–	–	–	–	–	–	–	–	–	N	N	N	N	N	N	–	–	–	–	–	–	–	–	–	–	–	–	–	–	–	–	–
Crystallaria asprella (crystal darter)	–	–	–	–	–	–	–	–	X	–	–	–	–	–	–	–	–	–	–	N	N	N	N	–	–	–	–	N	N	N	N	N	N	–	N	–	–	–	–	–	–	–
Etheostoma acuticeps (sharphead darter)	–	–	–	–	–	–	–	–	X	–	–	–	–	–	–	–	–	–	–	–	–	–	–	–	–	–	N	–	–	–	–	–	–	–	–	–	–	–	–	–	–	–
E. aquali (coppercheek darter)	–	–	–	–	X	–	–	X	–	–	–	–	–	–	–	–	–	–	–	–	–	–	–	–	–	N	–	–	–	–	–	–	–	–	N	–	–	–	–	–	–	–
E. asprigene (mud darter)	–	–	–	–	–	–	–	–	–	–	–	–	–	–	–	–	–	–	–	–	–	N	N	N	N	N	–	–	N	N	–	–	N	–	–	–	–	–	–	–	–	–

Appendix 1. Continued.

TAXA	Federal E	T	PE	PT	C1	C2	AFS E	T	SC	1	2	3	4	5	6	7	8	9	10	11	12	13	14	15	16	17	18	19	20	21	22	23	24	25	26	27	28	29	30	31	32	33
E. baileyi (emerald darter)	-	-	-	-	-	-	-	-	-	-	-	-	-	-	-	-	-	-	-	-	-	-	-	-	-	-	-	-	-	-	-	-	-	-	-	-	-	N	-	-	-	-
E. barbouri (teardrop darter)	-	-	-	-	-	-	-	-	-	-	-	-	-	-	-	-	-	-	-	-	-	-	-	-	-	-	-	-	-	-	-	-	-	-	-	-	-	N	-	-	-	-
E. barrenense (splendid darter)	-	-	-	-	-	-	-	-	-	-	-	-	-	-	-	-	-	-	-	-	-	-	-	-	-	-	-	-	-	-	-	-	-	-	-	-	-	N	-	-	-	-
E. bellator (warrior darter)	-	-	-	-	-	X	-	-	-	-	-	-	-	-	-	-	-	-	-	-	-	-	-	-	-	N	-	-	-	-	-	-	-	-	-	-	-	-	-	-	-	-
E. bellum (orangefin darter)	-	-	-	-	-	-	-	-	-	-	-	-	-	-	-	-	-	-	-	-	-	-	-	-	-	-	-	-	-	-	-	-	-	-	-	-	-	N	-	-	-	-
E. blennioides (greenside darter)	-	-	-	-	-	-	-	-	-	N	-	-	-	-	-	-	-	-	-	-	-	-	-	-	-	-	-	-	-	N	N	N	-	N	N	-	N	N	N	N	N	N
E. blennius (blenny darter)	-	-	-	-	-	-	-	-	-	-	-	-	-	-	-	-	-	-	-	-	-	-	-	-	-	-	-	-	-	-	-	-	-	N	N	N	-	-	-	-	-	-
E. boschungi (slackwater darter)	-	X	-	-	-	-	-	X	-	-	-	-	-	-	-	-	-	-	-	-	-	-	-	-	-	-	-	-	-	-	-	-	-	-	N	-	-	-	-	-	-	-
E. brevirostrum (holiday darter)	-	-	-	-	-	X	-	-	X	-	-	-	-	-	-	-	-	-	-	-	-	-	-	-	N	-	-	-	-	-	-	-	-	-	-	-	-	-	-	-	-	-
E. caeruleum (rainbow darter)	-	-	-	-	-	-	-	-	-	I	-	-	-	-	-	-	-	-	-	-	-	-	-	-	-	-	-	-	-	N	N	N	N	N	N	N	N	N	N	N	N	N
E. camurum (bluebreast darter)	-	-	-	-	-	-	-	-	-	-	-	-	-	-	-	-	-	-	-	-	-	-	-	-	-	-	-	-	-	N	N	N	-	N	N	N	N	N	N	N	-	-
E. chermocki (vermilion darter)	-	-	-	-	-	X	-	-	-	-	-	-	-	-	-	-	-	-	-	-	-	-	-	-	-	-	N	-	-	-	-	-	-	-	-	-	-	-	-	-	-	-
E. chienense (relict darter)	X	-	-	-	-	-	-	-	-	-	-	-	-	-	-	-	-	-	-	-	-	-	-	-	-	-	-	-	-	-	-	-	-	-	-	-	-	-	-	-	-	-
E. chlorobranchium (greenfin darter)	-	-	-	-	-	-	-	-	-	-	-	-	-	-	-	-	-	-	-	-	-	-	-	-	-	-	-	-	-	-	-	N	N	-	-	-	-	-	-	-	-	-
E. chlorosoma (bluntnose darter)	-	-	-	-	-	-	-	-	-	-	-	-	-	-	-	-	-	N	N	N	N	N	N	N	N	N	-	-	-	-	-	-	-	-	-	-	-	-	-	-	-	-
E. chuckwachatte (lipstick darter)	-	-	-	-	-	-	-	-	-	-	-	-	-	-	-	N	-	-	-	-	-	-	-	-	-	-	-	-	-	-	-	-	-	-	-	-	-	-	-	-	-	-
E. cinereum (ashy darter)	-	-	-	-	-	X	-	-	X	-	-	-	-	-	-	-	-	-	-	-	-	-	-	-	-	-	N	-	-	-	-	-	-	-	N	N	-	-	-	-	-	-
E. collis (Carolina darter)	-	-	-	-	-	-	-	-	-	-	-	N	N	N	N	N	-	-	-	-	-	-	-	-	-	-	-	-	-	-	-	-	-	-	-	-	-	-	-	-	-	-
E. colorosum (coastal darter)	-	-	-	-	-	-	-	-	-	-	-	-	-	-	N	-	-	-	-	-	-	-	-	-	-	-	-	-	-	-	-	-	-	-	-	-	-	-	-	-	-	-
E. coosae (Coosa darter)	-	-	-	-	-	-	-	-	-	-	-	-	-	-	-	N	-	-	-	-	-	-	-	-	-	-	-	-	-	-	-	-	-	-	-	-	-	-	-	-	-	-
E. corona (crown darter)	-	-	-	-	-	X	-	-	-	-	-	-	-	-	-	-	-	-	-	-	-	-	-	-	-	-	-	-	-	-	-	-	-	N	-	-	-	-	-	-	-	-
E. crossopterum (fringed darter)	-	-	-	-	-	-	-	-	-	-	-	-	-	-	-	-	-	-	-	-	-	-	-	-	-	-	-	-	-	-	-	N	N	-	N	-	N	-	N	-	-	-

Appendix 1. Continued.

TAXA	Federal						AFS			Drainage Units																																	
	E	T	PE	PT	C1	C2	E	T	SC	1	2	3	4	5	6	7	8	9	10	11	12	13	14	15	16	17	18	19	20	21	22	23	24	25	26	27	28	29	30	31	32	33
E. davisoni (Choctawhatchee darter)	–	–	–	–	–	–	–	–	–	–	–	–	–	–	–	–	–	–	–	–	–	–	–	N	–	–	–	–	–	–	–	–	–	–	–	–	–	–	–	–	–	–
E. ditrema (coldwater darter)	–	–	–	–	X	–	–	X	–	–	–	–	–	–	–	–	–	–	–	–	–	–	–	–	N	–	–	–	–	–	–	–	–	–	–	–	–	–	–	–	–	–
E. douglasi (Tuskaloosa darter)	–	–	–	–	–	X	–	–	–	–	–	–	–	–	–	–	–	–	–	–	–	–	–	–	–	–	N	–	–	–	–	–	–	–	–	–	–	–	–	–	–	–
E. duryi (blackside snubnose darter)	–	–	–	–	–	–	–	–	–	–	–	–	–	–	–	–	–	–	–	–	–	–	–	–	–	–	–	–	–	–	–	–	–	N	N	–	–	–	–	–	–	–
E. edwini (brown darter)	–	–	–	–	–	–	–	–	–	–	–	–	–	–	–	–	–	–	–	–	–	N	N	–	–	–	–	–	–	–	–	–	–	–	–	–	–	–	–	–	–	–
E. etnieri (cherry darter)	–	–	–	–	–	–	–	–	–	–	–	–	–	–	–	–	–	–	–	–	–	–	–	–	–	–	–	–	–	–	–	–	–	–	–	–	N	–	–	–	–	–
E. etowahae (Etowah darter)	X	–	–	–	–	–	–	–	–	–	–	–	–	–	–	–	–	–	–	–	–	–	–	N	N	–	–	–	–	–	–	–	–	–	–	–	–	–	–	–	–	–
E. flabellare (fantail darter)	–	–	–	–	–	–	–	–	–	N	N	N	N	N	N	N	–	–	–	–	–	–	–	–	–	–	–	–	–	–	–	–	–	N	N	N	N	N	N	N	N	N
E. flavum (saffron darter)	–	–	–	–	–	–	–	–	–	–	–	–	–	N	N	–	–	–	–	–	–	–	–	–	–	–	–	–	–	–	–	–	–	–	N	N	N	–	–	–	–	–
E. forbesi (Barrens darter)	–	–	–	–	–	X	–	–	–	–	–	–	–	–	–	–	–	–	–	–	–	–	–	–	–	–	–	–	–	–	–	–	–	–	–	N	–	–	–	–	–	–
E. fricksium (Savannah darter)	–	–	–	–	–	–	–	–	–	–	–	–	–	–	–	–	N	N	–	–	–	–	–	–	–	–	–	–	–	–	–	–	–	–	–	–	–	–	–	–	–	–
E. fusiforme (swamp darter)	–	–	–	–	–	–	–	–	–	N	N	–	N	N	N	N	N	N	N	N	N	N	N	N	–	N	N	N	N	N	N	N	N	–	N	I	N	N	N	N	N	N
E. gracile (slough darter)	–	–	–	–	–	–	–	–	–	–	–	–	–	–	–	–	–	–	–	–	–	–	–	–	–	–	N	N	N	–	N	N	N	–	N	–	N	N	–	–	–	–
E. histrio (harlequin darter)	–	–	–	–	–	–	–	–	–	–	–	–	–	–	–	–	–	N	N	–	–	–	–	–	N	N	N	N	N	N	N	N	N	–	N	N	–	–	N	–	–	–
E. hopkinsi (Christmas darter)	–	–	–	–	–	–	–	–	–	–	–	–	–	–	–	–	N	N	N	–	–	–	–	–	–	–	–	–	–	–	–	–	–	–	–	–	–	–	–	–	–	–
E. inscriptum (turquoise darter)	–	–	–	–	–	–	–	–	–	–	–	–	–	–	–	–	N	N	N	–	–	–	–	–	–	–	–	–	–	–	–	–	–	–	–	–	N	–	–	–	–	–
E. jessiae (blueside darter)	–	–	–	–	–	–	–	–	–	–	–	–	–	–	–	–	–	–	–	–	–	–	–	–	–	–	–	–	–	–	–	–	–	N	N	–	–	–	–	–	–	–
E. jordani (greenbreast darter)	–	–	–	–	–	–	–	–	–	–	–	–	–	–	–	–	–	–	–	–	–	–	–	–	N	N	–	–	–	–	–	–	–	–	–	–	–	–	–	–	–	–
E. kanawhae (Kanawha darter)	–	–	–	–	–	–	–	X	–	–	–	–	–	–	–	–	–	–	–	–	–	–	–	–	–	–	–	–	–	–	–	–	–	–	–	–	–	–	–	N	–	–
E. kennicotti (stripetail darter)	–	–	–	–	–	–	–	–	–	–	–	–	–	–	–	–	–	–	–	–	–	–	–	–	–	–	–	–	–	–	–	–	–	–	N	N	N	N	N	–	–	–
E. lachneri (Tombigbee darter)	–	–	–	–	–	–	–	–	–	–	–	–	–	–	–	–	–	–	–	–	–	–	–	–	–	–	N	–	–	–	–	–	–	–	–	–	–	–	–	–	–	–
E. longimanum (longfin darter)	–	–	–	–	–	–	–	–	–	–	N	–	–	–	–	–	–	–	–	–	–	–	–	–	–	–	–	–	–	–	–	–	–	–	–	–	–	–	–	–	–	–

Appendix 1. Continued.

TAXA	Federal						AFS			Drainage Units																															
	E	T	PE	PT	C1	C2	E	T	SC	1	2	3	4	5	6	7	8	9	10	11	12	13	14	15	16	17	18	19	20	21	22	23	24	25	26	27	28	29	30	31	32	33
E. luteovinctum (redband darter)	-	-	-	-	-	-	-	-	X	-	-	-	-	-	-	-	-	-	-	-	-	-	-	-	-	-	-	-	-	-	-	-	-	-	-	N	-	-	-	-	-	-
E. lynceum (brighteye darter)	-	-	-	-	-	-	-	-	-	-	-	-	-	-	-	-	-	-	-	-	-	-	-	-	-	-	-	-	-	-	-	-	-	-	-	-	-	N	-	N	-	-
E. maculatum (spotted darter)	-	-	-	-	-	X	-	-	X	-	-	-	-	-	-	-	-	-	-	-	-	-	-	-	-	-	-	-	-	-	-	-	-	-	-	-	-	N	N	N	-	-
E. mariae (pinewoods darter)	-	-	-	-	-	-	-	-	X	-	-	-	-	-	N	-	-	-	-	-	-	-	-	-	-	-	-	-	-	-	-	-	-	-	-	-	-	-	-	-	-	-
E. microlepidum (smallscale darter)	-	-	-	-	-	-	-	-	-	-	-	-	-	-	-	-	-	-	-	-	-	-	-	-	-	-	-	-	-	-	-	-	-	-	-	-	N	-	-	-	-	-
E. microperca (least darter)	-	-	-	-	-	-	-	-	-	-	-	-	-	-	-	-	-	-	-	-	-	-	-	-	-	-	N	N	N	N	N	N	N	-	-	-	-	-	-	-	-	-
E. neopterum (lollypop darter)	-	-	-	-	-	-	-	-	-	-	-	-	-	-	-	-	-	-	-	-	-	-	-	-	-	-	-	-	-	-	-	-	-	N	-	-	-	-	-	-	-	-
E. nigripinne (blackfin darter)	-	-	-	-	-	-	-	-	-	-	N	N	N	-	-	-	-	-	-	-	-	-	-	-	N	N	-	-	-	-	N	N	N	-	-	-	-	-	-	-	-	-
E. nigrum nigrum (johnny darter)	-	-	-	-	-	-	-	-	-	-	N	N	N	-	-	-	-	-	-	-	-	-	-	-	N	N	-	-	-	-	N	N	N	-	N	-	-	-	-	-	-	-
E. n. susanae (Cumberland johnny darter)	-	-	-	-	X	-	-	X	-	-	-	-	-	-	-	-	-	-	-	-	-	-	-	-	-	-	-	-	-	-	-	-	-	-	-	-	N	-	-	-	-	-
E. nuchale (watercress darter)	X	-	-	-	-	-	X	-	-	-	-	-	-	-	-	-	-	-	-	-	-	-	-	-	-	-	-	-	-	-	-	-	-	-	-	-	-	-	-	-	-	-
E. obeyense (barcheek darter)	-	-	-	-	-	-	-	-	-	-	-	-	-	-	-	-	-	-	-	-	-	-	-	-	-	-	-	-	-	-	-	-	-	-	-	N	-	-	-	-	-	-
E. okaloosae (Okaloosa darter)	X	-	-	-	-	-	-	X	-	-	-	-	-	-	-	-	-	-	-	-	-	-	-	N	-	-	-	-	-	-	-	-	-	-	-	-	-	-	-	-	-	-
E. olivaceum (dirty darter)	-	-	-	-	-	-	-	-	-	-	-	-	-	-	-	-	-	-	-	-	-	-	-	-	-	-	-	-	-	-	-	-	-	-	-	-	N	-	-	-	-	-
E. olmstedi (tessellated darter)	-	-	-	-	-	-	-	-	-	-	-	-	-	N	N	N	N	N	N	N	-	-	-	-	-	-	-	-	-	-	-	-	-	-	-	-	-	-	-	-	I	-
E. oophylax (guardian darter)	-	-	-	-	-	-	-	-	-	-	-	-	-	-	-	-	-	-	-	-	-	-	-	-	-	-	-	-	-	-	-	-	-	-	N	-	-	-	-	-	-	-
E. osburni (finescale saddled darter)	-	-	-	-	-	X	-	-	X	-	-	-	-	-	-	-	-	-	-	-	-	-	-	-	-	-	-	-	-	-	-	-	-	-	-	-	-	-	-	N	-	-
E. parvipinne (goldstripe darter)	-	-	-	-	-	-	-	-	-	-	-	-	-	-	-	-	-	-	-	-	-	-	-	-	-	-	-	-	-	-	-	-	-	-	N	-	-	-	-	-	-	-
E. percnurum (duskytail darter)	X	-	-	-	-	-	-	X	-	-	-	-	-	-	-	-	-	-	-	-	-	-	-	-	-	-	-	-	-	-	-	-	-	-	-	N	N	N	-	-	-	-
E. perlongum (Waccamaw darter)	-	-	-	-	-	-	-	-	-	-	-	-	-	-	-	-	-	-	-	-	-	-	-	-	-	-	-	-	-	-	-	-	-	-	-	-	-	-	-	-	-	-
E. podostemone (riverweed darter)	-	-	-	-	-	-	-	-	-	-	-	N	-	-	-	-	-	-	-	-	-	-	-	-	-	-	-	-	-	-	-	-	-	-	N	-	-	-	-	-	-	-
E. pseudovulatum (egg-mimic darter)	-	-	-	-	-	X	-	-	-	-	-	-	-	-	-	-	-	-	-	-	-	-	-	-	-	-	-	-	-	-	-	-	-	-	-	-	N	-	-	-	-	-

Appendix 1. Continued.

TAXA	Federal E	T	PE	PT	C1	C2	AFS E	T	SC	1	2	3	4	5	6	7	8	9	10	11	12	13	14	15	16	17	18	19	20	21	22	23	24	25	26	27	28	29	30	31	32	33
E. proeliare (cypress darter)	-	-	-	-	-	-	-	-	-	-	-	-	-	-	-	-	-	-	-	-	-	-	-	N	-	N	N	N	N	N	-	N	N	N	N	-	N	N	N	-	-	-
E. pyrrhogaster (firebelly darter)	-	-	-	-	-	-	-	-	X	-	-	-	-	-	-	-	-	-	-	-	-	-	-	-	-	-	-	-	-	-	-	-	N	-	-	-	-	-	-	-	-	-
E. rafinesquei (Kentucky snubnose darter)	-	-	-	-	-	-	-	-	-	-	-	-	-	-	-	-	-	-	-	-	-	-	-	-	-	-	-	-	-	-	-	-	-	-	-	-	N	-	-	-	-	-
E. ramseyi (Alabama darter)	-	-	-	-	-	-	-	-	-	-	-	-	-	-	-	-	-	-	-	-	-	-	-	-	-	N	-	-	-	-	-	-	-	-	-	-	-	N	-	-	-	-
E. raneyi (Yazoo darter)	-	-	-	-	-	-	-	-	-	-	-	-	-	-	-	-	-	-	-	-	-	-	-	-	-	-	-	-	-	-	-	N	-	-	-	-	-	-	-	-	-	-
E. rubrum (bayou darter)	X	-	-	-	-	-	-	X	-	-	-	-	-	-	-	-	-	-	-	-	-	-	-	-	-	-	-	-	-	N	-	-	-	-	-	-	-	-	-	-	-	-
E. rufilineatum (redline darter)	-	-	-	-	-	-	-	-	-	-	-	-	-	-	-	-	-	-	-	-	-	-	-	-	-	-	-	-	-	-	N	-	-	N	N	N	N	-	-	-	-	-
E. rupestre (rock darter)	-	-	-	-	-	-	-	-	-	-	-	-	-	-	-	-	-	-	-	-	-	-	N	-	N	N	-	-	-	-	-	-	-	-	-	-	-	-	-	-	-	-
E. sagitta (arrow darter)	-	-	-	-	-	-	-	-	-	-	-	-	-	-	-	-	-	-	-	-	-	-	-	-	-	-	-	-	-	-	N	-	-	N	-	-	N	-	N	-	-	-
E. saludae (Saluda darter)	-	-	-	-	-	-	-	-	-	-	-	-	-	-	-	-	-	-	-	-	-	-	-	-	-	-	-	-	-	-	-	-	-	-	-	-	-	-	-	-	-	-
E. sanguifluum (bloodfin darter)	-	-	-	-	-	-	-	-	-	-	-	-	-	-	-	N	-	-	-	-	-	-	-	-	-	-	-	-	-	-	-	-	N	-	-	-	-	-	-	-	-	-
E. scotti (Cherokee darter)	X	-	-	-	-	-	X	-	-	-	-	-	-	-	-	-	-	-	-	-	-	-	-	-	N	-	-	-	-	-	-	-	-	-	-	-	-	-	-	-	-	-
E. serrifer (sawcheek darter)	-	-	-	-	-	-	-	-	-	-	-	-	-	N	N	N	N	N	-	-	-	-	-	-	-	-	-	-	-	-	-	-	-	-	-	-	-	-	-	-	-	-
E. simoterum (Tennessee snubnose darter)	-	-	-	-	-	-	-	-	-	-	N	N	N	N	N	N	N	N	-	-	-	-	-	-	-	-	-	-	-	-	-	-	-	-	-	-	-	-	-	-	-	-
E. smithi (slabrock darter)	-	-	-	-	-	-	-	-	-	-	-	-	-	-	-	-	-	-	-	-	-	-	-	-	-	-	-	-	-	-	-	N	-	-	N	-	N	-	-	-	-	-
E. spectabile (orangethroat darter)	-	-	-	-	-	-	-	-	-	-	-	-	-	-	-	-	-	-	-	-	N	-	N	N	N	N	-	-	-	-	-	-	N	N	N	N	-	N	N	N	N	-	-
E. squamiceps (spottail darter)	-	-	-	-	-	-	-	-	-	-	-	-	-	-	-	-	-	-	-	-	-	-	-	-	-	-	-	-	-	-	N	N	N	-	-	N	-	N	-	-	-	-
E. stigmaeum (speckled darter)	-	-	-	-	-	-	-	-	-	-	-	-	-	-	-	-	-	-	-	-	-	-	-	-	-	-	-	-	-	-	-	-	-	-	-	-	-	-	-	-	-	-
E. striatulum (striated darter)	-	-	-	-	X	-	-	-	X	-	-	-	-	-	-	-	-	-	-	-	-	-	-	-	-	-	-	-	-	-	-	-	N	-	-	N	-	-	-	-	-	-
E. swannanoa (Swannanoa darter)	-	-	-	-	-	-	-	-	-	-	-	-	-	-	-	-	-	-	-	-	-	-	-	-	-	-	-	-	-	-	-	-	-	-	-	-	N	-	-	-	-	-
E. swaini (gulf darter)	-	-	-	-	-	-	-	-	-	-	-	-	-	-	-	-	-	-	-	-	N	N	-	-	N	N	-	-	-	-	N	N	N	N	N	-	-	-	-	-	-	-
E. tallapoosae (Tallapoosa darter)	-	-	-	-	-	-	-	-	-	-	-	-	-	-	-	-	-	-	-	-	-	-	-	-	-	-	-	-	-	-	-	-	-	-	-	-	-	-	-	N	-	-	-

Appendix 1. Continued.

TAXA	Federal E	T	PE	PT	C1	C2	AFS E	T	SC	1	2	3	4	5	6	7	8	9	10	11	12	13	14	15	16	17	18	19	20	21	22	23	24	25	26	27	28	29	30	31	32	33
E. thalassinum (seagreen darter)	-	-	-	-	-	-	-	-	-	-	-	-	-	-	-	N	-	-	-	-	-	-	-	-	-	-	-	-	-	-	-	-	-	-	-	-	-	-	-	-	-	-
E. tippecanoe (Tippecanoe darter)	-	-	-	-	-	-	-	-	-	-	-	-	-	-	-	-	-	-	-	-	-	-	-	-	-	-	-	-	-	-	-	-	-	-	N	N	N	N	N	N	N	-
E. trisella (trispot darter)	-	-	-	-	X	-	-	X	-	-	-	-	-	-	-	-	-	-	-	-	-	-	-	-	N	-	-	-	-	-	-	-	-	-	-	-	-	-	-	-	-	-
E. tuscumbia (Tuscumbia darter)	-	-	-	-	X	-	-	X	-	-	-	-	-	-	-	-	-	-	-	-	-	-	-	-	-	-	-	-	-	-	-	-	-	-	N	-	-	-	-	-	-	-
E. variatum (variegate darter)	-	-	-	-	-	-	-	-	-	-	-	-	-	-	-	-	-	-	-	-	-	-	-	-	-	-	-	-	-	-	-	-	-	-	-	-	-	-	N	N	N	N
E. virgatum (striped darter)	-	-	-	-	-	-	-	-	-	-	-	-	-	-	-	-	-	-	-	-	-	-	-	-	-	-	-	-	-	-	-	-	-	-	-	-	-	-	-	-	-	-
E. vitreum (glassy darter)	-	-	-	-	-	-	-	-	-	-	-	-	-	-	-	-	-	-	-	-	-	-	-	-	-	-	-	-	-	-	-	-	-	-	-	-	N	-	-	-	-	-
E. vulneratum (wounded darter)	-	-	-	-	-	-	-	-	-	-	-	-	-	-	-	-	-	-	-	-	-	-	-	-	-	-	-	-	-	-	-	-	-	-	-	N	-	-	-	-	-	-
E. wapiti (boulder darter)	X	-	-	-	-	-	-	X	-	-	-	-	-	-	-	-	-	-	-	-	-	-	-	-	-	-	-	-	-	-	-	-	-	-	N	-	-	-	-	-	-	-
E. whipplei (redfin darter)	-	-	-	-	-	-	-	-	-	-	-	-	-	-	-	-	-	-	-	-	-	N	N	-	-	-	-	-	-	-	-	-	-	-	-	-	-	-	-	-	-	-
E. zonale (banded darter)	-	-	-	-	-	-	-	-	-	-	-	-	-	-	-	N	N	N	N	N	-	-	-	-	-	-	N	N	N	N	N	N	N	N
E. zonifer (backwater darter)	-	-	-	-	-	-	-	-	-	-	-	-	-	-	-	N	N	-	-	-	-	-	-	-	-	-	-	-	-	-	-	-	-	-	-	-
E. zonistium (bandfin darter)	-	-	-	-	-	-	-	-	-	-	-	-	-	-	-	-	-	N	-	-	-	-	-	N	-	N	-	-	-	-	-	-	-	-	-	-
Etheostoma sp. cf. E. parvipinne (upland goldstripe darter)	-	-	-	-	-	-	-	-	-	-	-	-	-	-	-	-	-	N	-	-	-	-	-	-	-	-	-	-	-	-	-	-	-	-
Etheostoma sp. cf. E. stigmaeum (bluegrass darter)	-	-	-	-	-	-	-	-	-	-	-	-	-	-	-	-	-	-	-	-	-	-	-	-	-	-	-	-	N	-	-	-	-	-
Etheostoma sp. cf. E. stigmaeum (bluemask darter)	X	-	-	-	-	-	-	-	X	-	-	-	-	-	-	-	-	-	-	-	-	-	-	-	-	-	-	-	-	-	-	-	N	-	-	-	-	-
Etheostoma sp. cf. E. stigmaeum (clown darter)	-	-	-	-	-	-	-	-	-	-	-	-	-	-	-	-	-	-	-	-	-	-	-	-	-	-	N	-	-	-	-	-
Etheostoma sp. cf. E. stigmaeum (longhunt darter)	-	-	-	-	-	-	-	-	-	-	-	-	-	-	-	-	-	-	-	-	-	-	-	-	-	-	-	N	-	-	-	-
Perca flavescens (yellow perch)	-	-	-	-	-	-	-	-	-	I	I	I	I	I	I	I	-	I	-	-	-	-	I	I	I	-	-	-	-	-	-	-	-	-	I	I	I	I	I	-	I	I	I
Percina antesella (amber darter)	X	-	-	-	-	-	X	-	-	-	-	-	-	-	-	-	-	-	-	-	-	-	-	-	N	-	-	-	-	-	-	-	-	-
P. aurantiaca (tangerine darter)	-	-	-	-	-	-	-	-	-	-	-	-	-	-	-	-	-	-	-	-	-	-	-	-	-	-	N	-	-	-	-	-
P. aurolineata (goldline darter)	-	X	-	-	-	-	-	X	-	-	-	-	-	-	-	-	-	-	-	-	-	-	-	-	N	N	-	-	-	-	-	-

Appendix 1. Continued.

TAXA	Federal E	T	PE	PT	C1	C2	AFS E	T	SC	1	2	3	4	5	6	7	8	9	10	11	12	13	14	15	16	17	18	19	20	21	22	23	24	25	26	27	28	29	30	31	32	33
P. aurora (Pearl darter)	–	–	–	–	X	–	X	–	–	–	–	–	–	–	–	–	–	–	–	–	–	–	–	–	–	–	–	–	–	–	–	–	–	–	–	–	–	–	–	–	–	–
P. austroperca (southern logperch)	–	–	–	–	–	–	–	–	–	–	–	–	–	–	–	–	–	–	–	–	–	–	–	N	–	–	–	–	–	–	–	–	–	–	–	–	–	–	–	–	–	–
P. brevicauda (coal darter)	–	–	–	–	X	–	X	–	–	–	–	–	–	–	–	–	–	–	–	–	–	–	–	–	N	N	N	–	–	–	–	–	–	–	–	–	–	–	–	–	–	–
P. burtoni (blotchside logperch)	–	–	–	–	–	–	–	–	X	N	–	–	–	–	–	–	–	–	–	–	–	–	–	–	–	–	–	–	–	–	–	N	N	N	N	N	N	N	N	N	N	N
P. caprodes (logperch)	–	–	–	–	–	–	–	–	–	–	–	–	–	–	–	–	–	–	–	–	–	–	–	–	–	–	–	–	N	–	–	N	N	N	N	N	N	N	N	N	N	N
P. copelandi (channel darter)	–	–	–	–	–	–	–	–	–	–	–	–	–	–	–	–	–	–	–	–	–	–	–	–	–	–	–	–	–	–	–	–	–	–	N	–	N	N	N	N	N	N
P. crassa (Piedmont darter)	–	–	–	–	–	–	–	–	–	–	–	–	–	N	N	N	–	–	–	–	–	–	–	–	–	–	–	–	–	–	–	–	–	–	–	–	–	–	–	–	–	–
P. evides (gilt darter)	–	–	–	–	–	–	–	–	–	–	–	–	–	–	–	–	–	–	–	–	–	–	–	–	N	–	–	–	–	–	–	–	N	–	N	N	N	N	N	N	N	N
P. gymnocephala (Appalachia darter)	–	–	–	–	–	–	–	–	–	–	–	–	–	–	–	–	–	–	–	–	–	–	–	–	–	–	–	–	–	–	–	–	–	–	–	–	–	–	–	–	N	–
P. jenkinsi (Conasauga logperch)	X	–	–	–	–	–	X	–	–	–	–	–	–	–	–	–	–	–	–	–	–	–	–	–	N	–	–	–	–	–	–	–	–	–	–	–	–	–	–	–	–	–
P. lenticula (freckled darter)	–	–	–	–	–	–	X	–	–	–	–	–	–	–	–	–	–	–	–	–	–	–	–	–	N	N	N	N	–	–	–	–	–	–	–	–	–	–	–	–	–	–
P. macrocephala (longhead darter)	–	–	–	–	X	–	X	–	–	–	–	–	–	–	–	–	–	–	–	–	–	–	–	–	–	–	–	–	–	–	–	N	N	–	–	–	–	–	–	–	–	–
P. maculata (blackside darter)	–	–	–	–	–	–	–	–	–	–	–	–	–	–	–	–	–	N	N	N	N	N	N	N	N	N	N	–	N	N	N	N	–	N	–	N	N	N	N	N	N	N	N
P. nigrofasciata (blackbanded darter)	–	–	–	–	–	–	–	–	–	–	–	N	N	–	–	–	N	N	N	N	N	N	N	N	N	N	N	N	N	N	N	–	–	–	–	–	–	–	–	–	–	–
P. notogramma (stripeback darter)	–	–	–	–	–	–	–	–	–	N	N	–	–	–	–	–	–	–	–	–	–	–	–	–	–	–	–	–	–	–	–	–	–	–	–	–	–	–	–	–	–	–
P. ouachitae (saddleback darter)	–	–	–	–	–	–	–	–	–	–	–	–	–	–	–	–	–	–	–	–	–	N	N	N	N	N	N	N	N	N	N	–	–	–	–	–	–	–	–	–	–	–
P. oxyrhynchus (sharpnose darter)	–	–	–	–	–	–	–	–	–	–	–	–	–	–	–	–	–	–	–	–	–	–	–	–	–	–	–	–	–	–	–	–	–	–	–	–	–	N	–	–	–	–
P. palmaris (bronze darter)	–	–	–	–	–	–	–	–	–	–	–	–	–	–	–	X	–	–	–	–	–	–	–	–	–	–	–	–	–	–	–	–	–	–	–	–	–	–	–	–	–	–
P. peltata (shield darter)	–	–	–	–	–	–	–	–	–	N	N	N	N	–	–	–	–	–	–	–	–	–	–	–	–	–	–	–	–	–	–	–	–	–	–	–	–	–	–	–	–	–
P. phoxocephala (slenderhead darter)	–	–	–	–	–	–	–	–	–	–	–	–	–	–	–	–	–	–	–	–	–	–	–	–	–	–	–	–	–	–	N	–	N	–	N	–	N	N	N	N	N	–	N
P. rex (Roanoke logperch)	X	–	–	–	–	–	X	–	–	–	N	–	–	–	–	–	–	–	–	–	–	–	–	–	–	–	–	–	–	–	–	–	–	–	–	–	–	–	–	–	–	–
P. roanoka (Roanoke darter)	–	–	–	–	–	–	–	–	–	I	N	N	–	–	–	–	–	–	–	–	–	–	–	–	–	–	–	–	–	–	–	–	–	–	–	–	–	–	–	–	–	I	–

Appendix 1. Continued.

TAXA	Federal						AFS			Drainage Units																															
	E	T	PE	PT	C1	C2	E	T	SC	1	2	3	4	5	6	7	8	9	10	11	12	13	14	15	16	17	18	19	20	21	22	23	24	25	26	27	28	29	30	31	32	33
P. sciera (dusky darter)	–	–	–	–	–	–	–	–	–	–	–	–	–	–	–	–	–	–	–	–	–	–	–	–	N	N	N	N	N	N	N	N	N	N	N	N	N	N	N	N	N	N
P. shumardi (river darter)	–	–	–	–	–	–	–	–	–	–	–	–	–	–	–	–	–	–	–	–	–	–	–	–	N	N	N	N	N	–	N	N	N	N	N	N	N	N	N	–	–	N
P. squamata (olive darter)	–	–	–	–	–	X	–	X	–	–	–	–	–	–	–	–	–	–	–	–	–	–	–	–	–	–	–	–	–	–	–	–	–	–	–	N	N	–	–	–	–	–
P. stictogaster (frecklebelly darter)	–	–	–	–	–	–	–	–	–	–	–	–	–	–	–	–	–	–	–	–	–	–	–	–	–	–	–	–	–	–	–	–	–	–	–	–	–	N	–	–	–	–
P. tanasi (snail darter)	–	X	–	–	–	–	X	–	–	–	–	–	–	–	–	–	–	–	–	–	–	–	–	–	–	–	–	–	–	–	–	–	–	–	–	N	–	–	–	–	–	–
Percina sp. cf. P. caprodes (undescribed species 1)	–	–	–	–	–	–	–	–	–	–	–	–	–	–	–	–	–	–	–	–	–	–	–	–	–	–	N	N	N	N	–	–	–	–	–	–	–	–	–	–	–	–
Percina sp. cf. P. caprodes (undescribed species 3)	–	–	–	–	–	–	–	–	–	–	–	–	–	–	–	–	–	–	–	–	–	–	–	–	N	N	N	–	–	–	–	–	–	–	–	–	–	–	–	–	–	–
Percina sp. cf. P. macrocephala (bridled or muscadine darter)	–	–	–	–	–	X	–	X	–	–	–	–	–	–	–	–	–	–	–	–	–	–	–	–	N	N	N	–	–	–	–	–	–	–	–	–	–	–	–	–	–	–
Percina sp. cf. P. nigrofasciata (halloween darter)	–	–	–	–	–	X	–	–	–	–	–	–	–	–	–	–	–	–	–	–	–	–	N	–	–	–	–	–	–	–	–	–	–	–	–	–	–	–	–	–	–	–
Stizostedion canadense (sauger)	–	–	–	–	–	–	–	–	–	–	–	–	–	–	I	–	–	I	I	–	–	–	–	–	N	N	N	N	–	–	N	N	–	N	N	N	N	N	N	N	N	N
S. vitreum (walleye)	–	–	–	–	–	–	–	–	–	–	–	–	–	–	I	I	–	I	I	–	–	–	–	I	N	N	N	N	N	–	N	N	–	N	N	N	N	N	N	N	N	N
SCIAENIDAE – Drums																																										
Aplodinotus grunniens (freshwater drum)	–	–	–	–	–	–	–	–	–	–	–	–	–	–	–	–	–	–	–	–	–	–	–	N	N	N	N	N	N	N	N	N	N	N	N	N	N	N	N	N	N	N
CICHLIDAE – Cichlids																																										
Astronotus ocellatus (oscar)	–	–	–	–	–	–	–	–	–	–	–	–	–	–	–	–	–	–	I	–	–	–	–	–	–	–	–	–	–	–	–	–	–	–	–	–	–	–	–	–	–	–
Cichla ocellaris (peacock cichlid)	–	–	–	–	–	–	–	–	–	–	–	–	–	–	–	–	–	–	–	I	–	–	–	–	–	–	–	–	–	–	–	–	–	–	–	–	–	–	–	–	–	–
Cichlasoma bimaculatum (black acara)	–	–	–	–	–	–	–	–	–	–	–	–	–	–	–	–	–	–	–	I	–	–	–	–	–	–	–	–	–	–	–	–	–	–	–	–	–	–	–	–	–	–
C. citrinellum (Midas cichlid)	–	–	–	–	–	–	–	–	–	–	–	–	–	–	–	–	–	–	–	I	–	–	–	–	–	–	–	–	–	–	–	–	–	–	–	–	–	–	–	–	–	–
C. cyanoguttatum (Rio Grande cichlid)	–	–	–	–	–	–	–	–	–	–	–	–	–	–	–	–	I	I	I	I	–	I	–	–	–	–	–	–	–	–	–	–	–	–	–	–	–	–	–	–	–	–
C. meeki (firemouth)	–	–	–	–	–	–	–	–	–	–	–	–	–	–	–	–	–	–	–	I	–	–	–	–	–	–	–	–	–	–	–	–	–	–	–	–	–	–	–	–	–	–
C. octofasciatum (Jack Dempsey)	–	–	–	–	–	–	–	–	–	–	–	–	–	–	–	–	I	I	I	I	–	I	–	–	–	–	–	–	–	–	–	–	–	–	–	–	–	–	–	–	–	–
C. urophthalmus (Mayan cichlid)	–	–	–	–	–	–	–	–	–	–	–	–	–	–	–	–	–	–	–	I	–	–	–	–	–	–	–	–	–	–	–	–	–	–	–	–	–	–	–	–	–	–

Appendix 1. Continued.

TAXA	Federal E	PE	PT	C1	C2	AFS E	T	SC	1	2	3	4	5	6	7	8	9	10	11	12	13	14	15	16	17	18	19	20	21	22	23	24	25	26	27	28	29	30	31	32	33
Geophaghus surinamensis (redstriped eartheater)	-	-	-	-	-	-	-	-	-	-	-	-	-	-	-	-	-	-	-	I	-	-	-	-	-	-	-	-	-	-	-	-	-	-	-	-	-	-	-	-	-
Hemichromis letourneauxi (black aracara)	-	-	-	-	-	-	-	-	-	-	-	-	-	-	-	-	-	-	-	I	-	-	-	-	-	-	-	-	-	-	-	-	-	-	-	-	-	-	-	-	-
Oreochromis aureus (blue tilapia)	-	-	-	-	-	-	-	-	-	-	-	-	-	-	-	I	I	-	-	I	-	-	-	-	-	-	-	-	-	-	-	-	-	-	I	-	-	-	-	-	-
O. mossambicus (Mozambique tilapia)	-	-	-	-	-	-	-	-	-	-	-	-	-	-	-	I	I	-	-	I	-	-	-	-	-	-	-	-	-	-	-	-	-	-	-	-	-	-	-	-	-
Sarotherodon melanotheron (blackchin tilapia)	-	-	-	-	-	-	-	-	-	-	-	-	-	-	-	-	I	-	-	I	-	-	-	-	-	-	-	-	-	-	-	-	-	-	-	-	-	-	-	-	-
Tilapia mariae (spotted tilapia)	-	-	-	-	-	-	-	-	-	-	-	-	-	-	-	-	-	-	-	I	-	-	-	-	-	-	-	-	-	-	-	-	-	-	-	-	-	-	-	-	-
T. zilli (redbelly tilapia)	-	-	-	-	-	-	-	-	-	-	-	-	I	I	-	-	-	-	-	-	-	-	-	-	-	-	-	-	-	-	-	-	-	-	-	-	-	-	-	-	-
BELONTIIDAE – Gouramies																																									
Trichopsis vittata (croaking gourami)	-	-	-	-	-	-	-	-	-	-	-	-	-	-	-	-	-	-	-	I	-	-	-	-	-	-	-	-	-	-	-	-	-	-	-	-	-	-	-	-	-
COTTIDAE – Sculpins																																									
Cottus baileyi (black sculpin)	-	-	-	-	-	-	-	-	-	-	-	-	-	-	-	-	-	-	-	-	-	-	-	-	-	-	-	-	-	-	-	-	-	-	-	-	-	-	-	-	-
C. bairdi (mottled sculpin)	-	-	-	-	-	-	-	-	N	N	N	-	-	-	N	-	N	-	-	-	N	-	N	N	-	-	-	-	-	-	N	N	N	N	N	N	N	N	N	N	-
C. carolinae (banded sculpin)	-	-	-	-	-	-	-	-	-	-	-	-	-	-	-	-	-	N	N	-	-	-	-	-	-	-	-	-	N	N	N	N	-	-	-	-	-	-	-	N	-
C. cognatus (slimy sculpin)	-	-	-	-	-	-	-	-	N	-	-	-	-	-	-	-	-	-	-	-	-	-	-	-	-	-	-	-	-	-	-	-	-	-	-	-	-	-	-	-	-
C. girardi (Potomac sculpin)	-	-	-	-	-	-	-	-	N	N	-	-	-	-	-	-	-	-	-	-	-	-	-	-	-	-	-	-	-	-	-	-	-	-	-	-	-	-	-	-	-
C. pygmaeus (pygmy sculpin)	X	-	-	-	-	X	-	-	-	-	-	-	-	-	-	-	-	N	-	-	-	-	-	-	-	-	-	-	-	-	-	-	-	-	-	-	-	-	-	-	-
Cottus sp. cf. C. carolinae (Bluestone sculpin)	-	-	-	-	X	-	-	-	-	-	-	-	-	-	-	-	-	-	-	-	-	-	-	-	-	-	-	-	-	-	-	-	-	-	-	-	-	-	-	N	-

CHAPTER 6

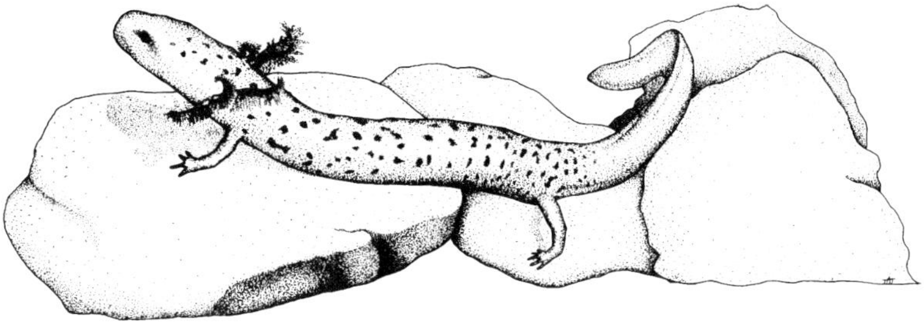

Imperiled Amphibians: A Historical Perspective

C. Kenneth Dodd, Jr.

Amphibians have been in and out of the news over the past few years because of the often unexplained disappearance of individual species or groups of species (Barinaga, 1990; Blaustein and Wake, 1990; Vitt et al., 1990; Wyman, 1990; Anonymous, 1991; Wake, 1991; Livermore, 1992, Blaustein et al., 1994c; Stebbins and Cohen, 1995). Amphibian declines or extinctions have been particularly apparent in the western United States (e.g., Bradford, 1991; Carey, 1993a; Fellers and Drost, 1993) and Australia (Richards et al., 1993), with scattered declines reported in Central and South America, Europe, and elsewhere (Vial and Saylor, 1993). Although much debate centers on natural population fluctuations (Pechmann et al., 1991; Blaustein, 1994; Pechmann and Wilbur, 1994) and their role in population viability (Sjogren, 1991a), there seems to be little doubt that amphibian populations are threatened by an ever expanding human population.

In this paper, I present an overview of the taxonomic diversity of the amphibians of the southeastern United States, the types of habitats used by amphibians, amphibian life history in relation to aquatic habitats, the types of studies that have been conducted on southeastern amphibians, and the status of and threats to particular species and populations. I define the southeastern United States to include an area from Virginia, West Virginia, and Kentucky, south through Florida and west to eastern Texas. As such, the region includes the contiguous southern Appalachians, southeastern Coastal Plain, Interior Highlands, and Edwards Plateau, all areas of important species richness and diversity.

TAXONOMIC REVIEW

Of the estimated 4,300 to 4,500 amphibian species worldwide (Vial and Saylor, 1993;

Aquatic Fauna in Peril: The Southeastern Perspective, edited by George W. Benz, and David E. Collins. 1997. Special Publication 1, Southeast Aquatic Research Institute, Lenz Design & Communications, Decatur, GA, 554 p.

Zug, 1993; McDiarmid, 1994), 147 species have been described from the southeastern United States. In addition to the described species, a number of species await formal taxonomic description, particularly in the salamander families Plethodontidae, Proteidae, and Sirenidae (P. Moler, Florida Game and Fresh Water Fish Commission, pers. comm.), and possibly in the frog family Ranidae (R. Franz, Florida Museum of Natural History, pers. comm.). Within North America, the Southeast has the greatest amphibian species richness (Kiester, 1971). Most of the native amphibians in the Southeast (68 percent) are salamanders, with 99 described species. The amphibian species richness of each southeastern state is shown in Figure 1.

Order Caudata

Of the seven salamander families in the southeastern United States, two (Amphiumidae and Sirenidae) are endemic to the region while two additional families (Ambystomatidae and Proteidae) have their greatest species richness in the Southeast. One of the three extant cryptobranchids occurs primarily in southern streams and rivers, whereas the other species (*Andrias* spp.) are found in Asia. The family Plethodontidae exhibits substantial diversity in the Southeast, although its greatest species richness occurs in the mountainous Neotropics of southern Mexico and Central America. The family Salamandridae is primarily Palearctic and Oriental in distribution, although all three known species of *Notophthalmus* are found in the Southeast.

The following salamander genera have their centers of distribution within the Southeast: *Cryptobranchus, Necturus, Amphiuma, Siren, Pseudobranchus, Leurognathus, Phaeognathus, Haideotriton, Stereochilus,* and *Typhlomolge*. Most or all species of *Notophthalmus, Desmognathus, Eurycea, Gyrinophilus, Plethodon,* and *Pseudotriton* also occur in the Southeast, although the ranges of individual species may extend substantially northward.

Order Anura

There are no endemic families of frogs in the southeastern United States, and only two genera (*Acris* and *Pseudacris*) have centers of species richness within the Southeast. The highest diversity (19 species) of southeastern frogs occurs within the Hylidae (treefrogs) followed by the Ranidae (true frogs: 14+ species) and the Bufonidae (toads: seven species). *Hypopachus* and *Syrrhophus* barely enter the coastal plain in Texas, whereas *Gastrophryne* and *Scaphiopus* are together represented by a total of five species, three of which barely enter the Southeast. In addition to the 48 native frog species, at least four exotic species (*Bufo marinus, Eleutherodactylus coqui, E. planirostris, Osteopilus septentrionalis*) have established breeding populations (all in Florida).

DISTRIBUTION AND HABITATS

Physiographic Regions and Centers of Species Diversity

Amphibians are found in all physiographic regions of the southeastern United States (Table 1). They are found from sea level to the tops of the highest Appalachian Mountains. Centers of species richness and endemism include the following: the Appalachian Mountains, particularly at higher elevations (salamanders, especially the family

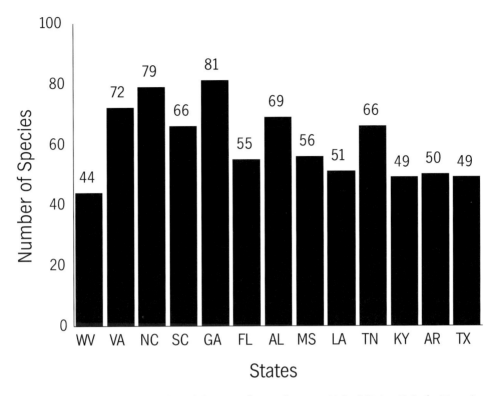

Figure 1. Species richness of amphibians in the southeastern United States. Data for Texas include only species found in the east Texas coastal plain.

Plethodontidae and the genus *Plethodon*); the Atlantic and Gulf of Mexico coastal plains (many salamanders and frogs, especially *Amphiuma, Siren, Pseudobranchus, Necturus, Haideotriton,* and *Pseudacris* species); the Interior Highlands, including the Boston, Ouachita, and Ozark mountains (many endemic salamanders); and the Edwards Plateau (many endemic cave and spring salamanders of the genera *Eurycea* and *Typhlomolge*) (Figure 2).

AQUATIC HABITATS

Amphibians are found in all types of aquatic wetlands (see Hackney et al., 1992, and references therein) except those associated with the saline waters along the coast. Even there, however, some species occasionally are found in brackish habitats (Neill, 1958; Christman, 1974). Selected references on amphibian species composition of southeastern aquatic environments include the following: Moler and Franz (1988), LaClaire and Franz (1991), Dodd (1992), and Cash (1994) for temporary ponds; Adams and Lacki (1993) for road-ruts; Turner and Fowler (1981) and Lacki et al. (1992) for ponds at former mine sites; Delis (1993) and O'Neill (1995) for wetlands in pine flatwoods; Mitchell et al. (1993) for saturated forested wetlands; Harris and Vickers (1984) and Vickers et al. (1985) for cypress domes; Pearson et al. (1987) for bayheads; Wright (1932), Delzell (1979), and Hall (1994) for large swamps; Dalrymple (1988) for wet prairies; Parker (1937) and Bancroft et al. (1983) for lakes; and Southerland (1986) for streams. Much information on amphibian use of aquatic habitats is contained in state or re-

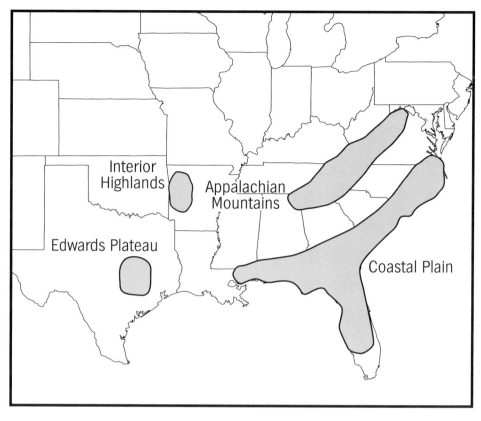

Figure 2. Centers of endemism and species richness (shaded areas) for the amphibian fauna of the southeastern United States.

gional books (e.g., Carr, 1940; Duellman and Schwartz, 1958; Ashton and Ashton, 1988; Dundee and Rossman, 1989; Gibbons and Semlitsch, 1991) as well as in numerous accounts of species in need of conservation (see Table 2).

Large, fully aquatic salamanders (*Cryptobranchus, Necturus*) typically are found in the larger rivers and streams, whereas small aquatic salamanders (*Desmognathus, Leurognathus, Eurycea*) frequent small streams and seeps. For these salamanders, larval development occurs within the stream and, after metamorphosis, adults live along the wet streamsides or among the gravelly substrate. Salamanders belonging to *Siren, Pseudobranchus,* and *Amphiuma* inhabit various types of vegetated ponds and mucky swamps. Newts and most *Ambystoma* species require temporary ponds to complete metamorphosis, and premature pond drying is an ever present threat to their development (Semlitsch, 1987; Pechmann et al., 1989; Dodd, 1993). Of course, even salamanders that do not require water to breed need moist environments to prevent desiccation.

As with salamanders, frogs use a variety of wetlands for reproduction. Most frog species have tadpoles which develop within ponds, lakes, wet prairies, or other lentic waters. Fewer species use streams, rivers, or swift flowing waters (e.g., *Rana heckscheri* in rivers, streams, and oxbows in addition to lentic waters). Some frogs are very habitat specific,

Table 1. Characteristics of the aquatic habitats and major ecosystems of native amphibians of the southeastern United States.[1]

Taxa	Number Species	Adult Habitat	Larval Habitat	Aquatic Habitats	Physiographic Provinces
Order Caudata — Salamanders					
Family Cryptobranchidae					
Cryptobranchus	1	A	A	R,LS	M,CUP,O
Family Proteidae					
Necturus	5?	A	A	R,LS,SS	CP
Family Amphiumidae					
Amphiuma	3	A	A	L,P,SW	CP
Family Sirenidae					
Pseudobranchus	2	A	A	L,P,SW	CP
Siren	2?	A	A	L,P,SW	CP
Family Ambystomatidae					
Ambystoma[2]	10	T,A	A	P	CP,P,M,O,CUP
Family Salamandridae					
Notophthalmus[2]	3	T,A	A	P	CP,P,M,CUP
Family Plethodontidae					
Desmognathinae					
Desmognathus	12	S,T	A,D	SS,SW	CP,P,M,O,CUP
Leurognathus	1	A	A	SS	M
Phaeognathus	1	T	D		CP
Plethodontinae					
Aneides	1	T	D		M,CUP
Eurycea	14?	A,T	A	SS,SW,C	CP,P,M,O,CUP,EP
Gyrinophilus	3?	S	A	SS,C	M,CUP
Haideotriton	1	A	A	C	CP
Hemidactylium	1	T	A	SW,SS	CP,P,M,O,CUP
Plethodon	33?	T	D		CP,P,M,O,CUP,EP
Pseudotriton	2?	S	A	SW,SS	CP,M,P,CUP
Stereochilus	1	A	A	SW	CP
Typhlomolge	2	A	A	C	EP
Typhlotriton	1	S	A	C,SS	O
Order Anura — Frogs					
Family Bufonidae					
Bufo	7	T	A	P,L,SW	CP,P,M,O,CUP,EP
Family Hylidae					
Acris	2	T	A	P,L	CP,P,M,O,CUP,EP
Hyla	8	T	A	P,L,SW	CP,P,M,O,CUP,EP
Pseudacris	9	T	A	P,L,SW	CP,P,M,O,CUP,EP
Family Microhylidae					
Gastrophryne	2	T	A	P	CP,P,O,CUP,EP
Hypopachus	1	T	A	P	CP
Family Leptodactylidae					
Syrrhophus	2	T	D		CP
Family Pelobatidae					
Scaphiopus	3	T	A	P	CP,P,O,CUP,EP

Table 1. Continued.

Taxa	Number Species	Adult Habitat	Larval Habitat	Aquatic Habitats	Physiographic Provinces
Family Ranidae					
Rana	14?	S,T	A	L,P,SW,R,LS,SS	CP,P,M,O,CUP,EP

[1] Adult habitat (T = terrestrial, S = semiaquatic, A = aquatic); Larval habitat (A = aquatic, D = direct development on land); Aquatic habitats (R = river, LS = large stream, SS = small stream, P = pond, L = lake, SW = swamp, bog or seep, C = cave); Physiographic provinces (CP = Coastal Plain, P = Piedmont, M = Appalachian Mountains, O = Ozark, Ouachita and Boston mountains, CUP = Cumberland Plateau, EP = Edwards Plateau). ? indicates that undescribed species are thought to be present.

[2] While most species have larvae that transform into adults, paedomorphic adults are not uncommon in some species or populations.

such as *Rana capito* and *Hyla gratiosa*, which require fishless temporary ponds for reproduction. Some species, such as *Bufo terrestris*, breed in a wide variety of wetland habitats.

TERRESTRIAL HABITATS

Although amphibians are usually associated with water, most species spend a substantial amount of time in terrestrial habitats. Individuals of some species often can be found at great distances from the nearest breeding ponds. For example, I have funnel-trapped many small frogs and salamanders in the harsh Florida sandhills 200 to greater than 800 m (656 to more than 2,624 feet) from the nearest water (Dodd, 1996). Franz et al. (1988) recorded a gopher frog (*Rana capito*) at a tortoise burrow 2 km (1.25 miles) from where the frog had been previously marked. Such long distance movements probably are not unusual. Greenberg (1993) captured southern toads (*Bufo terrestris*), eastern narrow-mouthed toads (*Gastrophryne carolinensis*), and eastern spadefoot toads (*Scaphiopus holbrooki*) in Florida sand pine scrub between 5 and 6 km (3.1 and 3.7 miles) from the nearest known water source.

Terrestrial refugia include caves (Saugey et al., 1988; Franz et al., 1994); burrows of tortoises (Jackson and Milstrey, 1989), pocket gophers, crayfish (especially by *Rana areolata* and *R. capito*) and other invertebrates; tree roots; rock crevices; surface debris; and probably many other subterranean habitats. Treefrogs often use arboreal retreats. Selected references on the use of terrestrial habitats by amphibians that require water to breed include Gibbons and Bennett (1974), Bennett et al. (1980), Semlitsch (1981), Campbell and Christman (1982), Pearson et al. (1987), Stout et al. (1988), Scott (1991), McCoy and Mushinsky (1992), and Dodd (1996).

AQUATIC AMPHIBIAN LIFE HISTORY

In North America, most amphibians have a biphasic life cycle consisting of an aquatic egg and larval stage, metamorphosis into a terrestrial adult, and migration back to water to breed and lay eggs. The time between metamorphosis and first breeding varies among species, although this period is usually one to four years (Duellman and Trueb, 1986). The life span of wild individuals also varies. For example, *Gastrophryne carolinensis* may live four or more years (Dodd, 1995a), whereas the hellbender may live greater than 25 years (Peterson et al., 1983). Generally, salamanders live longer than frogs, and larger species live longer than smaller species (Duellman and Trueb, 1986). Duellman and Trueb (1986) discussed life history variation and the factors that affect reproduction, life cycles, and other facets of amphibian biology.

There are exceptions to the "typical" amphibian life cycle. All non-hemidactyliine salamanders of the family Plethodontidae (i.e., *Aneides* and *Plethodon* species), two species of *Desmognathus* (*D. aeneus* and *D. wrighti*), and *Phaeognathus hubrichti* skip the aquatic larval stage (Table 1). Instead, eggs are laid on land in moist environments, the larval stage is passed within the egg, and the hatchling resembles a miniature adult.

Several salamanders, including all *Siren* spp., *Pseudobranchus* spp., *Necturus* spp., and *Typhlomolge* spp., some *Eurycea* spp., and *Haideotriton wallacei* and *Cryptobranchus alleganiensis*, are entirely aquatic and never leave the water or boggy wetlands. Eggs are deposited in vegetation, debris, or under rocks, young usually pass through a larval stage, and adults often retain larval features, such as exposed gills. *Amphiuma* spp. generally are aquatic, although eggs are deposited on land near water. Other species (*Ambystoma talpoideum, Notophthalmus* spp.) have individuals or populations that are facultative paedomorphs (that is, they become reproductively active while otherwise retaining larval phenotypes, and they never transform into adults while permanent water remains).

All native southeastern frogs, with the exception of the direct developing *Syrrhophus* spp., have a "typical" amphibian life cycle. Both of the introduced *Eleutherodactylus* spp. are direct developers with no aquatic life stage.

STUDIES AND LITERATURE ON IMPERILED SOUTHEASTERN AMPHIBIANS

Prior to the second half of the 20th century, most studies of the aquatic Amphibia of the southeastern United States focused on general distribution patterns, morphological systematics, and life history field observations. The literature stemming from those studies has been summarized in several major monographs and field guides (e.g., for Alabama see Mount, 1975; for Florida see Carr, 1940, and Ashton and Ashton, 1988; for Kentucky see Barbour, 1971; for Louisiana see Dundee and Rossman, 1989; for Texas see Dixon, 1987, and Garrett and Barker, 1987; for Virginia and the Carolinas see Martof et al., 1980; and for West Virginia see Green and Pauley, 1987). Books that will include extensive data on the biology of aquatic amphibians are in progress for the states of Tennessee and Virginia. In addition, separate herpetological bibliographies are available for the states of Florida (Enge and Dodd, 1992), Tennessee (Redmond et al., 1990), and Virginia (Mitchell, 1981).

Relatively recent concern for individual species has resulted in a series of books and journal articles which include a status assessment of actually or potentially imperiled aquatic amphibians. Reviews are available for West Virginia (Pauley and Canterbury, 1990), Virginia (Linzey, 1979; Pague and Mitchell, 1987; Terwilliger, 1991), North Carolina (Cooper et al., 1977), South Carolina (Harrison et al., 1979), Tennessee (Echternacht, 1980), Kentucky (Branson et al., 1981), Florida (McDiarmid, 1978; Moler, 1992d), Alabama (Mount, 1986c), and Arkansas (Reagan, 1974). Ashton (1976) provided a national checklist of amphibians and reptiles in need of conservation, and Bury et al. (1980) summarized

Table 2. Aquatic-dependent amphibians known or suspected of requiring conservation or management attention in the southeastern United States.[1]

Taxon	Threats — Rarity	States	Information Sources
Order Caudata — Salamanders			
Ambystoma cingulatum	habitat destruction	AL,FL,GA,SC	Ashton (1992); Palis (1992, 1993); M. Bailey, J. Palis, W. Seyle, J. McLemore (all pers. comm.); Means (1986c); Bury et al. (1980); Means et al. (1996)
A. mabeei	habitat destruction, forestry	VA	Pague and Mitchell (1991a)
A. maculatum	drought	GA	C. Camp (pers. comm.)
A. talpoideum	unknown, peripheral	AR,KY,NC,TN,VA	Echternacht (1980); Branson et al. (1981); Braswell (1977a); Pague and Mitchell (1991b); Reagan (1974); Trauth et al. (1993a)
A. texanum	rare?	AL	Folkerts (1986b)
A. tigrinum	locally rare, habitat destruction, exotics	AL,FL,VA	Mount (1986a); Travis (1992); Pague and Buhlmann (1991); M. Bailey (pers. comm.)
Amphiuma pholeter	rare?, siltation	AL,FL,GA	Bury et al. (1980); Means (1986d, 1992b)
A. tridactylum	unknown	KY	Branson et al. (1981)
Cryptobranchus alleganiensis	rare?, peripheral, habitat destruction, pollution, collecting	AL, AR, FL, GA, KY, MS NC, SC, TN, VA, WV	Redmond (1986); Pague (1991c); Echternacht (1980); Branson et al. (1981); Trauth et al. (1992, 1993b); Bruce (1977a); Bury et al. (1980); Reagan (1974); Nickerson and Mays (1973)
Desmognathus auriculatus	unknown	AL,FL,SC	Means (1986e); S. Christman, J. Harrison (both pers. comm.)

Table 2. Continued.

Taxon	Threats — Rarity	States	Information Sources
D. ochrophaeus	rare?	AL	Folkerts (1986c)
D. monticola	unknown, peripheral	AL,FL	Folkerts (1986a); Means (1992c)
D. quadramaculatus	peripheral, collecting	WV	Pauley and Canterbury (1990)
D. welteri	unknown	TN	Echternacht (1980)
Eurycea aquatica	habitat alteration	AL,TN	Bury et al. (1980)
E. longicauda	peripheral	NC	Bruce (1977b)
E. lucifuga	habitat destruction, collecting	WV	Pauley and Canterbury (1990)
E. multiplicata	habitat alteration, pesticides?	AR	Reagan (1974)
E. nana	habitat alteration	TX	Bury et al. (1980); USFWS (1984a)
E. soosorum	habitat destruction	TX	Chippindale et al. (1993)
E. tridentifera	rare?	TX	Bury et al. (1980)
E. tynerensis	habitat alteration	AR	Reagan (1974); Bury et al. (1980)
Gyrinophilus gulolineatus	habitat alteration, collection	TN	Echternacht (1980)
G. palleucus	unknown, habitat alteration	AL,TN	Simmons (1975); Ashton (1986); habitat alteration Echternacht (1980); Bury et al. (1980)
Haideotriton wallacei	rare	FL,GA	Bury et al. (1980); Means (1992d)
Hemidactylium scutatum	peripheral, unknown	AR,FL,KY,TN	Means (1992e); J. Palis (pers. comm.); Echternacht (1980); Branson et al. (1981); Reagan (1974); Saugey and Trauth (1991)
Leurognathus marmoratus	habitat destruction	VA	Gourley and Pague (1991)
Necturus sp.	habitat destruction	AL	Ashton and Peavy (1986); M. Bailey (pers. comm.)
N. lewisi	habitat alteration	NC	Stephan (1977); Bury et al. (1980)
Notophthalmus meridionalis	habitat destruction	TX	Judd (1985)

Table 2. Continued.

Taxon	Threats — Rarity	States	Information Sources
N. perstriatus	habitat destruction, drought	FL,GA	Christman and Means (1992); Dodd (1993); R. Franz (pers. comm.); Bury et al. (1980); Franz and Smith (1993); Dodd and LaClaire (1995)
Pseudobranchus striatus lustricolus	rare?	FL	Bury et al. (1980); Moler (1988, 1992c)
Pseudotriton montanus flavissimus	unknown	AL	Means (1986f)
P. ruber vioscai	unknown	AL	Means (1986g)
Siren intermedia	unknown	KY	Branson et al. (1981)
S. lacertina	rare?	AL	Mount (1986b)
Stereochilus marginatus	peripheral, forestry?	FL	Christman (1992); J. Palis (pers. comm.)
Typhlomolge rathbuni	habitat alteration	TX	Bury et al. (1980)
Typhlotriton spelaeus	pollution, collecting	AR	Reagan (1974)
Order Anura — Frogs			
Bufo boustonensis	habitat destruction	TX	Bury et al. (1980); USFWS (1984b)
B. quercicus	forestry	VA	Pague (1991a)
B. valliceps	rare?, peripheral	AR	Reagan (1974)
Hyla andersonii	habitat destruction	AL,FL,NC,SC	Means and Longden (1976); Mount (1980); Moler (1980, 1981); Cely and Sorrow (1983); Means (1986a, 1992a); Palmer (1977); Bury et al. (1980)
H. avivoca	unknown	AR, KY	Branson et al. (1981); Trauth (1992a)
H. cinerea	unknown	KY	Branson et al. (1981)
H. gratiosa	forestry, habitat destruction, rare?	KY,TN,VA	Echternacht (1980); Pague and Young (1991) Branson et al. (1981)
Pseudacris streckeri illinoensis	habitat destruction	AR	Bury et al. (1980); Trauth (1992b)
Rana areolata	unknown	KY	Branson et al. (1981)

Table 2. Continued.

Taxon	Threats — Rarity	States	Information Sources
R. capito aesopus	habitat destruction	FL,GA	Godley (1992); R. Franz, P. Moler, W. Seyle (all pers. comm.); Bury et al. (1980); Franz and Smith (1993)
R. c. capito	habitat destruction	GA,NC,SC	Braswell (1977b, 1993); S. Bennett, W. Seyle (both pers. comm.)
R. c. sevosa	habitat destruction	AL,FL,LA.MS	Bailey (1991); Dundee and Rossman (1989); M. Bailey (pers. comm.); Means (1986b)
R. okaloosae	rare?	FL	Moler (1985, 1992a)
R. palustris	peripheral	FL	Moler (1992b)
R. sylvatica	peripheral, drought	GA	C. Camp (pers. comm.)
R. virgatipes	peripheral, drought, habitat destruction, pollution	FL,VA	Means and Christman (1992); Pague (1991b)
Scaphiopus bombifrons	rare?	AR	Trauth (1989)
S. holbrooki	rare?	WV	Pauley and Canterbury (1990)

[1] Affiliations of personnel contributing information: Mark Bailey (Alabama Natural Heritage Program); Steve Bennett (South Carolina Wildlife and Marine Resources Department); Carlos Camp (Piedmont College); Steve Christman (Quincy, FL); Richard Franz (Florida Museum of Natural History); Julian Harrison (Charleston Museum); Jeffrey McLemore (South Carolina Nongame and Heritage Trust Program); Paul Moler (Florida Game and Fresh Water Fish Commission); John Palis (Jonesboro, IL); Win Seyle (U.S. Army Corps of Engineers).

the status of amphibians throughout the United States.

In generally assessing historical information about amphibians residing in the Southeast, endangered and threatened amphibian accounts were written by individuals familiar with the biology of the species (see Table 2). However, few assessments were based on thorough studies and none included long-term quantitative data. Symposia have seemed to highlight more of what was not known about a species than what was known. Edited proceedings have usually contained information on life history, distribution, status, and threats, whereas journal articles contained little background data.

Concern about the status of particular herpetofauna species or communities also has resulted in many inventory programs, but much of this information remains unpublished and generally unavailable. For example, intensive herpetofaunal inventories based on quantitative sampling were prepared for Lake Conway, Florida (Bancroft et al., 1983), the proposed Cross Florida Barge Canal route in the Ocala National Forest, the proposed phosphate mining area in the Osceola National Forest, and the St. Marks National Wildlife Refuge in Florida. Unfortunately, reports of the results of such surveys are difficult to obtain and often lack crucial details concerning site locations, sampling methods and intensity, and statistical analysis. Herpetofauna inventories of various other national forests (e.g., Pearson et al., 1987), military reservations (e.g., Williamson and Moulis, 1979), and state and private lands also exist for areas scattered throughout the Southeast. Herpetofaunal inventories are presently under way at Eglin Air Force Base, Florida; Ft. Stewart, Georgia; and Camp Blanding, Florida.

Recent examples of single species amphibian surveys include *Rana capito* in North Carolina (Braswell, 1993); *R. capito* and *Notophthalmus perstriatus* in Florida (Franz and Smith, 1993); *N. perstriatus* in Georgia (Dodd and LaClaire, 1995); and *Ambystoma cingulatum* in Florida (Palis, 1992, 1993) (also see Table 2). All southeastern states now have Natural Heritage Programs to assemble data on declining species. Some of these programs are well advanced in data analysis (e.g., Florida), whereas others are just getting started (e.g., Georgia).

In the 1970s, ecological studies generally became much more intensive and quantified, and often integrated field and laboratory work to examine hypotheses of species interactions. Although they did not initially begin as monitoring studies, the ecological studies at the Savannah River Site (SRS) in South Carolina (see Gibbons and Semlitsch, 1991, and references therein) and Hairston's studies of terrestrial salamander competition (Hairston and Wiley, 1993) in the southern Appalachians are the only studies with truly long-term continuous data sets in the Southeast. Only the SRS study has data on all of the aquatic amphibian species in the local community.

Other studies are available covering a shorter time span. Dodd (1992) systematically monitored the amphibian community at a temporary pond in north Florida sandhills from 1985 to 1990. H. Mushinsky (University of South Florida) and A. F. Scott (Austin Peay State University) have quantitatively monitored the amphibian community on a Florida sandhill and in north-central Tennessee, respectively, since the early 1980s, although these data are not yet published. Delis (1993) compared amphibian community changes from the 1970s to the 1990s in an area of west-central Florida undergoing urbanization. Other studies have monitored a single species in a region or at a single locality for various amounts of time (M. Bailey, Alabama Natural Heritage Program; J. Palis, Jonesboro, Illinois; W. Seyle, U.S. Army Corps of Engineers, all pers. comm.), but the results of such monitoring are generally not available.

In conclusion, the literature on potentially imperiled amphibians in the Southeast is scattered and based on few quantitative studies. Much information remains unpublished or is otherwise unavailable. Therefore, it is often impossible to assess the accuracy or thoroughness of completed work. The only long-term data set on continuously monitored aquatic-dependent amphibians in the Southeast is available from SRS. At SRS, much annual variation occurs in the number of reproductive adults visiting a wetland. Reproductive output also varies annually, even when substantial numbers of adults reproduce (Pechmann et al., 1991).

There are numerous published studies on the ecology of individual aquatic-dependent southeastern species or groups of species. Locations used for such studies could serve as monitoring sites to assess the status of the species and habitat since the original studies were completed. Examples of some original assessments include the work of Trauth et al. (1992) assessing the status of an Arkansas population of hellbenders (*Cryptobranchus alleganiensis*) previously studied in the mid-1980s and Dodd's (1991) study of the Red Hills salamander (*Phaeognathus hubrichti*). Few follow-up assessment studies have been undertaken.

THREATS TO SOUTHEASTERN AQUATIC SPECIES

Amphibians that depend on aquatic environments in the Southeast potentially are vulnerable to a great variety of threats, although few detailed studies have specifically considered such problems within the region. The integrity of both aquatic and terrestrial habitats is important to amphibian survival, even among species that never venture beyond a single habitat type. Furthermore, the various life history stages (eggs, larvae, young, adults) may be differentially susceptible or sensitive to environmental perturbations. Studies that assess only one phase of a species' life cycle (e.g., surveys only of breeding habitat) may overlook important ecological requirements of other life history phases. Although we tend to discuss conservation in terms of individual species, an ecosystem approach that is sensitive to all life history phases is necessary to ensure the habitat integrity that ultimately will continue to support individual species.

Literature references to southeastern aquatic-dependent amphibians that currently might be in need of some degree of management are provided in Table 2. Habitat destruction and alteration are the most commonly identified factors affecting species' status. There are many cases where a species appears rare but is geographically peripheral to the region in question, or its true status is unknown. There is only one case where a "mysterious" decline may have occurred regarding an aquatic species. The salamander *Desmognathus auriculatus* appears to have declined or disappeared from sections of the Atlantic Coastal Plain in South Carolina and peninsular Florida (S. Christman, Quincy, Florida; J. Harrison, Charleston Museum, both pers. comm.), but no systematic surveys have been undertaken. However, populations of coastal plain desmognathine salamanders are known to fluctuate substantially in numbers from one year to the next (B. Means, Coastal Plains Institute, pers. comm.). Some specific threats to aquatic amphibians are discussed briefly below.

Habitat Destruction and Alteration

Even before the arrival of Europeans, Native Americans exerted considerable influence upon southeastern landscapes. Villages formed in circular patterns were interconnected by corridors and surrounded by considerable amounts of buffer land used for hunting

(Hammett, 1992). Lands were used for agriculture and large areas were burned to clear land and to improve hunting. After colonization by Europeans, land clearing and ecosystem modification accelerated and have culminated in the present frenzy to redesign the landscape.

The Southeast has been rapidly increasing in human population for several decades, and its metropolitan areas are among the fastest growing population centers in the United States. In Florida alone, where more than 9 million acres (3,642,300 ha) of wetlands already have disappeared (Cerulean, 1991), the population increases by a net 900 new-comers each day. In Arkansas, 6 million of the original 10 million acres (2,428,200 of 4,047,000 ha) of Mississippi Delta wetlands have been converted to agricultural land (Smith et al., 1984). In a west-central peninsular Florida study, species richness was less in urbanized areas than in nearby pristine areas, and temporary pond breeding species disappeared entirely from the urbanized site (Delis, 1993). Although vast areas have been cleared in the Southeast for agriculture, industry, and urban use, there is virtually no assessment of the landscape effects of land conversion on amphibian populations. It seems evident, however, that habitat changes (see papers in Hackney et al., 1992; Boyce and Martin, 1993), and with them changes in aquatic amphibian populations, have been enormous.

Habitat alteration may occur without obvious large-scale topographic changes. For example, a massive boom in human population on the Edwards Plateau of Texas has increased the withdrawal of ground water from the Edwards Aquifer. As more and more water is withdrawn, water tables have decreased. In the future, springs and streams in this region are likely to dry completely, especially during periods of drought. This situation could lead to the loss of a unique aquatic biota that includes spring and cavernicolous salamanders (U.S. Fish and Wildlife Service, 1984a; Chippindale et al., 1993).

Habitat Fragmentation

Although habitat fragmentation affects biota in different ways (e.g., Mader, 1984), land use patterns resulting in fragmentation can influence amphibian population genetic structure (Reh and Seitz, 1990). Amphibian populations are most abundant when there is a mosaic of habitats located within a regional landscape (Mann et al., 1991). In such a context, metapopulations may develop which result in a dynamic equilibrium through time. However, if populations become overly fragmented, emigration and immigration may be inhibited or stopped, thus preventing recolonization from source populations. The effect of fragmentation on amphibians depends on the degree of isolation (Sjogren, 1991a). Small, isolated populations are particularly susceptible to environmental perturbations (Sjogren, 1991b) and to stochastic variation in demography that can lead to extinction even without external perturbations (Lande, 1988; Pimm et al., 1988). Isolation by habitat fragmentation thus becomes a threat to the regional persistence of species.

Forestry Practices

Most discussions of the effects of forestry on amphibians in the Southeast focus on salamanders in clearcuts (Blymer and McGinnes, 1977; Ash, 1988; Dodd, 1991; Petranka et al., 1993; Ash and Bruce, 1994; Petranka, 1994), although a few recent studies have examined amphibian communities in the coastal plain (Phelps, 1993; Dodd, 1995b; O'Neill, 1995; Phelps and Lancia, 1995; Means et al., 1996). Clearcutting reduces salamander populations because it eliminates shade, reduces forest litter (especially if litter is piled and burned), increases soil temperature, reduces soil moisture, and destroys wet-lands. Herbicides are frequently used in such operations, yet little is known of their effects on amphibians (but see Bidwell and Gorrie, 1995).

Depending on the type of site preparation, clearcutting practices also reduce or elimi-nate burrows and other hiding places needed by aquatic habitat-dependent amphibians when they are away from their breeding sites. For example, clearcutting an area adjacent to an *Ambystoma talpoideum* breeding pond in Louisiana lowered the survivorship of im-migrating adults using the clearcut site and displaced other adults to less suitable habitat (Raymond and Hardy, 1991). Other attributes which affect amphibian persistence after timber cutting include the status of amphibian populations prior to cutting, the type of cut (selective vs clear), the type of forest replanted, the size of the cut, the amount of time since last cut (Grant et al., 1994), and the distance to the nearest source populations. Mature southeastern pine plantations also support far fewer amphibians than adjacent deciduous forests (Bennett et al., 1980). In Florida sand pine scrub, clearcutting seems to mimic intensive wildfire; the richness and diversity of amphibians appear more dependent on the nearest water source for breeding than on the type of disturbance (Greenberg, 1993). However, clearcutting reduced amphibian species abundance in pine flatwoods tenfold by adversely affecting reproductive success (Enge and Marion, 1986). Regarding the effects of timbering, stream-dwelling species and their larvae have received little attention in the South-east, although adverse effects to stream-dwelling amphibians caused by logging in the Pacific Northwest are well documented (Bury and Corn, 1988; Corn and Bury, 1989).

On the southeastern Coastal Plain, vast pine plantations have replaced the native longleaf pine (*Pinus palustris*) savanna. During planting and site preparation, much of the land was ditched in an effort to speed water runoff. Literally thousands of acres of wetlands disap-peared or were substantially altered. Ditching occurred between ponds to facilitate water transfer; water essentially flowed downhill, although slowly, thus reducing available hydroperiods for amphibian larval development. A second type of ditching occurs around wetlands. Circumferential ditching results in lowered water tables with concomitant veg-etative changes, thus drastically altering or eliminating hydroperiods. Unditched ponds are more persistent than ditched ponds, and have greater amphibian species richness dur-ing dry periods (Harris and Vickers, 1984; Vickers et al., 1985). In addition, more aquatic amphibian species are associated with unditched ponds. This is especially important be-cause many temporary pond-breeding amphibians exhibit breeding site fidelity and other obligate breeding requirements which can be impacted by ditching.

The loss of the longleaf pine forest on the coastal plain of the southeastern United States has been dramatic (Means and Grow, 1985; Noss, 1989; Boyce and Martin, 1993; Stout and Marion, 1993; Ware et al., 1993). Concern for the survival of the coastal plain forest in Georgia was expressed at least as early as 1906 because of logging, turpentining, and land clearing for agriculture and "civilization" (Harper, 1906). Since the 1940s, old-growth longleaf pine forest has been converted to slash (*P. elliottii*) and loblolly (*P. taeda*) pine plantations throughout the Southeast. In southeast Georgia, for example, longleaf pine declined 36 percent between 1981 and 1988 to 230,000 acres (93,081 ha; see Johnson, 1988), whereas in southwest Georgia, longleaf pine declined four percent during these same years to 205,000 acres (82,963 ha)(Thompson, 1988). Today, less than one percent of the old growth longleaf pine forest remains (of the more than 70 million acres

[28,329,000 ha] present when Europeans colonized the continent). Most remaining forest is scattered and poorly managed. Even in national forests, longleaf pine has declined substantially (Means and Grow, 1985). In the last few decades, drastic changes probably have occurred in the composition and structure of the amphibian community in regions that formerly held longleaf pine (Dodd, 1995b; Means et al., 1996), but no baseline data exist to document the effects of this continuing massive landscape alteration.

Mining

Extensive coal strip mining is carried out in West Virginia, Virginia, Kentucky, Tennessee, and Alabama. In many instances, mining occurs directly through small streams or ponds, and mine tailings are pushed into the larger rivers. In Florida, vast areas have been strip-mined for phosphate. Mining not only destroys aquatic amphibian habitats outright, it also results in toxic pollution, decreased pH, and siltation of streams and rivers. Low pH combined with high levels of conductivity (an indication of the presence of pollutants) limit the presence of larval salamanders of the genus *Desmognathus* in mine-affected streams of the Cumberland Plateau (Gore, 1983). Paradoxically, amphibians have bred in strip mine ponds as long as the pH was not too low and toxic waste was prevented from entering the pond (Turner and Fowler, 1981; Lacki et al., 1992).

Transportation Corridors

Transportation corridors, especially roads, can have serious deleterious effects on amphibian populations (Langton, 1989). Road construction can lead to habitat destruction in both terrestrial and aquatic environments, and can negatively alter breeding habitats through increased siltation. Increased siltation can lead to increased amphibian mortality because of its own secondary effects. For example, nearly all aquatic life was eliminated downstream after U.S. Highway 441 was rebuilt in 1963 in the Great Smoky Mountains National Park. Toxic substances associated with leachates from roadfill were suspected as the cause. Laboratory experiments confirmed that roadfill leachates were toxic to larval shovel-nosed salamanders (*Leurognathus marmoratus*). The major components of the leachate responsible for toxicity included low pH combined with high heavy metal concentrations (Mathews and Morgan, 1982).

Roads may separate overwintering sites from breeding sites and increase mortality as animals attempt to cross. For example, Heine (1987) demonstrated that 26 vehicles per hour on one road was enough traffic to ensure that no toads successfully crossed. Road construction also can lead to habitat fragmentation, and in doing so can hinder immigration and emigration, and isolate populations (Laan and Verboom, 1990) leading to deleterious effects associated with small population size (Sjogren, 1991b). Furthermore, the noise levels and artificial lights associated with traffic may disrupt breeding activities. Noise makes it difficult to hear conspecifics or causes frogs to completely stop calling (author's pers. obs.). Bright artificial lighting can adversely affect frogs' abilities to detect and consume prey (Buchanan, 1993).

Climate Change

If climate changes, possibly in response to increasing levels of greenhouse gases, then there are bound to be changes in the diversity of southeastern amphibians. Most of our endemic species and species-rich amphibian communities are found on the higher elevations of mountains in the cool southern Appalachians and Ozarks, or in specialized coastal plain habitats, such as temporary ponds. Spring adapted salamanders of the Edwards Plateau are sensitive to alterations in ground water levels. These species would be particularly susceptible to climate changes which alter rainfall patterns or elevate mean annual temperatures. However, the potential for changes in amphibian diversity seems to have been overlooked in the climate change debate. For example, amphibians are mentioned, briefly, only twice in 26 chapters of a recent book which examines the effects of global warming on biological diversity (Peters and Lovejoy, 1992).

pH

The acidity of aquatic habitats can play a major role in limiting the distribution of amphibians. Decreased levels of pH in aquatic habitats may result from acidic precipitation or point-sources of pollution, such as abandoned mines. Acid concentration may increase steadily or come in pulses, such as during heavy rains or from snow melt. Although the Southeast has not experienced as many problems from acid rain as other parts of the United States, the acid content of our precipitation is increasing (Haines, 1979). For example, H+ increased 19-fold from 1955 to 1979 in Great Smoky Mountains National Park (Mathews and Larson, 1980). Bioassay results suggested that pH levels were near toxic to larval shovel-nosed salamanders, although not as toxic to adults (Mathews and Larson, 1980).

The literature on the effects of pH on amphibians is voluminous and complex (Freda, 1986; Dunson and Wyman, 1992). Low pH has different effects on different species of amphibians and, indeed, there may be intraspecific differences in pH sensitivity that varies geographically. Furthermore, these intraspecific differences may or may not have a genetic basis (Pierce and Wooten, 1992). In general, the eggs and developing larvae are the most sensitive life stages to low pH (< 4.5). A low pH alters the cellular chemical environment by disrupting the Na+ and Cl- balance both in terrestrial (Frisbie and Wyman, 1991) and aquatic life stages (Freda and Dunson, 1984). This, in turn, affects salamander spatial distribution since salamanders avoid soils of low pH (Wyman and Hawksley-Lescault, 1987; Freda and Taylor, 1992). Low pH also may impair the vitally important chemosensory system of amphibians (Griffiths, 1993) and inhibit larval feeding (Roudebush, 1988).

Low pH can also have indirect effects which can kill eggs, larvae, or even adults (Sadinski and Dunson, 1992). A low pH acts to inhibit amphibian egg capsule enlargement, and thus limits the space available to the growing embryo. In addition, high acidity inhibits proper jelly formation. Jelly allows spacing of the eggs within an egg mass which ensures that each developing embryo has an adequate oxygen supply (Seymour, 1994). If jelly does not form properly, death from anoxia results. Chronic or intermittent low pH also can disrupt environmental trophic interactions (Sadinski and Dunson, 1992), and can lead to problems associated with long-term environmental stress. For example, phytoplankton which are fed upon by tadpoles are also sensitive to low pH (Haines, 1981).

Toxic Substances

A great many substances are likely toxic to amphibians, at least during part of their life cycle. Toxicants need not be synthetic chemicals. For example, salt spread on roads during winter can affect the chemistry of amphibian breeding sites. Toxic chemicals can enter the environment in many ways, both intentionally and accidentally. There have been numerous instances of inadvertent release of toxic materials into aquatic habitats because of highway or railroad accidents.

Surprisingly little research has been done on the effects of toxic chemicals on amphibians, and even then most work has focused on only one part of the life cycle. Examples of toxic materials known to adversely affect amphibians include heavy metals (aluminum, mercury, selenium), pesticides (toxaphene, heptachlor, malathion, endrin, methoxychlor), herbicides (DEF, trifluralin, atrazine), fungicides (furanace, malachite green), phenols, carbon tetrachloride, and nitrite. Literature summaries are provided in Birge et al. (1980), Power et al. (1989), and Hall and Henry (1992).

Data on the level of toxic chemicals in wild populations of amphibians, much less those of the Southeast, are nearly non-existent. However, Hall et al. (1985) noted metabolites of DDT as well as PCBs (primarily chlordane constituents) in *Necturus lewisi* from the Tar and Neuse rivers, North Carolina. The herbicide atrazine was implicated as contributing to large frog (*Rana pipiens*) die-offs in Wisconsin (Hine et al., 1981).

In addition to direct effects, certain toxicants may affect amphibians differently depending on pH. For example, aluminum has adverse effects upon amphibians, but the level of adversity differs depending on species, life stage, and pH (Beattie and Tyler-Jones, 1992; Bradford et al., 1992; Jung and Jagoe, 1993). Lowered pHs amplify the toxicity of heavy metals to amphibians.

Endocrine Mimics

Many chlorinated chemicals (DDT, PCBs, etc.) have been dumped in huge quantities into the environment during the 20th century, and as they travel throughout food chains they become magnified in concentration. Chlorinated chemicals can act to impair development, block intracellular communication, and induce enzymes that break down hormones. In addition, many of these persistent compounds function, even in minute quantities, as hormones, especially mimicking estrogen. Some of the side effects of endocrine mimics are thyroid dysfunction, metabolic abnormalities, decreased fertility, birth deformities, abnormal sexual development, and immunosuppression (Carey and Bryant, 1995; Stebbins and Cohen, 1995). Although no specific examples exist yet for amphibians, xenobiotics have been implicated in partial sex reversals and gonadal feminization in a wild Florida population of American alligators (*Alligator mississippiensis*) (Guillette et al., 1994).

Amphibians are likely to be especially sensitive to the action of endocrine mimics because they are in close direct contact with chemicals in their environment, and the amphibian skin and egg capsule are highly permeable. Because hormones normally function in minute quantities and are vital to normal development (Hourdry, 1993), susceptibility to xenobiotics could be devastating during the complex changes that occur during hormonally-induced amphibian metamorphosis.

Ultraviolet-B Radiation

Recent evidence suggests ultraviolet-B (UV-B) radiation has adverse effects on amphibian larval hatching success and that sensitivity to UV-B varies among species (Blaustein et al., 1994a) or is exacerbated by low pH (Long et al., 1995). Species with high levels of photolyase (e.g., *Pseudacris* spp.), an enzyme involved in DNA repair of ultraviolet radiation damage, are less prone to the adverse effects of UV-B radiation than species with low levels of photolyase (e.g., *Bufo* spp., *Rana* spp.). Many populations of *Bufo* spp. and *Rana* spp. have declined in the western United States, whereas *Pseudacris triseriata* populations have not. Frog embryos (*Rana clamitans* and *R. sylvatica*) exposed to high levels of UV-B had higher rates of developmental abnormalities and increased mortality than controls which were shielded from UV-B (Grant and Licht, 1993). UV-B also can have detrimental effects on embryo growth. UV-B radiation has increased recently in the northern hemisphere because of ozone depletion (Blumthaler and Ambach, 1990; Kerr and McElroy, 1993). If UV-B adversely affects southern Appalachian anurans, toads (*Bufo* spp.) and true frogs (*Rana* spp.) would seem most likely to be affected.

Exotics, Predators, and Competitors

There is no literature on the effects of the many exotic fishes in southeastern waters on native herpetofauna. Fish may be both competitors and predators of amphibians, depending on life cycle stage (Bristow, 1991). They have been implicated in declines of western amphibians both as predators (Bradford, 1989) and as disease vectors (Blaustein et al., 1994b). Stocking of predatory fishes in ponds previously free of fish undoubtedly leads to a change in the amphibian community because many amphibians are defenseless against fish predators. Conversion of temporary ponds to permanent ponds by digging and blasting, followed by fish introductions, often leads to a loss of the temporary pond breeding species. The effects of exotic frogs, especially the marine toad (*Bufo marinus*) and Cuban treefrog (*Osteopilus septentrionalis*), on native amphibians are unknown, although anuran species richness was reduced in at least one area having marine toads, compared to a similar area without them (Rossi, 1981). Release of other exotics undoubtedly occurs with unknown effects. One south Florida tropical fish dealer reported selling 50,000 eastern newts in Florida that originated from outside the state (Enge, 1991). Many of these exotic newts undoubtedly were released intentionally or unintentionally.

Birds and mammals also may exact a substantial toll on amphibian populations, especially exotic cattle egrets, armadillos, and wild hogs. In addition, populations of some native species, such as raccoons, may become so large because of a lack of natural predators and adaptation to human surroundings that they in turn reduce amphibian populations beyond normal levels. The overabundance of some native species is an issue which biologists are only beginning to confront (Garrott et al., 1993).

Finally, there are few data on the effects of exotic invertebrates, especially imported red fire ants (*Solenopsis invicta*), on native amphibians. Ground-dwelling vertebrates are especially sensitive to this ravenous predator (Mount, 1981), and fire ants have been reported to kill endangered Houston toads (*Bufo houstonensis*) as they metamorphose (Freed and Neitman, 1988). Fire ants are especially abundant in the moist perimeter surrounding ponds and lakes, and they can float in mats across ponds from vegetation clump to vegetation clump. Fire ants have few predators and have expanded their range throughout the Southeast.

Collecting

Collecting specimens for the pet trade or biological laboratories probably has had some impact on local amphibian populations, but few data are available. Trauth et al. (1992) suspected that collection of hellbenders in the Spring River, Arkansas, contributed to observed population declines. From 1 July 1990 to 30 June 1991, 804 salamanders and 18,170 frogs were collected legally for the Florida pet trade (Enge, 1991). Included were 5,066 *Hyla cinerea*, 3,265 *Bufo terrestris*, 2,674 *Hyla gratiosa*, and 249 *Siren lacertina*. In 1992, 246 salamanders and 23,019 frogs were collected and sold in the pet trade in Florida

(Enge, 1993). Most sales went to New York, Pennsylvania, and Tennessee. Concern for the effect of biological supply house collection on frog populations is not new (Gibbs et al., 1971). In the early 1970s, U.S. frog suppliers shipped 9 million frogs (over 326,000 kg) per year. The number of frogs shipped by southeastern supply houses is unknown.

Loss or Decline of Associates

If species that are preyed upon by amphibians decline or disappear, amphibian populations may be expected to follow suit. The use of pesticides and the influence of toxics, pH, and habitat alteration all may be expected to affect amphibian prey populations. In addition, amphibians sometimes rely upon the burrows of other species for shelter when they are away from ponds. If these associated animals are eliminated, fewer shelters may be available. A few amphibians inhabit the burrows of specific associates. For example, gopher frogs (*Rana capito*) nearly always reside in sympatric gopher tortoise (*Gopherus polyphemus*) burrows when the frogs are not at breeding ponds. Yet, the number of gopher tortoises is estimated to have declined by 80 percent during the last 100 years (Auffenberg and Franz, 1982). The effect of the decline of tortoises and their sheltering burrows on gopher frogs is unknown.

Drought, Cold, and Disease

Drought, cold, and disease are natural factors that affect amphibian communities (e.g., Dodd, 1993, 1995a). Drought can lead to localized extirpation. Excessive cold can induce winterkill in torpid amphibians. Disease can wipe out populations. However, the chronic effects of these factors on amphibian populations, if any, remain unknown. Under pristine conditions, amphibian populations often may expand and contract in response to such natural variables affecting local distribution, thus forming a dynamic equilibrium (Sjogren, 1993a, 1993b). Under present human-dominated landscapes, however, populations may be so fragmented or under such a variety of stresses that they are unable to rebound from extrinsic environmental factors causing periodic population fluctuations. If many amphibian populations function as metapopulations, the long-term survival of local populations might be jeopardized by isolation from source populations coupled with natural environmental fluctuations.

In fact, "natural" factors may not be as natural as they first appear. For example, droughts may result from global climate change or they may be magnified by habitat alteration such as deforestation or overgrazing. The effects of disease also might be facilitated by human activity. Carey (1993a, 1993b) has proposed a model whereby sublethal stress (such as that associated with chronic low but sublethal pH, or high concentration of a toxicant, or increased UV-B radiation) induces either direct or indirect immunosuppression because of the prolonged elevation of adrenal cortical hormones. Depressed immunity makes the animal more prone to naturally occurring pathogens, such as red-leg disease causing bacteria (*Aeromonas* spp.), especially during periods of torpor. This model is consistent with observations on declining amphibians in many Rocky Mountain populations where amphibian populations have been known to decline gradually and then one year simply fail to emerge from hibernation.

A pathogenic fungus has been implicated recently in the decline and disappearance of *Bufo boreas* in the western United States (Blaustein et al., 1994b). The fungus (*Saprolegnia ferax*) is circumglobal in distribution and commonly occurs on fish. However, fish are not native to the high mountain habitats occupied by *B. boreas*, and the pathogen is thought to have been introduced when trout and salmon were stocked in high mountain streams and lakes. The same fungus has extirpated other frog populations in the U.S. and Europe (for a review of this topic see Blaustein et al., 1994b). Although the extent of amphibian fungal infections is unknown in the Southeast, every egg mass (*Rana* sp.) I examined during March 1994 in several ponds on Trail Ridge in southern Georgia was infected by an as yet unidentified fungus.

SUMMARY

The southeastern United States holds a rich temperate amphibian assemblage containing a great degree of endemism. Endemic species are especially well represented among the salamanders. A varied topography and complex geologic history have provided the necessary conditions that have resulted in this region's high level of speciation. However, the amphibians of this area, and particularly the fully aquatic species, face a multitude of threats to their long-term existence. These threats generally do not act independently, but instead act in concert to have potentially serious long-term effects. Many amphibian species have been identified as needing conservation programs and management, but few scientific studies have assessed direct effects to species or ecosystems. There also are few studies detailed enough to show trends or to separate unnatural trends from normal population fluctuations.

Although natural population fluctuations undoubtedly exist, it is extremely naive and certainly not objective to call simply for "more monitoring" (Pechmann and Wilbur, 1994). At a time when conservation related funding is nearly nonexistent and no agencies seem able to initiate long-term monitoring on a scale required to assess wide-ranging threats to amphibians, the call for more monitoring seems an effective mask for doing nothing. How can interest be generated in monitoring "common" or non-threatened species, much less communities and ecosystems, when programs directed at the conservation of critically endangered species are under-funded or not funded at all? Given the cumulative assaults on the biosphere in the late 20th century, I suggest Chicken Little is better in tune with biological and political reality than Nero with his fiddle (see Blaustein, 1994). Rome, after all, burned.

As Gibbons (1988) has discussed, a new attitude is needed toward the recognition of the importance of amphibians to ecosystem functioning. No longer can these species be assigned a role of non-importance in wildlife and land management. Attention must be focused on threats to species inasmuch as these threats may be symptomatic of serious environmental problems. We need to study the seemingly common species (Dodd and Franz, 1993), as well as the rare or endangered species. Our casual perceptions may not always give an accurate assessment of population status. Finally, we need an ecosystem, landscape, and watershed approach to understanding the role of amphibians in imperiled aquatic systems as well as adequate funding from private and governmental agencies (Mittermeier et al., 1992) to carry out necessary research and management programs.

ACKNOWLEDGEMENTS

I thank Ronn Altig, Dick Franz, Marian Griffey, and Stan Trauth for comments on the manuscript. Members of the southeastern Declining Amphibian Populations Task Force supplied some information used in this paper. I thank Dave Collins for inviting me to participate in the important imperiled aquatic fauna symposium. This paper is dedicated to the late Roger W. Barbour, who introduced me to the wonderful world of salamanders during my undergraduate days at the University of Kentucky.

REFERENCES

Adams, M. D., and M. J. Lacki. 1993. Factors affecting amphibian use of road-rut ponds in Daniel Boone National Forest. *Transactions of the Kentucky Academy of Science* **54**:13-16.

Anonymous. 1991. Declining amphibian populations — a global phenomenon? *Alytes* **9**:33-42.

Ash, A. N. 1988. Disappearance of salamanders from clearcut plots. *Journal of the Elisha Mitchell Scientific Society* **104**:116-122.

Ash, A. N., and R. C. Bruce. 1994. Impacts of timber harvesting on salamanders. *Conservation Biology* **8**:300-301.

Ashton, R. E., Jr. 1976. Endangered and threatened amphibians and reptiles in the United States. Herpetological Circular Number 5, Society for the Study of Amphibians and Reptiles, Lawrence, KS, 65 p.

Ashton, R. E., Jr. 1986. Tennessee cave salamander. In *Vertebrate Animals of Alabama in Need of Special Attention.* R. H. Mount (ed.). Alabama Agricultural Experiment Station, Auburn University, AL, p. 60-62.

Ashton, R. E., Jr. 1992. Flatwoods salamander. In *Rare and Endangered Biota of Florida, Volume III, Amphibians and Reptiles.* P. E. Moler (ed.). University Press of Florida, Gainesville, FL, p. 39-43.

Ashton, R. E., Jr., and P. S. Ashton. 1988. *Handbook of Reptiles and Amphibians of Florida, Part Three, The Amphibians.* Windward Publishing, Inc., Miami, FL.

Ashton, R. E., Jr., and J. Peavy. 1986. Black Warrior waterdog. In *Vertebrate Animals of Alabama in Need of Special Attention.* R. H. Mount (ed.). Alabama Agricultural Experiment Station, Auburn University, AL, p. 63-65.

Auffenberg, W., and R. Franz. 1982. The status and distribution of the gopher tortoise (*Gopherus polyphemus*). In *North American Tortoises: Conservation and Ecology.* R. B. Bury (ed.). Research Report Number 12, U.S. Fish and Wildlife Service, Washington, D.C., p. 95-126.

Bailey, M. A. 1991. The dusky gopher frog in Alabama. *Journal of the Alabama Academy of Sciences* **62**:28-34.

Bancroft, G. T., J. S. Godley, D. T. Gross, N. N. Rojas, D. A. Sutphen, and R. W. McDiarmid. 1983. The herpetofauna of Lake Conway: Species accounts. Miscellaneous Paper A-83-5, Aquatic Plant Control Research Program, U.S. Army Corps of Engineers, Vicksburg, MS, 252 p.

Barbour, R. W. 1971. *Amphibians and Reptiles of Kentucky.* University Press of Kentucky, Lexington, KY.

Barinaga, M. 1990. Where have all the froggies gone? *Science* **247**:1033-1034.

Beattie, R. C., and R. Tyler-Jones. 1992. The effects of low pH and aluminum on breeding success in the frog *Rana temporaria. Journal of Herpetology* **26**:353-360.

Bennett, D. H., J. W. Gibbons, and J. Glanville. 1980. Terrestrial activity, abundance and diversity of amphibians in differently managed forest types. *American Midland Naturalist* 103:412-416.

Bidwell, J. R., and J. R. Gorrie. 1995. Acute toxicity of a herbicide to selected frog species. Final Report, Western Australia Department of Environmental Protection, Perth, Western Australia, 9 p.

Birge, W. J., J. A. Black, and R. A. Kuehne. 1980. Effects of organic compounds on amphibian reproduction. Research Report Number 121, Water Resource Research Institute, University of Kentucky, Lexington, KY, 39 p.

Blaustein, A. R. 1994. Chicken Little or Nero's Fiddle: A perspective on declining amphibian populations. *Herpetologica* 50:85-97.

Blaustein, A. R., P. D. Hoffman, D. G. Hokit, J. M. Kiesecker, S. C. Walls, and J. B. Hays. 1994a. UV repair and resistance to solar UV-B in amphibian eggs: A link to population declines? *Proceedings of the National Academy of Science* 91:1791-1795.

Blaustein, A. R., D. G. Hokit, R. K. O'Hara, and R. A. Holt. 1994b. Pathogenic fungus contributes to amphibian losses in the Pacific Northwest. *Biological Conservation* 67:251-254.

Blaustein, A. R., and D. B. Wake. 1990. Declining amphibian populations: A global phenomenon? *Trends in Ecology and Evolution* 5:203-204.

Blaustein, A. R., D. B. Wake, and W. P. Sousa. 1994c. Amphibian declines: Judging stability, persistence, and susceptibility of populations to local and global extinction. *Conservation Biology* 8:60-71.

Blumthaler, M., and W. Ambach. 1990. Indication of increasing solar ultraviolet-B radiation flux in alpine regions. *Science* 248:206-208.

Blymer, M. J., and B. S. McGinnes. 1977. Observations on possible detrimental effects of clearcutting on terrestrial amphibians. *Bulletin of the Maryland Herpetological Society* 13:79-83.

Boyce, S. G., and W. H. Martin. 1993. The future of the terrestrial communities of the Southeastern United States. In *Biodiversity of the Southeastern United States: Upland Terrestrial Communities*. W. H. Martin, S. G. Boyce, and A. C. Echternacht (eds.). John Wiley and Sons, New York, NY, p. 339-366.

Bradford, D. F. 1989. Allotopic distribution of native frogs and introduced fishes in High Sierra Nevada lakes of California: Implication of the negative effect of fish introductions. *Copeia* 1989:775-778.

Bradford, D. F. 1991. Mass mortality and extinction in a high-elevation population of *Rana muscosa*. *Journal of Herpetology* 25:174-177.

Bradford, D. F., C. Swanson, and M. S. Gordon. 1992. Effects of low pH and aluminum on two declining species of amphibians in the Sierra Nevada, California. *Journal of Herpetology* 26:369-377.

Branson, B. A., D. F. Harker, Jr., J. M. Baskin, M. E. Medley, D. L. Batch, M. L. Warren, Jr., W. H. Davis, W. C. Houtcooper, B. Monroe, Jr., L. R. Phillippe, and P. Cupp. 1981. Endangered, threatened, and rare animals and plants of Kentucky. *Transactions of the Kentucky Academy of Science* 42:77-89.

Braswell, A. L. 1977a. Mole salamander. In *Endangered and Threatened Plants and Animals of North Carolina.* J. E. Cooper, S. S. Robinson, and J. B. Funderburg (eds.). North Carolina State Museum of Natural History, Raleigh, NC, p. 318-319.

Braswell, A. L. 1977b. Carolina gopher frog. In *Endangered and Threatened Plants and Animals of North Carolina.* J. E. Cooper, S. S. Robinson, and J. B. Funderburg (eds.). North Carolina State Museum of Natural History, Raleigh, NC, p. 323-324.

Braswell, A. L. 1993. Status report on *Rana capito capito* Le Conte, the Carolina gopher frog, in North Carolina. Unpublished Report submitted to the North Carolina Wildlife Commission, Raleigh, NC, 81 p.

Bristow, C. E. 1991. Interactions between phylogenetically distant predators: *Notophthalmus viridescens* and *Enneacanthus obesus. Copeia* 1991:1-8.

Bruce, R. C. 1977a. Hellbender. In *Endangered and Threatened Plants and Animals of North Carolina.* J. E. Cooper, S. S. Robinson, and J. B. Funderburg (eds.). North Carolina State Museum Natural Historical, Raleigh, NC, p. 316-317.

Bruce, R. C. 1977b. Long-tailed salamander. In *Endangered and Threatened Plants and Animals of North Carolina.* J. E. Cooper, S. S. Robinson, and J. B. Funderburg (eds.). North Carolina State Museum of Natural History, Raleigh, NC, p. 321-322.

Buchanan, B. W. 1993. Effects of enhanced lighting on the behavior of nocturnal frogs. *Animal Behavior* 45:893-899.

Bury, R. B., and P. S. Corn. 1988. Responses of aquatic and streamside amphibians to timber harvest: A review. In *Streamside Management: Riparian Wildlife and Forestry Interactions.* K. J. Raedeke (ed.). Contribution Number 59, Institute of Forest Research, University of Washington, Seattle, WA, p. 165-181.

Bury, R. B., C. K. Dodd, Jr., and G. M. Fellers. 1980. Conservation of the Amphibia of the United States: A review. Resource Publication 134, U.S. Fish and Wildlife Service, Washington, D.C., 34 p.

Campbell, H. W., and S. P. Christman. 1982. The herpetological components of Florida sandhill and sand pine scrub associations. In *Herpetological Communities.* N. J. Scott (ed.). Wildlife Research Report Number 13, U.S. Fish and Wildlife Service, Washington, D.C., p. 163-171.

Carey, C. 1993a. Hypothesis concerning the causes of the disappearance of boreal toads from the mountains of Colorado. *Conservation Biology* 7:355-362.

Carey, C. 1993b. The role of stress in amphibian declines and extinctions. Abstracts, Second World Congress of Herpetology, Adelaide, Australia, p. 48-49.

Carey, C., and C. J. Bryant. 1995. Possible interrelations among environmental toxicants, amphibian development, and decline of amphibian populations. *Environmental Health Perspectives* 103:13-17.

Carr, A. F., Jr. 1940. A contribution to the herpetology of Florida. Biological Science Series 3, University of Florida Publication, Gainesville, FL, p. 1-118.

Cash, W. B. 1994. Herpetofaunal diversity of a temporary wetland in the southeast Atlantic Coastal Plain. M.S. Thesis, Georgia Southern University, Statesboro, GA.

Cely, J. E., and J. A. Sorrow, Jr. 1983. Distribution, status and habitat of the Pine Barrens treefrog in South Carolina. Study Completion Report, South Carolina Wildlife Marine Resource Department, Columbia, SC, 55 p.

Cerulean, S. I. 1991. The Preservation 2000 Report. Florida's natural areas — what have we got to lose? The Nature Conservancy, Winter Park, FL, 74 p.

Chippindale, P. T., A. H. Price, and D. M. Hillis. 1993. A new species of perennibranchiate salamander (*Eurycea*: Plethodontidae) from Austin, Texas. *Herpetologica* **49**:248-259.

Christman, S. P. 1974. Geographic variation for salt water tolerance in the frog *Rana sphenocephala. Copeia* **1974**:774-778.

Christman, S. P. 1992. Many-lined salamander. In *Rare and Endangered Biota of Florida, Volume III, Amphibians and Reptiles.* P. E. Moler (ed.). University Press of Florida, Gainesville, FL, p. 58-61.

Christman, S. P., and D. B. Means. 1992. Striped newt. In *Rare and Endangered Biota of Florida, Volume III, Amphibians and Reptiles.* P. E. Moler (ed.). University Press of Florida, Gainesville, FL, p. 62-65.

Cooper, J. E., S. S. Robinson, and J. B. Funderburg (eds.). 1977. *Endangered and Threatened Plants and Animals of North Carolina.* North Carolina State Museum of Natural History, Raleigh, NC, 444 p.

Corn, P. S., and R. B. Bury. 1989. Logging in western Oregon: Responses of headwater habitats and stream amphibians. *Forest Ecology and Management* **29**:39-57.

Dalrymple, G. H. 1988. The herpetofauna of Long Pine Key, Everglades National Park, in relation to vegetation and hydrology. In *Management of Amphibians, Reptiles, and Small Mammals in North America.* R. C. Szaro, K. E. Severson, and D. R. Patton (eds.). General Technical Report RM-166, Forest Service, U.S. Depart ment of Agriculture, Washington, D.C., p. 72-97.

Delis, P. 1993. Effects of urbanization of the community of anurans of a pine flatwood habitat in west central Florida. M.S. Thesis, University of South Florida, Tampa, FL.

Delzell, D. E. 1979. A provisional checklist of amphibians and reptiles in the Dismal Swamp area, with comments on their range of distribution. In *The Great Dismal Swamp.* P. W. Kirk, Jr. (ed.). University Press of Virginia, Charlottesville, VA, p. 244-260.

Dixon, J. R. 1987. *Amphibians and Reptiles of Texas.* Texas A&M University Press, College Station, TX.

Dodd, C. K., Jr. 1991. The status of the Red Hills salamander *Phaeognathus hubrichti*, Alabama, USA, 1976-1988. *Biological Conservation* **55**:57-75.

Dodd, C. K., Jr. 1992. Biological diversity of a temporary pond herpetofauna in north Florida sandhills. *Biodiversity and Conservation* **1**:125-142.

Dodd, C. K., Jr. 1993. Cost of living in an unpredictable environment: The ecology of striped newts *Notophthalmus perstriatus* during a prolonged drought. *Copeia* **1993**:605-614.

Dodd, C. K., Jr. 1995a. The ecology of a sandhills population of the eastern narrow-mouthed toad, *Gastrophryne carolinensis*, during a drought. *Bulletin of the Florida Museum of Natural History* **38**:11-41.

Dodd, C. K., Jr. 1995b. Reptiles and amphibians in the endangered longleaf pine ecosystem. In *Our Living Resources. A Report to the Nation on the Distribution, Abundance, and Health of U.S. Plants, Animals, and Ecosystems.* E. T. LaRoe, G. S. Farris, C. E. Puckett, P. D. Doran, and M. J. Mac (eds.). National Biological Service, Washington, D.C., p. 129-131.

Dodd, C. K., Jr. 1996. Use of terrestrial habitats by amphibians in the sandhill uplands of north-central Florida. *Alytes* 14:42-52.

Dodd, C. K., Jr., and R. Franz. 1993. The need for status information on common herpetofaunal species. *Herpetological Review* 24:47-50.

Dodd, C. K., Jr., and L. V. LaClaire. 1995. Biogeography and status of the striped newt (*Notophthalmus perstriatus*) in Georgia, USA. *Herpetological Natural History* 3:37-46.

Duellman, W. E., and A. Schwartz. 1958. Amphibians and reptiles of southern Florida. *Bulletin of the Florida State Museum* 3:181-324.

Duellman, W. E., and L. Trueb. 1986. *Biology of Amphibians.* McGraw Hill Book Company, New York, NY.

Dundee, H. A., and D. A. Rossman. 1989. *The Amphibians and Reptiles of Louisiana.* Louisiana State University Press, Baton Rouge, LA.

Dunson, W. A., and R. L. Wyman (eds.). 1992. Symposium: Amphibian declines and habitat acidification. *Journal of Herpetology* 26:349-442.

Echternacht, A. C. 1980. Reptiles and amphibians. In *Tennessee's Rare Wildlife, Volume 1, The Vertebrates.* D. C. Eagar, and R. M. Hatcher (eds.). Tennessee Wildlife Resources Agency, Nashville, TN, p. D1-D33.

Enge, K. M. 1991. Herptile exploitation. Annual Performance Report, Florida Game and Fresh Water Fish Commission, Tallahassee, FL, 55 p.

Enge, K. M. 1993. Herptile use and trade in Florida. Final Performance Report July 1, 1990 - June 30, 1992, Florida Game and Fresh Water Fish Commission, Tallahassee, FL, 102 p.

Enge, K. M., and C. K. Dodd, Jr. 1992. An indexed bibliography of the herpetofauna of Florida. Technical Report Number 11, Nongame Wildlife Program, Florida Game and Fresh Water Fish Commission, Tallahassee, FL, 231 p.

Enge, K. M., and W. R. Marion. 1986. Effects of clearcutting and site preparation on herpetofauna of a north Florida flatwoods. *Forest Ecology and Management* 14:177-192.

Fellers, G. M., and C. A. Drost. 1993. Disappearance of the Cascades frog *Rana cascadae* at the southern end of its range, California, USA. *Biological Conservation* 65:177-181.

Folkerts, G. W. 1986a. Seal salamander (Coastal Plain population). In *Vertebrate Animals of Alabama in Need of Special Attention.* R. H. Mount (ed.). Alabama Agricultural Experiment Station, Auburn University, AL, p. 44.

Folkerts, G. W. 1986b. Small-mouthed salamander. In *Vertebrate Animals of Alabama in Need of Special Attention.* R. H. Mount (ed.). Alabama Agricultural Experiment Station, Auburn University, AL, p. 54-55.

Folkerts, G. W. 1986c. Mountain dusky salamander. In *Vertebrate Animals of Alabama in Need of Special Attention.* R. H. Mount (ed.). Alabama Agricultural Experiment Station, Auburn University, AL, p.59-60.

Franz, R., J. Bauer, and T. Morris. 1994. Review of biologically significant caves and their faunas in Florida and south Georgia. *Brimleyana* 20:1-109.

Franz, R., C. K. Dodd, Jr., and C. Jones. 1988. *Rana areolata aesopus* (Florida gopher frog). Movement. *Herpetological Review* 19:33.

Franz, R., and L. L. Smith. 1993. Distribution and status of the striped newt and Florida gopher frog in peninsular Florida. Unpublished Report submitted to the Florida Nongame Wildlife Program, Tallahassee, FL, 77 p. [two versions of this report were dated 1993, the second version was not issued until 1995 and it contains more data than the first version]

Freda, J. 1986. The influence of acidic pond water on amphibians: A review. *Water, Air and Soil Pollution* **30**:439-450.

Freda, J., and W. A. Dunson. 1984. Sodium balance of amphibian larvae exposed to low environmental pH. *Physiological Zoology* **57**:435-443.

Freda, J., and D. H. Taylor. 1992. Behavioral response of amphibian larvae to acidic water. *Journal of Herpetology* **26**:429-433.

Freed, P. S., and K. Neitman. 1988. Notes on predation on the endangered Houston toad, *Bufo houstonensis. Texas Journal of Science* **40**:454-456.

Frisbie, M. P., and R. L. Wyman. 1991. The effects of soil pH on sodium balance in the red-backed salamander, *Plethodon cinereus*, and three other terrestrial salamanders. *Physiological Zoology* **64**:1050-1068.

Garrett, J. M., and D. G. Barker. 1987. *A Field Guide to Reptiles and Amphibians of Texas.* Texas Monthly Press, Austin, TX.

Garrott, R. A., P. J. White, and C. A. V. White. 1993. Overabundance: An issue for conservation biologists? *Conservation Biology* **7**:946-949.

Gibbons, J. W. 1988. The management of amphibians, reptiles and small mammals in North America: The need for an environmental attitude adjustment. In *Management of Amphibians, Reptiles, and Small Mammals in North America.* R. C. Szaro, K. E. Severson, and D. R. Patton (eds.). General Technical Report RM-166, Forest Service, U.S. Department of Agriculture, Washington, D.C., p. 4-10.

Gibbons, J. W., and D. H. Bennett. 1974. Determination of anuran terrestrial activity patterns by a drift fence method. *Copeia* **1974**:236-243.

Gibbons, J. W., and R. D. Semlitsch. 1991. *Guide to the Reptiles and Amphibians of the Savannah River Site.* University of Georgia Press, Athens, GA.

Gibbs, E. L., G. W. Nace, and M. B. Emmons. 1971. The live frog is almost dead. *Bioscience* **21**:1027-1034.

Godley, J. S. 1992. Gopher frog. In *Rare and Endangered Biota of Florida, Volume III, Amphibians and Reptiles.* P. E. Moler (ed.). University Press of Florida, Gainesville, FL, p. 15-19.

Gore, J. A. 1983. The distribution of desmognathine larvae (Amphibia: Plethodontidae) in coal surface mine impacted streams of the Cumberland Plateau USA. *Journal of Freshwater Ecology* **2**:13-24.

Gourley, E. V., and C. A. Pague. 1991. Shovel-nosed salamander. In *Virginia's Endangered Species.* K. Terwilliger (ed.). McDonald and Woodward Publishing Company, Blacksburg, VA, p. 435-436.

Grant, B. W., K. L. Brown, G. W. Ferguson, and J. W. Gibbons. 1994. Changes in amphibian biodiversity associated with 25 years of pine forest regeneration: Implications for biodiversity management. In *Biological Diversity: Problems and Challenges.* S. K. Majumdar, F. J. Brenner, J. E. Lovich, J. F. Schalles, and E. W. Miller (eds.). Pennsylvania Academy of Science, Easton, PA, p. 354-367.

Grant, K. P., and L. E. Licht. 1993. Effects of ultraviolet radiation on life history parameters of frogs from Ontario, Canada. Abstracts, Second World Congress of Herpetology, Adelaide, Australia, p. 101.

Green, N. B., and T. K. Pauley. 1987. *Amphibians and Reptiles in West Virginia.* University of Pittsburgh Press, Pittsburgh, PA.

Greenberg, C. H. 1993. Effect of high-intensity wildfire and silvicultural treatments on biotic communities of sand pine scrub. Ph.D. Dissertation, University of Florida, Gainesville, FL.

Griffiths, R. A. 1993. The effect of pH on feeding behavior in newt larvae (*Triturus*: Amphibia). *Journal of Zoology, London* 231:285-290.

Guillette, L. J., Jr., T. S. Gross, G. Masson, J. M. Matter, H. F. Percival, and A. R. Woodward. 1994. Developmental abnormalities of the gonad and abnormal sex hormone concentrations in juvenile alligators from contaminated and control lakes in Florida. *Environmental Health Perspectives* 102:680-688.

Hackney, C. T., S. M. Adams, and W. H. Martin (eds.). 1992. *Biodiversity of the Southeastern United States: Aquatic Communities.* John Wiley and Sons, New York, NY.

Haines, B. 1979. Acid precipitation in southeastern United States: A brief review. *Georgia Journal of Science* 37:185-191.

Haines, T. A. 1981. Acidic precipitation and its consequences for aquatic ecosystems: A review. *Transactions of the American Fisheries Society* 110:669-707.

Hairston, N. G., Sr., and R. H. Wiley. 1993. No decline in salamander (Amphibia: Caudata) populations: A twenty-year study in the southern Appalachians. *Brimleyana* 18:59-64.

Hall, R. J. 1994. Herpetofaunal diversity of the Four Holes Swamp, South Carolina. Resource Publication 198, National Biological Survey, Washington, D.C., 43 p.

Hall, R. J., R. E. Ashton, Jr., and R. M. Prouty. 1985. Pesticide and PCB residues in the Neuse River waterdog, *Necturus lewisi. Brimleyana* 10:107-109.

Hall, R. J., and P. F. P. Henry. 1992. Assessing effects of pesticides on amphibians and reptiles: Status and needs. *Herpetological Journal* 2:65-71.

Hammett, J. E. 1992. The shapes of adaptation: Historical ecology of anthropogenic landscapes in the Southeastern United States. *Landscape Ecology* 7:121-135.

Harper, R. M. 1906. A phytogeographical sketch of the Altamaha Grit Region of the coastal plain of Georgia. *Annals of the New York Academy of Science* 17:1-415.

Harris, L. D. and C. R. Vickers. 1984. Some faunal community characteristics of cypress ponds and the changes induced by perturbations. In *Cypress Swamps*. K. C. Ewel, and H. T. Odum (eds.). University Presses of Florida, Gainesville, FL, p. 171-185.

Harrison, J. R., J. W. Gibbons, D. H. Nelson, and C. L. Abercrombie, III. 1979. Status report: Amphibians. In *Proceedings of the First South Carolina Endangered Species Symposium*. D. M. Forsythe, and W. B. Ezell, Jr. (eds.). South Carolina Wildlife and Marine Resources Department, Columbia, SC, p. 73-78.

Heine, G. 1987. Einfache Meß- und Rechenmethode zur Ermittlung der Überlebenschance wandernder Amphibien beim Überqueren von Straßen. *Beihefte zu den Veröffentlichungen Naturschutz und Landschaftspflege Baden-Württemberg* 41:473-479.

Hine, R. L., B. L. Les, and B. F. Hellmich. 1981. Leopard frog populations and mortality in Wisconsin, 1974-76. Technical Bulletin Number 122, Wisconsin Department of Natural Resources, Madison, WI, 39 p.

Hourdry, J. 1993. Passage to the terrestrial life in amphibians. II. Endocrine determinism. *Zoological Science* **10**:887-902.

Jackson, D. R., and E. G. Milstrey. 1989. The fauna of gopher tortoise burrows. Technical Report Number 5, Florida Nongame Wildlife Program, Tallahassee, FL, p. 86-98.

Johnson, T. G. 1988. Forest statistics for southeast Georgia, 1988. Resource Bulletin SE-104, Forest Service, U.S. Department of Agriculture, Washington, D.C., 53 p.

Judd, F. W. 1985. Status of *Siren intermedia texana, Notophthalmus meridionalis* and *Crotaphytus reticulatus*. Unpublished Report submitted to the U.S. Fish and Wildlife Service, Washington, D.C., 60 p.

Jung, R. E., and C. H. Jagoe. 1993. Effects of pH and aluminum on green treefrog (*Hyla cinerea*) tadpoles. Abstracts, Second World Congress of Herpetology, Adelaide, Australia, p. 136.

Kerr, J. B., and C. T. McElroy. 1993. Evidence for large upward trends of ultraviolet-B radiation linked to ozone depletion. *Science* **262**:1032-1034.

Kiester, A. R. 1971. Species density of North American amphibians and reptiles. *Systematic Zoology* **20**:127-137.

Laan, R., and B. Verboom. 1990. Effects of pool size and isolation on amphibian communities. *Biological Conservation* **54**:251-262.

Lacki, M. J., J. W. Hummer, and H. J. Webster. 1992. Mine-drainage treatment wetland as habitat for herpetofaunal wildlife. *Environmental Management* **16**:513-520.

LaClaire, L. V., and R. Franz. 1991. Importance of isolated wetlands in upland ecosystems. In *The Role of Aquatic Plants in Florida's Lakes and Rivers*. M. Kelly (ed.). Proceedings 2nd Annual Meeting of the Florida Lake Management Society, Winter Haven, FL, p. 9-15.

Lande, R. 1988. Genetics and demography in biological conservation. *Science* **241**:1455-1460.

Langton, T. E. S. (ed.). 1989. *Amphibians and Roads*. ACO Polymer Products Ltd., Shefford, England.

Linzey, D. W. (ed.). 1979. *Proceedings of the Symposium on Endangered and Threatened Plants and Animals of Virginia*. Center for Environmental Studies, Virginia Polytechnic Institute and State University, Blacksburg, VA, 665 p.

Livermore, B. 1992. Amphibian alarm: Just where have all the frogs gone? *Smithsonian Magazine* **1992**(10):113-120.

Long, L. E., L. S. Saylor, and M. E. Soulé. 1995. A pH/UV-B synergism in amphibians. *Conservation Biology* **9**:1301-1303.

Mader, H.-J. 1984. Animal habitat isolation by roads and agricultural fields. *Biological Conservation* **29**:81-96.

Mann, W., P. Dorn, and R. Brandl. 1991. Local distribution of amphibians: The importance of habitat fragmentation. *Global Ecology and Biogeography Letters* **1**:36-41.

Martof, B. S., W. M. Palmer, J. R. Bailey, and J. R. Harrison, III. 1980. *Amphibians and Reptiles of the Carolinas and Virginia*. University of North Carolina Press, Chapel Hill, NC.

Mathews, R. C., Jr., and G. L. Larson. 1980. Monitoring aspects of acid precipitation and related effects on stream systems in the Great Smoky Mountains National Park. Proceedings 1st Conference of the Society of Environmental Toxicology and Chemistry, Washington, D.C., 18 p.

Mathews, R. C., Jr., and E. L. Morgan. 1982. Toxicity of Anakeesta Formation leachates to shovel-nosed salamander, Great Smoky Mountains National Park. *Journal of Environmental Quality* 11:102-106.

McCoy, E. D., and H. R. Mushinsky. 1992. Rarity of organisms in the sand pine scrub habitat of Florida. *Conservation Biology* 6:537-548.

McDiarmid, R. W. (ed.). 1978. *Rare and Endangered Biota of Florida, Volume III, Amphibians and Reptiles.* University Presses of Florida, Gainesville, FL.

McDiarmid, R. W. 1994. Amphibian diversity and natural history: An overview. In *Measuring and Monitoring Biological Diversity: Standard Methods for Amphibians.* W. R. Heyer, M. A. Donnelly, R. W. McDiarmid, L.-A. C. Hayek, and M. S. Foster (eds.). Smithsonian Institution Press, Washington, D.C.

Means, D. B. 1986a. Pine barrens treefrog. In *Vertebrate Animals of Alabama in Need of Special Attention.* R. H. Mount (ed.). Alabama Agricultural Experiment Station, Auburn University, AL, p. 29-30.

Means, D. B. 1986b. Dusky gopher frog. In *Vertebrate Animals of Alabama in Need of Special Attention.* R. H. Mount (ed.). Alabama Agricultural Experiment Station, Auburn University, AL, p. 30-31.

Means, D. B. 1986c. Flatwoods salamander. In *Vertebrate Animals of Alabama in Need of Special Attention.* R. H. Mount (ed.). Alabama Agricultural Experiment Station, Auburn University, AL, p. 42-43.

Means, D. B. 1986d. One-toed amphiuma. In *Vertebrate Animals of Alabama in Need of Special Attention.* R. H. Mount (ed.). Alabama Agricultural Experiment Station, Auburn University, AL, p. 56-57.

Means, D. B. 1986e. Southern dusky salamander. In *Vertebrate Animals of Alabama in Need of Special Attention.* R. H. Mount (ed.). Alabama Agricultural Experiment Station, Auburn University, AL, p. 58-59.

Means, D. B. 1986f. Gulf Coast mud salamander. In *Vertebrate Animals of Alabama in Need of Special Attention.* R. H. Mount (ed.). Alabama Agricultural Experiment Station, Auburn University, AL, p. 62.

Means, D. B. 1986g. Southern red salamander. In *Vertebrate Animals of Alabama in Need of Special Attention.* R. H. Mount (ed.). Alabama Agricultural Experiment Station, Auburn University, AL, p. 62-63.

Means, D. B. 1992a. Pine Barrens treefrog. In *Rare and Endangered Biota of Florida, Volume III, Amphibians and Reptiles.* P. E. Moler (ed.). University Press of Florida, Gainesville, p. 20-25.

Means, D. B. 1992b. One-toed amphiuma. In *Rare and Endangered Biota of Florida, Volume III, Amphibians and Reptiles.* P. E. Moler (ed.). University Press of Florida, Gainesville, FL, p. 34-38.

Means, D. B. 1992c. Seal salamander. In *Rare and Endangered Biota of Florida, Volume III, Amphibians and Reptiles.* P. E. Moler (ed.). University Press of Florida, Gainesville, FL, p. 44-48.

Means, D. B. 1992d. Georgia blind salamander. In *Rare and Endangered Biota of Florida, Volume III, Amphibians and Reptiles.* P. E. Moler (ed.). University Press of Florida, Gainesville, FL, p. 49-53.

Means, D. B. 1992e. Four-toed salamander. In *Rare and Endangered Biota of Florida, Volume III, Amphibians and Reptiles.* P. E. Moler (ed.). University Press of Florida, Gainesville, FL, p.54-57.

Means, D. B., and S. C. Christman. 1992. Carpenter frog. In *Rare and Endangered Biota of Florida, Volume III, Amphibians and Reptiles.* P. E. Moler (ed.). University Press of Florida, Gainesville, FL, p. 26-29.

Means, D. B., and G. Grow. 1985. The endangered longleaf pine community. *ENFO (Florida Conservation Foundation)* **1985**(September):1-12.

Means, D. B., and C. L. Longden. 1976. Aspects of the biology and zoogeography of the Pine Barrens treefrog (*Hyla andersonii*) in northern Florida. *Herpetologica* **32**:117-130.

Means, D. B., J. G. Palis, and M. Baggett. 1996. Effects of slash pine silviculture on a Florida population of flatwoods salamander. *Conservation Biology* 10:426-437.

Mitchell, J. C. 1981. A bibliography of Virginia amphibians and reptiles. *Smithsonian Herpetological Information Service* 50:1-51.

Mitchell, J. C., S. Y. Erdle, and J. F. Pagels. 1993. Evaluation of capture techniques for amphibian, reptile, and small mammal communities in saturated forested wetlands. *Wetlands* **13**:130-136.

Mittermeier, R. A., J. L. Carr, I. R. Swingland, T. B. Werner, and R. B. Mast. 1992. Conservation of amphibians and reptiles. In *Herpetology: Current Research on the Biology of Amphibians and Reptiles.* K. Adler (ed.). Contributions to Herpetology Number 9, Society for the Study of Amphibians and Reptiles, Oxford, OH, p.59-80.

Moler, P. E. 1980. The Florida population of the Pine Barrens treefrog (*Hyla andersonii*). A status review. Unpublished Report submitted to the U.S. Fish and Wildlife Service, Atlanta, GA, 44 p.

Moler, P. E. 1981. Notes on *Hyla andersonii* in Florida and Alabama. *Journal of Herpetology* 15:441-444.

Moler, P. E. 1985. A new species of frog (Ranidae: *Rana*) from northwestern Florida. *Copeia* 1985:379-383.

Moler, P. E. 1988. Correction of the type locality of the Gulf Hammock dwarf siren, *Pseudobranchus striatus lustricolus. Florida Field Naturalist* **16**:12-13.

Moler, P. E. 1992a. Florida bog frog. In *Rare and Endangered Biota of Florida, Volume III, Amphibians and Reptiles.* P. E. Moler (ed.). University Press of Florida, Gainesville, FL, p. 30-33.

Moler, P. E. 1992b. Pickerel frog. In *Rare and Endangered Biota of Florida, Volume III, Amphibians and Reptiles.* P. E. Moler (ed.). University Press of Florida, Gainesville, FL, p. 66-69.

Moler, P. E. 1992c. Gulf Hammock dwarf siren. In *Rare and Endangered Biota of Florida, Volume III, Amphibians and Reptiles.* P. E. Moler (ed.). University Press of Florida, Gainesville, FL, p. 77-80.

Moler, P. E. (ed.). 1992d. *Rare and Endangered Biota of Florida, Volume III, Amphibians and Reptiles.* University Press of Florida, Gainesville, FL.

Moler, P. E., and R. Franz. 1988. Wildlife values of small, isolated wetlands in the southeastern coastal plain. In *Proceedings of the Third Nongame and Endangered Wildlife Symposium.* R. R. Odum, K. A. Riddleberger, and J. C. Ozier (eds.). Georgia Department of Natural Resources, Social Circle, GA, p. 234-241.

Mount, R. H. 1975. *Reptiles and Amphibians of Alabama.* Agriculture Experiment Station, Auburn University, Auburn, AL.

Mount, R. H. 1980. Distribution and status of the Pine Barrens treefrog, *Hyla andersonii,* in Alabama. Unpublished Report submitted to the U.S. Fish and Wildlife Service, Jackson, MS, 31 p.

Mount, R. H. 1981. The red imported fire ant, *Solenopsis invicta* (Hymenoptera: Formicidae) as a possible serious predator on some native southeastern vertebrates: Direct observations and subjective impressions. *Journal of the Alabama Academy of Science* **52**:71-78.

Mount, R. H. 1986a. Eastern tiger salamander. In *Vertebrate Animals of Alabama in Need of Special Attention.* R. H. Mount (ed.). Alabama Agriculture Experiment Station, Auburn University, AL, p. 55-56.

Mount, R. H. 1986b. Greater siren. In *Vertebrate Animals of Alabama in Need of Special Attention.* R. H. Mount (ed.). Alabama Agriculture Experiment Station, Auburn University, AL, p. 65-66.

Mount, R. H. (ed.). 1986c. *Vertebrate Animals of Alabama in Need of Special Attention.* Alabama Agriculture Experiment Station, Auburn University, Auburn, AL.

Neill, W. T. 1958. The occurrence of amphibians and reptiles in saltwater areas, and a bibliography. *Bulletin of Marine Science Gulf and Caribbean* **8**:1-97.

Nickerson, M. A., and C. E. Mays. 1973. The hellbenders: North American "giant salamanders." Publications in Biology and Geology Number 1, Milwaukee Public Museum, Milwaukee, WI, p. 1-106.

Noss, R. F. 1989. Longleaf pine and wiregrass: Keystone components of an endangered ecosystem. *Natural Areas Journal* **9**:211-213.

O'Neill, E. D. 1995. Amphibian and reptile communities of temporary ponds in a managed pine flatwoods. M.S. Thesis, University of Florida, Gainesville, FL.

Pague, C. A. 1991a. Oak toad. In *Virginia's Endangered Species.* K. Terwilliger (ed.). McDonald and Woodward Publishing Company, Blacksburg, VA, p. 423-424.

Pague, C. A. 1991b. Carpenter frog. In *Virginia's Endangered Species.* K. Terwilliger (ed.). McDonald and Woodward Publishing Company, Blacksburg, VA, p. 426-427.

Pague, C. A. 1991c. Hellbender. In *Virginia's Endangered Species.* K. Terwilliger (ed.). McDonald and Woodward Publishing Company, Blacksburg, VA, p. 443-445.

Pague, C. A., and K. A. Buhlmann. 1991. Eastern tiger salamander. In *Virginia's Endangered Species.* K. Terwilliger (ed.). McDonald and Woodward Publishing Company, Blacksburg, VA, p. 431-433.

Pague, C. A., and J. C. Mitchell. 1987. The status of amphibians in Virginia. *Virginia Journal of Science* **38**:304-318.

Pague, C. A., and J. C. Mitchell. 1991a. Mabee's salamander. In *Virginia's Endangered Species.* K. Terwilliger (ed.). McDonald and Woodward Publishing Company, Blacksburg, VA, p. 427-429.

Pague, C. A., and J. C. Mitchell. 1991b. Mole salamander. In *Virginia's Endangered Species.* K. Terwilliger (ed.). McDonald and Woodward Publishing Company, Blacksburg, VA, p. 429-431.

Pague, C. A., and D. A. Young. 1991. Barking treefrog. In *Virginia's Endangered Species.* K. Terwilliger (ed.). McDonald and Woodward Publishing Company, Blacksburg, VA, p. 424-426.

Palis, J. G. 1992. Distribution of the flatwoods salamander, *Ambystoma cingulatum*, on the Apalachicola and Osceola National Forests, Florida. Unpublished Report submitted to the Florida Natural Areas Inventory, Tallahassee, FL, 13 p.

Palis, J. G. 1993. A status survey of the flatwoods salamander, *Ambystoma cingulatum*, in Florida. Unpublished Report submitted to the U.S. Fish and Wildlife Service, Jackson, MS, 29 p.

Palmer, W. 1977. Pine Barrens treefrog. In *Endangered and Threatened Plants and Animals of North Carolina.* J. E. Cooper, S. S. Robinson, and J. B. Funderburg (eds.). North Carolina State Museum Natural History, Raleigh, NC, p. 313-314.

Parker, M. V. 1937. Some amphibians and reptiles from Reelfoot Lake. *Journal of the Tennessee Academy of Science* 12:60-86.

Pauley, T. K., and R. A. Canterbury. 1990. Amphibians and reptiles of special concern in West Virginia. In *Endangered and Threatened Species in West Virginia.* A. R. Buckelew, Jr. (ed.). Special Publication Number 2, Brooks Bird Club, Triadelphia, WV, p. 38-43.

Pearson, H. A., R. R. Lohoefener, and J. L. Wolfe. 1987. Amphibians and reptiles on longleaf-slash pine forests in southern Mississippi. In *Ecological, Physical, and Socioeconomic Relationships within Southern National Forests.* H. A. Pearson, F. E. Smeins, and R. E. Thill (eds.). General Technical Report SO-68, Forest Service, U.S. Department of Agriculture, New Orleans, LA, p. 157-165.

Pechmann, J. H. K., D. E. Scott, J. W. Gibbons, and R. D. Semlitsch. 1989. Influence of wetland hydroperiod on diversity and abundance of metamorphosing juvenile amphibians. *Wetlands Ecology and Management* 1:3-11.

Pechmann, J. H. K., D. E. Scott, R. D. Semlitsch, J. P. Caldwell, L. J. Vitt, and J. W. Gibbons. 1991. Declining amphibian populations: The problem of separating human impacts from natural fluctuations. *Science* 253:892-895.

Pechmann, J. H. K., and H. M. Wilbur. 1994. Putting declining amphibians populations in perspective: Natural fluctuations and human impacts. *Herpetologica* 50:65-84.

Peters, R. L., and T. E. Lovejoy (eds.). 1992. *Global Warming and Biological Diversity.* Yale University Press, New Haven, CT.

Peterson, C. L., R. F. Wilkinson, Jr., M. S. Topping, and D. E. Metter. 1983. Age and growth of the Ozark hellbender (*Cryptobranchus alleganiensis bishopi*). *Copeia* 1983:225-231.

Petranka, J. W. 1994. Response to impact of timber harvesting on salamanders. *Conservation Biology* 8:302-304.

Petranka, J. W., M. E. Elridge, and K. E. Haley. 1993. Effects of timber harvesting on southern Appalachian salamanders. *Conservation Biology* 7:363-370.

Phelps, J. P. 1993. The effect of clearcutting on the herpetofauna of a South Carolina blackwater bottomland. M.S. Thesis, North Carolina State University, Raleigh, NC.

Phelps, J. P., and R. A. Lancia. 1995. Effects of a clearcut on the herpetofauna of a South Carolina bottomland swamp. *Brimleyana* 22:31-45.

Pierce, B. A., and D. K. Wooten. 1992. Genetic variation in tolerance of amphibians to low pH. *Journal of Herpetology* **26**:422-429.

Pimm, S. L., H. L. Jones, and J. Diamond. 1988. On the risk of extinction. *American Naturalist* **132**:757-785.

Power, T., K. L. Clark, A. Harfenist, and D. B. Peakall. 1989. A review and evaluation of the amphibian toxicological literature. Research Report Series Number 61, Canadian Wildlife Service, Ottawa, ON, 222 p.

Raymond, L. R., and L. M. Hardy. 1991. Effects of a clearcut on a population of the mole salamander, *Ambystoma talpoideum*, in an adjacent unaltered forest. *Journal of Herpetology* **25**:509-512.

Reagan, D. P. 1974. Threatened native amphibians of Arkansas. In *Arkansas Natural Area Plan.* Arkansas Department of Planning, Little Rock, AR, p. 93-99.

Redmond, W. H., Jr. 1986. Eastern hellbender. In *Vertebrate Animals of Alabama in Need of Special Attention.* R. H. Mount (ed.). Alabama Agricultural Experiment Station, Auburn University, AL, p. 31-33.

Redmond, W. H., A. C. Echternacht, and A. F. Scott. 1990. Annotated Checklist and Bibliography of Amphibians and Reptiles of Tennessee (1835 through 1989). Miscellaneous Publication Number 4, Center for Field Biology, Austin Peay State University, Clarksville, TN, 173 p.

Reh, W., and A. Seitz. 1990. The influence of land use on the genetic structure of populations of the common frog *Rana temporaria*. *Biological Conservation* **54**:239-249.

Richards, S. J., K. R. McDonald, and R. A. Alford. 1993. Declines in populations of Australia's endemic tropical rainforest frogs. *Pacific Conservation Biology* **1**:66-77.

Rossi, J. V. 1981. *Bufo marinus* in Florida: Some natural history and its impact on native vertebrates. M.A. Thesis, University of South Florida, Tampa, FL.

Roudebush, R. E. 1988. A behavioral assay for acid sensitivity in two desmognathine species of salamanders. *Herpetologica* **44**:392-395.

Sadinski, W. J., and W. A. Dunson. 1992. A multilevel study of effects of low pH on amphibians of temporary ponds. *Journal of Herpetology* **26**:413-422.

Saugey, D. A., G. A. Heidt, and D. R. Heath. 1988. Utilization of abandoned mine drifts and fracture caves by bats and salamanders: Unique subterranean habitat in the Ouachita Mountains. In *Management of Amphibians, Reptiles, and Small Mammals in North America.* R. C. Szaro, K. E. Severson, and D. R. Patton (eds.). General Technical Report RM-166, U.S. Forest Service, U.S. Department of Agriculture, Washington, D.C., p. 64-71.

Saugey, D. A., and S. E. Trauth. 1991. Distribution and habitat utilization of the four-toed salamander, *Hemidactylium scutatum*, in the Ouachita Mountains of Arkansas. *Proceedings of the Arkansas Academy of Science* **45**:88-91.

Scott, A. F. 1991. The herpetofauna of Barnett Woods Natural Area, Montgomery County, Tennessee. *Journal of the Tennessee Academy of Science* **66**:85-88.

Semlitsch, R. D. 1981. Terrestrial activity and summer home range of the mole salamander (*Ambystoma talpoideum*). *Canadian Journal of Zoology* **59**:315-322.

Semlitsch, R. D. 1987. Relationship of pond drying to the reproductive success of the salamander *Ambystoma talpoideum*. *Copeia* **1987**:61-69.

Seymour, R. S. 1994. Oxygen diffusion through the jelly capsules of amphibian eggs. *Israel Journal of Zoology* **40**:493-506.

Simmons, D. D. 1975. The evolutionary ecology of *Gyrinophilus palleucus*. M.S. Thesis, University of Florida, Gainesville, FL.

Sjogren, P. 1991a. Extinction and isolation gradients in metapopulations: The case of the pool frog (*Rana lessonae*). *Biological Journal of the Linnean Society* **42**:135-147.

Sjogren, P. 1991b. Genetic variation in relation to demography of peripheral pool frog populations (*Rana lessonae*). *Evolutionary Ecology* **5**:248-271.

Sjogren, P. 1993a. Metapopulation dynamics and extinction in pristine habitats: A demographic explanation. Abstracts, Second World Congress of Herpetology, Adelaide, Australia, p. 244.

Sjogren, P. 1993b. Applying metapopulation theory to amphibian conservation. Abstracts, Second World Congress of Herpetology, Adelaide, Australia, p. 244-245.

Smith, K. L., W. F. Pell, J. H. Rettig, R. H. Davis, and H. W. Robison. 1984. *Arkansas's Natural Heritage.* August House Publishers, Little Rock, AR.

Southerland, M. T. 1986. The effects of variation in streamside habitats on the composition of mountain salamander communities. *Copeia* **1986**:731-741.

Stebbins, R. C., and N. W. Cohen. 1995. *A Natural History of Amphibians.* Princeton University Press, Princeton, NJ.

Stephan, D. L. 1977. Neuse River waterdog. In *Endangered and Threatened Plants and Animals of North Carolina.* J. E. Cooper, S. S. Robinson, and J. B. Funderburg (eds.). North Carolina State Museum of Natural History, Raleigh, NC, p. 317-318.

Stout, I. J., and W. R. Marion. 1993. Pine flatwoods and xeric pine forests of the southern (lower) Coastal Plain. In *Biodiversity of the Southeastern United States: Lowland Terrestrial Communities.* W. H. Martin, S. G. Boyce, and A. C. Echternacht (eds.). John Wiley and Sons, New York, NY, p. 373-446.

Stout, I. J., D. R. Richardson, and R. E. Roberts. 1988. Management of amphibians, reptiles, and small mammals in xeric pinelands of peninsular Florida. In *Management of Amphibians, Reptiles, and Small Mammals in North America.* R. C. Szaro, K. E. Severson, and D. R. Patton (eds.). General Technical Report RM-166, Forest Service, U.S. Department of Agriculture, Washington, D.C., p. 98-108.

Terwilliger, K. (ed.). 1991. *Virginia's Endangered Species.* McDonald and Woodward Publishing Company, Blacksburg, VA.

Thompson, M. T. 1988. Forest statistics for southwest Georgia, 1988. Resource Bulletin SE-102, Forest Service, U.S. Department of Agriculture, Washington, D.C., 53 p.

Trauth, S. E. 1989. Distribution of the Plains spadefoot toad, *Scaphiopus bombifrons*, in the Arkansas River valley of central Arkansas. Final Report submitted to the Arkansas Nongame Preservation Committee, Little Rock, AR, 11 p.

Trauth, S. E. 1992a. Distributional survey of the bird-voiced treefrog, *Hyla avivoca* (Anura: Hylidae), in Arkansas. *Proceedings of the Arkansas Academy of Science* **46**:80-82.

Trauth, S. E. 1992b. 1992 field survey of the Illinois chorus frog, *Pseudacris streckeri illinoensis*, from Clay County, Arkansas. Final Report submitted to the Missouri Department of Conservation, Jefferson City, MO, 8 p.

Trauth, S. E., J. D. Wilhide, and P. Daniel. 1992. Status of the Ozark hellbender, *Cryptobranchus bishopi* (Urodela: Cryptobranchidae), in the Spring River, Fulton County, Arkansas. *Proceedings of the Arkansas Academy of Science* 46:83-86.

Trauth, S. E., B. G. Cochran, D. A. Saugey, W. R. Posey, and W. A. Stone. 1993a. Distribution of the mole salamander, *Ambystoma talpoideum* (Urodela:Ambystomatidae), in Arkansas with notes on paedomorphic populations. *Proceedings of the Arkansas Academy of Science* 47:154-156.

Trauth, S. E., J. D. Wilhide, and P. Daniel. 1993b. The Ozark hellbender, *Cryptobranchus bishopi*, in Arkansas: Distributional survey for 1992. *Bulletin of the Chicago Herpetological Society* 28:81-85.

Travis, J. 1992. Eastern tiger salamander. In *Rare and Endangered Biota of Florida, Volume III, Amphibians and Reptiles.* P. E. Moler (ed.). University Press of Florida, Gainesville, FL, p. 70-76.

Turner, L. J., and D. K. Fowler. 1981. Utilization of surface mine ponds in East Tennessee by breeding amphibians. Office of Biological Services 81/08, U.S. Fish and Wildlife Service, Washington, D.C., 13 p.

U.S. Fish and Wildlife Service. 1984a. The San Marcos Recovery Plan for San Marcos River endangered and threatened species. U.S. Fish and Wildlife Service, Albuquerque, NM, 109 p.

U.S. Fish and Wildlife Service. 1984b. Recovery Plan for the Houston toad (*Bufo houstonensis*). U.S. Fish and Wildlife Service, Albuquerque, NM, 73 p.

Vial, J. L., and L. Saylor. 1993. The status of amphibian populations. A compilation and analysis. Working Document Number 1, Declining Amphibian Populations Task Force, International Union for the Conservation of Nature and Natural Resources/Species Survival Commission, Corvalis, OR, 98 p.

Vickers, C. R., L. D. Harris, and B. F. Swindel. 1985. Changes in herpetofauna resulting from ditching of cypress ponds in coastal plains. *Forest Ecology and Management* 11:17-29.

Vitt, L. J., J. P. Caldwell, H. M. Wilbur, and D. C. Smith. 1990. Amphibians as harbingers of decay. *BioScience* 40:418.

Wake, D. B. 1991. Declining amphibian populations. *Science* 253:860.

Ware, S., C. Frost, and P. D. Doerr. 1993. Southern mixed hardwood forest: The former longleaf pine forest. In *Biodiversity of the Southeastern United States: Lowland Terrestrial Communities.* W. H. Martin, S. G. Boyce, and A. C. Echternacht (eds.). John Wiley and Sons, Inc., New York, NY, p. 447-493.

Williamson, G. K., and R. A. Moulis. 1979. Survey of reptiles and amphibians on Fort Stewart and Hunter Army Airfield. Unpublished Report submitted to the U.S. Army, Fort Stewart, GA, 343 p.

Wright, A. H. 1932. *Life-histories of Frogs of Okefinokee Swamp, Georgia.* MacMillan Company, New York, NY.

Wyman, R. L. 1990. What's happening to the amphibians? *Conservation Biology* 4:350-352.

Wyman, R. L., and D. S. Hawksley-Lescault. 1987. Soil acidity affects distribution, behavior, and physiology of the salamander *Plethodon cinereus. Ecology* 68:1819-1827.

Zug, G. R. 1993. *Herpetology: An Introductory Biology of Amphibians and Reptiles.* Academic Press, San Diego, CA.

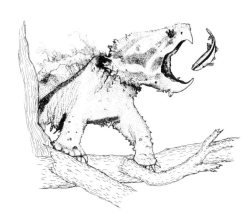

Imperiled Aquatic Reptiles of the Southeastern United States: Historical Review and Current Conservation Status

Kurt A. Buhlmann and J. Whitfield Gibbons

The purpose of our review of southeastern aquatic reptiles is to provide a benchmark on population status and trends as we currently understand them. In the future, ecologists and conservation biologists may be able to evaluate whether improvements have been made in the status of these species or if society has allowed continued declines.

For this review, we define the southeastern United States as encompassing all of North Carolina, South Carolina, Georgia, Florida, Alabama, Mississippi, Louisiana, Arkansas, Tennessee, and Kentucky. In addition, we include taxa from the Coastal Plain of Virginia, the Tennessee River drainages of western Virginia, and the "boot heel" (Mississippi Lowlands) region of southeastern Missouri.

Nearly 200 species of reptiles inhabit the United States and Canada in the form of turtles, snakes, lizards, and crocodilians. Clearly, the Southeast is a region where reptiles are in great abundance (Figure 1). Because of its wealth of wetland habitats, the Southeast is also the historical home of most of the aquatic reptiles in North America (Figure 2). The southeastern U.S. contains the greatest diversity of freshwater turtles (Harless and Morlock,

Aquatic Fauna in Peril: The Southeastern Perspective, edited by George W. Benz, and David E. Collins. 1997. Special Publication 1, Southeast Aquatic Research Institute, Lenz Design & Communications, Decatur, GA, 554 p.

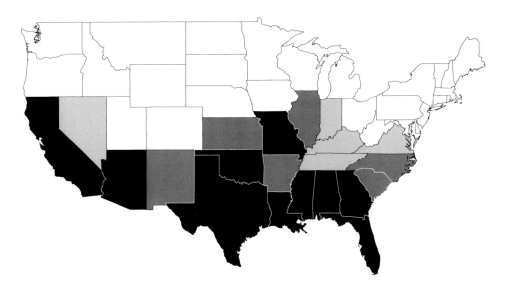

Figure 1. Numerical abundance of all native reptile species by state across the lower continental United States. Black = 70 or more species; dark gray = 60-69 species; light gray = 50-59 species; white = less than 50 species.

1979; Iverson, 1992) with up to 17 species occurring in one area (Bury, 1979; Figure 3). Twenty-three species of aquatic turtles are known from Alabama (Lydeard and Mayden, 1995). In comparison, fewer than ten species are found throughout the Northeast, with no more than eight occurring together (Figure 3). Only one aquatic turtle species is native to the Pacific coastal region. The Southeast also contains 17 aquatic snake species (Ernst and Barbour, 1989). In contrast, only four species of aquatic snakes are found in the Northeast, three of which also occur in the Southeast.

Generally, aquatic reptiles can be grouped into one of three categories (Table 1). Permanently aquatic species are those that spend almost their entire time in the water (i.e., they only leave water to nest or bask). Most river turtles such as *Graptemys* ssp., *Macroclemys temminckii*, and *Sternotherus minor* are in this category. Semi-aquatic species inhabit wetland habitats but may engage in overland travel, hibernate on land, or forage terrestrially. Some species of turtles (e.g., *Clemmys guttata* and *Deirochelys reticularia*) and snakes (*Agkistrodon piscivorous* and most *Nerodia* ssp.) fit this category. Marginally aquatic species live primarily on land but are often common in the vicinity of wetland habitats. These include the snakes *Thamnophis sauritus* and *Crotalus horridus atricaudatus* and the lizards *Ophisaurus ventralis* and *Eumeces anthracinus*. We acknowledge that these categories are somewhat arbitrary and other herpetologists might choose to classify several of the species differently.

For the purposes of determining "imperiled" status as an operational category for this review, we have relied heavily on the ranking system designed by The Nature Conservancy and used by all state Natural Heritage Programs (Table 2). Natural Heritage Program methodology requires that each taxon be given a global rank (G1-G5), where G1 is extremely rare throughout the range of the taxon and G5 denotes very common. Likewise, each state assigns a state rank (S1-S5) to all taxa within its boundary. For example, in Virginia,

Table 1. Numbers of imperiled aquatic reptile species exhibiting various associations with aquatic environments within the southeastern United States.

Aquatic Association [1]	Turtles	Snakes	Lizards	Crocodilians	Totals
Permanently aquatic	19	8	0	0	27
Semi-aquatic	7	5	0	2	14
Marginally aquatic	0	4	2	0	6
Totals	26	17	2	2	47

[1] For definitions of aquatic associations see text.

the chicken turtle (*D. reticularia*) is ranked G5S1 indicating the species' perceived common status due to its wide global range (G5) but very limited occurrence in Virginia (S1). The yellow-blotched sawback turtle (*Graptemys flavimaculata*) has a rank of G2 (global) and S2 (state) indicating its restricted global occurrence in one river system in Mississippi.

HISTORICAL DISTRIBUTION AND ABUNDANCE

From approximately 1725 until the middle 1800s, numerous prominent naturalists described the fauna and flora of North America (Adler, 1979). Although we have been able to gain an appreciation of the natural landscape from early botanists, information on the abundances and habitats of reptiles is sparse. Early emphasis on the herpetofauna of North America focused on descriptive taxonomy and any available population data are largely anecdotal (McIlhenny, 1935; Ditmars, 1936; Dellinger and Black, 1938; Cagle, 1953; Martof, 1956). For example, an early American naturalist and conservationist from Louisiana, E. A. McIlhenny (1872-1949), wrote in 1935 (McIlhenny, 1935; page 116), "alligators are not in immediate danger [of extinction], but it is extremely doubtful if they ever again will be an attractive feature of our waterways, as they were during the latter part of the last century." Ditmars (1936; page 4) stated, "Very large alligators are so rare nowadays that a specimen twelve feet long must be considered a giant. There was a time in Florida — long since gone — when alligators fourteen and fifteen feet long were no great rarity." Rarely, the early naturalists wrote about perceived declines of other animals. In Florida, as early as the 1930s, snake populations were regarded as declining due to proliferation of "motor roads" and the spread of fires (Ditmars, 1939).

When historical information was available on individual species, we added it to the *Species Accounts* section of this chapter. However, making definitive statements about population trends was difficult because of the frequent anecdotal nature of most of the historical data. Furthermore, modern survey techniques have shown some animals to be more abundant than previously thought by early naturalists, and have led to a better understanding of habitat and behavior.

HABITAT MODIFICATION

Since European settlement 400 years ago, the landscape of the southeastern United

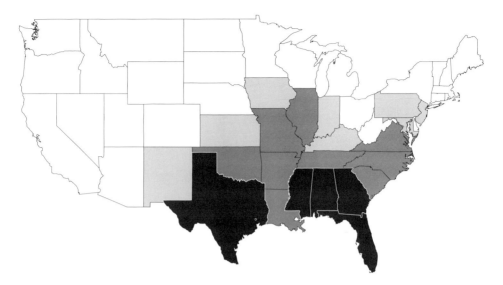

Figure 2. Numerical abundance of aquatic reptiles species by state across the lower continental United States. Black = 35 or more species; dark gray = 25-34 species; light gray = 15-24 species; white = less than 15 species.

States has been a progressive alteration of terrestrial and aquatic ecosystems. A large percentage of the Coastal Plain physiographic region was originally dominated by fire-maintained longleaf pine (*Pinus palustris*) communities. Between 1773 and 1777, William Bartram explored the Carolinas, Georgia, and Florida (Bartram [1791] 1980). He described virgin forests of oaks, hickories, yellow poplar, and pine, as well as wetlands and open savannas. On several occasions he traveled by horse through forests of huge spreading live oaks with open understories. Bartram described viewing an oval wetland (probably a Carolina bay) with a large expanse of grassy marsh on one side and a forest of towering cypress on the other in which numerous parrots (presumably the extinct Carolina parakeets) foraged. Coastal Plain rivers were bordered by forests of bottomland hardwoods and bald cypress (*Taxodium distichum*). These meandering rivers with their sandy bottoms were filled with tree snags (Benke, 1990).

Unfortunately, the majority of the longleaf pine forest has been logged, replanted in monocultures of loblolly or slash pine, and managed on 20-year rotations. Lands supporting longleaf pine-wiregrass (*Aristida stricta*) or longleaf pine-bluestem (*Andropogon* sp.) had declined to less than one-sixth of their original extent by 1946 and to less than ten percent today (Frost et al., 1986). Other previously forested lands are now in agriculture or have been urbanized. The loss of forest cover is illustrated in stark reality when one examines Landsat photographs. For example, the forested 300 square mile (777 km²) Savannah River Site (SRS), in South Carolina, is easily recognizable on a photograph that encompasses an expanse including New Jersey and Florida. The SRS is clearly distinguishable from the surrounding predominantly agricultural landscape.

Many of the natural Coastal Plain wetlands have been filled, ditched and drained, or left isolated in a fragmented landscape. In Virginia alone during 1950-1970, 57 percent

Table 2. Definitions of Natural Heritage State Rarity Ranks. Analogous Global Ranks (G1-G5, GU) would have the same definitions except that they would refer to rarity throughout the entire range of a species. Ranks should not be interpreted as legal designations.

Rank	Definition
S1	extremely rare, usually five or fewer occurrences in state; very vulnerable to extirpation
S2	very rare; usually between 6 and 20 occurrences in state; susceptible to extirpation
S3	rare to uncommon; usually between 21 and 100 occurrences in state; may be vulnerable to large scale disturbances
S4	uncommon to common; usually more than 100 occurrences in state; not usually vulnerable to immediate threats
S5	very common; demonstrably secure under present conditions
SU	status uncertain; this status is often warranted because of insufficient data associated with low search effort or cryptic nature of the species

of the state's freshwater wetlands were lost: 45 percent to agriculture, 27 percent to development, and the remainder to man-made ponds, reservoirs, and other causes (Tiner, 1987). Hefner and Brown (1984) reported wetland losses in the Southeast at a rate of about 385,471 acres per year (156,000 ha per year), with a total loss of about 7.4 million acres (3 million ha), 84 percent of the national total (Richardson and Gibbons, 1993).

The majority of bottomland hardwood forests were logged during the last century and 400-year-old cypress swamps have been replaced with red maple, sweetgum, and blackgum woods. Cypress does not regenerate well on sites that have been both logged and burned (Gunderson, 1984). Bottomland floodplain forests in the Southeast have also been destroyed incrementally through conversion to agriculture and diking for flood control (Sharitz and Mitsch, 1993). Sharitz and Gibbons (1982) provided detailed descriptions of the logging and draining of such huge tracts as Great Dismal Swamp in Virginia and Green Swamp in North Carolina. Gosselink and Lee (1989) reported an overall loss of 69 percent of bottomland hardwood wetlands throughout the continental U.S. since European settlement. The original extent of southern bottomland hardwood forests was thought to be 17.7 million acres (about 7.2 million ha); the current extent is 6.6 million acres (about 2.7 million ha), a 63 percent decline. MacDonald et al. (1979) estimated a 78 percent loss of forested wetlands in the Mississippi River floodplain. Fifty percent of Louisiana's forested wetlands have been lost (Turner and Craig, 1980).

The facilitation of navigation has resulted in channelization and de-snagging operations of most large Coastal Plain rivers. Benke (1990) noted that although humans have been modifying streams and rivers for centuries, major alterations really began in the 1930s with water projects for flood control, navigation, water supply, and electricity. In his review, Benke (1990) reported that only 42 free-flowing rivers greater than 124 miles (200 km) in length remained in the continental U.S. The Southeast has the greatest remaining length of high quality rivers but also the least amount of government protection (Benke, 1990).

On the Piedmont of Georgia, the oak-hickory-loblolly pine forests have been harvested several times (Skeen et al., 1993). Although the last century saw most of this region used

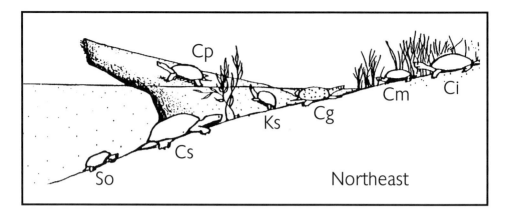

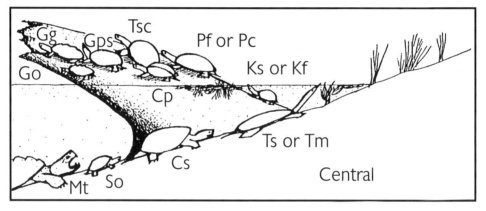

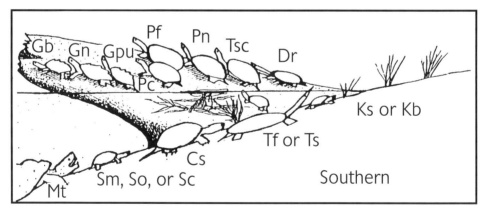

Figure 3. Abundance of aquatic turtle species in three geographic regions of the United States (northeastern, central, southern). Abbreviations: Cg = *Clemmys guttata*, Ci = *C. insculpta*, Cm = *C. muhlenbergii*, Cp = *Chrysemys picta*, Cs = *Chelydra serpentina*, Dr = *Deirochelys reticularia*, Gb = *Graptemys barbouri*, Gg = *G. geographica*, Gn = *G. nigrinoda*, Go = *G. ouachitensis*, Gps = *G. pseudogeographica*, Gpu = *G. pulchra*, Kb = *Kinosternon baurii*, Kf = *K. flavescens*, Ks = *K. subrubrum*, Mt = *Macroclemys temminckii*, Pc = *Pseudemys concinna*, Pf = *P. floridana*, Pn = *P. nelsoni*, Tsc = *Trachemys scripta*, Sc = *Sternotherus carinatus*, Sm = *S. minor*, So = *S. odoratus*, Tf = *Trionyx ferox*, Tm = *T. mutica*, Ts = *T. spinifera*. Note: not all *Graptemys* and *Pseudemys* spp. are found in the same habitats. Modified from Harless and Morlock (1979; page 593; *In* Bury, 1979), nomenclature follows Ernst et al., 1994. Modified and reprinted with permission from R. B. Bury.

for cotton and tobacco, recent uses have included short-term timber rotation and urbanization. As a result of inappropriate farming and logging practices, most of the original topsoil has been lost, leaving the red clay subsoil to erode into streams and rivers. Piedmont rivers were once gravel- and cobble-bottomed and flowed clear. They currently have mud bottoms and flow red-brown with silt and sediments.

Mountain forests have been logged and streams and rivers impacted by runoff, siltation, and pollution. The once majestic American chestnut-dominated forests are gone, the result of a fungus that was imported with ornamental trees around 1900. Chestnut accounted for 50 to 80 percent of the canopy in forests in the Smoky Mountains (Shelford, 1963). Runoff from mining operations has polluted many biologically diverse streams, especially in the Cumberland Plateau physiographic region, and is associated with declines in fish and freshwater mollusk faunas (Williams et al., 1993). Mountain bogs and fens in the Appalachian region have been ditched, drained, and otherwise impacted by farming and cattle grazing.

In summary, the landscape today is vastly different from the one Europeans encountered 400 years ago. The disappearance and modification of natural habitats is correlated with declines of the natural biodiversity, including aquatic reptiles.

SPECIES ACCOUNTS OF IMPERILED AQUATIC REPTILES

This section does not treat all taxa of aquatic reptiles in the southeastern United States. To be included, a taxon had to have a Natural Heritage Program (NHP) rank of S1, S2, or S3 in at least one of the southeastern states in which it occurs or be protected at the state or federal level (e.g., endangered, threatened, special concern, candidate). A designation of candidate (C) by the U.S. Fish and Wildlife Service indicates that enough information exists to support proposals to list the particular species as threatened or endangered and future listing is anticipated. Candidate species (C) were formerly Category 1 (C1) species, while those species formerly listed as Category 2 (C2) no longer have an official federal designation (U.S. Federal Register, 1996). Any taxon that was ranked as S4 or S5 was considered not to be of conservation concern or not to be imperiled at this time. By using this approach, our species counts can be used as benchmarks to gauge future declines or improvements in the status of imperiled species. For each species discussed, The Nature Conservancy's global (G) rank is given following the first use of the scientific name.

Crocodilians

AMERICAN ALLIGATOR — *Alligator mississippiensis* — G5

The American alligator is federally listed as threatened due to similarity of appearance with the American crocodile. Although once threatened with global extinction, alligator populations have increased concomitantly with protection measures, such as a ban on alligator products and regulated hunting. In Arkansas, the alligator is ranked S3 and the distribution of the animal has been altered due to stocking programs (Arkansas Natural Heritage Program, unpublished data). In North Carolina, the alligator is ranked S3 and is state listed as threatened.

AMERICAN CROCODILE — *Crocodylus acutus* — G2

The American crocodile is federally listed as endangered. The Florida Natural Areas Inventory ranks the American crocodile as S1 and it is state listed as endangered. The American crocodile was confirmed as occurring in Florida in 1875. Between then and 1936, 70 specimens were collected between Lake Worth and Cape Sable (Ditmars, 1936). To protect this species, anti-poaching laws need to be enforced, habitat encroachment needs to be reduced, and mortality associated with road traffic needs to be lowered. King et al. (1982) estimated the Florida population at 200 to 500 individuals. Currently, fewer than 200 to 400 animals, including 25 breeding females, remain in Everglades National Park and Crocodile Lake National Wildlife Refuge.

Lizards

EASTERN GLASS LIZARD — *Ophisaurus ventralis* — G5

The eastern glass lizard is ranked S1 and listed as threatened in Virginia, where it is found in coastal grassy freshwater swales between dunes and is a peripheral species at the northern edge of its range (Mitchell and Pague, 1991). We have found eastern glass lizards around the borders of Carolina bay wetlands in South Carolina. Martof (1956) considered them uncommon in Georgia. Louisiana ranks this lizard as S2 (Louisiana Natural Heritage Program, 1996).

COAL SKINK — *Eumeces anthracinus* — G5

The southern coal skink (*Eumeces anthracinus pluvialis*) is ranked S3 in Florida and is included in this review because it is marginally aquatic. It occurs around the borders of acidic wetlands in pine flatwoods and has been observed to retreat into shallow water and hide under bottom rubble (Means, 1992).

Snakes

NORTHERN WATER SNAKE — *Nerodia sipedon* — G5

The Carolina salt marsh snake (*Nerodia sipedon williamengelsi*) is ranked S3 and is listed as special concern in North Carolina. It is limited to salt marshes of the southern Outer Banks and Pamlico and Core sounds in North Carolina (H. LeGrand, North Carolina Natural Heritage Program, pers. comm.).

SOUTHERN WATER SNAKE — *Nerodia fasciata* — G5

The broad-banded water snake (*Nerodia fasciata confluens*) is ranked S1 and state listed as endangered in Kentucky, at the northern periphery of its range. Wetland drainage and destruction are causing the decline of this subspecies (Kentucky Nature Preserves Commission, unpublished data).

SALT MARSH SNAKE — *Nerodia clarkii* — G4

The U.S. Fish and Wildlife Service (USFWS) formerly listed the salt marsh snake (*Nerodia clarkii*) as C2. The Gulf salt marsh snake (*Nerodia clarkii clarkii*), ranked S3 in Florida, inhabits brackish coastal habitats on the Gulf Coast and is threatened by degradation of habitat, including development, and oil spills. Insecticides, such as those used in mosquito control, may be affecting the Gulf salt marsh snake (Florida Natural Areas Inventory, unpublished data). The Gulf salt marsh snake is ranked S2S3 in Mississippi and surveys are currently being conducted (T. Mann, Mississippi Natural Heritage Program, pers. comm.). The Gulf salt marsh snake is ranked S1S2 in Alabama (Alabama Natural Heritage Program, 1996). The Atlantic salt marsh snake (*N. c. taeniata*) is ranked S1 in Florida and is listed as threatened by the USFWS and the state of Florida (Kochman and Christman, 1992; Florida Natural Areas Inventory, 1995). Atlantic salt marsh snakes only occur in Volusia County, on the Atlantic coast in Florida, and require pristine brackish and salt marshes (Florida Natural Areas Inventory, unpublished data).

PLAINBELLIED WATER SNAKE — *Nerodia erythrogaster* — G5

Recently, the USFWS proposed the copperbellied water snake (*Nerodia erythrogaster neglecta*) as threatened (U.S. Fish and Wildlife Service, 1993). The copperbellied water snake is ranked SU and is state listed as threatened in Tennessee, where only five localities for its presence are known (Tennessee Division of Natural Heritage, unpublished data). Populations in Tennessee display traits that may indicate intergradation with the yellowbellied water snake (*N. e. flavigaster*) (Tennessee Division of Natural Heritage, 1996). The copperbellied water snake is a northern subspecies that occurs in disjunct colonies throughout its range. Major threats to the subspecies include the drainage of wetlands and agricultural activities, primarily in Tennessee, Kentucky, Illinois, Indiana, and Ohio. Kentucky ranks the copperbellied water snake as S2S3 and lists it as special concern. Only 14 occurrences are known in Kentucky, and wetland destruction is considered the cause of this snake's decline (Kentucky Nature Preserves Commission, unpublished data).

MISSISSIPPI GREEN WATER SNAKE — *Nerodia cyclopion* — G5

Sparse population information is available for the Mississippi green water snake. Ditmars (1936) considered the snake rare in the Mississippi Valley. The Nature Conservancy ranks it as G5, yet most states within its range consider it to be rare (Florida S1; Arkansas S2; Alabama S2; Tennessee S1; Kentucky S1). Missouri listed the Mississippi green water snake as endangered as a consequence of drastic reductions in cypress swamps (Johnson, 1987). No recent confirmations for the species have been reported in Missouri where the snake is presently listed as extirpated (Missouri Natural Heritage Database, 1995). The Mississippi green water snake is near the northern edge of its range in Kentucky, with the drainage of wetlands and agricultural runoff contributing to its decline (Kentucky Nature Preserves Commission, unpublished data). The Mississippi green water snake is ranked S1 and considered in need of management in Tennessee (Tennessee Division of Natural Heritage, 1996). The Mississippi green water snake was considered abundant in Louisiana by Dundee and Rossman (1989).

FLORIDA GREEN WATER SNAKE — *Nerodia floridana* — G5

The Florida green water snake is ranked S2 and considered a species of concern in South Carolina. The species exhibits a much greater level of habitat specificity than other water snakes, seeming to prefer ponds with water lilies and relatively permanent water (S. Bennett, South Carolina Heritage Trust, pers. comm.). The two known South Carolina populations occur on the Savannah River Site and the Charleston Naval Weapons Station. These snakes seem slow to recolonize wetlands that have dried, making them susceptible to local extinctions (Seigel et al., 1995). Alabama ranks the Florida green water snake as SU (Alabama Natural Heritage Program, 1996). The species is ranked S2 in Georgia where it seems to prefer prairies in the Okefenokee Swamp, sinkhole lakes, and Carolina bays with open canopies (Georgia Natural Heritage Program, unpublished data). Martof (1956) considered this snake uncommon to common in Georgia. The South Carolina populations appear to be disjunct from the Georgia populations by several hundred kilometers (Conant and Collins, 1991), but the reason for this gap is unclear. Using allozyme electrophoresis, Thompson (1994) found no differences between the South Carolina and nearest Georgia populations.

STRIPED CRAYFISH SNAKE — *Regina alleni* — G5

The striped crayfish snake is ranked S2 in Georgia, with the northernmost distributional records being from the Okefenokee Swamp. Godley (1980) determined that the striped crayfish snake is active at night, feeding on crayfish, dragonfly nymphs, and dwarf sirens (*Pseudobranchus striatus*). Ditmars (1939) considered the animal rare, a designation possibly linked to this snake's nocturnal behavior which makes it poorly known.

CRAYFISH SNAKE — *Regina rigida* — G5

Crayfish snakes occur around pond edges in vegetation, in freshwater tidal marshes, in floodplains, and in flatwoods ponds where they eat crayfish. The Gulf crayfish snake (*R. r. sinicola*) is ranked S2 in Arkansas and S3 in Mississippi. The glossy crayfish snake (*R. r. rigida*) is ranked S1 in Virginia and is known only from one disjunct population in a seemingly pristine freshwater tidal marsh (Richmond, 1940; Buhlmann et al., 1993b). In North Carolina, where it is known from marshes and cypress ponds (North Carolina Natural Heritage Program, unpublished data), the glossy crayfish snake is ranked S3. Ditmars (1939) considered this snake rare because it was infrequently encountered. Martof (1956) considered the glossy crayfish snake uncommon in Georgia.

GRAHAM'S CRAYFISH SNAKE — *Regina grahamii* — G5

Although poorly known, Graham's crayfish snake has been found along the margins of ponds, streams, sloughs, bayous, and swamps (Neill, 1958; Conant and Collins, 1991). This snake is ranked S2 in Arkansas where populations are believed to be declining because of the removal of tree snags, channelization of streams, and destruction of wetland habitat (Arkansas Natural Heritage Program, unpublished data).

QUEEN SNAKE — *Regina septemvittata* — G5

Populations of the queen snake (*Regina septemvittata*) in the Boston Mountains of Arkansas are disjunct from the remainder of the species' range (Conant and Collins, 1991). The USFWS previously listed this disjunct population as C2, and it is ranked S1 in Arkansas (Arkansas Natural Heritage Commission, 1996). Ernst and Barbour (1989) stated that queen snakes prefer clean, unpolluted streams with abundant crayfish populations. They also suggested that snake populations may be reduced as a result of water pollution and acid rain, which affects crayfish populations. In Arkansas, most streams inhabited by queen snakes exhibit water pollution from cattle pastures, poultry operations, and human occupation (Trauth, 1991).

KIRTLAND'S SNAKE — *Clonophis kirtlandi* — G2

The USFWS formerly listed Kirtland's snake as C2. Kirtland's snake may be declining throughout its range due to the drainage of prairie marshland over the last two centuries (Kentucky Nature Preserves Commission, unpublished data). This northern and midwestern species reaches the southern periphery of its range in Kentucky, where it is ranked S1 and is state listed as endangered (Kentucky Nature Preserves Commission, 1995). The Kentucky Nature Preserves Commission has five historic records from 1946-1968 and one verified record in the 1980s. Ditmars (1936; page 172) stated, "in some districts the species is as abundant as the garter snake."

BLACK SWAMP SNAKE — *Seminatrix pygaea* — G5

The black swamp snake is an inhabitant of thick vegetation in ponds and sluggish streams. The Carolina swamp snake (*Seminatrix pygaea paludis*) is ranked SU and considered a species of concern in South Carolina. It is ranked S3 in North Carolina. The North Florida swamp snake (*S. p. pygaea*) is ranked S3 in Georgia and populations are likely becoming more disjunct as habitat between cypress ponds and other wetlands becomes increasingly fragmented. The North Florida swamp snake is ranked S2 in Alabama.

EASTERN RIBBON SNAKE — *Thamnophis sauritus* — G5

The Florida Natural Areas Inventory Program recognizes a unique population of the peninsula ribbon snake (*Thamnophis sauritus sackeni*) in the lower Florida Keys in which individuals possess a yellow to orange mid-dorsal stripe. This population is ranked S1 and is state listed as threatened (Florida Natural Areas Inventory, 1995). Protection of the remaining permanent freshwater ponds on the lower Florida Keys will be necessary for this population to persist (Weaver and Christman, 1992). The eastern ribbon snake (*T. s. sauritus*) is ranked S2S3 and listed as special concern in Kentucky where it is declining due to loss of wetland habitat (Kentucky Nature Preserves Commission, unpublished data).

WESTERN RIBBON SNAKE — *Thamnophis proximus* — G5

The western ribbon snake (*Thamnophis proximus proximus*) reaches the most eastern periphery of its range in Kentucky where it is ranked S1S2 and state listed as threatened. Population declines in Kentucky are attributed to wetland losses (Kentucky Nature Preserves Commission, unpublished data).

RAINBOW SNAKE — *Farancia erythrogramma* — G5

The South Florida rainbow snake (*Farancia erythrogramma seminola*) is ranked S1 in Florida and represents a disjunct taxon known only from three specimens collected in 1949 and 1952 in one creek in Glades County, Florida (Moler, 1992). The South Florida rainbow snake, if it still exists, is probably threatened as a result of pollution from agricultural runoff. The eastern rainbow snake (*F. e. erythrogramma*) is ranked S2 and is state listed as endangered in Mississippi. Declines are believed due to channelization, siltation, and pollution (Mississippi Department of Fisheries, Wildlife, and Parks, 1992). Other states consider the eastern rainbow snake to be marginally rare (Georgia S3, Alabama S3, Louisiana S2). Habitat degradation of small streams and the draining of wetlands as well as a peripheral distribution (Louisiana) are cited as causes of concern or reasons for the species' rarity (S. Shively, Louisiana Natural Heritage Program, pers. comm.). Martof (1956) considered them uncommon in Georgia. Mitchell (1994) considered the species secure in Virginia despite its spotty occurrence.

MUD SNAKE — *Farancia abacura* — G5

The western mud snake (*Farancia abacura reinwardtii*) is ranked S3 and listed as special concern in Kentucky where it reaches the northeastern periphery of its range. Declines are probably the result of wetland drainage, logging, and channelization in the western Kentucky coal field area (Kentucky Nature Preserves Commission, unpublished data). Missouri lists the western mud snake as a "watchlist" species because of its peripheral occurrence at the northern edge of its range (Missouri Natural Heritage Database, 1995). Ditmars (1939) found these snakes most abundant in cypress swamps of the Gulf states.

CANEBRAKE RATTLESNAKE — *Crotalus horridus atricaudatus* — G5

The canebrake rattlesnake is ranked S1 and state listed as endangered in Virginia (Roble, 1996). Declines have been attributed to direct killing, destruction of forested wetlands, and an ever-expanding road network (Mitchell, 1994). Persecution by humans has resulted in declines of this snake throughout its range. Based on recent research using radio-telemetry, large tracts of land are required by this species (A. L. Savitzky, Old Dominion University, pers. comm.). Florida ranks the canebrake rattlesnake as S3 (Florida Natural Areas Inventory, 1995).

Turtles

ALLIGATOR SNAPPING TURTLE — *Macroclemys temminckii* — G3G4

The USFWS formerly listed the alligator snapping turtle as C2, and the turtle is now a species of concern in every state within its range. Ditmars (1936) found alligator snapping turtles common in the Mississippi River, as did Martof (1956) in Georgia. However, Pritchard (1989) documented the extensiveness of the alligator snapping turtle fishery and the effect that unregulated harvest has had on this slow-to-mature, long-lived organism. Arkansas ranks the alligator snapping turtle as SU, and anecdotal information suggests that most harvested individuals are being taken to the Louisiana meat market (Pritchard, 1989). Florida ranks the alligator snapping turtle as S3 and attributes declines to habitat degradation and direct harvest (Florida Natural Areas Inventory, unpublished data). Mississippi ranks the turtle as S3, and state law prohibits a commercial fishery for it. However, an illegal fishery exists with the catch going to Louisiana, and alligator snapping turtles in Mississippi also incur mortality in the poorly regulated trotline fishery (T. Mann, Mississippi Natural Heritage Program, pers. comm.). Georgia populations have suffered from commercial exploitation, as have Louisiana and Alabama populations (Pritchard, 1989). Tennessee populations might be declining due to dredging and the channelization of streams (Tennessee Division of Natural Heritage, unpublished data). Other state rankings are as follows: Georgia S3, state listed as threatened; Alabama S3, state listed as protected; Kentucky S1S2, state listed as threatened; Louisiana S3; Missouri S1, state listed as rare.

STRIPE-NECKED MUSK TURTLE — *Sternotherus minor* — G5

The stripe-necked musk turtle (*Sternotherus minor peltifer*) is ranked S2 in Virginia. North Carolina ranks it as S1 and lists it as a species of special concern. In those states, it is limited to streams of the upper Tennessee River drainage. These streams, which once harbored some of the most diverse mollusk faunas in the world, have been impacted by fly ash spills, heavy metals, acid mine drainage, and sewage. Stripe-necked musk turtles have heavy crushing jaws and feed on freshwater mussels and snails. They will likely continue to decline as their food source disappears. Stripe-necked musk turtles reach the western periphery of their range in Louisiana, where they are ranked S1.

RAZORBACK MUSK TURTLE — *Sternotherus carinatus* — G5

The razorback musk turtle is ranked S2 in Arkansas and its continued existence requires the maintenance of aquatic systems of the Coastal Plain, including riverine pools and slow-moving streams (Arkansas Natural Heritage Program, unpublished data). The razorback musk turtle is ranked S1 in Alabama, due to its recent discovery in the Alabama portion of the Escatawpa River (Blankenship et. al., 1995).

FLATTENED MUSK TURTLE — *Sternotherus depressus* — G2

The flattened musk turtle is federally listed as threatened (U.S. Fish and Wildlife Service, 1992). Alabama ranks this turtle as S2 and lists it as protected. The species seems to be doing well in only a few streams and is declining or non-existent in most of its historic range (M. Bailey, Alabama Natural Heritage Program, pers. comm.). The flattened musk turtle is an Alabama endemic that is confined to permanent streams of the upper Black Warrior River system above the Fall Line (Mount, 1975; Mount, 1981; U.S. Fish and Wildlife Service, 1992). The food of flattened musk turtles consists primarily of mollusks (Mount, 1981). Historically, the Black Warrior River system supported 45 species of unionid mussels. A 1975 survey found 18 species, and a 1990 survey by the USFWS found only two species (U.S. Fish and Wildlife Service, 1992). Six major impoundments have been built along the river and water quality degradation as a result of row-crop agricultural activity, timbering, urban drainage, poultry farms, feedlots, and coal mines has been documented (Dodd, 1990). Locust Fork, the largest and longest Black Warrior tributary, once contained the bulk of the *S. depressus* populations. Locust Fork is now degraded along its entire length as a result of heavy siltation associated with mines, although some turtles still occur there (K. Dodd, National Biological Service, pers. comm.). The flattened musk turtle is also threatened by disease and collection for the pet trade (Dodd, in press).

STRIPED MUD TURTLE — *Kinosternon baurii* — G5

The striped mud turtle is ranked SU and considered of special concern in South Carolina. In Virginia (S4), North Carolina (S3), and Georgia (S3), the species appears restricted to high quality riverine floodplain forests and blackwater cypress swamps and streams, and it is not found in man-made habitats or silted wetlands. In Florida, a unique population called the Key mud turtle is ranked S2 and occurs in permanent and temporary freshwater ponds on some islands of the lower Florida Keys. Rapid development is depleting the water table and thus threatening these ponds. Florida lists this population as endangered (Dunson, 1992).

COMMON MAP TURTLE — *Graptemys geographica* — G5

Although widespread in its distribution, the common map turtle is in a peripheral portion of its range in southwest Virginia where it is ranked S2S3 (Mitchell, 1994; Roble, 1996). The species is found in the same streams and subjected to the same threats as *Sternotherus minor peltifer*. The common map turtle is also in a peripheral portion of its range in northwest Georgia, where it is known only from the Conasauga River. Georgia ranks the common map turtle as S1 and lists it as rare (Georgia Natural Heritage Program, 1996). These turtles are associated with moving water systems. Human activities have dammed many rivers, removed the tree snags used for basking, and dredged the bottoms that harbor the mollusks that comprise a large portion of the diet of map turtles. Although the time has passed for us to know with certainty what historical population levels were, most ecologists familiar with map turtles would generally concur that their numbers have decreased and that most populations now appear on a downward trend.

BARBOUR'S MAP TURTLE — *Graptemys barbouri* — G2

The USFWS formerly listed Barbour's map turtle as C2. Barbour's map turtle is endemic to the Appalachicola River system. This range includes the Appalachicola in Florida, the Flint River in Georgia, and the Chattahoochee River in Georgia and Alabama. In Florida, where this species is ranked S2 and listed as special concern, the largest populations are found in alluvial and spring-fed rivers, such as the Chipola, and other clear, limestone-bottomed streams with an abundance of mollusks and fallen trees (Florida Natural Areas Inventory, unpublished data). In Georgia, Barbour's map turtle is also ranked S2 and is state listed as threatened. It occurs in the Flint River upstream to Lake Blackshear, where individuals are being affected by an unknown shell disease. Lovich et al. (1996) suggested that exposure to toxic chemicals may be causing the observed shell dermatitis. Other basking species in Lake Blackshear, notably *Trachemys scripta* and *Pseudemys concinna* are also similarly afflicted, suggesting a relationship between the causal agent and shell drying. In the Chattahoochee River along the Georgia-Alabama line, threats include channelization, dredging, and pollution that affects both the turtles and mollusks. Collection for the pet trade has also been heavy. Alabama ranks Barbour's map turtle as S2 and lists it as protected. Martof (1956) considered Barbour's map turtle uncommon to common in Georgia.

ALABAMA MAP TURTLE — *Graptemys pulchra* — G4

The Alabama map turtle is ranked S2 in Mississippi and is declining in numbers due to degraded riverine water quality in the Tombigbee River system (T. Mann, Mississippi Natural Heritage Program, pers. comm.). It is in a peripheral portion of its range in northwest Georgia, where it is only known from the Conasauga River (Santhuff and Wilson, 1990). Georgia ranks it as S1 and lists it as rare. The global range of the Alabama map turtle is confined to the Tombigbee and Alabama river systems that empty into Mobile Bay.

PASCAGOULA MAP TURTLE — *Graptemys gibbonsi* — G3

The Pascagoula map turtle was recently described as a new species and was previously considered to be a variant of *Graptemys pulchra* (Lovich and McCoy, 1992). The species is confined to large to medium-sized rivers of the Pascagoula and Pearl river systems, including the Leaf, Chickasawhay, and Bogue Chitto in Mississippi and eastern Louisiana. Louisiana ranks the Pascagoula map turtle as S3. In Louisiana, Dundee and Rossman (1989) considered populations of *G. pulchra* (now designated as *G. gibbonsi*) to be declining as a result of habitat degradation of the Pearl River system. These impacts include channelization for navigation and discharges of industrial effluent, particularly from the paper industry.

ESCAMBIA MAP TURTLE — *Graptemys ernsti* — G2

The Escambia map turtle was recently described as a new species, and like *Graptemys gibbonsi*, was previously considered to be a variant of *G. pulchra* (Lovich and McCoy, 1992). This species is ranked S2 in both Florida and Alabama and occurs in large to medium-sized river systems that empty into Pensacola Bay, including the Escambia, Conecuh, Yellow, and Shoal rivers of southern Alabama and western Florida. It is absent from streams that lack freshwater mollusks and is probably threatened by a variety of pollutants, including heavy metals, and by channelization (Florida Natural Areas Inventory, unpublished data). Shealey (1992) considered populations of *G. pulchra* (now designated as *G. ernsti*) to be rare in the Escambia and Yellow river drainages in Florida.

RINGED SAWBACK TURTLE — *Graptemys oculifera* — G2

The ringed sawback turtle is federally listed as threatened. This species is ranked S2 and is state listed as endangered in Mississippi and ranked S2 in Louisiana. The decline in numbers of the ringed sawback turtle has been attributed to habitat modification and water quality deterioration in the Pearl and Bogue Chitto rivers, reservoir construction, channelization, de-snagging for navigation, siltation and subsequent loss of invertebrate food sources (S. Shively, Louisiana Natural Heritage Program, pers. comm.). On the Pearl River, fewer ringed sawback turtles were found downstream than upstream of Jackson, Mississippi, a major industrial and urban area. Poorer downstream water quality, which may impact the prey base, was suggested as the cause (Jones and Hartfield, 1995). Cagle (1953) found that ringed sawback turtles specialized and fed on aquatic insects that were associated with log snags.

YELLOW-BLOTCHED SAWBACK TURTLE — *Graptemys flavimaculata* — G2

The yellow-blotched sawback turtle is federally listed as threatened. It is endemic to the Pascagoula River system in Mississippi where it is ranked S2 and is state listed as endangered. Threats to this species are similar to those of the other *Graptemys* spp. and include profiteering in the pet trade, shooting of basking turtles, pollution, removal of snags, and channelization. In addition, high nest mortality as a result of increased flooding and inundation of sandbars and predation by fish crows (*Corvus ossifragous*), as well as low fecundity have been reported (LaClaire, 1995; Seigel and Brauman, 1995).

BLACK-KNOBBED SAWBACK TURTLE — *Graptemys nigrinoda* — G3

The black-knobbed sawback turtle (*Graptemys nigrinoda nigrinoda*) is ranked S2 and is state listed as endangered in Mississippi and is ranked S3 in Alabama. Collection for the pet trade, shooting of basking turtles, the elimination of snags and sandbars, and channelization in the Tenn-Tom Waterway of the Tombigbee River are the probable causes related to the apparent decline in numbers (T. Mann, Mississippi Natural Heritage Program, pers. comm.). The delta map turtle (*G. n. delticola*) is ranked S2 in Alabama, where it is restricted primarily to the delta of the Mobile and Tensaw river systems (Conant and Collins, 1991).

DIAMONDBACK TERRAPIN — *Malaclemys terrapin* — G5

The northern diamondback terrapin (*Malaclemys terrapin terrapin*), which ranges from Massachusetts to North Carolina, was formerly listed as C2 by the USFWS, and is ranked S3 and listed as special concern in North Carolina. Its status is undetermined in Virginia (Mitchell, 1991). North Carolina ranks the Carolina diamondback terrapin (*M. t. centrata*) as S3 and lists it as special concern. The mangrove diamondback terrapin (*M. t. rhizophorarum*) is ranked S2 in Florida and is restricted to mangrove habitats in the Florida Keys. It has been eliminated on most islands linked by U.S. Highway 1. As of 1982 it was still common around stands of black mangroves (Wood, 1992). The Mississippi diamondback terrapin (*M. t. pileata*) was formerly listed as C2 by the USFWS. Alabama ranks it as S2 and state protected and Louisiana ranks is as S2. The Texas diamondback terrapin (*M. t. littoralis*) occurs in Louisiana and Texas and was formerly listed as C2 by the USFWS. General degradation of salt marsh habitats, road associated mortality of nesting females, and drownings associated with crab pots are likely causes of population declines in all diamondback terrapin sub-species (Seigel and Gibbons, 1995).

BOG TURTLE — *Clemmys muhlenbergii* — G3

The USFWS formerly listed the southern populations of the bog turtle as C2. This secretive turtle occurs in mountain meadows and bogs of the southern Blue Ridge in Virginia, Tennessee, North Carolina, South Carolina, and Georgia. The largest populations exist in North Carolina and Virginia, where the turtle is ranked S2 and is state listed as threatened (North Carolina) and S1 and state listed as endangered (Virginia). The draining of wetlands, ditching of meadows, overgrazing, prevention of beaver activity, development, illegal collecting for the pet trade, and lack of environmental education among landowners and law enforcement personnel are cumulatively contributing to the decline of these turtles. Opportunities for metapopulation management and protection exist in both Virginia and North Carolina (Herman, 1988; Buhlmann et al., in press). In South Carolina, where the bog turtle is known from only two sites, which consist of impounded streams and beaver ponds, the turtle is ranked S1 and is state listed as threatened. Surveys of several classic montane bogs have failed to discover any specimens (S. Bennett, South Carolina Natural Heritage Trust, pers. comm.). Succession and tree canopy closure pose threats to bog turtle populations. Georgia ranks the bog turtle as S1 and lists it as threatened. The species has been reported from only three sites within Georgia, but survey work is ongoing (D. Herman, Zoo Atlanta, pers. comm.). Protection is currently being sought for the two known sites in Tennessee (B. Tryon, Knoxville Zoo, pers. comm.) where the bog turtle is ranked S1 and state listed as threatened.

SPOTTED TURTLE — *Clemmys guttata* — G5

Although not generally recognized as a species in decline, we suggest that populations of spotted turtles are imperiled. In the southeastern United States, spotted turtles inhabit blackwater cypress swamps, coastal plain wetlands, sinkhole ponds, and pine flatwoods ponds. South Carolina considers the spotted turtle as a species of concern (South Carolina Heritage Trust, 1996). Georgia ranks the spotted turtle as S3S4 (Georgia Natural Heritage Program, 1996).

Populations in Florida (S3) are found in shallow woodland pools in wet pine flatwoods and are often disjunct from other populations. The species is suffering from population declines in the Coastal Plain of Virginia because of urban development, the destruction of wetlands in association with logging operations, and wetland drainage for agriculture. Martof et al. (1980) considered this turtle particularly vulnerable to habitat disruption resulting from drainage and development. The International Union for the Conservation of Nature (IUCN) recognizes the spotted turtle as a species in need of regulation due to the large volume of individuals involved in the pet trade. Unfortunately, spotted turtles can still be collected legally throughout much of their range. In North Carolina, 543 were known to have been recently removed in a single year (A. Braswell, North Carolina State Museum of Natural History, pers. comm.). If that many are known to have been removed, then certainly some multiple of that number was actually taken. Ditmars (1936) described this turtle as abundant.

CHICKEN TURTLE — *Deirochelys reticularia* — G5

The western chicken turtle (*Deirochelys reticularia miaria*) is ranked S2 in Arkansas and has been declining in numbers due to loss of shallow weedy ponds and swamps (Arkansas Natural Heritage Commission, unpublished data). The western chicken turtle is also found in cypress-bordered ponds in southeast Missouri where it is ranked S1 and is state listed as endangered. The turtle had not been verified in Missouri since 1962, until several individuals were found during 1995 field surveys (Buhlmann and Johnson, 1995). The floodplain swamps in the Missouri Bootheel region, where these turtles historically occurred, have been almost completely destroyed for agriculture. The eastern chicken turtle (*D. r. reticularia*) is ranked S1 and is state listed as endangered in Virginia. There, one disjunct population exists at the northern periphery of the species' range in interdunal cypress ponds in a state park and natural area where no opportunities exist for immigration or emigration (Buhlmann, 1995). North Carolina ranks the eastern chicken turtle as S3 and considers it to be significantly rare (LeGrand and Hall, 1995). Chicken turtles are locally abundant in Carolina bays on the Savannah River Site in South Carolina (Buhlmann and Gibbons, authors' unpublished data). Martof (1956) considered the eastern chicken turtle common in Georgia. In general, terrestrial movement is common in this species and road associated mortality is high.

PAINTED TURTLE — *Chrysemys picta* — G5

The southern painted turtle (*Chrysemys picta dorsalis*) is ranked S3 and listed as special concern in Kentucky. It is threatened by wetlands modification at the northern periphery of its range (Kentucky Nature Preserves Commission, unpublished data). It is also in a peripheral portion of its northern range in adjacent southeast Missouri, but appears secure at present (T. Johnson, Missouri Department of Conservation, pers. comm.).

RIVER COOTER — *Pseudemys concinna* — G5

The Suwannee cooter (*Pseudemys concinna suwanniensis*) is ranked S3 in Florida. Densities of these river turtles are presently less than they were historically (D. Jackson, Florida Natural Areas Inventory, pers. comm.). Major rivers in which this subspecies occurs have been degraded by dredging, impoundment, mining, and other sources of pollution. Large numbers of these turtles were once harvested for human consumption (Jackson, 1992). Carr (1940) reported that in the 1930s enormous aggregations of Suwannee cooters foraged on the flats off the mouth of the Suwannee River. Recently, Seidel (1994) proposed that *P. c. suwanniensis* be elevated to specific status, although this designation has been questioned by Jackson (1995). The status of the hieroglyphic cooter (*P. c. hieroglyphica*) is undetermined in Virginia, where it is recorded only from the Holston River in the extreme southwestern portion of the state (Mitchell, 1991).

ALABAMA REDBELLIED TURTLE — *Pseudemys alabamensis* — G1

This turtle is an Alabama endemic ranked S1, state listed as protected, and federally listed as endangered. It is restricted to the lower Mobile Bay and tributary streams in Mobile and Baldwin counties (Ernst et al., 1994). It reaches its greatest abundance in the uppermost portion of Mobile Bay in fresh to moderately brackish water that supports an abundance of submergent vegetation (Mount, 1975). The numbers of juvenile Alabama redbellied turtles apparently declined between 1970 and 1983 (Dobie and Bagley, 1990). Nesting was previously thought to be confined to one island, but is now known to occur on several spoil banks and along a causeway in Mobile Bay (D. Nelson, University of South Alabama, pers. comm.). Development, pollution, collecting for the pet trade, and a limited range are cited as causes for concern (Ernst et al., 1994).

FLORIDA REDBELLIED TURTLE — *Pseudemys nelsoni* — G5

Relatively abundant in Florida, the Florida redbellied turtle reaches the northern edge of its range in the Okefenokee Swamp in southeastern Georgia where it is ranked S2.

MISSISSIPPI REDBELLIED TURTLE — *Pseudemys* sp. — G1

This undescribed redbellied turtle was formerly listed as C2 by the USFWS. It is a Mississippi endemic that is restricted to the lower Pascagoula River (J. Dobie, Auburn University, unpublished data). It is ranked S1 and state listed as endangered in Mississippi. Threats to this turtle likely include those mentioned previously for *Graptemys flavimaculata*. Prior to 1950, shrimp trawlers reported capturing large numbers of "cooters" in the Mississippi Sound and this species may have been formerly abundant there (Mississippi Department of Wildlife, Fisheries, and Parks, 1992). All-terrain vehicles have been implicated as responsible for the disturbance of this turtle's nesting beaches. Morphological differences suggest that the Mississippi red-bellied turtle is unique from the Alabama red-bellied turtle, but the biochemical genetic differences are currently unresolved (C. Lydeard, University of Alabama, pers. comm.).

SLIDER TURTLE — *Trachemys scripta* — G5

In Virginia, the Cumberland slider (*Trachemys scripta troosti*) exists at the northeastern margin of its range (Mitchell, 1994) and is ranked S1. In Virginia it is known only from the Holston River and probably faces the same water pollution threats as already described for *Sternotherus minor peltifer* and *Graptemys geographica*. Tennessee ranks the Cumberland slider as S3S4. In Louisiana, at least 25 turtle farms have been reported to remove 100,000 mature individuals of the red-eared slider (*T. s. elegans*) from the wild annually (Warwick, 1986; Warwick et al., 1990). Data support the hypothesis that harvesting of adult sliders is having a significant impact on turtle populations in southern Louisiana. Turtles from harvested sites were significantly smaller in body size than turtles from protected sites (Close and Seigel, in press). The International Union for the Conservation of Nature is considering regulations restricting trade in this species, as large numbers are exported annually to Asian markets for food and European countries as pets. Populations of red-eared sliders have become established outside of their native range due to pet releases (Moll et al., in press). Many populations of yellow bellied sliders (*T. s. scripta*) from southeastern Virginia display morphological characteristics that indicate genetic influence from *T. s. elegans* (Mitchell, 1994).

FLORIDA SOFTSHELL TURTLE — *Trionyx (Apalone) ferox* — G5

The Florida softshell turtle reaches its northernmost range in South Carolina in ponds, lakes, and rivers of the Combahee and Savannah river system (Martof et al., 1980). This species is not well known in South Carolina and has been ranked SU and listed as special concern. At the western edge of its range in Alabama, it is ranked S2 and is state listed as protected. This softshell inhabits lakes, big clear water springs, permanent ponds, and occasionally slow-moving stretches of rivers (Conant and Collins, 1991). Recent information suggests that Florida softshell turtles are being harvested in Florida and shipped to Japan for food (Ft. Pierce Tribune, 1996).

SMOOTH SOFTSHELL TURTLE — *Trionyx (Apalone) mutica* — G5

In Florida, the Gulf Coast smooth softshell turtle (*Trionyx mutica calvata*) is ranked S2 and has a limited distribution that includes the Escambia River. This subspecies also occurs in the Pearl and Tombigbee rivers in Mississippi, two parishes in Louisiana (ranked S3), and in the Conecuh, Escambia, and Mobile Bay drainages in Alabama. Although the species has been poorly surveyed, habitat degradation in the big rivers may be a concern (S. Shively, Louisiana Natural Heritage Program, pers. comm.). The midland smooth softshell turtle (*T. m. mutica*) is found in the Ohio River in Kentucky where riverine water quality might be a concern and where it is ranked S3 and listed as special concern. In a study of both *T. mutica* and spiny softshell turtles (*T. spinifera*), Doody (1995) found that flooding of sandbars resulted in nest mortality. These results suggest that increases in flooding as a result of channelization may contribute to population declines. Doody (1995) also found that 21 percent of all predated nests were destroyed by introduced fire ants (*Solenopsis* sp.).

SPINY SOFTSHELL TURTLE — *Trionyx (Apalone) spinifera* — G5

The eastern spiny softshell turtle (*Trionyx spinifera spinifera*) is ranked S2 in Virginia, and it is ranked S1 and is listed as special concern in North Carolina. In those states, it inhabits rivers of the Tennessee River drainage, specifically the Clinch, Holston, Powell, and French Broad rivers, and Copper Creek. Threats to this species include poor water quality in rivers and are generally the same as those described previously for *Sternotherus minor peltifer* and *Graptemys geographica*. The Gulf Coast spiny softshell turtle (*T. s. aspera*) is ranked S3 in North Carolina where it reaches the northern edge of its range in southcentral river systems.

CAUSES OF DECLINES

Worldwide, the great majority of documented reptilian extinctions directly attributable to human-related disturbance have been on islands (Case et al., 1992). A minimum of 60 Holocene (Recent) reptile extinctions (13 percent on continents) are known to have occurred, compared to 115 extinctions of mammals (64 percent on continents), and 171 extinctions of birds (ten percent on continents). On continents, reptiles and birds have fared better than mammals, but birds have suffered more than either of the other groups on islands, judged on the basis of documented occurrences and disappearances. Overall, reptiles appear to have been slightly more resilient to human disturbance than birds or mammals (Case et al., 1992). For example, in striking contrast to the severely depleted mammalian megafauna, only three reptilian extinctions in North America (tortoise, *Geochelone wilsonii*; horned lizard, *Phrynosoma josecitensis*; and a large rattlesnake, *Crotalus potterensis*) are known from the approximately 130 fossil species described from the continental United States since the Pleistocene (about 10,000 years before the present) (Moodie and Van Devender, 1979). All of these reptiles were terrestrial, and the disappearance of none has been confirmed to have been in response to human environmental impacts.

However, many reptile species are clearly not faring well today. For example, Lydeard and Mayden (1995) considered 43 percent of Alabama's freshwater turtles to be imperiled. Lovich (1995) considered 45 percent of the total United States turtle species to require conservation action. We consider 62 percent of the total aquatic reptile fauna in the southeastern United States to be at some risk of extinction or significantly declining in numbers in at least a portion of their range (Table 3).

Peripheral Taxa

In this review we have included taxa that are rare or threatened due to their peripheral occurrences in one or more of the states in the Southeast. Generally, most of these taxa have wide distributions, occur in a variety of habitat types, and are not threatened globally. For example, in Kentucky, the broad-banded water snake (*Nerodia fasciata confluens*) and the southern painted turtle (*Chrysemys picta dorsalis*) are threatened by wetlands modification. Both taxa currently appear secure further south. In Georgia, the striped crayfish snake (*Regina alleni*), and the Florida redbellied turtle (*Pseudemys nelsoni*) reach their northernmost distributions in the Okefenokee Swamp and are considered rare due to their limited state distribution. Both taxa seem to be common in Florida. At the northern extent of its range, in extreme southeastern Virginia, the eastern glass lizard (*Ophisaurus ventralis*) occurs only in freshwater wetlands between coastal dunes (Mitchell, 1994). Eastern glass lizards occur in a wide range of habitats further south.

The identification and protection of taxa at the fringes of their ranges are important for conservation. Populations of species that exist at the edge of their ranges are likely to exhibit genetic differences from populations at the center because different selection pressures may be acting on them. These populations may already be physiologically stressed and therefore susceptible to human disturbance. Conversely, natural selection may function most strongly on fringe populations and hence these populations may have great importance for the long-term continuance of evolutionary processes. The rate of evolutionary change in a population is proportional to the amount of genetic diversity available (Fisher, 1930). Therefore, the reduction of intraspecific genetic diversity, as possibly caused by the extinction of peripheral or fringe populations, may limit the future ability of said species to survive under changing environmental conditions (Meffe and Carroll, 1994).

Commercial Exploitation

The decline of the alligator snapping turtle (*Macroclemys temminckii*) is a direct result of

Table 3. Numbers of aquatic reptile taxa (all recognized species and subspecies) occurring within the southeastern United States that fall into imperiled or unimperiled categories. Imperiled taxa are defined as taxa of conservation concern in at least one southeastern state within which they occur. Percent of total taxa reported in parentheses.

Group	Total Taxa	Imperiled Taxa	Presumed Unimperiled
Crocodilians	2	2 (100)	0 (0)
Lizards	2	2 (100)	0 (0)
Snakes	39	22 (56.4)	17 (43.6)
Turtles	57	36 (63.2)	21 (36.8)
Totals	100	62 (62)	38 (38)

unregulated or poorly regulated harvest (Sloan and Lovich, 1995). Congdon et al. (1994) have shown that populations of common snapping turtles (*Chelydra serpentina*) cannot withstand continued cropping of adults. Removal of long-lived, slow-growing animals with life history strategies aimed at replacement reproduction spread out over the lifetimes of the animals will cause a population decline (Congdon et al., 1993). Based on the reports of continued harvest and continued degradation of riverine systems, the future looks grim for alligator snapping turtles. Other turtles, primarily *Graptemys* ssp., *Clemmys guttata*, and *Clemmys muhlenbergii* have been exploited for the pet trade. Removal of individuals from populations that are already reduced because of human degradation of habitat represents another additive impact on populations. Even presently abundant species (e.g., *Trachemys scripta elegans*) should be considered of concern in some instances because of the vast numbers being removed from the wild and shipped to other countries.

Wetland Habitat Destruction

Destruction and alteration of wetland habitats, which include Carolina bays, cypress swamps, bottomland hardwoods, pine flatwoods ponds, mountain bogs, and salt marshes, have resulted in population declines of 34 aquatic snake and turtle taxa. The fragmentation and isolation of remaining wetlands subject populations to a greater risk of extinction through the loss of immigration and emigration opportunities, inbreeding, and random environmental perturbations.

Taxa at greatest risk from wetland habitat losses include the green water snakes (*Nerodia cyclopion* and *N. floridana*), copperbellied watersnake (*N. erythrogaster neglecta*), swamp snake (*Seminatrix pygaea*), rainbow snake (*Farancia erythrogramma*), and the glossy crayfish snake (*Regina rigida rigida*). Turtles at risk for the same reasons include the spotted turtle (*Clemmys guttata*), bog turtle (*C. muhlenbergii*), and chicken turtle (*Deirochelys reticularia*). The alteration, development, and pollution of salt marsh and mangrove swamp habitats have been shown to be the primary causes of declines in the salt marsh snakes *Nerodia clarkii* and *N. sipedon williamengelsi*, diamondback terrapins (*Malaclemys terrapin*), and American crocodile (*Crocodylus acutus*).

River Degradation

Overall, 22 southeastern reptile taxa (20 turtles, two snakes) show declines attributable to river and stream degradation. Among the most imperiled are species endemic to single or a few river systems. The map turtles (*Graptemys* spp.) are characterized by great taxonomic diversity and drainage-specific endemism, primarily Coastal Plain drainages along the Gulf of Mexico coast from the Appalachicola River in Florida to the Guadalupe River in Texas (Lovich and McCoy, 1992). Seven of the 13 species are restricted to single drainage systems.

Pollution, channelization, shooting, harvesting, and disease are all causes for declines of map turtles. In general, some of the musk turtles (*Sternotherus* spp.), the alligator snapping turtle (*Macroclemys temminckii*), and several *Pseudemys* spp. are imperiled for the same reasons. The documented declines in riverine fish faunas often parallel declines in riverine reptile faunas. Declines in fish species in large polluted rivers have often been attributed to chronic, sub-lethal pollution, which cause fish to disappear gradually as they produce fewer young, grow more slowly, and die from stress-related diseases (Moyle and Leidy, 1992). Many river fishes assimilate heavy metals and pesticides in their tissues. Aquatic turtles with relatively longer lifespans have been poorly studied with regard to chronic exposure to pollutants.

Sheldon (1988) stated that the best protection strategy for rivers would be to focus conservation efforts on the largest tributaries that contain their original faunas in as many regions as possible. In our assessment, river-dwelling reptiles are at the highest level of imperiled status and should be considered a high conservation priority.

Habitat Fragmentation

The opportunity for populations to exchange genetic material and find appropriate habitat when their current habitat becomes unsuitable is critical for their long-term persistence. Alteration of terrestrial habitats due to clearcutting, farming, highway construction, and other forms of development has left many wetland habitats isolated in a surrounding hostile landscape matrix. Riverine habitats are subject to fragmentation because reservoirs inhibit or stop the movement of individuals and isolate riffle habitats between deep lake habitats.

Populations of organisms that live in wetland habitats must be able to migrate to other wetland locations when their current habitats become unsuitable due to natural causes such as succession and drought. For example, slider turtle (*Trachemys scripta*) data showed that during a drought starting in 1985, most individuals exited Ellenton Bay, a typical Carolina bay habitat on the SRS, and moved toward water in a nearby beaver pond. When the drought ended, the turtles began to return (Burke et al., 1995).

During the drying period of 1986 through 1988 at Ellenton Bay, more than 189 snakes of three species were captured at the drift fence as they departed the area (Seigel et al., 1995). Banded water snakes (*Nerodia fasciata*) apparently left the site in direct response to low water levels, whereas swamp snakes (*Seminatrix pygaea*) left due to the absence of small fish (*Gambusia* sp.) and salamander (*Ambystoma* sp.) prey. Few green water snakes (*Nerodia floridana*) were recorded leaving, and the snakes that remained presumably perished. However, all species are again present at this site. The green water snake, unobserved at Ellenton Bay for five years post-drought, was first seen again in the spring of 1993, but numbers are less than pre-drought.

Turtles originally marked in Ellenton Bay were captured in a variety of more permanent aquatic sites during the next few years after the aforementioned period of drought, some up to 3.1 miles (5 km) away. If the neighboring aquatic habitats had been unavailable for these turtles to inhabit throughout the period of drought, the Ellenton Bay population would perhaps have been completely eliminated in response to this natural climatic event. Although we have no data on the exact dispersal patterns of snakes, we assume that many also weathered the drought by emigrating from Ellenton Bay to find temporary sanctuaries in nearby bodies of permanent water.

Loss of Surrounding Upland Habitats

Many aquatic reptiles require the adjacent terrestrial habitat at certain seasons. For example, the exact locations of nests and terrestrial hibernation sites of mud turtles (*Kinosternon subrubrum*) were recorded by Burke and Gibbons (1995) in South Carolina. All locations were outside the federal wetland delineation line. Likewise, most individuals in a nearby population of chicken turtles (*Deirochelys reticularia*) wintered in forested upland habitats 164-820 feet (50-250 m) from the wetland delineation margin of a Carolina bay (K. A. Buhlmann and J. W. Gibbons, authors' unpublished data). Understanding the natural history, including specific habitat needs, of wetland species is crucial for effective conservation planning (Buhlmann et. al., 1993a).

Natural Disasters

The diamondback terrapin (*Malaclemys terrapin*) serves as an example of the resilience of at least one native species to what humans regard as a severe natural disaster. In 1990, Hurricane Hugo hit the southeast coast around Charleston, South Carolina. Its commercial impact was catastrophic, yet its impact on terrapins was inconsequential. Until 1990, researchers at Savannah River Ecology Lab had captured and marked more than 500 terrapins in the tidal creeks and marshes around Kiawah Island, close to the focal point of the storm. Post-hurricane recaptures suggest that the diamondback terrapins in this healthy population were unaffected on a population level (J. W. Gibbons, author's unpublished data). This may not have been the case if the terrapins were already declining in numbers due to destruction of the marsh habitat and removal for commercial purposes.

Lack of Ecological Knowledge

Regrettably, we know so little about many species of aquatic reptiles that we can only speculate on the best ways to provide protection. Reptiles are often secretive creatures that require special capture techniques. Simply documenting their presence is not always easy. The SRS in South Carolina has been one of the most intensively studied tracts of land for reptiles in North America and gives some insight into this problem. More than 50,000 reptiles of 57 species have been captured during the past 41 years, and the species list is still growing. Freeman (1955) recorded 44 species; Duever (1967) 49; Gibbons (1977) 50; Gibbons and Patterson (1978) 51; and Gibbons and Semlitsch (1991) 57. Had aquatic habitats on the SRS been degraded or destroyed rather than protected since the 1950s, the presence of many of these species would probably have gone unrecognized.

Simply documenting a species' presence is only the first step toward ecological understanding. State and federal agencies should fund basic research including an inventory of the nation's biodiversity. It is also the responsibility of educators at the university level to explain the value of protecting biodiversity to the general public and to politicians.

SUMMARY

Turtles are declining in both number of species and total numbers at alarming rates through-out the world (Ernst and Barbour, 1989). Worldwide, losses have been attributed to causes that include the collecting of eggs, juveniles, and adults for the pet trade and human food consumption. Long-lived species with delayed sexual maturity and low reproductive rates cannot sustain continued high levels of harvest and maintain stable populations. Destruction and deterioration of natural habitats has led to reduced population sizes and to the fragmentation and isolation of remaining populations. For reptiles, the ever-increasing web of roads that spans the landscape serves to increase the probability of mortality for individuals of many species, leading to eventual local population reductions or extinctions.

We found that 35.5 percent of our list of imperiled aquatic reptiles are threatened be-cause of the continuing, cumulative abuse sustained by river systems. Another 37.1 per-cent are declining due to loss of Coastal Plain wetland habitats, 1.6 percent due to loss of mountain wetlands, 13.0 percent due to losses of brackish and salt marshes, and 3.2 per-cent due to loss of prairie wetlands.

If we are serious about protecting biodiversity and halting wildlife population declines in the Southeast, several intellectually simple, yet politically difficult changes must be made. First, the destruction and alteration of remaining wetlands must cease. The idea that landowners have the right to do whatever they wish to the natural resources on their land needs to be re-thought and openly addressed. Secondly, river environments must be restored and protected. Our river-dwelling reptile fauna is the most immediately imper-iled reptile group. The cumulative effects of industrial wastes, pesticides, herbicides, oil runoff, inappropriate and careless farming practices, and other environmental insults could ultimately relegate the rivers to little more than shipping canals. The cumulative effects of this abuse have resulted not only in declines of aquatic fauna but also present a real threat to human health as well. Downstream of almost every effluent discharge point is a drink-ing water intake. If people truly understood the dangers they face from the current treat-ment of our rivers, major changes could be made. Lastly, and possibly most important, human population growth must be controlled. The human population cannot keep grow-ing exponentially (Meffe et al., 1993). People require space and resources that displace wildlife. The population problem is a concern that most choose to ignore, but it is the rooted cause of most, if not all, of our environmental problems.

ACKNOWLEDGEMENTS

The following state biologists were invaluable in providing expertise and information about southeastern aquatic reptiles: Cindy Osborne, Arkansas Natural Heritage Commis-sion; Steve Bennett, South Carolina Department of Natural Resources; David J. Printiss and Dale R. Jackson, both Florida Natural Areas Inventory; Tom Mann, Mississippi Natural Heritage Program; Greg Krakow, Georgia Natural Heritage Program; David I. Withers, Tennessee Ecological Services Division; Tom Bloom, Kentucky State Nature Preserves Commission; Megan G. Rollins, Steven M. Roble, and Christopher H. Hobson, all Virginia Division of Natural Heritage; Tom R. Johnson, Missouri Department of Conservation; Harry LeGrand, North Carolina Natural Heritage Program; Mark Bailey, Alabama Natural Heritage

Program; Steve Shively, Louisiana Natural Heritage Program; and Melissa Morrison, TNC, Eastern Heritage Task Force. The manuscript was improved with comments from J. C. Mitchell, R. A. Seigel, D. Collins, G. W. Benz, S. McKeon and M. Plummer. Funding for manuscript preparation was provided by contract number DE-AC09-76SR00-819 between the U.S. Department of Energy and the University of Georgia's Savannah River Ecology Laboratory.

REFERENCES

Adler, K. 1979. A brief history of herpetology in North America before 1900. Herpetology Circular Number 8, Society for the Study of Amphibians and Reptiles, Athens, OH, 40 p.

Alabama Natural Heritage Program. 1996. Rare species inventory list. Department of Conservation and Natural Resources, Montgomery, AL, 26 p.

Arkansas Natural Heritage Commission. 1996. Inventory animal list. Arkansas Natural Heritage Commission, Little Rock, AR, 9 p.

Bartram, W. [1791] 1980. *William Bartram Travels.* Reprint, Peregrine Smith, Inc., Salt Lake City, UT.

Benke, A. C. 1990. A perspective on America's vanishing streams. *Journal of the North American Benthological Society* 9:77-88.

Blankenship, E. L., M. A. Bailey, K. Schnuelle, and B. Hauge. 1995. Geographic distribution: *Sternotherus carinatus. Herpetological Review* 26:106-107.

Buhlmann, K. A. 1995. Habitat use, terrestrial movements, and conservation of the turtle, *Deirochelys reticularia* in Virginia. *Journal of Herpetology* 29:173-181.

Buhlmann, K. A., and T. R. Johnson. 1995. Geographic distribution: *Deirochelys reticularia miaria. Herpetological Review* 26:209.

Buhlmann, K. A., J. C. Mitchell, and C. A. Pague. 1993a. Amphibian and small mammal abundance and diversity in saturated forested wetlands and adjacent uplands of southeastern Virginia. In *Proceedings of a Workshop on Saturated Forested Wetlands in the Mid-Atlantic Region: The State of the Science.* S. D. Eckles, A. Jennings, A. Spingarn, and C. Wienhold (eds.). U.S. Fish and Wildlife Service, Annapolis, MD, p. 1-7.

Buhlmann, K. A., J. C. Mitchell, and M. G. Rollins. in press. New approaches for the conservation of bog turtles, *Clemmys muhlenbergii*, in Virginia. In *Proceedings of the Symposium: Conservation and Management of Tortoises and Freshwater Turtles.* J. van Abbema (ed.). American Museum of Natural History, New York, NY.

Buhlmann, K. A., A. H. Savitzky, B. A. Savitzky, and J. C. Mitchell. 1993b. Geographic distribution: Glossy crayfish snake (*Regina rigida*). *Herpetological Review* 24:156-157.

Burke V. J., and J. W. Gibbons. 1995. Terrestrial buffer zones and wetland conservation: A case study of freshwater turtles in a Carolina bay. *Conservation Biology* 9:1365-1369.

Burke, V. J., J. L. Greene, and J. W. Gibbons. 1995. The effect of sample size and study duration on metapopulation estimates for slider turtles (*Trachemys scripta*). *Herpetologica* 51:451-456.

Bury, R. B. 1979. Population ecology of freshwater turtles. In *Turtles: Perspectives and Research*. M. Harless, and H. Morlock (eds.). John Wiley and Sons, New York, NY, p. 571-602.

Cagle, F. R. 1953. The status of the turtle *Graptemys oculifera* (Baur). *Zoologica* **38**:137-144.

Carr, A. F., Jr. 1940. A contribution to the herpetology of Florida. *University of Florida Biology Science Series* **3**:1-118.

Case, T. J., D. T. Bolger, and A. D. Richman. 1992. Reptilian extinctions: The last ten thousand years. In *Conservation Biology*. P. L. Fiedler, and S. K. Jain (eds.). Chapman and Hall, New York, NY, p. 91-125.

Close, L. M., and R. A. Seigel. in press. Differences in size structure among populations of red-eared sliders (*Trachemys scripta*) subjected to different levels of harvesting. *Chelonian Conservation Biology*.

Conant, R., and J. T. Collins. 1991. *A Field Guide to Reptiles and Amphibians of Eastern and Central North America*. Houghton Mifflin Company, Boston, MA.

Congdon, J. D., A. F. Dunham, and R. C. van Loben Sels. 1993. Delayed sexual maturity and demographics of Blanding's turtles (*Emydoidea blandingii*): Implications for conservation and management of long-lived organisms. *Conservation Biology* **7**:826-833.

Congdon, J. D., A. E. Dunham, and R. C. van Loben Sels. 1994. Demographics of common snapping turtles (*Chelydra serpentina*): Implications for conservation and management of long-lived organisms. *American Zoologist* **34**:397-408.

Dellinger, S. C., and J. D. Black. 1938. Herpetology of Arkansas. *Occasional Papers of the University of Arkansas Museum* **16**:1-47.

Ditmars, R. L. 1936. *The Reptiles of North America*. Doubleday, Doran and Company, Inc., New York, NY.

Ditmars, R. L. 1939. *A Field Book of North American Snakes*. Doubleday, Doran and Company, Inc., New York, NY.

Dobie, J. L., and F. M. Bagley. 1990. Alabama red-bellied turtle (*Pseudemys alabamensis*) recovery plan. U.S. Fish and Wildlife Service, Atlanta, GA, 17 p.

Dodd, C. K., Jr. 1990. Effects of habitat fragmentation on a stream-dwelling species, the flattened musk turtle *Sternotherus depressus*. *Biological Conservation* **54**:33-45.

Dodd, C. K., Jr. in press. Species account: Flattened musk turtle (*Sternotherus depressus*). In *Conservation Biology of Freshwater Turtles*. P. C. H. Pritchard, and A. G. L. Rhodin (eds.). Chelonian Research Foundation, Lunenburg, MA.

Doody, J. S. 1995. A comparative study of two syntopic species of softshell turtles (*Apalone mutica* and *Apalone spinifera*) in southcentral Louisiana. M.S. Thesis, Southeastern Louisiana University, Hammond, LA.

Duever, M. J. 1967. Distributions in space and time of reptiles on the Savannah River Plant in South Carolina. M.S. Thesis, University of Georgia, Athens, GA.

Dundee, H. A., and D. A. Rossman. 1989. *The Amphibians and Reptiles of Louisiana*. Louisiana State University Press, Baton Rogue, LA.

Dunson, W. A. 1992. Striped mud turtle. In *Rare and Endangered Biota of Florida. Volume III. Amphibians and Reptiles*. P. E. Moler (ed.). University Press of Florida, Gainesville, FL, p. 105-110.

Ernst, C. H., and R. W. Barbour. 1989. *Turtles of the World*. Smithsonian Institution Press, Washington, D.C.

Ernst, C. H., J. E. Lovich, and R. W. Barbour. 1994. *Turtles of the United States and Canada*. Smithsonian Institution Press, Washington, D.C.

Fisher, R. A. 1930. *The Genetical Theory of Natural Selection*. Clarendon Press, Oxford, U.K.

Florida Natural Areas Inventory. 1995. Tracking lists of special plants and lichens, invertebrates, vertebrates, and natural communities. Florida Natural Areas Inventory, Tallahassee, FL, 51 p.

Freeman, H. W. 1955. Amphibians and reptiles of the SRP Area, Chelonia. *University of South Carolina Publication Series III* 1:227-238.

Frost, C. C., J. Walker, and R. K. Peet. 1986. Fire-dependent savannas and prairies of the Southeast: Original extent, preservation status and management problems. In *Wilderness and Natural Areas in the Eastern United States: A Management Challenge*. D. L. Kulhavy, and R. N. Conner (eds.). Center for Applied Studies, School of Forestry, Stephen F. Austin St. University, Nacogdoches, TX, p. 348-357.

Ft. Pierce Tribune. 1996. Bandits rack up enemies. 3 May 1996 edition, Ft. Pierce Tribune, Ft. Pierce, FL, p. A1, A5.

Georgia Natural Heritage Program. 1996. Special concern animals of Georgia. Georgia Department of Natural Resources, Social Circle, GA, 5 p.

Gibbons, J. W. 1977. Snakes of the Savannah River Plant with information about snakebite prevention and treatment. Publication SRO-NERP-01, Savannah River Environmental Research Park Program, Aiken, SC, 26 p.

Gibbons, J. W., and K. K. Patterson. 1978. The reptiles and amphibians of the Savannah River Plant. Publication SRO-NERP-02, Savannah River Environmental Research Park Program, Aiken, SC, 24 p.

Gibbons, J. W., and R. D. Semlitsch. 1991. *Guide to the Reptiles and Amphibians of the Savannah River Site*. The University of Georgia Press, Athens, GA.

Godley, J. S. 1980. Foraging ecology of the striped swamp snake, *Regina alleni*, in southern Florida. *Ecological Monographs* 50:411-436.

Gosselink, J. G., and L. C. Lee. 1989. Cumulative impact assessment in bottomland hardwood forests. *Wetlands* 9:89-174.

Gunderson, L. H. 1984. Regeneration of cypress in logged and burned stands at Corkscrew Swamp Sanctuary, Florida. In *Cypress Swamps*. K. C. Ewel, and H. T. Odum (eds.). University Presses of Florida, Gainesville, FL, p. 349-357.

Harless, M., and H. Morlock. 1979. *Turtles: Perspectives and Research*. John Wiley and Sons, New York, NY.

Hefner, J. M., and J. D. Brown. 1984. Wetlands trends in the southeastern United States. *Wetlands* 4:1-11.

Herman, D. W. 1988. Status of the bog turtle, *Clemmys muhlenbergii* (Schoepff), in the southeastern United States. Unpublished Report submitted to the Conservation and Research Committee, Friends of the Atlanta Zoo, Atlanta, GA, 11 p.

Iverson, J. B. 1992. *A Revised Checklist with Distribution Maps of the Turtles of the World*. privately printed, Earlham College, Richmond, IN.

Jackson, D. R. 1992. River cooter. In *Rare and Endangered Biota of Florida. Volume III. Amphibians and Reptiles*. P. E. Moler (ed.). University Press of Florida, Gainesville, FL, p. 166-170.

Jackson, D. R. 1995. Systematics of the *Pseudemys concinna-floridana* complex (Testudines: Emydidae): An alternative interpretation. *Chelonian Conservation Biology* 1:329-333.

Johnson, T. R. 1987. *The Amphibians and Reptiles of Missouri.* Missouri Department of Conservation, Jefferson City, MO.

Jones, R. L., and P. D. Hartfield. 1995. Population size and growth in the turtle *Graptemys oculifera. Journal of Herpetology* 29:426-436.

Kentucky Nature Preserves Commission. 1995. Endangered, threatened, special concern, and historic plants and animals of Kentucky. Kentucky Nature Preserves Commission, Frankfort, KY, 16 p.

King, F. W., H. W. Campbell, and P. E. Moler. 1982. Review of the status of the American crocodile. In *Crocodiles — 5th Working Meeting of the IUCN/SSC Crocodile Specialist Group.* F. W. King (ed.). International Union for the Conservation of Nature, Gland, Switzerland, p. 84-98.

Kochman, H. I., and S. P. Christman. 1992. Atlantic salt marsh snake. In *Rare and Endangered Biota of Florida. Volume III. Amphibians and Reptiles.* P. E. Moler (ed.). University Press of Florida, Gainesville, FL, p. 111-116.

LaClaire, L. 1995. New clues in map turtle decline. *Endangered Species Bulletin* 10(2):1-15.

LeGrand, H. E., Jr., and S. P. Hall. 1995. Natural heritage program list of the rare animal species of North Carolina. North Carolina Natural Heritage Program, Department of Environment, Health, and Natural Resources, Raleigh, NC, 67 p.

Louisiana Natural Heritage Program. 1996. Animals of special concern. Louisiana Department of Wildlife and Fisheries, Baton Rouge, LA, 4 p.

Lovich, J. E. 1995. Turtles. In *Our Living Resources: A Report to the Nation on the Distribution, Abundance, and Health of U.S. Plants, Animals, and Ecosystems.* E. T. LaRoe, G. S. Farris, C. E. Puckett, P. D. Doran, and M. J. Mae (eds.). National Biological Service, U.S. Department of the Interior, Washington, D.C., p. 118-121.

Lovich, J. E., S. W. Gotte, C. H. Ernst, J. C. Harshbarger, A. F. Laemmerzahl, and J. W. Gibbons. 1996. Prevalence and histopathology of shell disease in turtles from Lake Blackshear, Georgia. *Journal of Wildlife Diseases* 32:259-265.

Lovich, J. E., and C. J. McCoy. 1992. Review of the *Graptemys pulchra* group (Reptilia: Testudines: Emydidae), with descriptions of two new species. *Annals of the Carnegie Museum* 61:293-315.

Lydeard, C., and R. L. Mayden. 1995. A diverse and endangered aquatic ecosystem of the southeast United States. *Conservation Biology* 9: 800-805.

MacDonald, P. O., W. E. Frayer, and J. K. Clauser. 1979. *Documentation, Chronology, and Future Projections of Bottomland Hardwood Habitat Losses in the Lower Mississippi Alluvial Plain. Volumes 1 and 2.* U.S. Fish and Wildlife Service, Washington D.C.

Martof, B. S. 1956. *Amphibians and Reptiles of Georgia.* University of Georgia Press, Athens, GA.

Martof, B. S., W. M. Palmer, J. R. Bailey, and J. R. Harrison III. 1980. *Amphibians and Reptiles of the Carolinas and Virginia.* The University North Carolina Press, Chapel Hill, NC.

McIlhenny, E. A. 1935. *The Alligator's Life History.* Christopher Publishing House, Boston, MA.

Means, D. B. 1992. Southern coal skink. In *Rare and Endangered Biota of Florida. Volume III. Amphibians and Reptiles.* P. E. Moler (ed.). University Press of Florida, Gainesville, FL, p. 219-222.

Meffe, G. K., and C. R. Carroll. 1994. *Principles of Conservation Biology.* Sinauer Associates, Inc., Sunderland, MA.

Meffe, G. K., A. H. Ehrlich, and D. Ehrenfeld. 1993. Human population control: The missing agenda. *Conservation Biology* 7: 1-3.

Mississippi Department of Fisheries, Wildlife, and Parks. 1992. *Endangered Species of Mississippi.* Mississippi Department of Fisheries, Wildlife, and Parks, Jackson, MS.

Missouri Natural Heritage Database. 1995. Rare and endangered species checklist of Missouri. Missouri Department of Conservation, Jefferson City, MO, 31 p.

Mitchell, J. C. 1991. Amphibians and reptiles. In *Virginia's Endangered Species.* K. Terwilleger (coordinator). The McDonald and Woodward Publishing Company, Blacksburg, VA, p. 411-423.

Mitchell, J. C. 1994. *The Reptiles of Virginia.* Smithsonian Institution Press, Washington, D.C.

Mitchell, J. C., and C. A. Pague. 1991. Eastern glass lizard. In *Virginia's Endangered Species.* K. Terwilleger (coordinator). The McDonald and Woodward Publishing Company, Blacksburg, VA, p. 464-466.

Moler, P. F. 1992. South Florida rainbow snake. *In Rare and Endangered Biota of Florida. Volume III. Amphibians and Reptiles.* P. E. Moler (ed.). University Press of Florida, Gainesville, FL, p. 251-253.

Moll, D., K. A. Buhlmann, and J. W. Gibbons. in press. Species account: Slider turtle (*Trachemys scripta*). In *Conservation Biology of Freshwater Turtles.* P. C. H. Pritchard, and A. G. L. Rhodin (eds.). Chelonian Research Foundation, Lunenburg, MA.

Moodie, K. B., and T. R. Van Devender. 1979. Extinction and extirpation in the herpetofauna of the southern high plains, with emphasis on *Geochelone wilsonii* (Testudinae). *Herpetologica* **35**:198-206.

Mount, R. H. 1975. *The Reptiles and Amphibians of Alabama.* Agricultural Experiment Station, Auburn University, Auburn, AL.

Mount, R. H. 1981. The status of the flattened musk turtle, *Sternotherus minor depressus* (Tinkle and Webb). Unpublished Report submitted to the U.S. Fish and Wildlife Service, Jackson, MS, 119 p.

Moyle, P. B., and R. A. Leidy. 1992. Loss of biodiversity in aquatic ecosystems: Evidence from fish faunas. In *Conservation Biology.* P. L. Fiedler, and S. K. Jain (eds.). Chapman and Hall, New York, NY, p. 127-169.

Neill, W. T. 1958. The occurrence of amphibians and reptiles in saltwater areas, and a bibliography. *Bulletin of Marine Science Gulf and Caribbean* 8:1-97.

Pritchard, P. C. H. 1989. *The Alligator Snapping Turtle, Biology and Conservation.* Milwaukee Public Museum, Milwaukee, WI.

Richardson, C. J., and J. W. Gibbons. 1993. Pocosins, Carolina bays, and mountain bogs. In *Biodiversity of the Southeastern United States: Lowland Terrestrial Communities.* W. H. Martin, S. G. Boyce, and A. C. Echternacht (eds.). John Wiley and Sons, Inc., New York, NY, p.257-310.

Richmond, N. D. 1940. *Natrix rigida* (Say) in Virginia. *Herpetologica* 2:21.

Roble, S. M. 1996. Natural heritage resources of Virginia: Rare animal species. Natural Heritage Technical Report 96-11, Division of Natural Heritage, Virginia Department of Conservation and Recreation, Richmond, VA, 23 p.

Santhuff, S. D., and L. A. Wilson. 1990. Geographic distribution: *Graptemys pulchra*. *Herpetological Review* **21**:39.

Seidel, M. E. 1994. Morphometric analysis and taxonomy of cooter and red-bellied turtles in the North American genus *Pseudemys* (Emydidae). *Chelonian Conservation Biology* **1**:117-130.

Seigel, R. A., and R. J. Brauman. 1995. Reproduction and nesting of the yellow-blotched map turtle, *Graptemys flavimaculata*. Unpublished Report, Mississippi Department of Wildlife, Fisheries, and Parks, Jackson, MS, 35 p.

Seigel, R. A., and J. W. Gibbons. 1995. Workshop on the ecology, status, and management of the diamondback terrapin (*Malaclemys terrapin*), Savannah River Ecology Laboratory, 2 August 1994: Final results and recommendations. *Chelonian Conservation Biology* **1**:240-243.

Seigel, R. A., J. W. Gibbons, and T. K. Lynch. 1995. Temporal changes in reptile populations: Effects of a severe drought on aquatic snakes. *Herpetologica* **51**:424-434.

Sharitz, R. R., and J. W. Gibbons. 1982. The ecology of southeastern shrub bogs (pocosins) and Carolina bays: A community profile. FWS/OBS-82/04, Division of Biological Services, U.S. Fish and Wildlife Service, Washington, D.C., 93 p.

Sharitz, R. R., and W. J. Mitsch. 1993. Southern floodplain forests. In *Biodiversity of the Southeastern United States: Lowland Terrestrial Communities*. W. H. Martin, S. G. Boyce, and A. C. Echternacht (eds.). John Wiley and Sons, Inc., New York, NY, p. 311-372.

Shealey, R. M. 1992. Alabama map turtle. In *Rare and Endangered Biota of Florida. Volume III. Amphibians and Reptiles*. P. E. Moler (ed.). University Press of Florida, Gainesville, FL, p. 200-203.

Sheldon, A. L. 1988. Conservation of stream fishes: Patterns of diversity, rarity, and risk. *Conservation Biology* **2**:149-156.

Shelford, V. E. 1963. *The Ecology of North America*. University of Illinois Press, Urbana, IL.

Skeen, J. N., P. D. Doerr, and D. H. Van Lear. 1993. Oak-Hickory-Pine Forests. In *Biodiversity of the Southeastern United States: Upland Terrestrial Communities*. W. H. Martin, S. G. Boyce, and A. C. Echternacht (eds.). John Wiley and Sons, Inc., New York, NY, p. 1-35.

Sloan, K. N., and J. E. Lovich. 1995. Exploitation of the alligator snapping turtle, *Macroclemys temminckii*, in Louisiana: A case study. *Chelonian Conservation Biology* **1**:221-222.

South Carolina Heritage Trust. 1996. Rare, threatened, and endangered species of South Carolina. Wildlife and Marine Resources Department, Columbia, SC, 12 p.

Tennessee Division of Natural Heritage. 1996. Rare vertebrates of the state of Tennessee. Department of Environment and Conservation, Nashville, TN, 9 p.

Thompson, J. S. 1994. Genetic variation of the allopatric populations of the Florida green water snake (*Nerodia floridana*) through allozyme electrophoresis. M.S. Thesis, Southeastern Louisiana University, Hammond, LA.

Tiner, R. W., Jr. 1987. Mid-Atlantic wetlands: A disappearing natural treasure. U.S. Fish and Wildlife Service, Newton Corner, MA, 28 p.

Trauth, S. E. 1991. Distribution, scutellation, and reproduction in the queen snake, *Regina septemvittata* (Serpentes: Colubridae), from Arkansas. *Proceedings of the Arkansas Academy of Science* **45**:103-106.

Turner, R. E., and N. J. Craig. 1980. Recent area changes in Louisiana's forested wetland riparian habitat. *Louisiana Academy of Science* **43**:61-78.

U.S. Federal Register. 1996. Endangered and threatened species, plant and animal taxa; proposed rule. *U.S. Federal Register* **61**(40):7596-7613.

U.S. Fish and Wildlife Service. 1992. Regional news: Region 4. *Endangered Species Technical Bulletin* **17**(3-8):10-11.

U.S. Fish and Wildlife Service. 1993. Northern copperbellied watersnake. *Endangered Species Technical Bulletin* **18**(4):14.

Warwick, C. 1986. Red-eared terrapin farms and conservation. *Oryx* **20**:237-240.

Warwick, C., C. Steedman, and T. Holford. 1990. Ecological implications of the red-eared turtle trade. *Texas Journal of Science* **42**:419-422.

Weaver, W. G., and S. P. Christman. 1992. Florida ribbon snake. In *Rare and Endangered Biota of Florida. Volume III. Amphibians and Reptiles*. P. E. Moler (ed.). University Press of Florida, Gainesville, FL, p. 162-164.

Williams, J. D., M. L. Warren, Jr., K. S. Cummings, J. L. Harris, and R. J. Neves. 1993. Conservation status of freshwater mussels of the United States and Canada. *Fisheries* **18**(9):6-22.

Wood, R. C. 1992. Mangrove terrapin. In *Rare and Endangered Biota of Florida. Volume III. Amphibians and Reptiles*. P. E. Moler (ed.). University Press of Florida, Gainesville, FL, p. 204-209.

CHAPTER 8

Birds of the Southeastern United States: A Historical Perspective

James G. Dickson

Historic freshwater aquatic and wetland ecosystems of the southeastern United States were predominantly rivers and streams and associated natural bottomland forests. These systems have been drastically altered through the creation of reservoirs via damming, through other alterations of water courses and their associated forests, and through conversion to other uses. In this chapter I will address historical aspects of bird communities of southeastern aquatic systems by considering the original composition of forested wetlands, the changes that have been wrought to them, and how these changes have most probably influenced bird communities.

BOTTOMLAND FORESTS

Pre-colonial bottomlands generally were portrayed by early naturalists as diverse landscapes, where forests of varying tree ages were interspersed with openings (Dickson, 1991). These forests contained a greater variety of tree ages than commonly found in present-day second-growth forests, and they contained many big and old trees, as well as decaying and fallen trees. Mast production in mature forests was high.

Pre-colonial forests typically were not stable, as they were influenced by a mixture of natural plant succession and other factors such as Native Americans, flooding, insects, diseases, ice and wind storms, and fires (Figure 1). Disturbance had, and has today, a major influence on the composition of southeastern forests. As such, the influences of

Aquatic Fauna in Peril: The Southeastern Perspective, edited by George W. Benz, and David E. Collins. 1997. Special Publication 1, Southeast Aquatic Research Institute, Lenz Design & Communications, Decatur, GA, 554 p.

Figure 1. A flooded riverbottom. Historic southeastern river systems have been extensively modified with accompanying effects on associated avian fauna. In many areas, human modifications to waterways and wetlands have reduced or eliminated natural cycles of seasonal flooding.

disturbance frequently created forest openings and set back plant succession.

Oak (*Quercus*)-gum (*Nyssa*)-cypress (*Taxodium*) forests predominated in the pre-colonial bottoms, though exact forest composition depended on site and other influences (Putnam et al., 1960). Eight general forest types have been recognized in the region. Cypress-tupelo gum (*N. aquatica*) and overcup oak (*Q. lyrata*)-bitter pecan (*Carya aquatica*) forests were widely distributed throughout the wettest areas. Cottonwood (*Populous*) and willow (*Salix*) type forests usually pioneered river fronts where hackberry (*Celtis*)-elm (*Ulmus*)-ash (*Fraxinus*) typically succeeded them. Sweetgum (*Liquidambar styraciflua*)-water oak (*Q. nigra*) forests were found throughout bottoms in areas with intermediate levels of moisture. The white oak-red oak-miscellaneous type forests occupied the higher bottomland ridges. Other moist site forests such as bays, pocosins, and wet prairies occurred in eastern parts of the region. Palmetto was dense in places, and cane (*Arundinaria gigantea*) formed dense thickets. In 1900, President Theodore Roosevelt described miles of cane on ridges in Louisiana bottoms so dense that other vegetation was choked out and cutting with a bush-knife was the only way to gain access (Roosevelt, 1908). Detailed descriptions of some specific remnant old-growth forests were presented by Wharton (1977).

Since pre-colonial times, there have been extensive losses of bottomland forests of the Southeast. Of the original ten million ha (24,704,661 acres) of Mississippi River delta forests only about 3 million ha (7,412,898 acres) remained by the early 1970s (Sternizke, 1976). Most of the forests have been converted to row crops or pasture. In some locations, reservoirs have inundated vast areas of bottomlands. For example in eastern Texas, Toledo Bend and Sam Rayburn reservoirs now occupy more than 100,000 ha (247,096 acres), much of which was once bottomland hardwood forests. From 1975 to 1986, remaining bottomland forests in eastern Texas declined by 12 percent (McWilliams and Lord, 1988). Likewise, the entire Tennessee River system has been dammed, resulting in extensive losses of native hardwood forests. Man has significantly influenced the forests that remain. Almost all have been repeatedly harvested, and stands existing today are typically dominated by trees not selected previously for harvest and by species favored by high natural regeneration capabilities.

STAND SUITABILITY FOR BIRDS

Bottomland forest stands vary in suitability as bird habitat depending on stand structure and other characteristics. In general, bird communities are associated with stand and foliage characteristics (Shugart and James, 1973). Hydroperiod also influences bird habitat and bird communities in hydric forests (Swift et al., 1984). In these forests, flooding provides nutrients and soil into riparian systems and influences physical site characteristics including vegetation and animal communities. Bottomland ridges, formed from past flooding and soil accretion, normally have diverse vertical foliage layers and diverse bird faunas. Low lying sites that are frequently flooded and have little understory and limited vertical structure support a less diverse bird community. In these areas, extended flooding during the growing season can kill trees and eliminate most foliage near the ground. This is detrimental to ground-nesting birds, such as Kentucky warblers (*Oporornis formosus*), and wintering ground foragers, such as white-throated sparrows (*Zonotrichia albicollis*) (Dickson and Noble, 1978). Conversely, extended flooding may create habitat for aquatic birds, such as the double-crested cormorant (*Phalacrocorax auritus*). Flooding may also help protect colonial nesters from mammalian predators, and kill trees which may provide woodpecker and wood duck cavity nests and woodpecker foraging sites in the short-term.

BREEDING BIRD COMMUNITIES

Historic riparian forests probably harbored abundant and diverse breeding bird communities as indicated by recent studies of bird communities in mature stands. For instance, in a relatively recent study of Louisiana oak-gum floodplain birds, about half the species of summer birds were neotropical migrants and about half were permanent residents (Dickson, 1978a). The proportion of migrant breeders was lower than that found in more northerly, and seasonally harsher areas.

In eastern Texas, estimated bird density was higher in a mature bottomland hardwood stand (1,050 per km^2 = 2,720 per square mile) than in a pine (835 per km^2 = 2,163 per square mile) or pine-hardwood stand (422 per km^2 = 1,093 per square mile) (Anderson, 1975). Bird species richness and diversity were similar in the bottomland hardwood and pine-hardwood stands, but higher than in the pine stand. Results of bird censuses from six pine, four pine-hardwood, and three bottomland stands in the Louisiana-East Texas area yielded similar results (Dickson, 1978b). Bird densities in the mature bottomland hardwoods were two to four times greater than densities in the upland pine and pine-hardwoods of different ages. Flooded forests also supported more birds than upland forests in the Midwest (Stauffer and Best, 1980) and in New England (Swift et al., 1984).

Riparian oak-gum-cypress forests provided and still provide important or critical habitat for many species which have evolved with these forests (Dickson 1978a, 1978b, 1988; Hamel, 1992). Breeding bird censuses (Dickson et al., 1980) showed that yellow-billed cuckoos (*Coccyzus americanus*), Acadian flycatchers (*Empidonax virescens*), tufted titmice (*Parus bicolor*), Carolina wrens (*Thryothorus ludovicianus*), red-eyed vireos (*Vireo olivaceus*), and northern cardinals (*Cardinalis cardinalis*) were consistently abundant in mature oak-gum-cypress forests. Other species regularly inhabit these stands (Table 1), and some have strong associations with this forest habitat. Many long-legged waders nest and forage in aquatic woodlands. Wood storks (*Mycteria americana*), which are now endangered, nest in tall cypress and hardwoods, and feed in associated aquatic systems. Purple gallinules (*Porphyrula martinica*) and common moorhens (*Gallinula chloropus*) also are found in aquatic habitats.

Several raptors inhabit riparian hardwood forests. Mississippi (*Ictinia mississippiensis*) and American swallow-tailed (*Elanoides forficatus*) kites, bald eagles (*Haliaeetus leucocephalus*), and ospreys (*Pandion haliaetus*) frequent this habitat, and red-shouldered hawks (*Buteo lineatus*) and barred owls (*Strix varia*) prefer forested wetlands. Bald eagle and osprey populations previously have declined, apparently due to egg shell thinning caused by pesticide accumulations. Restriction of pesticides seems to have benefited these, and probably other raptors as well.

Many species of birds excavate cavities in decayed trees for nests, and other birds use already excavated cavities. Decayed wood also harbors avian arthropod prey. There was probably a high density of cavity nesters in the pristine forests, where decayed and dead trees were numerous (Tomialojc, 1991). For example, in the early 1900s in Louisiana, Theodore Roosevelt thought that woodpeckers were characteristic species of the bottoms (Roosevelt, 1908). The ivory-billed woodpecker (*Campephilus principalis*), now probably extinct in North America, once thrived in old oak-gum forests, foraging on recently dead trees (Tanner, 1942). Cavity nesting birds, such as American kestrel (*Falco sparverius*), great crested flycatcher (*Myiarchus crinitus*), and red-headed woodpecker (*Melanerpes erythrocephalus*), were abundant in early forests in eastern Texas (Truett and Lay, 1984).

Many vireos and warblers associated with mature bottomland forests must have been abundant in pre-colonial forests. Red-eyed and yellow-throated vireos (*Vireo flavifrons*) inhabit canopy foliage and white-eyed vireos (*Vireo griseus*) inhabit low, shrubby foliage in riparian forests. Many warblers live in riparian habitats, some with special affinities. Prothonotary (*Prontonotaria citrea*), Swainson's (*Limnothlypis swainsonii*), northern parula (*Parula americana*), Kentucky, and hooded (*Wilsonia citrina*) warblers are strongly associated with bottomland habitat. Prothonotary warblers nest in cavities, often in small flood-killed trees. Northern parulas nest in Spanish moss (*Tillandsia usneoides*) in moist woods in the South. The Swainson's warbler is associated primarily with understory thickets of southern river floodplains and the southern Appalachian Mountains (Meanly, 1971). Habitat of the rare (or extinct) Bachman's warbler (*Vermivora bachmanii*) includes bottomlands and headwater swamps subject to disturbances (Hooper and Hamel, 1977). Both Swainson's and Bachman's warblers were historically associated with cane thickets, which were once extensive in southern bottomland forests (Meanly, 1971). Kentucky and hooded warblers usually are found in the moist understory of bottomland hardwoods

(Dickson and Noble, 1978), as well as in other habitats. Other warblers often found in forested riparian stands include black-and-white (*Mniotilta varia*), worm-eating (*Helmitheros vermivorus*), yellow-throated (*Dendroica dominica*), ovenbird (*Seiurus aurocapillus*), American redstart (*Setophaga ruticilla*), and Louisiana waterthrush (*Seiurus motacilla*) (Hamel et al., 1982).

Bird community composition of forest openings and young brushy stands, which were probably common in pre-colonial forests, would have been quite different than that of mature stands. Species associated with early successional vegetation, such as the yellow-breasted chat (*Icteria virens*), indigo bunting (*Passerina cyanea*), painted bunting (*Passerina circis*), prairie warbler (*Dendroica discolor*), common yellowthroat (*Geothlypis trichas*), white-eyed vireo, and northern cardinal (*Cardinalis cardinalis*) would have been characteristic. William Bartram in his travels through the pre-colonial Southeast noted birds associated with early successional stands, such as the yellow-breasted chat and blue linnet (indigo bunting) (Van Doren, 1928).

WINTER BIRD COMMUNITIES

Densities of wintering birds probably were very high in historic mature forests. Many species were probably attracted to the diverse forests and the abundant, high-energy acorns produced by large oaks. The oak-dominated bottoms at one time supported over one billion passenger pigeons (Truett and Lay, 1984). The demise of old-growth forests due to logging and overharvest coupled with the species' social reproductive behavior, probably caused this pigeon's extinction. Carolina parakeets were widely distributed in southern old-growth forests, where they fed on the fruits of giant bald cypress and other species (Van Doren, 1928). The depredation of settlers' crops and an unwary nature rendered the parakeet vulnerable to the gun (Truett and Lay, 1984).

Recent studies have shown that mature southern riparian forests support dense bird populations during the critical winter period. Many species, such as common grackles (*Quiscalus quiscula*) and red-headed woodpeckers, feed extensively on acorns in oak stands. For example, in a mature oak-gum stand in Louisiana, monthly estimated winter bird populations ranged from 1,400 to 2,000 birds per km^2 (3,626 to 5,180 per square mile) (Dickson, 1978a). Winter visitors dominated the bird community, comprising 79 to 89 percent of the total number of birds, and 55 to 60 percent of the total number of species. Mean winter density of white-throated sparrows approached 500 per km^2 (1,295 per square mile). Winter monthly population estimates for common grackles varied between approximately 100 and 1,000 per km^2 (259 and 2,590 per square mile) (Dickson, 1978a). Red-headed woodpeckers, which inhabit forest openings during the breeding season, were common during winter. Yellow-bellied sapsuckers (*Sphyrapicus varius*), blue jays (*Cyanocitta cristata*), brown thrashers (*Toxostoma rufum*), American robins (*Turdus migratorius*), hermit thrushes (*Catharus guttatus*), and ruby-crowned kinglets (*Regulus calendula*) were other common winter birds.

WILD TURKEY

The diverse forests of the pre-colonial Southeast supported abundant wild turkeys. In the late 1700s, William Bartram described the countryside near coastal St. Augustine as a

Table 1. List of bird species present in southeastern oak-gum-cypress forests. [1]

Permanent Residents

double-crested cormorant	pileated woodpecker
American anhinga	red-bellied woodpecker
great blue heron	red-headed woodpecker
green heron	hairy woodpecker
little blue heron	downy woodpecker
cattle egret	great crested flycatcher
great egret	eastern phoebe
snowy egret	blue jay
tricolored heron	American crow
black-crowned night-heron	fish crow
yellow-crowned night-heron	Carolina chickadee
wood stork	tufted titmouse
glossy ibis	white-breasted nuthatch
white ibis	Carolina wren
wood duck	marsh wren
turkey vulture	gray catbird
black vulture	brown thrasher
Cooper's hawk	blue-gray gnatcatcher
red-shouldered hawk	white-eyed vireo
short-tailed hawk	black-and-white warbler
bald eagle	northern parula
osprey	yellow-throated warbler
wild turkey	prairie warbler
limpkin	ovenbird
black rail	common yellowthroat
king rail	American redstart
purple gallinule	eastern meadowlark
common moorhen	red-winged blackbird
mourning dove	boat-tailed grackle
eastern screech-owl	common grackle
great horned owl	brown-headed cowbird
barred owl	northern cardinal
ruby-throated hummingbird	indigo bunting
belted kingfisher	painted bunting
northern flicker	rufous-sided towhee

Breeding Season Residents

American swallow-tailed kite	eastern wood-pewee
Mississippi kite	barn swallow
yellow-billed cuckoo	purple martin
chimney swift	wood thrush
Acadian flycatcher	yellow-throated vireo

Table 1. Continued.

Breeding Season Residents — continued

red-eyed vireo	Louisiana waterthrush
prothonotary warbler	Kentucky warbler
Swainson's warbler	yellow-breasted chat
worm-eating warbler	hooded warbler
Bachman's warbler	summer tanager
black-throated green warbler	blue grosbeak

Winter Residents

mallard	ruby-crowned kinglet
hooded merganser	water pipit
sharp-shinned hawk	cedar waxwing
northern harrier	European starling
Virginia rail	solitary vireo
sora	orange-crowned warbler
yellow rail	yellow-rumped warbler
American woodcock	northern waterthrush
short-eared owl	rusty blackbird
whip-poor-will	purple finch
yellow-bellied sapsucker	pine siskin
tree swallow	Savannah sparrow
brown creeper	grasshopper sparrow
house wren	Le Conte's sparrow
winter wren	white-throated sparrow
sedge wren	fox sparrow
American robin	Lincoln's sparrow
hermit thrush	swamp sparrow
golden-crowned kinglet	song sparrow

[1] Modified from Hamel et al. (1982), scientific names of listed birds can be found in American Ornithologists' Union (1983).

"universal shout" for hundreds of miles from the turkey cocks at dawn (Van Doren, 1928; page 89). Native Americans in the Southeast apparently had little trouble harvesting these birds, and turkeys were used for food and adornments (Mosby and Handley, 1943). Early colonists made extensive use of turkeys as a food staple (Mosby and Handley, 1943). Turkeys remained abundant into the nineteenth century when hunting for market became common. By the late 1800s, serious declines had occurred throughout virtually all of the southeastern range of the eastern wild turkey.

The wild turkey has made a remarkable comeback, and now numbers some 4 million in the United States. Better protection, maturing of the forests, and trap and transplant of wild turkeys have been responsible for this return (Figure 2).

Present riparian forests are prime habitat for the wild turkey as they often provide the

Figure 2. Wild turkey, apparently very abundant in much of the pre-colonial forests, were exploited and extirpated from most of the region. With help from trap-transplant programs, wild turkeys have now been restored throughout much of the Southeast.

only mature forested habitat in substantially altered landscapes. Wild turkeys use stream-side zones extensively as travel corridors and foraging areas, where they feed on soft and hard mast (Burk et al., 1990).

WATERFOWL

Riparian forests are prime habitat for several waterfowl species during some life stages. Wood ducks, appropriately named, are associated closely with forested wetlands. They wintered by the millions in southern flooded bottoms, and were drastically reduced by indiscriminate harvest in the last part of the 1800s and early 1900s. Since this time they have recovered substantially (Bellrose, 1990). Wood ducks nest in tree cavities. Prior to the nesting season females feed extensively on high protein macroinvertebrates in flooded forests (Batema et al., 1985). Although mallards do not normally nest in forested wetlands in the South, they winter regularly there. Mallards, as well as wood ducks, feed extensively on acorns produced in many bottomland oak stands, and certainly these species have suffered as a result of the loss of bottomland hardwoods. The hooded merganser (*Lophodytes cucullatus*), green-winged teal (*Anas crecca*), gadwall (*Anas strepera*), and American wigeon (*Mareca americana*) are other species that use flooded bottoms during winter.

IMPOUNDMENTS

While forest-associated birds have dwindled as their wooded habitat has been reduced, other species associated with aquatic systems probably have benefited from impoundments. Impoundments have drastically altered duck habitat. Suitability for waterfowl depends on the water regime, which controls aquatic vegetation (duck habitat) and determines duck species distribution and relative abundance (Johnson and Swank, 1981). As a result of the conversion of flooded bottoms to reservoirs, some species of diving ducks, such as ring-necked ducks (*Athya collaris*), canvasbacks (*Aythya valisineria*), buffleheads (*Bucephala albeola*), and ruddy ducks (*Oxyura jamaicensis*) may have benefited from the increase in open water conditions. In eastern Texas now, canvasbacks and ring-necked ducks are very abundant on reservoirs during winter and spring (M. Conway, Stephen F. Austin State University, pers. comm.). Before reservoirs existed in this region, these birds probably were uncommon.

Bald eagles, white pelicans (*Pelecanus erythrorhynchos*), and double-crested cormorants feed extensively on forage fish in open water and appear to have increased in numbers in recent years. Great egrets (*Casmerodius albus*), great blue (*Ardea herodias*), snowy (*Egretta thula*), and tricolored herons (*Egretta tricolor*), and other birds forage regularly around the extensive edges of impoundments, as well as a variety of other shallow water sites. American coots (*Fulica americana*) use lakes with aquatic vegetation and appear to have increased as a result of the creation of impoundments. For example, American coots are now very abundant on East Texas reservoirs during all seasons except summer (M. Conway, Stephen F. Austin State University, pers. comm.). Forster's terns (*Sterna forsteri*) and ring-billed gulls (*Larus delawarensis*) forage regularly on man-created, large impoundments. Also, some small shore birds, such as least sandpipers (*Calidris minutilla*) and killdeer (*Charadrius vociferus*) use impoundments when the shallow edges are exposed. These two species are very common wintering birds now along edges of East Texas reservoirs (B. Willhouse, Stephen F. Austin State University, pers. comm.). Wintering horned (*Podiceps auritus*) and pied-billed (*Podilymbus podiceps*) grebes also make regular use of man-made impoundments. Extensive flooding kills trees, and some cavity nesting species, such as red-headed woodpeckers, tree swallows (*Tachycineta bicolor*), and great crested flycatcher, use flood-killed trees for nesting sites until they fall.

CONCLUSIONS

Freshwater ecosystems throughout the Southeast have been drastically altered. While there were abundant and diverse bird communities in historic riparian forests, bird communities changed as forests were cut and converted to other land uses or allowed to develop into second-growth forests. Species that are faring well today include those associated with open water, some generalists that have benefited from forest cutting, and birds benefiting from protection and restoration. Forest-associated species, particularly those with low tolerance to human activities, low reproductive rates, or with narrow niches, have declined in numbers, and a few have become extinct. To secure these delicate ecosystems and their components, the few remaining old-growth forests should be maintained in an old-growth state, especially large remaining areas and old-growth corridors. In addition, some second-growth forests should be allowed to mature and some early successional stands should be maintained where they are limited. Representative species that have been extirpated should be restored. Ecosystem research should be expanded to increase our knowledge of the complex systems as well as to develop methods to protect and maintain their function and values.

REFERENCES

American Ornithologists' Union. 1983. *Check-list of North American birds, 6th Edition.* Port City Press, Baltimore, MD.

Anderson, R. M. 1975. Bird populations in three kinds of eastern Texas forests. M.S. Thesis, Stephen F. Austin State University, Nacogdoches, TX.

Batema, D. L., G. S. Henderson, and L. H. Fredrickson. 1985. Wetland invertebrate distribution in bottomland hardwoods as influenced by forest type and flooding regime. In *Proceedings of the Central Hardwoods Conference.* J. O. Dawson, and K. A. Majeruf (eds.). Department of Forestry, University of Illinois, Urbana-Champaign, IL, p. 196-202.

Bellrose, F. E. 1990. The history of wood duck management. In *Proceedings 1988 North American Wood Duck Symposium.* L. H. Fredrickson, G. V. Burger, S. P. Havera, D. A. Grober, R. E. Kirby, and T. S. Taylor (eds.). St. Louis, MO, p. 13-20.

Burk, J. D., G. A. Hurst, D. R. Smith, B. D. Leopold, and J. G. Dickson. 1990. Wild turkey use of streamside management zones in loblolly pine plantations. *Proceedings of the National Wild Turkey Symposium* 6:84-89.

Dickson, J. G. 1978a. Seasonal bird populations in a south central Louisiana bottom-land hardwood forest. *Journal of Wildlife Management* 42:875-883.

Dickson, J. G. 1978b. Forest Bird communities of the bottomland hardwoods. In *Proceedings of the Workshop: Management of Southern Forests for Nongame Birds.* R. M. DeGraaf (technical coordinator). General Technical Report SE-14, U.S. Forest Service, Asheville, NC, p. 66-73.

Dickson, J. G. 1988. Bird communities in oak-gum-cypress forests. In *Bird Conserva-tion 3.* J. A. Jackson (ed.). International Council for Bird Preservation, University of Wisconsin Press, Madison, WI, p. 51-62.

Dickson, J. G. 1991. Birds and mammals of pre-colonial southern old-growth forests. *Natural Areas Journal* 11:26-33.

Dickson, J. G., R. N. Conner, and J. H. Williamson. 1980. Relative abundance of breeding birds in forests in the Southeast. *Southern Journal of Applied Forestry* 4:174-179.

Dickson, J. G., and R. E. Noble. 1978. Vertical distribution of birds in a Louisiana bottomland hardwood forest. *Wilson Bulletin* 90:19-30.

Hamel, P. B. 1992. Land manager's guide to birds of the South. The Nature Conser-vancy, Chapel Hill, NC.

Hamel, P. B., H. E. LeGrand, Jr., M. R. Lennartz, and S. A. Gauthreaux, Jr. 1982. Bird-habitat relationships on southeastern forest land. General Technical Report SE-22, U.S. Forest Service, Asheville, NC, 417 p.

Hooper, R. G., and P. B. Hamel. 1977. Nesting habitat of Bachman's Warbler — A review. *Wilson Bulletin* 89:373-379.

Johnson, F. A., and W. G. Swank. 1981. Waterfowl habitat selection on a multipurpose reservoir in East Texas. *Proceedings of the Annual Conference of the Southeastern Association of Fish and Wildlife Agencies* 35:38-48.

McWilliams, W. H., and R. G. Lord. 1988. Forest resources of East Texas. Resource Bulletin SO-136, U.S. Forest Service, New Orleans, LA, 61 p.

Meanly, B. 1971. Natural history of the Swainson's Warbler. North American Fauna Number 69, U.S. Department of the Interior, Washington, D.C., 90 p.

Mosby, H. S., and C. O. Handley. 1943. The wild turkey in Virginia: Its status, life history and management. Virginia Commission of Game and Inland Fisheries, Richmond, VA.

Putnam, J. A., G. M. Furnival, and J. S. McKnight. 1960. Management and inventory of southern hardwoods. Agriculture Handbook 181, U.S. Forest Service, U.S. Government Printing Office, Washington, D.C.

Roosevelt, T. 1908. In the Louisiana Canebrakes. Scribners Magazine. [Reprinted in 1962 as Wildlife Education Bulletin 59, Louisiana Wildlife and Fisheries Commission, Baton Rouge, LA, 11 p.]

Shugart, H. H., Jr., and D. James. 1973. Ecological succession of breeding bird populations in northwestern Arkansas. *Auk* 90:62-77.

Stauffer, D. F., and L. B. Best. 1980. Habitat selection by birds of riparian communities: Evaluating effects of habitat alterations. *Journal Wildlife Management* 44:1-15.

Sternitzke, H. S. 1976. Impact of changing land use on delta hardwood forests. *Journal of Forestry* 74:25-17.

Swift, B. L., J. S. Larson, and R. M. DeGraaf. 1984. Relationship of breeding bird density and diversity to habitat variables in forested wetlands. *Wilson Bulletin* 96:48-59.

Tanner, J. T. 1942. The Ivory-billed woodpecker. National Audubon Society Resource Paper Number 1, National Audubon Society, New York, NY, 111 p.

Tomialojc, L. 1991. Characteristics of old growth in the Bialowieza Forest, Poland. *Natural Areas Journal* 11:7-18.

Truett, J. C., and D. W. Lay. 1984. *Land of Bears and Honey: A Natural History of East Texas.* University of Texas Press, Austin, TX.

Van Doren, M. (ed.). 1928. *The Travels of William Bartram.* Dover Publications, New York, NY.

Wharton, C. H. 1977. The natural environments of Georgia. Georgia Department of Natural Resources, Atlanta, GA.

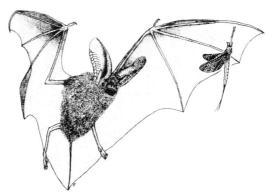

CHAPTER 9

Imperiled Mammalian Fauna of Aquatic Ecosystems in the Southeast: A Historical Perspective

Michael J. Harvey and Joseph D. Clark

About 100 species of mammals are endemic to the southeastern United States, an area of diverse habitat types and high biodiversity. Many of these species are either formally considered aquatic or semi-aquatic, or they are otherwise closely associated with aquatic ecosystems. In the southeastern United States, greater than 80 percent of mammalian species are listed in some category of concern throughout all or at least a portion of their ranges (i.e., endangered, threatened, under review for possible listing as endangered or threatened, species of special concern, species deemed in need of management, etc.). Almost all of these species are imperiled because their populations have declined to dangerously low levels due to habitat loss, habitat degradation, or other human-related factors. Most imperiled mammal taxa can be categorized as belonging to one of two general groups: habitat generalists or habitat specialists. Typically, habitat generalists have become imperiled mainly due to human exploitation, while habitat specialists have suffered primarily from habitat loss or habitat degradation.

The passage of the U.S. Endangered Species Act of 1973 resulted in an increased need

Aquatic Fauna in Peril: The Southeastern Perspective, edited by George W. Benz, and David E. Collins. 1997. Special Publication 1, Southeast Aquatic Research Institute, Lenz Design & Communications, Decatur, GA, 554 p.

for information concerning distribution and status of all native species. However, relatively little is known concerning the historical distribution and current status of many mammalian taxa, and this is particularly so for small non-game species. In this chapter we provide species accounts of mammals commonly associated with aquatic ecosystems that we consider to be imperiled in the southeastern United States. In these accounts we have included information which we feel is valuable toward best understanding the threats that challenge each considered taxon.

SPECIES ACCOUNTS

West Indian Manatee — *Trichechus manatus*

The endangered West Indian manatee inhabits shallow coastal waters, estuaries, and rivers along the coast of the southeastern United States, throughout the Caribbean region, along the eastern coast of Central America, and on the northeastern coast of South America to Brazil (Odell, 1982). Florida is essentially the northern extent of its range, although individuals have occasionally been reported as far north as New Jersey on the Atlantic coast and as far west as Texas along the Gulf of Mexico coast (U.S. Fish and Wildlife Service, 1978). These extremely docile aquatic herbivores have a very low reproductive potential, and females are thought to give birth to a single calf at three- to five-year intervals. Longevity in the wild may reach 40-50 years. Manatees spend a major portion of their time feeding, and they may consume 10 to 15 percent of their body weight daily (Odell, 1982).

Historically, populations of West Indian manatees were severely reduced by hunting for meat, bone, hides, and fat (Bertram and Bertram, 1973; Peterson, 1974). More recently, they have suffered because of pollution, flood-control dams, and injuries from accidents with pleasure boats and barges. In Florida, collisions with pleasure boats appear to be the major identifiable cause of manatee mortality (Hartman, 1971). A number of other factors related to rapidly increasing coastal development appear to threaten manatee populations. Censusing these large mammals is surprisingly difficult. In 1985, however, at least 1,200 West Indian manatees were estimated to winter in Florida (Reynolds and Wilcox, 1986; O'Shea, 1988), where most of the United States population congregates.

Florida Panther — *Puma concolor coryi*

The endangered Florida panther formerly occurred throughout the southeastern United States from central South Carolina through Tennessee, to northwestern Arkansas and south to the Gulf of Mexico. During the 1970s, the Florida panther was thought to be extinct, along with the remainder of the other subspecies of pumas in the eastern United States. During that decade, however, the existence of a population in and around Big Cypress National Preserve in southern Florida was confirmed.

The Florida panther is not restricted to aquatic ecosystems, but because of human pressures, this subspecies now survives only in habitats consisting of sawgrass prairies, cypress and oak hammocks, and permanently flooded wetlands. The density of white-tailed deer is relatively low in these habitats, and in these places panthers subsist primarily on feral hogs. Florida panthers require large home ranges: up to 260 km² (100 square miles) for females and 1,040 km² (approximately 400 square miles) for males (Maehr, 1990). Because these panthers move extensively, they are extremely sensitive to habitat fragmentation (Harris, 1985). The current range of the Florida panther encompasses some 800,000 ha (1,976,773 acres), and includes public lands of a national wildlife refuge, a national park and national preserve, a state preserve, a wildlife management area, and a Seminole reservation. About 50 percent of the Florida panther's range is on private land (Maehr, 1992a). Only 30-50 Florida panthers survive in the wild.

River Otter — *Lutra canadensis*

This semi-aquatic carnivore is classified as an Appendix II species under the Convention of International Trade in Endangered Species of Flora and Fauna. Until a few years ago, this classification was intended only for species that could become threatened if international trade was not strictly regulated. Today, the river otter is listed in Appendix II due to its status as a "look-alike" for pelts of endangered species of otters from South America and Africa.

The river otter was once abundant throughout most of the United States and was an important furbearer to colonial trappers (Schorger, 1970). Populations of river otters have been extirpated from much of their original range, partly due to indiscriminate, unregulated trapping (Godman, 1826; Flower and Lydekker, 1891; Duplaix and Simon, 1976) and losses of habitat (Park, 1971; Fimreite and Reynolds, 1973). During the 1950s and 1960s, not only was the quantity of suitable habitat diminished for river otters, but the quality was as well, due to the extensive use of DDT, heptachlor, dieldrin, and certain heavy metals (Clark et al., 1981). It is likely that bioaccumulation of those pollutants in this semi-aquatic species resulted in lowered reproduction or decreased survival. By the mid-20th century, river otters were common only in coastal regions of the southeastern United States.

Everglades Mink — *Mustela vison mink*

The Everglades mink, under review for listing as endangered or threatened, is an isolated population of mink and is considered common in portions of the Everglades and Big Cypress National Park (Humphrey, 1992b). Water-control projects, resulting in changes in water levels, saltwater intrusion into the aquifer, altered fire regimes, and oxidation of peat soils, likely have been detrimental to this subspecies. Destruction of natural habitat to increase citrus production appears to be the greatest current threat to the Everglades mink. However, several major habitat tracts suitable to this mink are protected through federal ownership.

Florida Black Bear — *Ursus americanus floridanus*

Major concentrations of Florida black bears occur in and around the Okefenokee National Wildlife Refuge in southern Georgia; Apalachicola National Forest, Osceola National Forest, and Ocala National Forest in the northern portion of Florida; and Big Cypress National Preserve in southern Florida. Estimates of current populations range from 500 to 1,000 individuals. Populations of black bears in Florida are probably the most fragmented in North America, and although the larger populations appear stable, extirpation of the smaller, more isolated populations probably will continue (Maehr, 1992b). Loss of suitable habitat, including cypress and hardwood swamps, represents the major threat to Florida black bears. Poaching and mortality caused by accidents with roadway traffic are also important factors in fringe populations due to this subspecies' low reproductive and recruitment rates (Maehr, 1992b).

Louisiana Black Bear — *Ursus americanus luteolus*

Historically, the Louisiana black bear was abundant in the lower Mississippi delta. However, due to the extensive loss of bottomland hardwoods caused by land clearing and human exploitation, the range of this subspecies has been severely restricted. Black bear populations are known to exist in the Atchafalaya River basin and Tensas National Wildlife Refuge in Louisiana. However, an introduction of *U. a. americanus* from Minnesota into Louisiana during the 1960s prompted debate among biologists over whether or not the Louisiana subspecies currently exists in its historic form.

The most important threat to the Louisiana black bear is continued loss of its habitat, although bear deaths caused by poaching and automobile collisions have also been documented and may represent significant mortality factors (Weaver, 1992). Populations have been estimated at greater than 60 bears in the Tensas River basin and greater than 30 bears in the Atchafalaya basin (Weaver, 1992).

Key Deer — *Odocoileus virginianus clavium*

The endangered Key deer historically occurred only at low densities in the Florida Keys, due to the dominance of mature forested lands. It is likely that hurricanes were a major influence on populations of Key deer, by operating to periodically create earlier successional-stage vegetation which was beneficial to this subspecies (Hardin et al., 1984).

The hunting of deer reduced the Key deer population to near extinction until it was banned by the Florida Legislature in 1939. The Key Deer National Wildlife Refuge was established in the early 1950s and a protection plan was developed. The Key deer population was estimated to be between 200 and 250 individuals in 1974 on Big Pine Key, with 100 to 150 deer estimated to live on 22 other keys (Klimstra et al., 1974). The overall population has apparently declined since that time (Hardin et al., 1984), and human-related destruction of deer habitat is no doubt an important factor responsible for this decline. However, the primary factor threatening the Key deer is mortality from collisions with automobiles (Klimstra et al., 1974; Klimstra, 1985), accounting for about 80 percent of all deaths.

Lower Keys Marsh Rabbit — *Sylvilagus palustris hefneri*

The endangered lower keys marsh rabbit is present on several of the lower Flordia Keys (Howe, 1988). Recent records include Big Pine, Hopkins, Sugarloaf, Welles, Saddlebunch, Geiger, and Boca Chica keys, and remaining populations are highly fragmented (Wolfe, 1992). The lower keys marsh rabbit has apparently been extirpated from several other keys. This subspecies is also commonly known as the "Playboy bunny" since its original description was partially funded by the Playboy Foundation (Wolfe, 1992).

The lower keys marsh rabbit prefers marshes and adjacent low vegetative cover, especially grasses and sedges. However, it is sometimes found in more upland areas such as grassy fields and tropical hammocks (Wolfe, 1992). The greatest threat to this rabbit has been the destruction of its habitat for use by humans. Highway traffic and predation by domestic and feral pets also have caused extensive mortality.

Round-tailed Muskrat — *Neofiber alleni*

This muskrat species of special concern is restricted to Florida and southeastern Georgia (Wassmer and Wolfe, 1983). Preferred habitat is shallow marshes with emergent vegetation such as maidencane and pickerelweed (Lefebvre and Tilmant, 1993). By far the greatest threat to the round-tailed muskrat has been the extensive destruction of its original wetland habitat. However, fragmentation of remaining habitat no doubt has also played a role in the demise of this species, as isolated populations are extremely vulnerable to destruction by fluctuations in water levels.

Lower Keys Rice Rat — *Oryzomys palustris natator*

The endangered lower keys rice rat (or marsh rice rat) is widespread in the lower Florida Keys, but apparently absent from the upper and middle Florida Keys (Schwartz, 1952; Goodyear, 1987). This rat's primary habitat is the upland-to-marine interface (Goodyear, 1987), and it is most abundant in tidal marshes (Wolfe, 1985, 1990). The primary threat to the lower keys rice rat is the destruction and fragmentation of its habitat for human development.

Key Largo Woodrat — *Neotoma floridana smalli*

The endangered Key Largo woodrat is endemic to Key Largo, Florida (Sherman, 1955; Schwartz and Odum, 1957). This woodrat is primarily found in deciduous forest habitats and usually is absent from deforested and oldfield areas. The primary threat to the Key Largo woodrat is the destruction of its forest habitat for human developments (Humphrey, 1992a). In the early 1980s, over 4,000 housing units were under construction or approved for construction on Key Largo, and certainly some of this construction impacted this woodrat.

Florida Saltmarsh Vole — *Mlcrotus pennsylvanicus dukecampbelli*

The endangered Florida saltmarsh vole is known only from Island Field Marsh along the shore of Waccasassa Bay, Levy County, Florida. It appears to be restricted to areas near the edge of patches of black rush and in patches of seashore saltgrass (Woods, 1992). The main threat to the survival of this vole is flooding of habitat during catastrophic weather such as hurricanes. Destruction and fragmentation of habitat by coastal development have also posed threats.

Key Largo Cotton Mouse — *Peromyscus gossypinus allapaticola*

The endangered Key Largo cotton mouse is restricted to the northern half of Key Largo, Florida (Barbour and Humphrey, 1982). This species' preferred habitat is deciduous forest in the dry-tropical-forest life zone (Holdridge, 1967). Human-related development and the resulting destruction and fragmentation of forest habitat has been the main threat to the survival of this mouse.

Alabama Beach Mouse — *Peromyscus polionotus ammobates*

The endangered Alabama beach mouse occurs only along the coast in Alabama, where its habitat consists of sand dunes along beaches. Destruction and fragmentation of this habitat by human development has been the greatest threat to this mouse's survival. Between 1921 and 1983, commercial and residential developments and human recreational activities destroyed over 60 percent of the habitat of this beach mouse (Holliman, 1983). Tropical storms also have resulted in mortality and habitat destruction.

Anastasia Island Beach Mouse — *Peromyscus polionotus phasma*

The endangered Anastasia Island beach mouse occurs only on Anastasia Island, Florida.

Substantial populations remain at each end of the island, with small populations scattered along its length (Humphrey et al., 1987). These mice are restricted to sand dunes vegetated mainly by sea oats and dune panic grass, and also to the adjoining scrub, characterized by oaks, sand pine, and palmetto. Habitat loss and fragmentation caused by human developments have been primary factors in the demise of this subspecies. Predation by domestic house cats and competition from house mice, which have colonized the dunes, also have had a detrimental impact on this mouse.

Choctawhatchee Beach Mouse — *Peromyscus polionotus allophrys*

The endangered Choctawhatchee beach mouse is endemic to coastal dunes and historically was present as almost a continuous population along the coastal dunes between the entrances to Choctawhatchee and Saint Andrew bays, Florida. Currently, only two, or possibly three, small disjunct populations survive (Holler, 1992a). Optimal habitat consists of the primary and secondary dunes vegetated by sea oats, beach grass, and bluestem. Habitat loss caused by real estate development has been the single most important factor endangering this mouse subspecies (Bowen, 1968).

Perdido Key Beach Mouse — *Peromyscus polionotus trissyllepsis*

The endangered Perdido Key beach mouse is endemic to the coastal dunes between Perdido Bay, Alabama and Pensacola Bay, Florida. It currently occupies only 1.9 km (1.2 miles) of habitat at Gulf State Park, Alabama and 11 km (6.8 miles) of habitat at Gulf Islands National Seashore, Florida. It is considered the most endangered of the five endangered subspecies of beach mice (Holler, 1992b). Loss of habitat to real estate development and storm damage has resulted in the endangered status of this mouse. Vulnerability of remaining habitat and populations to storm damage is the greatest present threat to this subspecies' survival (Holler, 1992b).

Southeastern Beach Mouse — *Peromyscus polionotus niveiventris*

The threatened southeastern beach mouse is endemic to coastal dunes from south of Ponce Inlet in Volusia County to Hollywood Beach in Broward County, Florida. This subspecies' principal habitat is the sea oats zone of coastal dunes, but grassland and open sandy areas with scattered shrubs are also occupied in some locations. Cumulative effects of real estate development, house cats, and house mice appear to render otherwise suitable habitat uninhabitable to this mouse, and in addition, erosion of beaches has destroyed significant mouse habitat (Stout, 1992).

Saint Andrew Beach Mouse — *Peromyscus polionotus peninsularis*

The endangered Saint Andrew beach mouse is endemic to coastal dune habitat from the Saint Joseph spit in Gulf County to the entrance of Saint Andrew Bay in Bay County, Florida. The only substantial population remaining is in an 8 km (five mile) strip of high dunes at the northern end of the spit in Saint Joseph Peninsula State Park. A small population also exists on Crooked Island East in Bay County. Real estate development has destroyed and fragmented this subspecies' habitat in many areas. Foot and vehicle traffic associated with recreational activities on sand dunes has resulted in serious erosion of the remaining mouse habitat (James, 1992).

Gray Bat — *Myotis grisescens*

The endangered gray bat inhabits cave regions of Arkansas, Missouri, Kentucky, Tennessee, and Alabama, with occasional colonies and individuals found in adjacent states. Gray bats are cave residents year-round. Approximately 95 percent of all gray bats hibernate in only eight caves; two in Tennessee, three in Missouri, and one each in Kentucky, Alabama, and Arkansas (Harvey, 1992).

During summer, female gray bats form maternity colonies of a few hundred to thousands of individuals, often in caves containing streams. Male gray bats, along with non-reproductive females, form summer bachelor colonies in caves. Summer caves, especially those occupied by maternity colonies, rarely are located greater than 3 km (about two miles) from rivers or lakes. Each summer colony occupies a home range that often contains several roosting caves scattered along as much as 80 km (50 miles) of river or lake shore. Gray bats forage for insects primarily over water. Mayflies are apparently a major part of the diet, but like most bat species, they often feed on other insects as well.

Gray bat populations have suffered from habitat destruction, vandalism, disturbance to hibernation and maternity colonies by humans, pesticides, and other chemical toxicants. Population declines have been estimated at 89 percent in Kentucky, 72 to 81 percent in Missouri, 61 percent in Arkansas, and 76 percent in Tennessee and Alabama (Tuttle, 1979).

Indiana Bat — *Myotis sodalis*

The endangered Indiana bat occurs in the eastern United States from Oklahoma, Iowa, and Wisconsin east to Vermont, and south to northwestern Florida. Distribution is associated with major cave regions and areas north of cave regions. About 85 percent of the remaining Indiana bat population hibernates at only seven locations: two caves and a mine in Missouri, two caves in Indiana, and two caves in Kentucky (Harvey, 1992). During summer, female Indiana bats form small maternity colonies of at most 100 individuals, usually under loose tree bark, primarily in wooded streamside habitat. Indiana bats usually forage for insects near foliage of streamside and floodplain trees.

Populations of Indiana bats continue to decline in size in spite of recovery efforts. Destruction of foraging and roosting habitat, vandalism, disturbance to hibernating colonies, and chemical toxicants have all likely played a role in this decline. Population estimates at major cave hibernacula indicated a 34 percent decline in numbers of individuals from 1983 to 1989 (Harvey, 1992).

Star-nosed Mole — *Condylura cristata*

This semi-aquatic mole occurs in the southeastern United States only in the Appalachian Mountains and along the Atlantic coast as far south as Georgia. It inhabits damp or muddy soil. Some tunnels constructed by this mole lead directly into water, and this species is an excellent swimmer. Food consists of aquatic insects, crustaceans, small fish, and annelids (van Zyll de Jong, 1983). The star-nosed mole can be considered imperiled in the southeastern United States because of its limited distribution and restrictive habitat type.

Dismal Swamp Southeastern Shrew — *Sorex longirostris fisheri*

The threatened Dismal Swamp southeastern shrew occurs only in the Dismal Swamp National Wildlife Refuge in southeastern Virginia and adjacent portions of the swamp in

North Carolina (French, 1980). The primary threat to this shrew has been the destruction of its swamp habitat, which is more accurately described as a wooded peat bog. The original Dismal Swamp has been reduced in size by roughly 85 percent since about 1900.

Water Shrew — *Sorex palustris*

This semi-aquatic shrew occurs in the southeastern United States only at higher elevations in the Appalachian Mountains. The water shrew is an excellent swimmer and feeds primarily on aquatic insects, other aquatic invertebrates, and small fish (van Zyll de Jong, 1983). This shrew can be considered imperiled in the southeastern United States because of its very limited distribution.

CONCLUSION

The aquatic, semi-aquatic, or otherwise aquatic habitat dependent mammal taxa discussed in this paper are considered imperiled for a number of reasons, almost all of which are human related. Destruction, alteration, and fragmentation of habitat, along with other forms of environmental degradation, are no doubt the foremost causes of imperilment (summarized in Table 1). Quite likely, some of these taxa will be extirpated in the foreseeable future unless immediate steps are taken to arrest or reverse current trends. The question is, "beach houses or beach mouses?"

Table 1. Summary of imperiled aquatic, semi-aquatic, and otherwise aquatic habitat associated mammal taxa of the southeastern United States, their level of imperilment, and the primary reasons for their imperilment.

Order: Family:	Species/Subspecies Common Name[1]	Aquatic Association: Regional Location	Level of Imperilment	Primary Cause of Imperilment
Sirenia: Trichechidae:	West Indian manatee	Aquatic: southeast U.S. coast, estuaries & rivers	Endangered	Habitat loss & alteration, hunting, pollution, boat traffic related mortalities
Carnivora: Felidae:	Florida panther	Closely associated: FL	Endangered	Habitat loss & fragmentation, road traffic related mortalities
Mustelidae:	river otter	Semi-aquatic: throughout southeastern U.S.	Threatened locally	Habitat loss, trapping, pollution[2]
	Everglades mink	Semi-aquatic: FL	Threatened locally	Habitat loss & alteration, pollution
Ursidae:	Florida black bear	Closely associated: FL & GA	Threatened locally	Habitat loss, poaching, road traffic related mortalities
	Louisiana black bear	Closely associated: LA	Threatened locally	Habitat loss, poaching
Artiodactyla: Cervidae:	Key deer	Closely associated: FL	Endangered	Habitat loss, hunting, road traffic related mortalities
Lagomorpha: Leporidae:	lower keys marsh rabbit	Closely associated: FL	Endangered	Habitat loss, road traffic related mortalities, predation caused by pets

Table 1. Continued.

Order: Family:	Species/Subspecies Common Name [1]	Aquatic Association: Regional Location	Level of Imperilment	Primary Cause of Imperilment
Rodentia: Muridae:	round-tailed muskrat	Semi-aquatic: FL & GA	Threatened locally	Habitat loss & alteration
	lower keys rice rat	Closely associated: FL	Endangered	Habitat loss & fragmentation
	Key Largo woodrat	Closely associated: FL	Endangered	Habitat loss & fragmentation
	Florida saltmarsh vole	Closely associated: FL	Endangered	Habitat loss & fragmentation
	Key Largo cotton mouse	Closely associated: FL	Endangered	Habitat loss & fragmentation
	Alabama beach mouse	Closely associated: AL	Endangered	Habitat loss & fragmentation, storm related habitat damage
	Anastasia Island beach mouse	Closely associated: FL	Endangered	Habitat loss & fragmentation, predation caused by pets
	Choctawhatchee beach mouse	Closely associated: FL	Endangered	Habitat loss & fragmentation
	Perdido Key beach mouse	Closely associated: AL & FL	Endangered	Habitat loss & fragmentation, storm related habitat damage
	southeastern beach mouse	Closely associated: FL	Threatened	Habitat loss & fragmentation, storm related habitat damage, beach erosion
	Saint Andrew beach mouse	Closely associated: FL	Endangered	Habitat loss & fragmentation, beach erosion

Table 1. Continued.

Order: Family:	Species/Subspecies Common Name [1]	Aquatic Association: Regional Location	Level of Imperilment	Primary Cause of Imperilment
Chiroptera: Vespertilionidae:	Indiana bat	Closely associated: southeastern U.S.	Endangered	Habitat loss, human disturbance, vandalism, chemical toxicants
	gray bat	Closely associated: southeastern U.S.	Endangered	Habitat loss, human disturbance, vandalism, chemical toxicants
Insectivora: Talpidae:	star-nosed mole	Semi-aquatic: Appalachian Mtns. & Atlantic coastal states	Threatened locally	Habitat loss, limited distribution
Soricidae:	Dismal Swamp southeastern shrew	Closely associated: VA & NC	Threatened	Habitat loss
	water shrew	Semi-aquatic: Appalachian states	Threatened locally	Habitat loss, limited distribution

[1] For scientific names refer to text.

[2] As explained in text, part of the reason this species is regulated is due to the fact that it looks like some other imperiled otter species.

REFERENCES

Barbour, D. B., and S. R. Humphrey. 1982. Status and habitat of the Key Largo woodrat and cotton mouse (*Neotoma floridana smalli* and *Peromyscus gossypinus allapaticola*). *Journal of Mammalogy* **63**:144-148.

Bertram, G. C. L., and C. K. R. Bertram. 1973. The modern Sirenia: Their distribution and status. *Biological Journal of the Linnaean Society* **5**:297-338.

Bowen, W. W. 1968. Variation and evolution of Gulf coast populations of beach mice, *Peromyscus polionotus. Bulletin of the Florida State Museum, Biological Science* **12**:1-91.

Clark, J. D., J. H. Jenkins, P. B. Bush, and E. B. Moser. 1981. Pollution trends in river otter in Georgia. *Proceedings of the Annual Conference of the Southeastern Association of Fish and Wildlife Agencies* **35**:71-79.

Duplaix, N., and N. Simon. 1976. *World Guide to Mammals.* Crown Publishers, Inc., New York, NY.

Fimreite, N., and L. M. Reynolds. 1973. Mercury contamination in fish of northwestern Ontario. *Journal of Wildlife Management* **37**:62-68.

Flower, W. H., and R. Lydekker. 1891. *An Introduction to the Study of Mammals Living and Extinct.* Adam and Charles Black, London.

French, T. W. 1980. *Sorex longirostris. Mammalian Species* **143**:1-3.

Godman, J. D. 1826. *American Natural History, Volume I.* H. C. Carey and I. Lea, Philadelphia, PA.

Goodyear, N. C. 1987. Distribution and habitat of the silver rice rat, *Oryzomys argentatus. Journal of Mammalogy* **68**:692-695.

Hardin, J. W., W. D. Klimstra, and N. J. Silvy. 1984. Florida Keys. In *White-tailed Deer: Ecology and Management.* Lowell K. Halls (ed.). Stackpole Books, Harrisburg, PA, p. 381-390.

Harris, L. D. 1985. *The Fragmented Forest: Island Biogeography Theory and the Preservation of Biotic Diversity.* University of Chicago Press, Chicago, IL.

Hartman, D. S. 1971. Behavior and ecology of the Florida manatee, *Trichechus manatus latirostris* (Harlan), at Crystal River, Citrus County. Ph.D. Dissertation, Cornell University, Ithaca, NY.

Harvey, M. J. 1992. Bats of the eastern United States. Arkansas Game and Fish Commission, Little Rock, AR.

Holdridge, L. R. 1967. *Life Zone Ecology.* Tropical Science Center, San Jose, Costa Rica.

Holler, N. R. 1992a. Choctawhatchee beach mouse. In *Rare and Endangered Biota of Florida: Volume I, Mammals.* S. R. Humphrey (ed.). University Press of Florida, Gainesville, FL, p. 76-86.

Holler, N. R. 1992b. Perdido Key beach mouse. In *Rare and Endangered Biota of Florida: Volume I, Mammals.* S. R. Humphrey (ed.). University Press of Florida, Gainesville, FL, p. 102-109.

Holliman, D. C. 1983. Status and habitat of Alabama Gulf Coast beach mice *Peromyscus polionotus ammobates* and *P. p. trissyllepsis. Northeast Gulf Science* **6**:121-129.

Howe, S. E. 1988. Lower Keys marsh rabbit status survey. Report submitted to the U.S. Fish and Wildlife Service, Jacksonville, FL, 8 p.

Humphrey, S. R. 1992a. Key Largo woodrat. In *Rare and Endangered Biota of Florida: Volume I, Mammals.* S. R. Humphrey (ed.). University Press of Florida, Gainesville, FL, p. 119-130.

Humphrey, S. R. 1992b. Southern Florida population of mink. In *Rare and Endangered Biota of Florida: Volume I, Mammals.* S. R. Humphrey (ed.). University Press of Florida, Gainesville, FL, p. 319-327.

Humphrey, S. R., W. H. Kern, Jr., and M. E. Ludlow. 1987. Status survey of seven Florida mammals. Report submitted to the U.S. Fish and Wildlife Service, Jacksonville, FL, 39 p.

James, F. C. 1992. St. Andrew beach mouse. *In Rare and Endangered Biota of Florida: Volume I, Mammals.* S. R. Humphrey (ed.). University Press of Florida, Gainesville, FL, p. 87-93.

Klimstra, W. D. 1985. The Key deer. *Florida Naturalist* **58** (4):2-5.

Klimstra, W. D., J. W. Hardin, N. J. Silvy, B. N. Jacobson, and V. A. Terpening. 1974. Key deer investigations final report: December 1967-June 1973. Southern Illinois University, Carbondale, IL, 184 p.

Lefebvre, L. W., and J. T. Tilmant. 1993. Round-tailed muskrat. In *Rare and Endangered Biota of Florida: Volume I, Mammals.* S. R. Humphrey (ed.). University Press of Florida, Gainesville, FL, p. 276-286.

Maehr, D. S. 1990. Tracking Florida's panthers. *Defenders* **65** (5):9-15.

Maehr, D. S. 1992a. Florida panther distribution and conservation strategy. Final Report, Florida Game and Fresh Water Fish Commission, Tallahassee, FL, 24 p.

Maehr, D. S. 1992b. Florida black bear. In *Rare and Endangered Biota of Florida: Volume I, Mammals.* S. R. Humphrey (ed.). University Press of Florida, Gainesville, FL, p. 265-275.

Odell, D. K. 1982. Manatee. In *Wild Mammals of North America: Biology, Management, and Economics.* J. A. Chapman, and G. A. Feldhamer (eds.). Johns Hopkins University Press, Baltimore, MD, p. 828-837.

O'Shea, T. J. 1988. The past, present, and future of manatees in the southeastern United States: Realities, misunderstandings, and enigmas. In *Proceedings of the Third Southeastern Nongame and Endangered Wildlife Symposium.* R. R. Odom, K. A. Riddleberger, and J. C. Ozier (eds.). Georgia Department of Natural Resoures, Game and Fish Division, Social Circle, GA, p. 184-204.

Park, E. 1971. *The World of the Otter.* J. B. Lippincott Co., New York, NY.

Peterson, S. L. 1974. Man's relationship with the Florida manatee, *Trichechus manatus latirostris* (Harlan): An historical perspective. M. A. Thesis, University of Michigan, Ann Arbor, MI.

Reynolds, J. E., III, and J. R. Wilcox. 1986. Distribution and abundance of the West Indian manatee, *Trichechus manatus*, around selected Florida power plants following winter cold fronts: 1984-85. *Biological Conservation* **38**:103-113.

Schorger, A. W. 1970. The otter in early Wisconsin. *Wisconsin Academy of Science, Arts and Letters, Transactions* **58**:129-146.

Schwartz, A. 1952. The land mammals of southern Florida and the upper Florida Keys. Ph.D. Dissertation, University of Michigan, Ann Arbor, MI.

Schwartz, A., and E. P. Odum. 1957. The woodrats of the eastern United States. *Journal of Mammalogy* **38**:197-206.

Sherman, H. B. 1955. Description of a new race of woodrat from Key Largo, Florida. *Journal of Mammalogy* **36**:113-120.

Stout, I. J. 1992. Southeastern beach mouse. In *Rare and Endangered Biota of Florida: Volume I, Mammals.* S. R. Humphrey (ed.). University Press of Florida, Gainesville, FL, p. 242-249.

Tuttle, M. D. 1979. Status, cause of decline, and management of endangered gray bats. *Journal of Wildlife Management* **43**:1-17.

U.S. Fish and Wildlife Service. 1978. Administration of the Marine Mammal Protection Act of 1972, June 22, 1977 to March 31, 1978. U.S. Fish and Wildlife Service, Washington, D.C., 80 p.

van Zyll de Jong, C. G. 1983. Handbook of Canadian mammals: l, Marsupials and insectivores. National Museum of Natural Sciences, Ottawa, Ontario, Canada.

Wassmer, D. A., and J. L. Wolfe. 1983. New Florida localities for the round-tailed muskrat. *Northeast Gulf Science* **6**:197-199.

Weaver, K. M. 1992. Louisiana status report. *Eastern Black Bear Workshop* **11**:16-21.

Wolfe, J. L. 1985. Population ecology of the rice rat (*Oryzomys palustris*) in coastal marshes. *Journal of Zoology* **205**(A):235-244.

Wolfe, J. L. 1990. Environmental influences on the distribution of rice rats (*Oryzomys palustris*) in coastal marshes. *Florida Science* **53**:81-84.

Wolfe, J. L. 1992. Lower Keys marsh rabbit. In *Rare and Endangered Biota of Florida: Volume I, Mammals.* S. R. Humphrey (ed.). University Press of Florida, Gainesville, FL, p. 71-75.

Woods, C. A. 1992. Lower Keys marsh rabbit. In *Rare and Endangered Biota of Florida: Volume I, Mammals.* S. R. Humphrey (ed.). University Press of Florida, Gainesville, FL, p. 131-139.

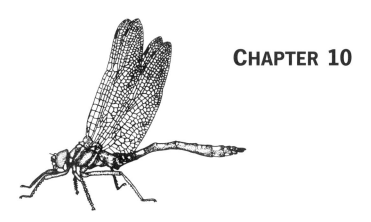

CHAPTER 10

Aquatic Insect Resource Management

Kenneth J. Tennessen

M anaging natural resources specifically to ensure the continued existence of any aquatic insect has yet to become a reality. Weighted down by the pest stigma, insects have garnered relatively little visibility or clout in the realm of species protection. Consequently, past protective measures and management practices have been directed at a few vertebrate and even fewer invertebrate species. Yet on a number of species basis, 95 percent of the world's fauna is composed of invertebrates, and roughly 70 to 80 percent of this fauna is composed of insects alone (Wilson, 1988). The species richness and enormous population sizes of invertebrates prompted E. O. Wilson to contend that invertebrates drive our planet's living systems. If we are going to maintain the biological diversity of this world, we must plan for the well-being of invertebrates. Considering that biological diversity is largely a function of insect species richness and that many aquatic insects are imperiled (Morse et al., 1997), work in this area is sadly overdue.

In the southeastern United States (Alabama, Arkansas, Florida, Georgia, Kentucky, Louisiana, Mississippi, North Carolina, South Carolina, Tennessee, Virginia), there are more than 4,200 species of aquatic insects known to science. At the regional conference where an oral version of this chapter was presented, the grand total of all species addressed was roughly 6,000. Aquatic invertebrates (insects, decapod crustaceans, and molluscs) accounted for at least 5,000 of these, which was more than 80 percent of the total. Of course, this percentage is an underestimate given that not all invertebrate groups were considered (e.g., non-decapod crustaceans, annelids, bryozoans, nematodes, rotifers). Furthermore, there certainly are aquatic invertebrate species awaiting discovery in the Southeast.

Although our knowledge of aquatic insect distributions, population sizes, and habitat requirements is incomplete, it is apparent that some aquatic insect species are imperiled. Morse et al. (1997) considered 153 species in just four orders of aquatic insects as rare and

Aquatic Fauna in Peril: The Southeastern Perspective, edited by George W. Benz, and David E. Collins. 1997. Special Publication 1, Southeast Aquatic Research Institute, Lenz Design & Communications, Decatur, GA, 554 p.

vulnerable to extirpation. This number is 12.6 percent of the 1,212 species contained in these orders known to occur in the Southeast. If this percentage is applicable to the other orders of aquatic insects (beetles, hemipterans, dipterans, etc.), then of the approximately 4,200 species in the Southeast, over 500 may be imperiled. Morse et al. (1997) suspect that at least three species (two stoneflies and one caddisfly) may have been extirpated from the southern Appalachian Mountains. However, many insect species occupy small, unusual habitats that are hard to find, and there are few entomologists searching for certain groups. Therefore, we cannot say whether certain species are extinct, rare, in danger of extinction, or whether they still exist as undiscovered populations.

The degradation of our nation's streams is clearly associated with human population density and activity. Where humankind has been most active, watersheds and their associated biota have often suffered. Increasing human populations will mean further demand for space, natural resources, and recreation, and will be accompanied by further degradation of our streams and lakes and the drainage and pollution of our wetlands. Morse et al. (1997) pointed out that we do not know if aquatic insect species now considered to be in peril are rare because of natural restrictions or because of human activities. However, we can predict that further disturbance to their habitats probably will hasten population declines. The continued existence of some species over the next few decades appears questionable. Recently, even some once-common stream species have drastically declined in numbers. Clearly something must be done to protect insect species and their habitats if we are going to maintain the biological diversity of the southeastern United States.

AQUATIC INSECT MANAGEMENT

One step that has been taken toward protecting aquatic insects is the maintenance of a federal listing of endangered species. In the U.S. Federal Register dated November 15, 1994 (U.S. Fish and Wildlife Service, 1994), 198 species of aquatic insects were proposed for possible addition to the threatened and endangered species list. Of these, 73 species occur in the southeastern United States. The status of most of these candidate species is unsettled, and much time is being spent gathering information necessary to make listing category decisions. Regarding actual listings, 29 insect species are now federally listed as threatened or endangered species. Most of these are terrestrial beetles and butterflies. Only two aquatic species, *Ambrysus amargosus*, a naucorid bug known only from Nevada, and *Somatochlora hineana*, a dragonfly which occurs in the Great Lakes region, are on the threatened and endangered (T&E) list.

The U.S. Endangered Species Act as it pertains to insects is administered by the U.S. Fish and Wildlife Service. For each species that becomes listed as threatened or endangered, a species recovery plan aimed at de-listing the species is prepared. A suggestion to amend the Act has been made to allow the listing of many species that share a single ecosystem. This would be a step to shift emphasis from management of single species to management of habitat (Opler, 1993). Although species listing is a positive step that ultimately can afford protection, many species that have not as yet been proposed for listing and which contribute the bulk of biodiversity are declining in numbers due to the widespread disturbance of our running waters.

The actual management of aquatic habitats to benefit aquatic insects is only beginning to be considered, and few examples are available for discussion. Field activities aimed at enhancing habitats for other aquatic taxa, such as stream restoration for fish, probably benefit certain insect groups. However, these efforts do not take into account key differences in the life histories and habitat requirements of various aquatic insects (Stewart and Stark, 1988). In general, to enhance stream habitat to maximize insect diversity, a strong emphasis should be placed on providing habitat diversity and bank and substrate stabilization. Specific protection or enhancement efforts will require knowledge of the target species' life cycle and habitat requirements, both in the immature and adult stages. In providing conditions for a specific insect, care must be taken not to alter the habitat in such a way that would be detrimental to other rare species.

Of course, a species approach to aquatic insect management requires two limited resources — time and money. Research on habitat requirements of individual species is beset with difficulties and uncertainties, and is time-consuming. Unfortunately, time may be something endangered species lack. Furthermore, securing sufficient funds to carry out imperiled species projects can be difficult. In contrast, habitat protection or improvement plans can often be relatively more timely and less costly in achieving results. They often can also be more readily accepted by the parties that are affected by them.

Because of the biological and sociological complexities associated with managing aquatic insects, we will need to skillfully build upon our successes and learn from our mistakes regarding the methods we use to realize improvement. Below I will briefly discuss several habitat management projects to illustrate some of the types of problems that such projects can pose to insects.

Case 1. Damselflies and the Controlled Burning of Australian Marshes

Hemiphlebia mirabilis is a small, rare damselfly once thought to be extinct. According to New (1993), it is now listed as a threatened taxon (in accordance with the Victoria Flora and Fauna Guarantee Act of 1988) because of population loss and decline associated with agricultural practices and modifications to river flow and flooding regimes. It is the only species in the family Hemiphlebiidae, and it has several interesting ancestral characteristics important in studies of the evolution of the Zygoptera. With its habitat limited to seasonal swamps that are found on sandy heathland, *H. mirabilis* is a weak flier that depends on emergent aquatic vegetation for cover and as a substrate in which it lays eggs. At one of its major known population sites, controlled burning in a mosaic pattern was used to prevent successional progression of vegetation and promote earlier seral stages, while also preventing a build-up of dead vegetation on the ground which could fuel more intense, unintentional fires (New, 1993). However, it appears that the burning was intended to create food for vertebrates, and was not necessarily intended to provide continued suitable habitat for the damselfly. In 1987, a "controlled" fire spread to the site of the largest colony of *H. mirabilis*, destroying the vegetation. No damselflies were seen in the area for two years following the burn. A few individuals were observed during the third year after the burn, and recently, numbers have increased nearly to the level present prior to the fire.

Study of this situation reveals several critical points. First, careful burning of patches of the surrounding habitat can be an important management tool regarding species like *H. mirabilis* because fires can prevent the maturation of the shrubby trees which can be responsible for the long-term drying of swamps. Secondly, *H. mirabilis* can withstand even drastic temporary alterations of its habitat if there are nearby locations from which individuals can immigrate when habitat conditions again become favorable. Of course the widescale reduction in the habitat of *H. mirabilis* makes the last mentioned possibility extremely tenuous, and underlines the vulnerability of this species. Together, the above experiences illustrate the need to carefully monitor habitat alteration projects and to consider the long-term effects they might cause.

Case 2. Re-establishment of Prairie Habitat in Illinois

In a small area of northeastern Illinois, there is a particular site being managed to restore mid-western prairie habitat. This is accomplished mainly by periodic controlled burning and removal of trees and shrubs. Within this area, a rare dragonfly (Hine's emerald, *Somatochlora hineana*) inhabits an unusual microhabitat, namely shallow, spring-fed sheet flow, and narrow streamlets through calcareous (dolomitic) cattail marsh. This dragonfly was once thought to be extinct, but a few isolated colonies have been found recently in northeastern Illinois and eastern Wisconsin (Cashatt, 1991). *Somatochlora hineana* was recently placed on the T&E list (Beattie, 1995), partly because of its apparent extirpation from previously known localities in Ohio and Indiana.

For two main reasons, the cut-and-burn management practice at the Illinois location creates concern regarding whether the future survival of *S. hineana* is being considered. First, burning of the wetlands may directly destroy dragonfly individuals if aestivating nymphs occur in dry peat/muck or if the shallow habitat is overheated. Furthermore, this species' distribution may be limited in part by water chemistry (Vogt and Cashatt, 1994), and an additional problem might be created if burning temporarily changes the water chemistry where eggs are laid and nymphs develop. Secondly, removal of nearby trees and shrubs denies adult dragonflies access to preferred perching sites, as well as to mating and foraging areas. This last issue underscores the importance of the terrestrial environment to an aquatic insect species.

The most pressing need regarding *S. hineana* is the immediate protection of the wetlands area, as well as research aimed at developing management strategies that will ensure continued existence of the species' required habitat. Close communication and cooperation among all concerned parties along with a monitoring program are needed to manage the site properly for the continued existence of the variety of organisms now present.

Case 3. Weir Project, South Fork of the Holston River, Tennessee

In an effort to improve levels of dissolved oxygen (DO) and minimum flow in the South Fork Holston River in northeastern Tennessee, the Tennessee Valley Authority (TVA) constructed an aerating labyrinth weir (completed in December, 1991) 2 km (about 1.2 miles) downstream from the South Holston Dam. This was the first project under TVA's Lake Improvement Plan (Hauser, 1993). DO levels have improved from 1.5-3.0 mg per l upstream of the weir and from 6.0-8.7 mg per l downstream, and a minimum flow of 2.55 cms is usually maintained between electricity generating periods. Rainbow trout have been stocked below the weir, and the monitoring of benthic organisms downstream of the South Holston weir has been conducted.

The impoverished macroinvertebrate fauna in the tailwaters below the South Holston Dam, characterized by low taxonomic diversity and a predominance of stress-tolerant species, is characteristic of hypolimnetic release areas. The minimum flow regime established now provides a more constant habitat for benthic insects. Eleven aquatic insect taxa have been collected immediately downstream of the weir and about twice that number in the 1.6 km (one mile) stretch further downstream (Yeager et al., 1993). However, only two EPT taxa[1] were found. Despite a slight increase in biodiversity below the weir compared to the area immediately upstream, there was still a much lower diversity of aquatic insects than would be expected in a river of this size in eastern Tennessee. Moreover, blackfly (Diptera: Simuliidae) production below the weir was extremely high, and was undoubtedly a response to continuous flow combined with the high organic productivity of the upstream lake water.

This example illustrates the need for monitoring the response of aquatic life to supposed habitat improvements. It also raises the question, is altering one or two physical/chemical parameters adequate to improve habitat and enhance biodiversity? Other questions follow. What can be done about nutrient overloading in rivers, especially when conditions are optimum for large populations of pest insects to be produced? What factors other than low DO, low flows, and nutrient loading are responsible for depressing desirable aquatic insects in tailwaters of large dams? Solving these problems would help reinstate well-balanced communities in rivers below reservoirs, of which there are many river-miles in the southeastern United States.

Case 4. Walker Branch State Natural Area, Tennessee

Walker Branch is a tributary of Mud Creek, flowing through an ecotone between an upland area and big river bottomland in Hardin County, Tennessee. The area is a mosaic of aquatic habitat types, including wooded hillside seeps, first-order runs, shaded and partly open second-order streams, larger slow-flowing and pooled streams, and swampy wetlands with bald cypress and Tupelo gum. Disturbance from past farming and logging activities is still evident, although the area has experienced considerable regrowth and habitat recovery. The diversity of Odonata I found while collecting there between 1979 and 1982 prompted me to suggest that the area be looked at by other biologists and perhaps be considered for some type of protection. Besides the great number of Odonata species I found (nearly 40), the combination of rare and unusual species at this site is not easily found elsewhere. In addition to rare insects, several state-listed plants were also found, including *Iris brevicaulis*, *Carex lacustris*, and *Malanthium virginicum*.

The area in which the seeps and cypress wetlands lie is designated to be purchased by the Tennessee Wildlife Resources Agency and registered as a state natural area known as Walker Branch Hills. This positive action is mainly being realized due to efforts by staff at the Tennessee Department of Environment and Conservation. No development or publicity of the area is proposed, in hope of keeping human visitation to a minimum. The seeps I surveyed constitute only a small part of the area, 0.81 ha (roughly two acres). They are vulnerable to trampling and are still recovering from past disturbance. However, prospects are now good for the continued existence of this rich community of dragonflies and other species. This case is a rare example of an important natural area being discovered and eventually protected because of its aquatic insect fauna.

---

[1] EPT stands for the three aquatic insect orders Ephemeroptera, Plecoptera, and Trichoptera. EPT counts are generally used as a measure of taxa richness and hence stream quality. An EPT value less than 10 generally indicates a stream in poor biotic condition.

Case 5. *Gomphus sandrius* — The Tennessee Clubtail

The clubtail dragonfly, *Gomphus sandrius,* is unusual in that it has the most restricted distribution known within the entire *Gomphus* species complex. It occurs in only five tributary streams of the Duck River in a 150 km² (about 60 square miles) area of the Central Basin south of Nashville, Tennessee. Population sizes are small, estimated to be one to six individuals per 30 m (about 100 feet) depending on the stream and locality (Tennessen, 1994). The streams this clubtail inhabits are shallow and slow-flowing, with bedrock and gravel bottoms. Nymphs of *G. sandrius* occupy gravel bars consisting of mixed particle sizes that accumulate downstream of rock fissures and small islands of water willows. The surrounding lands are heavily used as pastureland for cattle, with some fields cropped for hay. Cattle have access to the streams and surface runoff contributes organic waste and perhaps agricultural chemicals to the streams. Removal of much of the riparian vegetation undoubtedly has raised water temperatures and increased algal growth and sediment input.

Although *G. sandrius* is on the federal candidate T&E list and a status survey for this species has been conducted (Tennessen, 1994), a decision to list it has not been made. Populations at several of the streams appear to have declined since discovery of the species, but because aquatic insect population size is difficult to estimate, longer periods of time often are needed to discover trends. It is possible that T&E status would not benefit *G. sandrius,* because the species might be faced with a range of adversities that place it close to extinction. Furthermore, forcing regulations on private landowners often generates entirely new sets of problems. An alternative and perhaps more timely approach to prevent further damage to these streams is to form cooperative agreements with the local citizenry. By showing landowners the benefits of improved water quality and stream habitat, and involving them in decisions on what can be done to lessen agricultural impacts, their help can be enlisted for the benefit of all forms of aquatic life, including the Tennessee clubtail.

CONFLICTING LEGISLATION

Roberts (1993) pointed out that the mandates of the U.S. Endangered Species Act (ESA) conflict with those of the U.S. Mosquito Abatement Act (MAA). He illustrated this by applying a strict interpretation of these acts to two situations as follows:

   Example 1.   A wildlife biologist trying to manage a wetland to support an endangered aquatic or semi-aquatic species inevitably might create conditions that produce mosquitoes. This would be in violation of the MAA, which states that aquatic habitats that support mosquito production are public nuisances to be legally abated.

   Example 2.   A vector biologist trying to control mosquitoes in a wetland could negatively affect an aquatic or semi-aquatic endangered species. This would be in violation of the ESA.

Such dilemmas result from various specialized disciplines considering environmental management independently rather than working together toward a more harmonious approach. Ecosystems are complex, integrated systems, and Roberts (1993) warned that attempts at piecemeal solutions to many environmental problems are bound to fail. Section 7 of the ESA requires federal agencies to consult with the U.S. Fish and Wildlife

Service concerning any activity which may adversely affect listed species, and this at least provides a gateway for interagency cooperation. Cooperation between biologists and resource managers during the initial planning stages of projects is especially critical.

Of course, the issue of public health and human rights versus animal protection and animal rights is often at the heart of conflicting legislation, and taking inflexible sides on such matters sets up confrontation scenarios which can thwart lasting achievements. However, through cooperation aimed at trying to resolve or otherwise minimize apparent differences, rewards can often be realized which benefit the greatest number of involved parties. As an example, while no insect species that has been implicated in the transmission of human disease is currently considered endangered or threatened, if such an instance is identified, the insect would not be afforded protection under the ESA.

CLOSING THOUGHTS ON THE MANAGEMENT OF INSECT RESOURCES

In contrast to the present gloomy state of affairs regarding the protection of imperiled aquatic insects, the future can bring brightness through education and change. Our industrial, capitalistic society, which put a man on the moon before adopting a national environmental policy, has become conscious of its environment, and a large faction cares for or at least appreciates the other living things around them. The term "biodiversity" is being used outside biological circles by politicians and the general public, and understanding of its importance is being commonly gained. We are in the process of looking at aquatic species and their habitats in hopes of identifying what is in danger of being lost forever. The federal government is concerned with endangered species, including candidate aquatic insects, and is attempting to rectify some of its own past assaults on our rivers. Private citizens are becoming involved in clean-up and restoration activities, and a majority of people express the desire for a "healthy" environment.

On the other hand, the world's human population continues to increase at an alarming rate. Globally, the human population is increasing at about 10,000 people per hour, or 93 million people per year (source: "People Count," a TBS television production aired August 29, 1994). In the United States, the 1994 census was 261 million, and this number is projected to increase by 25 percent to 326 million by the year 2020 (Campbell, 1994). In the 11 southeastern states considered in this chapter, the population will increase from approximately 60.9 to 78.2 million by the year 2020, a 28 percent jump in just 25 years. The Southeast will remain the most densely populated region in the country. Florida currently has the highest population within the Southeast (about 14 million people) and the greatest projected rate of increase (estimated to be about 36 percent from 1995 to 2020).

More people will place greater demands on natural resources, increase demands for living space, and increase encroachment on natural habitats. Many people desire lakefront or streamside property and most seek high standards of living. These demands often result in water quality reductions and habitat degradation. Protecting species requires a constant vigil, because losses are irrecoverable. Increased human habitation of remote areas can result in a greater number of species whose ranges are fragmented or otherwise diminished in size. For many, it is extremely disturbing and ironic that although we have instituted more policies to prevent or regulate the degradation of our waters over the last 20 years than ever before, more damage seemingly has occurred during this period than ever before.

How do we satisfy the needs of our rapidly growing human population and still keep aquatic habitats capable of supporting other life forms? The solution lies in getting appropriate agencies and affected organizations and individuals in watersheds concerned with local projects and to work through cooperative efforts. Where regulation might fail, communication, education, and recruiting stakeholders can often succeed. We need to instill and foster an appreciation of all forms of life at an early age through education, both formal and by example. The belief that other living things were put here for our use must be challenged. Furthermore, we need to educate everyone of the benefits of protecting habitats and maintaining the levels of biodiversity that are still present. By stressing the importance of habitat protection and its benefits to society as well as to the natural world, even skeptical parties might be persuaded to become good stewards of nature. The integrated ecosystem approach to environmental management was recommended by the U. S. National Research Council (1992) in a proposal to embark on a major national aquatic ecosystem restoration program.

I suggest that we might benefit from a more proper term than "resource management" for trying to improve aquatic habitats. To manage means to handle, direct, govern, or control in action or use. This concept is difficult to apply to human tinkering with natural systems. Furthermore, some might question the goodness of human control regarding a workable philosophy in dealing with ecosystems. The term resource management also implies knowledge of how to change things to achieve particular goals. Lastly, the term "resource" carries a connotation that there is something in it for people. A term that is more neutral and also connotes resources for all living things is "habitat."

Terms such as "habitat manipulation" and "habitat alteration" do not imply that we can control the outcome of our actions. After all, a lack of knowledge concerning an organism's requirements and responses to change reduces our management efforts to trying to manipulate one or two environmental variables and then observing the outcome. The term "restoration" also seems inappropriate, as it means to bring back to a former, original, or normal condition. We have changed many of our larger streams so drastically (by damming, dredging, etc.) that they arguably cannot be restored to their original conditions. Strictly adhered to, habitat restoration of a large system where a reservoir is now in place would dictate that the dam be removed, allowing the river to resume its natural dynamic state. Of course, many problems would result from removal of large dams (e.g., flooding, bank cutting and other forms of erosion) such that this action might lead to new forms of environmental disaster. It might be more prudent to try to improve existing reservoirs and remaining river stretches by re-establishing riparian vegetation and conducting other bank stabilization projects, by reviewing dredging proposals, and by preventing livestock, organic wastes, and toxicants from entering water courses. Monitoring programs should be initiated to document that natural processes are being maintained in our rivers.

The next ten years will probably be critical regarding the overall fate of our aquatic insect fauna in the Southeast. A heightened public awareness of stream biodiversity and its importance will be needed to abate the negative pressures impacting our streams. People from all disciplines will be needed to work together using integrated approaches to maintain watersheds as natural functioning systems. How will we be able to measure our success in these matters? Some will count the numbers of species being removed from the federal T&E list. Some may tally the number of river kilometers improved. I hope to go to a stream, pick up some submerged rocks, and see many various mayflies, stoneflies, caddisflies, and dragonflies crawling on them.

ACKNOWLEDGEMENTS

I thank Paul Hartfield (U.S. Fish and Wildlife Service) for discussions on approaches to habitat protection and alteration, and also for reviewing a draft of this chapter. I am indebted to Dr. Joseph C. Cooney, Martin K. Painter, Chris Ungate, and Bruce Yeager (all Tennessee Valley Authority) for criticisms, comments, and information used in this chapter. Dr. Everett D. Cashatt (Illinois State Museum) and Tom E. Vogt (The Nature Conservancy) provided input to the case study on prairie habitat in Illinois. Dr. John C. Morse (Clemson University) provided direction and encouragement. Lastly, I want to publicly recognize the native peoples of this country who were wise stewards of the lands and waters for thousands of years prior to the habitation of North America by Europeans.

REFERENCES

Beattie, M. H. 1995. Rules and regulations. *U.S. Federal Register* **60**(17):5267-5273.

Campbell, P. R. 1994. *Population Projections for States, by Age, Race, and Sex: 1993 to 2020.* Current Population Reports, P25-1111, U.S. Bureau of the Census, United States Government Printing Office, Washington, D.C., 40 p.

Cashatt, E. D. 1991. A vulnerable species, the Ohio emerald dragonfly. *The Living Museum* **53**(2):29-30.

Hauser, G. E. 1993. South Holston labyrinth weir operation and maintenance plan. Report No. WR28-1-21-104R1, Tennessee Valley Authority, Norris, TN, 28 p.

Morse, J. C., B. P. Stark, W. P. McCafferty, and K. J. Tennessen. 1997. Southern Appalachian and other southeastern streams at risk: implications for mayflies, dragonflies and damselflies, stoneflies, and caddisflies. In *Aquatic Fanua in Peril: the Southeastern Perspective.* G. W. Benz and D. E. Collins (eds.). Special Publication 1, Southeast Aquatic Research Institute, Lenz Design & Communications, Decatur, GA, p. 17-42.

New, T. R. 1993. *Hemiphlebia mirabilis* Selys: recovery from habitat destruction at Wilsons Promontory, Victoria, Australia, and implications for conservation management (Zygoptera: Hemiphlebiidae). *Odonatologica* **22**:495-502.

Opler, P. A. 1993. The US Endangered Species Act: conservation and research for aquatic insects. *Aquatic Conservation: Marine and Freshwater Ecosystems* **3**:289-291.

Roberts, F. C. 1993. The Endangered Species Act and vector control legislation: reconcilable? *Journal of the Florida Mosquito Control Association* **64**:41-45.

Stewart, K. W., and B. P. Stark. 1988. Nymphs of North American stonefly genera (Plecoptera). Volume XII, The Thomas Say Foundation, Entomological Society of America, USA, 460 p.

Tennessen, K. J. 1994. Status survey for *Gomphus sandrius* and *Ophiogomphus acuminatus* (Insecta: Odonata: Gomphidae). Report for Cooperative Agreement No. 14-16-0004-89-953, U.S. Fish and Wildlife Service, Asheville, NC, 53 p.

U.S. Fish and Wildlife Service. 1994. Endangered and threatened wildlife and plants; animal candidate review for listing as endangered or threatened species; proposed rule. *U.S. Federal Register* **59**(219):58982-59028.

U.S. National Research Council. 1992. *Restoration of Aquatic Ecosystems: Science, Technology, and Public Policy.* National Academy Press, Washington, D.C.

Vogt, T. E., and E. D. Cashatt. 1994. Distribution, habitat, and field biology of *Somatochlora hineana* (Odonata: Corduliidae). *Annals of the Entomological Society of America* **87**:599-603.

Wilson, E. O. 1988. The current state of biological diversity. In *Biodiversity.* E. O. Wilson, and F. M. Peter (eds.). National Academy of Science Press, Washington, D.C., p. 3-18.

Yeager, B. L., T. A. McDonough, and D. A. Kenny. 1993. Growth, feeding, and movement of trout in South Holston tailwater. Report WM-94-003, Tennessee Valley Authority, Norris, TN, 29 p.

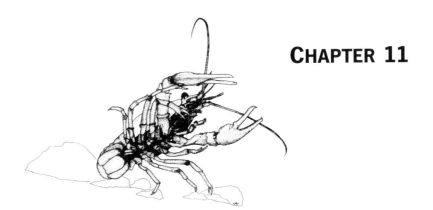

CHAPTER 11

Resource Management of Freshwater Crustaceans in the Southeastern United States

Guenter A. Schuster

I t has been estimated that only about 10 percent of all extant species of crustaceans occur in freshwater (Bowman and Abele, 1982; Covich and Thorp, 1991). However, the freshwater crustaceans consist of a variety of taxonomic groups (Table 1) that may be found in almost any type of freshwater habitat. Freshwater crustaceans can be found in coldwater springs, small to large order streams, in underground caverns and burrows, in a variety of lentic habitats (from swamps and marshes to ponds and lakes), and even in temporary aquatic habitats such as autumnal and vernal pools.

The southeastern region of North America has played an important role in the evolution of several crustacean groups (Holsinger, 1969, amphipods; Steeves, 1969, isopods; Hobbs, 1969, crayfish; Hart and Hart, 1969, ostracods). It has been proposed that at least one group, the crayfish genus *Cambarus*, has had the Cumberland Plateau as the center of its radiation (Hobbs, 1969). In addition, several crayfish genera (Hobbs, 1989) and many other crustacean species (e.g., Hobbs, 1942, 1981, 1989; Bouchard, 1972) are endemic to specific regions in the Southeast. Distribution maps in Hobbs (1989) clearly show that the crayfish genera *Barbicambarus* (found in Kentucky and Tennessee), *Bouchardina* (found in Arkansas), *Distocambarus* (found in Georgia and South Carolina), *Hobbseus* (found in Alabama and Mississippi), and *Troglocambarus* (found in Florida) are all endemic to the Southeast. Crustacean groups other than crayfishes also have southeastern endemic spe-

Aquatic Fauna in Peril: The Southeastern Perspective, edited by George W. Benz, and David E. Collins. 1997. Special Publication 1, Southeast Aquatic Research Institute, Lenz Design & Communications, Decatur, GA, 554 p.

Table 1. Major crustacean taxa living in the southeastern United States.[1]

Taxon	Common Names
Class Branchiopoda	
Order Conchostraca	clam shrimp
Order Cladocera	water fleas
Order Anostraca	fairy shrimp
Class Branchiura	fish lice
Class Copepoda	copepods
Order Cyclopoida	
Order Harpacticoida	
Order Poecilostomatoida	
Order Siphonostomatoida	
Class Malacostraca	crabs, crayfish, shrimps
Order Amphipoda	side swimmers
Order Decapoda	decapods
Family Atyidae	cave shrimp
Family Cambaridae	crayfishes
Order Isopoda	isopods
Order Mysidacea	mysids
Class Ostracoda	seed shrimp

[1] Nomenclature follows Ruppert and Barnes, 1994.

cies (e.g., Frey, 1986, cladocera; Holsinger, 1986, amphipoda). In fact, most of the southeastern species that are considered candidates for listing as endangered or threatened (C2) (U.S. Fish and Wildlife Service [USFWS], 1991) show a very high degree of endemism (i.e., one or two known localities), and that may, at least in part, be the reason for their C2 status.

Hobbs (1992) categorized freshwater crustaceans ecologically into cave dwellers (isopods, amphipods, and decapods), surface dwellers (most groups have representatives of these), and burrowers (mostly crayfishes). Hobbs (1992) further categorized cave dwellers according to how much of their life cycle is actually spent in the cave (i.e., troglobites, trogloxenes, and troglophiles). The surface water dwellers are restricted typically either to lotic or lentic habitats, and may be part of the benthic (e.g., isopods, amphipods, and crayfishes), nektonic (e.g., shrimp), or planktonic (e.g., copepods and cladocerans) communities in those habitats (Covich and Thorp, 1991). Freshwater crustaceans are considered ecologically important members of the communities to which they belong, and may fulfill a variety of functions within their communities. Some are predators, some are herbivores, some are parasites, while many, such as crayfishes, are omnivores, and may comprise a large part of the biomass of a community (Covich and Thorp, 1991).

Because of the long-term degradation of fresh waters, it should not come as a surprise that some freshwater crustacean species are having problems surviving. Currently, the USFWS (1993) lists 13 species of freshwater crustaceans as either endangered or threatened, seven (54 percent) of which are from the Southeast (Table 2). In addition, a number of southeastern crustaceans have C2 status (i.e., no conclusive data on biological vulnerability and threat are currently available and further study is necessary; USFWS, 1991), for which listing as either endangered or threatened is possibly appropriate (Table 3).

Table 2. Crustacean species from the southeastern United States that are federally listed as endangered (E) or threatened (T).[1]

Species	State	Status	Habitat
Cambarus aculabrum (crayfish)	AR	E	caves
C. zophonastes (crayfish)	AR	E	caves
Orconectes shoupi (crayfish)	TN	E	surface water
Palaemonias alabamae (shrimp)	AL	E	caves
P. ganteri (shrimp)	KY	E	caves
Palaemonetes cummingi (shrimp)	FL	T	caves
Lirceus usdagalum (isopod)	VA	E	caves

[1] Tabled information obtained from USFWS, 1993.

A number of taxonomic groups (Classes Branchiopoda, Branchiura, Copepoda; Order Mysidaecea) have no species currently listed or being considered for possible listing (USFWS, 1991, 1993). The primary reason is not that these species are currently doing well, but that, in fact, we do not have enough information about their distributions and population dynamics to make a judgment about their conservation status.

IMPEDIMENTS TO CRUSTACEAN RESOURCE MANAGEMENT

Cultural and Scientific Bias

Crustaceans, like most other animal groups, suffer because of the positive bias associated with the so called "charismatic megafauna" (i.e., large and easily identifiable species such as the grizzly bear or the bald eagle). It is clear that this bias exists both in our culture and in science. Culturally, the field of crustacean resource management completely revolves around the economically important crustaceans for which a fisheries industry has been developed. This of course includes a variety of freshwater species of shrimp and crayfish which are raised as bait and human food.

In a book edited by Holdrich and Lowery (1988), which specifically dealt with the biology and management of crayfish species, not one chapter was dedicated to the conservation of these crustaceans. Hart and Clark (1989) provided approximately 11,000 citations for crayfishes under a variety of subject headings, but did not have a heading entitled "conservation." These are not oversights, but are instead reflections of the lack of scientific work that has been done in the conservation of freshwater crustaceans. If very little has been written about relatively well-known species such as crayfishes, then it is easy to see why next to nothing has been done for relatively obscure groups such as fairy shrimp or water fleas.

Taxonomy and Systematics

One of the main obstacles for the protection of lesser-known species is the current need for taxonomic experts who can identify various species. Many freshwater crustaceans are microscopic, or at least a microscope is necessary for their identification. In some freshwa-

Table 3. Number of C2 crustacean species in the southeastern United States in various taxonomic groups. [1]

Taxa	Number
Amphipoda	20
Decapoda	36
Cambarinae	36
Cambarus	10
Distocambarus	1
Fallicambarus	7
Hobbseus	1
Orconectes	4
Procambarus	13
Isopoda	7
Ostracoda	3
Total	66

[1] Tabled information obtained from USFWS, 1991.

ter crustacean groups, the taxonomy has been fairly well resolved (i.e., crayfishes and shrimps), although new species are often found annually. However, in some groups the taxonomy is still in great flux. A common idea expressed in recently published crustacean taxonomic keys is that for many of these taxa much is left to do, and that species and sometimes even generic level identification is often very tenuous (Williams, 1972, isopods; Frey, 1986, cladocerans; Holsinger, 1986, amphipods; Delorme, 1991, ostracodes; Dodson and Frey, 1991, branchiopods). When experts can not easily and reliably identify species, or even genera, then species protection is nearly impossible. This is a common problem in many invertebrate groups, and it will not be resolved easily, since fewer taxonomists are being trained to work with these difficult to identify taxa.

Distribution Information

The delineation of species' ranges obviously requires the ability of trained taxonomists to identify field collected specimens (Frey, 1986). In addition to the identification problems mentioned above, distribution data sometimes is lacking for taxonomically sound groups simply because of inadequate field work. In some groups, cladocerans for example (Frey, 1986), older distribution records are suspect because of recent reinterpretation of the taxonomy of the group. The only way to resolve these problems is to initiate extensive faunal inventories. Unfortunately, such inventories historically have not been well-supported through adequate funding.

Life History Data

Even for the best-known groups of freshwater crustaceans, the life history of most species has not been studied in detail. For example, of the over 300 species of crayfishes and shrimps in North America north of Mexico only about 20 have had their life histories studied (Hobbs, 1991). Researchers and resource managers often are left to extrapolate about the biology of a species based on the few studies that have been done on other related species. An example is the recovery plan (Biggins, 1989) for the federally listed endangered species, the Nashville crayfish (*Orconectes shoupi*). Under the heading of "Description, Ecology and Life History," Biggins (1989; page 2) stated: "However, some life history data does exist, and some speculations can be made based on this species' similarities to other crayfish… Like many crayfish, this species probably feeds on a variety of organic material, both plant and animal." This points out the lack of hard data available for most species, even for species that have already been federally listed.

Destruction, Degradation, and Fragmentation of Habitat

In recent years much has been written about the loss of aquatic habitats. Two primary causes of aquatic habitat destruction and fragmentation include the construction of dams and stream channelization. Both of these activities are prevalent in the Southeast, especially in states such as Alabama, Kentucky, North Carolina, and Tennessee. Almost all of the major stream systems of the Southeast have been impounded, channelized, drained or otherwise manipulated. This has resulted in the changing of these systems from typical lotic to lentic or semilentic systems (Adams and Hackney, 1992). Soballe et al. (1992) listed 144 major reservoirs for the Southeast. Tennessee has the most with 26, followed by Alabama and North Carolina with 19 each, and Kentucky with 17 (Soballe et al., 1992).

The effects of dams and channelization are well-known (Mulholland and Lenat, 1992; Soballe et al., 1992). Dams may create multiple impacts both upstream and downstream. Impoundments and channelization act as agents of habitat destruction and fragmentation, playing important roles in altering temperature regimes, natural water level fluctuations (both in surface and ground waters), physicochemical processes, deposition of fine particulate matter, erosion patterns downstream, and community composition.

As noted above, it has become increasingly clear that the southeastern region has played an important role in the evolution of several crustacean groups (Holsinger, 1969, amphipods; Steeves, 1969, isopods; Hobbs, 1969, crayfish; Hart and Hart, 1969, ostracods). Therefore, it stands to reason that the widespread habitat destruction caused by damming and channelization has and will have major impacts on these groups and will play an important role in the future management plans for these species. Unfortunately, changes in biogeography caused by habitat destruction make it difficult or impossible to interpret the historical ranges of impacted species, and thus knowledge concerning our natural heritage can become forever lost and unavailable for restoration efforts.

Habitat degradation may be the result of either point- (such as effluent from a pipe) or nonpoint-sources (such as agricultural runoff) of pollution. Habitat degradation is often difficult to document and its impact on species may be insidious and long-term. Habitat degradation may also play an important role in future management of freshwater crustaceans in that its effects may need to be mitigated in order to protect and/or restore some crustacean species.

Introduced Species

For the purposes of this discussion, introduced or non-indigenous species have been divided into two main categories. The first category includes other crustaceans that may be closely related to some native species. The second category includes non-crustacean species that may have an impact on native freshwater crustaceans. Through competition for resources, the first category often has greater impacts on the native fauna than does the second category of introduced species (Capelli, 1975).

Probably the best examples of introduced crustaceans come from the crayfishes. Crayfishes have been used both for food and bait for many years and, therefore, have been widely introduced. For example, *Procambarus clarkii* has been introduced on all continents except Australia and Antarctica (Huner, 1988). The effects of some such introductions have been widely documented. In Wisconsin *Orconectes rusticus* has had a serious impact on the native *O. virilis* and *O. propinquus* populations (Capelli, 1975). *Orconectes limosus* was introduced in Europe, and it has since been reported that it has all but eliminated many of the native species (Laurent, 1988). The introduction of *Pacifasticus leniusculus* and *Orconectes virilis* into California streams inhabited by *P. fortis*, the Shasta crayfish, has resulted in a serious decline of *P. fortis* (Hogger, 1988). In the Southeast, Biggins (1989) pointed out that *Orconectes shoupi*, a federally listed endangered species, may be at risk because of an impending invasion of *O. placidus*, a much more successful crayfish, from adjacent watersheds.

Even though there are many other examples of problems associated with the introduction of non-indigenous crayfishes in the Southeast, fisheries research continues to pursue species that may be exploited for culturing. A recent study on the red claw crayfish (*Cherax quadricarinatus*) from Australia is an example of such on-going fisheries research (Webster et al., 1994).

Non-crustacean introductions that have impacted native freshwater crustaceans range from fishes, which are potential predators, to zebra mussels (*Dreissena polymorpha*). Zebra mussels have been observed to attach to the exoskeleton of crayfish, and in doing so may potentially cause all sorts of biological problems (O'Neill and MacNeill, 1989). Leitheuser and Holsinger (1983) and Leitheuser (1988) reported that introduced rainbow trout (*Oncorhynchus mykiss*) eat *Palaemonias ganteri*, the Mammoth Cave shrimp, which is a federally listed endangered species known only from the Mammoth Cave system in Kentucky. Even though this predatory behavior was first reported over a decade ago (Leitheuser and Holsinger, 1983), trout are still being introduced into the Green River in the vicinity of Mammoth Cave National Park in order to maintain a put-and-take trout fishery (J. Axon, Kentucky Department of Fish and Wildlife Resources, pers. comm.). This situation has obvious management and recovery implications for the shrimp, and the solution here seems quite clear. The established trout should be eradicated from waters confluent with the cave and the reintroduction of rainbow trout to the cave should be halted.

Reconciliation of Biology, Politics, and Economics

In the course of managing for an endangered or threatened species, social and political considerations often become crucial stumbling blocks, and they must be considered before a management plan can be implemented. This is often very hard for biologists, who often are not very politically active or prone to thinking about large scale economic issues. The biological and physical needs of species are sometimes relatively more easily defined. However, convincing the general public that a species deserves protection can be very difficult. The first question usually asked is, "What good is it?" Often there is a compelling need to justify the existence of a species according to how useful it is to humans. Along with this, there often must be appeasement of numerous local, state, and federal agencies, and many citizen groups as well as industry, all of whom may have their own agendas which ultimately may harm nature. This set of circumstances of course is not unique to crustacean management, but is something that must be faced with all species that need protection.

MAMMOTH CAVE SHRIMP — A POSSIBLE WORST CASE SCENARIO

The Mammoth Cave shrimp may represent the best or the worst case scenario depending on your point of view for crustacean management. As mentioned above, this species is restricted in distribution to the caves in and around Kentucky's Mammoth Cave National Park. Logically, one would assume that this would afford the shrimp a great deal of protection, but ironically it does not.

Biological Profile

The following biological profile (mainly taken from Leitheuser and Holsinger [1983], Lisowski [1983], and Leitheuser [1988]) provides important life history information that has impact on the management of the Mammoth Cave shrimp. *Palaemonias ganteri* belongs to the family Atyidae. Its closest relative is *Palaemonias alabamae*, another endangered cave shrimp that is restricted to caves in Alabama (USFWS, 1991). The Mammoth Cave shrimp lives within nine distinct groundwater basins in the Mammoth Cave National Park, Kentucky vicinity, and at least three of these basins are outside of the Park. Within its preferred habitat of deep pools with minimal currents, the shrimps have been observed filter feeding and skimming food (mostly detritus) off the water surface.

The Mammoth Cave shrimp is dioecious. However, the average instantaneous sex ratio, the number of reproductive periods, and the time to sexual maturity are all unknown. These shrimp have been observed carrying 1 to 30 eggs, and it is thought that their longevity is probably 10 to 15 years. Lisowski (1983) indicated that there may have been recent declines in this shrimp population due to local groundwater pollution and hydrological changes in the cave system caused by dams on the Green River, both upstream and downstream of the Park boundaries. Leitheuser (1988) estimated the population size to be between 7,000 and 10,000. *Palaemonias ganteri* belongs to a community that also includes *Amblyopsis spelaea* (northern cavefish), *Typhlichthys subterraneus* (southern cavefish), *Orconectes pellucidus* (cave crayfish), and the aquatic cave snail *Antroselates spiralis*.

Like all troglobites (i.e., species restricted to caves), *P. ganteri* has certain biological characteristics which are associated with species known as K-strategists (Hobbs, 1992). These features include small population size, late age to maturity, low fecundity, large hatching size, and increased longevity. When these characteristics are combined with a very restrictive required habitat, management and protection of such species become very difficult problems.

Mammoth Cave Shrimp Management Problems

Even though most of the *P. ganteri* populations are known to occur within the Mammoth Cave National Park, this species is not well-protected from anthropogenic changes to its environment. Because of the hydrogeology of the area, activities outside of the Park (i.e., outside the sphere of its legal protection) may have devastating impacts on the fauna that lives within the cave system. Lisowski (1983) indicated that declines in *P. ganteri* population size were linked to water pollution that originated outside of the Park, and to two dams (lock and dam number 6 and the Green River Dam; respectively downstream and upstream of the Park) that greatly influence hydrological events within the caves.

Leitheuser (1988) described four toxic spills in the area of the Park that could also have had serious impacts on the cave fauna. Three spills were along Interstate 65 adjacent to the Park boundaries: 1980, cyanide salts; 1985, cresol; and 1985, synthetic solvents. Additionally, in 1985 a local train derailment spilled pesticides and methyl alcohol. Leitheuser (1988) also discussed the possible impacts of area petroleum wells that have leaked oil and gas in the past into the cave system. In addition, local agriculture has had impacts on local water quality via pesticides, herbicides, fertilizers, siltation, and livestock runoff (W. Sampson, Kentucky Division of Water, pers. comm.). There has also been a history of poor sewage treatment in the area (Lisowski, 1983; Leitheuser, 1988). This includes inadequate or poor treatment of the sewage of surrounding municipalities and the extensive use of septic systems which, because of the karst topography, drain directly or at least very quickly into the underlying cave system.

In addition to the above anthropogenic problems, the Park also has been subjected to the introduction of a non-indigenous species. As mentioned above, Leitheuser and Holsinger (1983) and Leitheuser (1988) both discussed the possible impacts of the introduction of the rainbow trout. Leitheuser observed trout eating cave shrimp in Pike Spring, one of the groundwater basins inhabited by *P. ganteri*. He indicated that the trout population was relatively small, but was well-established. Leitheuser and Holsinger (1983) indicated that trout were released by the Kentucky Department of Fish and Wildlife Resources as an on-going trout fisheries put-and-take program. As of this writing, the trout continue to be released monthly from April to November in the tailwaters of Nolin Lake Dam (Edmonson County), which is just downstream of the Park, and monthly from April to July in Lynn Camp Creek (Hart County), upstream of the Park (J. Axon, Kentucky Department of Fish and Wildlife Resources, pers. comm.). Leitheuser (1988) suggested that a trout survey should be conducted to determine the distribution of trout in the Park, and he indicated that it may become necessary to both stop the introductions and to remove trout from the river.

As in most endangered species cases, political activity can often become intense, and numerous federal, state, and local agencies as well as a variety of citizen groups become involved in the attempt to resolve the issue. In the case of *P. ganteri*, there are at least five federal agencies, four state agencies, five citizen groups as well as a number of local city and county governments, that are involved (Table 4). It is indeed a challenging proposition to bring such a diversity of interest groups toward a consensus about how best to protect the Mammoth Cave shrimp. In fact, some of these groups and agencies seem to be opposed to the protection of *P. ganteri*, and the reasons for this opposition appear varied. As Salwasser (1991) pointed out, it is very important for us to recognize that the issues of biodiversity are political issues, and that generally they are very complex with no simple solutions. One of the most challenging issues then is to reconcile the differences of all of these groups and arrive at a workable and acceptable management plan.

Another important management problem, again not unique to crustacean management, is the implementation of the species recovery plans. In the case of the Mammoth Cave shrimp, a recovery plan was prepared in 1988 (Leitheuser, 1988), but to date limited funds have been appropriated to fund the plan (D. Biggins, USFWS, pers. comm.). The plan outlines in detail the recovery tasks as well as a time schedule for their completion. However, without the necessary funding the recovery goals cannot be achieved.

A greater commitment must be made to fund recovery plans, especially for non-charis-

Table 4. Groups involved in *Palaemonias ganteri* management decisions.[1]

Group
Federal Agencies:
U.S. Fish and Wildlife Service
National Park Service
U.S. Department of Agriculture
U.S. Army Corps of Engineers
Soil Conservation Service
State Agencies:
Department of Fish and Wildlife Resources
Division of Water
State Nature Preserves Commission
Department of Agriculture
Local Agencies:
Caveland Sanitation Authority
Private Citizen Groups:
International Union for the Conservation of Nature and Natural Resources
Trout Unlimited
National Speleological Society
American Cave Conservation Association
Cave Research Foundation

[1] Information from Leitheuser and Holsinger (1983) and Leitheuser (1988).

matic microfauna species. It is clear that the distribution of these funds is often skewed in favor of larger, more noticeable species, as exemplified by funding to assist spotted owls and bald eagles. There must be a more equitable distribution of funds so that lesser publicized species also benefit.

The reason for noting the Mammoth Cave shrimp here as a possible worst case scenario is that virtually all of the problems associated with endangered species management are present. These include habitat alteration and destruction, point- and nonpoint-source water pollution, an introduced species, politics, and inadequate funding of the recovery plan. The biology of the species (i.e., low fecundity, small population size, extremely small range of distribution, etc.) also introduces additional management problems. That is not to say that any of these problems are unique to this one species, but rather *P. ganteri* embodies many of the problems that are common to all endangered species. If the list of the USFWS (1991, 1993) endangered, threatened, and C2 crustacean species is reviewed, it is apparent that many of the problems associated with *P. ganteri* are also common to other crustaceans. Six of the seven listed species (see Table 2) are restricted to living in caves, and many of the C2 species (see Table 3) are also cave dwellers.

FUTURE OF FRESHWATER CRUSTACEAN MANAGEMENT

As Soule (1985) observed, conservation biology currently is an exercise in crisis control. Most often species are not placed on the endangered species list until they are virtually on the edge of extinction, which is the ultimate crisis for any species. One of the main problems with crisis management, as pointed out by Meffe and Carroll (1994), is the search for a "quick fix" when actually long-term stewardship of the environment is what is needed. Meffe and Carroll (1994) maintain that there are five basic principles associated with good conservation management:

1) critical ecological processes must be maintained,
2) goals and objectives are the result of understanding the ecology of the system,
3) whatever threats exist must be minimized, and whatever benefits exit must be maximized,
4) evolutionary processes must be maintained, and
5) management mument must have minimal intrusion into the system.

These five principles are all logical and straightforward. However, their implementation may be extremely difficult. Since the complicated relationships among species and their environments are just being realized, there is still a great deal that needs to be learned about ecosystems before predictable and effective management plans can be set in place.

Meffe and Carroll (1994) pointed out that scale is a very important consideration for the conservation of endangered species. Both biological (population or community) and physical (habitat or landscape) scales need to addressed. In the past the greatest emphasis has always been at the species level. This is the whole philosophy behind the U.S. Endangered Species Act (ESA). It is clear, however, that in most cases this probably is not the most effective level of management. The well-being of the spotted owl, for example, depends on the well-being of the old growth forest in which it lives. Management of the owl cannot take place unless the whole system is managed.

The same principle is true in the management of the Mammoth Cave shrimp, and probably all other imperiled aquatic cave organisms. In order to protect this and other cave species, it is not enough to deal with the immediate habitat. The entire drainage of the cave system must be managed. This of course is a formidable task for a cave system that is more than 777 km (483 miles) long, as such the Mammoth Cave system. The staff of Mammoth Cave National Park is currently taking on the difficult task of trying to understand this complex system (Mammoth Cave National Park, 1994), and ultimately their work may result in an overall management plan that will protect not only the cave shrimp, but all other fauna and flora of the Park. For smaller cave systems the task may not be quite as daunting, but there may be greater land use and land ownership problems in these cases.

Logically, the same rationale should be used for the management of surface dwelling species. Entire drainage systems must be managed rather than individual habitats within the systems. It does very little good to protect a segment of a stream if the water quality upstream of this so-called protected area is subject to development or degradation. Ecosystem conservation is really the only logical way by which we can expect to save individual imperiled species and communities. That is not to say we should do away with the ESA, for the recognition of imperiled species raises the red flag and alerts us that entire systems are not well.

For freshwater crustaceans there are a number of specific problems that stand in the way of the development of adequate management plans. Some of the most serious problems that need to be addressed include the following.

1) There is a tremendous need to train taxonomists to work with these groups of animals. For some of the more "obscure" crustacean groups there are few if any taxonomic experts. Even for better known groups, such as the crayfishes, there are only a few

active workers, and death of even an individual (such as the recent passing of Dr. Horton H. Hobbs, Jr.) can produce a huge void.

2) Associated with the above, there is a need to produce reliable contemporaneous species level keys for all groups, as well as a need to educate and train people to use and update these keys as needed. For most crustacean groups, taxon identification is not merely a matter of learning a few terms, but it also usually involves a great deal of microscopy experience to develop the necessary skills.

3) Intensive inventories are needed in the Southeast for freshwater crustaceans in order to better understand the distribution and status of each species. Inventories are not just needed for listed and C2 species, but for all crustacean species. It is amazing that the exact distribution of many, if not most, species is still unknown.

4) Intensive life history studies need to be done on all federally listed and C2 crustacean species.

5) There is a need for money to support conservation work. It does no good to draw up elaborate recovery plans if they will not be adequately funded. There must be a more equitable distribution of research and management funds to benefit all species.

ACKNOWLEDGEMENTS

I thank Dick Biggins (Asheville, NC), Bob Butler (Jacksonville, FL) and Paul Hartfield (Jackson, MS) (all U.S. Fish and Wildlife Service) for graciously providing me with literature I would otherwise not have seen. I thank James Axon (Kentucky Fish and Wildlife Resources) and Bill Sampson (Kentucky Division of Water) for providing information for this paper. I also thank Donald Batch, Branley Branson, Amy Bruendermann, Eve Kimsey, and Greg Pond (all Eastern Kentucky University) and Ron Cicerello (Kentucky State Nature Preserves Commission) for critically reading various versions of this manuscript. Lastly, I dedicate this paper to Dr. David Etnier (University of Tennessee), my mentor and friend. Over the years his enthusiasm and love for aquatic organisms have touched hundreds of students. I thank him for the influence he has had on my life and career, and I am proud to say I am one of his students.

REFERENCES

Adams, S. M., and C. T. Hackney. 1992. Ecological Processes in southeastern United States aquatic ecosystems. In *Biodiversity of the Southeastern United States: Aquatic Communities.* C. T. Hackney, S. M Adams, and W. H. Martin (eds.). John Wiley and Sons, New York, NY, p. 3-17.

Biggins, R. G. 1989. Recovery plan for Nashville crayfish (*Orconectes shoupi*), First Revision. U.S. Fish and Wildlife Service, Atlanta, GA, 16 p.

Bouchard, R. W. 1972. A contribution to the knowledge of Tennessee crayfish. Ph.D. Dissertation, University of Tennessee, Knoxville, TN.

Bowman, T. E., and L. G. Abele. 1982. Classification of the recent Crustacea. In *The Biology of Crustacea. Volume 1. Systematics, the Fossil Record, and Biogeography.* L. G. Abele (ed.). Academic Press, New York, NY, p. 1-27.

Capelli, G. M. 1975. Displacement of northern Wisconsin crayfish by *Orconectes rusticus. Limnology and Oceanography* 27:741-745.

Covich, A. P., and J. H. Thorp. 1991. Crustacea: Introduction and Peracarida. In *Ecology and Classification of North American Freshwater Invertebrates*. J. H. Thorp, and A. P. Covich (eds.). Academic Press, New York, NY, p. 665-689.

Delorme, D. L. 1991. Ostracoda. In *Ecology and Classification of North American Freshwater Invertebrates*. J. H. Thorp, and A. P. Covich (eds.). Academic Press, New York, NY, p. 691-722.

Dodson, S. I., and D. G. Frey. 1991. Cladocera and other Branchiopoda. In *Ecology and Classification of North American Freshwater Invertebrates*. J. H. Thorp, and A. P. Covich (eds.). Academic Press, New York, NY, p. 723-786.

Frey, D. G. 1986. The non-cosmopolitanism of chydorid Cladocera: Implications for biogeography and evolution. In *Crustacean Biogeography*. R. H. Gore, and K. L. Heck (eds.). A. A. Balkema, Rotterdam, p. 237-256.

Hart, C. W., Jr., and J. Clark. 1989. *An Interdisciplinary Bibliography of Freshwater Crayfishes.* Smithsonian Institution Press, Washington, D.C.

Hart, C. W., Jr., and D. G. Hart. 1969. Evolutionary trends in the ostracod family Entocytheridae, with notes on the distributional patterns in the southern Appalachians. In *The Distributional History of the Biota of the Southern Appalachians, Part 1: Invertebrates.* P. C. Holt, R. L. Hoffman, and C. W. Hart, Jr. (eds.). Virginia Polytechnic Institute, Blacksburg, VA, p. 179-190.

Hobbs, H. H. Jr. 1942. The crayfishes of Florida. University of Florida Publications, Biological Sciences Series, Number 3, Gainesville, FL.

Hobbs, H. H., Jr. 1969. On the distribution and phylogeny of the crayfish genus *Cambarus*. In *The Distributional History of the Biota of the Southern Appalachians, Part 1: Invertebrates.* P. C. Holt, R. L. Hoffman, and C. W. Hart, Jr. (eds.). Virginia Polytechnic Institute, Blacksburg, VA, p. 93-178.

Hobbs, H. H., Jr. 1981. The crayfishes of Georgia. *Smithsonian Contributions to Zoology* 318:1-549.

Hobbs, H. H., Jr. 1989. An illustrated checklist of the American crayfishes (Decapoda: Astacidae, Cambaridae and Parastacidae). Smithsonian Institution Press, Washington, D.C.

Hobbs, H. H., III. 1991. Decapoda. In *Ecology and Classification of North American Freshwater Invertebrates*. J. H. Thorp, and A. P. Covich (eds.). Academic Press, New York, NY, p. 823-858.

Hobbs, H. H., III. 1992. Caves and Springs. In *Biodiversity of the Southeastern United States: Aquatic Communities*. C. T. Hackney, S. M Adams, and W. H. Martin (eds.). John Wiley and Sons, New York, NY, p. 59-131.

Hogger, J. B. 1988. Ecology, population biology and behaviour. In *Freshwater Crayfish: Biology, Management and Exploitation*. Holdrich, D. M., and R. S. Lowery (eds.). Chapman and Hall, London, p. 114-144.

Holdrich, D. M., and R. S. Lowery, R. S (eds.). 1988. *Freshwater Crayfish: Biology, Management and Exploitation*. Chapman and Hall, London.

Holsinger, J. R. 1969. Biogeography of the freshwater amphipod crustaceans (Gammaridae) of the central and southern Appalachians. In *The Distributional History of the Biota of the Southern Appalachians, Part 1: Invertebrates.* P. C. Holt, R. L. Hoffman, and C. W. Hart, Jr. (eds.). Virginia Polytechnic Institute, Blacksburg, VA, p. 19-50.

Holsinger, J. R. 1986. Zoogeographic patterns of North American subterranean amphipod crustaceans. In *Crustacean Biogeography.* R. H. Gore, and K. L. Heck (eds.). A. A. Balkema, Rotterdam, p. 85-106.

Huner, J. V. 1988. *Procambarus* in North America and elsewhere. In *Freshwater Crayfish: Biology, Management and Exploitation.* Holdrich, D. M., and Lowery, R. S. (eds.). Chapman and Hall, London, p. 239-261.

Laurent, P. J. 1988. *Austropotamobius pallipes* and *A. torrentium*, with observations on their interaction with other species in Europe. In *Freshwater Crayfish: Biology, Management and Exploitation.* Holdrich, D. M., and Lowery, R. S. (eds.). Chapman and Hall, London, p. 341-364.

Leitheuser, A. T. 1988. Recovery plan for Kentucky cave shrimp (*Palaemonias ganteri* Hay). U.S. Fish and Wildlife Service, Atlanta, GA, 47 p.

Leitheuser, A. T., and J. R. Holsinger. 1983. Ecological analysis of the Kentucky cave shrimp, *Palaemonias ganteri* Hay, Mammoth Cave National Park (Phase IV). Final Report submitted to the United States Department of the Interior, National Park Service, Atlanta, GA, 70 p.

Lisowski, E. A. 1983. Distribution, habitat, and behavior of the Kentucky cave shrimp, *Palaemonias ganteri* Hay. *Journal of Crustacean Biology* 3:88-92.

Mammoth Cave National Park. 1994. *Proceedings of Mammoth Cave National Park's Third Science Conference.* Mammoth Cave National Park and Cave Research Foundation, Mammoth Cave, KY, 295 p.

Meffe, G. K., and C. R. Carroll. 1994. *Principles of Conservation Biology.* Sinauer Associates, Inc., Sunderland, MA.

Mulholland, P. J., and D. R. Lenat. 1992. Streams of the southeastern piedmont, Atlantic drainage. In *Biodiversity of the Southeastern United States: Aquatic Communities.* C. T. Hackney, S. M Adams, and W. H. Martin (eds.). John Wiley and Sons, New York, NY, p. 193-231.

O'Neill, C. R., Jr., and D. B. MacNeill. 1989. *Dreissena polymorpha* an unwelcome new Great Lakes invader. Sea Grant Cooperative Extension Fact Sheet, Cornell University, Ithaca, NY, 11 p.

Ruppert, E. E., and R. D. Barnes. 1994. *Invertebrate Zoology, Sixth Edition.* Saunders College Publishing, New York, NY.

Salwasser, H. 1991. Roles for land and resource managers in conserving biological diversity. In *Challenges in the Conservation of Biological Resources.* D. J. Decker, M. E. Krasney, G. R. Goff, C. R. Smith, and D. W. Gross (eds.). Westview Press, Boulder, CO, p. 11-32.

Soballe, D. M., B. L. Kimmel, R. H. Kennedy, and R. F. Gaugush. 1992. Reservoirs. In *Biodiversity of the Southeastern United States: Aquatic Communities.* C. T. Hackney, S. M Adams, and W. H. Martin (eds.). John Wiley and Sons, New York, NY, p. 421-474.

Soule, M. E. 1985. What is conservation biology? *Bioscience* 35:727-734.

Steeves, H. R., Jr. 1969. The origin and affinities of the troglobitic asellids of the southern Appalachians. In *The Distributional History of the Biota of the Southern Appalachians, Part 1: Invertebrates.* P. C. Holt, R. L. Hoffman, and C. W. Hart, Jr. (eds.). Virginia Polytechnic Institute, Blacksburg, VA, p. 51-66.

U.S. Fish and Wildlife Service. 1991. Endangered and threatened wildlife and plants; animal candidate review for listing as endangered or threatened species, proposed rule. *U.S. Federal Register* 56:58804-58836.

U.S. Fish and Wildlife Service. 1993. Endangered and threatened wildlife and plants. United States Government Printing Office, Washington, D.C., 40 p.

Webster, C. D., L. S. Goodgame-Tiu, J. H. Tidwell, and D. B. Rouse. 1994. Evaluation of practical feed formulations with different protein levels for juvenile red claw crayfish (*Cherax quadricarinatus*). *Transactions of the Kentucky Academy of Sciences* 55:108-112.

Williams, W. D. 1972. Freshwater isopods (Asellidae) of North America. United States Biota of Freshwater Ecosystems Identification Manual Number 7, Environmental Protection Agency, Cincinnati, OH, 45 p.

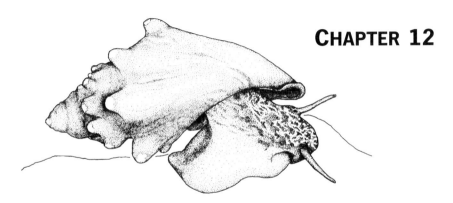

CHAPTER 12

Management of Native Mollusk Resources

John J. Jenkinson and Robert M. Todd

I n the historical perspective paper on aquatic mollusks included in this volume, Neves et al. (1997) review the diversity and current status of southeastern freshwater snails, clams, and mussels. The intent of our report is to review what has been done in past years to manage these freshwater mollusks and what could be done to manage them in the future.

This discussion uses an extremely broad definition of management as it applies to aquatic mollusk resources. We have chosen to include descriptions of all sorts of actual or potential activities which could lead to greater protection or enhancement of native aquatic mollusks. We have excluded purely taxonomic studies from this review because they rarely have advanced our understanding of the habitat, life history, or ecological requirements of these animals.

As you read on, it will become obvious that nearly all of this review deals with the large native freshwater mussels (Superfamily Unionoidea). Neves et al. (1997) indicated that several fingernail clams (Family Sphaeriidae) and many more freshwater snails (in the Orders Mesogastropoda and Basommatophora) occur in southeastern streams; however, as of yet, these groups have received little or no management attention.

On the other hand, a wide variety of information is available concerning freshwater mussel management, and the proceedings of two important mussel management meetings (Rasmussen, 1980; Cummings et al., 1993) have been extremely valuable in the preparation of this review. A new annotated bibliography on mussel reproduction and propagation (Watters, 1994) also has been extremely helpful in finding and organizing the contributions of various authors.

Given the regional focus of the symposium in which this paper was presented, this review of mollusk management activities has intentionally adopted a southeastern perspective. The work of southeastern researchers and projects in this region are used as examples whenever possible. This approach both carries out the symposium theme and

Aquatic Fauna in Peril: The Southeastern Perspective, edited by George W. Benz, and David E. Collins. 1997. Special Publication 1, Southeast Aquatic Research Institute, Lenz Design & Communications, Decatur, GA. 554 p.

indicates the relatively broad scope and depth of mussel research in this part of the United States. As we report, the diversity of aquatic mollusk problems and projects in the Southeast rival the diversity of the region's species.

MANAGEMENT OF AQUATIC GASTROPODS

As indicated by Neves et al. (1997), rivers and streams in the southeastern United States support an extremely diverse snail fauna, at least as diverse as this region's native mussel fauna. Southeastern aquatic snails have suffered from the alteration of streams and watersheds at least as much as the mussels (Stein, 1976; Neves et al., 1997). However, in spite of the losses of snail habitat and populations, little or no effort has been given to managing these resources. Protection of southeastern aquatic snails has not occurred, probably because none of the native snails have economic value; none but one are large or gaudy enough for most people to notice; and, until 1993, none had been listed as a federal endangered or threatened species.

In the absence of economic reasons, human interest, or regulatory requirements to protect them, the native freshwater snails have been left to the few naturalists and academicians who have become interested in them. Identification of many aquatic snail species is still extremely difficult either because so little careful attention has been given to the task or because these animals really do not follow our rules on the distinctions between species. At the moment, resource managers are faced with uncertainty regarding which snail species they should be concerned about, and they have no compelling reasons to spend either time or money on any of them.

There is one obvious exception to these generalities about freshwater snails. The spiny riversnail, *Io fluvialis*, is the largest gastropod found in North American rivers and streams. The snails presently grow up to 50 mm (about two inches) in length. As the common name implies, many individuals of this species have obvious conical spines on their shells which make them look like out-of-place marine murex or whelks. Natural populations of this species survive only in parts of the Powell, Clinch, and Nolichucky rivers in Tennessee and Virginia, but the species' former range extended down the mainstem Tennessee River to near Muscle Shoals, Alabama (Stansbery and Stein, 1976). Tennessee River *Io* specimens, which were as much as 60 mm (about 2.4 inches) long and very obviously spined, often wash or are dug out of Native American refuse heaps along the river banks. Years ago, the spiny river snail was adopted as the symbol of the American Malacological Union, and since 1977 this species has been a candidate for federal listing as an endangered or threatened species (U.S. Fish and Wildlife Service, 1977a).

The reason for bringing *Io fluvialis* into this discussion is that the species has benefited from an intentional management effort. In 1978 and 1979, Ahlstedt and other Tennessee Valley Authority (TVA) staff transplanted spiny river snails from the Clinch River to sites on the North Fork Holston River (Ahlstedt, 1991). That Holston River tributary once had supported an *Io* population, but those snails and most other aquatic species had been extirpated by discharges from an upstream chemical plant. After the plant ceased operation and the site was reclaimed, TVA had documented that life in the river was starting to recover. Sampling near the North Fork Holston River transplant sites since 1979 has indicated a steady increase in spiny river snail numbers and the populations are beginning to spread in the river (Ahlstedt, 1991). This appears to be the first intentional transplant of an American aquatic snail species, and it also represents a documented management success. Apparently, we know at least one method of managing aquatic snails but, so far, do not have the incentive to take on the task.

MANAGEMENT OF NATIVE MUSSELS

Most members of the general public know very little about the large freshwater mussels which are native to Interior Basin and southeastern streams. However, within a fairly small community of mussel biologists, commercial fishermen, game managers, exporters, and jewelers, freshwater mussels constitute an extremely important American resource. From various perspectives, native mussels have substantial commercial value and ecological significance. Both of these reasons have led to activities intended to protect, preserve, or enhance mussel resources (our definition of resource management).

Beginning with the earliest contacts with Native Americans, European explorers have known that attractive and potentially valuable pearls could be found in North American mussels (Dickinson, 1968). Unfortunately, the chances of discovering valuable pearls in native mussels have always been extremely low. Also, in the absence of a nearby market, the value of pearls was often established by someone willing to buy them. Waves of pearl hunting have occurred rather consistently all across the eastern United States since colonial times (Kunz, 1898b). The pearl hunters and buyers had an obvious interest in native mussels as the source for what they sought; however, that interest did not result in any documented attempts to manage mussel stocks.

Around 1890, George Boepple, a German immigrant, recognized that the shells of many North American mussel species were extremely good raw materials for making inexpensive, durable buttons (O'Hara, 1980). He adapted European button technology to use this new resource and started making pearl buttons near Muscatine, Iowa. Within the decade, pearl button factories were in operation all along the upper Mississippi River. Almost as quickly, mussel resources adjacent to the button factories were depleted and a nationwide market developed for high-quality button shells. The annual commercial harvest of button shells jumped from literally zero in the late 1880s to thousands of tons by 1910 (Figure 1).

After World War II, plastic buttons became available and the pearl button industry declined and disappeared, only to be replaced by another commercial use for mussel shell. The cultured pearl industry developed in post-war Japan and, since the 1960s, has become a major international enterprise (Ward, 1985). North American mussels are crucial to this industry because beads made from these shells are tolerated by marine pearl oysters and retain the thin layers of pearly material which the oysters deposit on them. The market for native mussel shells created by the cultured pearl industry has increased both the number of commercial mussel fishermen and the harvest pressure on surviving mussel populations (Figure 2).

A very different reason for managing native mussel resources began in 1976 when the U.S. Fish and Wildlife Service (USFWS) added the first mussel species to the federal list of endangered wildlife (U.S. Fish and Wildlife Service, 1976). Subsequent research has demonstrated that major mussel habitats have been severely modified and important components of the native mussel fauna are near extinction. Sections of the U.S. Endangered Species Act require federal agencies to determine if their actions will further jeopardize

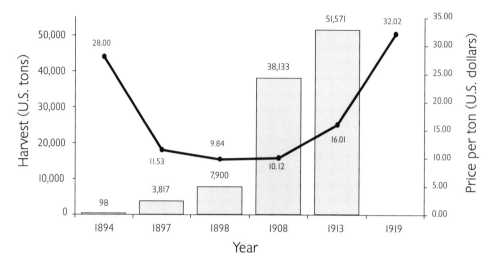

Figure 1. Known weight in U.S. tons (bars) of the commercial mussel harvest in the United States and the average prices paid in U.S. dollars per ton (line) to mussel fishermen during the first three decades of the pearl button industry (data from Smith, 1899; Coker, 1919).

listed species. More broadly than that, the public interest which has been generated as species have been added to the endangered or threatened lists has encouraged many individuals and organizations to investigate why so many species are in peril and what can be done to prevent or reverse the threat of extinction.

The various types of activities which have been implemented or proposed to protect and enhance mussel resources could be presented in several different ways. The following semi-historical approach indicates both the ideas which have been proposed and the context in which they developed.

U.S. Bureau of Fisheries

In the mid-1890s, less than five years after the button industry started, mussel resources in the Mississippi River near the Muscatine, Iowa, factories had become obviously depleted. Button manufacturers requested assistance from the U.S. Fish Commission (later called the U.S. Bureau of Fisheries and, later still, the U.S. Fish and Wildlife Service). This request started a 40-year federal program of research and scientific inquiry focused on commercially important native mussels.

As this program began, the existing status of the resource and commercial interest in native mussels were documented in three Bureau of Fisheries reports. Apparently without leaving New York, George F. Kunz, a well-known gem and pearl expert, produced both a short and a long report on pearls and pearl fisheries in the United States (Kunz, 1898a, 1898b). Charles T. Simpson, curator of mollusks at the U.S. National Museum, wrote a non-technical description of the anatomy, ecology, life history, and problems facing native mussels in the United States (Simpson, 1899). Hugh M. Smith, then a fisheries biologist with the Bureau, went to the button manufacturing area and produced a detailed report on the mussel fishery and pearl button industry as it existed at the time (Smith, 1899).

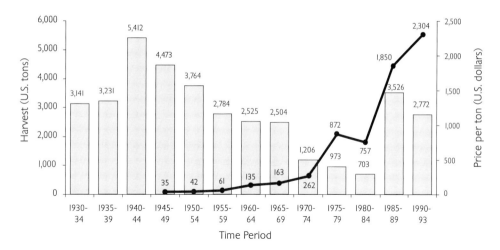

Figure 2. Five-year average harvest weights in U.S. tons (bars) and purchase prices in U.S. dollars per ton (line) for the commercial mussel fishery in the state of Tennessee (data from Hargis, 1968; Todd, 1993; Hubbs, 1995; TVA, unpublished reports).

Regardless of its short length, the Simpson report (loc. cit.) clearly presented what was then known about mussel biology and life history. Information contained in both the Simpson and Smith reports (both loc. cit.) presented their initial concepts about management activities required to sustain the commercial fishery and protect mussel resources.

During the next four decades, the Bureau of Fisheries supported a wide range of research projects in four broad categories: biology and life history studies, resource surveys, propagation work, and identification of protection measures. Initially, much of this research was conducted at the Fairport Biological Station located along the Mississippi River near the center of the button industry. The program quickly grew, however, to include more and more rivers across the nation.

LIFE HISTORY STUDIES

State-of-the-art biological and life history studies (e.g., Figure 3) were conducted by a variety of individuals in close association with others working under different sponsorships. Between 1900 and 1920, Bureau-supported studies confirmed that most native mussels had separate sexes (Lefevre and Curtis, 1912) and that shell rings could be used as approximate indicators of age (Isley, 1914). Other Bureau projects demonstrated that mussel larvae (glochidia) could be identified by their size and shape (Surber, 1914, 1915) and that the larvae of almost all species had to spend some time as obligate parasites, generally on fish, before they could develop into adults (Lefevre and Curtis, 1912). The findings of many Bureau studies were summarized in a non-technical report (Coker et al., 1921) which made much of this information available to the button industry and state resource managers. After 1921, Bureau-supported researchers working on life history projects focused on narrower topics such as mussel feeding mechanisms and food (Churchill and Lewis, 1924) and comparisons of growth rates at different locations (Chamberlain, 1931). Most of what is known today concerning the ecological and life history characteristics of native mussels was discovered during these Bureau of Fisheries studies.

Figure 3. View of U.S. Bureau of Fisheries laboratory at North La Crosse, Wisconsin (from Lefevre and Curtis, 1912). This photograph was probably taken in 1908.

RESOURCE SURVEYS

Biologists working on mussel projects for the Bureau of Fisheries had obvious interest in where mussel stocks existed because of their close association with the constant demands of the button industry. Once mussel resources on the upper Mississippi River were depleted, mussel fishermen and Bureau biologists literally searched the nation for high-quality button shells. Between 1912 and 1915, Bureau of Fisheries reports were published on the status of mussel stocks in over 15 important watersheds or larger regions of the nation. In addition to documenting the quality of commercial mussel stocks present at that time, reports such as "The Mussel Resources of the Illinois River" (Danglade, 1914) and "The Mussels of the Cumberland River and its Tributaries" (Wilson and Clark, 1914) provided distribution and abundance benchmarks to which many subsequent studies have been compared.

PROPAGATION WORK

From the beginning, the chief purpose of the Bureau of Fisheries's work on native mussels was to find ways to replace stocks of species harvested to make buttons. After it was confirmed that virtually all larval mussels must spend some time as parasites on fish before they could develop into adults, Lefevre and Curtis began a long series of experiments on ways to increase recruitment success. The essential features of their artificial propagation technique were published in 1912 (Lefevre and Curtis, 1912) and, by 1921, had become a standardized procedure (Coker et al., 1921). Each year from some time before 1919 (Smith, 1919) until 1930 (Jones, 1950), Bureau employees infected thousands of fish with millions of glochidia before releasing them into the Mississippi and many other rivers. Fish infections were stopped for several years during the 1930s, but the techniques were improved and infections were resumed to some degree at least as recently as 1950 (Jones, 1950).

In addition to the release of infected fish, Bureau staff also began to culture juvenile mussels which had been transformed on fish (Figure 4). Experiments on juvenile mussel culture were described by Howard (1922) and at least one mass transplant of juvenile mussels was made into Virginia waters in 1926 (Higgins, 1928).

Interest in both fish infections and juvenile mussel culture was reduced substantially in the late 1920s because new considerations were coming into play. In 1926, Ellis used experimental work on mussel blood as a starting point in developing a way to transform glochidia into juvenile mussels without the use of a fish host (Ellis and Ellis, 1926). This artificial propagation of mussels offered the possibility of rearing large numbers of juveniles without having to deal with difficult and, for some mussel species, unknown fish hosts.

In the late 1920s, the emphasis of Bureau mussel work was focused on perfecting this artificial culture technique, and some laboratory-scale successes were reported (Higgins, 1930, 1931). Very soon, however, Ellis and other Bureau staff found that protozoans and pollution were severely reducing the percentage of viable glochidia in female mussel gills. Field studies conducted in the Mississippi and other major rivers indicated that although protozoans occurred in many locations, siltation and pollution were affecting much larger amounts of previous mussel habitat (Ellis, 1931a). While Bureau-sponsored research on artificial propagation continued for several years (at Columbia, Missouri and Fort Worth, Texas), Ellis and associated staff shifted their focus to exploring the broad range of pollution and sedimentation effects on aquatic life. By 1938, the Bureau of Fisheries annual report on scientific research excluded any mention of mussel propagation activities (Higgins, 1939).

PROTECTION MEASURES

Also from the beginning, biologists working with the Bureau of Fisheries attempted to encourage the states and commercial interests to protect existing mussel stocks. Both of the initial Bureau studies on mussels (Simpson, 1899) and the button industry (Smith, 1899) included recommendations for actions which would help prevent further depletion of mussel resources. Smith prefaced his list of recommendations with a clear statement of where the authority to implement any protection measures resided:

"… It should, however, be understood that the perpetuation of this important industry depends wholly on the joint action of the States concerned, and that the General Government and the U.S. Fish Commission are entirely without jurisdiction" (Smith, 1899; page 313).

The recommendations proposed by Smith included minimum size restrictions (by species), closed seasons (when mussels were spawning), establishment of pollution controls, prohibitions on interstate shipment of shells, and reduction of shell waste during button production.

Fifteen years later, another Bureau biologist offered a second set of recommendations on

Figure 4. U.S. Bureau of Fisheries staff examining a juvenile mussel culture basket in a pond at the Fairport Biological Station, probably in 1919 (from Coker et al., 1921).

protecting mussel resources (Coker, 1914). By this time the Bureau had completed many of its surveys and life history studies and had started stocking infected fish in a number of areas. Bureau staff also had come to realize that any results achieved through propagation could be quickly undone by strong harvest pressure, especially in the absence of state protection measures. Coker recommended the imposition of a single minimum size limit for all species (two inches [about 5 cm] in greatest dimension), rotating closure of large river reaches for several years to allow mussel stocks to recuperate, and state enforcement authority. He also suggested the states adopt a mussel fishing license fee to cover the cost of enforcing compliance with these laws. In 1919, the Bureau assisted in drafting model legislation for the states to encourage uniform and adequate protection of mussel resources (Smith, 1919).

In 1931, results from the propagation and pollution research led the Bureau of Fisheries to radically modify their recommendations to the states. Ellis and his coworkers had concluded that "Extensive and rapid reduction, amounting in many places almost to extermination, of the mussel fauna is to be expected if the erosion and pollution problems are not solved" (Ellis, 1931b; page 10). Acting on these findings, the Bureau recommended the states eliminate all restrictions on mussel harvesting so that existing mussel stocks could be used before they were lost (Carlander, 1954). While some lingering Bureau of Fisheries mussel research projects continued for a few more years and a few commercial mussel projects were conducted later (see below), this conclusion and recommendation signaled the end of extensive Bureau-sponsored research on commercial mussel species.

State Management Activities

During the early years of the button industry, in spite of the recommendations from the Bureau of Fisheries, most states did not attempt to regulate the mussel harvest. By the late 1910s, however, many mussel-producing states recognized that mussel stocks were severely depleted and they began implementing harvest regulations (Waters, 1980). Those states, most of which were located along the upper Mississippi River, instituted license fees, set minimum size limits, and restricted harvest gear. Some closed areas to harvest for a time. Although some improvements in mussel stocks were observed in a few areas, all stocks generally continued to decline. In light of these failing efforts and the emerging understanding of siltation and pollution effects on mussels, in 1931 when the Bureau recommended elimination of all harvest restrictions, most states quickly adopted the new position to use the remaining resource rather than waste what would soon be gone anyway.

Between the mid-1930s and early 1960s (or in some instances the 1970s), very few states paid much attention to mussel resources or the mussel harvest. A few states, such as Kentucky, continued to license mussel fishermen, required annual harvest reports, and took other actions to protect commercial mussel resources (Crowell and Kinman, 1993). Most states realized that the button industry was declining but did not appreciate the impact of the new market for shells to supply the cultured pearl industry.

Another change which occurred between the 1930s and 1970s was the substantial modification of nearly all the large rivers which once supported extensive mussel populations. By the late 1970s, hydropower facilities had been constructed at practically every feasible site on the continent's mainstem rivers except in Alaska and northern Canada (Stanford and Ward, 1979). Initial assumptions were that low flow conditions and increased sedimentation would eliminate all mussel stocks in the various impoundments (Ellis, 1931a). When mussel harvesting resumed after World War II and pre-impoundment mussel stocks were found to persist in many areas, those assumptions were presumed to be incorrect. For several years, the commercial harvest increased to meet a growing pearl culture demand, but price also increased as high-quality shell became more difficult to find (Figure 2).

In the early 1950s, the struggling pearl button industry once again requested federal assistance to investigate the status of the mussel resource and recommend measures to increase stocks of valuable mussels (Scruggs, 1960). The USFWS conducted a two-year study of mussel stocks at selected sites on the Tennessee River which, since the war, had become the most important source of freshwater shell. That study concluded that populations of the most important commercial species (*Pleurobema cordatum*) were being extensively harvested but were experiencing almost no recruitment, possibly because impoundment had made radical changes in big-river habitats (Scruggs, 1960).

In 1963, with the encouragement of the states and several shell companies, TVA conducted an evaluation of mussel stocks all along the mainstem Tennessee River in Kentucky, Tennessee, and Alabama (Isom, 1966, 1969). Results of that evaluation indicated that suitable mussel habitat persisted only in 33 percent of the river reach studied. In those areas, overharvesting was causing a rapid depletion of the mussel resources. TVA recommended the three states adopt regulations to control the harvest, establish sanctuaries where harvesting should not occur, and conduct life history studies to find out why important commercial species were not reproducing (Isom, 1966).

This time the states were quick to respond. In 1965, Kentucky restricted mussel harvesting to daylight hours, defined legal harvest methods, imposed a minimum size limit of 2.5 inches (6.35 cm), and created a sanctuary in the Tennessee River immediately downstream from Kentucky Dam (Crowell and Kinman, 1993). Also in 1965, Tennessee passed enabling legislation to issue licenses and began regulating the mussel harvest. Those regulations included license requirements for both mussel fishermen and buyers, a size limit of 2.5 inches (6.35 cm), gear restrictions, daylight harvesting only, and establishment of sanctuaries (Todd, 1993). In 1966, Alabama passed enabling legislation and started regulating its mussel harvest along similar lines (Isom, 1969).

By the mid-1970s, the upper Mississippi River states were conducting mussel surveys to determine the status of their remaining mussel stocks. These surveys were prompted by concerns over poor water quality conditions, ongoing channel maintenance activities, levee construction, and likely overharvest of the mussel resource.

In 1985, the five upper Mississippi River states met to determine what actions were necessary to prevent further resource declines. These managers recommended increasing the minimum legal size limits, reducing the length of the harvest season, and implementing a harvest reporting system. They also recommended that the states try to make their regulations as uniform as possible. Most of these recommendations were implemented by the states by 1992 (Thiel and Fritz, 1993).

The middle states of the Mississippi River Valley also were reevaluating mussel management policies during the later 1980s. Reports of mussel die-offs and increased harvest pressure stimulated these states to obtain information regarding their mussel resources. Most states did not have the necessary information regarding their mussel stocks to make informed management decisions, and many states decided to close their waters to mussel harvest until such information could be collected. Kentucky, Oklahoma, and Tennessee closed some productive areas to commercial musseling to slow the harvest and protect the resource. Tennessee also funded surveys to determine the current state of its mussel resources (Bates and Dennis, 1985).

In the early 1990s, many states implemented more restrictive regulations regarding commercial musseling. Several states increased the minimum size limits on commercial species, limited which species could be harvested, closed waters thought to be experiencing overharvest, shortened the harvest season, instituted mussel harvest reporting procedures, restricted the types of gear which could be used for mussel harvest, and limited access to the fishery. These more restrictive regulations were aimed at protecting mussels until they were old enough to reproduce, reducing the take of non-marketable shells, minimizing the impact on non-target species, providing data on the harvest trends, and reducing the number of fishermen (Todd, 1993).

Endangered Species Act Effects

Management interest in native mussels probably would have remained focused only on species with commercial value if mussels had never been added to the federal lists of endangered or threatened species. However, some native mussels have been declared endangered species, and the management of mussel resources has changed tremendously because of this.

The U.S. Endangered Species Act (ESA) was passed in 1973. In addition to establishing formal lists of endangered and threatened wildlife and plants, this law requires federal agencies to ensure that activities they conduct, fund, or authorize do not jeopardize the continued existence of species on either the endangered or threatened lists. The law also establishes procedures for states to receive federal funds to protect and enhance listed species (U.S. Fish and Wildlife Service, 1992).

The first group of native mussel species was added to the endangered species list in 1976 (U.S. Fish and Wildlife Service, 1976). Eighteen of the 23 species in that group occur in one or more of the southeastern states. One additional mussel species was listed as endangered in 1977; it also occurs in southeastern states (U.S. Fish and Wildlife Service, 1977b). Other mussels were not added to either the endangered or threatened federal lists until 1985; however, there has been a steady stream of listings since then (Figure 5).

The federal listing of 24 endangered mussel species had a dramatic effect on several federal and state agencies, especially in the southeastern states. Because of their roles in developing and maintaining water projects, the U.S. Army Corps of Engineers and TVA now had new responsibilities: first, to find out whether endangered mussels (and other listed species) were present where projects were being proposed and, second, to determine what they should or could do to avoid impacting those species. The USFWS, charged with implementing the ESA inland, also needed up-to-date distribution and life history information to protect each listed species and enough expertise in impact assessment to evaluate the proposals being made by other federal agencies.

State agencies were faced with a slightly different situation. A wide variety of projects which involved federal funds or required federal permits were now being evaluated for impacts on species (mussels as well as other groups) that many state biologists knew little or nothing about. In addition, federal biologists or their contractors were surveying streams all across the states, gathering information on mussels, fish, and other species which had been studied very little because they had no commercial or sport value. Beyond that, the ESA provided a new source of federal funds to study local fish and wildlife, once appropriate state programs were established.

This new emphasis on all native mussels caused by the ESA listings spawned a variety of research efforts not unlike those started by the Bureau of Fisheries almost a century before. The primary difference associated with this new wave of research on mussel life histories, distribution surveys, propagation efforts, and protection measures was that these studies were focused on rare or non-commercial species. In addition, these projects were not being conducted by a single organization, but by individuals working for a variety of organizations, often with different missions.

LIFE HISTORY STUDIES

While there had been a steady trickle of mussel life history studies since the 1930s (e.g., Stein, 1968; Yokley, 1972), the pace of this work started to increase in the late 1970s, and the focus shifted toward endangered species. Between 1981 and 1985, TVA biologists conducted a series of fish infection experiments focused on identifying hosts for two endangered mussel species. The results of that work (Hill, 1986; Yeager and Neves, 1986) established one or more hosts for seven mussel species, including two listed endangered species and three species which were candidates for listing. Neves and students working at Virginia Polytechnic Institute started fish host identification studies about the same time and, so far, have identified hosts for at least ten mussel species (Neves, 1991; Watters, 1994). Others also have started filling this information gap for different species (e.g.,

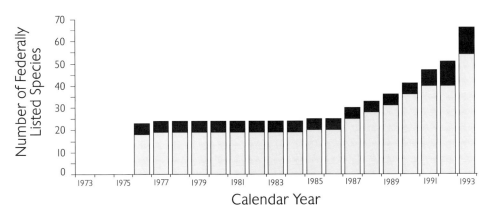

Figure 5. Year-by-year counts of federal endangered and threatened aquatic mollusks known from the southeastern states (depicted by height of gray bars) and from the United States as a whole (depicted by height of black bars) (data from various U.S. Fish and Wildlife Service publications).

Parker et al., 1984; Buchanan, 1987; Gordon and Layzer, 1993).

In addition to fish host identifications, a number of recent projects or observations have explored other mussel life history and ecological relationships. During the early 1980s, TVA spent a substantial amount of time and effort attempting to identify the essential characteristics of endemic (Cumberlandian) mussel habitat (Jenkinson and Heuer, 1986). Others have begun to explore a variety of new topics, including juvenile mussel habitat preferences (Yeager et al., 1993), special reproductive behaviors of gravid females (Buchanan, 1987), and population dynamics (Payne and Miller, 1989).

DISTRIBUTION SURVEYS

Updating distribution and abundance information have been essential components of the new emphasis on all mussel species. Only a few workers had conducted detailed distribution surveys since the 1930s (e.g., Isom and Yokley, 1968; Starrett, 1971), and the status of the entire fauna was extremely poorly known. Starting in the late 1970s, relatively traditional surveys of smaller streams, such as the Meramec River in Missouri (Buchanan, 1980), several rivers in Mississippi (e.g., Hartfield and Jones, 1990), and smaller rivers in the Tennessee Basin (Ahlstedt, 1986; Jenkinson and Ahlstedt, 1988), have provided updated information on mussel populations in many streams. The widespread availability of scuba and other diving equipment in recent years also has made it possible to conduct detailed surveys of mussel resources in the largest rivers (e.g., Pardue, 1981; Sickel, 1985).

PROPAGATION

A new wave of interest in mussel propagation began in 1982 when a TVA biologist and contractor announced they had used an artificial medium to produce juvenile mussels without the involvement of a fish host (Isom and Hudson, 1982). While it is still not possible to turn a gill full of mussel larvae into 50 or 100 thousand yearling mussels ready to be stocked in some stream, this potential has led to a variety of research projects using juvenile mussels (e.g., Dimock and Wright, 1993). The ability to produce known-age juveniles of at least one species also has made it possible to start conducting standardized toxicity tests on native mussels (Wade, 1990). The results of such studies are beginning to indicate that native mussels have very different tolerances to many pollutants than the standard fish or arthropod test organisms (Wade et al., 1993).

PROTECTION MEASURES

Protection and, more recently, enhancement measures for the full spectrum of native mussel species now include a variety of approaches. Resource management agencies have reduced the number of species which can be harvested to those most important to the industry and have restricted the harvest to those areas which can withstand the losses (e.g., Todd, 1993). Some states are carefully selecting minimum size limits which will allow animals to spawn before they can be harvested. Mussel sanctuaries have been established in areas with few commercial species, in part to minimize impacts on non-commercial species. Information guides produced by states and others help mussel harvesters learn more about the legal species and mussels in general. Strategies are now being pursued by some states to establish and maintain a stable mussel harvest without affecting the long-term survival of all mussel species (e.g., Hubbs, 1995).

Federal agencies also have begun to take protection and enhancement action in a variety of different ways. Recovery plans for endangered and threatened species, prepared or sponsored by the USFWS, have highlighted research and/or enhancement needs (e.g., U.S. Fish and Wildlife Service, 1984). In 1992, TVA started improving habitat conditions for mussels and other aquatic life downstream from its tributary dams by adopting minimum releases and by beginning to correct seasonal low dissolved oxygen levels (Davis and Brock, 1994). Specific habitat improvements (Miller, 1983) and reintroductions (Jenkinson, 1983; Sheehan et al., 1989) have been made to restore or accelerate the recovery of degraded mussel communities. A number of agencies and organizations are beginning to work together to address various types of nonpoint-source pollution to restore degraded stream water and habitat quality (Water Quality 2000, 1994). Native mussels, especially endangered species, are often the intended benefactors of these activities (Master, 1993). The USFWS also has enhanced public education and interest in native mussels by sponsoring the production of a high-quality videotape and a poster about them (Helfrich, 1993; Helfrich et al., 1993).

THE FUTURE OF MOLLUSK MANAGEMENT

Anyone unfamiliar with the current status of freshwater mollusks might assume the preceding history of commercial mussel management activities and new emphasis on non-commercial species should mean that native mussels, if not all freshwater mollusks, are now being carefully managed and protected from further harm. Unfortunately, that is not the case. Results of various studies conducted during the last 20 years indicate that commercial species and many non-commercial mussels are still declining, both in terms of their distributions and numbers of individuals (Williams et al., 1993).

Two recent evaluations present similar views on the current status of North American mussel resources. In a 1992 "A State-of-the-Unionids Address," Neves concluded the following:

"The freshwater mussel fauna of the United States is in serious trouble. Of the

297 species and subspecies recognized, 21 species (7%) are presumed extinct, 42 (15%) are federally listed as endangered or threatened, and 69 (23%) are candidates for federal protection. The highly diverse endemic mussel fauna of the southeastern United States is in greatest jeopardy, with depressed population levels today reflecting transgressions to rivers decades earlier" (Neves, 1993; page 1).

Williams et al. (1993) reported similar statistics for the United States and Canada. They also summarized the existing threats and likely future for mussels as follows:

"The primary reasons for the decline of freshwater mussels are habitat destruction from dams, channel modification, siltation, and the introduction of nonindigenous mollusks. The high numbers of imperiled freshwater mussels in the United States and Canada . . . portend a trajectory toward an extinction crisis that, if unchecked, will severely impoverish one of our richest components of aquatic biodiversity" (Williams et al., 1993; page 6).

If the native freshwater mussels and other aquatic mollusks are to survive, several types of management activities will have to be conducted. From our perspective, four broad categories of such need to be addressed: habitat protection, population enhancements, harvest controls, and public appreciation. Each of these categories is briefly explored below.

Habitat Protection

It is becoming increasingly clear that the presence of a diverse, reproducing mussel community indicates that important physical, chemical, and biological features of the habitat have been stable for a long time, at least several decades. The protection of existing native mussel communities will require the identification and perpetuation of the full set of habitat features which are essential to their survival. If mussel populations or communities are to be restored in an area, these essential habitat features will have to be present and expected to persist for decades.

At the present time, we know the general concepts but lack specifics on the habitat features which are essential for mussel species survival. Careful, broad spectrum evaluations of good mussel habitats should help identify these features, especially if the results can be compared to a variety of habitats where diverse mussel communities no longer exist. Pioneering habitat studies conducted by TVA (Jenkinson and Heuer, 1986) and Layzer (e.g., Cochran and Layzer, 1993) appear to be valuable examples of such research; however, much more work on this topic is urgently needed.

Population Enhancements

Even before there is reasonable assurance that suitable mussel habitat will continue to be available, a variety of techniques must be developed to protect or augment mussel species reduced to very few populations or individuals. If possible, fish hosts should be identified for all species so that essential habitat features for both the mussels and these fishes can be protected. Where required combinations of habitat features are present, fish and mussel life cycles are very likely to continue without the need for human intervention.

When the surviving stock of a mussel species is extremely small or does not appear to be reproducing in nature, some form of artificial propagation will have to be used to save that species from extinction. Results from various propagation experiments suggest that it should be possible to transform the larvae and raise the juveniles of most mussel species. However, there are still a number of improvements which must be made before these techniques can be expected to work consistently. If a large-scale artificial propagation technique were to become available, a tremendous variety of restoration, enhancement, genetic study, and commercial possibilities could begin.

Regardless of whether artificial propagation techniques are perfected soon, it may be necessary to develop ways to store mussel genetic and reproductive material before some species are lost completely. Genetic material, gametes, and embryos of other animals and plants have been frozen and revived to develop normally (Ballou, 1992). If appropriate cryopreservation techniques could be developed for mussels and other aquatic mollusks, the unique characteristics of species and populations could be saved for possible future study and, hopefully, for eventual reintroductions into streams.

Harvest Controls

State agencies are becoming increasingly more knowledgeable about the biology of various mussel species sought by commercial fishermen. If the commercial fishery is to survive, habitats and mussel populations will have to be carefully managed to balance both the needs of the mussels and the desires of the harvesters. To achieve such a balance, the states will have to monitor recruitment and growth rates of current and potential commercial stocks as well as the extent and intensity of the commercial harvest. Management activities based on these data could include selective closing of areas to harvesting, varying legal minimum size limits on particular species, and imposing substantial financial and license penalties for illegal activities. Adoption of uniform size limits by all states would simplify law enforcement activities and reduce confusion among the commercial harvesters.

Public Appreciation

None of the preceding management activities is likely to be conducted or to be particularly successful if it does not have at least some level of public support. Native mussels (and other aquatic mollusks) are not cuddly, generally appreciated, or fun to watch. Their abundance or absence in a stream, however, can and should convey an important message about the quality of that water. Given the sizable, and growing, human population in the southeastern states, the resident aquatic mollusks may not survive much longer in the absence of substantial public support. Interestingly, current information also suggests that human populations in the southeastern states may not have sufficient potable water to meet their future needs if the deterioration of rivers and streams is not stopped.

Federal agencies, state agencies, and other organizations must make the public more aware of the value of aquatic diversity, especially as it relates to water quality. Public comments about faunal posters, environmental brochures, nature talks, and the like suggest that people are willing to appreciate and support resource management once they learn of its relevance. Attractive nature posters, interesting videotapes, and engaging exhibits can expose people to the unique communities which exist in their local creeks. Well-written brochures, carefully planned demonstrations, and involving workshops can provide non-professionals with the information they need to evaluate land- and water-use activities on their own. A coordinated, long-term awareness program could turn passive public curiosity about what is in the water into widespread support for the protection and restoration of aquatic mollusks as residents of valuable stream ecosystems.

Zebra Mussel Invasion

If all four of the preceding categories of management activities were implemented and nothing else interfered, southeastern native mollusks and the natural communities in which they live would survive and flourish. The management categories just described all consist of activities which agencies or groups of individuals could conduct, if they possessed enough resolve, time, and effort. Unfortunately, there is another threat to southeastern mollusks over which we have little or no control. That threat is two closely related species of zebra mussel (*Dreissena polymorpha* and *D. bugensis*). These bivalve mollusks were introduced into North America in the mid-1980s, probably from one or more locations near the Caspian Sea. Zebra mussels are spread as larvae floating in the water or as adults attached to boats and barges. As adults, zebra mussels live attached to virtually any firm substrate and, where habitat conditions are favorable, they can occur by the thousands per square meter (Claudi and Mackie, 1994).

The chief threat zebra mussels pose to native mollusks is that they readily attach to exposed parts of mussel and snail shells, often in such large numbers that they interfere with normal feeding and movement activities. In Lake Erie, where zebra mussels were first found in 1988, native mussel populations have been virtually extirpated by zebra mussel encrustations (Haag et al., 1993).

Zebra mussels were first observed in the Southeast in the lower Tennessee River in 1991. By 1993, the species had been spread up the Tennessee to Fort Loudoun Dam (near Knoxville) and down the Mississippi River to near New Orleans. Projections are that zebra mussels will eventually spread to virtually all of the large, navigable rivers in the Southeast (Strayer, 1991). If that happens, and if zebra mussels establish large populations, they could destroy the remaining mussel and snail populations in those southeastern rivers. Zebra mussels also are likely to eventually spread to tributary reservoirs and smaller streams. Whether such populations will become large enough to impact the native mollusks in those areas is not yet clear.

At present, there do not appear to be any significant predators, other natural controlling agents, or artificial ways of suppressing zebra mussel populations which would not harm components of natural aquatic communities. Once zebra mussels are introduced to an area, we can only wait and watch to see what impacts they will have. In at least some areas, large zebra mussel populations may extirpate the few native mollusks which have survived the habitat modifications, harvest pressure, and other assaults we have inflicted.

SUMMARY

This review of management activities affecting native aquatic mollusks, primarily freshwater mussels, has covered considerable calendar time and subject matter. American interest in protecting and augmenting native mussel stocks began approximately 100 years ago when the shells of some mussel species were recognized to have commercial value as the raw material used by the pearl button industry. Today, mussel shell is still an important raw material, except now shell beads are used as nuclei for cultured pearls.

Twice during this 100-year period considerable emphasis has been given to research on native freshwater mussels: first between about 1900 and 1930 when button shells were becoming increasingly hard to find and, second, starting in the late 1970s after passage of the U.S. Endangered Species Act. Both times, the research effort focused on learning more about the habitat requirements, life histories, and existing distribution of various mussel species. Both times, new propagation techniques were developed and new protection measures were devised to prevent and, hopefully, reverse the further depletion of existing mussel stocks.

Today, native aquatic mollusks seem to be closer to extinction as a group than ever before. Commercial mussel resources are still harvested; however, decreasing mussel populations and increasing prices have combined to reduce the acceptable options available to both the harvesters and the state regulatory agencies. Non-commercial mussel and, probably, most snail species now exist only in small percentages of their former ranges, generally where the habitats have survived extensive degradation by sedimentation and impoundment. In many of these stream habitats, resident mollusk populations are declining, but the specific reasons for the declines are not known. Most federal and state agencies, especially in the Southeast, are aware of the plight of these mollusk resources, but the general public is barely aware that these animals even exist.

A variety of research and management actions have been identified which could help protect and restore native aquatic mollusks. More precise identification of the specific habitat features important to various mussel species could lead to the protection or restoration of stream reaches where mollusks and other members of diverse aquatic communities could survive. Identification of mussel fish hosts and the perfection of artificial propagation techniques could help insure the survival of existing mussel populations and provide ways to prevent the extinction of species reduced to only a few individuals. Adoption of biologically based harvest regulations could protect mussel populations while providing a sustainable level of mussel harvest. Public education programs, supported and coordinated by a variety of organizations, could help citizens to realize that the current plight of native mollusks should be viewed as a warning about the potential loss of stream ecosystems and all of the species they support, including us.

During the last 100 years, interested Americans have learned a great deal about the native mollusk resources in our streams and what we should do to protect and enhance them. Those management activities, if implemented, could prevent species extinctions, restore commercial stocks, and improve the overall quality of the water we use. Several agencies are already working to make this happen and, with increased public support, success could be possible. But, even then, our native aquatic mollusks would still be threatened by an exotic biological threat, the zebra mussel invasion.

REFERENCES

Ahlstedt, S. A. 1986. Cumberlandian mollusk conservation program activity 1: Mussel distribution surveys. TVA/ONRED/AWR-86/15, Tennessee Valley Authority, Norris, TN, 125 p.

Ahlstedt, S. A. 1991. Reintroduction of the spiny riversnail *Io fluvialis* (Say, 1825) (Gastropoda: Pleuroceridae) into the North Fork Holston River, southwest Virginia and northeast Tennessee. *American Malacological Bulletin* 8:139-142.

Ballou, J. D. 1992. Potential contribution of cryopreserved germ plasma to the preservation of genetic diversity and conservation of endangered species in captivity. *Cryobiology* **29**:19-25.

Bates, J. M., and S. D. Dennis. 1985. Mussel resource survey, state of Tennessee. Technical Report No. 85-4, Tennessee Wildlife Resources Agency, Nashville, TN, 125 p.

Buchanan, A. C. 1980. Mussels (Naiades) of the Meramec River Basin, Missouri. Aquatic Series Number 17, Missouri Department of Conservation, Columbia, MO, 70 p.

Buchanan, A. C. 1987. Aspects of the life history of the Curtis' pearly mussel, *Epioblasma florentina curtisi* (Utterback, 1915). Final Report, Endangered Species Project SE-3-2, Missouri Department of Conservation, Columbia, MO, 21 p.

Carlander, H. B. 1954. A history of fish and fishing in the upper Mississippi River. Upper Mississippi River Conservation Committee, Rock Island, IL, 96 p.

Chamberlain, T. K. 1931. Annual growth of fresh-water mussels. *Bulletin of the U.S. Bureau of Fisheries* **46**:713-739.

Churchill, E. P., and S. I. Lewis. 1924. Food and feeding in fresh-water mussels. *Bulletin of the U.S. Bureau of Fisheries* **39**:439-471.

Claudi, R., and G. L. Mackie. 1994. *Practical Manual for Zebra Mussel Monitoring and Control.* Lewis Publishers, Boca Raton, FL.

Cochran, T. G. II, and J. B. Layzer. 1993. Effects of commercial harvest on unionid habitat use in the Green and Barren rivers, Kentucky. In *Conservation and Management of Freshwater Mussels.* K. S. Cummings, A. C. Buchanan, and L. M. Koch (eds.). Proceedings of a UMRCC symposium, 12-14 October 1992, St. Louis , MO, Upper Mississippi River Conservation Committee, Rock Island, IL., p. 61-65.

Coker, R. E. 1914. The protection of fresh-water mussels. Report of the Commissioner of Fisheries for 1912, Document Number 793, U.S. Bureau of Fisheries, Washington, D.C., 23 p.

Coker, R. E. 1919. Fresh-water mussels and mussel industries of the United States. *Bulletin of the U.S. Bureau of Fisheries* **36**:11-89.

Coker, R. E., A. F. Shira, H. W. Clark, and A. D. Howard. 1921. The natural history and propagation of fresh-water mussels. *Bulletin of the U.S. Bureau of Fisheries* **37**:75-181.

Crowell, E. F., and B. T. Kinman. 1993. Musseling in Kentucky: The first 200 years. In *Conservation and Management of Freshwater Mussels.* K. S. Cummings, A. C. Buchanan, and L. M. Koch (eds.). Proceedings of a UMRCC symposium, 12-14 October 1992, St. Louis , MO, Upper Mississippi River Conservation Committee, Rock Island, IL, p. 25-31.

Cummings, K. S., A. C. Buchanan, and L. M. Koch (eds.). 1993. *Conservation Management of Freshwater Mussels.* Proceedings of a UMRCC symposium, 12-14 October 1992, St. Louis , MO, Upper Mississippi River Conservation Committee, Rock Island, IL.

Danglade, E. 1914. The mussel resources of the Illinois River. Report of the Commissioner of Fisheries for 1913, Document Number 804, U.S. Bureau of Fisheries, Washington, D.C., 48 p.

Davis, J. L., and W. G. Brock. 1994. Status of TVA's reservoir releases improvement efforts. In *Proceedings and Extended Abstracts of the 1994 Annual Spring Symposium*, American Water Resources Association, Minneapolis, MN, p. 147-152.

Dickinson, J. Y. 1968. *The Book of Pearls*. Crown Publishers, Inc., New York, NY.

Dimock, R. V., and A. H. Wright. 1993. Sensitivity of juvenile freshwater mussels to hypoxic, thermal and acid stress. *Journal of the Elisha Mitchell Scientific Society* 109:183-192.

Ellis, M. M. 1931a. A survey of conditions affecting fisheries in the upper Mississippi River. Fisheries Circular Number 5, U.S. Bureau of Fisheries, Washington, D.C., 18 p.

Ellis, M. M. 1931b. Some factors affecting the replacement of the commercial freshwater mussels. Fisheries Circular Number 7, U.S. Bureau of Fisheries, Washington, D.C., 10 p.

Ellis, M. M., and M. D. Ellis. 1926. Growth and transformation of parasitic glochidia in physiological nutrient solutions. *Science* 64:579-580.

Gordon, M. E., and J. B. Layzer. 1993. Glochidial host of *Alasmidonta atropurpurea* (Bivalvia: Unionoidea, Unionidae). *Transactions of the American Microscopical Society* 112:145-150.

Haag, W. R., D. J. Berg, D. W. Garton, and J. L. Farris. 1993. Reduced survival and fitness in native bivalves in response to fouling by the introduced zebra mussel (*Dreissena polymorpha*) in western Lake Erie. *Canadian Journal of Fisheries and Aquatic Sciences* 50:13-19.

Hargis, H. L. 1968. Development of improved fishing methods for use in southeastern and south-central reservoirs. Completion Report 4-5-R-2, Tennessee Wildlife Resources Agency, Nashville, TN, 101 p.

Hartfield, P., and R. Jones. 1990. Population status of endangered mussels in the Buttahatchee River, Mississippi and Alabama, segment 1, 1989. Mississippi Department of Wildlife, Fisheries and Parks, Museum of Natural Science, Jackson, MS, 35 p.

Helfrich, L. A. (producer). 1993. *Help Save America's Pearly Mussels* [videotape]. Virginia Polytechnic Institute and State University, Blacksburg, VA.

Helfrich, L. A., R. J. Neves, and R. G. Biggins (producers). 1993. *Help Save America's Pearly Mussels* [poster]. Virginia Polytechnic Institute and State University, Blacksburg, VA.

Higgins, E. 1928. Progress in biological inquiries, 1926. Report of the Commissioner of Fisheries for 1927, Document Number 1029, U.S. Bureau of Fisheries, Washington, D.C., p. 555-556.

Higgins, E. 1930. Progress in biological inquiries, 1928. Report of the Commissioner of Fisheries for the Fiscal Year 1929, Document Number 1068, U.S. Bureau of Fisheries, Washington, D.C., p. 670-673.

Higgins, E. 1931. Progress in biological inquiries, 1929. Report of the Commissioner of Fisheries for the Fiscal Year 1930, Document Number 1096, U.S. Bureau of Fisheries, p. 1119-1121.

Higgins, E. 1939. Progress in biological inquiries, 1938. Report of the Commissioner of Fisheries for the Fiscal Year 1939, Administrative Report Number 35, U.S. Bureau of Fisheries, Washington, D.C., p. 73-77.

Hill, D. M. (compiler). 1986. Cumberlandian mollusk conservation program activity 3: Identification of fish hosts. TVA/ONRED/AWR-86/17, Tennessee Valley Authority, Norris, TN, 57 p.

Howard, A. D. 1922. Experiments in the culture of fresh-water mussels. *Bulletin of the U.S. Bureau of Fisheries* **38**:63-89.

Hubbs, D. W. 1995. 1993 Statewide commercial mussel report. Fisheries Report 95-15, Tennessee Wildlife Resources Agency, Nashville, TN, 63 p.

Isley, F. B. 1914. Experimental study of the growth and migration of fresh-water mussels. Report of the Commissioner of Fisheries for 1913, Document Number 792, U.S. Bureau of Fisheries, Washington, D.C., 24 p.

Isom, B. G. 1966. The mussel resource of the Tennessee River. Tennessee Valley Authority, Norris, TN, 32 p.

Isom, B. G. 1969. The mussel resource of the Tennessee River. *Malacologia* 7:397-425.

Isom, B. G., and R. G. Hudson. 1982. In vitro culture of parasitic freshwater mussel glochidia. *Nautilus* **96**:147-151.

Isom, B. G., and P. Yokley. 1968. The mussel fauna of Duck River in Tennessee, 1965. *American Midland Naturalist* **80**:34-42.

Jenkinson, J. J. 1983. Status report on the Tennessee Valley Authority Cumberlandian mollusk conservation program. In *Report of Freshwater Mussels Workshop, 26-27 October 1982.* A. C. Miller (compiler). U.S. Army Engineer Waterways Experiment Station, Vicksburg, MS, p. 79-83.

Jenkinson, J. J., and S. A. Ahlstedt. 1988. Quantitative reassessment of the freshwater mussel fauna in the Powell River, Tennessee and Virginia. Tennessee Valley Authority, Knoxville, TN, 28 p.

Jenkinson, J. J., and J. H. Heuer. 1986. Cumberlandian mollusk conservation program activity 9: Selection of transplant sites and habitat characterization. TVA/ONRED/AWR-86/23, Tennessee Valley Authority, Knoxville, TN, 120 p.

Jones, R. O. 1950. Propagation of fresh-water mussels. *Progressive Fish-Culturist* **12**:13-25.

Kunz, G. F. 1898a. A brief history of the gathering of fresh-water pearls in the United States. *Bulletin of the U.S. Bureau of Fisheries* **17**:321-330.

Kunz, G. F. 1898b. The fresh-water pearls and pearl fisheries of the United States. *Bulletin of the U.S. Bureau of Fisheries* **17**:375-426.

Lefevre, G., and W. C. Curtis. 1912. Studies on the reproduction and artificial propagation of fresh-water mussels. *Bulletin of the U.S. Bureau of Fisheries* **30**:105-201.

Master, L. L. 1993. Information networking and the conservation of freshwater mussels. In *Conservation and Management of Freshwater Mussels.* K. S. Cummings, A. C. Buchanan, and L. M. Koch (eds.). Proceedings of a UMRCC symposium, 12-14 October 1992, St. Louis , MO, Upper Mississippi River Conservation Committee, Rock Island, IL, p. 126-130.

Miller, A. C. 1983. A gravel bar habitat for mussels on the Tombigbee River near Columbus, Mississippi. In *Report of Freshwater Mussels Workshop, 26-27 October 1982.* A. C. Miller (compiler). U.S. Army Engineer Waterways Experiment Station, Vicksburg, MS, p. 65-78.

Neves, R. J. 1991. Mollusks. In *Virginia's Endangered Species.* K. Terwilliger (ed.). McDonald and Woodward Publishing Co., Blacksburg, VA, p. 251-320.

Neves, R. J. 1993. A state-of-the-unionids address. In *Conservation and Management of Freshwater Mussels.* K. S. Cummings, A. C. Buchanan, and L. M. Koch (eds.). Proceedings of a UMRCC symposium, 12-14 October 1992, St. Louis , MO, Upper Mississippi River Conservation Committee, Rock Island, IL, p. 1-10.

Neves, R. J., A. E. Bogan, J. D. Williams, S. A. Ahlstedt, and P. W. Hartfield. 1997. Status of aquatic mollusks in the southeastern United States: A downward spiral of diversity. In *Aquatic Fauna in Peril: The Southeastern Perspective.* G. W. Benz, and D. E. Collins (eds.). Special Publication 1, Southeast Aquatic Research Institute, Lenz Design & Communications, Decatur, GA, p. 43-86.

O'Hara, M. G. 1980. The founding and early history of the pearl button industry. In *Proceedings of the UMRCC Symposium on Upper Mississippi River Bivalve Mollusks, May 1979.* J. L. Rasmussen (ed.). Upper Mississippi River Conservation Committee, Rock Island, IL, p 3-10.

Pardue, W. J. 1981. A survey of the mussels (Unionidae) of the Upper Tennessee River - 1978. *Sterkiana* 71:41-51.

Parker, R. S., C. T. Hackney, and M. F. Vidrine. 1984. Ecology and reproductive strategy of a south Louisiana freshwater mussel, *Glebula rotundata* (Lamarck) (Unionidae: Lampsilini). *Freshwater Invertebrate Biology* 3:53-58.

Payne, B. S., and A. C. Miller. 1989. Growth and survival of recent recruits to a population of *Fusconaia ebena* (Bivalvia: Unionidae). *American Midland Naturalist* 121:99-104.

Rasmussen, J. L. (ed.). 1980. *Proceedings of the UMRCC Symposium on Upper Mississippi River Bivalve Mollusks, May 1979.* Upper Mississippi River Conservation Committee, Rock Island, IL.

Scruggs, G. D. 1960. Status of fresh-water mussel stocks in the Tennessee River. Special Scientific Report — Fisheries Number 370, U.S. Fish and Wildlife Service, Washington, D.C., 41 p.

Sheehan, R. J., R. J. Neves, and H. E. Kitchel. 1989. Fate of freshwater mussels transplanted to formerly polluted reaches of the Clinch and North Fork Holston Rivers, Virginia. *Journal of Freshwater Ecology* 5:139-149.

Sickel, J. B. 1985. Biological assessment of the freshwater mussels in the Kentucky Dam tailwaters of the Tennessee River. Kentucky Division of Water, Frankfort, KY, 42 p.

Simpson, C. T. 1899. The pearly fresh-water mussels of the United States; their habits, enemies, and diseases, with suggestions for their protection. *Bulletin of the U.S. Bureau of Fisheries* 18:279-288.

Smith, H. M. 1899. The mussel fishery and pearl-button industry of the Mississippi River. *Bulletin of the U.S. Bureau of Fisheries* 18:289-314.

Smith, H. M. 1919. Fresh water mussels: A valuable national resource without sufficient protection. Economic Circular Number 43, U.S. Bureau of Fisheries, Washington, D.C., 5 p.

Stanford, J. A., and J. V. Ward. 1979. Stream regulation in North America. In *The Ecology of Regulated Streams.* J. V. Ward, and J. A. Stanford (eds.). Plenum Press, New York, NY, p.215-236.

Stansbery, D. H., and C. B. Stein. 1976. Changes in the distribution of *Io fluvialis* (Say, 1825) in the upper Tennessee River system (Mollusca: Gastropoda: Pleuroceridae). *Bulletin of the American Malacological Union* 1976:28-33.

Starrett, W. C. 1971. A survey of the mussels (Unionacea) of the Illinois River: A polluted stream. *Illinois Natural History Survey Bulletin* **30**:263-403.

Stein, C. B. 1968. Studies in the life history of the naiad *Amblema plicata* (Say, 1817). *Annual Report of the American Malacological Union* **1968**:46-47.

Stein, C. B. 1976. Gastropods. In *Endangered and Threatened Plants and Animals of Alabama.* H. Boschung (ed.). Bulletin Number 2, Alabama Museum of Natural History, Tuscaloosa, AL, p. 21-41.

Strayer, D. L. 1991. Projected distribution of the Zebra Mussel, *Dreissena polymorpha*, in North America. *Canadian Journal of Fisheries and Aquatic Science* **48**:1389-1395.

Surber, T. 1914. Identification of the glochidia of fresh-water mussels. Report of the Commissioner of Fisheries for 1912, Document Number 771, U.S. Bureau of Fisheries, Washington, D.C., 10 p.

Surber, T. 1915. Identification of the glochidia of fresh-water mussels. Report of the Commissioner of Fisheries for 1914, Document Number 813, U.S. Bureau of Fisheries, Washington, D.C., 9 p.

Thiel, P. A., and A. W. Fritz. 1993. Mussel harvest regulations in the upper Mississippi River system. In *Conservation and Management of Freshwater Mussels.* K. S. Cummings, A. C. Buchanan, and L. M. Koch (eds.). Proceedings of a UMRCC symposium, 12-14 October 1992, St. Louis , MO, Upper Mississippi River Conservation Committee, Rock Island, IL, p. 11-18.

Todd, R. M. 1993. Tennessee's commercial musseling regulations. In *Conservation and Management of Freshwater Mussels.* K. S. Cummings, A. C. Buchanan, and L. M. Koch (eds.). Proceedings of a UMRCC symposium, 12-14 October 1992, St. Louis, MO, Upper Mississippi River Conservation Committee, Rock Island, IL, p. 32-37.

U.S. Fish and Wildlife Service. 1976. Endangered status for 159 taxa of animals. *U.S. Federal Register* **41**:24062-24067.

U.S. Fish and Wildlife Service. 1977a. Endangered and threatened wildlife and plants: Proposed endangered or threatened status for 41 species of U.S. fauna. *U.S. Federal Register* **42**:2507-2515.

U.S. Fish and Wildlife Service. 1977b. Endangered and threatened wildlife and plants: Determination that the tan riffle shell is an endangered species. *U.S. Federal Register* **42**:42351-42353.

U.S. Fish and Wildlife Service. 1984. Tan riffleshell pearly mussel recovery plan. U.S. Fish and Wildlife Service, Atlanta, GA, 59 p.

U.S. Fish and Wildlife Service. 1992. Endangered and threatened species of the southeast United States (the red book). U.S. Government Printing Office, Washington, D.C., various pages in 2 volumes.

Wade, D. C. 1990. Screening toxicity evaluation of Wheeler Reservoir sediments using juvenile freshwater mussels (*Anodonta imbecillis* Say) exposed to sediment interstitial water. TVA/WR/AB-90/13, Tennessee Valley Authority, Muscle Shoals, AL, 28 p.

Wade, D. C., R. G. Hudson, and A. D. McKinney. 1993. Comparative response of *Ceriodaphnia dubia* and juvenile *Anodonta imbecillis* to selected complex industrial whole effluents. In *Conservation and Management of Freshwater Mussels.* K. S. Cummings, A. C. Buchanan, and L. M. Koch (eds.). Proceedings of a UMRCC symposium, 12-14 October 1992, St. Louis , MO, Upper Mississippi River Conservation Committee, Rock Island, IL, p. 109-112.

Ward, F. 1985. The pearl. *National Geographic* 168(2):192-223.

Water Quality 2000. 1994. Evaluation of a watershed approach to clean water: A site visit to the Tennessee Valley Authority and an evaluation of their clean water initiative. Water Quality 2000, Alexandria, VA, 29 p.

Waters, S. J. 1980. The evolution of mussel harvest regulations on the upper Mississippi River. In *Proceedings of the UMRCC Symposium on Upper Mississippi River Bivalve Mollusks, May 1979.* J. L. Rasmussen (ed.). Upper Mississippi River Conservation Committee, Rock Island, IL, p. 191-201.

Watters, G. T. 1994. An annotated bibliography of the reproduction and propagation of the Unionoidea (primarily of North America). Miscellaneous Contributions Number 1, Ohio Biological Survey, Columbus, OH, 158 p.

Williams, J. D., M. L. Warren, Jr., K. S. Cummings, J. L. Harris, and R. J. Neves. 1993. Conservation status of freshwater mussels of the United States and Canada. *Fisheries* 18(9):6-22.

Wilson, C. B., and H. W. Clark. 1914. The mussels of the Cumberland River and its tributaries. Report of the Commissioner of Fisheries for 1912, Document No. 781, U.S. Bureau of Fisheries, Washington, D.C., 63 p.

Yeager, B. L., and R. J. Neves. 1986. Reproductive cycle and fish hosts of the rabbit's foot mussel, *Quadrula cylindrica strigillata* (Mollusca: Unionidae) in the upper Tennessee River drainage. *American Midland Naturalist* 116:329-340.

Yeager, M. M., D. S. Cherry, and R. J. Neves. 1993. Interstitial feeding behavior of juvenile unionid mussels. *Bulletin of the Association of Southeastern Biologists* 40:113.

Yokley, P. 1972. Life history of *Pleurobema cordatum* (Rafinesque, 1820) (Bivalvia: Unionacea). *Malacologia* 11:351-364.

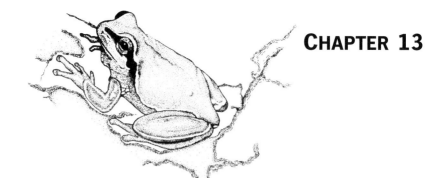

CHAPTER 13

Amphibians in Peril: Resource Management in the Southeast

Linda V. LaClaire

I n this chapter I will review past and current resource management programs that have benefited amphibians in the southeastern United States and management strategies that could be used to conserve the Southeast's imperiled amphibian fauna. Many of the projects and concepts discussed here are relatively new and much of the information provided was obtained from the "gray" literature (e.g., various federal, state or private agency reports) or from unpublished data. Nonetheless, this information provides a significant foundation upon which to build the consensus needed to ensure that the modest strides made in amphibian management will continue. Conservation of our imperiled amphibian fauna will require a commitment from resource managers to include amphibians in management planning at local, regional, national, and global levels.

Amphibian life histories grade from those that are totally aquatic to those that are entirely terrestrial; however, all amphibian species require a moist environment. Management efforts needed to protect the watersheds and wetlands inhabited by aquatic amphibians are often the same ones required to protect the moist woodland environments that are home to many terrestrial amphibians. Moreover, because water quality in wetlands is often dependent on conditions prevailing in surrounding terrestrial habitats, and because many amphibians depend on both aquatic and terrestrial habitats, the management of aquatic and terrestrial habitats can seldom be separated from one another when considering conservation measures aimed at amphibian resources. It is for this reason that this chapter will consider all imperiled amphibians in the southeastern United States, no matter what their degree of connection to aquatic habitats. The southeastern United States is

Aquatic Fauna in Peril: The Southeastern Perspective, edited by George W. Benz, and David E. Collins. 1997. Special Publication 1, Southeast Aquatic Research Institute, Lenz Design & Communications, Decatur, GA, 554 p.

defined as the region composed by the states of Alabama, Arkansas, Florida, Georgia, Kentucky, Louisiana, Mississippi, North Carolina, South Carolina, and Tennessee.

In this chapter, management is considered in broad terms as those techniques and activities which strive to maintain the continuity of ecological and evolutionary processes (O'Connell and Noss, 1992). Because habitat loss is the primary threat to imperiled amphibians in the Southeast, the development of effective habitat management plans is crucial for amphibian conservation. Unfortunately, few management projects have been specifically directed at amphibian species or populations in the Southeast or elsewhere throughout the United States.

Most amphibian management has involved species listed under the Endangered Species Act or those species listed by individual states. Priorities determining the allocation of management resources are often based on these federal and state lists (Master, 1991). In the past, the federal candidate species list (U.S. Fish and Wildlife Service, 1994b) was used to identify species that may be biologically vulnerable and in need of active management. However, the U.S. Fish and Wildlife Service (1996) has revised its list of candidate taxa to include only those species which have been proposed for listing or which were previously considered Category 1 candidates. Category 1 candidates were those species for which sufficient data were available to support a proposed rule, but issuance of the rule was precluded by other listing activity. Category 2 candidates, those species which were being assessed for biological vulnerability and threat, are no longer included on the candidate list; these taxa are considered species of concern. Another prioritization system has been developed by The Nature Conservancy (TNC) in cooperation with the Natural Heritage Data Center Network (NHDCN) (NHDCN, 1993). Numeric ranks given for species with potential global biological vulnerability include: G1 = critically imperiled; G2 = imperiled; G3 = rare or uncommon; and G4 = widespread, abundant, and apparently secure, but with cause for long-term concern. This system has been used to develop lists of species with ranked levels of imperilment (TNC and the International Network of Natural Heritage Programs and Conservation Data Centers, 1996).

In the following discussion I will consider "imperiled" amphibians of the Southeast to be those species which are listed under the Endangered Species Act or by a state management agency, former federal Category 2 candidate species, and G1-G3 TNC/NHDCN ranked species (see Table 1). While extensive data are not available to support declines in all of these species, there is general concern among biologists that without effective management these amphibians will truly be in peril.

Under the Endangered Species Act, only one southeastern amphibian is listed, the Red Hills salamander (Phaeognathus hubrichti) (U.S. Fish and Wildlife Service, 1994a). An additional 15 amphibian species (12 salamanders and three frogs) were formerly considered federal Category 2 candidates (U.S. Fish and Wildlife Service, 1994b). Six of the ten states in the Southeast (Florida, Georgia, Mississippi, North Carolina, South Carolina, and Tennessee) have lists of state protected amphibian species. Twenty-six salamanders and six frogs are on these lists. The current list compiled by TNC and the Natural Heritage Program ranks 20 salamanders and two frogs as critically imperiled, imperiled, or rare and uncommon. There is considerable overlap between these lists, as many species appear on more than one list (see Table 1). Counting each species only once, the total number of imperiled amphibians equals 46, including 39 salamanders and seven frogs (see Table 2). The total number of native amphibian species known to occur in the South-

Table 1. Imperiled amphibian fauna of the southeastern United States.[1] This list contains amphibians listed under the Endangered Species Act and other species of concern (former Category 2 candidate species), as well as those listed by a state, or ranked as G1-G3 by The Nature Conservancy and Natural Heritage Programs (TNC). STATE LIST CATEGORIES: WM = wildlife in need of management; R = rare; SC = species of special concern; T = threatened; E = endangered; NL = not listed; - = not resident in state. FEDERAL RANK: SC = species of concern (former Category 2 candidate species); T = threatened; NR = not ranked. TNC RANK: G3 = rare or uncommon; G2 = imperiled; G1 = critically imperiled; Q = taxonomy questioned; ? = ranking inexact; NR = not ranked.

Amphibian Taxa	State Lists										Federal Rank	TNC Rank
	AL	AR	FL	GA	KY	LA	MS	NC	SC	TN		
SALAMANDERS												
Cryptobranchidae												
Cryptobranchus alleganiensis (eastern hellbender)	NL	NL	-	R	NL	-	NL	SC	NL	WM	SC	G3[2]
Proteidae												
Necturus sp. (Black Warrior waterdog)	NL	-	-	-	-	-	-	-	-	-	SC	G2
N. lewisi (Neuse River waterdog)	-	-	-	-	-	-	-	SC	-	-	NR	G3
N. maculosus (mudpuppy)	NL	-	-	NL	NL	NL	NL	SC	-	NL	NR	NR
Amphiumidae												
Amphiuma pholeter (one-toed amphiuma)	NL	-	NL	R	-	-	-	-	-	-	NR	G3
Sirenidae												
Pseudobranchus striatus belli (Everglades dwarf siren)	-	-	NL	-	-	-	-	-	-	-	NR	G3?
P. s. lustricolus (Gulf hammock dwarf siren)	-	-	NL	-	-	-	-	-	-	-	SC	NR
P. s. spheniscus (slender dwarf siren)	-	-	NL	NL	-	-	-	-	-	-	NR	G3?
P. s. striatus (broad-striped dwarf siren)	-	-	NL	NL	-	-	-	-	T	-	NR	G3?

Table 1. Continued.

Amphibian Taxa	State Lists										Federal Rank	TNC Rank
	AL	AR	FL	GA	KY	LA	MS	NC	SC	TN		
Ambystomatidae												
Ambystoma cingulatum (flatwoods salamander)	NL	-	NL	R	-	-	-	-	E	-	SC	G2/G3
A. talpoideum (mole salamander)	NL	NL	NL	NL	NL	NL	NL	SC	NL	WM	NR	NR
A. tigrinum tigrinum (eastern tiger salamander)	NL	NL	NL	NL	NL	NL	NL	T	NL	NL	NR	NR
Salamandridae												
Notophthalmus perstriatus (striped newt)	-	-	NL	R	-	-	-	-	-	-	SC	G2/G3
Plethodontidae												
Desmognathinae												
Desmognathus aeneus (seepage salamander)	NL	-	-	NL	-	-	-	NL	-	NL	SC	NR
D. apalachicolae (Apalachicola dusky salamander)	NL	-	NL	NL	-	-	-	-	-	-	NR	G3
D. brimleyorum (Ouachita dusky salamander)	-	NL	-	-	-	-	-	-	-	-	SC	NR
D. santeetlah (Santeetlah dusky salamander)	-	-	-	-	-	-	-	NL	-	NL	NR	G3/Q
D. welteri (Black Mtn. dusky salamander)	-	-	-	-	NL	-	-	-	-	WM	NR	NR
Phaeognathus hubrichti (Red Hills salamander)	T	-	-	-	-	-	-	-	-	-	T	NR
Plethodontinae												
Aneides aeneus (green salamander)	NL	-	-	R	NL	-	E	E	NL	WM	SC	NR

Table 1. Continued.

Amphibian Taxa	State Lists										Federal Rank	TNC Rank
	AL	AR	FL	GA	KY	LA	MS	NC	SC	TN		
Eurycea aquatica (dark-sided salamander)	NL	-	-	NL	-	-	-	-	-	-	SC	NR
E. junaluska (Junaluska salamander)	-	-	-	-	-	-	-	SC	-	NL	SC	G2/Q
E. longicauda longicauda (longtail salamander)	NL	NL	NL	-	NL	-	-	SC	-	NL	NR	NR
E. lucifuga (cave salamander)	NL	NL	NL	-	NL	-	E	-	-	NL	NR	NR
E. quadridigitata (dwarf salamander; silver morph)	-	NL	-	-	-	NL	-	SC	-	-	NR	NR
E. tynerensis (Oklahoma salamander)	-	NL	-	-	-	-	-	-	-	-	NR	G3
Gyrinophilus palleucus (Tennessee cave salamander)	NL	-	-	NL	-	-	-	-	-	T	SC	G2
G. porphyriticus porphyriticus (spring salamander)	NL	-	-	NL	NL	-	E	NL	-	NL	NR	NR
Haideotriton wallacei (Georgia blind salamander)	-	-	SC	T	-	-	-	-	-	-	SC	G2
Hemidactylium scutatum (four-toed salamander)	NL	NL	NL	NL	NL	NL	NL	SC	NL	WM	NR	NR
Plethodon aureolus (Tellico salamander)	-	-	-	-	-	-	-	NL	-	NL	NR	G2/G3/Q
P. caddoensis (Caddo Mountain salamander)	-	NL	-	-	-	-	-	-	-	-	NR	G2
P. dorsalis (zigzag salamander)	NL	NL	NL	-	NL	-	NL	SC	-	NL	NR	NR
P. fourchensis (Fourche Mountain salamander)	-	NL	-	-	-	-	-	-	-	-	NR	G2

Table 1. Continued.

Amphibian Taxa	State Lists										Federal Rank	TNC Rank
	AL	AR	FL	GA	KY	LA	MS	NC	SC	TN		
P. kisatchie (Louisiana slimy salamander)	–	NL	–	–	–	NL	–	–	–	–	NR	G3/Q
P. ouachitae (Rich Mountain salamander)	–	NL	–	–	–	–	–	–	–	–	NR	G2/G3
P. petraeus (Pidgeon Mountain salamander)	–	–	–	R	–	–	–	–	–	–	NR	G1/G2
P. teyahalee (southern Appalachian salamander)	–	–	–	NL	–	–	–	NL	NL	NL	NR	G3/Q
P. websteri (Webster's salamander)	NL	–	–	NL	–	NL	NL	–	E	–	NR	NR
P. wehrlei (Wehrle's salamander)	–	–	–	–	NL	–	–	T	–	NL	NR	NR
P. welleri (Weller's salamander)	–	–	–	–	–	–	–	SC	–	NL	NR	NR
P. yonahlossee[3] (Yonahlossee salamander)	–	–	–	–	–	–	–	SC	–	NL	NR	NR
FROGS												
Hylidae												
Hyla andersonii (Pine Barrens treefrog)	NL	–	SC	–	–	–	–	–	T	–	NR	NR
H. gratiosa (barking treefrog)	NL	–	NL	NL	NL	NL	NL	NL	NL	WM	NR	NR
Pseudacris brachyphona (mountain chorus frog)	NL	–	NL	–	NL	–	NL	SC	–	NL	NR	NR
P. streckeri illinoensis (Illinois chorus frog)	–	NL	–	–	NL	–	–	–	–	–	SC	NR

Table 1. Continued.

Amphibian Taxa	State Lists										Federal Rank	TNC Rank
	AL	AR	FL	GA	KY	LA	MS	NC	SC	TN		
Ranidae												
Rana capito aesopus (Florida gopher frog)	-	-	SC	NL	-	-	-	-	-	-	SC	G3
R. c. capito (Carolina gopher frog)	-	-	-	NL	-	-	-	SC	NL	-	SC	NR
R. c. sevosa (dusky gopher frog)	NL	-	SC	-	-	NL	E	-	-	-	SC	G3
R. heckscheri (river frog)	NL	-	NL	NL	-	-	NL	SC	NL	-	NR	NR
R. okaloosae (Florida bog frog)	-	-	SC	-	-	-	-	-	-	-	SC	G2

[1] Species names and distributions based on Conant and Collins, 1991.

[2] Arkansas and Missouri populations only.

[3] Listed in North Carolina as *Plethodon longicrus*, the crevice salamander.

east is 126 (Conant and Collins, 1991). Therefore, the imperiled species represent 37 percent of the total amphibian fauna of the Southeast, with 45 percent of salamander and 18 percent of frog species being imperiled.

AMPHIBIAN RESOURCE MANAGEMENT IN THE SOUTHEAST

Over the past several years, herpetologists have begun sharing their observations on declining amphibian populations with the general public (Blaustein and Wake, 1990; Vitt et al., 1990; Livermore, 1992; Yoffe, 1992). The dramatic population declines seen in some areas of the world have not been demonstrated in the Southeast. Granted, range-wide historical data are few and generally not comprehensive enough to provide an adequate baseline with which to compare current distributions. However, given the destruction, degradation, and fragmentation of imperiled amphibian habitats in the Southeast, there can be little doubt that the distribution of many species has probably contracted from historical levels (Vial and Saylor, 1993; Pechmann and Wilbur, 1994).

The management of amphibians as a resource to be protected, in the traditional sense of wildlife management, has only recently been addressed (Szaro et al., 1988). Wildlife management has historically targeted game and other species which have a perceived economic value (Schemnitz, 1980). Amphibians generally do not fall into this category, and thus they have typically been ignored. Additional reasons for the limited management activities focusing on amphibians include a lack of information on the regional fauna; scarce resource dollars for management which are often specifically targeted for birds, mammals, or fish (e. g., Pittman/Robertson funds to states); a perception that amphibians are common and do not require management; and a general attitude that amphibians are not as important a component of ecosystems as other vertebrates. Further neglect may be a consequence of difficulties associated with studying fauna which are inactive for large portions of the day or year (Scott and Seigel, 1992). Lastly, most herpetologists do not have a background in resource management, and they seldom have directly participated in the development of resource management strategies.

Although the implementation of amphibian resource management is in its infancy, resource managers are beginning to show an interest in amphibians. This interest is being supported by researchers who are providing information to assist in planning management strategies (Seehorn, 1982; Dodd and Charest, 1988; Gibbons, 1988; Szaro et al., 1988; Dodd, 1991; Scott and Seigel, 1992; Dodd, 1993; Bookhout, 1994; Dodd and LaClaire, 1995; deMaynadier and Hunter, 1995; Dupuis et al., 1995). This link between managers and scientists is being strengthened in several ways. For example, a manual for wildlife managers that addresses management of both amphibians and reptiles is being developed by the U.S. Forest Service in cooperation with The Nature Conservancy (M. Robertson, U.S. Forest Service, pers. comm.). Scientific assessment methods to reliably determine amphibian rarity or commonness have also recently been standardized and made generally available (Jones, 1986; Corn and Bury, 1990; Heyer et al., 1994). In spite of this progress, the incorporation of amphibians into resource management plans remains rare, and funds for amphibian management projects are usually difficult to obtain from resource management agencies.

Although amphibians have generally been overlooked in the past, they have benefited when resource management strategies incidentally protected their habitats. In a few in-

Table 2. Summary of numbers of imperiled amphibians in the southeastern United States.

Amphibian Group	Federal Listed Species	Federal Species of Concern	State Listed Species	Species With TNC Global Rank[1]	Total Number[2]
Salamanders	1	12	26	20	39
Frogs	0	3	6	2	7

[1] This category reflects ranking systems of The Nature Conservancy and Natural Heritage Data Center Network.

[2] Total Number will be less than the sum of each row due to overlap in categories (see Table 1).

stances, amphibian populations and their habitats have been specifically targeted for protection, usually as a result of federal or state regulations.

LEGISLATION AND REGULATION AS MANAGEMENT TOOLS

Legal protection afforded by federal and state regulations has been the basis for amphibian resource management. Federal legislation which may afford protection for amphibian resources includes the Clean Water Act, the Endangered Species Act, the Fish and Wildlife Coordination Act, the National Environmental Policy Act, the National Forest Management Act, and the National Wild and Scenic Rivers Act. As mentioned above, six southeastern states have non-game regulations which provide protection for state-listed species, and all ten southeastern states require scientific or commercial permits to collect at least some species of non-game wildlife. These permits can be denied on the basis of species rarity. There are also local zoning and land-use regulations which may offer some protection for amphibian resources.

The implementation of most environmental legislation has been reactive rather than pro-active (see Karr, 1990; Doppelt et al., 1993). For example, the intent of the Endangered Species Act is to provide a means to conserve the ecosystems upon which endangered and threatened species depend and to provide a program for the conservation of those species. Implementation of the Endangered Species Act often results in protecting individuals of a particular species on a case by case basis, but conservation of the habitats and ecosystems in which these species live has rarely been accomplished (Clark et al., 1994). Some legislation, such as the Clean Water Act, can target habitat directly. In general, enforcement of such environmental regulations is difficult and often directed towards only the most blatant violators.

Each of the six acts of federal legislation outlined below are intended, at least in part, to protect the quality of the environment and, as a result, have applicability to amphibian protection and management. The Clean Water, the Fish and Wildlife Coordination, and the National Wild and Scenic Rivers acts, specifically address protection of water resources. The Endangered Species, the National Environmental Protection, and the National Forest Management acts, address protection of species, protection of the human environment, and protection of our national forests and their resources, respectively.

The Clean Water Act (CWA) provides for the restoration and maintenance of the chemical, physical, and biological integrity of the Nation's lakes, rivers, streams, and coastal waters. The CWA specifically regulates the discharge of any pollutant or the discharge of dredge or fill material into all waters of the United States including adjacent wetland ecosystems. Section 404 of the CWA defines a permit program to control dredging or filling activities. The U.S. Army Corps of Engineers (COE) has permit authority over waters of the United States (i.e., all waters affecting interstate and foreign commerce and translated by the U.S. Environmental Protection Agency [EPA] as any wetland habitat used by migratory birds). The EPA has an oversight role in promulgating guidelines for the permit program and has the authority to veto permits. The COE can issue General Permits for activities "similar in nature" and having minimal individual or cumulative adverse effects. One of these General Permits, Nationwide Permit 26, authorizes any dredge or fill activity in headwaters and isolated wetlands provided less than ten acres (approximately four ha) are impacted. In waters other than traditionally navigable waters, states may displace COE permitting (Blumm and Zaleha, 1989) and determine the size of wetlands to be regulated under dredge and fill permits. Many wetlands used for amphibian breeding are smaller than the size designated as jurisdictional by Nationwide Permit 26 or by state agencies.

The Fish and Wildlife Coordination Act (FWCA) was promulgated to allow development of water resources while conserving wildlife resources and environmental quality. The intent of the FWCA is to give wildlife conservation a coequal purpose or objective in federally funded or permitted water resource development proposals or projects. Federal agencies planning projects to develop water resources (e.g., the COE) must consult with the U.S. Fish and Wildlife Service and state game and fish agencies prior to seeking authorization for the action. The planning agency must give full consideration to measures recommended by these agencies to mitigate impacts to wildlife resources. This provides opportunity for amphibian management issues to become part of the decision-making review process. The agency carrying out the development project makes the final decision on wildlife mitigative measures, however.

The National Wild and Scenic Rivers Act (WSRA) created a system for designation and preservation of free-flowing rivers on private, state, or federal lands. A separate federal law is required for each Wild and Scenic River segment protected. Management areas for these congressionally designated rivers generally include adjacent corridors; however, the average acreage per river mile may not exceed 320 acres (about 130 ha) within the designated segment (Doppelt et al., 1993). Federal land management agencies must preserve designated river segments within their jurisdiction in free-flowing condition, protect water quality, and fulfill other national conservation purposes (e.g., protection of wildlife). The federal managing agency decides how best to protect the value of a river, but must consult with the EPA and state water pollution control authorities. Three rivers in the southern Appalachian Mountains have been designated Wild and Scenic Rivers under this Act. Implementation of the WSRA may benefit amphibians living in these watersheds. The three rivers are the Chattooga River in Georgia, North Carolina, and South Carolina, the Obed River in Tennessee, and the headwaters of the New River in North Carolina (Wallace et al., 1992).

The Endangered Species Act (ESA) specifically addresses the conservation of endangered species and the ecosystems on which they depend. Implementation of this Act is initiated by determining if a species meets the criteria to be designated an endangered or threatened species. This determination is made by reviewing a species' status based on the following five factors: the present or threatened destruction, modification, or curtailment of its habitat or range; the overutilization for commercial, recreational, scientific, or educational purposes; disease or predation factors; the inadequacy of existing regulatory mechanisms; and other natural or man-made factors affecting the species' continued existence. Once a species is placed on the Endangered Species List, the ESA provides a number of methods to protect it and its habitat. Recovery Plans are developed and implemented for listed species. Legal protection provided by the ESA is described under Section 7 (actions of or supported by government agencies shall not jeopardize endangered species), Section 9 ("take" of endangered species is prohibited), and Section 10 (an incidental take permit may be obtained if an approved Habitat Conservation Plan has been developed). Section 6 of the Act describes provisions for states to receive federal funds to perform research on candidate and listed species. Management issues can be addressed through use of these funds, but in most cases research is in response to a need for status surveys or recovery tasks outlined in Recovery Plans. All states in the Southeast have Section 6 agreements with the U. S. Fish and Wildlife Service which require the states to provide protection for federally listed species.

The National Environmental Policy Act (NEPA) provides guidelines for federal agencies to follow in the course of performing their various activities. The laws, regulations, and policies of the United States must be administered in accordance with the policies of NEPA. Specifically, federal agencies are required to consult with each other when planning actions that may significantly affect the quality of the human environment. Consultation must occur prior to approval of projects, and a statement of environmental impacts that are likely to result from the actions must be formulated. The federal agency with the lead on the action must prepare an Environmental Impact Statement with input from the public, state and local governments, and all federal agencies with legal jurisdiction or special expertise. The Act offers the opportunity for input from agencies with the lead for natural resource protection, such as the U.S. Fish and Wildlife Service, in the development of mitigative measures which can offset impacts of the proposed action. These measures may provide a direct benefit to imperiled amphibians.

The National Forest Management Act (NFMA) governs stewardship of national forests which is the responsibility of the U.S. Forest Service. The major focus of NFMA is on interdisciplinary land management planning, including procedures for public participation in the decision making process. Forest management plans must provide for multiple uses of national forest lands and must incorporate the values of watersheds and fish and wildlife into planning documents. Guidelines are provided for the following: obtaining inventory data on the various renewable resources in order to maintain the diversity of plant and animal communities; allowing timber harvest only where water bodies are protected from detrimental changes in water temperature, blockage of flow, and deposits of sediment; and, ensuring that harvesting methods are carried out in a manner consistent with the protection of soil, watersheds, and fish and wildlife. As a result of NFMA, amphibian status surveys and research projects are being funded to provide data for improving resource management plans for national forests.

SPECIFIC MANAGEMENT PROGRAMS BENEFITING IMPERILED AMPHIBIANS

The development of resource management programs for imperiled amphibians has been hindered by the limited data available on species' distributions and population sizes. In order to improve this situation, distribution and status surveys of some southeastern amphibians have been initiated by state non-game and heritage programs, The Nature Conservancy, the U.S. Fish and Wildlife Service, the U.S. Forest Service, the U.S. Department of Defense, and individual herpetologists. Funding for surveys has been provided by private landowners, state non-game programs, and by federal agencies. The Alabama Natural Heritage Program and the U.S. Fish and Wildlife Service have initiated the Alabama Herpetological Atlas Project to provide baseline data on reptiles and amphibians in Alabama. These efforts represent the beginnings of a region-wide database on amphibian distribution and abundance.

Specific management projects for imperiled amphibians are discussed below. Since resource management funds are not generally allocated solely for imperiled amphibians, total dollars spent directly for amphibian management could be provided for only a few of the projects discussed. Most of these management programs are ongoing and are being modified as results dictate. Of course, their success or failure cannot be judged until adequate long-term monitoring studies (at least a generation time for each species) have been completed.

Amphibian Management on Federal Lands

Resource management addressing amphibians has generally been tied to timber management on federal lands by the U.S. Forest Service and the Department of Defense. Timber management on these lands has most commonly focused on communities or ecosystems. In some cases, specific actions which benefit amphibians have been included. These include strategies to maintain moist environments and to protect wetland and stream habitats. Streamside management zones and timber harvests, limited to single tree selection, have been used to maintain forest canopy and soil moisture at a level more suitable to imperiled amphibians than would clearcut harvests. Many pond breeding amphibians require temporary wetlands for reproduction. Management actions used to protect these ponds have included the prescribed burning of temporary wetlands, the termination of fish stocking, the curtailment of the use of breeding ponds as fire breaks, and the creation of temporary ponds.

Studies have been undertaken on a number of national forests in different states to examine the effects of different harvest methods and successional impacts on amphibian and reptile populations. Additional studies have focused on surveys for imperiled amphibians on lands managed by the U.S. Forest Service and the Department of Defense. These studies have provided information that will be used in developing timber management plans.

Many federally owned lands in the Southeast have suitable habitat for three imperiled amphibians endemic to areas historically dominated by longleaf pine forests: the gopher frog (*Rana capito*), the striped newt (*Notophthalmus perstriatus*), and the flatwoods salamander (*Ambystoma cingulatum*). Managers of these federal lands have, or plan to, tailor their resource management plans to include measures to protect these amphibians.

A project has been undertaken in the Conecuh National Forest of Alabama to restore Nellie Pond, a breeding site of the dusky gopher frog (*Rana capito sevosa*). Due to the relatively recent introduction of predaceous fish to the pond by fishermen, tadpoles of the gopher frog, which historically bred in this ephemeral pond, were no longer surviving to metamorphosis. In 1992, U.S. Forest Service personnel drained the pond, removed as many fish as possible, and used rotenone to kill the remaining fish. The pond refilled naturally. Signs were erected to inform the public of the importance of maintaining the pond without a fish community. Public hearings were held to receive public input. Dusky gopher frog eggs were collected from a nearby pond and were raised in a laboratory until they were large tadpoles. They were then introduced into Nellie Pond, and during subsequent monitoring, metamorphic frogs were observed exiting the pond. Continued monitoring will be needed to determine the long-term success of this project. The project cost, approximately $11,000, was supported in part by a timber sale resulting from slash pine thinning of the surrounding habitat (R. Lint, U.S. Forest Service, pers. comm.). In addition to funding the project, the timber thinning improved the habitat for the resident upland-dwelling adult dusky gopher frogs.

The only breeding pond for the dusky gopher frog in Mississippi occurs in the DeSoto National Forest. Projects have been funded by the U.S. Forest Service and the U.S. Fish and Wildlife Service to study gopher frog life history and to improve the pond habitat for this species. Forest management plans since 1994 have incorporated the needs of the frog and will continue to be adapted as new data become available.

In Florida, status surveys have been conducted for the Florida gopher frog (*Rana capito aesopus*) and the striped newt in the Ocala National Forest (ONF) (Telford, 1993). In addition to these surveys, a study of the effects on amphibians of different timber cutting regimes around selected temporary ponds in the ONF has been initiated (K. Greenberg, U.S. Forest Service, pers. comm.). Results of these studies will be incorporated into resource management plans for the forest. Additional surveys have been funded by the U.S. Forest Service and the U.S. Fish and Wildlife Service to determine the distribution of the flatwoods salamander, formerly considered a Category 2 federal candidate species, in Florida's Apalachicola National Forest (Palis, 1992, 1993, 1995a) and Osceola National Forest (Palis, 1992; D. Printiss, Florida Natural Areas Inventory, pers. comm.). These distribution data will be used to help formulate resource management plans for the salamander on both of these national forests.

The U.S. Department of Defense (DOD) has funded surveys for rare vertebrates, including the three aforementioned longleaf pine endemic amphibians, on a number of military bases in the Southeast. Surveys on Camp Blanding in Florida have been conducted by biologists with the Florida Natural Heritage Program. Management steps to enhance populations of the Florida gopher frog and striped newt were included in their summary report (Hipes and Jackson, 1994). A faunal survey for rare vertebrates on Fort Benning in Georgia was initiated in 1994 and will continue through 1997 (P. Laumeyer, U.S. Fish and Wildlife Service, pers. comm.). Prior to this study, a breeding site for the imperiled dusky gopher frog had been found on the base. For this reason, biologists conducting the surveys are especially interested in searching for additional localities for the gopher frog and other rare amphibians. Data collected during the survey will be used in future Fort Benning resource management plans. Biologists with The Nature Conservancy, funded by DOD, have surveyed Fort Stewart in Georgia for rare plants and animals including the Carolina gopher frog (*Rana capito capito*), the striped newt, and the flatwoods salamander (K. Lutz, The Nature Conservancy, pers. comm.). The distribution information generated by this study is being used to help develop a resource management plan (L. Swindell, DOD, pers. comm.). Additional studies on flatwoods salamander and striped newt life histories will continue through the year 2000 to determine how best to manage for these species on Fort Stewart (L. Swindell, DOD, pers. comm.).

A five-year Natural Resources Management Plan has been developed by the DOD for Eglin Air Force Base in Florida (Department of Defense, 1993). The goals of the plan are to protect plant communities and to restore ecosystem function and viability through careful land management. Eglin Air Force Base encompasses what may be the largest remaining, relatively intact longleaf pine/turkey oak forest in the United States. The presence of the federally listed red-cockaded woodpecker has focused planning on the restoration and maintenance of the sandhill community. The longleaf pine sandhills and flatwoods at Eglin Air Force Base are also habitat for the dusky gopher frog and the flatwoods salamander. Population surveys and identification of temporary pond breeding sites used by these two imperiled amphibians have been completed (Palis, 1995b). Habitat restoration, as described in the management plan, will benefit both species.

The U.S. Department of Energy (DOE) has funded long-term studies on reptiles and amphibians at the DOE Savannah River Site (SRS) in South Carolina. A considerable database has been developed for the site by researchers at the Savannah River Ecology Laboratory (SREL) (see Gibbons and Semlitsch, 1991). The U.S. Forest Service manages the forest on the SRS for timber production. Portions of the SRS have been set aside for protection, but at present there are no specific management goals for imperiled amphibians (B. Jarvis, U.S. Forest Service, pers. comm.). A project started at the site in the late 1980s provided potential benefits to imperiled amphibians through the creation of several temporary ponds as replacements for a pond that was destroyed. This attempt to replace the destroyed wetland with newly created ones of equal value was only partially successful (J. Pechmann, SREL, pers. comm.). The new ponds were dug near the periphery of the construction site and the location of the original wetland. Re-creating the original hydrologic conditions was problematic. Initially, the created ponds drained more frequently and remained dry for longer periods of time than the original temporary pond. Later, when liners were used to create an impervious bottom layer, the ponds became too permanent. As a result, species composition differed in the created ponds from the original wetland. Uncommon species, formerly present in the destroyed pond, were not recorded in the created ponds.

Projects on national forest lands in the southern Appalachian Mountains, which are habitat for a number of imperiled amphibians (see Table 3), are being carried out in the Daniel Boone National Forest in Kentucky, and the Nantahala and Pisgah national forests in North Carolina. In the Daniel Boone National Forest, traditional wildlife ponds have been created for many years for use by the resident deer population. U.S. Forest Service biologists, interested in managing for amphibians, modified the design of these ponds by varying their depth and shape, and by adding logs and branches to encourage colonization by amphibians. Eight of these newly created ponds were monitored during the first year (1994) after construction. Six species of frogs and two species of salamanders were found in the ponds, including an imperiled species, the mountain chorus frog (*Pseudacris brachyphona*) (J. MacGregor, U.S. Forest Service, pers. comm.).

On the Nantahala and Pisgah national forests, a study of the distribution and habitat of the Junaluska salamander (*Eurycea junaluska*) was completed in 1995. The results of this study will be used in the development of a conservation strategy for this imperiled species. Discussion of a multi-agency conservation agreement was initiated in May 1996 between the U.S. Forest Service, the U.S. Fish and Wildlife Service, the North Carolina Depart-

Table 3. Imperiled amphibian fauna of the southern Appalachian Mountains. All = endemic, Part = part of range within southern Appalachian Mountains.

Taxon	All	Part
SALAMANDERS		
Plethodontidae		
Desmognathinae		
Desmognathus aeneus, seepage salamander		X
D. santeetlah, Santeetlah dusky salamander	X	
D. welteri, Black Mountain dusky salamander		X
Plethodontinae		
Aneides aeneus, green salamander		X
Eurycea aquatica, dark-sided salamander	X	
E. junaluska, Junaluska salamander	X	
E. longicauda longicauda, longtail salamander		X
E. lucifuga, cave salamander	X	
Gyrinophilus palleucus, Tennessee cave salamander		X
G. porphyriticus, spring salamander		X
Hemidactylium scutatum, four-toed salamander		X
Plethodon aureolus, Tellico salamander		X
P. dorsalis, zigzag salamander		X
P. petraeus, Pidgeon Mountain salamander	X	
P. teyahalee, southern Appalachian salamander	X	
P. websteri, Webster's salamander		X
P. wehrlei, Wehrle's salamander		X
P. welleri, Weller's salamander	X	
P. yonahlossee, Yonahlossee salamander[1]	X	
FROGS		
Hylidae		
Pseudacris brachyphona, mountain chorus frog		X

[1] Listed in North Carolina as *Plethodon longicrus*, the crevice salamander.

ment of Transportation, and a regional power company (R. McClanahan, U.S. Forest Service, pers. comm.). Additionally, a database on the distribution of another imperiled species, the green salamander (*Aneides aeneus*), has been compiled for these two national forests. Using this database, timber operations are modified when needed, on a case by case basis, to ensure that green salamanders and their habitat are protected (R. McClanahan, U.S. Forest Service, pers. comm.).

The Ouachita Mountains of Arkansas and Oklahoma are also habitat for a number of imperiled amphibians. Two imperiled species, the Fourche Mountain salamander (*Plethodon fourchensis*) and the Caddo Mountain salamander (*P. caddoensis*), are endemic to Arkansas and virtually all of their habitat occurs within the Ouachita National Forest. Both species occur on steep wooded slopes and are vulnerable to reductions in soil moisture. The U.S. Fish and Wildlife Service, the U.S. Forest Service, and the Arkansas Game and Fish Commission have developed a memorandum of understanding for each species to benefit their conservation. Since 1993, these three agencies have been working together to determine the distribution of these salamanders and to monitor their populations. In addition, timber harvest and selective forest thinning have been restricted in streamside management zones and on slopes greater than 35 degrees to protect salamander habitat. The management of these salamanders has been incorporated into the larger, ecosystem-level Ouachita National Forest Management Plan.

Additional research in the Ouachita National Forest, part of the Ouachita Mountains Management Research Project, examines the distribution of amphibians and reptiles in the forest. Cooperators on this project, which was initiated in 1992 and continues through 1997, include the U.S. Forest Service, Weyerhaeuser Company, Oklahoma State University, the University of Arkansas, and the National Council of the Paper Industry for Air and Stream Improvement, Inc. (NCASI) (B. Wigley, NCASI, pers. comm.). Data on amphibian and reptile species abundance and community composition are being collected at both the forest-stand level and landscape-level in four watersheds with different histories of silviculture and intensity of timber management. A study of forest stands compares surveys on sites managed under three different regimes: single-tree selection (not clearcut), even-age management (clearcut, burn, replant), and eighty-year mature forest. Results of the surveys will be used to examine the effects of forest succession on the distribution of amphibians and reptiles (D. Crosswhite, Oklahoma State University, pers. comm.). A landscape-level study used satellite imagery to classify habitats from which different size study plots were chosen. The study plots are being censused to determine amphibian and reptile community composition. These data will be used to compare amphibian population diversity in different size patches and to determine if certain patches have higher value than others for amphibians. Geographic Information System (GIS) methods are being tested as a technique to make predictions about species composition on forest patches. The results of these studies will be used in preparing a management plan for the Ouachita National Forest in 1997 or 1998. This plan will encompass management for imperiled amphibians as well as other rare vertebrates (R. Perry, U.S. Forest Service, pers. comm.).

The U.S. Department of the Army, Corps of Engineers is planning a study at Haines Island Park in Alabama on the federally threatened Red Hills salamander (*Phaeognathus hubrichti*) (B. Peck, COE, pers. comm.). The study will focus on the development of a management plan to promote the recovery of the Red Hills salamander. An additional study at the site, initiated in 1995 and funded by the U.S. Fish and Wildlife Service, is testing the feasibility of using implanted passive integrated transponder (PIT) tags to monitor salamanders. This technique shows promise for use in mark and recapture studies and as a method to study burrow use by the animals. Data from this study will be valuable in determining management strategies for the Red Hills salamander.

Amphibian Management on Private and State Lands

While most amphibian management has been the result of forest management on public lands, some management has been directed at imperiled amphibians on private lands. Principles of conservation biology have rarely been used as guidance for private land-use planners. However, some private landowners are beginning to incorporate ecological principles into economic land-use decisions. O'Connell and Noss (1992) outlined ecological criteria for use in developing appropriate management plans and general methods for monitoring the effectiveness of those programs. Private land management plans that have accommodated both land-use objectives and the needs of rare species often use mitigation, restoration, and compensation to meet these goals. Projects directed at protection or enhancement of imperiled amphibian populations on private lands have been undertaken by the International Paper Timberlands Operating Company, Ltd. in Alabama; The Nature Conservancy in North Carolina; the National Council of the Paper Industry for Air and Stream Improvement, Inc. in Alabama, Florida, and Georgia; and a development company in Florida.

The International Paper Timberlands Operating Company, Ltd. (IPTOC) has developed a Habitat Conservation Plan (HCP) for the federally threatened Red Hills salamander in Conecuh and Monroe counties in Alabama (International Paper Timberlands Operating Company, Ltd., 1993). The plan was developed in cooperation with the U.S. Fish and Wildlife Service as part of an application for an incidental take permit under Section 10 of the ESA. The ESA defines the term "take" as meaning to harass, harm, pursue, hunt, shoot, wound, kill, trap, capture, collect, or to attempt to engage in any such conduct. Section 10 of the ESA allows issuance of permits if a taking is incidental to, and not the purpose of, the carrying out of an otherwise lawful activity. The underlying philosophy of an HCP is that resource management on private lands (e.g., silviculture) and endangered species management objectives can be integrated for the benefit of both. The cost for developing the IPTOC plan was between 50,000 and 75,000 dollars, and included costs for species surveys, plan preparation, and training of field personnel (J. McGlincy, IPTOC, pers. comm.).

The primary form of incidental take under the aforementioned Section 10 permit is habitat modification resulting from timber harvesting activities. To address this issue, results of habitat and population surveys were used to classify Red Hills salamander habitat as optimal, suboptimal, or marginal. The HCP includes provisions to minimize take by only allowing forest management activities in marginal salamander habitat and to avoid and mitigate the impacts of take by establishing high-value habitat areas totaling 4,500 acres (about 1,821 ha) where no timber harvesting will occur. These habitats represent 92 percent of all occupied Red Hills salamander habitat on IPTOC lands. In forested buffer zones, adjacent to the areas where no harvest will occur, timber harvesting may occur, but a 50 percent canopy cover will be maintained. The plan includes methods for ongoing habitat and species monitoring and procedures for implementing contingency plans and amending the HCP. The permit allows incidental take for a 30-year period, with a comprehensive review conducted every ten years.

The North Carolina field office of The Nature Conservancy, in cooperation with the North Carolina Herpetological Society and the North Carolina State Museum of Natural Sciences (NCSMNS), has worked to improve breeding habitat for the Carolina gopher frog on properties they manage in the state. The imperiled Carolina gopher frog is listed as a species of special concern in North Carolina. The project involved altering the hydrology of one pond and it required creating two ponds on TNC properties, and creating one pond on North Carolina Department of Agriculture property (A. Braswell, NCSMNS, pers. comm.). The five-year project was directed by the NCSMNS and funded by the U.S. Fish and Wildlife Service at a cost of approximately 10,000 dollars.

The existing pond was converted from a permanent pond to a temporary pond by removing the resident fish and adjusting the contour to allow the pond to dry completely. The three created ponds were dug in areas of suitable habitat. They were inoculated with aquatic vegetation, a nutrient source, and gopher frog tadpoles from local populations.

Metamorphic frogs were observed leaving two of the created ponds, but thus far, no adults have returned to the ponds to breed (A. Braswell, NCSMNS, pers. comm.).

Difficulties were encountered in this project when trying to establish ponds of a temporary nature. The converted fish pond remains too permanent and may require more modifications to make it shallower and to allow it to dry completely on a seasonal basis. One of the created ponds may be too ephemeral. Although no gopher frog breeding has been observed in any of the four ponds, the eastern tiger salamander (*Ambystoma tigrinum tigrinum*), listed as threatened in North Carolina, has bred in the converted pond. Many other amphibian species have also used the ponds for breeding.

The National Council of the Paper Industry for Air and Stream Improvement, Inc., a non-profit research organization associated with the forest products industry, is conducting several amphibian research projects which may provide benefits to southeastern imperiled amphibians. One of these projects involves studies on the effects of various timber practices on amphibians and wetlands at a site in Alachua County in Florida. Imperiled amphibians are not specifically targeted in this project; however, researchers hope the results of the study will provide a means to integrate the needs of sustainable industrial forestry with those of maintaining biodiversity (B. Wigley, NCASI, pers. comm.).

A second research project, funded by participating American Forest and Paper Association member timber companies and conducted by NCASI, targets three imperiled longleaf pine endemics, the gopher frog, the striped newt, and the flatwoods salamander, on lands owned or managed by the timber companies. Potential breeding sites for these three species are being surveyed within selected counties of Alabama, Georgia, and Florida. The three-year project was initiated in 1995. Once the surveys are completed, it is hoped that the distribution data from the study will be used by the timber companies to develop resource management plans that protect these three species.

In Lake and Sumter counties in Florida, the development plan for a 3,200 acre (about 1,295 ha) residential area, The Villages of Lake Sumter, included on-site protection for the Florida gopher frog. The protection was achieved through mitigation and compensation resulting from the Development of Regional Impact (DRI) review process required by the state of Florida for large scale development projects (R. McCann, Florida Game and Fresh Water Fish Commission, pers. comm.). Within the development, a 126.2 acre (about 51 ha) preserve was created to protect a number of vertebrate species including the gopher tortoise, the burrowing owl, and the southeastern kestrel. Part of the preserve (33.2 acres or about 13.4 ha), including a 0.25 acre (about 0.1 ha) sinkhole pond breeding site, has been set aside to protect the Florida gopher frog. Habitat restoration on the preserve, which was formerly part of a cattle ranch, occurred as development of the site progressed. This included exotic vegetation removal, mowing, and burning. A wildlife habitat management plan written for the preserve, as part of a conservation easement, contains restrictions on land-use in the preserve and habitat management requirements, including ones specifically addressing the gopher frog. The Florida Game and Fresh Water Fish Commission (FGFWFC) holds the conservation easement on the property which gives the FGFWFC interest in the title. The development company must adhere to the management plan as outlined in the easement. Management activities are intended to be financially supported in perpetuity through a homeowners' association fee. Parts of the management plan addressing the gopher frog include monitoring the water quality and hydrology of the gopher frog breeding pond, protecting the pond from residential and golf course drainage, monitoring frog activity at the breeding pond, managing the upland areas used by the gopher frog with prescribed burning, and providing information to the public on the frog and the importance of protecting its habitat (R. Ashton, Applied Technology and Management, Inc., pers. comm.).

FUTURE OF AMPHIBIAN MANAGEMENT IN THE SOUTHEAST

In the future, successful management of amphibian resources in the Southeast will require a coordinated effort between land managers on both public and private lands. Fortunately, there is a growing awareness within federal and state agencies and private organizations about the importance of protecting our native amphibian fauna. The development of quality management plans will require the expertise of herpetologists, the skill of resource managers, the support of public citizens, and the creativity and cooperation of all parties involved.

Ideally, the development of most amphibian management plans should begin with an inventory and threat assessment of the amphibian community of concern. High priority species and habitats, as well as research needs should be identified during this inventory and threat assessment. Site-specific, single-species or ecosystem conservation strategies must be based on the threats to these species and habitats and should consider changes in species distributions and population status. Resource management plans should include criteria to determine effectiveness and measures of progress, as well as provisions to allow for modifications as new management information becomes available. Once a plan has been formulated, funding should be provided at a level sufficient to fully implement the management plan and to complete long-term monitoring studies.

Determining the distribution of imperiled amphibians and the threats they face can be difficult and time consuming. State non-game and heritage programs, The Nature Conservancy, the U.S. Fish and Wildlife Service, and interested herpetologists have begun surveys to determine the distribution and status of many imperiled amphibians in the Southeast. Additional data on amphibian status and distribution can be found by searching museum records and by gathering anecdotal information from experienced herpetologists. The Declining Amphibian Populations Task Force of the International Union for the Conservation of Nature/Species Survival Commission (IUCN/SSC) has developed a database called FROGLOG to summarize available information. Data from all of these sources have been used to prioritize species and communities that are imperiled (Natural Heritage Data Center Network, 1993). More rigorous methodologies, such as that developed by Millsap et al. (1990) in Florida, are needed for assessing priorities for research and monitoring based on species imperilment.

The difficulty in assessing priorities becomes apparent when looking at the literature published on the status of amphibian populations in the Southeast. There is a growing body of work documenting population declines on sites where habitats have been degraded or destroyed (Vickers et al., 1985; Enge and Marion, 1986; Ash, 1988; Dodd, 1991; Raymond and Hardy, 1991; Petranka et al., 1993; Phelps and Lancia, 1995; Means et al., 1996). The long-term effects of these declines to the species involved are unclear (Ash and Bruce, 1994). Clearly, when the habitat of a given population is destroyed, that population has gone or will shortly go extinct. Many species may be unable to recolonize areas after local extinctions, especially when unsuitable habitat exists between the extinct population and extant populations. In cases where the habitat is degraded but population stability is documented, the stability may simply reflect the persistence of long-lived individuals (Blaustein et al., 1994). On the other hand, several long-term studies have demonstrated that wide fluctuations in population numbers may be characteristic of amphibians (Pechmann et al., 1991; Hairston and Wiley, 1993). Also, many amphibians can survive prolonged drought or lack of food, and they may persist for long periods if the essential aspects of their habitat can be protected (Scott and Seigel, 1992). Long-term population studies, for at least one complete generation turnover of the monitored population, will be needed to determine the significance of declines and to critically assess the imperilment of many southeastern amphibians (Franklin, 1989; Blaustein et al., 1994). In the case of some amphibians, these studies may need to be extended to 15 or more years.

Other research needs will become evident after inventories and threat assessments are completed. Herpetologists from the public and private sectors need to become actively involved in studies that involve resource management of imperiled amphibians. Data are needed for use in the development of population and habitat viability models. For example, habitat requirements (both adult and larval), spatial use, and population structure are relatively unknown for many species. Research is also needed on the taxonomy and ecology of imperiled amphibians. Groups such as the plethodontids, *Necturus* spp., *Pseudobranchus* spp., and the ranid complexes may contain more species than presently described. Virtually nothing is known of the genetic diversity of rare amphibian populations (Stiven and Bruce, 1988). Without basic information about a species' biology, conservation programs will be based on assumptions that may not ensure the protection of amphibian populations (see Scott and Seigel, 1992; Underwood, 1995). The best available scientific information is needed to develop sound conservation strategies. This information should be continually updated to identify and investigate new management techniques and to critically assess the value of current conservation activities.

Species with specialized habitats or very limited distributions, such as the Red Hills salamander or the Fourche and Caddo mountain salamanders discussed above, can be protected by developing site specific management plans with a narrow focus. Other wide-ranging species may occur in multiple states and will require a management plan directed at ecosystem or watershed protection. The following discussion outlines management plan development for three areas which could improve conservation of a large portion (30 of 46 species) of the imperiled amphibians in the Southeast, namely, the southern Appalachian Mountains, the Mobile River Basin, and the longleaf pine forest ecosystem. A watershed management approach can be used to develop a conservation plan for both the southern Appalachian Mountains and the Mobile River Basin. A plan developed for the forests of the longleaf pine ecosystem will involve land-use management across watersheds, as well as wetlands management within geographically separated forests.

Southern Appalachian Mountains

The southern Appalachian region encompasses portions of Alabama, Georgia, Kentucky, North and South Carolina, and Tennessee. The imperiled amphibian fauna in this region, within the Blue Ridge and Ridge and Valley physiographic provinces, includes one frog and 19 salamanders (see Table 3). The frog is the mountain chorus frog and the salamanders are species within six genera of the family Plethodontidae. Eight of the salamanders are endemic to the southern Appalachian Mountains. These 20 amphibians inhabit areas adjacent to or in association with high-gradient streams. The streams are the headwaters of many major river systems, and the water originating from these watersheds is an important resource for major metropolitan areas (Wallace et al., 1992). Since rivers are open, directional systems, protection of any segment requires protection of the entire upstream network along with the surrounding landscape (Sedell et al., 1990). Within the southern Appalachian Mountains, watershed impacts occur as a result of forestry and surface mining activities, and industrial, agricultural, and municipal waste-water inputs.

A management plan for imperiled amphibians in watersheds throughout the Southern Appalachian Mountains should begin with a forest management plan. Aquatic amphibians and terrestrial species with aquatic larval stages are sensitive to degraded stream and wetland quality. Completely terrestrial southern Appalachian salamanders are sensitive to modifications in prevailing temperature, humidity, or soil moisture because adults lack lungs and gas exchange must occur through moist skin (Duellman and Trueb, 1986). Clearcutting and large-scale canopy removal can have negative effects on the quality of both aquatic and terrestrial habitats. Vegetation removal increases stream flow and water temperatures and reduces the input of coarse woody debris and other organic matter after cutting. Reductions in the quality of aquatic habitats can also occur through sedimentation. Loss of soil stability and sedimentation results from logging and associated practices such as road building (Anderson et al., 1976). In addition, where the forest has been removed, streams are decoupled from self-regulatory mechanisms within the watershed and they become more hydrologically unstable (Sedell et al., 1990). The quality of terrestrial habitats is reduced when canopy removal eliminates shading and increases temperatures and moisture loss at the soil surface.

Habitat destruction and degradation resulting from timbering operations may create problems for long-term survival of imperiled amphibians (Kramer et al., 1993; Petranka et al., 1993). Several studies in the southern Appalachian Mountains have demonstrated declines in salamander numbers after clearcutting (Ash, 1988; Petranka et al., 1993; Ash, 1994). Petranka et al. (1993) found that numbers of salamanders on study plots in the Pisgah National Forest in North Carolina were five times higher in mature forest stands than in clearcuts. Species richness also was higher in the mature stands. Clearcuts contained, on average, about 50 percent of the species found in mature forest sites. Ash (1988, 1994) studied a site in Nantahala National Forest near Highlands, North Carolina, for over 15 years. Salamanders were surveyed on two clearcut and two control plots. Numbers of Jordan's salamanders (*Plethodon jordani*) collected on clearcut plots ranged from 40 percent of the number on forested plots during the first summer after cutting to zero the fourth summer. By the sixth year after cutting, salamanders had returned to clearcut plots and by the fifteenth year, salamander numbers exceeded 50 percent of those found on forested plots.

Additional threats to imperiled amphibians can occur through impacts to the watershed resulting from surface mining and associated acid mine drainage, industrial and municipal wastes, and acid precipitation (Wallace et al., 1992). Numerous conflicts exist between commercial and other economic interests, private citizens, and the federal government over land and stream use in the southern Appalachian Mountains. Watershed protection in this sensitive area will require compromise and cooperation between these groups. There are strong, vested economic considerations in continuing practices that contribute to environmental degradation. In many cases, adequate knowledge exists to sharply curtail much of the stream degradation; however, it has been difficult to transfer technology from researchers to those engaged in forestry, agriculture, and development (Wallace et al., 1992). Public education is needed to provide alternatives to harmful practices and to demonstrate the long-term benefits of quality water resources. Public involvement at the local level is imperative. Cooperation is needed between the private sector and government agencies to share responsibility for both water quality degradation and improvement. Adequate laws must be enacted to protect water quality. In addition to regulation, government could support water quality improvement practices undertaken by the private sector through tax breaks or other economic incentives.

To protect imperiled amphibians in the Blue Ridge and Ridge and Valley physiographic provinces of the southern Appalachian Mountains, a region-wide conservation plan is needed. Core areas within the region, and connecting linkages or corridors of habitat for exchange of individuals and their genes, should be defined for each species (Mitchell, 1994; Dupuis et al., 1995). Streamside management zones may act as refugia and centers of dispersal on sites where timber has been harvested (Foley, 1994). Recommendations to preserve cool, moist habitats within harvested areas include maintaining logs and snags as moist microhabitats and retaining some understory as a source of shade (Dupuis et al., 1995). The core areas should be protected from further degradation by the maintenance of natural riparian and hardwood forest areas and reduction of fragmentation, isolation, and edge effects (Mitchell, 1994). A plan of this scope will also require public education on the importance of conservation efforts to protect the habitat and its imperiled species.

The U.S. Fish and Wildlife Service (1995) has completed an ecosystem management plan of this scope for the Southern Appalachian Ecosystem (SAE). Many of the components described above have been incorporated into the plan. The purpose of the plan is to outline goals, objectives, and strategies to protect and restore U.S. Fish and Wildlife Service (USFWS) trust resources and ecological integrity within the SAE. A number of initiatives are described in the plan which, if implemented, would benefit imperiled amphibians. These include strategies for projects on aquatic systems, riparian restoration, declining amphibian populations, education and outreach, and wetland restoration. The USFWS is just one of many partners whom share responsibility for ecosystem health. Additional partners include other federal agencies (e.g., U.S. Forest Service, U.S. National Park Service), state and local agencies, communities, organizations, and corporate and other private landowners. The four major goals and objectives in the SAE plan are as follows:

1) Protect, restore, and enhance habitats and essential processes necessary to maintain healthy biological diversity in SAE. The objective is to reverse the decline of communities and species groups most "at risk" through an inventory and assessment of threats, then initiate the development and implementation of protection, management, and monitoring strategies for high priority species and habitats.

2) Promote and support compatible and sustainable uses of ecosystem resources. The objective is to reduce the overuse and/or exploitation of biological and cultural resources and emphasize cooperation through partnerships to develop strategies to increase compliance with federal and state regulations.

3) Increase public knowledge and support for ecosystem resources and their management. The objective is to promote stewardship of ecosystem resources, emphasizing cooperation built via partnerships.

4) Increase the coordination and cooperation among agencies and organizations. The objective is to enhance the effective and efficient management of our shared natural resources.

Mobile River Basin

The Mobile Basin includes the Mobile, Tombigbee-Black Warrior, and Alabama-Coosa-Tallapossa river systems. Total drainage area prior to the construction of the Tennessee Tombigbee Waterway included more than half of the state of Alabama and portions of Georgia, Mississippi, and Tennessee (Livingston, 1992). Two imperiled amphibians occur in this drainage, the Black Warrior waterdog (*Necturus* sp.), and the one-toed amphiuma (*Amphiuma pholeter*). Water quality and the habitat of these two aquatic species have been degraded in the Mobile River Basin due to impoundment; channelization; dredging; coal, sand, and gravel mining; industrial and municipal discharge; and nonpoint discharge and run-off. All streams surveyed by Bailey (1992, 1995) for the waterdog, which occurs in the Black Warrior River system, showed some degree of degradation from sedimentation, and many appeared to be biologically depauperate. Bailey (1995) felt that surface mining was probably the greatest threat to the integrity of waterdog habitat, and that prospects for the long-term survival of the species were poor unless conditions in the watershed improved.

The Mobile River Basin ecosystem has been severely degraded. As a result, at least 18 species of mussels and 32 species of aquatic snails are presumed to have gone extinct, mostly within the past few decades. The Jackson, Mississippi field office of the U.S. Fish and Wildlife Service has initiated development of a recovery plan draft to address water quality improvement measures for the benefit of all federally listed aquatic flora and fauna in the Mobile River Basin. There are currently 32 aquatic animal and plant species in the basin that are listed under the ESA (U.S. Fish and Wildlife Service, 1994a). The primary objective of the plan under development is to protect the Basin's aquatic flora and fauna by achieving ecosystem stabilization. Actions presented in the draft plan to achieve this objective include the following:

1) Protection of habitat integrity and water quality by full and appropriate implementation of federal and state regulations.
2) Development and implementation of Best Management Practices and Water Quality Plans for construction, agriculture, urban, and suburban activities that affect aquatic ecosystems.
3) Development and implementation of Watershed Management Plans that address problems specific to watersheds occupied by listed species.
4) Development, funding, and implementation of programs that educate and directly involve the general public in ecosystem recovery.
5) Basic research on life history, ecology, anatomy, taxonomy, contaminant sensitivities, and propagation of listed and candidate species.
6) Reintroduction of listed and endemic species into restored habitats, as appropriate.
7) Monitoring of listed species populations.
8) Coordination of ecosystem and species recovery efforts.

Many of the needs and objectives of the Mobile River Basin Draft Recovery Plan are similar to those previously discussed for the southern Appalachian Mountains, including stressing the need for public education and cooperation between government agencies and the private sector. Improvements in water quality have been made in the Mobile River Basin, in part due to government regulation. These regulations alone, however, can't provide adequate protection to the imperiled species of the Mobile River Basin. It has become obvious that the public will have to become directly involved if the flora and fauna of the Basin, including its imperiled amphibians, are to be protected. Government agencies can provide support through conservation agreements, on-site guidance and assistance, and funds for stream protection and restoration. Water quality problems can be addressed through federal government funded research and the development of alternative practices.

In addition to this cooperation, both private and public entities need to formulate strategies to improve water quality through local actions. Individuals and organizations will need to enlist support for programs at the local level and to encourage individual- and community-based responsibility for the protection of water resources. Organizations already in existence, such as The Nature Conservancy, Alabama Natural Heritage Program, River Watch, Adopt-a-Stream, and others, could take the lead in encouraging public involvement. Government sponsored projects such as the construction of impoundments, channelization, and dredging should require assessments of need and alternatives, and economic analyses including assessments of costs associated with environmental impacts. Federal agencies such as the COE and the EPA need to fulfill their obligations to maintain and improve water quality within the Basin.

Conservation and management strategies focused on imperiled amphibians should prioritize streams within the Mobile River Basin based on occurrences of rare fauna and potential for restoration. Drainage Management Plans could then be designed to implement stream restoration and species specific management. State and federal regulatory agencies should be encouraged to enforce current water quality and mining regulations within these drainages. Through a cooperative effort between the public and private sector, Best Management Practices should be developed to address nonpoint discharge and run-off within an ecosystem context.

Longleaf Pine Forest Ecosystem

The longleaf pine forest ecosystem was once the predominant vegetative community of the southeastern Coastal Plain and stretched from Virginia to Texas (Means, 1988). Longleaf pine communities in pre-settlement times covered 60-80 million acres (roughly 24.3-32.4 million ha), over 60 percent of the upland area of the coastal plain (Croker, 1979; Ware et al., 1993). Today these communities cover less than 2 percent of their original distribution (Ware et al., 1993). The original longleaf pine stands ranged across a wide spectrum of environmental conditions from wet, poorly drained flatwoods to well-drained high pine or dry sandhills (Boyce and Martin, 1993). Urban development and conversion to agriculture have eliminated large portions of this ecosystem. Wetlands, integrated within the longleaf pine ecosystem, have been lost through ditching, draining, filling, and lowering of the water table. Intensive forestry has changed the once open longleaf pine stands to dense loblolly and slash pine plantations and second-growth hardwoods. Most of the longleaf pine ecosystem that remains is second-growth and degraded by logging, turpentining, grazing, intensive site preparation, and fire suppression (Noss, 1988).

The gopher frog, the striped newt, the flatwoods salamander, and two subspecies of dwarf siren (*Pseudobranchus striatus*) are imperiled amphibians endemic to longleaf pine forests. An additional five imperiled amphibians, three salamander species and two frog species, would also benefit from protection of the longleaf pine habitat (Table 4).

Habitat changes in the longleaf pine ecosystem could have significant impacts on the distribution and abundance of imperiled amphibians. Grant et al. (1994) compared amphibian communities on even-aged pine plantations in South Carolina in four age-classes (one, three, eight, and 26 years). First-year pine plantations had the lowest species richness and the 26-year-old plantations had the highest. Enge and Marion (1986) examined the effects of clearcutting and site preparation on amphibian community dynamics in pine flatwoods forest in Florida. Clearcutting decreased reproductive success, reducing species abundance by a factor of ten. Means and Moler (1979) studied the imperiled Pine Barrens treefrog (*Hyla andersonii*) in seepage bogs in the Florida panhandle. They found that the seepage habitat could be destroyed by woody shrub succession resulting from fire suppression. Another study in Florida implicated the conversion of longleaf pine savannas to bedded slash pine plantations in the decline of a local flatwoods salamander population (Means et al., 1996). In a few cases, however, forestry practices such as clearcutting may mimic some natural processes. Campbell and Christman (1982) suggested that these techniques may substitute for the hot, lightning-ignited crown fires to which sand pine stands are adapted. Researchers studying amphibian populations within the longleaf pine ecosystem need to become familiar with current and past forest management practices (site preparation, regeneration method, rotation time, etc.) in different longleaf pine habitats (deMaynadier and Hunter, 1995). Studies can then be conducted to isolate and evaluate the impacts of various practices on imperiled amphibians and to provide information to land managers for use in development of resource management plans.

At present, imperiled amphibians are benefiting from protection afforded other species with which they share their terrestrial habitat (e.g., the federally threatened gopher tortoise and eastern indigo snake, and the endangered red-cockaded woodpecker). Maintenance of longleaf pine habitat for amphibians will also require wetlands conservation. The imperiled dwarf sirens are totally aquatic. The other imperiled longleaf pine species, except for the pine barrens tree frog, require temporary ponds in which to breed. The ponds required by these species are typically devoid of large predaceous fish and dry completely on a cyclic basis, generally during the summer months (Moler and Franz, 1987; LaClaire and Franz, 1991). These temporary ponds are very sensitive to changes in hydrology (LaClaire, 1992). In order to protect these sites, the practice of using the pond basins as recipient sites for road run-off or for slash disposal during timbering operations should be terminated. Bedding, ditching, and harvesting of hardwoods in pond basins should be curtailed whenever possible to maintain pond function (Vickers et al., 1985; Dodd and LaClaire, 1995). The hydrology of the area surrounding these ponds should not be altered, or the capacity of the basin to hold water may be compromised. In addition, fires should be allowed to burn completely across dry pond basins in order to maintain the wetland plant community necessary for nutrient cycling and amphibian egg attachment and larval development (LaClaire, 1995).

Most of the remaining acres of longleaf pine habitat are on private lands and are rapidly being converted to slash and loblolly pine or developed for residential or industrial use (Means and Grow, 1985). Efforts are being made by the U.S. Fish and Wildlife Service to assist the private timber industry in the formation of Habitat Conservation Plans which will allow for the needs of industrial forestry and for conservation of endangered species

Table 4. Imperiled amphibian fauna of the longleaf pine ecosystem. All = endemic, Part = part of range within longleaf pine ecosystem.

Taxon	All	Part
SALAMANDERS		
Ambystomatidae		
Ambystoma cingulatum, flatwoods salamander	X	
A. talpoideum, mole salamander		X
A. tigrinum tigrinum, tiger salamander		X
Salmandridae		
Notophthalmus perstriatus, striped newt	X	
Sirenidae		
Pseudobranchus striatus spheniscus, slender dwarf siren	X	
P. s. striatus, broad-striped dwarf siren	X	
FROGS		
Hylidae		
Hyla andersonii, Pine Barrens treefrog		X
H. gratiosa, barking treefrog		X
Ranidae		
Rana capito, gopher frog	X	

on industry lands. Public education programs are also underway in several states to demonstrate the benefits of planting and managing for longleaf pine to the small private landowner.

Primary obligation for protection of longleaf pine communities in public ownership rests with the U.S. Forest Service and the U.S. Department of Defense. The national forests of the Southeast contain about 700,000 acres (some 283,290 ha) of longleaf pine, representing one percent of the original longleaf pine community (Means and Grow, 1985). The DOD also has considerable acreage of longleaf pine habitat. For example, Eglin Air Force Base has 400,641 forested acres (about 162,140 ha) of which 81 percent are, or were historically, longleaf pine dominated sandhill communities (Department of Defense, 1993). The U.S. Forest Service and the DOD have re-oriented resource management programs toward an ecosystem-based approach.

To benefit imperiled amphibians, a longleaf pine ecosystem plan should include strategies for the following: re-establishing longleaf pine on appropriate sites; single tree selection timber harvesting to retain soil moisture; reducing soil disturbance during site preparation; maintaining the existing hydrology of temporary pond breeding sites; protecting streamside management zones; retaining downed logs, stumps, and snags as microhabitats; and using summer controlled burning (Means and Grow, 1985; Means, 1988; LaClaire, 1992; Dodd and LaClaire, 1995; Dupuis et al., 1995).

A region-wide plan is needed to protect the remaining longleaf pine ecosystem. A recent meeting hosted in 1994 by the U.S. Forest Service brought together a group of resource managers and researchers working in longleaf pine communities. This meeting highlighted the importance of a group effort to address protection and management of the remaining longleaf pine ecosystem. Development and coordination of a plan could be organized by working groups in each state. The working groups could then network with The Nature

Conservancy, the U.S. Forest Service, the U.S. Fish and Wildlife Service, state heritage programs, other state and federal agencies, and private timber companies which have an interest in the status of longleaf pine communities and rare and endangered species.

CONCLUSIONS

There are 46 species of imperiled amphibians in the southeastern United States. Historically, resource management on public and private lands has not targeted amphibians, and their protection has been incidental to management for other resources. Recently, however, more emphasis has been placed on managing habitats and ecosystems which include imperiled amphibians.

There are many state and federal agencies and private conservation organizations that need to work together to implement resource management plans to conserve imperiled amphibians. Amphibian management in the Southeast will require status assessments, research, ecosystem management strategies (including long-term monitoring plans), and public participation to protect imperiled southeastern amphibians. Public involvement is crucial. Without the commitment of private landowners to conservation, amphibian management efforts can realize only minimal success. Legislation and regulations, no matter how worthwhile, will be effective only when the public perceives the good associated with them.

Most land available to imperiled amphibians in the Southeast is in private ownership. For example, timber companies own millions of acres that are often the only undeveloped sites large enough to maintain viable populations of amphibians and other wildlife. Increased efforts are needed to encourage conservation through mutual cooperation between the public and private sectors. As federal agencies, such as the U.S. Forest Service, the U.S. Fish and Wildlife Service, and others, shift from resource management to ecosystem management, rich opportunities for effective partnerships should develop. If these partnerships are nourished, they will provide tremendous opportunities to grow broad-based conservation support for imperiled amphibians as well as other plants and animals.

REFERENCES

Anderson, H. W., M. D. Hoover, and K. G. Reinhart. 1976. Forests and water: Effects of forest management on floods, sedimentation and water supply. General Technical Report PSW-GTR-18, Pacific Southwest Forest and Range Experiment Station, Forest Service, U.S. Department of Agriculture, Berkeley, CA, 118 p.

Ash, A. N. 1988. Disappearance of salamanders from clearcut plots. *Journal of the Elisha Mitchell Science Society* **104**:116-122.

Ash, A. N. 1994. Disappearance and return of salamanders to clearcut plots in the southern Blue Ridge Mountains. In *Proceedings of the Fifth Annual Southern Appalachian Man and the Biosphere Conference*. (Abstracts). Hendersonville, NC, p. 13.

Ash, A. N., and R. C. Bruce. 1994. Impacts of timber harvesting on salamanders. *Conservation Biology* **8**:300-301.

Bailey, M. A. 1992. Black Warrior waterdog status survey: Final report 1991-92. Unpublished Report submitted to the U.S. Fish and Wildlife Service, Atlanta, GA, 27 p.

Bailey, M. A. 1995. Black Warrior waterdog survey, 1994-95. Unpublished Report submitted to the U.S. Fish and Wildlife Service, Atlanta, GA, 27 p.

Blaustein, A. R., and D. B. Wake. 1990. Declining amphibian populations: A global phenomenon? *Trends in Ecology and Evolution* 5:203-204.

Blaustein, A. R., D. B. Wake, and W. P. Sousa. 1994. Amphibian declines: Judging stability, persistence, and susceptibility of populations to local and global extinctions. *Conservation Biology* 8:60-71.

Blumm, M. C., and D. B. Zaleha. 1989. Federal wetlands protection under the Clean Water Act: Regulatory ambivalence, intergovernmental tension, and a call for reform. *University of Colorado Law Review* 60:695-772.

Bookhout, T. A. (ed.). 1994. *Research and Management Techniques for Wildlife and Habitat, 5th Edition.* The Wildlife Society, Bethesda, MD.

Boyce, S. G., and W. H. Martin. 1993. The future of the terrestrial communities of the southeastern United States. In *Biodiversity of the Southeastern United States: Upland Terrestrial Communities.* W. H. Martin, S. G. Boyce, and A. D. Echternacht (eds.). John Wiley and Sons, Inc., New York, NY, p. 339-366.

Campbell, H. W., and S. P. Christman. 1982. The herpetological components of Florida sandhill and sand pine scrub association. In *Herpetological Communities.* N. J. Scott, Jr. (ed.). Wildlife Research Report 13, Fish and Wildlife Service, U.S. Department of the Interior, Washington, D.C., p. 163-171.

Clark, T. W., R. P. Reading, and A. L. Clarke. 1994. *Endangered Species Recovery: Finding the Lessons, Improving the Process.* Island Press, Washington, D.C.

Conant, R., and J. T. Collins. 1991. *A Field Guide to Reptiles and Amphibians of Eastern and Central North America.* Houghton Mifflin Company, Boston, MA.

Corn, P. S., and R. B. Bury. 1990. Sampling methods for terrestrial amphibians and reptiles. General Technical Report PNW-GTR-256, Forest Service, U.S. Department of Agriculture, Portland, OR, 34 p.

Croker, T. C., Jr. 1979. The longleaf pine story. *Journal of Forestry History* 1979 (January):32-43.

deMaynadier, P. G., and M. L. Hunter. 1995. The relationship between forest management and amphibian ecology: A review of the North American literature. *Environmental Review* 3:230-261.

Department of Defense. 1993. Natural resources management plan, Eglin Air Force Base. U.S. Department of the Air Force, Eglin Air Force Base, FL, 235 p.

Dodd, C. K., Jr. 1991. The status of the Red Hills salamander *Phaeognathus hubrichti*, Alabama, USA, 1976-1988. *Biological Conservation* 55:57-75.

Dodd, C. K., Jr. 1993. Strategies for snake conservation. In *Snakes: Ecology and Behavior.* R. A. Seigel, and J. T. Collins (eds.). McGraw-Hill, Inc., New York, NY, p. 363-393.

Dodd, C. K., Jr., and B. G. Charest. 1988. The herpetological community of temporary ponds in north Florida sandhills: Species composition, temporal use, and management implications. In *Management of Amphibians, Reptiles, and Small Mammals in North America.* R. E. Szaro, K. E. Severson, and D. R. Patton (eds.). General Technical Report RM-166, Forest Service, U.S. Department of Agriculture, Fort Collins, CO, p. 87-97.

Dodd, C. K., Jr., and L. V. LaClaire. 1995. Biogeography and status of the striped newt (*Notophthalmus perstriatus*) in Georgia, USA. *Herpetological Natural History* 3:37-46.

Doppelt, B., M. Scurlock, C. Frissell, and J. Karr. 1993. *Entering the Watershed.* Island Press, Washington, D.C.

Duellman, W. E., and L. Trueb. 1986. *Biology of Amphibians.* McGraw-Hill Book Company, New York, NY.

Dupuis, L. A., J. J. M. Smith, and F. Bunnell. 1995. Relation of terrestrial-breeding amphibian abundance to tree-stand age. *Conservation Biology* 9:645-653.

Enge, K. M., and W. R. Marion. 1986. Effects of clearcutting and site preparation on herpetofauna of a north Florida flatwoods. *Forest Ecology Management* 14:177-192.

Foley, D. H. 1994. Short-term response of herpetofauna to timber harvesting in conjunction with streamside management zones in seasonally-flooded bottomland-hardwood forests of southeast Texas. M.S. Thesis, Texas A&M University, College Station, TX.

Franklin, J. E. 1989. Importance and justification of long-term studies in ecology. In *Long-term Studies in Ecology.* G. E. Likens (ed.). Springer Publishing Company, New York, NY, p. 3-19.

Gibbons, J. W. 1988. The management of amphibians, reptiles and small mammals in North America: The need for an environmental attitude adjustment. In *Management of Amphibians, Reptiles, and Small Mammals in North America.* R. C. Szaro, K. E. Severson, and D. R. Patton (eds.). General Technical Report RM-166, Forest Service, U.S. Department of Agriculture, Fort Collins, CO, p. 4-10.

Gibbons, J. W., and R. D. Semlitsch. 1991. *Guide to the Reptiles and Amphibians of the Savannah River Site.* The University of Georgia Press, Athens, GA.

Grant, B. W., Brown, K. L., Ferguson, G. W., and J. W. Gibbons. 1994. Changes in amphibian biodiversity associated with 25 years of pine forest regeneration: Implications for biodiversity management. In *Biological Diversity: Problems and Challenges.* S. K. Majumdar, F. J. Brenner, J. E. Lovich, J. F. Schalles, and E. W. Miller (eds.). The Pennsylvania Academy of Science, Philadelphia, PA, p. 355-367.

Hairston, M. G., Sr., and R. H. Wiley. 1993. No decline in salamander (Amphibia: Caudata) populations: A twenty-year study in the southern Appalachians. *Brimleyana* 18:59-64.

Heyer, W. R., M. A. Donnelly, R. W. McDiarmid, L.-A. C. Hayek, and M. S. Foster. 1994. *Measuring and Monitoring Biological Diversity: Standard Methods for Amphibians.* Smithsonian Institution Press, Washington, D.C.

Hipes, D., and D. Jackson. 1994. Rare vertebrate survey of Camp Blanding Training Site. Florida Natural Areas Inventory and The Nature Conservancy, Tallahassee, FL, 66 p.

International Paper Timberlands Operating Company, Ltd. 1993. Red Hills salamander habitat conservation plan. U.S. Fish and Wildlife Service, Jackson, MS, 32 p.

Jones, K. B. 1986. Amphibians and reptiles. In *Inventory and Monitoring of Wildlife Habitat.* A. Y. Cooperrider, R. J. Boyd, and H. R. Stuart (eds.). Bureau of Land Management Service Center, U.S. Department of the Interior, Denver, CO, p. 267-290.

Karr, J. R. 1990. Biological integrity and the goal of environmental legislation: Lessons for conservation biology. *Conservation Biology* 4:244-250.

Kramer, P., N. Reichenbach, M. Hayslett, and P. Sattler. 1993. Population dynamics and conservation of the Peaks of Otter salamander, *Plethodon hubrichti. Journal of Herpetology* 27:431-435.

LaClaire, L. V. 1992. Ecology of temporary ponds in north-central Florida. M.S. Thesis, University of Florida, Gainesville, FL.

LaClaire, L. V. 1995. Vegetation of selected upland temporary ponds in north and north-central Florida. *Bulletin of the Florida Museum of Natural History* **38**:69-96.

LaClaire, L. V., and R. Franz. 1991. Importance of isolated wetlands in upland landscapes. In *Proceedings of the Second Annual Meeting.* M. Kelly (ed.). Florida Lake Management Society, Winter Haven, FL, p. 9-15.

Livermore, B. 1992. Amphibian alarm: Just where have all the frogs gone? *Smithsonian Magazine* 1992(October):113-120.

Livingston, R. J. 1992. Medium-sized rivers of the gulf coastal plain. In *Biodiversity of the Southeastern United States: Aquatic Communities.* C. T. Hackney, S. M. Adams, and W. H. Martin (eds.). John Wiley and Sons, New York, NY, p. 351-386.

Master, L. L. 1991. Assessing threats and setting priorities for conservation. *Conservation Biology* **5**:559-563.

Means, D. B. 1988. Management recommendations for the gopher tortoise in the longleaf pine ecosystem. In *Gopher Tortoise Habitat Management: Strategies and Options.* C. K. Dodd, Jr. (ed.). Proceedings of the Sixth Annual Meeting of the Gopher Tortoise Council, Florida Museum of Natural History, Gainesville, FL, p. 41-56.

Means, D. B., and G. Grow. 1985. The endangered longleaf pine community. ENFO Report, Environmental Information Center of the Florida Conservation Foundation, Inc., Winter Park, FL, 12 p.

Means, D. B., and P. E. Moler. 1979. The pine barrens treefrog: Fire, seepage bogs, and management implications. In *Proceedings of the Rare and Endangered Wildlife Symposium.* R. R. Odum, and L. Langers (eds.). Technical Bulletin WL-4, Game and Fish Division, Georgia Department of Natural Resources, Atlanta, GA, 77-83.

Means, D. B., J. G. Palis, and Mary Baggett. 1996. Effects of slash pine silviculture on a Florida population of flatwoods salamander. *Conservation Biology* **10**:426-437.

Millsap, B. A., J. A. Gore, D. E. Runde, and S. I. Cerulean. 1990. Setting priorities for the conservation of fish and wildlife species in Florida. *Wildlife Monographs* **111**:1-57.

Mitchell, J. C. 1994. Habitat conservation assessment for the Cow Knob salamander (*Plethodon punctatus*) in the George Washington National Forest. Report submitted to the U.S. Fish and Wildlife Service, Annapolis, MD, and the George Washington National Forest, Harrisonburg, VA, 16 p.

Moler, P. E., and R. Franz. 1987. Wildlife values of small, isolated wetlands in the Southeastern Coastal Plain. In *Proceedings of the Third Southeastern Nongame and Endangered Wildlife Symposium.* R. R. Odom, K. A. Riddleberger, and J. C. Ozier (eds.). Georgia Department of Natural Resources, Atlanta, GA, p. 234-241.

Natural Heritage Data Center Network. 1993. Perspectives on species imperilment, Revised printing. The Nature Conservancy, Arlington, VA, 40 p.

Noss, R. F. 1988. The longleaf pine landscape of the Southeast: Almost gone and almost forgotten. *Endangered Species Update* **5**:1-6.

O'Connell, M. A., and R. F. Noss. 1992. Private land management for biodiversity conservation. *Environmental Management* **16**:435-450.

Palis, J. G. 1992. Distribution of the flatwoods salamander, *Ambystoma cingulatum*, on the Apalachicola and Osceola National Forests, Florida. Unpublished Report submitted to the Florida Natural Areas Inventory, Tallahassee, FL, 19 p.

Palis, J. G. 1993. A status survey of the flatwoods salamander, *Ambystoma cingulatum*, in Florida. Unpublished Report submitted to the U.S. Fish and Wildlife Service, Jackson, MS, 36 p.

Palis, J. G. 1995a. A survey of the flatwoods salamander (*Ambystoma cingulatum*) breeding sites east of the Apalachicola River, Florida. Unpublished Report submitted to the U.S. Fish and Wildlife Service, Jackson, MS, 40 p.

Palis, J. G. 1995b. Distribution and breeding biology of the flatwoods salamander (*Ambystoma cingulatum*) and gopher frog (*Rana capito*) on Eglin Air Force Base, Florida. Florida Natural Areas Inventory, Tallahassee, FL, 46 p. + appendices.

Pechmann, J. H. K., D. E. Scott, R. D. Semlitsch, J. P. Caldwell, L. J. Vitt, and J. W. Gibbons. 1991. Declining amphibian populations: The problem of separating human impacts from natural fluctuations. *Science* 253:892-895.

Pechmann, J. H. K., and H. M. Wilbur. 1994. Putting declining amphibian populations in perspective: Natural fluctuations and human impacts. *Herpetologica* 50:65-84

Petranka, J. W., M. E. Elridge, and K. E. Haley. 1993. Effects of timber harvesting on southern Appalachian salamanders. *Conservation Biology* 7:363-370.

Phelps, J. P., and R. A. Lancia. 1995. Effects of a clearcut on the herpetofauna of a South Carolina bottomland swamp. *Brimleyana* 22:31-45.

Raymond, L. R., and L. M. Hardy. 1991. Effects of a clearcut on a population of the mole salamander, *Ambystoma talpoideum*, in an adjacent unaltered forest. *Journal of Herpetology* 25:509-512.

Schemnitz, S. D. (ed.). 1980. *Wildlife Management Techniques Manual.* The Wildlife Society, Washington, D.C.

Scott, N. J., Jr., and R. A. Seigel. 1992. The management of amphibian and reptile populations: Species priorities and methodological and theoretical constraints. In *Wildlife 2001: Populations.* D. R. McCullough, and R. H. Barrett (eds.). Elsevier Applied Science, New York, NY, p. 343-367.

Sedell, J. R., G. H. Reeves, R. R. Hauer, J. A. Stanford, and C. P. Hawkins. 1990. Role of refugia in recovery from disturbances: Modern fragmented and disconnected river systems. *Environmental Management* 14:711-724.

Seehorn, M. E. 1982. Reptiles and amphibians of southeastern national forests. Forest Service, U.S. Department of Agriculture, Atlanta, GA, 84 p.

Stiven, A. E., and R. C. Bruce. 1988. Ecological genetics of the salamander *Desmognathus quadramaculatus* from disturbed watersheds in the Southern Appalachian Biosphere Reserve Cluster. *Conservation Biology* 2:194-205.

Szaro, R. E., K. E. Severson, and D. R. Patton (eds.). 1988. *Management of Amphibians, Reptiles, and Small Mammals in North America.* General Technical Report RM-166, Forest Service, U.S. Department of Agriculture, Fort Collins, CO, 458 p.

Telford, S. 1993. Breeding sites for the gopher frog and the striped newt in the Ocala National Forest, and the discovery of a possibly undescribed species of frog apparently restricted to the forest. Unpublished Report submitted to staff at Ocala National Forest, Ocala, FL, 29 p.

The Nature Conservancy and the International Network of Natural Heritage Programs and Conservation Data Centers. 1996. Biological and conservation databases. The Nature Conservancy, Arlington, VA, 58 p.

Underwood, A. J. 1995. Ecological research and (research into) environmental management. *Ecological Applications* 5:232-247.

U.S. Fish and Wildlife Service. 1994a. Endangered and threatened wildlife and plants. 50 CFR 17.11 and 17.12. U.S. Government Printing Office, Washington, D.C., 42 p.

U.S. Fish and Wildlife Service. 1994b. Endangered and threatened wildlife and plants: Animal candidate review for listing as endangered or threatened species, proposed rule. *U.S. Federal Register* 50 CFR, Part 17, **59**(219):58982-59028.

U.S. Fish and Wildlife Service. 1995. Ecosystem management plan for the southern Appalachian ecosystem. Asheville Field Office, U.S. Fish and Wildlife Service, Asheville, NC, 15 p.

U.S. Fish and Wildlife Service. 1996. Endangered and threatened species, plant and animal taxa; proposed rule. *U.S. Federal Register* 50 CFR, Part 17, **61**(40):7596-7613.

Vial, J. L., and L. Saylor. 1993. The status of amphibian populations: A compilation and analysis. Working Document Number 1, IUCN/SSC Declining Amphibian Populations Task Force, Corvallis, OR, 98 p.

Vickers, C. R., L. D. Harris, and B. F. Swindel. 1985. Changes in herpetofauna resulting from ditching of cypress ponds in coastal plains. *Forest Ecology Management* 11:17-29.

Vitt, L. J., J. P. Caldwell, H. M. Wilbur, and D. C. Smith. 1990. Amphibians as harbingers of decay. *BioScience* **40**:418.

Wallace, J. B., J. R. Webster, and R. L. Lowe. 1992. High-gradient streams of the Appalachians. In *Biodiversity of the Southeastern United States: Aquatic Communities.* C. T. Hackney, S. M. Adams, and W. H. Martin (eds.). John Wiley and Sons, New York, NY, p. 133-192.

Ware, S., C. Frost, and P. D. Doerr. 1993. Southern mixed hardwood forest: The former longleaf pine forest. In *Biodiversity of the Southeastern United States: Lowland Terrestrial Communities.* W. H. Martin, S. G. Boyce, and A. C. Echternacht (eds.). John Wiley and Sons, New York, NY, p. 447-493.

Yoffe, E. 1992. Silence of the frogs. *New York Times Magazine* **1992**(December 13):36-39, 64, 66, 76.

CHAPTER 14

Birds of the Southeastern United States: Resource Management Programs

Robert P. Ford, Robert J. Cooper, Douglas L. Helmers,
John E. Cely, Robert M. Hatcher, Don H. Orr,
and Mark S. Woodrey

A quatic systems are critical habitats for many bird species. Open water habitats are used by waterfowl, coots, grebes, and loons; mudflats and shorelines are used by shorebirds and wading birds. Freshwater and saltwater marshes are used by wading birds, rails, and some songbirds; and bottomland forests are used by a variety of songbirds, waterfowl, raptors, and others. The southeastern United States contains significant areas regarding the management and conservation of Western Hemisphere birds. For many species, the Southeast provides an important link between boreal breeding habitats and tropical winter habitats. Some birds may occur in the Southeast only in the winter, others only during the summer, and many are permanent residents.

Of the many habitats used by birds in the Southeast, perhaps none are more important and threatened with destruction or degradation than aquatic habitats. Between 1950 and 1970, over 30 percent of the remaining wetlands in the Lower Mississippi Valley were lost (Mitsch and Gosselink, 1986). This same region has lost an average of 67,000 ha (165,554 acres) of wetlands per year (Tiner, 1984). Other extreme examples of habitat loss include North Carolina pocosins, which have declined by an average rate of 17,600 ha (43,489 acres) per year, and Louisiana coastal marshes, which have declined by an average rate of 10,000 ha (24,709 acres) per year (Tiner, 1984).

Aquatic Fauna in Peril: The Southeastern Perspective, edited by George W. Benz, and David E. Collins. 1997. Special Publication 1, Southeast Aquatic Research Institute, Lenz Design & Communications, Decatur, GA, 554 p.

It is difficult to demonstrate a direct causal relationship between declines in bird populations and any particular factor, and this is especially true for migratory species that use different and widely separated habitats. However, habitat losses such as those mentioned above have been implicated in the declines of bird populations, and the correlations between the declining abundance of many bird species and habitat loss are extremely suggestive (e.g., Robbins et al., 1986; Howe et al., 1989).

Various approaches used to address resource management concerns can be placed in two broad categories: narrowly-focused reactive programs and broad-based proactive programs. Narrowly focused management programs are usually species-specific approaches, are usually reactive, and are usually designed to facilitate crisis management of species threatened or endangered with extinction.

Broad-based programs involve a habitat-based approach to conserve species assemblages, or groups of species that share similar habitats. Similar to ecosystem management (Grumbine, 1994), these programs are often proactive and designed to halt population declines before a species, or a group of species, becomes critically endangered. Maintenance of ecosystem function is also stressed (Grumbine, 1994). Necessarily, these programs require a landscape view of conservation and require partnership development between public and private parties.

In this chapter, we discuss a number of bird management programs with narrow focus, plus three broad-based management programs that are international in scope and that target populations of migratory birds: the North American Waterfowl Management Plan, the Western Hemisphere Shorebird Reserve Network, and the Neotropical Migratory Bird Conservation Program (commonly called Partners in Flight). Each of the programs will be discussed in relation to important physiographic provinces in the Southeast, with emphasis on the Mississippi River Alluvial Valley.

SPECIES SPECIFIC MANAGEMENT PROGRAMS

The following programs are examples of vital recovery projects for threatened or endangered bird species or species whose populations are declining throughout the Southeast. The programs described do not include all of the endangered bird programs for imperiled birds of aquatic habitats. Instead, the examples provided range from highly visible and popular recovery projects (e.g., large birds of prey) to poorly funded projects that focus on species whose biology is largely unknown (e.g., rails).

Bald Eagle — *Haliaeetus leucocephalus*

Population declines of bald eagle in the Southeast from about 1945 to 1975 were principally due to reproductive failures caused by contamination by chlorinated hydrocarbon pesticides (see Mulherin et al., 1970). Throughout the region, these declines were often severe, and they reduced eagle populations to levels which ranged from 0-75 percent of historical values. The nesting status in the Southeast was summarized by Wood et al. (1988).

The following perspective for bald eagles is based largely on a Tennessee Wildlife Resources Agency questionnaire sent to state wildlife agencies in 14 states in January of 1994. The questionnaire requested information about hacking (described below) and other management programs, as well as observed nesting success. Survey results discussed here represent all 14 states, and all of these states except Maryland and Virginia occur in the Southeastern Bald Eagle Recovery Region.

At the time of the aforementioned survey, the bald eagle was listed as federally endangered in 43 of 50 states. For the Southeastern Bald Eagle Recovery Region, criteria required before a listing change to threatened status could be made were the existence of 600 or more occupied breeding areas distributed over nine of the 12 states of the Southeastern Recovery Region, the existence of an overall reproductive rate of greater than 1.5 young per successful nest, and the maintenance of these biological parameters on average over a period of at least three years (Murphy, 1984). In 1995, the U.S. Fish and Wildlife Service changed the status of the bald eagle from endangered to threatened in all 48 contiguous states (U.S. Fish and Wildlife Service, 1995a).

The hacking technique, in which young birds are removed from the nest where they were born, or from captive breeding populations, and relocated to artificial nests in historic parts of their range, has been used to successfully restore nesting populations of many raptor species (Cade and Temple, 1977). Since 1979, 614 young bald eagles have been released from hack sites in seven of 14 states surveyed (Table 1). Southeastern hacking efforts began in Georgia in 1979 (see Hammer et al., 1981). Tennessee has released 230 eagles through 1993, the most of any southeastern state. Bald eagle hacking continued in 1994 in Georgia, northern Louisiana, and Tennessee.

The large proportion of occupied nests found in close proximity to hack sites in Tennessee (see Hatcher, 1991) indicates that hacking has been successful. Furthermore, even greater nesting activity is predicted for the future since most of the eagle hack releases have been in recent years, and on the average, successful nesting does not occur until these birds reach five years of age. Tennessee's successful nests have the potential to increase from 15 in 1993 to about 42 by the year 2000. Actual increases in Tennessee and elsewhere will be governed largely by the availability of suitable habitat, the amounts of disturbance by humans, and the educational successes associated with these factors (Hatcher, 1991).

Osprey — *Pandion haliaetus*

The widely used pesticide DDT and other organochlorines were the primary cause of drastic drops in osprey productivity by the early 1970s. After the use of DDT was restricted in 1972, osprey populations stabilized and began to increase at most locations. Osprey are most common near the Chesapeake Bay and along the Atlantic and Gulf coasts of the Southeast. Large inland reservoirs also provide potential osprey habitat. Osprey currently nest in 12 southeastern states. As of this writing, osprey carry special concern or threatened status in seven states, and active hacking programs exist in several southeastern states (Table 2).

Open-topped live or dead trees are preferred natural nest sites for osprey throughout the Southeast. However, these birds are notable for their attraction to man-made structures, including navigation markers and powerline towers. Man-made nest platforms of 1 m² (about 11 square feet) and approximately 6 m (about 20 feet) above the ground have proven attractive osprey nesting locations across the country. These structures have allowed managers to provide potential nest sites in areas that lack sufficient natural ones and to relocate pairs of nesting birds away from excessive disturbances (Martin et al., 1986). The acceptance of man-made nests by ospreys also allows nest substitutions to help mitigate problems associated with nesting activity about hazardous or conflicting-use, man-made structures (Martin et al., 1986).

Table 1. Bald eagle hacking and nesting status, by state, in the southeastern United States from 1979 through 1993. Results are based on responses to a 1994 Tennessee Wildlife Resources Agency survey of state wildlife agencies.

State	Hacking No. Birds	Years	No. of Successful Nests 1982	1988	1993	1993 Ave. Fledges Per Successful Nest	Nest Recovery Goal
AL	91	1985-91	0	0	6	1.2	10
AR	unknown		0	0	9	1.7	10
FL	0		240	276	447	1.5	400[1]
GA	84	1979-93	1[2]	5	14	1.2	20
KY	0		0	0	6	2.0	5[1]
LA	30	1992-93	14[2]	24	62	1.5	40[1]
MD	0		46[2]	77	135[2]		
MO	74	1981-90	0	3	3	2.2	
MS	76	1986-92	0	1	8	1.6	10
NC	29	1983-88	0	1	3	2.0	10
SC	0		17[2]	41	63	1.6	51[1]
TN	230	1980-93	0	8	15	1.7	15[1]
VA	0		37[2]	65	100	1.8	85[2]
WV	0		0	1	2	2.0	2[1]
Total	614	1979-93	355+	502+	633+	1.5	

[1] Have reached state recovery goals, assuming approximately 75 percent of occupied nests are successful.

[2] Estimate.

In 1993, over half of Tennessee's 51 osprey nests were located on Watts Bar Lake, and of these, approximately 66 percent occurred on nesting platforms and 27 percent occurred on other man-made structures (B. Anderson, Tennessee Wildlife Resources Agency, unpubl. data). On the Kentucky portion of Land Between the Lakes, all 14 osprey nests were located on either platforms or other man-made structures (T. Evans, Tennessee Valley Authority, pers. comm.). As indicated by the aforementioned Tennessee Wildlife Resources Agency's 1994 questionnaire, Tennessee and Georgia reported that future osprey management measures will focus on the installation of nesting platforms and will include an initiative to provide technical assistance to others interested in constructing and installing platforms.

Rails

Of all North American rallids, seven are considered game species: American coot (*Fulica americana*), common moorhen (*Gallinula chloropus*), purple gallinule (*Porphyrula martinica*), king rail (*Rallus elegans*), clapper rail (*R. longirostris*), Virginia rail (*R. limicola*), and sora (*Porzana carolina*). Yellow rails (*Coturnicops noveboracensis*) and black rails (*Laterallus jamaicenses*) have not been game species since the late 1960s (Eddleman et al., 1988). Despite some efforts to perform survey work and telemetry research, notably in Florida (Runde et al., 1990) and South Carolina (Cely et al., 1993), rail management can best be characterized as underfunded and based on limited life history information (Tacha and Braun, 1994).

Eddleman et al. (1988) summarized available information on rails and identified conservation problems. Because these birds are wetland species commonly found associated

Table 2. Osprey hacking and nesting status, by state, in the southeastern United States. Results are based on responses to a 1994 Tennessee Wildlife Resources Agency survey of state wildlife agencies.

State	Conservation Status	Hacking		Number of Breeding Pairs	
		No. Birds	Years	1988	1993
AL	special concern[1]	77	1982-88	9	unknown
AR	special concern[1]	unknown		1	unknown
FL	special concern[1]	0		1750	unknown
GA		23	1987-90	105	unknown
KY		92	1981-89	0	unknown
LA	special concern[1]	0		6	unknown
MO		4	1980s	0	0
MS	special concern[1]	0		40+	unknown
NC		0		450	unknown
SC	special concern[1]	0		500	1000
TN	threatened[2]	165	1980-89	33	51
VA		0		1300	unknown
WV		126	1983-93	1	2

[1] Species of special concern in the state.

[2] Threatened species in the state.

with marshes, rails have suffered much loss of habitat. Furthermore, as most rails are migratory, habitat losses can impact these species throughout the annual cycle. Pesticides and other contaminants might also impact rails, although pollution effects on these birds are little-known at this time (Eddleman et al., 1988; Tacha and Braun, 1994).

Three rail species are the focus of this section. Black rails and yellow rails are small, secretive, rarely seen, and highly sought by birders. King rails, typically inhabitants of freshwater marshes, were fairly common permanent residents over much of their south-eastern range 30 to 50 years ago (Sprunt and Chamberlain, 1949; Ripley, 1977). However, many observers consider the species to be experiencing serious population declines in recent years (Reid et al., 1994). Eddleman et al. (1988) recently considered king rails threatened outside of Florida and Louisiana. From 1976 to 1982 the National Audubon Society's Blue List included king rails as a species suspected to be in trouble, and in 1986, king rails were listed as a species of special concern. In the Carolinas and Georgia, LeGrand (1991) reported king rails as "quite scarce" away from tidewater marshes. A recent survey of marsh birds in South Carolina, using tape-recorded playback calls, amplified the concern of declining king rail populations. Only seven king rails were found at inland coastal sites (e.g., the Atlantic Coastal Plain), and none occurred at more than 50 Piedmont sites despite the presence of suitable habitat (Cely et al., 1993).

Yellow rails are strictly winter visitors in the Southeast, a time when they are found primarily in moist coastal grasslands and marshes. Little is known of their wintering status, distribution, and habitat needs. Cursory surveys in South Carolina have documented yellow rails at a few sites in shallow-flooded Carolina bays, featuring grasses and sedges (wet depression meadows), from October through January (J. Cely, South Carolina Wildlife and Marine Resources Department, pers. obs.). However, their presence has been erratic and is apparently dependent on water levels and rainfall. The coastal prairies and high marsh of Texas and Louisiana may support the highest densities of a yellow rail wintering population.

Black rails are federal candidates for threatened or endangered listing (Category 2), and they are also migratory nongame birds of management concern (U.S. Fish and Wildlife Service, 1995b). Except during migration, the southeastern range of this secretive species is apparently confined to tidal marshes and a few inland sites (Potter et. al., 1980). Black rails have been located using tape playbacks during the nesting season in the upper reaches of shallow-flooded tidal marshes, as well as in high marshes in coastal waterfowl impoundments (Runde et al., 1990; Cely et al., 1993), but few nests have been found in the region. The wintering status of black rails in the Southeast is unclear, but they apparently occur from Florida and the Gulf Coast north to New Jersey.

Although few, if any, resource management programs specifically target rails in the Southeast, these birds partially benefit from extensive waterfowl management efforts by federal, state, and private entities. For example, the majority of marsh birds present in one survey were associated with waterfowl management areas in South Carolina (Cely et al., 1993). Rail management, with some considerations, can be compatible with most waterfowl management practices. Eddleman et al. (1988) noted that rails preferred shallower marshes with denser emergent vegetation than those typically managed for waterfowl. Flooding and de-watering regimes for waterfowl can affect rail management. To best benefit rails, flooding during fall migration should commence earlier than usual for waterfowl and continue later into the spring.

Fire can play a significant role in rail management. Prescribed marsh fires, designed to keep marshes open and remove excessive dead vegetation, can be detrimental if not enough cover for rails remains. Damp meadows, high marsh, and drier transition marsh habitats, preferred by yellow rails and black rails, are often susceptible to replacement by woody plants without periodic burning or other disturbances.

Yellow rails and black rails are among the most sought after species by ever growing numbers of bird watchers, and this fact is added justification for higher priority rail management and research efforts in the Southeast. These birds could play leading roles in Watchable Wildlife Programs and other forms of ecotourism (see Mitchell and Hatcher, 1993). For example, the marsh buggy tours for yellow rails at Anahuac National Wildlife Refuge in Texas were extremely popular with the birding public. Although marsh buggy tours were discontinued in 1987 due to impacts on marsh vegetation, a successful scaled down version has been substituted in the 1990s. Wildlife management agencies could cultivate new constituencies by developing partnerships with bird watchers that have a high interest in black rails and yellow rails. Refuges could utilize volunteer bird watchers to survey and document rail occurrences and to serve as guides.

Low cost management practices can be implemented for rails. First, to investigate the status and distribution of yellow rails in the Southeast, managers and others may consider a region-wide census of state and federal refuges using volunteers on a Yellow Rail Day in winter. Such a snapshot census could be carried out in conjunction with local Christmas Bird Counts. For black rails, a similar one-day volunteer survey could be conducted in May or June. These surveys could be coordinated through a regional U.S. Fish and Wildlife Service office and individual state wildlife agencies.

Although king rail populations may be declining more dramatically than other marsh birds, interest in this species among bird watchers is not as high as for the aforementioned rails. Therefore, to monitor king rails, managers might use a combination of professional and volunteer surveys, including assistance from waterfowl associations, hunt clubs, and groups that work in king rail habitat. Surveys should be concentrated at sites of known historical occurrence for rails, especially inland wetlands. If suitable populations can be located, detailed investigations of nesting and population ecology should be initiated.

Sandhill Crane — *Grus canadensis*

Six subspecies of sandhill crane are currently recognized, five of which occur in the United States (U. S. Fish and Wildlife Service, 1991; Tacha et al., 1994). The sixth sub-species, the endangered, nonmigratory Cuban sandhill crane (*G. c. nesiotes*) occurs in Cuba and the Isle of Pines. Of the three migratory subspecies, the greater sandhill crane (*G. c. tabida*) is commonly found wintering in the Southeast. The Florida sandhill crane (*G. c. pratensis*) and the Mississippi sandhill crane (*G. c. pulla*) are nonmigratory and nest in the southeastern United States (U. S. Fish and Wildlife Service, 1991). Both of these sandhill crane subspecies were listed as rare in 1968 by the U.S. Fish and Wildlife Service. After its recognition as a subspecies (Aldrich, 1972), the Mississippi sandhill crane was listed as an endangered species by the U.S. Fish and Wildlife Service (1973).

Currently, 115 to 120 free-ranging Mississippi sandhill cranes reside on and around the Mississippi Sandhill Crane National Wildlife Refuge in Jackson County, Mississippi. Of these, about 90 are captive reared birds released through a reintroduction program at the refuge. Prior to augmentation with captive-reared birds, wild population numbers were less than 40 individuals with no more than eight breeding pairs per year, and an average of less than five pairs (S. Hereford, U.S. Fish and Wildlife Service, pers. comm.). During the last three to four years, an average of six breeding pairs per year have nested on the refuge, and since captive-reared birds have entered the breeding population, an average of seven pairs have nested annually (S. Hereford, U.S. Fish and Wildlife Service, unpubl. data). However, chick productivity of these nesting attempts has been very low, with only two wild-reared chicks being fledged each year since 1991 (S. Hereford, U.S. Fish and Wild-life Service, pers. comm.).

Mississippi sandhill cranes nest in Lower Coastal Plain wet, pine savanna habitats. His-toric population declines of these cranes have likely been caused indirectly or directly by habitat loss and increased rates of various forms of mortality (U. S. Fish and Wildlife Service, 1991). For example, in recent history, indirect loss of savanna habitats has oc-curred via the suppression of wildfires, which has allowed the establishment of plants such as gallberry (*Ilex glabra* and *I. coriacea*). These plants make the savanna unsuitable for crane nesting. Direct loss of habitat resulted from conversion to pine plantations during the 1950s and 1960s. During this period, thousands of acres of wet savanna were drained and planted with slash pine (*Pinus elliotii*) seedlings (U. S. Fish and Wildlife Service, 1991; Tacha et al., 1994). Reports of crane shootings, particularly in the 1960s and 1970s, though sporadic, resulted in mortality rates which may have exceeded natural recruitment rates for the popula-tion. Increased natural mortality caused by predation on adults and nestlings continues to restrict crane population growth (S. Hereford, U.S. Fish and Wildlife Service, unpubl. data).

Challenges to the recovery of the Mississippi sandhill crane population are many. The recovery objective regarding this subspecies is to maintain a genetically viable, stable, self-sustaining, free-living population (U. S. Fish and Wildlife Service, 1991). Actions needed to recover the subspecies include the following: improvement of the quality and quantity of nesting habitat on or near the Mississippi Sandhill Crane National Wildlife Refuge; increasing natural recruitment in the wild population; minimizing human disturbance (especially to nesting cranes); continued restoration, improvement, and maintenance of feeding and roosting habitats; and limiting or negating contact with potential toxins (U. S. Fish and Wildlife Service, 1991). Results of a 1992 workshop on population and habitat viability assessment indicated that efforts aimed at habitat restoration, reducing mortality, and increasing reproduction are essential to the continued existence of this species (Seal and Hereford, 1994).

Least Tern — *Sterna antillarum*

Least terns are listed by the U.S. Fish and Wildlife Service as migratory nongame birds of management concern throughout the United States (U. S. Fish and Wildlife Service, 1995b). Though fairly common in coastal areas, there is moderate concern for this species throughout the Southeast. Reasons for this concern include apparent population declines and this species' use of geographically restricted coastal areas for breeding. Coastal habitats, particularly in the Southeast, are under tremendous pressure associated with land development and human disturbance (Cullitan et al., 1990). Development of coastal habitats restricts the availability of suitable least tern breeding sites and it predisposes these birds to disturbance. Human disturbance at suitable nesting areas has been documented to cause entire colonies of nesting least terns to fail.

Of more immediate concern in the Southeast is a population of least terns which nest in interior regions. The interior least tern (*S. a. athalassos*) nests in low numbers on barren sandbars (Smith and Renken, 1993) along the Mississippi, Missouri, Arkansas, Ohio, Red, Rio Grande, Platte, and other river systems in the central United States (Hardy, 1957; U. S. Fish and Wildlife Service, 1985; Sidle et al., 1988; Whitman, 1988). In 1985, the interior least tern was listed as a federally endangered subspecies throughout its range (U. S. Fish and Wildlife Service, 1985). Southern states included under the federal listing are Arkansas, Kentucky, Louisiana, Mississippi, Tennessee, and Texas. These states also list the interior least tern as endangered under state law.

Surveys conducted by the U.S. Army Corps of Engineers (e.g., Rumancik, 1993) and the Missouri Department of Conservation (Smith and Renken, 1991, 1993) found about half of the rangewide population of interior least terns, estimated by Kirsch (1992), to be 6,800 birds between Cairo, Illinois and Vicksburg, Mississippi (Sidle et al., 1988). Kirsch (1992) analyzed productivity data from studies of breeding interior least terns to estimate population trends at several geographic scales. Population trends were strongly positive for the entire population, as well as for populations in the Mississippi River drainage. Population trends for the Missouri River and Platte River drainage basins were not significantly different from zero.

Interior least terns nest from May through July. Threats to this subspecies include the loss of riverine sandbar nesting habitat because of high water during annual floods and channelization and impoundment of rivers (U. S. Fish and Wildlife Service, 1990). The federal recovery plan aims at establishing a stable population over ten years of 7,000 birds divided among five river drainage basins (U.S. Fish and Wildlife Service, 1990). Current recovery activities include ongoing investigations of population trends and habitat requirements throughout the breeding range of interior least terns, management of reservoir and river water levels when possible to benefit terns (i.e., expose sandbars when seasonally appropriate), education programs to develop public awareness, and protection of nesting areas in places where public use is high (U. S. Fish and Wildlife Service, 1990).

BROAD-BASED PROACTIVE MANAGEMENT PROGRAMS

In contrast to the species-specific programs discussed above, more proactive, broad-based management programs have in some instances been implemented prior to the point when a bird species becomes so rare that it must be protected to ensure its survival. The three programs described below represent such broad-based programs, and as such they benefit more species, are implemented over wider geographic areas, and generally seem more economical in comparison to species-specific management programs.

North American Waterfowl Management Plan

Waterfowl had been intensively managed for many years prior to the initiation of the North American Waterfowl Management Plan in 1986. Throughout the Southeast, state and federal wildlife agencies had acquired, developed, and intensively managed hundreds of refuges and management areas. In this region, management efforts have historically focused on providing wintering habitat for the dabbling duck group, which includes the mallard (*Anas platyrhynchos*) and other ducks that feed in shallow water, and breeding habitat for wood ducks (*Aix sponsa*). Canada goose (*Branta canadensis*) has been the featured species of most goose habitat management efforts. Thousands of habitat acres that are managed by private individuals and organizations are critically important to waterfowl. Treaties and laws that protect waterfowl have been enacted, and state and federal governments work together each year to implement and enforce hunting regulations designed to sustain and increase breeding populations.

While the efforts described above have been beneficial, waterfowl populations have generally declined because of the continual loss of breeding, migration, and wintering habitat in Canada and the United States. To address these declines, the North American Waterfowl Management Plan (NAWMP) was approved by Canada and the United States in 1986. This program sets waterfowl population goals and identifies the actions needed to achieve those goals. Because it was recognized that the total cost of achieving the NAWMP's goals was beyond the capability of government, the plan recommends that partnerships between public and private organizations be formed to share in the effort to restore waterfowl populations to levels of the 1970s by protecting about 2,428,200 ha (approximately 6 million acres) of priority habitat (U.S. Department of Interior and Canadian Wildlife Service, 1986).

Priority waterfowl habitat areas in the Southeast are the Lower Mississippi River Valley (LMV), the Gulf Coast, and the Middle-Upper Atlantic Coast. The LMV habitat program was initiated in 1989 with a goal to "Provide an adequate quantity, quality and distribution of migration and wintering habitat on public and private lands to ensure that the LMV Joint Venture area can support a wintering population of at least 8.6 million ducks and 1.0 million geese during the years of normal precipitation" (Lower Mississippi Valley Joint Venture Management Board, 1990; page 6).

Contributions from the private sector have been significant; the federal government contributed $16,809,789, state governments contributed $1,847,574, and private interests contributed $909,306 for habitat management in the LMV during 1993 (Loesch et al., 1994).

The habitat program in the Southeast has been successful not only because of the additional habitat that has been provided, but also because it has shown that creating partnerships between the private and public sectors can be extremely beneficial and cost effective when managing waterfowl. Furthermore, partnerships create a new awareness and interest within private groups and among individuals. For example, in the Lower Mississippi Valley Joint Venture, 114,696 ha (283,409 acres) of wetlands have been protected, 46,635 ha (115,233 acres) of wetlands have been restored or enhanced, and active water management occurs on 24,436 ha (60,380 acres) of private lands (Loesch et al., 1994).

This program is young, and it is still too early to have produced significant changes toward achieving its waterfowl population goals. The program will continue through at least the year 2000, and the available resources are expected to increase each year. NAWMP activities in the other two priority areas (Gulf Coast and Middle-Upper Atlantic) have also been commendable.

Waterfowl management in the Southeast should continue with programs that improve habitat in high priority areas, while seeking to expand into other areas that are also important to waterfowl. As overall continental waterfowl populations increase, so will Southeast populations. Predation rates on nesting females are very high on the breeding grounds and significantly affect the continental population of waterfowl, particularly ducks. Improving nesting habitat on breeding grounds should increase nesting success and ultimately strengthen duck populations.

Western Hemisphere Shorebird Reserve Network

Shorebirds are a diverse group, with 80 species, primarily of the families Scolopacidae and Charadriidae occurring throughout the world. Body size ranges from the 20 g (0.7 ounce) least sandpiper (*Calidris minutilla*) to the greater than 500 g (17.6 ounce) double-striped thick-knee (*Burhinus bistriatus*) and oystercatchers (*Haematopus* spp.). In addition to their morphological diversity, shorebirds also exploit diverse habitats, ranging from coastal beaches and marshes, to mud flats and freshwater wetlands, to grasslands and savannas. Their annual migrations can cover 30,000 km (18,642 miles) round trip, taking them from the tip of South America's Tierra del Fuego to the Arctic tundra and boreal forest breeding grounds found in Alaska and Canada. These birds depend intimately on the continued availability of several critical wetland areas to provide food and resting places during their international migrations. So important are these stopover locations that the elimination of one wetland along a migratory pathway could translate into a major population disruption for an entire species.

The Western Hemisphere Shorebird Reserve Network (WHSRN), based at the Manomet Bird Observatory in Massachusetts, is a voluntary collaboration of private and government organizations committed to protecting shorebirds and their wetland habitats. The WHSRN program began in 1985 to address the alarming declines in shorebird numbers. Via this program, critical stopover sites used by large concentrations of migratory shorebirds are identified and provided international recognition. The Network uses shorebird conservation to raise awareness of the intense international cooperation needed to protect wildlife habitat, and to endorse the need for a global perspective to conserve the planet's natural ecosystems and biological diversity. Specific sites are incorporated into this program based upon biological criteria and voluntary nomination by landowners or managers.

WHSRN was initiated as a result of decades of research by the Manomet Bird Observatory, the Academy of Natural Sciences of Philadelphia, and the Canadian Wildlife Service, that suggested that many shorebird populations were declining (Howe et al., 1989). Through research it became apparent that to protect shorebirds, a strategy was needed to protect migration stopover habitats in areas where they were most threatened.

Although many gaps still exist in our knowledge of shorebird migrations, the WHSRN uses data from the International Shorebird Survey, the Pacific Flyway Program, the U.S. Fish and Wildlife Service, the Canadian Wildlife Service, and other sources to identify the most important shorebird stopover areas. These locations can then be nominated for inclusion as part of the Shorebird Reserve Network. The Network extends international recognition to member sites and fosters improved conservation management that benefits shorebirds.

WHSRN recognizes four categories of sites with locations in seven countries across the hemisphere. Sites are placed in one of four categories: hemispheric sites include 500,000 shorebirds or 30 percent of a flyway population, international sites include 100,000 shorebirds or 15 percent of a flyway population, regional sites include 20,000 shorebirds or five percent of a population, endangered species registry sites include important locations for endangered species and no minimum population is required. These sites encompass about 5 million ha (12,354,830 acres) of wetlands, affecting about 30 million shorebirds. Although this program benefits shorebirds, these populations are still at risk because the WHSRN actually extends no legal protection to critical sites.

WHSRN unites wildlife agencies, private conservation groups, and other organizations across the Americas to solve the conservation problems negatively affecting migratory shorebirds and their habitat. The success of WHSRN's collaborative and hemispheric approach to a global environmental challenge, such as the conservation of migratory shorebird populations, is one model for the international management approach needed to confront the crucial environmental problems that exist today. WHSRN has become a widely respected hemispheric effort, especially in Latin America, and has initiated and developed local wetland groups along with new international, national, and local wetlands policies.

WHSRN is also active in the North American Waterfowl Management Plan to manage and protect shorebird habitats. A shorebird habitat management manual has been prepared by WHSRN to help integrate the management of wetlands for shorebirds (Helmers, 1992). WHSRN is currently collaborating with federal, state, and private agencies to organize training workshops for natural resource managers throughout the United States. The objective of these workshops is to provide information that can be used to integrate shorebird management into traditional wetland management practices. Workshops provide resource managers with many of the tools needed to enhance the availability of shorebird habitat.

WHSRN's shorebird and wetland conservation activities have enhanced public and political conservation awareness, and have elevated important issues into national and international policy arenas. Myers et al. (1987) suggested similar conservation programs for other migratory species that pass through various bottlenecks during migration. These species could include several species of birds of prey, large wading birds, cetaceans, anadromous fishes, and large terrestrial mammals.

Neotropical Migratory Bird Conservation Program — Partners in Flight

Long-term population declines of many songbirds have been summarized from a variety of data sources including the Breeding Bird Survey (Robbins et al., 1986), Breeding Bird Census (Hall, 1964), and independent research projects (e.g., Hagan and Johnston, 1992). Specifically, Breeding Bird Survey data indicated recent declines in many bird species groups, including populations of long-distance, or neotropical migratory birds (Robbins et al., 1986; see also Hagan and Johnston, 1992; Finch and Stangel, 1993).

Neotropical migrants are birds that nest in North America and spend the nonbreeding season in Mexico, Central or South America, or the Caribbean. These attributes differentiate them from migrants in general, which include birds that winter in southern North America but breed in northern North America, and neotropical birds, which include species that spend their entire lives in neotropical areas. Over 160 species of birds are classified as neotropical migrant landbirds (Finch, 1991), with major groups including raptors (birds of prey), cuckoos, caprimulgids, swifts, hummingbirds, flycatchers, swallows, thrushes, vireos, warblers, tanagers, orioles, buntings, grosbeaks, and some sparrows.

In response to recognized population declines of songbirds and associated public concern (e.g., Terborgh, 1989), the National Fish and Wildlife Foundation hosted an international meeting in Atlanta, Georgia in late 1990. Representatives attended from federal, state, and local governments, large and small non-government organizations, and universities. From this meeting, the "Partners in Flight — Aves de las Americas" Neotropical Migratory Bird Conservation Program began. The goals of the Partners in Flight initiative are as follows: determine the status and specific causes of neotropical migratory bird population declines, maintain stable populations of these species, and reverse declining population trends through habitat restoration and management (Finch and Stangel, 1993).

During the first two years of the initiative (1991-1993), approximately 114 projects were funded by about 3 million dollars of National Fish and Wildlife Foundation funds privately matched by 5.3 million dollars. Most of these projects have taken place in the United States, but some work has been carried out in tropical wintering areas. Many federal agencies have signed a memorandum of understanding to manage and conserve neotropical migrants; those with extensive responsibilities for wetlands and aquatic systems in the Southeast include the U.S. Department of Defense (Army Corps of Engineers), the Tennessee Valley Authority, the U.S. Fish and Wildlife Service, and the U.S. Forest Service.

The national Partners in Flight is organized into regional working groups (northeast, southeast, midwest, and west) containing subsets based on four topics: information and education, management, research, and monitoring. Hunter et al. (1993) have provided strategies for prioritization of species, species assemblages, and habitats by physiographic province. The development of species and habitat priorities has enhanced the establishment of goals and objectives. Many states, such as Tennessee (see Ford and Cooper, 1993), have initiated five-year plans for conservation and management of neotropical migrants. One focus of the southeast working group has been to address issues and ultimately manage neotropical migrants at the physiographic province level, which transcends traditional state boundaries.

Pertinent to aquatic systems is the Mississippi Alluvial Valley physiographic province. The Mississippi Valley bottomland hardwood forests and other wetlands are important habitats for birds. Recently, daily checklists from ten sites in the Mississippi Valley included 174 bird species. Of those, 39 species were breeding neotropical migrants and 41 were transient species (Smith et al., 1993). To date, conservation and management activities in the Mississippi Valley have been primarily associated with inventorying, monitoring, and research as applied to forest management. A landscape level management plan is currently being developed and will be integrated with developing waterfowl and shorebird management objectives. This plan will primarily address the need for quality nesting habitats.

Nesting habitats have been the primary focus of Partners in Flight. Yet, little is known about the importance of habitat during the migratory period, and the importance of stopover habitats has been overlooked in most conservation strategies involving long-distance migratory birds (Moore and Woodrey, 1993). The availability of suitable stopover habitats is critical when birds must replenish depleted fat reserves, respond to unfavorable weather, and avoid predation (Moore et al., 1993).

Many species migrating through the Southeast make a nonstop migration of greater than 1,000 km (621 miles) across the Gulf of Mexico in 18 to 24 hours. Forested coastal habitats may be crucial to landbird migrants in the fall, because they provide a place to develop energy reserves for the flight across the Gulf, and in the spring because they provide a place to rest and replenish energy reserves following a trans-Gulf flight (Moore et al., 1990).

Rapid urban and rural development in coastal zones throughout the Southeast is a conservation problem (Moore et al., 1990). By the year 2010, coastal populations are likely to have grown from 80 million to 127 million people, an increase of about 60 percent. In the Southeast, the northern coast of the Gulf of Mexico is expected to follow this trend (Cullitan et al., 1990), and as a result, possibly the most important migratory stopover areas of the Nearctic-Neotropcial migration system in the southeastern United States appear in critical need of protection.

As with the other broad, proactive programs described here, private landowners are an integral part of the Partners in Flight program. Workshops concerning the simultaneous management of forests and birds, and conflict resolution have been held in several physiographic provinces, including the Mississippi Valley (Smith and Pashley, 1994), the Coastal Plain, and the Interior Low Plateaus. The forest products industry is funding significant research and management of their own volition, including at least one ecosystem management initiative in the Interior Low Plateaus region of Kentucky, Tennessee, and Alabama. The Anderson-Tully Co., a forest products industry, published a breeding bird field manual for managers of bottomland hardwood forests (Anderson-Tully Co., 1994). This manual identifies important habitat types, seral stages, life history characteristics, and beneficial silvicultural activities for various bird species found in bottomland hardwood forests. These types of conservation activities demonstrate a positive move away from the highly confrontational atmosphere that has often surrounded endangered species management in many areas of the country.

FUNDING PROBLEMS

One serious problem that has always thwarted the management of nongame species is the lack of a consistent, reliable funding source. The adequate management of nongame species will never be realized until a reliable funding mechanism is developed to support it. Along these lines, annual funds obtained via the excise tax associated with the Pittman-Robertson and Dingle-Johnson Acts serve as an excellent model of success. A similar user pay-user benefit surcharge levied at the manufacturer level on birdseed, feeders, field guides, binoculars, and other items associated with observing wildlife as a form of recreation could provide the necessary sustained funding to drive ecosystem management programs. Such a surcharge is currently being proposed by the International Association of Fish and Wildlife Agencies and a large coalition of users. The acceptance of this initiative, commonly known as Teaming With Wildlife, is vital for state leadership in developing conservation, management, and research programs for nongame species, and conservation education programs for the public.

SUMMARY

Narrowly focused, or single species, management programs for aquatic birds in peril, such as bald eagle, osprey, least tern and sandhill crane, involve intensive efforts such as creation and protection of nesting sites and artificial rearing of birds. Although these programs are necessary, effective, and often benefit other species, they are also extremely expensive regarding benefits obtained per species and per individual. Furthermore, private landowners often fear these programs because there is often little room for compromise or experimentation in terms of simultaneous management of exploited resources and imperiled fauna. Hence, via such programs landowners sometimes can lose control over certain aspects of management of their own lands.

Broad-based approaches to wildlife management are oriented towards large-scale habitat conservation that helps multiple species. Adopting ecosystem management, these programs are proactive, embracing the philosophy that the best way to approach the imperiled species problem is to keep species and habitats from becoming endangered. Because of the large geographic scale often involved, partnerships between the public and private sectors are encouraged. The North American Waterfowl Management Plan (NAWMP) has been exemplary in this regard. To date, the broad-based programs described above have afforded land managers and owners the opportunity to provide proactive input into the overall plan, simultaneously manage their land resource for traditional objectives as well as the groups of species in question, and maintain greater control over the various management objectives of their lands. Administrators also prefer this approach because it is more cost and labor efficient. For example, creation of flooded grasslands and emergent marshes under the NAWMP also benefits rails, bald eagles, osprey, and other species as well.

Along with creating a sustainable funding source, we recommend the following program needs for adequate conservation and management of imperiled birds which use aquatic habitats:

1) increased inventory, monitoring, and research efforts focusing on bird populations to better determine species in need of management;
2) increased funding levels for single species management until recovery goals are met, and the addition of other imperiled species as necessary to prevent extinction or local extirpation;
3) increased financial support for existing broad-based proactive programs, and integrated management of multiple species and species assemblages as a step toward ecosystems management;
4) prioritization and development of a broad-based proactive program for rails which increases inventories, monitoring, and research on these species and which uses research findings to drive management actions;
5) increased inventory, monitoring, and research of important stopover habitats during

migration periods and integration of the data thus obtained into international, national, regional, physiographic province, and local management plans; and

6)   increased support and encouragement for research programs designed to investigate the assumptions of management priorities.

REFERENCES

Aldrich, J. 1972. A new subspecies of sandhill crane from Mississippi. *Proceedings of the Biological Society of Washington* 85:63-70.

Anderson-Tully Company. 1994. *Breeding Bird Field Manual: A Guide for Bottomland Hardwood Forest Managers.* Anderson-Tully Co., Memphis, TN.

Cade, T., and S. A. Temple. 1977. Cornell University falcon programme. In *Proceedings On World Conference on Birds of Prey.* R. D. Chancellor (ed.). International Council on Bird Preservation, Vienna, p. 353-369.

Cely, J. E., D. P. Ferral, and B. A. Glover. 1993. Marsh bird survey final report. South Carolina Wildlife and Marine Resources Department, Columbia, SC, 38 p.

Cullitan, T. J., M. A. Warren, T. R. Goodspeed, D. G. Remer, C. M. Blackwell, and J. J. McDonough, III. 1990. Fifty years of population change along the nation's coasts 1960-2010. Coastal Trends Series, Report No. 2, Strategic Assessment Branch, National Oceanic and Atmospheric Association, Rockville, MD, 41 p.

Eddleman, W. R., F. L. Knopf, B. Meanly, F. A. Reid, and R. Zembal. 1988. Conservation of North American rallids. *Wilson Bulletin* 100(3):438-475.

Finch, D. M. 1991. Population ecology, habitat requirements, and conservation of neotropical migratory birds. General Technical Report RM-205, Forest Service, U.S. Department of Agriculture, Fort Collins, CO, 23 p.

Finch, D. M., and P. W. Stangel (eds.). 1993. Status and management of neotropical migratory birds. General Technical Report RM-229, Rocky Mountain Forest and Range Experiment Station, Forest Service, U.S. Department of Agriculture, Fort Collins, CO, 422 p.

Ford, R. P., and R. J. Cooper. 1993. Tennessee partners in flight: Birds and biodiversity. *Tennessee Wildlife* 16:5-12.

Grumbine, R. E. 1994. What is ecosystem management? *Conservation Biology* 8:27-38.

Hagan, J. M. III, and D. W. Johnston (eds.). 1992. *Ecology and Conservation of Neotropical Migrant Landbirds.* Smithsonian Press, Washington, D.C.

Hall, G. A. 1964. Breeding-bird censuses — why and how. *Audubon Field Notes* 18:413-416.

Hammer, D. A., J. L. Mechler, and R. M. Hatcher. 1981. Restoration of bald eagle populations in the Mid-South. In *Proceedings of Biology and Management of Bald Eagle and Osprey Symposium.* D. M. Bird, N. Y. Seymor, and J. M. Gerrard (eds.). MacDonald Raptor Research Center, McGill University, Raptor Research Foundation, Quebec, p. 107-125.

Hardy, J. 1957. The least tern in the Mississippi Valley. *Publication of Museum of Michigan State University, Biological Service* 1:1-60.

Hatcher, R. M. 1991. Computer model projections of bald eagle nesting in Tennessee. *Journal of Tennessee Academy of Science* 66:225-228.

Helmers, D. L. 1992. *Shorebird Management Manual.* Western Hemisphere Shorebird Reserve Network, Manomet, MA.

Howe, A., P. H. Geissler, and B. A. Harrington. 1989. Population trends of North American shorebirds based on the International Shorebird Survey. *Biological Conservation* 49:189-199.

Hunter, W. C., M. F. Carter, D. N. Pashley, and K. Barker. 1993. The Partners in Flight species prioritization scheme. *In* General Techical Report RM-229, Rocky Mountain Forest and Range Experiment Station, Forest Service, U.S. Department of Agriculture, Fort Collins, CO, p. 109-119.

Kirsch, E. M. 1992. Population trends and possible immigration/emigration patterns in the interior population of least terns (*Sterna antillarium*). Unpublished Report, Endangered Species Office, U.S. Fish and Wildlife Service, Twin Cities, MN, 42 p.

LeGrand, H. E., Jr. 1991. South Atlantic coast report. American Birds 45(1):88-91.

Loesch, C. R., K. J. Reinecke, and C. K. Baxter. 1994. The Lower Mississippi Valley Joint Venture 1993 Evaluation Plan. North American Waterfowl Management Plan, U.S. Fish and Wildlife Service, Vicksburg, MS, 34 p.

Lower Mississippi Valley Joint Venture Managment Board. 1990. Conserving waterfowl and wetlands: The Lower Mississippi Valley Joint Venture. North American Waterfowl Management Plan, U.S. Fish and Wildlife Service, Vicksburg, MS, 32 p.

Martin, C. O., W. A. Mitchell, and D. A. Hammer. 1986. Osprey nest platforms. Section 5.1.6, Technical Report EL-86-21, Wildlife resources management manual, U.S. Army Corps of Engineers, Vicksburg, MS, 25 p.

Mitchell, L. J., and R. M. Hatcher. 1993. Development of a statewide watchable wildlife program and wildlife viewing guide in Tennessee. *Proceedings of the Annual Conference of the Southeastern Association of Fish and Wildlife Agencies* 47:757-766.

Mitsch, W. J., and J.G. Gosselink. 1986. *Wetlands.* Van Nostrand Reinhold, New York, NY.

Moore, F. R., S. A. Gauthreaux, P. Kerlinger, and T. R. Simons. 1993. Stopover habitat: management implications and guidelines. In *Status and management of neotropical migratory birds.* D. M. Finch, and P. W. Stangel (eds.). General Technical Report RM-229, U.S. Department of Agriculture, Forest Service, Rocky Mountain Forest and Range Experiment Station, Ft. Collins, CO, p. 58-69.

Moore, F. R., P. Kerlinger, and T. R. Simons. 1990. Stopover on a Gulf Coast barrier island by spring trans-gulf migrants. *Wilson Bulletin* 102:487-500.

Moore, F. R., and M. S. Woodrey. 1993. Stopover habitat and its importance in the conservation of landbird migrants. *Proceedings of the Annual Conference of the Southeastern Association of Fish and Wildlife Agencies* 47:447-459.

Mulherin, B. M., W. L. Reickel, L. N. Locke, P. G. Lamont, A. A. Belisle, E. Chromartic, G. E. Galey, and R. M. Proupy. 1970. Organochlorine residue and autopsy results in bald eagles: 1962-1968. *Pesticide Monitoring Journal* 4:141-144.

Murphy, T. M. 1984. Southeastern states bald eagle recovery plan. South Carolina Wildlife and Marine Resources Department, Columbia, SC, 63 p.

Myers, J. P., R. I. G. Morrison, P. T. Z. Antas, B. A. Harrington, T. E. Lovejoy, M. Sallaberry, S. E. Senner, and A. Tarak. 1987. Conservation strategy for migratory species. *American Scientist* 75:18-26.

Potter, E. F., J. F. Parnell, and R. P. Teulings. 1980. *Birds of the Carolinas*. University of North Carolina Press, Chapel Hill, NC.

Reid, F. A., B. Meanly, and L. H. Frederickson. 1994. King rail. In *Migratory Shore and Upland Game Bird Management in North America*. T. C. Tacha, and C. E. Braun (eds.). International Association of Fish and Wildlife Agencies, Washington, D.C., p. 181-191.

Ripley, S. D. 1977. *Rails of the World*. D. R. Godine Publications, Boston, MA.

Robbins, C. S., D. Bystrak, and P. H. Geissler. 1986. The breeding bird survey: Its first fifteen years, 1965-1979. Resource Publication No. 157, U.S. Fish and Wildlife Service, Washington, D.C., 196 p.

Rumancik, J. P., Jr. 1993. Survey of the interior least tern on the Mississippi River from Cape Girardeau, Missouri to Vicksburg, Mississippi. Unpublished Report, U.S. Army Corps of Engineers, Memphis, TN, 14 p.

Runde, D. E., P.D. Southall, J.A. Hovis, R. Sullivan, and R. B. Renken. 1990. Recent records and survey methods for the black rail in Florida. *Florida Field Naturalist* 18(2):33-35.

Seal, U. S., and S. Hereford. 1994. Mississippi sandhill crane *Grus canadensis pulla* population and habitat viability assessment workshop report. IUCN/SSC Captive Breeding Specialist Group, MN, 146 p.

Sidle, J. G., J. J. Dinan, M. P. Dryer, J. P. Rumancik, Jr., and J. W. Smith. 1988. Distribution of the least tern in interior North America. *American Birds* 42:195-201.

Smith, J. W., and R. B. Renken. 1991. Least tern nesting habitat in the Mississippi River Valley adjacent to Missouri. *Journal of Field Ornithology* 62:497-504.

Smith, J. W., and R. B. Renken. 1993. Reproductive success of least terns in the Mississippi River Valley. *Colonial Waterbirds* 16:39-44.

Smith, W. P., P. B. Hamel, and R. P. Ford. 1993. Mississippi Alluvial Valley forest conversion: Implications for eastern North American avifauna. *Proceedings of the Annual Conference of the Southeast Association of Fish and Wildlife Agencies* 47:460-469.

Smith, W. P., and D. N. Pashley. 1994. A workshop to resolve conflicts in the conservation of migratory landbirds in bottomland hardwood forests. General Technical Report SO-114, U.S. Forest Service, New Orleans, LA, 37 p.

Sprunt, A., Jr., and E. B. Chamberlain. 1949. South Carolina bird life. University of South Carolina Press, Columbia, SC.

Tacha, T. C., and C. E. Braun (eds.). 1994. *Migratory Shore and Upland Gamebird Management in North America*. International Association of Fish and Wildlife Agencies, Washington, D.C.

Tacha, T. C., S. A. Nesbitt, and P. A. Vohs. 1994. Sandhill crane. In *Migratory Shore and Upland Gamebird Management in North America*. T. C. Tacha, and C. E. Braun (eds.). International Association of Fish and Wildlife Agencies, Washington, D.C., p. 77-94.

Terborgh, J. 1989. *Where Have All the Birds Gone?* Princeton University Press, Princeton, NJ.

Tiner, R. W. 1984. Wetlands of the United States: Current status and recent trends. National Wetlands Inventory, U.S. Fish and Wildlife Service, Washington, D.C., 59 p.

U.S. Department of the Interior and Canadian Wildlife Service. 1986. North American waterfowl management plan. U.S. Fish and Wildlife Service, Washington, D.C., 19 p.

U.S. Fish and Wildlife Service. 1973. Amendments to lists of endangered fish and wildlife. *U.S. Federal Register* **38**:14678.

U.S. Fish and Wildlife Service. 1985. Interior population of the least tern determined to be endangered. *U.S. Federal Register* **50**:21784-21792.

U.S. Fish and Wildlife Service. 1990. Recovery plan for the interior population of the least tern (*Sterna antillarum*). U.S. Fish and Wildlife Service, Twin Cities, MN, 90 p.

U.S. Fish and Wildlife Service 1991. Mississippi sandhill crane *(Grus canadensis pulla)* recovery plan. U.S. Fish and Wildlife Service Atlanta, GA, 42 p.

U.S. Fish and Wildlife Service. 1995a. Bald eagle reclassification: Final rule. *U.S. Federal Register* **60** (**133**): 36000-36010.

U.S. Fish and Wildlife Service. 1995b. Migratory nongame birds of management concern in the United States: The 1995 list. Final Report, Office of Migratory Bird Management, Washington, D.C., 22 p.

Whitman, P. L. 1988. Biology and conservation of the endangered interior least tern: A literature review. *Biological Report of the U.S. Fish and Wildlife Service* 88(3):1-22.

Wood, P. B., D. A. Buehler, and M. A. Byrd. 1988. Bald eagle. In *Proceedings of Southeast Raptor Management Symposium and Workshop.* B. G. Pendleton (ed.), Institute for Wildlife Research, Scientific and Technical Series No. 14, Blacksburg, VA, p. 13-21.

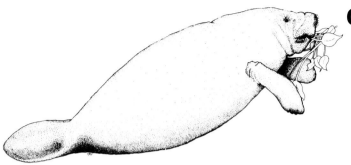

CHAPTER 15

Imperiled Mammalian Fauna of Aquatic Ecosystems in the Southeast: A Management Perspective

Joseph D. Clark and Michael J. Harvey

Management of imperiled mammals associated with aquatic ecosystems in the southeastern United States ranges from almost no management for some species to intensive, high-profile programs for others. Aquatic mammals are notoriously difficult to census because they are often secretive, trap-wary, relatively rare, or have extensive movement patterns. As a result, conservation efforts aimed at these animals often have been greatly hampered by a general lack of comprehensive population data. Historically, certain high-profile, "flagship" species have been the primary beneficiaries of management efforts. One of the earliest examples involves beaver, *Castor canadensis*, which had been reduced to a low ebb due to unregulated harvest and were subsequently live-trapped by state game officials in the 1940s and repatriated throughout the southeastern states. The success of this restocking program has exceeded expectations, and today beaver numbers have reached what many consider to be nuisance proportions in most states. Similar restocking stories can be told for muskrats (*Ondatra zibethicus*) and, to a limited extent, for river otters (*Lutra canadensis*).

Unfortunately, other imperiled species of lesser economic or recreational value have not

Aquatic Fauna in Peril: The Southeastern Perspective, edited by George W. Benz, and David E. Collins. 1997. Special Publication 1, Southeast Aquatic Research Institute, Lenz Design & Communications, Decatur, GA, 554 p.

been as fortunate. Efforts to conserve these lower-profile species have been minimal or conservation problems so immense that their complete recovery has been unsuccessful. Wilson (1992) suggested that 20 percent of all species on earth may be lost to extinction in the next four decades. If this disaster should occur, it would rival the greatest geological extinction episodes. Certainly, conservationists need to explore new methods for preserving mammalian diversity.

In this chapter we will discuss the resource management history of aquatic mammals which are imperiled in the Southeast. In doing so we define an aquatic mammal as any mammal that is directly or indirectly associated with aquatic ecosystems. Imperiled mammals are any mammalian species, subspecies, or population listed as endangered, threatened, or of special concern on any state or federal list, and also includes mammals experiencing long-term population declines or significant range contractions.

MANAGEMENT PROFILES

West Indian Manatee — *Trichechus manatus*

There are many gaps in our knowledge of this mysterious mammal. Most research on this manatee has been conducted in Florida and may not accurately portray the animal's biology in other parts of its range (Odell, 1982). Although census techniques often are unreliable for manatees, in 1985 at least 1,200 West Indian manatees were accounted for at Florida wintering areas (Reynolds and Wilcox, 1986; O'Shea, 1988), where almost the entire U.S. population congregates.

Major factors resulting in declines of West Indian manatees primarily relate to increased mortality, which can have a marked impact on populations due to the low reproductive capability of the species. Historically, hunting for meat, bone, hides, and fat have caused severe reduction of *T. manatus* populations (Bertram and Bertram, 1973; Peterson, 1974). In Florida, where this manatee has been protected since 1893, poaching still occurs.

Presently, the major source of manatee mortality in Florida is associated with human activities, particularly boating (Hartman, 1974). A carcass salvage program in Florida documented 337 manatee deaths from 1974 to 1979. Of these manatee mortalities, 36 percent were associated with human activities, of which 22 percent were due to boat collisions, eight percent were associated with human structures (primarily flood control dams), and six percent were associated with other human-related factors (Odell and Reynolds, 1979). To attempt to mitigate those losses, 1978 Florida legislation restricted some boating activities in areas of wintering manatee congregations. Since this legislation was enacted, sanctuaries have been designated, boating speeds have been reduced, and public awareness programs have been initiated. Despite these efforts, however, the number of manatees killed by boats has doubled during the past decade (O'Shea, 1988).

Another potential problem for *T. manatus* is that power plants and other industrial activities have created artificially warm effluents that may attract and keep this species north of its historical winter range (Hartman, 1974). These unnatural conditions may create "ecological traps" for manatees that are subsequently exposed to cold waters when the heated effluents are periodically turned off during winter. In addition, dredge and fill operations associated with coastal development have resulted in a dramatic decline in marine vegetation and, thus, manatee food resources.

Many traditional techniques for studying large mammals often are not feasible for manatees, and consequently, much of manatee biology remains a mystery. Habitat management plans are hampered by inadequate knowledge of manatee migration routes, food habits, and physiology. The reproductive ecology of *T. manatus* also is poorly understood.

In addition to protection afforded by the 1973 U.S. Endangered Species Act, the West Indian manatee is also protected by the 1972 U.S. Marine Mammal Protection Act. While manatee numbers at wintering sites have increased in the last two decades (O'Shea and Ludlow, 1992), overall projections based on population structure data suggest a continued decline (Packard, 1985). Unfortunately, the future for the West Indian manatee remains uncertain.

Florida Panther — *Puma concolor coryi*

During the early 1970s there was considerable opinion that the Florida panther was extinct, along with the remainder of the other mountain lion populations in the eastern United States. Although the existence of a population of these felids in south Florida was eventually confirmed, some 20 years later it remains one of the rarest mammals in the world. Recovery of this cat has been hampered by numerous problems, including collisions with automobiles, disease (e.g., rabies, mercury poisoning), inbreeding, and most importantly, accelerated habitat loss due to urban and agricultural development.

Although the Florida panther is probably better suited to more terrestrial habitats, intense pressure to develop land in Florida has caused the range of this cat to be reduced to those aquatic environments that are not readily suitable for human uses. The aquatic habitats where panthers currently exist are generally of poor quality and include sawgrass prairies, cypress and oak hammocks, and permanently flooded wetlands. Soils in these habitats are typically thin and relatively sterile, and white-tailed deer (*Odocoileus virginianus*) densities are low. Feral hogs (*Sus scrofa*) constitute the bulk of the diet of the cats in these areas, and these exotic animals, therefore, are a critical food item (Maehr, 1990). The best panther habitats in south Florida are drier, more fertile, and consist mostly of oak or pine. However, these sites are the most sought after for conversion to citrus, cattle, and vegetable production, and these activities are often incompatible with panther conservation.

Research on Florida panthers began in the early 1980s with efforts to learn more about the basic life history and habitat requirements of this species. Researchers discovered that some panthers travel as much as 32 km (19.9 miles) per night and home ranges can be up to 260 km² (100 square miles) for females and 1,040 km² (402 square miles) for males (Maehr, 1990). Mortalities of panthers from automobile collisions prompted state officials to reduce nighttime speed limits within panther habitat and to install underpasses along Interstate 75 and State Road 29.

Because panther ranges typically include multiple public and private land ownerships, coordination of Florida panther management efforts is essential. About half of the Florida panther population occurs on 800,000 ha (1,976,773 acres) of land consisting of a national wildlife refuge, a national park, a national preserve, a state reserve, a wildlife management area, and two Indian reservations. The remaining panthers are found on private lands (Maehr, 1992a). The large home ranges of these cats and this mixture of land ownership and management responsibility creates a significant management challenge. As a result, the Florida Panther Interagency Committee (FPIC) was formed in 1986 to provide a coordinated, unified recovery program (Jordan, 1990).

Panthers are sensitive to habitat fragmentation due to their large home ranges and extensive movement patterns. Furthermore, the small population size (30 to 50 panthers) and limited genetic variability theoretically subject this subspecies to a high risk of extinction in the next few decades. Analyses indicate that the present panther population is losing genetic diversity at a rate of three to seven percent per generation, with extinction probable within 25 to 40 years (Jordan, 1990). In 1989, the FPIC determined that a captive population was essential to any successful recovery program for the Florida panther. Objectives of maintaining a captive population are to provide security against extinction, preserve and manage genetic resources, and provide a source of animals for population re-establishment (Jordan, 1991).

The objective of the Florida Panther Recovery Plan is to achieve three viable populations within the subspecies' historic range (U.S. Fish and Wildlife Service, 1987). Twenty-four candidate release sites across the Southeast were evaluated using biological and sociological criteria, and 14 of those were selected as potential re-establishment locations (Jordan, 1994). Sites in the lower coastal plain of Alabama and Mississippi, along the Arkansas/Louisiana state line, and along the lower Apalachicola River (Florida) were deemed best re-establishment areas. An effort is currently underway to evaluate releases of Texas mountain lions (*P. c. stanleyana*) in southeastern Georgia and northeastern Florida. Although the evaluation is preliminary, the onset of deer hunting season in the autumn of 1988 seems to have resulted in dramatic dispersals and direct mortalities of the initially reintroduced lions (Belden and Hagedorn, 1993). Subsequent releases, however, have met with better success (C. Belden, Florida Game and Fresh Water Fish Commission, pers. comm.).

In addition, the FPIC has recommended that several female Texas mountain lions be introduced into the south Florida panther population to bolster regional genetic diversity. The request was recommended as the preferred alternative by the U.S. Fish and Wildlife Service (USFWS), and tentative plans are to augment the Florida panther population during the winter of 1994-95.

River Otter — *Lutra canadensis*

River otter populations have been extirpated from much of their original range, partly due to indiscriminate, unregulated trapping (Godman, 1826; Flower and Lydekker, 1891; Duplaix and Simon, 1976) and habitat losses (Park, 1971; Fimreite and Reynolds, 1973). In recent times, not only has the quantity of suitable otter habitat declined, but the quality has as well, due to the extensive use of DDT, heptachlor, dieldrin, and certain heavy metals during the 1950s and 1960s (Clark et al., 1981). It is likely that bioaccumulation of those pollutants in this semi-aquatic carnivore resulted in lowered reproduction or decreased survival. By the mid-20th century, river otters were only common in coastal regions of the Southeast.

Management of river otters may include total protection, reintroduction into areas where population extirpation has occurred, protection of habitat, and where appropriate, regulation and monitoring of the otter harvest (Toweill and Tabor, 1984). Habitats for river otters have significantly improved due to beaver population resurgence following reintroductions between the 1920s and 1950s. During this period, a number of game agencies developed restoration programs for beaver, with beavers being trapped and released throughout the Southeast. Beaver populations increased dramatically over the next 40 years as did the wetlands they created. Beaver ponds are excellent habitats for otters and, where otters were present, they exploited those habitats. Due to bans on many environmental contaminants, conservative trapping regulations, and the return of the beaver, river otter populations have increased dramatically throughout the Southeast. Some states (e.g., Missouri, Tennessee, Kentucky, and North Carolina) have initiated river otter restoration programs whereby otters are translocated (often using stock obtained from out-of-state sources) to establish populations. For example, reintroduction programs in Tennessee and Kentucky have obtained otters from coastal Louisiana (Melquist and Dronkert, 1987).

The river otter is classified as an Appendix II species under the Convention of International Trade in Endangered Species of Flora and Fauna. Until a few years ago, this classification was intended only for species that could become threatened if international trade was not strictly regulated. Today, the river otter is listed in Appendix II due to its status as a "look-alike" of pelts of endangered South American and African species of otters. The Appendix II classification requires that pelts of river otters be marked with permanent tags before export from their state of origin. State agencies are responsible for keeping accurate records of pelts tagged each year, and those records are submitted to the USFWS annually, along with a recommendation for continued export based on biological data.

River otters are difficult to capture and handle. Radio telemetry transmitters have to be implanted surgically and tagging for mark-recapture is unwieldy. Censusing methods are often inaccurate. Melquist and Hornocker (1979) developed a number of techniques for capturing and radio tracking otters, and several telemetry studies have subsequently been conducted. Nevertheless, there is still a poor understanding of population numbers and trends. Furthermore, because movements can be extreme and habitats inaccessible, little is known about river otter reproductive and mortality rates, and this makes it difficult to develop reliable population models for management purposes.

The river otter is classified as a game species and is trapped in almost all southeastern states. Louisiana leads the nation in production of river otter pelts (Deems and Pursley, 1978). In other southeastern states, river otter populations are generally increasing, again, due largely to the effect of more suitable habitat created by increasing numbers of beavers. Despite this, river otters are susceptible to overharvest due to their low reproductive rates and because their habitat is restricted to watercourses. Therefore, harvest management of river otters is necessarily implemented in a conservative fashion. Because otters can sometimes impact fisheries and aquaculture, occasional damage control at fish ponds and boat docks is required.

Everglades Mink — *Mustela vison mink*

The Everglades mink is an isolated population of a southeastern subspecies and is considered common in portions of the Everglades and Big Cypress Swamp (Humphrey, 1992d). Water control projects at the Everglades and Big Cypress Swamp have affected the population, but the consequences have been difficult to document. These control projects have resulted in changes in water levels, saltwater intrusion into the aquifer, altered fire regimes, and oxidation of peat soils. However, the greatest current threat to the Everglades mink is the potential for conversion of private lands within Big Cypress for citrus production.

This mink is under review for listing by the USFWS. Major tracts of mink habitat are currently under federal ownership, primarily by the National Park Service. In 1989, the U.S. Congress ordered the Army Corps of Engineers to restore the natural water flow to Everglades National Park. This massive restoration project should have positive long-term consequences for this population of mink.

Florida and Louisiana Black Bears — *Ursus americanus floridanus* and *U. a. luteolus*

Major concentrations of Florida black bears occur in and around the Okefenokee National Wildlife Refuge in south Georgia; Apalachicola National Forest, Osceola National Forest, and Ocala National Forest in the northern portion of Florida; and Big Cypress National Preserve in south Florida. Population estimates range from 500 to 1,000 (Maehr, 1992b). Black bear populations in Florida are probably the most fragmented in North America, and although the larger populations are stable, extirpation of the smaller, more isolated populations will probably continue to occur. Loss of suitable habitats, including cypress and hardwood swamps, represents the major threat to Florida black bears. Poaching and road-associated mortality are also important factors in fringe populations due to low reproductive and recruitment rates (Maehr, 1992b).

Hunting of selected northern populations of Florida black bears was prohibited in 1994, and the USFWS has proposed listing the subspecies as threatened (Wooding, 1992). An aggressive capture-release program is conducted by the Florida Game and Fresh Water Fish Commission (FGFWFC) to reduce conflicts between bears and beekeepers (Maehr, 1983). In addition to a need to protect critical habitats, other measures such as placing bear crossing signs along roads and building highway underpasses for use by bears and panthers have been undertaken.

The Louisiana black bear was historically abundant in the lower Mississippi Delta, but because of the loss of more than 80 percent of bottomland hardwood habitats due to human exploitation, the range of this subspecies has been severely restricted. The translocation of *Ursus americanus americanus* from Minnesota into Louisiana during the 1960s prompted debate over whether the subspecies currently exists in its historic form. Populations of black bears are known to exist in the Atchafalaya River Basin and Tensas National Wildlife Refuge in Louisiana. The most important threat to *U. a. luteolus* is continued habitat loss, although mortality from poaching and collisions with automobiles have also been documented and may be significant mortality factors (Weaver, 1992).

The Louisiana black bear was designated as threatened by the USFWS in 1992, and populations were estimated to be greater than 60 in the Tensas River Basin and greater than 30 in the Atchafalaya River Basin at that time (Weaver, 1992). Although no formal statewide management plan exists for this subspecies, a number of studies are underway to determine its population status and habitat requirements. The Louisiana black bear weighs heavily in management plans on the national wildlife refuge. The Louisiana Forestry Association initiated the formation of a Black Bear Conservation Committee (BBCC) in 1990 to develop a coordinated approach to bear conservation. Today, the BBCC consists of representatives from a broad array of landowners, state and federal agencies, private conservation groups, the forest industry, representatives of agricultural interests, and the academic community. The BBCC coordinates its efforts through the USFWS.

The BBCC has published habitat management guidelines for the Louisiana black bear, and a management plan is being developed to serve as a template for the recovery program. Furthermore, regional research needs have been developed and prioritized, and a southeastern bear mapping project has been completed. The BBCC has been successful in obtaining funding for these and other projects, and it was recognized by the Louisiana Wildlife Federation as the 1991 Conservation Group of the Year.

Key Deer — *Odocoileus virginianus clavium*

The earliest historic accounts of Key deer were by Spanish explorers in 1575, and the subspecies then occurred only at low densities due to the dominance of mature forested lands in the Florida Keys (Hardin et al., 1984). Hurricanes undoubtedly played a major role in periodically creating earlier successional stage vegetation that was more beneficial to this deer. The Florida Legislature banned the hunting of Key deer in 1939 because of their near annihilation, but this measure was largely ineffective. The Key Deer National Wildlife Refuge was established in the early 1950s, and a protection plan was developed by the Boone and Crockett Club (Hardin et al., 1984). In 1957, a 2,400-ha (5,930-acre) refuge was established, and the subspecies was placed on the federal endangered species list in 1967 and thus was given full protection under the U.S. Endangered Species Act in 1973. The Key deer population was estimated at 300 to 400 individuals in 1974 (Klimstra et al., 1974), but it appears to have subsequently declined to 250 to 300 (Hardin et al., 1984).

The Key deer is especially vulnerable to urban development associated with tourism and residential housing. Projections are that by the 21st century, almost all private land on Big Pine Key (where 65 to 70 percent of all Key deer reside) will be developed, supporting a human population of 6,800 to 10,800 (Klimstra, 1985). A major habitat component for Key deer is fresh water, which is present during the dry season on only a few of the larger keys. Therefore, residential development of the larger keys, especially near water holes, would have an especially adverse impact on this deer.

The Key deer also is vulnerable to mortalities caused by road traffic, and this accounts for about 80 percent of all deaths (Klimstra, 1985). Ditches created for mosquito control are common on the larger keys, and these have caused the drowning of about 18 percent of marked fawns in one study (Hardin, 1974). Killing by free-ranging dogs also appears to be an important mortality factor (Klimstra, 1992), and this will likely increase along with the human population of the keys.

Key deer respond quickly and favorably to habitat management efforts. Prescribed fire (Klimstra, 1986), enlargement of water holes (Klimstra, 1992), and filling segments of mosquito ditches all benefit this subspecies. Although highway speed limits have been reduced in the region, the numbers of collisions between Key deer and automobiles have not declined. Apparently efforts to reduce traffic speeds were not adequate due to increasing numbers of vehicles on these roads.

A Key deer recovery plan was developed and approved in 1980 (Klimstra et al., 1980), and it identified the greatest obstacle to Key deer conservation as residential and commercial land development. Recommendations made in the plan were to protect habitat by designating and properly identifying inviolate areas, to control visitor access and reduce speed limits on roads, and to acquire and preserve additional land for wildlife (particularly No Name Key). When nuisance problems occur, the plan recommends that deer be selectively removed and translocated to appropriate unpopulated keys. The plan strongly suggests, however, that animals from zoological parks not be used to restock Key deer ranges due to the possibility that the integrity of the remnant genetic stock might be compromised. Hardin et al. (1984; page 390) cautioned that, "the predicted increase in competition for land use … likely will reduce the Key deer population, possibly to its precarious status of the 1950s."

Lower Keys Marsh Rabbit — *Sylvilagus palustris hefneri*

This subspecies of marsh rabbit apparently has always been localized, with numbers relatively stable at 200 to 400 individuals (Howe, 1988). However, populations are fragmented, and it has disappeared from several of the lower Florida Keys. This subspecies is also known as the "Playboy bunny" because its recent description was partially funded by the Playboy Foundation (Wolfe, 1992). The greatest threat to the lower keys marsh rabbit is habitat loss associated with land development. This animal is listed as endangered by the USFWS and the FGFWFC. The most immediate management action to assist this subspecies should be habitat acquisition and preservation. Studies of population structure also should be conducted because virtually nothing is known about the population dynamics of this marsh rabbit.

Round-tailed Muskrat — *Neofiber alleni*

Also known as the Florida water rat, the abundance of the round-tailed muskrat rises and falls with long-term water level fluctuations and associated changes in habitat. Florida's statewide population of this muskrat probably has declined in recent years due to freshwater and brackish wetland losses (Lefebvre and Tilmant, 1992), and the species apparently has adapted to sugarcane field habitats.

Although no specific management or conservation measures for the round-tailed muskrat have been taken, preservation of the Okefenokee Swamp in Georgia and Payne's Prairie and the Everglades in Florida has undoubtedly been beneficial for the species. Little is known about the population biology of this species.

Florida Rice Rat — *Oryzomys palustris natator*

Rice rats are present throughout the Florida mainland but are absent from the upper Florida Keys. The Florida rice rat is a localized population of rice rats endemic to the lower keys, and it is imperiled. This subspecies is in jeopardy largely due to human population expansion. Few data exist on numbers of these rice rats, and population trends are unknown (Humphrey, 1992c).

As with other imperiled mammal populations of the lower keys, the principal threat to this rice rat lies in conversion of habitats for human use. The USFWS has proposed to list this population of rice rats as endangered, and it is currently listed as such by the FGFWFC.

Key Largo Woodrat — *Neotoma floridana smalli* and Key Largo Cotton Mouse — *Peromyscus gossypinus allapaticola*

Not long ago, extrapolations of density estimates to available habitat on Key Largo (Florida) suggested a potential population size of about 6,500 Key Largo woodrats and 18,000 Key Largo cotton mice (Humphrey, 1988). However, efforts to find either animal in some suitable but isolated habitats have since been unsuccessful. The Key Largo woodrat and cotton mouse both inhabit dry tropical forest, and Key Largo woodrats do not appear to tolerate deforested or oldfield sites.

The major threat to both of these subspecies is forest conversion, and they do not appear to be particularly susceptible to other threats (e.g., predation by house cats and competition with the black rat, *Rattus rattus*), as are many other endangered rodents on island habitats. The major threat to these subspecies occurred in the early 1980s when over

4,000 housing units on Key Largo were approved or under construction. However, by restricting numbers of electrical hook-ups for housing units, planners kept similar housing developments in check on the proposed Crocodile Lake National Wildlife Refuge. Unfortunately, other areas were not so fortunate. In 1983, the USFWS issued a biological opinion that the proposed electrical hook-ups (and the subsequent housing units) would jeopardize the Key Largo woodrat. Since then, little pressure for residential development in upland areas on Key Largo has occurred (Humphrey, 1992b).

The Key Largo woodrat and the Key Largo cotton mouse are on both federal and state endangered species lists, and most of the habitat of these two subspecies is within proposed state and federal land acquisitions. A comprehensive Habitat Conservation Plan was developed by the state of Florida for the area, and although the plan has never been implemented, it has had a positive conservation impact by depreciating land values. Via translocations, populations of both species were established on Lignumvitae Key in the early 1970s. However, these populations subsequently declined, and no woodrats or cotton mice are known to exist there today (Humphrey, 1992b).

Florida Saltmarsh Vole — *Microtus pennsylvanicus dukecampbelli*

This vole subspecies has a limited distribution and is characterized by densities that shift radically depending on time of year and other rodent competitors in the saltmarsh community (Woods, 1992). Only one male was captured in each of 1987 and 1988 trapping attempts, and subsequent capture efforts have been unsuccessful. The greatest threat to the Florida saltmarsh vole is flooding due to storms, high tides, or high winds. In 1985, Hurricane Elena apparently resulted in a dramatic population decline of these voles. The problem of flooding is exacerbated due to development of adjacent upland habitats where the voles normally seek refuge when the saltmarshes are inundated. The USFWS has published a notice of intent to list the Florida saltmarsh vole as endangered. Conservation measures to assist this subspecies should include an intensive search for other suitable habitats and uplands adjacent to vole habitats should be protected from development. Woods (1992) recommended that consideration be given to a captive breeding program to supply individuals for possible repatriation.

Beach Mice — *Peromyscus polionotus allophrys, P. p. ammobates, P. p. niveiventris, P. p. peninsularis, P. p. phasma*, and *P. p. trissyllepsis*

Choctawhatchee (*Peromyscus polionotus allophrys*), Alabama (*P. p. ammobates*), St. Andrew (*P. p. peninsularis*), Anastasia Island (*P. p. phasma*), and Perdido Key (*P. p. trissyllepsis*) beach mice are all listed as federally endangered, whereas the southeastern beach mouse (*P. p. niveiventris*) is listed as threatened by the USFWS. Habitat requirements for all these beach mice are similar and, consequently, they are vulnerable to many of the same impacts. The most important decimating factor is habitat loss, mostly due to coastal development and damage to sand dunes from pedestrian travel and recreational vehicles (Bowen, 1968). Direct loss of populations during tropical storms, predation by domestic cats, genetic isolation, and competition with house mice (*Mus musculus*) all have played some role in the declining status of these beach mice (Holler, 1992a, 1992b).

By 1968, more than two-thirds of the habitat available for the Choctawhatchee beach mouse had been lost to coastal development (Bowen, 1968). In 1979, the population was greater than 178 at Topsail Hill and greater than 357 on Shell Island, Florida (Humphrey and Barbour, 1981). The population on Shell Island has appeared stable (Meyers, 1983), but the population at Topsail Hill may have declined. A translocation program from 1987 to 1988 resulted in a small, persistent population at Grayton Beach, Florida. Four areas of critical beach mouse habitat (totaling 20.2 linear km [about 13 miles]) have been identified in Florida, 14 km (8.7 miles) of which is in public ownership.

Between 1921 and 1983, commercial and residential development and human recreational activities destroyed over 60 percent of beach mouse habitat in Alabama (Holliman, 1983). Today, the Alabama beach mouse is found on the Fort Morgan Peninsula in Alabama, with the exception of Gulf State Park at the peninsula's east end. Hill (1989) conducted extensive trapping studies on the Fort Morgan Peninsula and found that house cats and house mice were more common at Gulf State Park than at other localities along the peninsula. Along with habitat acquisition, Hill (1989) recommended placing hay bales or snow fencing along low-lying (blowout) areas to reduce damage to dunes by storms. Installation of boardwalks to reduce human-associated damage to dunes and reducing house mouse and cat populations also was recommended.

The southeastern beach mouse is the most widely distributed of the imperiled beach mice, and its density increased on Merritt Island, Florida from 1975 to 1979 (Extine and Stout, 1987). This mouse is found in modest numbers on Atlantic coast beaches along the lower two-thirds of Florida, and populations appear stable although certain sections contain only fragmentary populations (Stout, 1992).

The St. Andrew beach mouse was estimated at about 500 individuals within the St. Joseph Peninsula State Park, Florida, with only a few tracks being seen outside the park (James, 1992). A smaller population persists on Tyndall Air Force Base, but its status is undetermined. Military exercises have damaged the sand dune habitats there.

Substantial populations of the Anastasia Island beach mouse exist, though numbers have been greatly reduced in recent decades (Humphrey, 1992a). This beach mouse exists in good numbers at each end of Anastasia Island; however, the habitat in between is privately owned and fragmented, and numbers of mice there are few. This subspecies was listed as federally endangered in 1989, and currently the best undeveloped habitat on Anastasia Island is under federal ownership. A number of individuals were introduced to a small barrier island in South Carolina, but the effort was not successful, partly due to severe predation by owls. Another population was established on the South Carolina coast, but it appears to be suffering from inbreeding depression (Ramsey, 1973).

The Perdido Key beach mouse is the most endangered of the five beach mice subspecies listed by the USFWS (Holler, 1992b). In 1979, populations of 26 and 52 mice were estimated respectively at Gulf State Park in Alabama and on Gulf Islands National Seashore, Florida (Humphrey and Barbour, 1981). By 1986, the mice were known to exist only on Gulf State Park (Holler et al., 1989). Perdido Key beach mice have since been reintroduced to Gulf Islands National Seashore from Gulf State Park, and this new population appears to be viable.

Besides state and federal listing as endangered or threatened subspecies, critical habitat has been designated for most of these beach mice. As such, these subspecies are given consideration in management decisions on all public lands. There currently is a repatriation program for Choctawhatchee and Perdido Key beach mice, and captive breeding populations for the former have been established (Holler, 1992a). Efforts are underway to establish additional breeding populations for many of these mice, but it may be necessary to remove domestic cats and house mice prior to reintroduction. Unfortunately, due to the extensive loss of coastal habitat, it may never be possible to remove these subspecies from protection under the U.S. Endangered Species Act.

Gray Bat — *Myotis grisescens* and Indiana Bat — *Myotis sodalis*

Although gray bats are currently thought to number about 1.5 million individuals, their numbers have dramatically decreased in recent years. About 95 percent of all gray bats hibernate in only eight caves in Tennessee, Missouri, Kentucky, Alabama, and Arkansas (Harvey, 1992). The Indiana bat numbers about 400,000 individuals, and 85 percent of these hibernate in seven caves in Missouri, Indiana, and Kentucky, and nearly half of these winter in just two caves. Estimates at a major hibernaculum have indicated a 34 percent decline from 1983 to 1989. Both of these bat species forage primarily over water, and thus they are closely linked with aquatic environments.

Gray and Indiana bats have narrow habitat requirements and exhibit strong site fidelity. They are sensitive to noise, lights, and other human disturbance, and human intrusion into hibernacula can result in mortality due to increased energy expenditure (Tuttle, 1979). Disturbance to summer colonies can cause bats to abandon caves. Furthermore, stream impoundment, forest clearing, and siltation may cause secondary impacts to gray and Indiana bat populations, although little is known about how stream impacts affect bats.

Disturbance to roosting habitats is considered the most significant negative impact to these two bat species, and efforts to gate caves to exclude humans have been initiated. However, even the gating itself has caused bats to abandon some caves.

Gray and Indiana bats are federally listed as endangered species. Since listing, wildlife agencies and conservation groups have purchased or protected several important maternity and hibernation caves (Tuttle, 1987). Gating designs have been improved and bats are returning to some of the previously abandoned caves. Bats are routinely monitored to determine effects of management efforts.

Dismal Swamp Southeastern Shrew — *Sorex longirostris fisheri*

The Dismal Swamp southeastern shrew is found in a very restricted range in the Great Dismal Swamp area of North Carolina and Virginia. Almost nothing is known concerning this subspecies' ecological relationship with the closely allied subspecies *S. l. longirostris* (French, 1980). The Dismal Swamp southeastern shrew has been listed as an endangered species by the USFWS, and much of its habitat is under federal protection within the Great Dismal Swamp National Wildlife Refuge which is managed by the U.S. Department of the Interior.

CONCLUSIONS AND RECOMMENDATIONS

The disproportionate representation of species endemic to Florida discussed above is due largely to impacts caused by humans. However, it also has come about because of biological mechanisms that affect speciation. Both of these issues are central to endangered species management, and they each must be understood if patterns of imperilment are to be considered in a manner that facilitates conservation management. Florida and

California have received more intensive pressures for urban and agricultural development than any other states in the continental United States. This factor alone probably would have resulted in dramatic decreases in biodiversity in these states. However, due to its peninsular shape and its fragmented aquatic habitats, isolation of Florida's mammal populations has occurred and has possibly resulted in high rates of genetic divergence, resulting in the wide array of subspecies present within the state. Some of these subspecies that are currently listed as federally endangered have been rare yet relatively stable in numbers for many decades. As a result, habitat modification which accompanies human land development has the potential for accelerated losses of diversity in this rich and fragile biotic assemblage. In essence, Florida represents a microcosm for endangered species management. Both spatially and temporally, efforts in Florida may foreshadow successes or failures of endangered species management elsewhere in North America.

Maintenance of biological diversity is a tremendous challenge in Florida, a state where geographical and climatological characteristics have produced high mammal diversity, yet even higher demand for citrus fruit, cattle, row crops, and urban development. Most of Florida's endangered mammals are associated with aquatic environments because these animals are extremely sensitive to slight changes in hydrology, pollution, and temperature, and because the unique natural beauty of their habitat places intense developmental pressure on it by humans. It is in such areas that land managers are faced with the enormous challenge of keeping the classic "oldfield-savannah-forest" successional sequence from being transformed into what has been called the "oldfield-orange groves-cities" sequence (Humphrey, 1992e).

In Florida and elsewhere, the single-species paradigm for endangered species conservation has been at best inequitable and at worst ineffective (Tasse, 1993). Success of single-species conservation programs are not always correlated with the amount of resources directed toward them. The Florida panther, which has served as a flagship species with a high-profile and intensive management program, continues to decline, whereas others, such as the river otter, have recovered with proportionately fewer resources allocated toward their restoration. The current approach is inequitable because, for example, almost 50 percent of endangered species funding in North America disbursed by the USFWS currently assists ten high-profile species, with the remaining 467 imperiled species receiving the remaining funds (Figure 1; LaRoe, 1993). While much of this funding has been appropriately directed toward important species in critical and immediate peril, it is certain that many little-known species are being overlooked.

The increasing loss of biological diversity will require an approach that is more clearly linked with ecological systems. Many of the mammal species discussed above are vulnerable to the same threats in the same habitats. The protection of additional wetland habitats in the lower Florida Keys and along Atlantic and Gulf Coast beaches, for example, would be beneficial for many of the imperiled mammals we have listed here. The endangered species scenario (consisting of listing, subsequent restrictions on land use, the inevitable litigation, etc.) repeated over and over again is an inefficient approach to conserving imperiled aquatic mammals. More importantly, this process often does not result in adequate long-term protection of the ecosystems in jeopardy, and it is generally agreed that most taxa became imperiled due to habitat or ecosystem dysfunction.

One, perhaps more equitable, approach has been termed "ecosystem management," and LaRoe (1993) lists three reasons why its time has come. First, resource management prob-

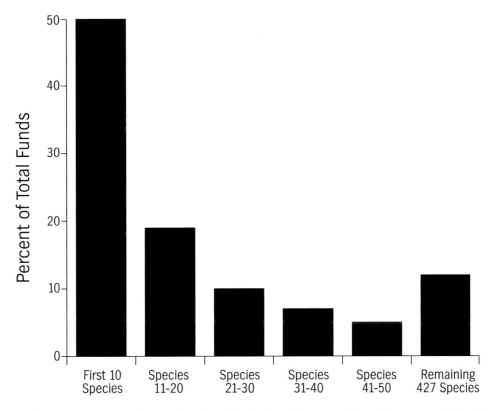

Figure 1. Distribution of U.S. Fish and Wildlife Service dollar expenditures (as a percent of total funds) for domestic endangered species conservation efforts (species placed in groups from most expensive to least expensive) for federal fiscal year 1990 (adapted from LaRoe, 1993).

lems today are much more complex than they were even a decade ago. Global issues such as increasing air pollution, increasing ultraviolet radiation, and global climate change, for example, were hardly considered at that time. Second, because issues concerning biological diversity usually transcend jurisdictional lines, a landscape approach to conservation is warranted. We no longer can afford to manage species solely within the jurisdictional boundaries of the state, federal, or private land manager for whom we are employed. We have to operate in the context of surrounding land uses, and too often this has been ignored. Finally, ecosystem management is more cost efficient than the single-species approach. We will never be able to address the inequities of the single-species approach unless we can redirect our focus to ecosystems and the species they contain.

There will be new challenges to carry out such an ecosystem approach. For example, state and federal agencies will be required to work together in a landscape context toward a common goal. However, various state and federal agencies may have different goals, clienteles, and funding sources. State wildlife agencies, for example, typically are almost solely supported by hunters and fishermen (via license sales and taxes on sporting goods), yet these agencies have played a major role in endangered species conservation. They have had to do so while remaining responsive to their funding source, i.e., the sportsmen. By and large, this has been a responsibility that the agencies and sportsmen have gladly accepted, but there have been and will be instances of conflicting interests and goals regarding endangered species management. The inter-jurisdictional consensus building required for ecosystem management will be an immense challenge.

To some, ecosystem management means "natural regulation" or "no management." This strict interpretation and implementation could have catastrophic consequences. The fact that the globe has changed dramatically due to the actions of humans necessitates that these altered areas be actively managed. Species compositions have changed, the vegetation and soils have been altered, hydrology has been changed, etc., and these human impacts will require management to achieve the desired objectives for the ecosystem. There will always be hard decisions to be made, and as always, those will involve trade-offs. Any change in habitat (even something as simple as a stand of trees that is allowed to mature) will positively affect some species and negatively affect others. Managers need to be able to predict those responses and make appropriate choices based on land management objectives that are identified by humans.

Finally, ecosystem management implies that single-species management is no longer appropriate. That need not be the case. If humans decide that recovery of an endangered species is a primary management objective for an ecosystem, a single-species emphasis can still be built into the management plan.

At projected rates, species will soon become extinct faster than they can be reviewed and listed (LaRoe, 1993). Therefore, resource managers must take an anticipatory approach. It is more efficient to conserve a species while it is still abundant than when it becomes imperiled. The concept of ecosystem management offers a framework for *a priori* endangered species management. Hopefully the implementation of this concept will help reverse the terrible tide of imperilment that jeopardizes many mammals associated with aquatic systems throughout the Southeast.

ACKNOWLEDGEMENTS

We express our gratitude to the Tennessee Aquarium for inviting us to present a version of this paper at their imperiled aquatic fauna conference, and for their generous hospitality during the symposium. We also wish to thank the American Society of Mammalogists for loaning some slides of small mammals from their slide library, and J. W. Hardin for loaning slides of Key deer used for the presentation.

REFERENCES

Belden, R. C., and B. W. Hagedorn. 1993. Feasibility of translocating panthers into northern Florida. *Journal of Wildlife Management* 57:388-397.

Bertram, G. C. L., and C. K. R. Bertram. 1973. The modern Sirenia: Their distribution and status. *Biological Journal of the Linnaean Society* 5:297-338.

Bowen, W. W. 1968. Variation and evolution of Gulf Coast populations of beach mice, *Peromyscus polionotus. Bulletin of the Florida State Museum, Biological Science* 12:1-91.

Clark, J. D., J. H. Jenkins, P. B. Bush, and E. B. Moser. 1981. Pollution trends in river otter in Georgia. *Proceedings of the Annual Conference of the Southeastern Association of Fish and Wildlife Agencies* **35**:71-79.

Deems, E. F., and D. Pursley. 1978. *North American Furbearers: Their Management, Research and Harvest Status in 1976.* International Association of Fish and Wildlife Agencies Publication, University of Maryland, College Park, MD.

Duplaix, N., and N. Simon. 1976. *World Guide to Mammals.* Crown Publishers, Inc., New York, NY.

Extine, D. D., and I. J. Stout. 1987. Dispersion and habitat occupancy of the beach mouse, *Peromyscus polionotus niveiventris. Journal of Mammalogy* **68**:297-304.

Fimreite, N., and L. M. Reynolds. 1973. Mercury contamination in fish of northwestern Ontario. *Journal of Wildlife Management* **37**:62-68.

Flower, W. H., and R. Lydekker. 1891. *An Introduction to the Study of Mammals Living and Extinct.* Adam and Charles Black, London.

French, T. W. 1980. *Sorex longirostris. Mammalian Species* **143**:1-3.

Godman, J. D. 1826. *American Natural History, Volume I.* H. C. Carey and I. Lea, Philadelphia, PA.

Hardin, J. W. 1974. Behavior, socio-biology, and reproductive life history of the Florida Key deer, *Odocoileus virginianus clavium.* Ph.D. Dissertation, Southern Illinois University, Carbondale, IL.

Hardin, J. W., W. D. Klimstra, and N. J. Silvy. 1984. Florida Keys. In *White-tailed Deer: Ecology and Management.* Lowell K. Halls (ed.). Stackpole Books, Harrisburg, PA, p. 381-390.

Hartman, D. S. 1974. Distribution, status and conservation of the manatee in the United States. Contract 14-16-008-748, U.S. Fish and Wildlife Service, National Technical Information Service, Springfield, VA, 246 p.

Harvey, M. J. 1992. Bats of the eastern United States. Arkansas Game and Fish Commission, Little Rock, AR.

Hill, E. A. 1989. Population dynamics, habitat, and distribution of the Alabama beach mouse. M.S. Thesis. Auburn University, Auburn, AL.

Holler, N. R. 1992a. Choctawhatchee beach mouse. In *Rare and Endangered Biota of Florida: Volume I, Mammals.* S. R. Humphrey (ed.). University Press of Florida, Gainesville, FL, p. 76-86.

Holler, N. R. 1992b. Perdido Key beach mouse. In *Rare and Endangered Biota of Florida: Volume I, Mammals.* S. R. Humphrey (ed.). University Press of Florida, Gainesville, FL, p. 102-109.

Holler, N. R., D. W. Mason, R. M. Dawson, T. Simons, and M. C. Wooten. 1989. Reestablishmet of the Perdido Key beach mouse (*Peromyscus polionotus trisyllepsis*) on Gulf Islands National Seashore. *Conservation Biology* **3**:397-404.

Holliman, D. C. 1983. Status and habitat of Alabama Gulf Coast beach mice *Peromyscus polionotus ammobates* and *P. p. trissyllepsis. Northeast Gulf Science* **6**:121-129.

Howe, S. E. 1988. Lower Keys marsh rabbit status survey. Report submitted to the U.S. Fish and Wildlife Service, Jacksonville, FL, 8 p.

Humphrey, S. R. 1988. Density estimates of the Key Largo woodrat and cotton mouse (*Neotoma floridana smalli* and *Peromyscus gossypinus allapaticola*), using the nested grid approach. *Journal of Mammalogy* **69**:524-531.

Humphrey, S. R. 1992a. Anastasia Island beach mouse. In *Rare and Endangered Biota of Florida: Volume I, Mammals.* S. R. Humphrey (ed.). University Press of Florida, Gainesville, FL, p. 94-101.

Humphrey, S. R. 1992b. Key Largo woodrat. In *Rare and Endangered Biota of Florida: Volume I, Mammals.* S. R. Humphrey (ed.). University Press of Florida, Gainesville, FL, p. 119-130.

Humphrey, S. R. 1992c. Lower Keys population of rice rat. In *Rare and Endangered Biota of Florida: Volume I, Mammals.* S. R. Humphrey (ed.). University Press of Florida, Gainesville, FL, p. 300-309.

Humphrey, S. R. 1992d. Southern Florida population of mink. In *Rare and Endangered Biota of Florida: Volume I, Mammals.* S. R. Humphrey (ed.). University Press of Florida, Gainesville, FL, p. 319-327.

Humphrey, S. R. (ed.). 1992e. *Rare and Endangered Biota of Florida: Volume I, Mammals.* University Press of Florida, Gainesville, FL.

Humphrey, S. R., and D. B. Barbour. 1981. Status and habitat of three subspecies of *Peromyscus polionotus* in Florida. *Journal of Mammalogy* **62**:840-844.

James, F. C. 1992. St. Andrew beach mouse. In *Rare and Endangered Biota of Florida: Volume I, Mammals.* S. R. Humphrey (ed.). University Press of Florida, Gainesville, FL, p. 87-93.

Jordan, D. B. 1990. A proposal to issue endangered species permits to capture select Florida panthers (*Felis concolor coryi*) for the establishment of a captive population. Draft Environmental Assessment, U.S. Fish and Wildlife Service, Gainesville, FL, 66 p.

Jordan, D. B. 1991. A proposal to establish a captive breeding population of Florida panthers. Final Supplemental Environmental Impact Statement, U.S. Fish and Wildlife Service, Atlanta, GA, 65 p.

Jordan, D. B. 1994. Final preliminary analysis of some potential Florida panther population reestablishment sites. Final Report, U.S. Fish and Wildlife Service, University of Florida, Gainesville, FL, 11 p.

Klimstra, W. D. 1985. The Key deer. *Florida Naturalist* **58**(4):2-5.

Klimstra, W. D. 1986. Controlled burning in habitat management: Some observations, National Key Deer Refuge. Unpublished Final Report, Cooperative Wildlife Research Laboratory, Southern Illinois University, Carbondale, IL, 35 p.

Klimstra, W. D. 1992. Key deer. In *Rare and Endangered Biota of Florida: Volume I, Mammals.* S. R. Humphrey (ed.). University Press of Florida, Gainesville, FL, p. 201-215.

Klimstra, W. D., J. W. Hardin, M. D. Carpenter, and S. Jenkusky. 1980. Florida Key deer recovery plan. U.S. Fish and Wildlife Service, Washington D.C., 52 p.

Klimstra, W. D., J. W. Hardin, N. J. Silvy, B. N. Jacobson, and V. A. Terpening. 1974. Key deer investigations final report: December 1967-June 1973. Southern Illinois University, Carbondale, IL, 184 p.

LaRoe, E. T. 1993. Implementation of an ecosystem approach to endangered species conservation. *Endangered Species Update* **10/11**:3-6.

Lefebvre, L. W., and J. T. Tilmant. 1992. Round-tailed muskrat. In *Rare and endangered biota of Florida: Volume I, Mammals.* S. R. Humphrey (ed.), University Press of Florida, Gainesville, FL, p. 276-286.

Maehr, D. S. 1983. Black bear depredation on beeyards in Florida. In *First Eastern Wildlife Damage Control Conference.* D. J. Decker (ed.). Ithaca, NY, p. 133-135.

Maehr, D. S. 1990. Tracking Florida's panthers. *Defenders* 65(5):9-15.

Maehr, D. S. 1992a. Florida panther distribution and conservation strategy. Final Report, Florida Game and Fresh Water Fish Commission, Tallahassee, FL, 24 p.

Maehr, D. S. 1992b. Florida black bear. In *Rare and Endangered Biota of Florida: Volume I, Mammals.* S. R. Humphrey (ed.). University Press of Florida, Gainesville, FL, p. 265-275.

Melquist, W. E., and A. E. Dronkert. 1987. River otter. In *Wild Furbearer Management and Conservation in North America.* M. Novak, J. A. Baker, M. E. Obbard, and B. Malloch (eds.). Ontario Ministry of Natural Resources, Toronto, p. 626-641.

Melquist, W. E., and M. G. Hornocker. 1979. Development and use of a telemetry technique for studying river otter. In *Proceedings of the Second International Conference on Wildlife Biotelemetry.* F. M. Long (ed.). Laramie, WY, p. 104-114.

Meyers, J. M. 1983. Status, microhabitat, and management recommendations for *Peromyscus polionotus* on Gulf Coast beaches. Unpublished Report submitted to the U. S. Fish and Wildlife Service, Atlanta, GA, 29 p.

Odell, D. K. 1982. Manatee. In *Wild Mammals of North America: Biology, Management, and Economics.* J. A. Chapman, and G. A. Feldhamer (eds.). Johns Hopkins University Press, Baltimore, MD, p. 828-837.

Odell, D. K., and J. E. Reynolds. 1979. Observations on manatee mortality in south Florida. *Journal of Wildlife Management* 43:572-577.

O'Shea, T. J. 1988. The past, present, and future of manatees in the southeastern United States: Realities, misunderstandings, and enigmas. In *Proceedings of the Third Southeastern Nongame and Endangered Wildlife Symposium.* R. R. Odom, K. A. Riddleberger, and J. C. Ozier (eds.). Georgia Department of Natural Resources, Game and Fish Division, Social Circle, GA, p. 184-204.

O'Shea, T. J., and M. E. Ludlow. 1992. Florida manatee. In *Rare and Endangered Biota of Florida: Volume I, Mammals.* S. R. Humphrey (ed.). University Press of Florida, Gainesville, FL, p. 190-200.

Packard, J. M. 1985. Preliminary assessment of uncertainty involved in modeling manatee populations. Manatee Population Research Report Number 9, Technical Report Number 8-9, Florida Cooperative Fish and Wildlife Research Unit, University of Florida, Gainesville, FL, 19 p.

Park, E. 1971. *The World of the Otter.* J. B. Lippincott Co., New York, NY.

Peterson, S. L. 1974. Man's relationship with the Florida manatee, *Trichechus manatus latirostris* (Harlan): An historical perspective. M.A. Thesis, University of Michigan, Ann Arbor, MI.

Ramsey, P. R. 1973. Spatial and temporal variation in genetic structure of insular and mainland populations of *Peromyscus polionotus.* Ph.D. Dissertation. University of Georgia, Athens, GA.

Reynolds, J. E., III, and J. R. Wilcox. 1986. Distribution and abundance of the West Indian manatee, *Trichechus manatus*, around selected Florida power plants following winter cold fronts: 1984-85. *Biological Conservation* **38**:103-113.

Stout, I. J. 1992. Southeastern beach mouse. In *Rare and Endangered Biota of Florida: Volume I, Mammals.* S. R. Humphrey (ed.). University Press of Florida, Gainesville, FL, p. 242-249.

Tasse, J. 1993. For skeptics only. *Endangered Species Update (Special Issue)* **10**:1-2.

Toweill, D. E., and J. E. Tabor. 1984. River otter. In *Wild Mammals of North America: Biology, Management, and Economics.* J. A. Chapman, and G. A. Feldhamer (eds.). Johns Hopkins University Press, Baltimore, MD, p. 688-703.

Tuttle, M. D. 1979. Status, cause of decline, and management of endangered gray bats. *Journal of Wildlife Management* **43**:1-17.

Tuttle, M. D. 1987. Endangered gray bat benefits from protection. *Endangered Species Technical Bulletin* **21**(3):4-5.

U.S. Fish and Wildlife Service. 1987. Florida panther recovery plan. Prepared by the Florida Panther Interagency Committee for the U.S. Fish and Wildlife Service, Atlanta, GA, 75 p.

Weaver, K. M. 1992. Louisiana status report. *Eastern Black Bear Workshop* **11**:16-21.

Wilson, E. O. 1992. *The Diversity of Life.* Belknap Press of Harvard University Press, Cambridge, MA.

Wolfe, J. L. 1992. Lower Keys Marsh Rabbit. In *Rare and Endangered Biota of Florida: Volume I, Mammals.* S. R. Humphrey (ed.). University Press of Florida, Gainesville, FL, p. 71-75.

Wooding, J. B. 1992. Florida status report. *Eastern Black Bear Workshop* **11**:12-13.

Woods, C. A. 1992. Southeastern beach mouse. In *Rare and Endangered Biota of Florida: Volume I, Mammals.* S. R. Humphrey (ed.). University Press of Florida, Gainesville, FL, p. 131-139.

CHAPTER 16

Status and Restoration of the Etowah River, an Imperiled Southern Appalachian Ecosystem

Noel M. Burkhead, Stephen J. Walsh,

Byron J. Freeman, and James D. Williams

"The last word in ignorance is the man who says of an animal or plant: 'What good is it?'" — Aldo Leopold, *A Sand County Almanac*

M ost concern by contemporary scientists and conservation groups about biodiversity loss focuses on regions of rich terrestrial diversity such as tropical rain forests. Much less attention is directed at the decline and loss of aquatic species, communities, and ecosystems, whether they are Amazonian, coral reef, or southern Appalachian (Lydeard and Mayden, 1995; Stiassny, 1996). Humans are emotionally biased towards terrestrial biotas and particularly towards those species that are warm-blooded and endearing — the so-called "charismatic megafauna." It is lamentable that this emotional bias is transferred to the intellectual arena by what science is funded and which resources receive protection (Warren et al., 1997). Relatively few resource managers and science leaders are aware of the rich temperate freshwater biodiversity in rivers of the southeastern United States, or of the alarming levels of imperilment of these systems.

Aquatic Fauna in Peril: The Southeastern Perspective, edited by George W. Benz, and David E. Collins. 1997. Special Publication 1, Southeast Aquatic Research Institute, Lenz Design & Communications, Decatur, GA, 554 p.

North America north of Mexico harbors the richest temperate freshwater fish fauna in the world (Page and Burr, 1991) and therefore is an important global biodiversity resource. This ichthyofauna consists of about 800 species, of which some 490 species occur in the southeastern United States and about 349 inhabit the southern Appalachians. The Etowah River system harbors 91 native fishes (26 percent of the southern Appalachian fish fauna) and 14 introduced species. The southeastern United States is also rich in other aquatic faunas including freshwater mussels and snails (Neves et al., 1997), aquatic insects (Morse et al., 1997), and crayfishes (Taylor et al., 1996). The levels of extinction and imperilment of fishes and mollusks (mussels and snails) in southern states are truly disturbing: about 20 percent of the fish fauna (Williams et al., 1989; Warren and Burr, 1994; Walsh et al., 1995) and over 70 percent of the mollusk fauna (Neves et al., 1997) are in jeopardy. Although less is known about aquatic arthropods, we suspect that similar levels of decline exist in these animals as well. The fact that the arthropod diversity of the southeastern United States is so poorly known and we do not know the extent that the fauna is imperiled exemplifies a general lack of commitment to study of southeastern aquatic resources.

Causes of habitat destruction and aquatic faunal decline are discussed throughout this volume. The ultimate causes are ignorance and greed in the overall way society perceives and exploits the Earth's finite natural resources. The consequences of this exploitation are exacerbated by human population size and its continued exponential growth. However, there is basis for hope that society will make commitments and take actions necessary to retain most of the existing biodiversity. Humans have clearly advanced in our moral commitment to the natural world (Nash, 1989). Based on the success of nature television programming, more Americans are concerned now than ever before about the intrinsic values of biodiversity.

Relative to biological conservation, the traditional roles of scientists have been as theoreticians with few real data, prognosticators of doom and gloom, or scribes of decline. Conservation science has matured into a focused, multidisciplinary field that incorporates elements of systematics, ecology, population biology, and genetics to study the causes and patterns of biological simplification, and is beginning to offer scientifically-based solutions to restoring damaged biological systems. Many conservation scientists now recognize that communicating only with other scientists or exclusively relying on government agencies to solve onerous and often politically charged environmental problems is simply not working. Furthermore, at the local level, civic leaders and resource managers are often incapacitated by capricious changes in political will. If meaningful changes are going to occur to correct the most blatant abuses of our aquatic resources, scientists must repackage and effectively communicate their esoteric knowledge directly to the public (Tangley, 1994).

In this paper, we use the Etowah River of north Georgia as a conceptual and practical model for restoration of an imperiled southern Appalachian river system. The terrestrial and aquatic components of the Etowah River watershed together compose the Etowah River ecosystem, and we emphasize that the streams in the watershed cannot be considered independently from the lands they drain. Freshwater fishes are primarily used herein to characterize the aquatic health of the river system because our knowledge of fishes is more comprehensive than any other taxonomic group of the southeastern aquatic fauna. However, because of significant imperilment and extirpation levels of mollusks, we also discuss their status in the Etowah River.

The Etowah River is representative of southern Appalachian river systems: it drains southern Appalachian physiography, it has relatively high aquatic diversity, and high fish endemism. It is beleaguered by a litany of environmental threats that are common to southern Appalachian river systems. As a result of habitat decline, the Etowah River system has lost many species and has others placed on state and federal endangered species lists. This contribution synthesizes original data and information from diverse sources. Via this synthesis, we hope to provide critical background information on the status of the Etowah River that will be useful for protection and recovery of this unique ecosystem.

METHODS

Records of fishes are largely based on about 250 collections made by ourselves and colleagues since 1989, but also include a relatively complete survey of national and regional museum holdings and a summary of literature records. Our initial survey work focused on determining the distribution of the threatened Cherokee darter and later expanded into a general survey of Etowah River fishes. Figure 1 depicts Etowah River collection sites (some recent collection sites are not shown).

Collections were made by seining, backpack shocking, boat shocking, and gill netting. All specimens were retained except for those of the most common or protected species. Most of the specimens collected during our surveys are housed at the Florida Museum of Natural History at the University of Florida (UF). Significant holdings of Etowah River fishes are also at the University of Georgia Museum of Natural History (UGAMNH) and the University of Tennessee at Knoxville (UT). Fish nomenclature is based on a combination of Robins et al. (1991), Mayden et al. (1992), and our interpretation of Coburn and Cavender (1992; page 333) regarding recognition of the minnow genera *Ericymba* and *Hybopsis*.

Ecological associations of imperilment for Etowah River fishes are derived from our ongoing study of imperilment patterns of southern Appalachian fishes. We summarized a subset of Etowah fish data from the southern Appalachian fauna to generally compare patterns of imperilment for Etowah River and southern Appalachian fishes. The southern Appalachian analysis is based on a matrix of 349 southern Appalachian fishes (contrasting non-imperiled versus imperiled species) and 46 ecological and zoogeographic attributes similar to a study by Angermeier (1995) for the Virginia fish fauna. Attributes were grouped into related categories, and the set of categories for Etowah River fishes included in this review are range size, vertical orientation in the water column, body size, and habitat size. The matrix for each category consists of species (rows) and attributes (columns).

For definitions of basin, drainage, and system, we use those of Page and Burr (1991). The Etowah River is actually a subsystem of the Coosa River system, but throughout this paper we refer to the Etowah River as a system. The usual definition of an endemic freshwater fish is a species that is restricted to a drainage (Jenkins and Burkhead, 1994), but here we restrict it to a species found only in one river system.

The category *range size* includes four attributes:

1. Wide-ranging — occurring throughout a large geographic area, such as the Southeast, in multiple drainages, and often in more than one basin.
2. Intermediate-ranging — occurring in more than one drainage within a basin, but sometimes occurring in geographically proximate portions of adjacent basins.
3. Localized — restricted to one or more river systems within one drainage, but sometimes occurring in limited portions of several drainages within one basin.

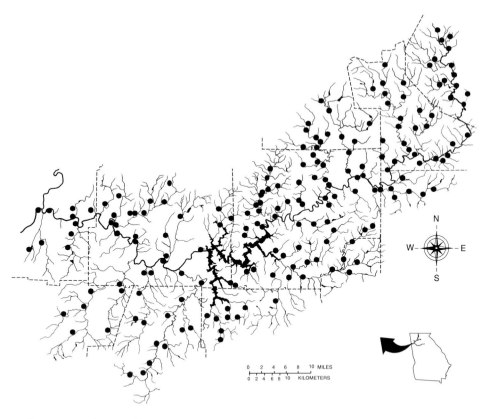

Figure 1. Distribution of fish collections made in the Etowah River from 1876 to present (some recent collections not shown); solid circles represent collection sites; county boundaries depicted by dashed lines.

4. Isolated — very restricted distribution, often occurring only at one or several sites within one or a few tributary systems, usually within one drainage.

No attempt was made to distinguish between species which have always been highly localized and others with relictual distributions (i.e., those having experienced range constrictions over geologic time).

The category *vertical orientation* in the water column is divided into two attributes:

1. Benthic — living on the bottom.
2. Non-benthic — living above the bottom.

Each attribute was averaged across three activities: feeding, spawning, and sheltering.

The category *body size* is divided into four attributes:

1. Very small — maximum adult length up to 75 mm (2.9 inches) total length (TL).
2. Small — maximum adult length from 76 to 150 mm (3.0 to 5.8 inches) TL.
3. Medium — maximum adult length from 151 to 400 mm (5.9 to 15.7 inches) TL.
4. Large — maximum adult size exceeding 400 mm (15.7 inches) TL.

The category *habitat size* association is represented by five attributes:

1. Headwater — tiny headwater or first order tributaries, or small springs that are usually less than 2 m (6.6 feet) wide (stream order is a system that characterizes the degree

of branching of a stream system; order number increases when two tributaries of the same order join);

2. Small Creek — usually first or second order streams less than 5 m (16.4 feet) in width.
3. Creek — streams ranging in average width from 5 to 15 m (16.4 to 49.2 feet).
4. Small River — streams ranging in average width from 16 to 99 m (52.5 to 324.8 feet).
5. Large River — streams with an average width of 100 m (328.1 feet) or more.

Our definition of the imperiled fishes and mussels, with few exceptions, includes species federally listed under the U.S. Endangered Species Act of 1973 as threatened or endangered (U.S. Federal Register, 1994a), Category 2 species (U.S. Federal Register, 1994b), and those listed as special concern, threatened, or endangered by Williams et al. (1989) and Williams et al. (1992b). Until intensive status surveys are made for the lined chub, burrhead shiner, frecklebelly madtom, and freckled darter, we regard their most appropriate status to be Category 2 (versus 3C in U.S. Federal Register, 1994b). Also included as a C2 species is an undescribed darter, *Percina* sp. cf. *P. macrocephala.* The populations of this species appear to be disjunct and confined to the upper Coosa River system.

We do not support the recent elimination by the U.S. Fish and Wildlife Service of Category 2 candidates from the Animal Candidate Review for Listing as Threatened or Endangered Species that is periodically published in the U.S. Federal Register. Contrary to the argument by Sayers (1996), we believe the C2 status to be a useful category equivalent to Special Concern status employed by the American Fisheries Society and by many states. In effect, this action orphans declining elements of the fauna from direct federal responsibility until they are in imminent jeopardy and merit listing as threatened or endangered.

Assignment of ecological attributes for species was based on published information. Because of incomplete life-history data on the southern upland fish fauna, matrix cells were scored as either present (1) or absent (0), and no cells were left blank. Body and range size categories had a single attribute score of "1" per species. Habitat size and vertical orientation categories frequently had multiple attributes scored as "1" for each species. For example, in the habitat size category, many species occupy creeks, small rivers, and large rivers, and in the vertical orientation category, some species feed at all depths in the water column. Where data for a species were unavailable, we scored cells based on knowledge of closely related taxa or on the morphology of the species in question. Approximately one-third of the fauna required estimating attribute cell scores. However, based on our knowledge of the fish fauna and experience in compiling an encyclopedic reference summarizing life-history data (Jenkins and Burkhead, 1994), on the whole we believe that our attribute assignments for missing data closely approximate reality. Matrices were summed by columns (attributes) for proportional comparisons of the imperiled and non-imperiled subsets of Etowah River and southern Appalachian fishes.

PHYSICAL AND BIOLOGICAL SETTING

"We do not inherit the land from our parents — we borrow it from our children."
— Native American adage

Physiography of the Etowah River

The Etowah River is one of four major headwater tributaries of the upper Coosa River system of the Mobile River drainage. The Etowah River joins the Oostanaula River in Rome, Georgia, to form the Coosa River (Figure 2).

Most of the Coosa River in Alabama is impounded; therefore much of the surviving biodiversity of this system is confined to major tributaries in Alabama and Georgia.

The Etowah River occurs entirely within Georgia; its headwaters originate in the southern boundary of the Blue Ridge and the river flows southwesterly through the Upland subsection of the Piedmont, the Talladega subsection of the Blue Ridge, and the Great Valley subsection of the Valley and Ridge provinces (Wharton, 1978; Figure 3).

County and principal tributary names are depicted in Figure 4. In the center of the watershed is Allatoona Reservoir, a large 4,800-ha (11,861-acre) hydroelectric and flood-control impoundment that was completed in 1949 by the U.S. Army Corps of Engineers (Martin and Hanson, 1966). Allatoona Dam is located in a narrow gorge in a zone of faults (Cressler et al., 1979) that, prior to impoundment, probably represented a natural transition area in the character of the river from rolling upland hills and isolated ridges to the valley floor of the Great Valley subsection. Geologically, this fault zone roughly delineates a transition from crystalline metamorphic rocks to sedimentary limestones (Wharton, 1978). Selected physical attributes of the Etowah River system are as follows: drainage area = 4,871 km^2 (3,027 square miles); drainage area above Allatoona Reservoir = 1,588 km^2 (987 square miles); elevation at mouth = 174 m (571 feet); maximum elevation = 769 m (2,523 feet); greatest stream order = 6; drainage pattern = dendritic; main channel length = 265 km (165 miles); impounded channel length = 51.8 km (32.2 miles); and average gradient = 2.2 m per km (11.6 feet per mile). Historically, the Etowah watershed was inhabited by Native Americans who occupied a major village at a site presently known as the Etowah Indian Mound, located below the Allatoona Dam site (van der Schalie and Parmalee, 1960). Remnants of Native American fish traps still exist in the main channel of the river above and below Allatoona Dam (Figure 5).

The Etowah River drains portions of 11 counties. Much of the land use in these counties is agricultural, but there are large cities within and adjacent to the watershed, most notably the sprawling Atlanta metropolitan area south of the system (Figure 6). Other large or moderate-sized cities are Rome, located at the mouth of the Etowah River; Cartersville, situated downstream from Allatoona Reservoir on the north side of the river; and Canton, on the south side of the river upstream from Allatoona Reservoir (Figure 6). In decreasing order, Fulton, Cobb, Floyd, and Cherokee are the most urbanized counties in the watershed.

The main channel and most tributaries of the Etowah River are constantly turbid as a result of soil erosion. During normal water levels, water color is typically brown or greenish, but during high water levels the water is orange-red, characteristic of the clay soils of

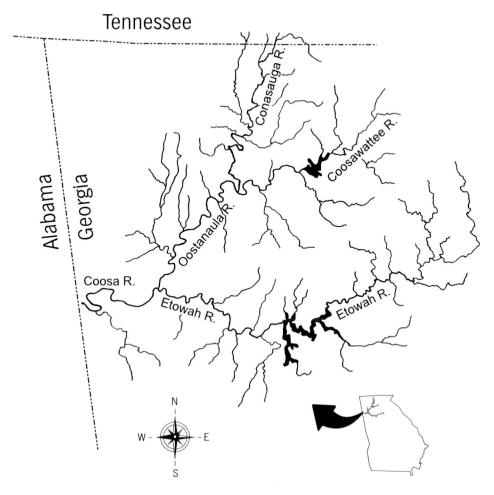

Figure 2. The upper Coosa River system of north Georgia and its major headwater tributaries.

the region. Little is known about the quality of the river prior to 1900. Jordan (1877) characterized a few tributaries of the lower Etowah River as clear with rocky bottoms as compared to the muddy waters of the Ocmulgee River of Georgia. In his autobiography, Jordan (1922) described the main channel of the Etowah River as muddy during a brief collecting trip in 1876. Given the physiography and surface geology of the drainage, there is little doubt that the Etowah River system was historically as clear as the upper Conasauga River, a sister tributary of the Etowah in the upper Coosa River system. By visiting the Conasauga River in northern Murray County, Georgia, or Polk County, Tennessee, one can see clear water conditions that undoubtedly existed in the Etowah River prior to extensive deforestation and land disturbance.

Status of the Aquatic Fauna

The Coosa River and its major tributaries, including the Etowah River, may hold the dubious distinction of having more recent extirpations and extinctions of aquatic organ-

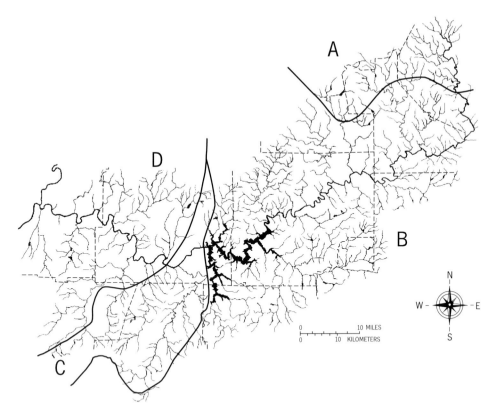

Figure 3. The Etowah River system: county boundaries depicted by dashed lines; physiographic boundaries depicted by solid bold lines; A = Blue Ridge province; B = upland subsection of the Piedmont province; C = Talladega subsection of the Blue Ridge province; D = Great Valley subsection of the Valley and Ridge province. The large impoundment in the center of the system is Allatoona Reservoir.

isms than any other equally-sized river system in the United States. Neves et al. (1997) document the recent mass extinction of 38 species of endemic aquatic snails in the Coosa River. We estimate the Etowah River has more imperiled fishes (17 spp.) and invertebrates (16 spp.) than any other river system of similar length in the southeastern United States (Table 1). The Conasauga River has the second highest number of imperiled species (ten fishes and 15 mollusks). The high levels of imperilment in the Etowah and Conasauga rivers result in large part from the diminution of the high biodiversity of the Coosa River system caused by extensive habitat loss such that only remnants of formerly more widespread assemblages survive in fragmented headwater systems. The high levels of imperilment of the aquatic fauna are not restricted to the relatively intact portions of the upper Coosa River system; many species are jeopardized throughout the entire Mobile River drainage (Lydeard and Mayden, 1995).

We tabulate 17 fishes as imperiled in the Etowah River: two each threatened or endangered, 12 C2 species, and one species on the Georgia state list but not on federal lists. Twelve Etowah River mussels are on federal lists: eight endangered, three threatened, and one C2 species. The mussel list includes five species (upland combshell, southern acornshell,

Table 1. Imperiled aquatic species in the Etowah River system. Status categories: C2 = may merit listing, but more data are needed to determine status; T = threatened; E = endangered. Asterisks denote fishes considered extirpated from the river system.

Common Name	Scientific Name	Federal	Georgia
		Status	
Fishes:			
lake sturgeon*	*Acipenser fulvescens*	C2	-
blue shiner*	*Cyprinella caerulea*	T	E
lined chub*	*Hybopsis lineapunctata*	C2	-
burrhead shiner*	*Notropis asperifrons*	C2	-
undescribed "blue sucker"*	*Cycleptus sp. cf. C. elongatus*	C2	-
frecklebelly madtom	*Noturus munitus*	C2	E
freckled madtom*	*N. nocturnus*	-	E
coldwater darter*	*Etheostoma ditrema*	C2	T
Etowah darter	*E. etowahae*	E	T
Cherokee darter	*E. scotti*	T	T
trispot darter*	*E. trisella*	C2	-
undescribed darter A	*E. sp. cf. E. brevirostrum*	C2	T
undescribed darter B	*E. sp. cf. E. brevirostrum*	C2	T
amber darter	*Percina antesella*	E	E
coal darter*	*P. brevicauda*	C2	-
freckled darter	*P. lenticula*	C2	E
undescribed darter C	*P. sp. cf. P. macrocephala*	C2[1]	-
Mussels:			
upland combshell	*Epioblasma metastriata*	E	E
southern acornshell	*E. othcaloogensis*	E	E
fine-lined pocketbook	*Lampsilis altilis*	T	T
orange-nacre mucket	*L. perovalis*	T	-
Tennessee heelsplitter	*Lasmigona holstonia*	C2	-
Alabama moccasinshell	*Medionidus acutissimus*	T	T
Coosa moccasinshell	*M. parvulus*	E	E
southern clubshell	*Pleurobema decisum*	E	E
southern pigtoe	*P. georgianum*	E	E
Warrior pigtoe	*P. rubellum*	E	-
ovate clubshell	*P. perovatum*	E	E
triangular kidneyshell	*Ptychobranchus greeni*	E	E
Snails:			
spindle elimia	*Elimia capillaris*	C2	-
coldwater elimia	*E. gerhardti*	C2	-
rough hornsnail	*Pleurocera foremani*	C2	-
Insects:			
Berners two-winged mayfly	*Heterocleon berneri*	C2	-
Totals:		33	19

[1] Status is our recommendation; not listed as such in U.S. Federal Register (1994b). The Alabama shad (*Alosa alabamae*), a species extirpated from the Etowah River system, may warrant future consideration as a C2 species.

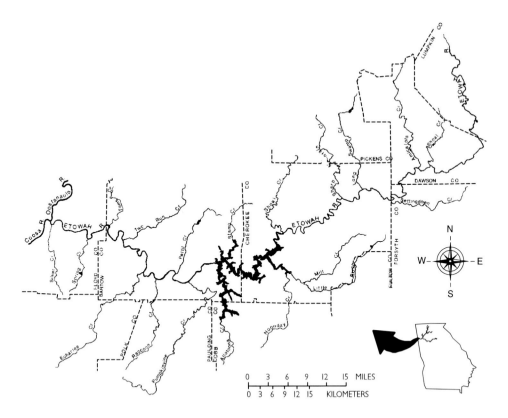

Figure 4. Counties and principal tributaries of the Etowah River system.

orange-nacre mucket, Coosa moccasinshell, and ovate clubshell) for which there are no museum records, but that are included based on literature or on probable occurrence given their distribution elsewhere in the Coosa River system. Additionally, three gastropods (snails) and one mayfly in the Etowah River are C2 species (Table 1).

Nine of the 17 imperiled fishes are believed to be extirpated. How much of the imperiled mussel species are extirpated is unknown. Combined, this beleaguered fauna overwhelmingly indicates that the Etowah River system has been and continues to be a system under severe stress and in need of immediate remedial attention.

Fish Fauna of the Etowah River

Our earliest knowledge of the fishes of the Etowah River is from collections made by the eminent ichthyologist David Starr Jordan and students in 1876 (Jordan, 1877, 1878; Jordan and Brayton, 1878). The first list of Etowah River fishes was included in a state list compiled by Dahlberg and Scott (1971). Additions to a list of the Etowah fish fauna, as range extensions or descriptions of new species, were made by Suttkus and Raney (1955), Richards and Knapp (1964), Ramsey and Suttkus (1965), Clemmer and Suttkus (1971), Williams and Etnier (1977), Bryant et al. (1979), Burr and Cashner (1983), Suttkus and Etnier (1991), Wood and Mayden (1993), Suttkus et al. (1994), and Bauer et al. (1995). The list of fishes presented herein is the most comprehensive tally to date of the Etowah River ichthyofauna.

Figure 5. Aerial photograph of the Etowah River below Allatoona Dam showing V-shaped fish traps constructed by Native Americans (photograph by Richard T. Bryant).

The total historic and present fish fauna of the Etowah River numbers approximately 105 species plus one stocked hybrid (striped bass × white bass) (Table 2). Uncertainty about the exact number of species inhabiting the Etowah River system relates to the former occurrence of species that may now be extirpated from the system (see *Fish Extirpations*), and to the taxonomic status of putative new taxa. Of the 105 species, 91 are native. Fifteen of the native species are extirpated from the system, 14 plus one hybrid are nonindigenous, and four are endemic to the Etowah River (Table 2). We consider this list provisional and likely to change in the future. The Conasauga River has long been considered to have the greatest fish and mussel diversity within the upper Coosa River system (Etnier and Starnes, 1994). Only recently has the Etowah River been identified as having an equally diverse, but greatly threatened aquatic fauna (Burkhead et al., 1992; Bauer et al., 1995). We now believe the Etowah River was historically a center of aquatic biodiversity in the eastern Mobile River drainage.

Level of Endemism

The most striking characteristic of the Etowah River ichthyofauna is its high level of fish endemism (four species). To compare the number of endemic fishes in the Etowah River system to that of other systems in the Mobile River drainage, we compared the proportion of endemic fishes to total fish species among the Black Warrior, Cahaba, Conasauga, and Etowah rivers (Table 3). In the tally of total species, we did not include nonindigenous species and marine invaders (except for diadromous forms) that are reported to have penetrated the upper Coosa system in western Alabama or Georgia (Dahlberg and Scott, 1971; Boschung, 1992). Sources of data were as follows: Black Warrior, Mettee et al. (1989); Cahaba, Pierson et al. (1989); and our data for the Conasauga and Etowah

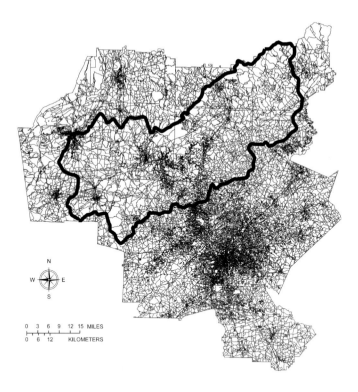

Figure 6. Centers of human population density within the Etowah River watershed taken from 1990 census data. Population centers are: at mouth of river — Rome; north side of river downstream from Allatoona Dam — Cartersville; huge center south of river — Atlanta; on south side of river upstream from Allatoona Reservoir — Canton. Bold perimeter line is the Etowah watershed boundary; bold line within the perimeter is the main channel of the Etowah River and Allatoona Reservoir.

rivers. The Black Warrior River has more endemics than the Etowah River (six versus four), but the drainage area of the Black Warrior River is nearly four times as large as that of the Etowah River, and the proportional differences of endemics for the Black Warrior versus Etowah (5.1 versus 4.4 percent) are close. The Etowah River is closest in drainage area to the Cahaba River but has twice the number of endemic fishes.

CRYPTIC FISH TAXA

All the presumed endemic species noted in Table 2 are recently described or recently discovered taxa. The Etowah darter (Figure 7A) was described in 1993 (Wood and Mayden, 1993), and the Cherokee darter (Figure 7C) in 1995 (Bauer et al., 1995). The remaining undescribed endemic fishes (two darters) were discovered by us in 1993 and 1994. Additionally, two undescribed minnows and one undescribed sucker are known or presumed to have occurred in the Etowah River. All these taxa are morphologically cryptic species similar to the nominal taxa with which they have long been placed. The detection of the undescribed darters was based on discovery of subtle but distinct differences between the two forms in male nuptial coloration. Although the study of these putative darter taxa is presently incomplete, we hypothesize that specific differences exist analogous to those of the greenbreast darter group analyzed by Wood and Mayden (1993). Recognition of these putative species is based on a greater level of systematic scrutiny of the Etowah fish fauna than has previously been applied, and parallels recognition of cryptic darter taxa by other ichthyologists in the Southeast (Boschung et al., 1992; Page et al., 1992).

FISH EXTIRPATIONS

Fifteen fish species, 16 percent of the native fauna, are considered to be extirpated from the river system (Table 2). A few of the extirpated forms are globally imperiled: lake sturgeon, blue shiner, and coldwater darter. Their extirpation from the Etowah River is not surprising given widespread habitat deterioration. At least two extirpations (American eel and lake sturgeon) were likely caused by multiple impoundments of the Coosa River system, including Allatoona Reservoir. However, the demise of much of the missing fauna is enigmatic because many of these species are generally regarded as tolerant or persistent species and occur in other degraded rivers. While we have no recent records for these species, we find it difficult to believe that some of them actually are extirpated (e.g., chain pickerel, lined chub, creek chubsucker, and blackspotted topminnow). Perhaps provisional listing here will promote their "rediscovery." Two suckers not included as extirpated are puzzling. The spotted sucker, a relatively tolerant and usually common species, has not been collected by us although it is known from the Etowah River (Beisser, 1989; year of capture not specified). Unknown from the Etowah River is the sometimes elusive river redhorse. We captured the river redhorse in the lower Oostanaula River and suspect that a low-density population persists in the lower Etowah River. Documentation for the extirpated fish fauna, as presently conceived, is as follows:

Lake sturgeon — This species is known from the Coosa and Oostanaula rivers (Boschung, 1992). One of us (BJF) heard an anecdotal report of someone catching a 1.5-m (4.9-feet) specimen with a pitchfork below the spillway dam in Cartersville in the late 1940s. The species is probably extirpated from Georgia and Alabama (Boschung, 1992).

American eel — Jordan and Brayton (1878) listed the American eel as "abundant" in the Alabama River system. A landowner informed one of us (BJF) that eels used to be common in the Etowah River above Allatoona Reservoir.

Alabama shad — Not known from the Etowah River. Boschung (1992) reported it from the Coosa River below Jordan Reservoir. We suspect that prior to multiple impoundments of the Coosa River, the Alabama shad probably occurred in the lower Etowah and Oostanaula rivers. The closely related American shad was known to penetrate the Blue Ridge in the James River in Virginia prior to construction of spillway dams at and above Richmond (Jenkins and Burkhead, 1994).

Blue shiner — One lot of this species at Cornell University (CU 1488) lists the following locality data: Etowah River, Jordan, October 1876. However, Jordan (1877) and Jordan and Brayton (1878) did not report the blue shiner from the Etowah River. Gibbs (1955) erroneously listed records of the blue shiner from the Little River in Cherokee County, Georgia; these were actually from the Little River in Cherokee County, Alabama. The blue shiner was historically distributed in the Oostanaula and Coosa rivers in the Valley and Ridge province (Gilbert et al., 1980). We believe it formerly occurred in the Etowah River system.

Figure 7. Cryptic species recently described from the Etowah River: A = Etowah darter, *Etheostoma etowahae* (male, 47 mm standard length, Etowah River, Lumpkin County, GA), similar to B = greenbreast darter, *E. jordani* (male, 58 mm standard length, Shoal Creek, Cleburne County, AL); C = Cherokee darter, *E. scotti* (male, 55 mm standard length, Shoal Creek, Dawson County, GA), similar to D = Coosa darter, *E. coosae* (male, 58 mm standard length, Moseley Spring, Chattooga County, GA) (photographs by N. M. Burkhead).

Lined chub — Jordan (1877) reported it as "abundant in all tributaries of the Etowah" In their list of material examined, Clemmer and Suttkus (1971) reported two localities for the lined chub above Allatoona Dam, and in their distribution map, the authors plotted another record below Allatoona Dam.

Burrhead shiner — Suttkus and Raney (1955) examined specimens at the United States National Museum collected by Jordan from the Etowah River (USNM 164968 and USNM 164969, one specimen each). These appear to be the last burrhead shiners collected from the Etowah River system.

"Blue sucker" (undescribed Mobile drainage form) — This interesting large-river sucker is not known from the Etowah River system. However, there were no extensive main-channel collections made in the upper Coosa, or lower Etowah and Oostanaula rivers prior to extensive impoundment of the Coosa River. Historically, the blue sucker probably penetrated the upper Coosa River system, including the lower reaches of the Etowah and Oostanaula rivers.

Creek chubsucker — Jordan (1877) reported it from the Etowah River, but later called it the lake chubsucker (Jordan, 1878). Because the mouth of the Etowah River is a significant distance above the Fall Line, we speculate that Jordan's record was based on creek chubsuckers.

Freckled madtom — In the Etowah River it is known from only one specimen collected in 1962 (UGAMNH 814). The freckled madtom is a widespread species within the Mississippi Embayment (Rhode, 1980). The Etowah River record represents the most upstream collection of the species in the Coosa River system.

Chain pickerel — Jordan (1877) reported it as abundant in tributary ponds of the lower Etowah River system. To our knowledge, no pickerels have since been captured from the Etowah River, thus indicating another enigmatic disappearance.

Blackspotted topminnow — There are no records of this species from the Etowah River. However, it is known from Big Dry Creek (Freeman, 1983), an Oostanaula tributary adjacent to the Etowah River. We consider it likely that the blackspotted topminnow historically resided in the Etowah River.

Coldwater darter — Jordan (1877) misidentified this species as "*Boleichthys elegans*" (Ramsey and Suttkus, 1965), stating that it was most common in Dykes Pond near Rome. Dykes Creek, presumably where Dykes Pond was located, presently contains a depauperate fish fauna, and no coldwater darters have been recently collected there. Although no other records of coldwater darters are known from the Etowah River, there are several large spring-fed tributaries in the Valley and Ridge portion of the system that may have supported coldwater darter populations.

Trispot darter — There are no records of this species from the Etowah River. It is known from the Valley and Ridge province of the Conasauga and Oostanaula rivers (Freeman, 1983), and we consider it very likely that the trispot darter formerly existed in the lower Etowah River in the same province.

Coal darter — This recently described darter (Suttkus et al., 1994) is not known from the Etowah River. The coal darter is a large-river species known from the main channel of the Coosa River above the Fall Line, and, like the undescribed "blue sucker," we presume it occurred historically in the lower Oostanaula and Etowah rivers.

River darter — There are no Etowah River records of this large-river species. Stiles and Etnier (1971) reported it from the Conasauga River far upstream from the mouth of the Etowah River;

Table 2. Fishes of the Etowah River system. Status symbols: N = native; PN = probably native; I = introduced (i.e., nonindigenous); PI = possibly introduced; EX = extirpated from system; E = exclusively endemic to the Etowah River system.

Family Name (No. Species) Scientific Name	Common Name	Status
Family Petromyzontidae (3 spp.)	**Lampreys**	
Ichthyomyzon castaneus	chestnut lamprey	N
I. gagei	southern brook lamprey	N
Lampetra aepyptera	least brook lamprey	N
Family Acipenseridae (1 sp.)	**Sturgeons**	
Acipenser fulvescens	lake sturgeon	N, EX
Family Lepisosteidae (1 sp.)	**Gars**	
Lepisosteus osseus	longnose gar	N
Family Hiodontidae (1 sp.)	**Mooneyes**	
Hiodon tergisus	mooneye	N
Family Anguillidae (1 sp.)	**Freshwater eels**	
Anguilla rostrata	American eel	N, EX
Family Clupeidae (3 spp.)	**Herrings**	
Alosa alabamae	Alabama shad	PN, EX
Dorosoma cepedianum	gizzard shad	N
D. petenense	threadfin shad	I
Family Cyprinidae (31 spp.)	**Minnows**	
Campostoma oligolepis	largescale stoneroller	N
C. pauciradii	bluefin stoneroller	N
Ctenopharyngodon idella	grass carp	I
Cyprinella caerulea	blue shiner	N, EX
C. callistia	Alabama shiner	N
C. lutrensis	red shiner	I
C. trichroistia	tricolor shiner	N
C. venusta	blacktail shiner	N
Cyprinus carpio	common carp	I
Ericymba buccata	silverjaw minnow	PN[1]
Hybopsis lineapunctata	lined chub	N, EX?
Hybopsis sp. cf. *H. winchelli*	undescribed chub	PN[1]
Luxilus chrysocephalus	striped shiner	N
L. zonistius	bandfin shiner	PN[1]
Lythrurus lirus	mountain shiner	N
Macrhybopsis sp. cf. *M. aestivalis*	undescribed chub	N
M. storeriana	silver chub	N
Nocomis leptocephalus	bluehead chub	N
N. micropogon	river chub	PI
Notemigonus crysoleucas	golden shiner	N
Notropis asperifrons	burrhead shiner	N, EX?
N. chrosomus	rainbow shiner	N
N. longirostris	longnose shiner	PN[1]
N. lutipinnis	yellowfin shiner	PI
N. stilbius	silverstripe shiner	N
N. xaenocephalus	Coosa shiner	N
Phenacobius catostomus	riffle minnow	N
Pimephales notatus	bluntnose minnow	I
P. vigilax	bullhead minnow	N
Rhinichthys atratulus	blacknose dace	N

Table 2. Continued.

Family Name (No. Species) Scientific Name	Common Name	Status
Semotilus atromaculatus	creek chub	N
Family Catostomidae (9 spp.)	**Suckers**	
Cycleptus sp. cf. *C. elongatus*	undescribed "blue" sucker	PN, EX
Erimyzon oblongus	creek chubsucker	N, EX?
Hypentelium etowanum	Alabama hog sucker	N
Ictiobus bubalus	smallmouth buffalo	N
Minytrema melanops	spotted sucker	N
Moxostoma carinatum	river redhorse	N
M. duquesnei	black redhorse	N
M. erythrurum	golden redhorse	N
M. poecilurum	blacktail redhorse	N
Family Ictaluridae (10 spp.)	**Bullhead catfishes**	
Ameiurus brunneus	snail bullhead	PN[1]
A. melas	black bullhead	N
A. natalis	yellow bullhead	N
A. nebulosus	brown bullhead	N
Ictalurus furcatus	blue catfish	N
I. punctatus	channel catfish	N
Noturus leptacanthus	speckled madtom	N
N. munitus	frecklebelly madtom	N
N. nocturnus	freckled madtom	N, EX?
Pylodictis olivaris	flathead catfish	N
Family Esocidae (1 sp.)	**Pikes**	
Esox niger	chain pickerel	N, EX?
Family Salmonidae (3 spp.)	**Trouts**	
Oncorhynchus mykiss	rainbow trout	I
Salmo trutta	brown trout	I
Salvelinus fontinalis	brook trout	I
Family Fundulidae (2 spp.)	**Killifishes**	
Fundulus olivaceus	blackspotted topminnow	PN, EX?
F. stellifer	southern studfish	N
Family Poeciliidae (1 sp.)	**Livebearers**	
Gambusia holbrooki	eastern mosquitofish	N
Family Cottidae (2 spp.)	**Sculpins**	
Cottus bairdi	mottled sculpin	N
C. carolinae	banded sculpin	N
Family Moronidae (3 spp.)	**Temperate basses**	
Morone chrysops	white bass	I
M. mississippiensis	yellow bass	I
M. saxatilis	striped bass	I
M. chrysops × *M. saxatilis*	hybrid	I
Family Centrarchidae (13 spp.)	**Sunfishes**	
Ambloplites ariommus	shadow bass	N
Lepomis auritus	redbreast sunfish	I
L. cyanellus	green sunfish	N
L. gulosus	warmouth	N
L. macrochirus	bluegill	N
L. megalotis	longear sunfish	N

Table 2. Continued.

Family Name (No. Species) Scientific Name	Common Name	Status
L. microlophus	redear sunfish	N
L. miniatus	redspotted sunfish	N
Micropterus coosae	redeye bass	N
M. punctulatus	spotted bass	N
M. salmoides	largemouth bass	N
Pomoxis annularis	white crappie	N
P. nigromaculatus	black crappie	N
Family Percidae (19 spp.)	**Perches**	
Etheostoma sp. cf. *E. brevirostrum*	Etowah undescribed darter	E
Etheostoma sp. cf. *E. brevirostrum*	Amicalola undescribed darter	E
E. coosae	Coosa darter	N
E. ditrema	coldwater darter	N, EX
E. etowahae	Etowah darter	E
E. jordani	greenbreast darter	N
E. rupestre	rock darter	N
E. scotti	Cherokee darter	E
E. stigmaeum	speckled darter	N
E. trisella	trispot darter	PN, EX
Percina sp. cf. *P. caprodes*	undescribed logperch	N
Percina sp. cf. *P. macrocephala*	undescribed darter	N
P. antesella	amber darter	N
P. brevicauda	coal darter	PN, EX
P. lenticula	freckled darter	N
P. nigrofasciata	blackbanded darter	N
P. palmaris	bronze darter	N
P. shumardi	river darter	PN, EX
Stizostedion vitreum	walleye	N
Family Sciaenidae (1 sp.)	**Drums**	
Aplodinotus grunniens	freshwater drum	N

[1] We tentatively regard the occurence of these species in the Etowah River to be the result of stream capture with the Chattahoochee River system *fide* Suttkus and Boschung (1990; page 61).

therefore, we conclude it formerly occurred in the lower main channel of the Etowah River.

Ecological Correlates of Fish Imperilment

Understanding shared biological patterns among declining and extinction-prone species is of strong interest to ecologists (Terborgh, 1974; Willis, 1974; Diamond, 1984; Angermeier, 1995; Parent and Schriml, 1995). For rheophilic freshwater fishes, life-history and ecological attributes such as range size, body size, habitat association, and vertical orientation in the water column are attributes for intuitively investigating correlates of imperilment. Herein we generally compare these attributes between the non-imperiled and imperiled fishes in southern Appalachia and the Etowah River. The results of the comparisons are discussed by category below. These comparisons do not establish causal mechanisms but they do allow possible inference for further lines of investigation. The

Table 3. Comparison of areas, species richness, and levels of endemism of four river systems of the Mobile River drainage. Data for native species (excluding nonindigenous and marine invading species) are from Mettee et al. (1989) and Pierson et al. (1989) for the Black Warrior and Cahaba river systems, and our unpublished data for the Conasauga and Etowah river systems.

River System	Drainage Area	Species:Endemics	Percent Endemic
Black Warrior	16,255 km² (6,274 sq. miles)	118:6	5.1
Cahaba	4,727 km² (1,825 sq. miles)	127:2	1.6
Conasauga	1,883 km² (727 sq. miles)	75:2	2.7
Etowah	4,871 km² (1,880 sq. miles)	91:4	4.4

results also contribute to a growing body of evidence that patterns of rarity and extinction are not isolated, random phenomena (Angermeier, 1995; Parent and Schriml, 1995). Lastly, understanding that associations of imperilment span shared suites of ecological adaptations in multiple, evolutionarily diverse families underscores the concept that single-species management is biologically inappropriate and fiscally wasteful.

We consider range size to be the most important correlate of imperilment. It is axiomatic that fishes with small ranges are generally more vulnerable to threats, because even small losses of habitat can be proportionally more serious than similar reductions in species with larger ranges (Moyle and Williams, 1990; Burkhead and Jenkins, 1991; Etnier and Starnes, 1991; Angermeier, 1995). This premise is independent of population density, although it is obvious that, of two species with similar small ranges, the species with the lowest population is potentially more vulnerable. Most non-imperiled species of the southern Appalachians and the Etowah River are wide- and intermediate-ranging, whereas most imperiled species are localized or geographically isolated (Figure 8). Proportional differences of localized and isolated range sizes between the non-imperiled and imperiled faunas are considerable. The species with the most restricted distributions in the Etowah River are the amber and the Etowah darters (federally endangered), and two undescribed darters (*Etheostoma* spp. cf. *E. brevirostrum*) that are Category 2 species (Table 1). The latter three species are exclusively endemic to the Etowah River. All of the environmentally degrading factors discussed below (see *Threats to the System*) can cause reductions in range size.

Benthic specialization is an important correlate of imperilment. Obligate benthic species — those that spawn, feed, and shelter on the stream bottom — compose a substantial fraction of the Etowah's imperiled fish fauna. Obligate benthic specialization occurs throughout the southern Appalachian and Etowah River fish faunas. The ratio of imperiled benthic fishes to imperiled non-benthic fishes is about 5:1, as opposed to about 2:1 for the same ratio among non-imperiled species in both the Etowah River and southern Appalachian faunas (Figure 9). Of the imperiled fishes in Table 1, 80 percent are obligate benthic species and the remaining ones are associated with the substrate by one or more critical life-history activities (spawning, feeding, or sheltering). The primary form of degradation and destruction of benthic habitats is elevated sedimentation, and the present effects of sedimentation may be heightened by pollutants bound to sediments (see *Threats to the System*).

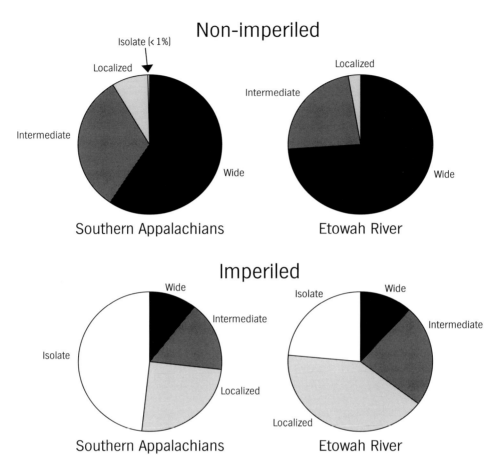

Figure 8. Relative range sizes of non-imperiled versus imperiled fish faunas of southern Appala-chia and the Etowah River.

Small body size is associated with imperilment in aquatic and terrestrial vertebrates (Diamond, 1984; Angermeier, 1995). For fishes this is partially because most eastern North American species are less than 150 mm (6 inches) in total length. However, a substantially greater proportion of very small- and small-sized species are imperiled versus medium- and large-sized species (Figure 10). Small body size in fishes is correlated with several other ecological attributes associated with imperilment: low intrinsic dispersal ca-pabilities, short longevity, benthic specialization, and generally reduced reproductive po-tential. Fifteen of 17 imperiled fishes (Table 1) are very small- and small-sized species. The lake sturgeon and the undescribed "blue sucker" are the only imperiled large-sized and medium large-sized species (that formerly occurred) in the Etowah River.

Because the southern upland fish fauna evolved in, and is primarily associated with lotic habitats, we examined flowing-water habitat associations of the imperiled and non-imperiled faunas to determine if differences exist. Prior to our analysis, we speculated that most of the imperiled species would be associated with headwaters, small creeks, and large rivers because of the high degree of degradation of those fluvial water bodies by agriculture and impoundment.

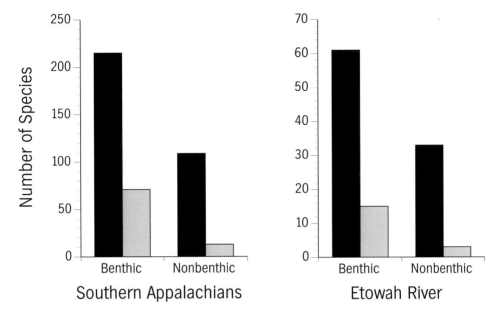

Figure 9. Benthic orientation of non-imperiled (black bars) versus imperiled (gray bars) fishes of southern Appalachia and the Etowah River. Numbers are averages of spawning, feeding, and sheltering activities for benthic versus non-benthic attributes.

Most species in the southern Appalachians and in the Etowah River occur in creeks and small rivers, habitat sizes that probably represent most of the total habitat area available. We found no large differences between frequency distributions of the non-imperiled and imperiled species (Figure 11). While it is impossible to state that there is an equal sampling effort across all habitat sizes, particularly with respect to large rivers, repeated sampling by multiple methods has yielded the best data available. We further realize that as imperiled species become rarer, the probability of detecting them significantly declines (Etnier, 1994). Given these constraints on the best data available, we feel these results imply that habitat degradation and destruction has been relatively ubiquitous across fluvial habitats; all sizes of habitats — small headwater creeks to large rivers — have been despoiled to some degree.

Mussel Fauna of the Etowah River

Like temperate freshwater fishes, freshwater mussels or clams (family Unionidae) are most diverse in the southeastern United States. Of the 297 freshwater mussel taxa recognized (281 species and 16 subspecies) in the United States and Canada (Turgeon et al., 1988), about 90 percent occur in the southeastern United States. About 17 percent (51 species) of this mussel fauna is known from the Etowah River system, where species historically occupied diverse habitats ranging from upland creeks to the main channel of the river.

Adult unionids range in size from 4 cm to more than 25 cm (1.6 inches to greater than 9.8 inches) and the largest may weigh 1 kg (2.2 pounds). Mussels are among the longest lived freshwater invertebrates; many species may live 20 to 40 years and a few species live more than 50 years. Freshwater unionids have a unique relationship with fishes in that

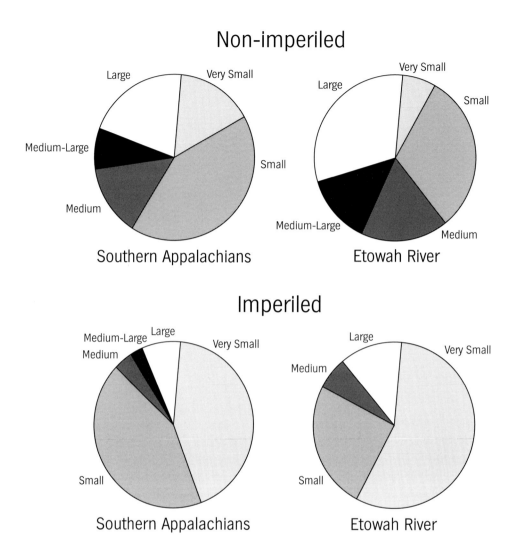

Figure 10. Relative body sizes of non-imperiled versus imperiled fish faunas of southern Appalachia and the Etowah River.

about 98 percent of all species require a fish host to complete their life cycles (Fuller, 1974; Hoggarth, 1992).

Mussels were historically common throughout freshwater ecosystems of the southeastern United States. Mussel declines during the past century parallel those of other freshwater organisms, notably snails, and fishes. Williams et al. (1992b) reported 213 species, about 72 percent of the United States mussel fauna, as endangered, threatened or of special concern, and 21 species (7 percent) as possibly extinct. The demise of this widespread and diverse fauna is primarily the result of habitat destruction and deteriorated water quality of southern rivers.

Our provisional list (Table 4) of mussels thought to have historically existed in the Etowah River is based on records from archeological digs, early collections, and inference from known mussel distributions throughout the remainder of the upper Coosa River system. Mussels were collected in the Etowah River watershed for centuries by Native Americans who used them for a variety of purposes, including food, tools, and jewelry. Mussels excavated from middens at the Etowah Mound Site in Bartow County were analyzed by van der Schalie and Parmalee (1960). Mussel collectors sampled the Etowah River in the early to mid-1800s and most of the shells were shipped to wealthy conchologists who maintained them in their personal collections or donated them to natural history museums.

The present outlook of the mussel fauna of the Etowah River is bleak. Burkhead et al. (1992) estimated that as many as 65 percent of the species may have been extirpated from the system. Mussels are susceptible to many pollutants and most species cannot survive in reservoirs (Fuller, 1974; Williams et al., 1992a). Decline of the Etowah River mussel fauna may have begun around the time of the first gold rush in the United States, in northern Georgia. Gold miners used mercury to coalesce gold fines. Mercury contamination in the Etowah River alluvial floodplain has been dated to 1830 in core sediment samples (Leigh, 1994).

Without a thorough and systematic survey for mussels we cannot know what percentage of the Etowah River mussel fauna survives. In over 200 fish collections that we have made since 1989, we have only observed valves of three dead native mussels. Our efforts to detect mussels — while certainly not a survey — have not been casual either. We have intentionally searched river banks while collecting and canoeing, and have walked islands (particularly where we camped) looking for valves in places where they might normally be observed.

Faunal Fragmentation

One of the most common patterns associated with extirpation is the fragmentation of a species' range into small, isolated subpopulations within the larger geographic area occupied by the species. Habitat and population fragmentation and the scales on which it can occur are summarized by Harris (1984) and Meffe and Carroll (1994). Fragmentation results from localized environmental degradation and exists at all spatial scales. Widespread losses of aquatic habitats in the southern Appalachians result largely from major impoundments, deforestation, urbanization, and chronic pollution, including sedimentation. Smaller-scale fragmentation occurs from scattered, localized habitat perturbations associated with a variety of anthropogenic activities such as small water supply or farm pond impoundments, isolated residential developments, riparian clearing, landfills, site-specific sedimentation, agricultural runoff, and urban sprawl along transportation routes near streams. While large-scale projects are typically evaluated for potential environmental impacts, many small-scale projects do not receive such attention. In the long run, extensive fragmentation by piecemeal habitat loss may actually harm aquatic species as much or more than large-scale, often controversial projects.

The biological consequences of population fragmentation involve genetic isolation and demographic effects. Genetic isolation can diminish population fitness (Soulé, 1980; Carson, 1983). However, even minimal emigration of a few individuals between insularized populations can maintain at least short-term population heterozygosity (Soulé, 1980). Emigration across relatively permanent barriers such as major dams can be considered "sweepstakes" dispersal, i.e., possible but not likely (Chesser, 1983), while intermittent dispersal across smaller stretches of degraded stream habitat may bolster insular heterozygosity. A pervasive problem in the Etowah River system, and other southern Appalachian

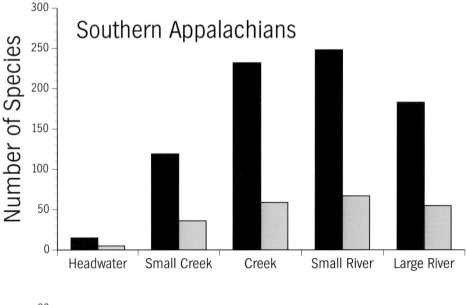

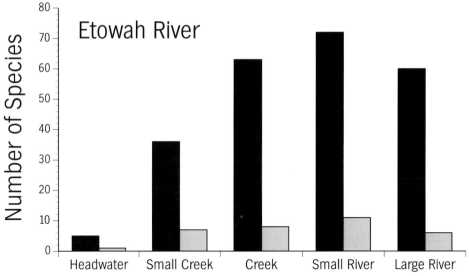

Figure 11. Frequency distribution of southern Appalachian and Etowah River fishes by habitat size; black bars = non-imperiled fishes, gray bars = imperiled fishes.

rivers, is that ever-increasing habitat loss continually decreases or eliminates temporal opportunities for fishes to disperse across degraded stream reaches. The efficacy of degraded stream habitats contributing to isolation of fish populations has been genetically demonstrated by reduced allele and genotype frequencies in populations of the spotfin shiner (*Cyprinella spiloptera*) separated by polluted stream reaches (Gillespie and Guttman, 1993), and morphologically demonstrated by the distinctiveness of disjoined populations in the California roach (*Hesperoleucas symmetricus*) (Brown et al., 1992).

Presently, we know little about the genetic consequences of extensive population fragmentation in southeastern fishes. In the Etowah River system, the distribution pattern of the threatened Cherokee darter suggests severe levels of insularization which warrant further investigation (Figure 12). Bauer et al. (1995) found significant differences in seven out of ten meristic characters between Cherokee darters inhabiting northern and southern tributaries of the Etowah River, suggesting that the degraded main channel of the river was acting as a barrier to dispersal of this tributary species. Barriers creating insularization in the Etowah River have existed for over 100 years as a main-channel spillway dam in Cartersville (Hall and Hall, 1921), and as severe sedimentation and pollution episodes dating to 1830 (Leigh, 1994).

Population responses to habitat fragmentation may contribute to extirpation and extinction more directly than genetic factors (Lande, 1988). Habitat fragmentation directly impacts population dynamics through changes in population size, Allee effects (density-triggered phenomena such as mass emigration or reduction of overall reproductive rates), changes in population structure, decline or extirpation of rare species and habitat specialists, and reduced ability of populations to respond to environmental stochasticity (Shaffer, 1981; Brown, 1984; Lande, 1988; Pimm et al., 1988).

In the Etowah River we have found anomalous distribution gaps of several fish species (e.g., rainbow shiner, Cherokee darter, and rock darter), constricted ranges (e.g., frecklebelly madtom), widespread extirpations (amber and Cherokee darters), and the persistence of a distinct guild of tolerant species in many areas throughout the watershed. A vexing aspect of habitat fragmentation is that rare species may require larger reaches of suitable habitat over time than they actually use at a given time. Freeman and Freeman (1994) discovered that the endangered amber darter, utilized only 40 percent of available suitable habitat during their study. These authors hypothesized that long-term population viability may depend on availability of the additional habitat to support populations during periods of random environmental variation, such as during droughts.

THREATS TO THE SYSTEM

> *"Large numbers of feathers, balls of fat approximately one inch in diameter,*
> *and chicken parts (wings and feathers) were floating downstream."*
> — Georgia Water Quality Control Board (1970)

All modern biologists studying riverine systems or their faunas in the southeastern United States are working on systems that have a history of episodic degradation that transcends several human generations. Sometimes certain southern streams are described as "pristine," but in most cases the modern application of this word is a misnomer.

The major threats to southern Appalachian rivers are impoundments, sedimentation, harmful agricultural practices, urbanization, and pollution. All of these degrading forces occur to some extent throughout the Etowah River watershed, and these anthropogenic impacts have been repeatedly identified as major causes of aquatic faunal decline and extinction throughout North America (Williams, 1981; Ono et al., 1983; Miller et al.,

Table 4. Provisional list of 51 native freshwater mussels (family Unionidae) from the Etowah River system based on: L = literature (van der Schalie and Parmalee, 1960; Hurd, 1974); M = museum records; and P = probable occurrence in the Etowah Drainage based on the species' distribution in the Coosa River system. Other symbols: I = imperiled (endangered, threatened, or special concern as treated by Williams et al., 1992b); E = federally endangered; T = federally threatened.

Scientific Name	Common Name	Source & Status
Amblema plicata perplicata	roundlake	L, M
Anodontoides radiatus	rayed creekshell	I, M
Ellipsaria lineolata	butterfly	I, L
Elliptio arca	Alabama spike	I, L, M
E. arctata	delicate spike	I, L, M
E. crassidens	elephant-ear	L, M
Epioblasma metastriata	upland combshell	E, L
E. othcaloogensis	southern acornshell	E, P
Fusconaia cerina	Gulf pigtoe	L
F. ebena	ebonyshell	L, M
Lampsilis altilis	fine-lined pocketbook	T, L, M
L. ornata	southern pocketbook	I, L, M
L. perovalis	orange-nacre mucket	T, P
L. straminea claibornensis	southern fatmucket	L, M
Lasmigona complanata alabamensis	Alabama heelsplitter	I, P
L. holstonia	Tennessee heelsplitter	I, L, M
Leptodea fragilis	fragile papershell	L, M
Ligumia recta	black sandshell	I, L
Medionidus acutissimus	Alabama moccasinshell	T, L, M
M. parvulus	Coosa moccasinshell	E, L
Megalonaias nervosa	washboard	L
Obliquaria reflexa	threehorn wartyback	L, M
Obovaria unicolor	Alabama hickorynut	I, L
Pleurobema altum	highnut	I, L, M
P. chattanoogaense	painted clubshell	I, M
P. decisum	southern clubshell	E, L, M
P. georgianum	southern pigtoe	E, L, M
P. hanleyanum	Georgia pigtoe	I, L, M
P. johannis	Alabama pigtoe	L, M
P. murrayense	Coosa pigtoe	I, L
P. nucleopsis	longnut	I, L, M
P. perovatum	ovate clubshell	E, P
P. rubellum	Warrior pigtoe	I, L, M
P. troschelianum	Alabama clubshell	I, L, M
Potamilus purpuratus	bleufer	L
Ptychobranchus greeni	triangular kidneyshell	E, L, M
Pyganodon grandis	giant floater	P
Quadrula asperata	Alabama orb	I, L, M
Q. metanevra	monkeyface	L
Q. rumphiana	ridged mapleleaf	I, L, M
Strophitus connasaugaensis	Alabama creekmussel	I , L, M
S. subvexus	southern creekmussel	I, L
Toxolasma parvus	lilliput	L, M
Tritogonia verrucosa	pistolgrip	L, M
Truncilla donaciformis	fawnsfoot	P
Uniomerus tetralasmus	pondhorn	L, M

Table 4. Continued.

Scientific Name	Common Name	Source & Status
Utterbackia imbecillis	paper pondshell	P
Villosa lienosa	little spectaclecase	L, M
V. nebulosa	Alabama rainbow	I, L, M
V. vanuxemensis umbrans	Coosa creekshell	I, L, M
V. vibex	southern rainbow	L, M

1989; Williams et al., 1989; Burkhead and Jenkins, 1991; Etnier and Starnes, 1991; Moyle and Leidy, 1992; Warren and Burr, 1994). Below we present data and observations of the effects of impoundment and sedimentation on the Etowah River and a less detailed discussion on the effects of pollution and urbanization.

Effects of Impoundments

The present assemblage of drainages, environments, and associated faunas of southern Appalachia began to assume their pre-European colonization configuration after the last glacial retreat at the beginning of the Holocene (10,000 years before present; Hackney and Adams, 1992). Major anthropogenic modifications to riverine habitats began with the arrival of European immigrants. The earliest alterations of North American rivers by European descendants were primarily canals and low-head spillway dams (Palmer, 1986). However, in the years spanning the 1930s to the late 1970s, approximately 144 large dams were constructed in the southeastern United States. Today, 98 percent of all southeastern rivers are blocked by at least one major dam, and some major rivers are nearly or completely impounded (Hackney and Adams, 1992; Soballe et al., 1992). Most large impoundments in the southern Appalachians are hydroelectric-flood control facilities, or are associated with hydrogeneration as pump-storage impoundments. Hydrogenerated electricity only produces about two to three percent of the energy used during peaking power consumption. These colossal edifices are clearly major landscape-scale causes of aquatic faunal decline, fragmentation, and extirpation in southern Appalachia, including the Etowah River. In addition to large impoundments, there are over a million farm pond impoundments on first- and second-order tributaries in the Southeast (Menzel and Cooper, 1992). Negative ecological effects vary between large and small impoundments as discussed below.

LARGE IMPOUNDMENTS

Large impoundments are not benign replacements of river sections with lakes. Rather, they are hybrid environments (Soballe et al., 1992) that lack the productive littoral zone of natural lakes and the mosaic of riffle-run-pool habitats characteristic of upland streams. Impoundments dramatically alter habitat and reduce biodiversity in the inundated river portion. Hydrogeneration creates episodic fluctuations in downstream flow levels, resulting in dramatic physicochemical changes of the river environment. These negative effects may extend for many kilometers below a large dam. The main deleterious effects of large impoundments include the following: 1) loss of system connectivity; 2) alteration or elimi-

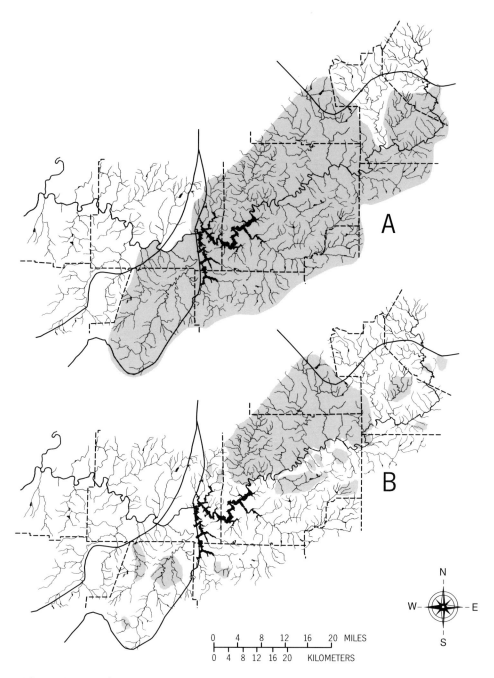

Figure 12. Range fragmentation of the Cherokee darter: A = hypothesized historical range prior to ca. 1830; B = fragmentation of present range based on extant populations sampled through 1992 (several recently discovered tributary populations within this range are omitted).

nation of natural flood cycles or natural low-water periods; 3) concentration of pollutants and sediments deposited in impounded reaches; 4) providing focal points for introductions of nonindigenous fishes; 5) alteration of nutrient cycling and natural trophic webs; 6) thermal alteration of the river below the dam by hypolimnotic water release; 7) bank destabilization and scouring or armoring (compacting and hardening to a crust-like layer) of downstream substrates; 8) truncation and isolation of tributaries entering the reservoir; and 9) changes in physicochemical parameters below the dam such as daily or seasonal reductions in dissolved oxygen (DO) (U.S. National Research Council, 1992; pages 200-201; Stanford and Ward, 1992, Table 5.1; Yeager, 1994).

Allatoona Reservoir has multiple negative effects on many species of native fishes and aquatic invertebrates. Besides permanently eliminating significant segments of the free-flowing Etowah River (ca. 52 river km; about 32.3 river miles) and lower portions of impounded tributaries, the reservoir has been an introduction point for several nonindigenous fishes (Beisser, 1989).

Water release from the dam apparently does not dramatically alter the natural temperature regimes of the river (Stokes et al., 1986). Water quality immediately below the dam was characterized as moderately polluted in 1969, based on low DO concentrations and reduced macroinvertebrate abundance and diversity (Georgia Water Quality Control Board, 1970). While sampling fish in early September 1993 we recorded a low DO of 2.7 parts per million (ppm) and detected the distinct odor of hydrogen sulfide. A persistent benthic boundary layer, high in hydrogen sulfide, occurs in deeper sections of Allatoona Reservoir (G. S. Beisser, Georgia Department of Natural Resources, pers. comm.). Water-level fluctuations in the Etowah River below the dam vary seasonally, weekly, and daily based on hydrogeneration demands. Figure 13 illustrates daily and weekly variations in discharge at a site just below the dam and at a site in the lowermost river during August and September 1994. Weekend reduction of discharges to base flows are evident. Daily fluctuations during these months were approximately 1.5 m (4.9 feet) at the upstream gauge and 1 m (3.3 feet) at the downstream gauge. These daily discharge variations create a highly unstable environment. The fluctuating water levels and associated velocities have scoured and armored the substrate throughout the upper one-third of the river below the dam. Large gravel, rubble, and small boulders of riffles are generally embedded in a matrix of sand and clay, eliminating most interstitial habitat available for macroinvertebrates.

Allatoona Reservoir seriously impacts the main-channel fish fauna below the dam (Figure 14). Only five species, all uncommon, were sampled immediately below the dam: one nonindigenous species (common carp) and four centrarchids. The numbers of fishes collected at sites downstream from the dam were strongly negatively correlated with proximity to the dam. Diversity of the ichthyofauna does not reach a downstream maximum until 64 river km (40 miles) below the dam.

The present downstream fauna probably differs substantially from the fauna that occurred historically in the vicinity of the dam site, and it is clearly unlike the main-channel fauna above the dam. The fish community below the dam is dominated by suckers (Catostomidae), large catfishes (Ictaluridae, excluding madtoms), and sunfishes (Centrarchidae), and there are notably fewer species of minnows (Cyprinidae) and darters (Percidae) than in the Etowah River upstream of Allatoona Reservoir. Nonindigenous species occurring only below the dam are red shiner and grass carp. Prior to construction

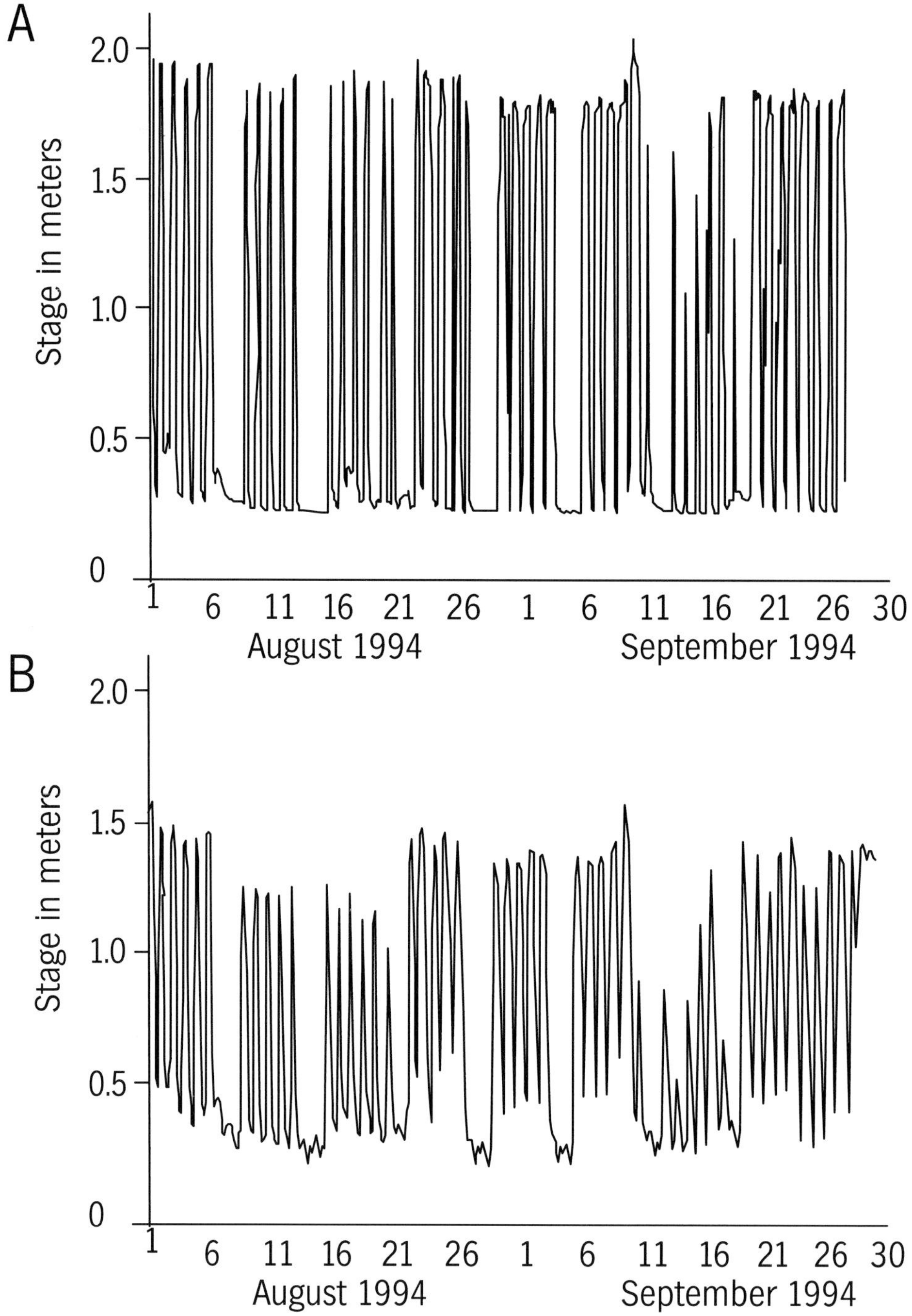

Figure 13. Hydrograph of the main-channel Etowah River: A = stage in meters measured at discharge gauge just below Allatoona Dam; B = stage in meters measured at discharge gauge at the Georgia State Route 746 bypass just upstream (east) of Rome.

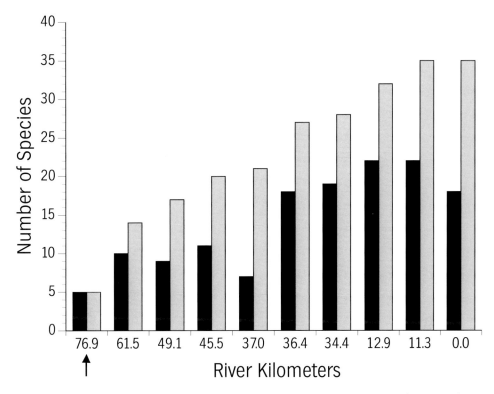

Figure 14. Relationship of number of Etowah River main channel fish species (black bars) and cumulative number of species (gray bars) to river kilometers below Allatoona Dam (location of dam indicated by arrow).

of the dam and associated changes, the total fauna of the lower Etowah River probably exceeded our estimated number of cumulative species by as much as 30 percent. The extirpated fauna probably included lake sturgeon, American eel, Alabama shad, undescribed Mobile "blue sucker," coal darter, river darter, and species surviving elsewhere in the system such as largescale stoneroller, Alabama shiner, silver chub, bluehead chub, riffle minnow, speckled madtom, frecklebelly madtom, greenbreast darter, rock darter, amber darter, and freckled darter.

Changes in the fish community structure in flow-regulated sections of the Tallapoosa River were reported by Kinsolving and Bain (1993) and Travnichek and Maceina (1994). Both studies presented evidence of faunal recovery and did not detect the extirpation level or degree of community replacement that we have observed in the Etowah River. The community shifts in the lower Etowah river may be partially due to increased large-river habitat and associated riverine species, e.g., mooneye, smallmouth buffalo, and blue catfish. We suspect that the increase in faunal composition in the lower Etowah River is explained by persistence or recolonization by a guild of relatively tolerant species — the macrohabitat generalists of Kinsolving and Bain (1993). Because our data are qualitative (presence or absence of species), we cannot document any shifts in biomass, but we have observed low abundance of most species in the main channel 30 to 40 km (18.6 to 25 miles) below the dam. Other factors that may also contribute to an increase in the total number of species in lower river segments are improved water quality by dilution from tributaries and progressive amelioration of fluctuating water levels. The fact that the Tallapoosa fish fauna shows greater recovery at similar distances below large hydropower dams than is evident in the lower Etowah, despite similar faunas in the two rivers (Table 2; Williams, 1965), suggests that additional factors may be causing faunal depression in the lower Etowah River. Diminution of the Etowah River fauna below Allatoona Dam may be the collective result of hydrogeneration, pollution, and sedimentation.

SMALL IMPOUNDMENTS

Small impoundments primarily include farm ponds and small, off-river water supply impoundments. Most farm ponds in the southeastern United States were constructed in the last 50 years and represent nearly 0.5 percent of the land surface (Menzel and Cooper, 1992). About half of the surface area of small inland water bodies (those less than 16 ha or 39.5 acres) in Georgia is farm ponds (Menzel and Cooper, 1992). The damaging effects of farm ponds on native fishes are similar to those summarized for large impoundments except for negative impacts associated with hydrogeneration (U.S. National Research Council, 1992; Stanford and Ward, 1992). In most southern river systems the sheer number of farm ponds and their role in tributary fragmentation has not been sufficiently evaluated. In Settingdown Creek, an upper Piedmont tributary of the Etowah River, there are at least 13 farm ponds on order 1 and 2 tributaries (Figure 15). Although we have not estimated the total number of farm ponds in the Etowah River watershed, we surmise the density of farm ponds elsewhere in the system, except perhaps in the Blue Ridge province, is similar to Settingdown Creek.

Small off-river water supply impoundments are becoming an attractive source of municipal water to growing communities and major metropolitan areas. Tentative plans proposed to construct a series of reservoirs around the greater Atlanta metropolitan area for future water supply. In the Etowah River watershed, plans exist to impound Yellow Creek in eastern Cherokee and western Dawson counties for water supply, and plans have been drafted for a similar impoundment on Sharp Mountain Creek (Figure 16). The Yellow Creek impoundment will eliminate a healthy population of the threatened Cherokee darter and further contribute to fragmentation of the system. Water supply reservoirs on tributaries may also affect water quality and flow in the main channel of the Etowah River, especially if water is released to augment flow and availability at downstream municipal water intakes during natural low-flow periods. Sharp Mountain Creek also harbors Cherokee darters and the endangered amber darter, and it is one of the few remaining large tributaries of the Etowah River system that is relatively undisturbed.

Sedimentation

Sedimentation in eastern North America is often characterized as a form of nonpoint-source pollution (Karr and Schlosser, 1977). Herein we focus heavily on sedimentation because it is a widespread and serious problem in many fluvial systems. Unnatural sedimentation rates began with European colonization of North America. Sedimentation rates of Atlantic slope rivers are estimated to be four to five times greater than rates prior to European colonization (Meade, 1969). Intensive early sedimentation of the southeastern Piedmont was particularly associated with cotton farming and slavery and the fact that land was cheaper than labor; nutrient-ex-

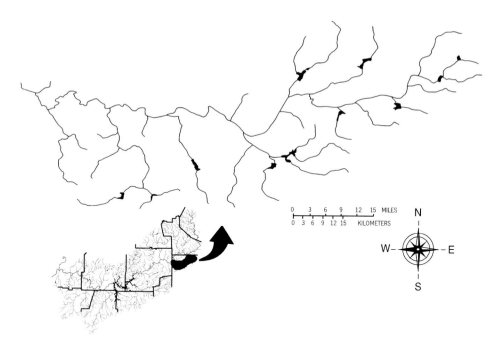

Figure 15. Density of farm ponds in the Settingdown Creek system in the upper Etowah River watershed. Farm ponds indicated by solid outlines.

hausted fields were cheaper to abandon than to reclaim and exposed fields were simply left to erode (Trimble, 1974). Abandoned cultivated fields that were stripped of top soils typically became deeply gullied and in some cases it took as long as 75 to 100 years for erosion to be stabilized by natural revegetation (Trimble, 1974). Although overall current levels of sedimentation may be less than those in the first half of this century (Georgia Erosion and Sedimentation Control Panel, 1995; Pimentel et al., 1995), vastly accelerated sedimentation remains a ubiquitous threat in all southern upland river systems. The economic costs of soil erosion are staggering. Throughout the United States the annual costs of water-caused soil erosion is estimated to be about 7.4 billion dollars and annual costs for all causes of soil erosion are estimated to be 44 billion dollars (Pimentel et al., 1995). These estimates, however, do not consider the biological impacts of sedimentation and their intangible costs on humans. Herein we define sedimentation, examine the historical and present-day causes in the Etowah River watershed, and briefly review its effects on aquatic organisms.

TYPES OF SEDIMENTATION

Some biologists have synonymously referred to sedimentation and siltation (e.g., Burkhead and Jenkins, 1991; Bogan, 1993). Siltation is a form of sedimentation that refers to the deposition of silts (finely particulate soils) on stream or lake bottoms. Sedimentation encompasses a size range of solid particles including silt, sand, gravel, cobble, etc. Sediment transport along the bottom and suspended in the water column is a natural fluvial process of all rivers. The amount of sediment transported through a stream system is dependent on the quantity of sediment eroded into a stream and on the ability of a stream to carry washed-in sediments to a

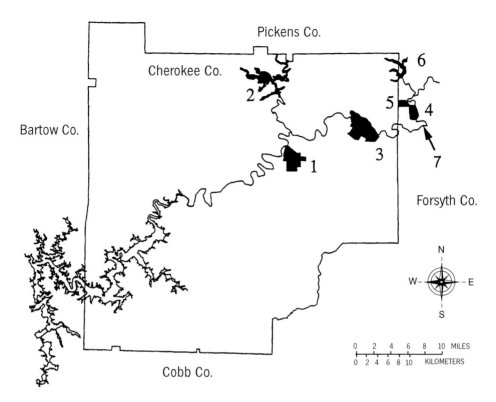

Figure 16. Locations of existing and future major threats to the Etowah River system centered around Cherokee County (boundary shown): 1 = active landfill; 2 = proposed water-supply impoundment on Sharp Mountain Creek; 3 = proposed golf course and housing development; 4 = proposed private landfill; 5 = Forsyth County landfill; 6 = proposed Yellow Creek water-supply reservoir; 7 = proposed site of water release of secondary-treated sewage from the Chattahoochee River watershed.

downstream outlet (Gordon et al., 1992). Increased sedimentation usually results from land-use practices that increase the amount of soil available to erosion. The total sediment load may be defined as the sum of bedload plus suspended bed-material load plus washload (Gordon et al., 1992). In southern upland streams bedload material consists of coarse substrates such as small rubble, gravel, and coarse sands that are moved along the bottom by rolling, sliding, or bouncing. Suspended bed-material load represents the smaller fractions of bedload that will remain in suspension for an appreciable time but that settle out when water velocity decreases. Washloads are the smallest sediments in particle size, such as fine sands, silts, and clays, and are readily suspended in low water velocity.

Washloads are considered supply-limited, i.e., dependent on bank or terrestrial sources of material, but are not limited by a stream's capacity to carry them in suspension. Bed-material load is capacity-limited, i.e., dependent on channel morphology, discharge, gradient, and substrate composition and configuration (Gordon et al., 1992). Habitat-destructive portions of the total sediment load are the suspended bed-material loads that fall out of suspension during periods of stable or diminished flows. These sediments, when excessive at a level above a stream's ability to flush them, can blanket the stream bottom and diminish the overall habitat complexity by filling interstitial spaces of the substrate. Fine silts, sands, and clays of the washload directly harm organisms by fouling mucous membranes of gills and egg surfaces. Species that are especially sensitive to high levels of sedimentation are those that evolved in upland streams where historic levels of sedimentation were usually low and water transparency was normally high.

CAUSES OF SEDIMENTATION

While geologists may consider sedimentation rates on temporal scales as large as one million to 100 million years (Meade et al., 1990), threats to southern Appalachian aquatic biodiversity due to increased sedimentation have only occurred in about the last 200 years. Prior to deforestation and early gold mining in the upper Coosa River system, the Etowah and Oostanaula rivers were probably as clear as the upper Conasauga River is today. Gold mining and associated erosion in the upper Etowah River caused the first major episode of sedimentation as early as 1830 (Leigh, 1994). Jordan (1922) described the main channel of the Etowah River as running muddy in 1876. A report by the Secretary of Agriculture to President Theodore Roosevelt described a correlation between poor logging practices and the clearing of mountain slopes to extensive sedimentation of southern Appalachian rivers (Wilson, 1902). We surmise that the Etowah River has been subjected to major sedimentation events since the 1830s, and has probably had greater-than-normal levels of sedimentation on a continual basis from the time the watershed was first settled by European immigrants.

Early deforestation within the Etowah watershed probably was not accompanied by efforts to abate sedimentation. By the early 20th century, upper Piedmont streams in Georgia, including the Etowah River, were exposed to extensive erosion from deforested uplands (Barrows et al., 1917). The solution to the resulting drainage problems was to ditch rivers and creeks to make them more efficient in transporting runoff (Barrows et al., 1917). The Soil Conservation Service (now the Natural Resources Conservation Service) channelized extensive areas of the Etowah River watershed. Bagby (1969) reviewed the deleterious consequences of channelization activities in Georgia including projects on 12 Etowah tributaries and the main river channel. The general effect of channelization on game fish populations was immortalized by the expression "you can't get no fishes in SCS ditches" (Bagby, 1969).

The location of land-disturbing activities is important relative to inherent erosion vulnerability of soils. Meade et al. (1990) reported that deeply weathered Piedmont soils in Georgia produced ten times greater sediment yields than the poorly consolidated sedimentary soils of the Coastal Plain. The Upland subsection of the Piedmont represents the largest province in the Etowah watershed (Figure 3). Little River, one of the largest tributaries of the Etowah River (Figure 4) occurring entirely within the Upland subsection of the Piedmont, is probably the tributary most degraded by sedimentation in the watershed.

Current causes of sedimentation in the Etowah watershed are primarily construction, mining, and agricultural activities. Construction practices that leave soils (primarily red clays and sands in the Etowah River watershed) exposed to rainfall significantly increase levels of sedimentation (see Figure 17). Most recent construction is directly or indirectly associated with urbanization, industrial growth, and strip development along transportation routes. Urbanization of the watershed, especially around the greater Atlanta metropolitan area, increases rainfall runoff and greatly exacerbates sedimentation and pollution within the Etowah River watershed.

Most types of mining greatly accelerate sedimentation of rivers (Meade et al., 1990). Mining for bauxite, gold, iron, limestone, marble, and ocher has occurred in the Etowah River watershed (Butts and Gildersleeve, 1948; Park, 1953; Leigh, 1994). In the 1960s, one mining company in the vicinity of Cartersville discharged up to 550 tons per day of mineral-washing wastes into the Etowah River (Mackenthun, 1969). We have observed waste material from marble quarries in streams near Tate in Pickens County. Excessive sedimentation in these and other streams has occurred from mining and related construction activities, and has been intensified by denuded or thinned riparian cover (Figure 18).

Agricultural activities that contribute to excessive sedimentation include row-crop farming, livestock grazing, and silviculture. The amount of sediment entering streams is positively correlated with the percent of the drainage area in croplands (Meade et al., 1990).

Clearing of riparian vegetation is a ubiquitous problem throughout agricultural areas of the Southeast (Karr and Schlosser, 1977; Armour et al., 1991; Welsch, 1991). This greatly increases erosion (Figure 19) and is exacerbated in the mountains where steep slopes increase runoff rates and bank destabilization (Figure 20). Erosion from farms also contributes to water pollution and eutrophication, particularly where riparian zones have been cleared. Vegetated riparian buffer strips are efficient traps for sediments and nutrients (Lowrance et al., 1984, 1984a, 1984b, 1985; Lowrance, 1992). Most of the row-crop and livestock farming in the Etowah River watershed occurs in Piedmont and Valley and Ridge province subsections of Cherokee, Bartow, and Paulding counties. Euharlee, Raccoon, and Pumpkinvine creeks (Figure 4) are heavily degraded by these land uses.

Forestry activities contribute significantly to sedimentation in upland and mountain streams through road construction and clearcutting (Schlosser, 1991; Franklin, 1992). Historically, the U.S. Forest Service has been reluctant to address sedimentation and hydrological changes of streams resulting from forestry practices on federal lands (Hewlett, 1984). However, the Forest Service is demonstrating a growing awareness of deleterious sedimentation problems relative to forestry practices (Welsch, 1991; U.S. Department of Agriculture, 1994). Prospects for increased sedimentation from forestry in the upper Etowah River watershed appear to be significant. Due to timber harvest restrictions elsewhere in the United States, the Southeast will likely face increased timber harvesting. However, in the Etowah River watershed, approximately 85 percent of the land is privately owned and timber quotas for federal lands may not have as great an impact as in other southern Appalachian watersheds. Nonetheless, the Chattahoochee National Forest encompasses some of the best remaining headwater streams of the Etowah River, and increased clearcutting would exacerbate existing sedimentation problems. Current timber harvesting in the Chattahoochee National Forest is causing a large sediment load in the main channel of the Etowah River near the border of the national forest at the Lumpkin County Route 72 bridge (authors' pers. obs.). Deep deposits of micaceous silts and sands are present at this site in pools, and gravel, rubble, and small boulders are embedded in a matrix composed of smaller sediments. The Georgia Forestry Commission recommends best management practices (BMP) for timber harvesting on private lands. The use of BMPs is not mandatory, and their effectiveness in reducing stream sedimentation from silviculture rests upon this voluntary compliance. Streamside management zones, which are an integral part of these BMPs, vary in width from 25 feet on warmwater streams to 100 feet on designated trout streams.

Figure 17. An example of destructive construction practices relative to soil conservation and abusive sedimentation of a tributary to Noonday Creek. Note the lack of sediment screens around the tributary. This site is immediately north of the junction of Chastain and Big Shanty roads, Kennesaw, GA, date 9 July 1991 (photograph by N. M. Burkhead).

DESTRUCTIVE CONSEQUENCES OF SEDIMENTATION

The destructive effects of excessive sedimentation on fluvially-adapted macroinvertebrates and fishes have been well documented. Excessive sedimentation destroys habitats by reducing habitat complexity and diversity. Substrates entombed by sediment lose vital habitat niches for macroinvertebrates, thereby reducing community and faunal complexity (Ellis, 1936; Cordone and Kelley, 1961; Chutter, 1969; Nuttall and Bielby, 1973; Brusven and Prather, 1974; Fuller, 1974; Rosenberg and Wiens, 1978; Quinn et al., 1992). Faunal decline caused by sedimentation diminishes trophic web complexity and the efficiency of nutrient cycling within the aquatic community. Fish biodiversity is similarly impoverished by the action of sedimentation that reduces substrate heterogeneity. Because fish diversity is positively correlated with habitat diversity (Gorman and Karr, 1978; Karr and Dudley, 1981), increased sedimentation is particularly harmful to benthic fishes (Berkman and Rabeni, 1987; see Figure 9). Moreover, catastrophic sedimentation events can cause fish kills (Hesse and Newcomb, 1982). A particularly noxious result of sedimentation is reduced reproductive success of benthic-spawning fishes (Peters, 1967; Muncy et al., 1979). Egg survival in trouts is positively correlated with intergravel permeability and increased particle size in the redd, and increased mortality is largely associated with hypoxia from eggs and larvae being smothered by fine silt (Chapman, 1988). Suffocation of eggs is probably the primary cause of pre-larval mortality of benthic-spawning riverine fishes.

Turbidity, caused by sediments suspended in the water column, reduces or eliminates

Figure 18. Abandoned marble quarry contributing to sedimentation of Cove Creek, Pickens County, GA (photograph by N. M. Burkhead).

Figure 19. Riparian loss and associated sedimentation at a site on Clear Creek, a small tributary draining pasture land in Bartow County, GA (photograph by N. M. Burkhead).

Figure 20. Bank-cutting and heavy sedimentation during a period of high runoff at a site on Mountain Creek at the confluence of Padgett and Town creeks, Pickens County, GA (photograph by S. J. Walsh).

light penetration thereby reducing primary photosynthetic productivity (Davies-Colley et al., 1992). Turbidity also affects sight-feeding fishes by diminishing their ability to detect prey. We speculate that many or some species exhibiting probable signs of sexual selection (such as the brilliant colors adorned by males of many species) may have reduced reproductive success in turbid water. Turbidity may also reduce the efficacy of a recently discovered, fascinating reproductive strategy in certain lampsiline mussels. Some species release superconglutinates — clusters of mussel larvae collectively mimicking the shape of a small fish or invertebrate attached to the end of a mucous strand — that sway and undulate in currents, acting as lures to potential host fishes (Haag et al., 1995). High turbidity would obviously reduce the ability of many fishes to detect such lures.

Pollution

Prior to the U.S. Clean Water Act of 1972 (CWA) and subsequent amendments, the Etowah River was moderately polluted in its middle and lower reaches, but sections upstream from Allatoona Reservoir were considered relatively healthy (Georgia Water Quality Control Board, 1970). Some of the most polluted sites in the river were immediately below poultry rendering plants. For example, the wet stream banks at a site in Blankets Creek below a poultry processing plant in Canton were literally "scarlet from the protruding bodies of millions of oligochaete worms" (Georgia Water Quality Control Board, 1970). Presently, the Etowah River is significantly improved from the most severe cases of obvious pollution that existed prior to the CWA. However, based on the tremendous decline and extirpation of the aquatic biota, the present status of water quality is probably not sufficient to maintain the existing fish and mussel biodiversity, and water quality is clearly below standards necessary to restore the river.

We are unaware of any ongoing systematic monitoring of water quality in the Etowah River system other than that associated with municipal sewage discharges and water supply intakes. Primary point-source discharges in the river include sewage, industrial, and poultry processing effluents. Nonpoint-sources of pollution include excessive sedimentation from multiple sources, agricultural runoff (including pesticides and nutrients), mercury and other trace metals, potential landfill leaching (see Figure 16), and polycyclic aromatic hydrocarbons. The latter class of pollutants are primarily associated with urban and industrial environments (Neff, 1985). In this regard there is a direct relevance to human health concerns in the watershed. Because pesticides and trace metals can bind and accumulate in sediments (Leland and Kuwabara, 1985; Nimmo, 1985), we are concerned that the deleterious effects of the severe sedimentation problem in the Etowah River may be worsened by contaminants.

A serious future pollution threat to the Etowah River is the proposed interbasin transfer of 42 million gallons per day (mgd) (1.74×10^8 lpd) of secondary-treated sewage wastewater from the Chattahoochee River to the upper Etowah River in Forsyth County, just above the mouth of Settingdown Creek (Figure 16). This project was halted, at least temporarily, by the 1996 Georgia Legislature (Senate Bill 500). This bill amends Georgia law to prohibit surface water interbasin transfers of "sewage, industrial waste, treated wastewater, or other wastes" unless the Director of the Georgia Department of Environmental Protection has established criteria that allow for pollutants which cause receiving waters or lakes below the point of discharge to fall below water quality standards. In other words, a simple reduction of the waste-level standards would allow for the transfer of treated sewage.

Using Forsyth County's estimate of phosphorous (P) concentrations in the effluent, a

10 mgd (3.79×10^7 lpd) discharge would contribute an additional 4,145 kg (9,138 pounds) P per year to the Etowah River and Allatoona Reservoir, and 17,520 kg (38,624 pounds) P per year for a 42 mgd discharge. Measurements by one of us (BJF, October 1991) of P/ PO_4 at the proposed introduction site were 0.0055 parts per million (ppm), and recent measurements of P/PO_4 from several Etowah River sites above the mouth of Settingdown Creek ranged from 0.0027 to 0.0122 ppm. A 42 mgd discharge would increase phosphorous during average flow conditions by 482 percent and by 1,682 percent during a 7Q10 flow (defined as the lowest flow on record measured during one week in a ten-year interval). The increases in nitrogen would be comparable. Clearly the proposed interbasin transfer would have a significant eutrophication effect on the Etowah River, and furthermore, the average temperature of the transferred wastewater would be 18.3° C (65° F), warmer than ambient water temperature in winter and cooler than ambient temperature in summer. Thus, the interbasin transfer would likely create additional stress and further contribute to habitat fragmentation of the Etowah River system by adding nutrient and thermal pollution.

The fact that the interbasin transfer could even be considered suggests that municipal and regional planners already view the Etowah River with little regard for its rich biological resources. In our opinion, a system-wide assessment of current water quality is critically needed, with special attention to the problem of contaminated sediments, and the establishment of a biological monitoring program for water quality standards.

Urbanization

The human population is projected to increase in the South by 31 percent by the year 2000 (Alig and Healy, 1987), and most of this growth will probably occur in major metropolitan areas. In few places does such projected growth approach the magnitude of the greater Atlanta area. Urban environments dramatically affect the physical characteristics of streams. Urbanization may increase sediment loads delivered to streams by as much as 100 percent (Meade et al., 1990). Because urban centers have large areas of impervious surfaces and infrastructure designed to efficiently transport water (e.g., gutters and storm drains), increased runoff rates enhance the transport of soils and other materials to stream channels (Hirsch et al., 1990). In Maryland streams, water quality impairment was first evidenced when watershed imperviousness reached 12 percent, and reduced water quality became severe when imperviousness reached 30 percent (Klein, 1979). Increased runoff rates in urban areas produce higher flood levels in short intervals, causing bank destabilization and erosion in outlet streams, and sometimes causing abrupt changes in channel morphology. Noonday Creek in Cobb County is an Etowah River tributary that drains an urban area (Figure 4). The substrates at sites we examined in Noonday Creek consisted entirely of clay and sand, 15 to 30 cm (5.9 to 11.8 inches) deep, covering the old gravel and rubble stream bottom. The substrate composition of streams in the Atlanta metropolitan area is also dominated by sand (Couch et al., 1995).

Streams draining urban landscapes typically have diminished, or significantly depleted, pollution-tolerant faunas (Duda et al., 1982; Weaver and Garman, 1994). Streams in the greater Atlanta metropolitan area have fewer native species, generally less than one-half, than intradrainage streams in predominately forested areas (Couch et al., 1995). The same Atlanta urban streams also have more nonindigenous species than similar streams in rural areas. Chemical by-products of urbanization, a plethora of chemicals ranging from used motor oil, paint products, and residential pesticides to PCBs leaked from transformers, have a variety of deleterious effects on aquatic organisms, including developmental abnormalities. Populations of the threatened Cherokee darter in Butler Creek, an Etowah River tributary in Cobb County, exhibited progressive interruption of the supratemporal canal (a sensory structure on the head) from the 1940s to present (Bauer et al., 1995). Interruption of the supratemporal canal is otherwise rare in subnose darters (Bauer et al., 1995), and may be a teratological phenomenon related to urban runoff.

Weaver and Garman (1994) suggested that urbanization represents a low-intensity disturbance of stream systems. While this is true relative to high-intensity disturbances such as large impoundments, catastrophic chemical spills, or point-source toxic discharges, the overall effects of urbanization can be equal to or more harmful to stream systems than high-intensity disturbances. The process of urbanization constitutes piecemeal habitat loss (see *Faunal Fragmentation*). The biological health of an urban stream depends on the type of urban environment the stream drains. Streams flowing through parks or semi-wooded residential areas with relatively intact riparian zones will retain more of their natural aquatic biota than streams flowing through concrete environments. The latter streams may be little more than culverts with faunas of hardy and pollution-tolerant organisms.

RESTORATION OF THE ETOWAH RIVER ECOSYSTEM

"Don't it always seem to go
That you don't know what you've got
Till it's gone
They paved paradise
And put up a parking lot..."
— Joni Mitchell, *Big Yellow Taxi*

Status: Endangered

During Earth Week 1996, the nonprofit environmental organization American Rivers, Inc., released its annual list of the top ten most endangered river systems of the United States. Included on this list were the Etowah and the adjacent Chattahoochee rivers. These two systems, inextricably linked by proposed interbasin water exchange and mutual environmental problems associated with growth and extractive resource use, have the dubious distinction of being among the most ecologically threatened rivers in the Southeast. This treatise is timely considering the inauspicious recognition of the Etowah River as one of the nation's most endangered river ecosystems. Herein, we provide an overview and summary of basic tenets of restoration ecology as applied to river systems and adjacent landscapes, and conclude with a variety of topics to be considered by all citizens and organizations with vested interests in the Etowah River watershed and other southern Appalachian rivers.

Overview and Definitions

Restoration ecology is an important and fast growing subdiscipline of conservation biology. Management of natural resources has long included aspects of habitat recovery, but only relatively recently has there been heightened attention to proactive, comprehensive restoration of habitats, communities, and ecosystems. The following examples illustrate some of the reasons for a greatly accelerated focus on riverine restoration ecology: 1. Even though the U.S. Clean Water Act was established over two decades ago, today nearly half of the nation's fresh waters fail to meet minimum water quality standards based on biological criteria; 2. Less than two percent of all lotic river miles in the United States currently receive federal protection under the 1968 U.S. National Wild and Scenic Rivers Act; 3. Principal objectives of the 1973 U.S. Endangered Species Act are to list, protect, and recover imperiled plants and animals, yet listing and recovery of most species and populations has lagged far behind discovery and recognition of jeopardized taxa, such that aquatic species, in particular, are now disappearing rapidly and ubiquitously (Doppelt et al., 1993; Warren and Burr, 1994; Mann and Plummer, 1995; Walsh et al., 1995).

As a consequence of the general failure of existing single-species management programs, most scientists now espouse greater conservation efforts toward multiple scales of biological complexity. Much of this shift in emphasis is a consequence of increasingly diminished global biodiversity and a greater realization that effective conservation programs must include protection of relatively healthy habitats and recovery of perturbed habitats. Emerging as a vital activity of more encompassing resource management, ecological restoration is a rational approach for recovering, reestablishing, and protecting native biotas (U.S. National Research Council, 1992; Doppelt et al., 1993; MacMahon and Jordan, 1994; Noss and Cooperrider, 1994).

Increasingly, restoration programs target entire ecosystems. Our concept of an ecosystem generally follows that of Whittaker (1975) and Odum (1993), and is broadly defined as an aggregate of communities and environments treated together as a functioning system of complementary relationships that transfer and circulate energy and matter. We stress that this definition includes all dynamic spatial and temporal processes that affect natural, interconnected terrestrial and aquatic assemblages. Additional, concise definitions related to riverine watersheds and riparian areas provided by Doppelt et al. (1993) are used similarly here, to encourage people to think about "riverine systems as complex, dynamic ecological and biological systems on a landscape scale." These authors use the terms "watershed ecosystem" and "riverine-riparian ecosystem" in a hierarchical sense; these definitions and other relevant terms are summarized in Table 5.

During its early growth, the field of restoration ecology has undergone extensive theoretical development. The objectives, scope, limitations, and feasibility of ecosystem restoration have been broadly examined. Considering the obstacles and complexity of restoration, some ecologists argue that successful restoration of seriously degraded habitats on a large scale is unlikely or impossible. Notwithstanding, most ecologists feel that restoration must be a common goal of future conservation activities. In southern Appalachia there is an acute need for riverine restoration to protect the remaining aquatic biodiversity of the region. For practical purposes, we adhere loosely to many proffered definitions of "restoration," "rehabilitation," "reclamation," "recovery," and related terms (U.S. National Research Council, 1992; MacMahon and Jordan, 1994). The term "restoration" itself is generally used to mean the return of an ecosystem to a close approximation of its condition prior to disturbance (U.S. National Research Council, 1992). Realistically, we acknowledge that few if any southern rivers may ever return to historic conditions or a reasonable semblance of that which existed prior to human settlement. Thus, we employ the term "restoration" as the sum of all processes and activities that serve to redirect an ecosystem on a trajectory toward a pre-disturbance state (MacMahon and Jordan, 1994). In practical terms, we believe the preferred endpoint should be to restore conditions that maximize biological evolutionary processes through space and time. The term "recovery" is also used here in a broad sense, to mean not only the return of natural conditions through passive processes (MacMahon and Jordan, 1994), but also through active human intervention such as programs to abate excessive sedimentation or to reintroduce extirpated species. We refer the reader to the following synoptic works, and references in each, for additional general information on ecological restoration and watershed management: Gore, 1985; Jordan et al., 1987; Naiman, 1992; U.S. National Research Council, 1992; Doppelt et al., 1993; Hesse et al., 1993; Cairns, 1994; MacMahon and Jordan, 1994; and Noss and Cooperrider, 1994.

The Etowah River watershed presents formidable challenges for ecological restoration due to a burgeoning human population and widespread negative environmental changes within the watershed and in northwestern Georgia. Below we present a general prospectus for planning, prioritizing, and initiating restoration activities within the Etowah River watershed. Our intent is to provide a general framework on which to eventually build a more detailed, consensus-based strategy for restoration and ecosystem management of aquatic resources in the Etowah River system. This framework should have direct application to restoration of other riverine systems throughout the southern Appalachians.

Restoration Goals, Limitations, and Planning

The National Research Council developed a checklist of important questions, goals, and criteria to be addressed prior to, during, and following any restoration program (U.S. National Research Council, 1992, Table 3.1; MacMahon and Jordan, 1994, Table 14.1). These central questions concern various aspects of each project's mission, planning, design, feasibility, scope, cost, post-restoration analysis, and long-term ecological and socio-economic benefits. However, restoration needs of the Etowah River are so extensive that many of the specific questions outlined by the U.S. National Research Council (1992) at present cannot be adequately addressed to determine the suitability and potential success of individual restoration projects within the watershed. Moreover, environmental protection of the Etowah River watershed has long been neglected and there have been no previous comprehensive efforts to identify and initiate ecosystem restoration programs. We feel that a top priority exists for coordination of local and regional assessments, planning, and management of growth and environmental protection within the Etowah River system. Better organization and communication than currently exists among all relevant parties is a necessary first step to initiating restoration projects within the ecosystem, since restoration efforts cannot be expected to succeed without enhanced coordination of resource management (Ford et al., 1990; Doppelt et al., 1993). Ultimately, successful recovery will not occur unless private citizens, the business sector, and government agencies unite with a mutual goal of restoring ecological integrity of the Etowah River watershed.

The restoration and watershed management goals that we envision for the Etowah River ecosystem are straightforward: to reverse as much as possible all conditions contributing to the decline of natural, physical, and biological resources and processes; to protect minimally disturbed areas, and; to stem future losses of biodiversity and diminution of ecosystem health. Given the magnitude of ecological degradation and the extent of urban and rural growth in the area, it is unrealistic from a practical standpoint to assume that comprehensive, system-wide ecological restoration throughout the Etowah River watershed is possible in the immediate foreseeable future. However, rather than adopting a minimalist approach to restoration, we believe the above stated objectives impart ultimate goals to strive for, and discourage compromising attitudes that certain portions of the drainage are unrecoverable, can be sacrificed, or excluded from restoration activities.

The greatest limitations facing restoration in the Etowah River watershed, as in most other systems, are fiscal constraints, the coordination of public and private interests, and the balancing of socioeconomic concerns. Meffe and Carroll (1994, page 492) define *sustainable development* as "human activities conducted in a manner that respects the intrinsic value of the natural world, the role of the natural world in human well-being, and the need for humans to live on the income from nature's capital rather than the capital itself." This is analogous to living on the dividends of one's investments rather than the principal itself; the term "sustainable development" is often grossly misunderstood and fallaciously misused by politicians and the corporate sector. The main threat to the biological and physical integrity of the Etowah River system is *unsustainable growth* in northwest Georgia. Ecological restoration efforts in the watershed will be successful over time only if there is acceptance of mutual responsibility and commitment by citizens, the business community, and government agencies to plan and better manage economic development, and, in our opinion, to seriously address consumptive resource use in the region.

Prudent analysis and planning of aquatic ecosystem restoration is fundamental to the success of any program. For the Etowah River watershed, the need for a unified, aggressive restoration and ecosystem management plan has never been greater than now. Various authors have discussed the value and nature of integrative planning processes and methods that involve policy analysts, decision makers, resource managers, and scientists (U.S. National Research Council, 1992; Doppelt et al., 1993). Most such programs would encompass all relevant economic, social, and environmental considerations early in the assessment process, while retaining significant flexibility (Holling, 1978). Recently, Doppelt et al. (1993) proposed a new approach to riverine restoration — the Rapid Biotic and Ecosystem Response — a concept founded on principles linking watershed dynamics, ecosystem function, and conservation biology. Their approach involves three integrated components. Initially, there is comprehensive identification and protection of remaining, relatively healthy tributaries, biotic refuges, riparian areas, floodplains, and biological "hot spots" throughout the entire ecosystem. This emphasizes protection and reduces the need for post-disturbance control or repair, thereby improving effectiveness and cost-efficiency. Second, restoration efforts are devoted to improved management of intervening areas between those that are protected, with a goal to eventually link healthy areas. A third concurrent step in the Rapid Biotic and Ecosystem Response is to actively involve local communities and citizens in implementing all the steps for planning and supporting environmentally sustainable economic development. This approach is urgently needed to begin ecological restoration of the Etowah River watershed.

Spatial Scales

Considerable debate exists concerning minimum reserve size for protected areas, extent and nature of habitat corridors, and appropriate scales for ecosystem management and restoration. Some of the most successful or widely publicized restoration projects have been relatively small in scale, on the order of a few hectares, and most riverine restoration projects are limited to rehabilitation of selected river sections to a predetermined state of structure and function (Gore and Shields, 1995). Moreover, many ecosystems are so severely degraded or overexploited that socioeconomic and other factors limit the practicality of comprehensive, large-scale restoration projects. Nevertheless, riverine restoration programs should ultimately be done on a watershed- or ecosystem-wide basis (e.g., Noss and Cooperrider, 1994). At the very least, restoration planning should encompass the entire ecosystem, even if initial restoration activities are limited to subsections. In fluvial ecosystems this is especially important, because environmental impacts in one part of the catchment may strongly affect other areas of the watershed. For example, mitigation of major sedimentation sources in upper portions of a watershed will positively affect downstream reaches.

Potential success of ecological restoration projects is directly related to spatial scale according to the following criteria: 1) The project area must be sufficiently large to ameliorate deleterious effects that boundary conditions may impose on interior aquatic functions. 2) Project managers must have control or influence over zones where major causes of ecological disturbance exist. 3) The area must be large enough to allow for monitoring and follow-up assessment of success. 4) A project must be affordable in size (U.S. National Research Council, 1992).

In the Etowah River system many environment-degrading land practices are widespread and restoration might best be approached on a watershed-wide basis, such as by establishing programs for reducing loss of riparian vegetation, nonpoint-source pollution, and sedimentation. Other problems are very site-specific and restoration could be enhanced by mitigation on a relatively small scale, such as upgrading sewage treatment facilities. A salient aspect of the planning process is to evaluate and rank river reaches and tributaries relative to their ecological status and restoration needs.

Restoration Framework

A fundamental premise of ecological restoration is that background information exists regarding predisturbance conditions of the ecosystem. While the precise historical structure of an ecosystem is seldom if ever known, some estimate can be made by extrapolating from conditions that persist or by comparison with similar systems. Unfortunately, ecologists rarely have sufficient baseline data to accurately reconstruct historical conditions or to evaluate community structure and dynamics on the basis of comparable systems. Ideally, planning a restoration project includes survey, inventory, and compilation of preliminary physical and biological data to assess progress and success. In practice, however, cost limitations and the degree of environmental change may preclude adequate pre-restoration analysis of existing or historic conditions. However, obvious ecologically-deleterious conditions do not require knowledge of predisturbance circumstances in order to begin fundamental steps of restoration, assuming disturbance causes are adequately understood and restoration goals have been established.

Crucial information about the Etowah River watershed is currently lacking. Basic biological and geophysical research is needed to determine present ecosystem structure and dynamics. Also needed are assessments of current land-use coverage and general environmental conditions, as well as a comprehensive review of all existing municipal and re-

Table 5. Definitions of physical and biological terms pertinent to riverine ecosystem restoration and management, slightly modified from Doppelt et al. (1993).

Term	Definition
biological diversity (biodiversity)	The variety of the world's biological elements and processes, represented and integrated over organizational levels from genes to landscapes.
biological hot spots	Intact riverine habitat patches that provide critical functions for biodiversity or the stream; ranging from microhabitats (such as individual pools or riffles) to larger sections of complex, healthy habitats.
biotic refuges (refugia)	Physical areas with healthy and relatively undisturbed habitats and processes that serve as refuges for biodiversity.
ecosystem simplification	The cumulative result of impacts causing large reductions in the life-supporting complexity and diversity of ecosystems.
riparian area	The transition zone between the flowing water and terrestrial ecosystems.
riverine-riparian biodiversity	All native aquatic and riparian organisms dependent on the riverine-riparian ecosystem.
riverine-riparian ecosystem	All the processes and elements that interact in the flowing water and riparian areas of the riverine system (often corresponding to the 100-year floodplain).
riverine system	An entire river network, including all tributaries, sloughs, side channels, and intermittent streams. The term *riverine* is used more restrictively than *aquatic* to mean only a natural flowing freshwater system.
watershed (catchment basin)	The entire physical area or basin drained by a stream or riverine system, separated from other watersheds by ridgetop boundaries.
watershed ecosystem	All of the elements and processes that interact within the watershed.

gional growth and development policies and plans. Several important initiatives are required for greater organization of resource management and restoration in the Etowah River watershed (Table 6). These initiatives mainly fall under general categories of political and socioeconomic review, ecosystem evaluation, restoration planning, and public education; these goals are common in any restoration program and need to be seriously addressed for the Etowah River ecosystem. To coordinate environmental reform across the watershed, we propose that a well-balanced organization be established to review, plan, and implement improved ecosystem management. An "Etowah Watershed Alliance," or similarly-named organization should be composed of individuals and groups representing diverse economic, environmental, and political interests, with a common goal of establishing healthy ecosystem management while striving for true sustainable development. Bolling (1994) provides important considerations in building a successful, interjurisdictional program for watershed protection and management.

Critical Research Needs

Whereas cooperative alliances, some planning, and initial restoration measures can be immediately implemented, critical research is needed for organized, cost-effective restoration throughout the Etowah River watershed. Research needs span multiple and complex areas, including species biology, community and system ecology, hydrology, fluvial geomorphology, and human demographic and socioeconomic issues. An exhaustive analysis of research priorities for the Etowah River watershed is beyond the scope and intent of this work, but we summarize the primary research deficiencies that need to be addressed in Table 7.

Basic research required to determine the current ecological health of the watershed are analyses of land-use coverage and determinations of biotic diversity, location, and abundance. Several valuable analytical tools are applicable for this assessment, including Aquatic Gap Analysis, Population Viability Analysis, and the Index of Biotic Integrity (Table 7). Surveys of aquatic macroinvertebrates are especially needed for incorporation in Aquatic Gap Analysis. There is a strong need for determining the impacts of habitat fragmentation on the genetic structure of metapopulations, and for evaluating habitat discontinuity and barriers to potential dispersal and recolonization capabilities of aquatic organisms. This is especially important for determining species at greatest risk and for identifying critical linkage areas to target for restoration. Basic autecological research to determine habitat requirements and life histories of selected species representing different ecological guilds is required for planning comprehensive restoration projects and in evaluating the recovery progress. Typical species-oriented restoration approaches focus on habitat rehabilitation for a few high-profile species. This type of restoration effort is often endorsed because ecological data are lacking for many species, or management is aimed toward game or protected species. Such efforts to optimize habitats for a few valued species may cause suboptimal conditions for other species or impair riverine ecology, and may therefore be inconsistent with goals of ecosystem management in maintaining or recovering biological integrity (Keenlyne, 1993; Sparks, 1995).

Important toxicological research should focus on elucidating the effects of sediments and both organic and inorganic contaminants on survivorship, reproductive success, and other ecological traits of aquatic species. These data are especially needed for the early life-history stages of riverine organisms in the Etowah River watershed. Experimental data are essential, since qualitative conclusions about the effects of sediments are often unsubstantiated by empirical data and do not improve scientific understanding of the biological basis for negative ecological impacts of sediments (Berkman and Rabeni, 1987). Toxicological studies should emphasize the synergistic effects of chemical pollutants and sediments that are often bound together during transport or deposition (Leland and Kuwabara, 1985; Nimmo, 1985).

There is an immediate need for determining physical structure and hydrological function of the Etowah River watershed to better understand ecological impacts. A preliminary analysis should be done to assess historical changes that have occurred and the current status and conditions of both aquatic and terrestrial resources. Pervasive riparian loss and sedimentation throughout the drainage indicate that a comprehensive geomorphological study is in order. Especially urgent is an analysis of sediment, contaminant, and nutrient transport throughout the system, so that sources and sinks can be identified and targeted for mitigation. Sediment sampling and transport modeling are increasingly essential to riverine restoration and watershed management (Gordon et al., 1992), and are imperative for the Etowah River watershed because of the highly erodible soils of the Piedmont province, riparian deforestation, and overall deteriorating water quality of Georgia's rivers (Meade et al., 1990; Georgia Erosion and Sedimentation Panel, 1995). We recommend that the Etowah River watershed be seriously considered for inclusion in the National Water-Quality Assessment (NAWQA) program of the U.S. Geological Survey. The NAWQA program evaluates physical and biological conditions of surface and groundwater resources, thereby providing critical baseline data necessary for resource assessment, restoration planning, and long-range monitoring of water quality. The recent addition of the Etowah River to the NAWQA program is especially timely due to the rapid rate of ecosystem decline in the Etowah River system, and imminent prospects for greatly accelerated demands on water resources in the greater Atlanta area.

The most challenging research needs for the Etowah River watershed involve socioeconomic issues. Because of highly fragmented and often conflicting government and private interests, there is currently no comprehensive ecosystem management of aquatic and terrestrial resources. In fact, we are unaware of any metropolitan areas in or adjacent to the watershed that consider principals of resource sustainability during economic planning. The first step in initiating ecosystem restoration of the Etowah River watershed is to review existing environmental policies at all levels, and to collectively draw together all public and private partners with vested economic and natural resource interests. Accordingly, we have listed in Appendix 1 many of the relevant organizations and government agencies with significant environmental responsibilities for the Etowah River watershed and general interests in environmental conservation. One function of a watershed coalition (see *Restoration Framework* above) would be to serve as a liaison between these diverse groups and to focus them on a unified, comprehensive approach to ecosystem management and restoration.

Watershed Priorities

Within the Etowah River watershed, as elsewhere throughout southern Appalachia, the following criteria are among the most important factors in considering specific riverine areas to target for restoration: 1. existing or historical biotic diversity and endemism; 2. nature and extent of ecological perturbations and degradation; 3. biological, physical, and socioeconomic value of restoring a specific area; 4. potential for success in restoring an area; and 5. cost effectiveness relative to improving overall health of the ecosystem.

The complex land-use pattern that surrounds the Etowah River provides a mosaic from which to identify and establish priority areas suitable for ecosystem protection and ecological restoration. General categorization of subregions of the Etowah River watershed based on environmental perturbation and existing fish diversity provides a general basis for targeting restoration areas (Figure 21). Relatively high-quality areas have the least ecosystem damage and retain the greatest degree of faunal diversity and endemism, or least extirpation of native taxa. These are primarily tributary headwaters in the upper portion of the watershed that have large, intact riparian zones forested with native hardwood species and where disturbances are generally least intensive. Included in this category are headwaters and adjacent lands of the Etowah River system, encompassing all or significant portions of Sharp Mountain Creek, Long Swamp Creek, Amicalola Creek, and Shoal Creek. Faunal diversity remains fairly high and endemic fishes (three species of snubnose darters and the Etowah darter) are found in these regions. Also placed in this category are two areas in the lower portion of the watershed, Spring Creek and Connesena Creek, which have undergone moderate habitat degradation but harbor species (rainbow shiner and blacknose dace) that are restricted or extirpated elsewhere in the Etowah River system and are otherwise rare or uncommon throughout the upper Coosa River system.

Consideration of the above regions as areas of relatively low restoration priority is not intended to diminish their ecological importance. Conversely, the least-perturbed areas of the Etowah River watershed are among those with the highest intrinsic biological, physical, and aesthetic value. For this reason, these are regions that should be protected through strong, proactive conservation measures. Protection of the relatively undisturbed and healthier headwaters, tributaries, riparian zones, and biological hot spots is essential to the future success of other restoration activities and is the first strategy in the Rapid Biotic and Ecosystem Response approach of Doppelt et al. (1993). Long-range monitoring of these areas should be done to ensure that negative environmental impacts are minimal, and the areas should be targeted for restoration efforts if present conditions deteriorate. Significant areas for long-term protection are in the headwaters of the Etowah River system within the Chattahoochee National Forest. The U.S. Forest Service should manage federal lands under its jurisdiction within the region by implementing Best Management Practices that beneficially contribute to overall ecosystem health (see *Remediation* below).

Of somewhat higher priority for riverine restoration within the Etowah River watershed are regions with moderate environmental degradation and faunal decline. These areas are in the upper-middle portion of the drainage, from Stamp Creek in northeastern Bartow County to the main channel and southern tributaries upstream of Allatoona Reservoir in the northern half of Cherokee County and southern portions of Pickens, Dawson, and Lumpkin counties. Also included in this category are headwaters of various lower Etowah River tributaries in Paulding, Polk, Floyd, and Bartow counties (Figure 21). These are largely rural, agricultural areas, although significant portions of Cherokee, Pickens, Dawson, and Lumpkin counties remain moderately forested with mixed hardwoods and conifers. The extreme lower Etowah River and Spring Creek have been detrimentally impacted by industrial development and urbanization near the city of Rome. In Cherokee County, there has been recent and rapid urban sprawl extending northward along a corridor centered around Interstate 575. Additionally, the planned northern perimeter loop of the interstate highway system will bring further development and associated negative impacts to the northcentral part of the watershed.

Restoration planning in the above moderately-impacted areas minimally should include three primary facets. First, immediate efforts should be made to evaluate present land-use coverage and to identify and secure protection for existing stream reaches with maximum physical and biological integrity and ecosystem health. Second, degraded stream sections that could potentially link the best-quality habitats should be identified, ranked, and targeted for specific cost-effective rehabilitation projects. Third, methods should be developed and implemented to abate, mitigate, and reverse the most pervasive causes of envi-

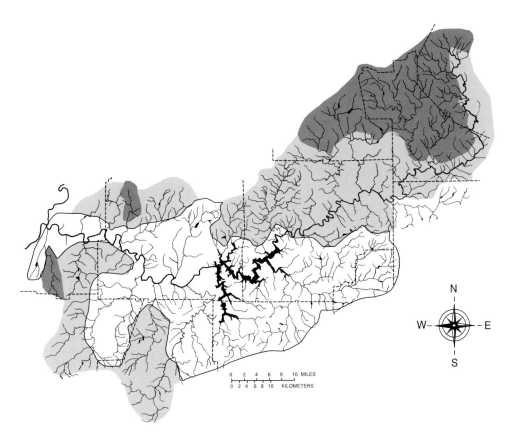

Figure 21. Ecological restoration priority areas of the Etowah River watershed. Heavy shading = areas with high faunal diversity and/or endemism, and lowest existing threats; light shading = areas of moderate faunal diversity and moderate existing threats; unshaded = areas of lowest faunal diversity and greatest habitat loss and degradation.

ronmental degradation, especially reducing the loss of riparian cover and improving control of sediments, nutrients, and pollutants emanating from farms, landfills, golf courses, and urban development. There should be careful scrutiny of existing and future proposed projects that are likely to have negative environmental impacts in these areas, with critical attention devoted to exploring economically viable alternatives. We suggest that serious consideration be given to a temporary moratorium on proposed water-supply impoundments in areas of the basin pending a comprehensive review of projected growth and water usage needs throughout the drainage. Research should also be initiatied on practical conservation measures and alternatives to construction of new reservoirs, and evaluation of long-range impacts of each additional proposed impoundment.

Restoration efforts within the moderately-impacted areas are critical for ecosystem recovery of the entire watershed, because continued ecological decline in tributary headwaters of these sections will further exacerbate detrimental impacts downstream. Further, these stream segments and riparian zones are critical linkage areas and their restoration is essential for health of the entire watershed. Moreover, restoration projects in these areas could be the most cost-effective, in terms of potential for rehabilitation success and overall positive impacts to the watershed relative to per capita expenditures.

Ecological conditions are most severely degraded in a large, central portion of the Etowah River watershed (Fig. 21). Included in this area are streams that have undergone faunal impoverishment and ecosystem simplification through habitat loss and cumulative effects listed under *Threats to the System*, primarily resulting from Allatoona Reservoir, urbanization, deforestation and destruction of riparian cover, industrial and agricultural pollution, widespread sedimentation, and eutrophication. Considerable growth in recent years between Marietta (Cobb County) and Cartersville (Bartow County) has contributed significantly to environmental decline in the central portion of the drainage, coupled with years of heavy agriculture. Etowah River tributaries in Fulton and Forsyth counties have been so severely modified by harmful agricultural effects, urbanization, and small impoundments, that sedimentation and other factors have reduced faunal diversity to a disturbance-tolerant guild, much like nearby streams in urban reaches of the upper Chattahoochee River system (Couch et al., 1995). Major Etowah River tributaries that fall in the high-disturbance category include Euharlee Creek, Petit Creek, Little River, Noonday Creek, and lower Pumpkinvine Creek. Additionally, direct tributaries flowing into Allatoona Reservoir, such as Stamp Creek and Allatoona Creek, have suffered extensive degradation and have depauperate faunas that are isolated from other tributaries of the drainage. Finally, Allatoona Reservoir has obliterated large sections of fluvial habitats and has a significant effect on the main channel fauna far downstream of the dam, as discussed under *Threats to the System*.

Restoration of heavily-disturbed areas presents some of the most challenging problems to ecosystem management in the Etowah River watershed. Many of the major degraded riverine segments are critical to ecosystem function and could provide major linkages between healthier regions of the watershed. These highly altered sectors are bound to primary economic development in the drainage, and their rehabilitation involves the greatest social, political, and financial obstacles. As the most seriously impacted riverine segments, these areas will require the greatest amount of work and time to successfully restore. Moreover, restoring these streams will not only be expensive, but some restored habitats, especially tributaries flowing into Allatoona Reservoir, will not be available to colonizing fishes from other tributaries or the main channel. Likewise, fish populations restored by introductions could not serve as sources to other tributaries or the main channel without human intervention. Thus, restoration projects in the most perturbed areas may not be the most economical or practical, and socioeconomic costs must be thoroughly evaluated relative to potential success for ecological restoration and the overall impact of improving ecosystem function.

Remediation

Based on the above review of restoration concepts and issues, we suggest the following measures for consideration as a starting point for comprehensive and organized restoration of the Etowah River watershed. We feel there is an urgency for certain immediate, remedial restoration activities to prevent continued ecological degradation and possible irreversible loss of biological diversity and ecosystem function. The following list of possible remedial measures for the Etowah River watershed is far from being exhaustive, but addresses some of the basic and most important restoration issues that we feel pertain to the Etowah River watershed. This outline is not intended to be a mandate or to establish

Table 6. List of major steps needed to develop a regional ecosystem restoration and management strategy for the Etowah River watershed.

---

a. Identify all appropriate individuals, institutions, industries, and agencies within the private and public sectors to participate in ecosystem management and restoration within the watershed (see Appendix 1).
b. Adopt and implement a comprehensive public education program.
c. Evaluate present status of aquatic and terrestrial biological and physical resources, including faunal surveys, basic ecological research, indices of biological integrity, and risk assessment.
d. Determine complete hydrologic discharge, removal, wastewater treatment, and water quality throughout the watershed, including a review of all existing residential and industrial wastewater and point-source permits.
e. Establish long-term water quality monitoring stations on all major tributaries and along the entire main channel of the Etowah River. In accordance with the National Water-Quality Assessment (NAWQA) program of the U.S. Geological Survey, critical sites should be established for modeling sediment transport and water quality.
f. Compile and analyze existing land-use data and proposed agricultural and municipal projects with potential adverse environmental impacts. A centralized data base would facilitate restoration planning and comprehensive resource management strategies.
g. Evaluate, adopt, and implement regional growth management plans for the multi-county metropolitan and rural corridors within and surrounding the Etowah River watershed.
h. Develop comprehensive assessment, planning, and monitoring programs for management of sustainable natural resources within the region. Coordinate local municipal, county, and state government agencies, industries, real estate speculators, and land-owners in developing a watershed-based environmental management plan.
i. Review and revise all local and regional regulatory policies governing environmental protection and natural resource management.
j. Identify, prioritize, target, and modify environmentally detrimental land-use practices. Revise urban zoning procedures.
k. Evaluate, rank, and establish individual geographic areas for pilot restoration projects.
l. Analyze and secure cooperative funding from all potential sources; establish a financial review panel for identifying and soliciting suitable funding sources.
m. Recruit and engage all available industries, agencies, conservation organizations, and private citizens in conducting and monitoring individual restoration projects.

---

priorities. Rather, it is intended to provide a focal point and catalyst for open debate, critical evaluation, and, hopefully, earnest public action devoted to ecosystem restoration efforts within the basin. All of the measures detailed below should be construed as viable options suitable for serious consideration and constructive scrutiny in an open forum of all public and private parties with vested interests in land-use and environmental issues of the Etowah River ecosystem.

 I. Organization of an ecosystem-protective coalition (Etowah Watershed Alliance).
   A. Assemble relevant private, business, and government interests (Appendix 1).
   B. Plan and conduct annual public conferences on socioeconomic and natural resource issues pertaining to the Etowah River watershed.
   C. Formulate short- and long-range plans for *sustainable development* within the watershed.

Table 7. Summary list of critical research needs for the Etowah River watershed.

ECOLOGICAL
Macro-scale
  Examine large-scale factors affecting distribution of both aquatic and terrestrial organisms of the watershed using Geographical Information System (GIS) technology to assess current and historic distribution patterns and to analyze present land-use coverage.
  Identify existing protected areas, biodiversity hot spots and unprotected but viable corridors and linkages using Aquatic Gap Analysis (Scott et al., 1987).
Meso-scale
  Analyze aquatic community structure and function using the Index of Biotic Integrity (IBI), a powerful multimetric tool for evaluating natural resource conditions and establishing a baseline of overall ecosystem health (Karr, 1981; 1991; Karr et al., 1986).
Population scale
  Assess select jeopardized taxa and species at risk using Population Viability Analysis (PVA), a quantitative model for examining the interrelationships among extinction likelihood, environmental variability, habitat availability, demographic stochasticity, and genetic factors (Soulé, 1987, Shaffer, 1990).
  Evaluate consequences of localized extirpation and population fragmentation on genetic variation of select imperiled and nonimperiled taxa.
Autecology
  Determine habitat needs of keystone and sensitive species.
  Obtain detailed ecological data for evaluating how changing environmental conditions may affect life history parameters.
Aquatic Toxicology
  Conduct bioassays of prevalent pesticides and pollutants, including possible synergistic interactions, on early life-history stages of fishes and aquatic invertebrates.
  Examine effects of sediments on reproductive success of native aquatic organisms.
  Review point-source pollution discharge permits for all industries, landfills, and other sources throughout the watershed, and identify significant contaminants and their causes.

GEOPHYSICAL
Macro-scale
  Determine historic changes in habitats throughout the watershed.
  Model sediment and nutrient transport in the entire drainage.
  Identify riparian coverage throughout the watershed.
  Establish sites throughout the watershed and implement routine sampling in accordance with the U.S. Geological Survey National Water-Quality Assessment (NAWQA) program.
Meso-scale
  Identify areas with the highest quality of physical habitat.
  Identify mainstem and tributary reaches that are highly degraded by sedimentation.
  Determine habitat connectivity at different stage levels in the main channel of the Etowah River and its major tributaries.

SOCIOECONOMIC
  Review all local, regional, state, and federal environmental policies and legislation pertaining to natural resources of the watershed.
  Review all water-use permits and determine viable alternatives for improving water conservation in the region, at all levels, from private citizens to industries and municipalities.

Table 7. Continued.

Critically review needs and plans for all large resource-altering projects, based on the best available growth projects, and explore feasibly sustainable alternatives.

Review procedures for determining site locations of environmentally threatening projects (e.g., landfills, factories), with special emphasis on selecting alternatives to sites within the floodplain.

Provide technical and financial assistance to farmers for converting to best agricultural practices.

Review economically viable alternatives to present silviculture methods in the watershed.

Determine the most cost effective and environmentally favorable methods for disposal of waste effluents from poultry farms and processing facilities.

II. Sedimentation abatement.
  A. Adopt and apply research, monitoring, and mitigation recommendations of the Georgia Erosion and Sedimentation Control Panel (1995).
  B. Involve existing programs of the U.S. Fish and Wildlife Service (Partners in Wildlife), the Natural Resources Conservation Service, the National Fish and Wildlife Foundation, The Nature Conservancy, and various public and private endowments to assist landowners in protecting and recovering riparian zones.
  C. Provide incentives and education to farmers for mitigating and abating sedimentation and topsoil erosion.
  D. Establish standards for vegetated riparian buffer strips along streams in each physiographic province.
  E. Encourage and provide incentives for private and business landowners to replant native vegetation in currently denuded riparian areas.
  F. Promote effective sediment-control measures during all types of building construction, roadway development, and other forms of habitat modification.
  G. Adopt and implement best management practices (e.g., Bisson et al., 1992; U.S. Department of Agriculture, 1994) on federal lands in the Chattahoochee National Forest with emphasis on protection of aquatic habitats.
    1. Plan, develop, and adapt management practices geared specifically toward ecological protection of southern Appalachian riverine resources.
    2. Investigate economically viable alternatives to cultivation of conifer monocultures that promote silviculture methods utilizing native hardwood species.
    3. Evaluate all clearcutting and road-building methods and implement harvest techniques that minimize sediment production.
    4. Promote fisheries management programs that favor diversity, abundance, and enjoyment of native aquatic communities without comprimising recreational, commercial, or tourism interests.
  H. Provide incentives to mitigate industrial and mining sources of sedimentation.
III. Minimizing impoundment and runoff effects.
  A. Investigate all potential ecological, socioeconomic, and associated costs and benefits that might pertain to construction of a re-regulation dam below Allatoona

Reservoir to mitigate flow pulses in the main river channel.

B. Evaluate potential feasibility of installing an air-injection system, or a suitable alternative, in Allatoona Dam to alleviate low dissolved oxygen and high hydrogen sulfide concentrations in the reservoir tailrace.

C. Conduct exhaustive reviews of existing and future water demands and reevaluate the necessity for new water-supply impoundments.

D. Educate, encourage, and provide incentives to private citizens and businesses to adopt beneficial water and energy conservation measures.

E. Investigate suitable alternatives to locating new urban developments, roadway construction, and other impervious surfaces near or adjacent to the main river channel and tributaries.

F. Create incentives for attracting low water-consumptive industries to the area.

IV. Pollution mitigation.

A. Upgrade all municipal sewage treatment facilities for tertiary treatment.

B. Review existing National Pollution Discharge Elimination System permits, and monitor minimum water quality standards for all licensed point-source discharges throughout the watershed.

C. Provide incentives to poultry farmers and processing facilities to alleviate negative impacts of waste disposal.

D. Discourage placement of any new landfills, golf courses, or sources of industrial pollutants adjacent to or near the main river channel or tributaries.

E. Explore alternatives to interbasin transfers of wastewater.

V. Ecosystem protection.

A. Review potential for seeking designation of Amicalola Creek as a National Wild and Scenic River.

B. Pursue opportunities for acquisition and protection of additional public lands.

C. Educate, encourage, assist, and empower private landowners, citizen groups, and conservation organizations in protecting local natural resources.

Education

Pervasive environmental deterioration of the Etowah River watershed is partly attributable to inadequate education about the value and significance of ecosystem protection and the benefits of sustainable development. Like many places elsewhere, a lack of awareness about the plight and importance of the Etowah River watershed contributes to continual disregard for the long-range effects of unsustainable exploitation of natural resources within the ecosystem. Ecological restoration cannot be expected to succeed without greater public education and galvanized support for a conservation agenda to protect the Etowah River watershed.

Improved education about the current status and future prospects of the Etowah River watershed encompasses two priorities: education of the general public, and education of policy makers and natural resource managers. Public education must include programs that purvey the current status and role of the watershed to overall ecosystem function, and how ecosystem health relates to long-term human welfare. Central to general education is the notion that public empowerment is essential to solving environmental problems. As stewards entrusted by the public, natural resource agencies and policy makers must be aware of all environmental issues affecting the watershed and must take strong responsibility and leadership in holistic ecosystem management.

Protection of the Etowah River watershed, like all other natural ecosystems, may require a fundamental change in how local citizens view their role in the global environment. Humans are as equally susceptible as many other organisms to disease, famine, natural disasters, and, especially, overpopulation. As sentient beings, there is a prevalent myopia that we are able to solve all technological, biological, and other challenges, and that materialistic gain and human welfare supersedes the environmental consequences of unsustained exploitation of natural resources. Yet, many environmental education programs fail to stress that human existence is ultimately and inextricably linked to a well-balanced global biosphere, comprised of functional and healthy ecosystems. As Rolston (1991) eloquently stated, "There is something overspecialized about an ethic, held by the dominant class of *Homo sapiens*, that regards the welfare of only one of several million species as an object and beneficiary of duty...about living in a reference frame in which one species takes itself as absolute and values everything else relative to its utility. If true to its specific epithet, which means wise, ought not *Homo sapiens* value this host of life as something that lays on us a claim to care for life in its own right?" If precious natural resources of the Etowah River system are to be saved, people in and around the watershed must cogently acknowledge that ecological protection and environmental sustainability are intrinsically valuable and essential for a healthy quality of life for all organisms within the ecosystem.

ACKNOWLEDGEMENTS

We are grateful to the Georgia Department of Natural Resources, especially G. S. Beisser and R. M. Gennings, for granting scientific collecting permits, field assistance, and technical support. The U.S. Fish and Wildlife Service provided most of the funding and technical assistance for surveys of the Cherokee and Etowah darters. Additional funding was also provided by the U.S. Forest Service. We especially thank the following individuals for aid in field work: M. M. Bentzien, R. T. Bryant, J. H. Chick, R. S. Cowles, A. Daniels, G. R. Dinkins, M. C. Freeman, C. R. Gilbert, A. G. Haines, D. C. Haney, G. Hill, M. H. Hughes, H. L. Jelks, T. Jones, J. M. Matter, P. W. Parmalee, J. Peterkin, C. E. Skelton, T. Smith, W. F. Smith-Vaniz, L. A. Somma, C. M. Timmerman, J. Troxel, and D. C. Weaver. M. C. Freeman kindly provided hydrographs and brought to our attention certain relevant literature. G. R. Dinkins and J.M. Pierson furnished many important recent fish records and accompanying collection data. J. T. Williams kindly loaned fishes from the U.S. National Museum of Natural History. K. W. Burkhead and L. G. Spinella generously assisted with editorial revisions. H. L. Jelks and D. C. Haney provided invaluable assistance in producing graphics, maps, and helping with editorial changes. M. C. Freeman and R. E. Sparks critically reviewed and greatly improved an earlier draft of the manuscript. Our work in the Etowah River system has benefited greatly over the years from discussions with R. G. Biggins, R. S. Butler, D. A. Etnier, M. C. Freeman, P. D. Hartfield, R. J. Larson, R. L. Mayden, and C. A.Williams. Lastly we thank J. A. Mann (Technical Information Service, National Biological Service) for always being pleasant, patient, and timely with our numerous literature requests. We regretfully apologize for inadvertently omitting others that have contributed substantially to this work

REFERENCES

Alig, R. J., and R. G. Healy. 1987. Urban and built-up land area changes in the United States: An empirical investigation of determinants. *Land Economics* **63**(3):215-226.

Angermeier, P. L. 1995. Ecological attributes of extinction-prone species: Loss of freshwater fishes of Virginia. *Conservation Biology* **9**:143-158.

Armour, C. L., D. A. Duff, and W. Elmore. 1991. The effects of livestock grazing on riparian and stream ecosystems. *Fisheries* **16**(1):7-11.

Bagby, G. T. 1969. Our ruined rivers. *Georgia Game and Fish* **4**:1-16.

Barrows, H. H., J. V. Phillips, and J. E. Brantly. 1917. Agricultural drainage in Georgia. *Geological Survey of Georgia Bulletin* **32**:1-122.

Bauer, B. H., D. A. Etnier, and N. M. Burkhead. 1995. *Etheostoma* (*Ulocentra*) *scotti* (Osteichthyes: Percidae), a new darter from the Etowah River system in Georgia. *Bulletin of the Alabama Museum of Natural History* **17**:1-16.

Beisser, G. S. 1989. The fish populations and sport fishery of Allatoona Reservoir, 1980-1987. D-J Final Report, Project F-36, Georgia Department of Natural Resources, Atlanta, GA, 70 p.

Berkman, H. E., and C. F. Rabeni. 1987. Effect of siltation on stream fish communities. *Environmental Biology of Fishes* **18**:285-294.

Bisson, P. A., T. P. Quinn, G. H. Reeves, and S. V. Gregory. 1992. Best management practices, cumulative effects, and long-term trends in fish abundance in Pacific northwest river systems. In *Watershed Management: Balancing Sustainability and Environmental Change*. R. J. Naiman (ed.). Springer Verlag, New York, NY, p. 189-232.

Bogan, A. E. 1993. Freshwater bivalve extinctions (Mollusca: Unionoida): A search for causes. *American Zoologist* **33**:599-609.

Bolling, D. M. 1994. *How to Save a River: A Handbook for Citizen Action*. Island Press, Washington, D.C.

Boschung, H. T. 1992. Catalogue of freshwater and marine fishes of Alabama. *Bulletin Alabama Museum of Natural History* **14**:1-266.

Boschung, H. T., R. L. Mayden, and J. R. Tomelleri. 1992. *Etheostoma chermocki*, a new species of darter (Teleostei: Percidae), from the Black Warrior River drainage of Alabama. *Bulletin Alabama Museum of Natural History* **13**:11-20.

Brown, J. H. 1984. On the relationship between abundance and distribution of species. *The American Naturalist* **124**:255-279.

Brown, L. R., P. B. Moyle, W. A. Bennett, and B. D. Quelvog. 1992. Implications of morphological variation among populations of California roach *Lavinia symmetricus* (Cyprinidae) for conservation policy. *Biological Conservation* **62**:1-10.

Brusven, M. A., and K. V. Prather. 1974. Influence of stream sediments on distribution of macrobenthos. *Journal of the Entomological Society of British Columbia* **71**:25-32.

Bryant, R. T., B. H. Bauer, M. G. Ryon, and W. C. Starnes. 1979. Distributional notes on fishes from northern Georgia with comments on the status of rare species. *Southeastern Fishes Council Proceedings* **2**:1-4.

Burkhead, N. M., and R. E. Jenkins. 1991. Fishes. In *Virginia's Endangered Species*. K. Terwilliger (coordinator). McDonald and Woodward Publishing Company, Blacksburg, VA, p. 321-409.

Burkhead, N. M., J. D. Williams, and B. J. Freeman. 1992. A river under siege. *Georgia Wildlife* **2**:10-17.

Burr, B. M., and R. C. Cashner. 1983. *Campostoma pauciradii*, a new cyprinid fish from southeastern United States, with a review of related forms. *Copeia* **1983**:101-116.

Butts, C., and B. Gildersleeve. 1948. Geology and mineral resources of the Paleozoic area in northwest Georgia. *Geological Survey of Georgia Bulletin* **54**:1-176.

Cairns, J., Jr. (ed.). 1994. *Rehabilitating Damaged Ecosystems, Volumes 1 and 2, 2nd Edition.* CRC Press, Boca Raton, FL.

Carson, H. L. 1983. The genetics of the founder effect. In *Genetics and Conservation: A Reference for Managing Wild Animal and Plant Populations.* C. M. Schonewald-Cox, S. M. Chambers, B. MacBryde, and W. L. Thomas (eds.). The Benjamin/ Cummings Publishing Company, Inc., Menlo Park, CA, p. 189-200.

Chapman, D. W. 1988. Critical review of variables used to define effects of fines in redds of large salmonids. *Transactions of the American Fisheries Society* **117**:1-21.

Chesser, R. K. 1983. Isolation by distance: Relationship to the management of genetic resources. In *Genetics and Conservation: A Reference for Managing Wild Animal and Plant Populations.* C. M. Schonewald-Cox, S. M. Chambers, B. MacBryde, and W. L. Thomas (eds.). The Benjamin/Cummings Publishing Company, Inc., Menlo Park, CA, p. 66-77.

Chutter, F. M. 1969. The effects of silt and sand on the invertebrate fauna of streams and rivers. *Hydrobiologia* **34**:57-76.

Clemmer, G. H., and R. D. Suttkus. 1971. *Hybopsis lineapunctata*, a new cyprinid fish from the upper Alabama River system. *Tulane Studies in Zoology and Botany* **17**:21-30.

Coburn, M. M., and T. M. Cavender. 1992. Interrelationships of North American cyprinid fishes. In *Systematics, Historical Ecology, and North American Freshwater Fishes.* R. L. Mayden (ed.). Stanford University Press, Stanford, CA, p. 328-373.

Cordone, A. J., and D. W. Kelley. 1961. The influences of inorganic sediment on the aquatic life of streams. *California Fish and Game* **47**:189-228.

Couch, C. A., J. C. DeVivo, and B. J. Freeman. 1995. What fish live in the streams of metropolitan Atlanta? Fact Sheet FS-091-95, National Water-Quality Assessment Program, U.S. Geological Survey, Atlanta, GA, 4 p.

Cressler, C. W., H. E. Blanchard, Jr., and W. G. Hester. 1979. Geohydrology of Bartow, Cherokee, and Forsyth counties, Georgia. *Georgia Geological Survey Information Circular* **50**:1-45.

Dahlberg, M. D., and D. C. Scott. 1971. The freshwater fishes of Georgia. *Bulletin of the Georgia Academy of Sciences* **29**:1-64.

Davies-Colley, R. J., C. W. Hickey, J. M. Quinn, and P. A. Ryan. 1992. Effects of clay discharges on streams. 1. Optical properties and epilithon. *Hydrobiologia* **248**:215-234.

Diamond, J. M. 1984. "Normal" extinctions of isolated populations. In *Extinctions.* M. H. Nitecki (ed.). The University of Chicago Press, Chicago, IL, p. 191-246.

Doppelt, B., M. Scurlock, C. Frissell, J. Karr, and Pacific Rivers Council. 1993. *Entering the Watershed: A New Approach to Save America's River Ecosystems.* Island Press, Washington, D.C.

Duda, A. M., D. R. Lenat, and D. L. Penrose. 1982. Water quality in urban streams-what can we expect. *Journal Water Pollution Control Federation* **54**:1139-1147.

Ellis, M. M. 1936. Erosion silt as a factor in aquatic environments. *Ecology* 17:29-42.

Etnier, D. A. 1994. Our southeastern fishes — what have we lost and what are we likely to lose. *Southeastern Fish Council Proceedings* **29**:5-9.

Etnier, D. A., and W. C. Starnes. 1991. An analysis of Tennessee's jeopardized fish taxa. *Journal of the Tennessee Academy of Science* **66**:129-133.

Etnier, D. A., and W. C. Starnes. 1994. *The Fishes of Tennessee.* University of Tennessee Press, Knoxville, TN.

Ford, K. E., K. A. Glatzel, and R. E. Piro. 1990. Watershed planning and restoration: Acheiving holism through interjurisdictional solutions. In *Environmental Restoration: Science and Strategies for Restoring the Earth.* J. J. Berger (ed.). Island Press, Washington, D.C., p. 312-327.

Franklin, J. F. 1992. Scientific basis for new perspectives in forests and streams. In *Watershed Management: Balancing Sustainability and Environmental Change.* R. J. Naiman (ed.). Springer-Verlag, New York, NY, p. 25-72.

Freeman, B. J. 1983. Final report on the status of *Etheostoma trisella*, the trispot darter, and *Percina antesella*, the amber darter, in the upper Coosa River system in AL, GA, TN. Unpublished Report submitted to the U. S. Fish and Wildlife Service, Asheville, NC, 21 p. + appendices.

Freeman, B. J., and M. C. Freeman. 1994. Habitat use by an endangered riverine fish and implications for species protection. *Ecology of Freshwater Fish* **3**:49-58.

Fuller, S. L. H. 1974. Clams and mussels (Mollusca: Bivalvia). In *Pollution Ecology of Freshwater Invertebrates.* C. W. Hart, Jr., and S. L. H. Fuller (ed.). Adacemic Press, New York, NY, p. 215-273.

Georgia Erosion and Sedimentation Control Panel. 1995. Erosion and sedimentation: Scientific and regulatory issues. Special Report to the Lt. Govenor, Georgia Board of Regents Scientific Panel on Evaluating the Erosion Measurement Standard Defined by the Georgia Erosion and Sedimentation Act, Atlanta, GA, 34 p.

Georgia Water Quality Control Board. 1970. Coosa River basin study. Georgia Water Quality Control Board, Atlanta, GA, 226 p.

Gibbs, R. H., Jr. 1955. A systematic study of the cyprinid fishes belonging to the subgenus *Cyprinella* of the genus *Notropis*. Ph.D. Dissertation, Cornell University, Ithaca, NY.

Gilbert, C. R., H. T. Boschung, and G. H. Burgess. 1980. *Notropis caeruleus* (Jordan). Blue shiner. In *Atlas of North American Freshwater Fishes.* D. S. Lee, C. R. Gilbert, C. H. Hocutt, R. E. Jenkins, D. E. McAllister, and J. R. Stauffer, Jr. (eds.). North Carolina State Museum of Natural History, Raleigh, NC, p. 244.

Gillespie, R. B., and S. I. Guttman. 1993. Correlations between water quality and frequencies of allozyme genotypes in spotfin shiner (*Notropis spilopterus*) populations. *Environmental Pollution* **81**:147-150.

Gordon, N. D., T. A. McMahon, and B. L. Finlayson. 1992. *Stream Hydrology: An Introduction for Ecologists.* John Wiley and Sons, New York, NY.

Gore, J. A. (ed.). 1985. *The Restoration of Rivers and Streams: Theories and Experience.* Butterworth Publishers, Boston, MA.

Gore, J. A., and F. D. Shields, Jr. 1995. Can large rivers be restored? *BioScience* **45**:142-152.

Gorman, O. T., and J. R. Karr. 1978. Habitat structure and stream fish communities. *Ecology* **59**:507-515.

Haag, W. R., R. S. Butler, and P. D. Hartfield. 1995. An extraordinary reproductive strategy in freshwater bivalves: Prey mimicry to facilitate larval dispersal. *Freshwater Biology* **34**:471-476.

Hackney, C. T., and S. M. Adams. 1992. Aquatic communities of the southeastern United States: Past, present, and future. In *Biodiversity of the Southeastern United States: Aquatic Communities.* C. T. Hackney, S. M. Adams, and W. H. Martin (eds.). John Wiley and Sons, Inc., New York, NY, p. 747-760.

Hall, B. M., and M. R. Hall. 1921. Third report on the water powers of Georgia. *Geological Survey of Georgia Bulletin* **38**:1-316.

Harris, L. D. 1984. *The Fragmented Forest: Island Biogeography Theory and the Preservation of Biotic Diversity.* The University of Chicago Press, Chicago, IL.

Hesse, L. W., and B. A. Newcomb. 1982. Effects of flushing Spencer Hydro on water quality, fish, and insect fauna in the Niobrara River, Nebraska. *North American Journal of Fisheries Management* **2**:45-52.

Hesse, L. W., C. B. Stalnaker, N. G. Benson, and J. R. Zuboy (eds.). 1993. *Proceedings of the Symposium on Restoration Planning for the Rivers of the Mississippi River Ecosystem.* Biological Report 19, National Biological Survey, U.S. Department of the Interior, Washington, D.C.

Hewlett, J. D. 1984. Forest cutting and water quality, quantity and timing in the Georgia Piedmont. In *A Conference on the Water Resources of Georgia and Adjacent Areas.* R. Arora, and L. L. Gorday (eds.). Bulletin 99, Georgia Geologic Survey, Atlanta, GA, p. 38-47.

Hirsch, R. M., J. F. Walker, J. C. Day, and R. Kallio. 1990. The influence of man on hydrologic systems. In *Surface Water Hydrology: The Geology of North America, Volume 0-1.* M. G. Wolman, and H. C. Riggs (eds.). The Geological Society of America, Boulder, CO, p. 329-359.

Hoggarth, M. A. 1992. An examination of the glochidia - host relationships reported in the literature for North American species of Unionacea (Mollusca: Bivalvia). *Malacology Data Net* **3**:1-30.

Holling, C. S. 1978. *Adaptive Environmental Assessment and Management.* John Wiley and Sons, New York, NY.

Hurd, J. C. 1974. Systematics and zoogeography of the Unionacean mollusks of the Coosa River drainage of Alabama, Georgia and Tennessee. Ph.D. Dissertation, Auburn University, AL.

Jenkins, R. E., and N. M. Burkhead. 1994. *The Freshwater Fishes of Virginia.* American Fisheries Society, Bethesda, MD.

Jordan, D. S. 1877. A partial synopsis of the fishes of upper Georgia. *Annals of the New York Lyceum of Natural History* **11**:307-377.

Jordan, D. S. 1878. A synopsis of the family Catostomidae. *Bulletin of the United States National Museum* **12**:97-230.

Jordan, D. S. 1922. *The Days of a Man, Being Memories of a Naturalist, Teacher and Minor Prophet of Democracy.* World Book, Yonkers-on-Hudson, New York, NY.

Jordan, D. S., and A. W. Brayton. 1878. On the distribution of the fishes of the Alleghany region of South Carolina, Georgia, and Tennessee, with descriptions of new or little known species. *Bulletin of the United States National Museum* 12:3-95.

Jordan, W. R., III, M. E. Gilpin, and J. D. Aber (eds.). 1987. *Restoration Ecology: A Synthetic Approach to Ecological Research*. Cambridge University Press, Cambridge, NY.

Karr, J. R. 1981. Assessment of biotic integrity using fish communities. *Fisheries* 6(6):21-27.

Karr, J. R. 1991. Biological integrity: A long-neglected aspect of water resource management. *Ecological Applications* 1:66-84.

Karr, J. R., and D. R. Dudley. 1981. Ecological perspective on water quality goals. *Environmental Management* 5:55-68.

Karr, J. R., K. D. Fausch, P. L. Angermeier, P. R. Yant, and I. J. Schlosser. 1986. Assessing biological integrity in running waters: A method and its rationale. *Illinois Natural History Survey Special Publication* 5:1-28.

Karr, J. R., and I. J. Schlosser. 1977. Impact of nearstream vegtation and stream morphology on water quality and stream biota. Ecological Research Series EPA-600/3-77-097, Environmental Protection Agency, Springfield, VA, 91 p.

Keenlyne, K. D. 1993. Resolving resource management conflicts between listed and unlisted species on large rivers. In *Proceedings of the Symposium on Restoration Planning for the Rivers of the Mississippi River Ecosystem*. L. W. Hesse et al. (eds.). Biological Report 19, National Biological Survey, U.S. Department of the Interior, Washington, D.C., p. 481-484.

Kinsolving, A. D., and M. B. Bain. 1993. Fish assemblage recovery along a riverine disturbance gradient. *Ecological Applications* 3:531-544.

Klein, R. D. 1979. Urbanization and stream water quality impairment. *Water Resources Bulletin* 15(4):948-963.

Lande, R. 1988. Genetics and demography in biological conservation. *Science* 241:1455-1460.

Leigh, D. S. 1994. Mercury storage and mobility in floodplains of the Dahlonega gold belt. Technical Completion Report Project 14-08-0001-G2013-(04), U.S. Geological Survey, U.S. Department of the Interior, Atlanta, GA, 41 p.

Leland, H. V., and J. S. Kuwabara. 1985. Trace metals. In *Fundamentals of Aquatic Toxicology: Methods and Applications*. G. M. Rand, and S. R. Petrocelli (eds.). Hemisphere Publishing Corporation, New York, NY, p. 374-415.

Lowrance, R. 1992. Groundwater nitrate and denitrification in a Coastal Plain riparian forest. *Journal of Environmental Quality* 21:401-405.

Lowrance, R., R. Leonard, and J. Sheridan. 1985. Managing riparian ecosystems to control nonpoint pollution. *Journal of Soil and Water Conservation* 40:87-91.

Lowrance, R. R., R. L. Todd, and L. E. Asmussen. 1984a. Nutrient cycling in an agricultural watershed: I. Phreatic movement. *Journal of Environmental Quality* 13:22-26.

Lowrance, R. R., R. L. Todd, and L. E. Asmussen. 1984b. Nutrient cycling in an agricultural watershed: II. Streamflow and artifical drainage. *Journal of Environmental Quality* 13:27-32.

Lowrance, R., R. Todd, J. Fail, Jr., O. Hendrickson, Jr., R. Leonard, and L. Asmussen. 1984. Riparian forests as nutrient filters in agricultural watersheds. *BioScience* 34:374-377.

Lydeard, C., and R. L. Mayden. 1995. A diverse and endangered aquatic ecosystem in the southeast United States. *Conservation Biology* 9:800-805.

Mackenthun, K. M. 1969. The practice of water pollution biology. Division of Technical Support, Federal Water Pollution Control Administration, U.S. Department of the Interior, U.S. Government Printing Office, Washingtion, D.C.

MacMahon, J. A., and W. R. Jordan, III. 1994. Ecological restoration. In *Principles of Conservation Biology.* G. K. Meffe, and C. R. Carroll (eds.). Sinauer Associates, Inc., Sunderland, MA, p. 409-438.

Mann, C. C., and M. Plummer. 1995. Is endangered species act in danger? *Science* 267:1256-1258.

Martin, R. O. R., and R. L. Hanson. 1966. Reservoirs in the United States. Water-Supply Paper 1838, U.S. Geological Survey, U.S. Government Printing Office, Washington, D.C., 115 p.

Mayden, R. L., B. M. Burr, L. M. Page, and R. R. Miller. 1992. The native freshwater fishes of North America. In *Systematics, Historical Ecology, and North American Freshwater Fishes.* R. L. Mayden (ed.). Stanford University Press, Stanford, CA, p.827-863.

Meade, R. H. 1969. Errors in using modern stream-load data to estimate natural rates of denudation. *Geological Society of America Bulletin* **80**:1265-1274.

Meade, R. H., T. R. Yuzyk, and T. J. Day. 1990. Movement and storage of sediment in rivers of the United States and Canada. In *Surface Water Hydrology: The Geology of North America, Volume 0-1.* M. G. Wolman, and H. C. Riggs (eds.). The Geological Society of America, Boulder, CO, p. 255-280.

Meffe, G. K., and C. R. Carroll (eds.). 1994. *Principles of Conservation Biology.* Sinauer Associates, Inc., Sunderland, MA.

Menzel, R. G., and C. M. Cooper. 1992. Small impoundments and ponds. In *Biodiversity of the Southeastern United States: Aquatic Communities.* C. T. Hackney, S. M. Adams, and W. H. Martin (eds.). John Wiley and Sons, Inc., New York, NY, p. 389-420.

Mettee, M. F., P. E. O'Neil, J. M. Pierson, and R. D. Suttkus. 1989. Fishes of the Black Warrior River system in Alabama. *Geological Survey of Alabama Bulletin* **133**:1-201.

Miller, R. R., J. D. Williams, and J. E. Williams. 1989. Extinctions of North American fishes during the past century. *Fisheries* 14(6):22-38.

Morse, J. C., B. P. Stark, W. P. McCafferty, and K. J. Tennessen. 1997. Southern Appalachian and other southeastern streams at risk: Implications for mayflies, dragonflies and damselflies, stoneflies, and caddisflies. In *Aquatic Fauna in Peril: The Southeastern Perspective.* G. W. Benz, and D. E. Collins (eds.). Special Publication 1, Southeast Aquatic Research Institute, Lenz Design & Communications, Decatur, GA, p. 17-42.

Moyle, P. B., and R. A. Leidy. 1992. Loss of biodiversity in aquatic ecosystems: Evidence from fish faunas. In *Conservation Biology: The Theory and Practice of Nature, Conservation, Preservation, and Management.* P. L. Fielder, and S. K. Jain (eds.). Chapman and Hall, New York, NY, p. 127-169.

Moyle, P. B., and J. E. Williams. 1990. Biodiversity loss in the temperate zone: Decline of the native fish fauna of California. *Conservation Biology* 4:275-284.

Muncy, R. J., G. J. Atchison, R. M. Bulkley, B. W. Menzel, L. G. Perry, and R. C. Summerfelt. 1979. Effects of suspended solids and sediment on reproduction and early life history of warmwater fishes: A review. Research and Development EPA-600/3-79-042, U.S. Environmental Protection Agency, Springfield, VA, 101 p.

Naiman, R. J. (ed.). 1992. *Watershed Management: Balancing Sustainability and Environmental Change.* Springer Verlag, New York, NY.

Nash, R. F. 1989. *The Rights of Nature. A History of Environmental Ethics.* University of Wisconsin Press, Madison, WI.

Neff, J. M. 1985. Polycyclic aromatic hydrocarbons. In *Fundamentals of Aquatic Toxicology: Methods and Applications.* G. M. Rand, and S. R. Petrocelli (eds.). Hemisphere Publishing Corporation, New York, NY, p. 416-454.

Neves, R. J., A. E. Bogan, J. D. Williams, S. A. Ahlstedt, and P. W. Hartfield. 1997. Status of aquatic mollusks in the southeastern United States: A downward spiral of diversity. In *Aquatic Fauna in Peril: The Southeastern Perspective.* G. W. Benz, and D. E. Collins (eds.). Special Publication 1, Southeast Aquatic Research Institute, Lenz Design & Communications, Decatur, GA, p. 43-86.

Nimmo, D. R. 1985. Pesticides. In *Fundamentals of Aquatic Toxicology: Methods and Applications.* G. M. Rand, and S. R. Petrocelli (eds.). Hemisphere Publishing Corporation, New York, NY. p. 335-373.

Noss, R. F., and A. Y. Cooperrider. 1994. *Saving Nature's Legacy: Protecting and Restoring Biodiversity.* Island Press, Washington, D.C.

Nuttall, P. M., and G. H. Bielby. 1973. The effect of china-clay wastes on stream invertebrates. *Environmental Pollution* 5:77-86.

Odum, E. P. 1993. *Ecology and Our Endangered Life Support Systems, 2nd Edition.* Sinauer Associates, Inc., Sunderland, MA.

Ono, R. D., J. D. Williams, and A. Wagner. 1983. *Vanishing Fishes of North America.* Stone Wall Press, Inc., Washington, D.C.

Page, L. M., and B. M. Burr. 1991. *A Field Guide to Freshwater Fishes.* Houghton Mifflin Company, Boston, MA.

Page, L. M., P. A. Ceas, D. L. Swofford, and D. G. Buth. 1992. Evolutionary relationships of the *Etheostoma squamiceps* complex (Percidae; Subgenus *Catonotus*) with descriptions of five new species. *Copeia* 1992:615-646.

Palmer, T. 1986. *Endangered Rivers and the Conservation Movement.* University of California Press, Berkeley, CA.

Parent, S., and L. M. Schriml. 1995. A model for the determination of fish species at risk based upon life-history traits and ecological data. *Canadian Journal of Fisheries and Aquatic Sciences* 52:1768-1781.

Park, C. F., Jr. 1953. Gold deposits of Georgia. *Georgia Geological Survey Bulletin* 60:60-67.

Peters, J. C. 1967. Effects on a trout stream of sediment from agricultural practices. *Journal of Wildlife Management* 31:805-812.

Pierson, J. M., W. M. Howell, R. A. Stiles, M. F. Mettee, P. E. O'Neil, R. D. Suttkus, and J. S. Ramsey. 1989. Fishes of the Cahaba River system in Alabama. *Geological Survey of Alabama Bulletin* 134:1-183.

Pimentel, D., C. Harvey, P. Resosudarmo, K. Sinclair, D. Kurz, M. McNair, S. Crist, L. Shpritz, L. Fitton, R. Saffouri, R. Blair. 1995. Environmental and economic costs of soil erosion and conservation benefits. *Science* 267:1117-1123.

Pimm, S. L., H. L. Jones, and J. Diamond. 1988. On the risk of extinction. *The American Naturalist* 132:757-785.

Quinn, J. M., R. J. Davies-Colley, C. W. Hickey, M. L. Vickers, and P. A. Ryan. 1992. Effects of clay discharges on streams. 2. Benthic invertebrates. *Hydrobiologia* 248:235-247.

Ramsey, J. S., and R. D. Suttkus. 1965. *Etheostoma ditrema*, a new darter of the subgenus *Oligocephalus* (Percidae) from springs of the Alabama River basin in Alabama and Georgia. *Tulane Studies in Zoology* 12:65-77.

Richards, W. J., and L. W. Knapp. 1964. *Percina lenticula*, a new percid fish, with a redescription of the subgenus *Hadropterus*. *Copeia* 1964:690-701.

Robins, C. R., R. M. Bailey, C. E. Bond, J. R. Brooker, E. A. Lachner, R. N. Lea, and W. B. Scott. 1991. *Common and Scientific Names of Fishes from the United States and Canada*. Special Publication 20, American Fisheries Society, Bethesda, MD.

Rohde, F. C. 1980. *Noturus nocturnus* Jordan and Gilbert. Freckled madtom. In *An Atlas of North American Freshwater Fishes*. D. S. Lee, C. R. Gilbert, C. H. Hocutt, R. E. Jenkins, D. E. McAllister, and J. R. Stauffer, Jr. (eds.). North Carolina State Museum of Natural History, Raleigh, NC, p. 466.

Rolston, H., III. 1991. Environmental ethics: Values in and duties to the natural world. In *Ecology, Economics, Ethics: The Broken Circle*. F. H. Bormann, and S. R. Kellert (eds.). Yale University Press, New Haven, CT, p. 73-96.

Rosenberg, D. M., and A. P. Wiens. 1978. Effects of sediment addition on macrobenthic invertebrates in a northern Canadian River. *Water Research* 12:753-763.

Sayers, R. 1996. Candidate notice is revised. *Endangered Species Bulletin* March/April 21(2):7.

Schlosser, I. J. 1991. Stream fish ecology: A landscape perspective. *BioScience* 41:704-712.

Scott, J. M., B. Csuti, J. D. Jacobi, and J. E. Estes. 1987. Species richness. *BioScience* 37:782-788.

Shaffer, M. L. 1981. Minimum population sizes for species conservation. *BioScience* 31:131-134.

Shaffer, M. L. 1990. Population viability analysis. *Conservation Biology* 4:39-40.

Soballe, D. M., B. L. Kimmel, R. H. Kennedy, and R. F. Gaugush. 1992. Reservoirs. In *Biodiversity of the Southeastern United States: Aquatic Communities*. C. T. Hackney, S. M. Adams, and W. H. Martin (eds.). John Wiley and Sons, Inc., New York, NY, p. 421-474.

Soulé, M. E. 1980. Thresholds for survival: Maintaining fitness and evolutionary potential. In *Conservation Biology: An Evolutionary-Ecological Persepective*. M. E. Soulé, and B. A. Wilcox (eds.). Sinauer Associates, Inc., Sunderland, MA, p. 151-169.

Soulé, M. E. (ed.). 1987. *Viable Populations for Conservation*. Cambridge University Press, Cambridge, NY.

Sparks, R. E. 1995. Need for ecosystem management of large rivers and their flood-plains. *BioScience* 45:168-182.

Stanford, J. A., and J. V. Ward. 1992. Management of aquatic resources in large catchments: Recognizing interactions between ecosystem connectivity and environmental disturbance. In *Watershed Management: Balancing Sustainability and Environmental Change*. R. J. Naiman (ed.). Springer-Verlag, New York, NY, p. 91-124.

Stiassny, M. L. J. 1996. An overview of freshwater biodiversity: with some lessons from African fishes. *Fisheries* 21(9):7-13.

Stiles, R. A., and D. A. Etnier. 1971. Fishes of the Conasauga River drainage, Polk and Bradley counties, Tennessee. *Journal of the Tennessee Academy of Science* 46:12-16.

Stokes, W. R., III., T. W. Hale, J. L. Pearman, and G. R. Buell. 1986. Water resources data Georgia, water year 1985. Report USGS/WRD/HD-86/264, U.S. Geological Survey, Doraville, GA, 389 p.

Suttkus, R. D., and H. T. Boschung. 1990. *Notropis ammophilus*, a new cyprinid fish from southeastern United States. *Tulane Studies in Zoology and Botany* 27:49-63.

Suttkus, R. D., and D. A. Etnier. 1991. *Etheostoma tallapoosae* and *E. brevirostrum*, two new darters, subgenus *Ulocentra*, from the Alabama River drainage. *Tulane Studies in Zoology and Botany* 28:1-24.

Suttkus, R. D., and E. C. Raney. 1955. *Notropis asperifrons*, a new cyprinid fish from the Mobile Bay drainage of Alabama and Georgia, with studies of related species. *Tulane Studies in Zoology* 3:1-33.

Suttkus, R. D., B. A. Thompson, and H. L. Bart, Jr. 1994. Two new darters, *Percina* (*Cottogaster*), from the southeastern United States, with a review of the subgenus. *Occasional Papers Tulane University Musuem of Natural History* 4:1-46.

Tangley, L. 1994. The importance of communicating with the public. In *Principles of Conservation Biology*. G. K. Meffe, and C. R. Carroll (eds.). Sinauer Associates, Inc., Sunderland, MA, p. 535-536 (Essay 18B).

Taylor, C. A., M. L. Warren, Jr., J. F. Fitzpatrick, Jr., H. H. Hobbs III, R. F. Jezerinac, W. L. Pflieger, and H. W. Robison. 1996. Conservation status of crayfishes of the United States and Canada. *Fisheries* 21(4):25-38.

Terborgh, J. 1974. Preservation of natural diversity: The problem of extinction prone species. *BioScience* 24:715-722.

Travnichek, V. H., and M. J. Maceina. 1994. Comparison of flow regulation effects on fish assemblages in shallow and deep water habitats in the Tallapoosa River, Alabama. *Journal of Freshwater Ecology* 9:207-216.

Trimble, S W. 1974. Man-induced soil erosion on the southern Piedmont 1700-1900. Soil Conservation Society of America, Anteny, IA, 180 p.

Turgeon, D. D., A. E. Bogan, E. V. Coan, W. K. Emerson, W. G. Lyons, W. L. Pratt, C. F. E. Roper, A. Scheltema, F. G. Thompson, and J. D. Williams. 1988. *Common and Scientific Names of Aquatic Invertebrates from the United States and Canada: Mollusks*. Special Publication 16, American Fisheries Society, Bethesda, MD.

U.S. Department of Agriculture. 1994. Protecting and restoring aquatic ecosystems: New directions for watershed and fisheries research in the USDA Forest Service. Forest Service, U.S. Department of Agriculture, Washington, D.C., 13 p.

U.S. Federal Register. 1994a. Endangered and threatened wildlife and plants. *U.S. Federal Register* 50 CFR (17.11 & 17.12):1-42.

U.S. **Federal Register. 1994b.** Endangered and threatened wildlife and plants; animal candidate review for listing as threatened or endangered; proposed rule. *U.S. Federal Register* **50** CFR, Part 17, Number 59:58982-59028.

U.S. **National Research Council. 1992.** *Restoration of Aquatic Ecosystems: Science, Technology, and Public Policy.* National Academy Press, Washington, D.C.

van der Schalie, H., and P. W. Parmalee. 1960. Animal remains from the Etowah Site, Mound C, Bartow County, Georgia. *The Florida Anthropologist* **8**:37-54.

Walsh, S. J., N. M. Burkhead, and J. D. Williams. 1995. Conservation status of southestern freshwater fishes. In *Our Living Resources 1995: A Report to the Nation on the Distribution, Abundance, and Health of U.S. Plants, Animals, and Ecosystems.* E. T. LaRoe (ed.). National Biological Service, U.S. Department of the Interior, Washington, D.C., p. 144-147.

Warren, M. L., Jr., P. L. Angermeier, B. M. Burr, and W. R. Haag. 1997. Decline of a diverse fish fauna: Patterns of imperilment and protection in the southeastern United States. In *Aquatic Fauna in Peril: The Southeastern Perspective.* G. W. Benz, and D. E. Collins (eds.). Special Publication 1, Southeast Aquatic Research Institute, Lenz Design & Communications, Decatur, GA, p. 105-164.

Warren, M. L., Jr., and B. M. Burr. 1994. Status of freshwater fishes of the United States: Overview of an imperiled fauna. *Fisheries* **19**(1):6-18.

Weaver, L. A., and G. C. Garman. 1994. Urbanization of a watershed and historical changes in a stream fish assemblage. *Transactions of the American Fisheries Society* **123**:162-172.

Welsch, D. J. 1991. Riparian forest buffers: Function and design for protection and enhancement of water resources. NA-PR-07-91, Northeastern Area, Forest Resources Management, U.S. Department of Agriculture, Radnor, PA, 20 p.

Wharton, C. H. 1978 [Reprinted 1989]. The natural environments of Georgia. *Georgia Geological Survey Bulletin* **114**:1-227.

Whittaker, R. H. 1975. *Communities and Ecosystems, 2nd Edition.* MacMillan Publishing Co., New York, NY.

Williams, J. D. 1965. Studies of the fishes of the Tallapoosa River system in Alabama and Georgia. M.S. Thesis, University of Alabama, Tuscaloosa, AL.

Williams, J. D. 1981. Threatened warmwater stream fishes and the Endangered Species Act: A review. In *The Warmwater Streams Symposium.* L. A. Krumholz (ed.). Southern Division, American Fisheries Society, Allen Press, Inc., Lawrence, KS, p. 328-337.

Williams, J. D., and D. A. Etnier. 1977. *Percina (Imostoma) antesella*, a new percid fish from the Coosa River system in Tennessee and Georgia. *Proceedings of the Biological Society of Washington* **90**:6-18.

Williams, J. D., S. L. H. Fuller, and R. Grace. 1992a. Effects of impoundments on freshwater mussels (Mollusca: Bivalvia: Unionidae) in the main channel of the Black Warrior and Tombigbee Rivers in western Alabama. *Bulletin Alabama Museum of Natural History* **13**:1-10.

Williams, J. D., M. L. Warren, Jr., K. S. Cummings, J. L. Harris, and R. J. Neves. 1992b. Conservation status of freshwater mussels of the United States and Canada. *Fisheries* **18**(9):6-22.

Williams, J. E., J. E. Johnson, D. A. Hendrickson, S. Contreras-Balderas, J. D. Williams, M. Navarro-Mendoza, D. E. McAllister, and J. E. Deacon. 1989. Fishes of North America endangered, threatened, or of special concern: 1989. *Fisheries* 14(9):2-20.

Willis, E. O. 1974. Population and local extinctions of birds on Barro Colorado Island, Panama. *Ecological Monographs* 44:153-169.

Wilson, J. 1902. Message from the President of the United States transmitting a report of the Secretary of Agriculture in relation to the forests, rivers, and mountains of the southern Appalachian Region. U.S. Government Printing Office, Washington, D.C., 210 p.

Wood, R. M., and R. L. Mayden. 1993. Systematics of the *Etheostoma jordani* species group (Teleostei: Percidae), with descriptions of three new species. *Bulletin Alabama Museum of Natural History* 16:31-46.

Yeager, B. L. 1994. Impacts of reservoirs on the aquatic environment of regulated rivers. TVA/WR-93/1, Resource Group Water Management, Tennessee Valley Authority, Norris, TN, 109 p.

Appendix 1. List of representative federal, state, and county agencies, development centers, environmental organizations, and foundations that may participate in restoration efforts in the Etowah River watershed.

FEDERAL OFFICES:

Natural Resource Conservation Service:
Gainesville Field Office: Lumpkin-Dawson-Forsyth, Federal Building, Rm. G-13, 126 Washington St. NE, Gainesville, GA 30501; phone 770 536-6981.
Rome Field Office: Polk-Floyd, 1401 Dean St., Suite F, Rome, GA 30161; phone 706 291-5651.

U.S. Department of Agriculture:
Forest Service:
Chattahoochee/Oconee National Forest, 1755 Cleveland Hwy., Gainesville, GA 30501; phone 770 536-0541.
1720 Peachtree Rd., NW, Suite 816, Atlanta, GA 30367-9102; phone 404 347-4082.
Natural Resources Conservation Service:
1401 Dean St., Suite I, Rome, GA 30161-6494; phone 706 291-5652.

U.S. Department of the Army:
South Atlantic Division, U.S. Army Corps of Engineers, 77 Forsyth Street SW, Rm. 313, Atlanta, GA 30335-6801; phone 404 331-4619.

U.S. Environmental Protection Agency:
61 Forsyth St., Atlanta, GA 30303; phone 404 562-8327.
980 College Station Rd., Athens, GA 30605; phone 706 546-3136.

U.S. Geological Survey:
Water Resources Division, National Water Quality Assessment:
Regional Office: 3850 Holcomb Bridge Rd., Norcross, GA 30092; phone 770 409-7700.
Georgia District Office: Peachtree Business Center, Suite 130, 3039 Amwiler Rd., Atlanta, GA 30360; phone 770 903-9100.
Biological Resources Division, Florida Caribbean Science Center:
7920 NW 71st St., Gainesville, FL 32653; phone 352 378-8181.

U.S. Fish and Wildlife Service:
4270 Norwich St., Brunswick, GA 31520; phone 921 265-9336.
1875 Century Blvd., Suite 400, Atlanta, GA 30345; phone 404 679-4000.
330 Richfield Ct., Asheville, NC 28806; phone 704 665-1195.
6620 South Point Dr., S., Suite 310, Jacksonville, FL 32216; phone 904 232-2580.

STATE OFFICES:

Georgia Adopt-A-Stream:
7 Martin Luther King Dr. SW, Suite 643, Atlanta, GA 30334; phone 404 656-4988.

Georgia Department of Natural Resources:
Floyd Towers East, 205 Butler St. SE, Suite 1058, Atlanta, GA 30334; phone 404 656-4708.
2070 U.S. Hwy. 278 SE, Social Circle, GA 30279; phone 770 918-6406.

Georgia Environmental Protection Division:
745 Gaines School Rd., Athens, GA 30605; phone 706 369-6376.
7 Martin Luther King Dr. SW, Suite 643, Atlanta, GA 30334; phone 770 659-4905.

Georgia Forestry Commission:
141 Willshire Rd., Rome, GA 30161; phone 706 295-6020.

Appendix 1. Continued.

Soil and Water Conservation Commission:
Coosa District, 700 East 2nd Ave, Suite J, Rome, GA 30161; phone 706 295-6131.
4310 Lexington Rd., Athens, GA 30605; phone 706 542-3065.

REGIONAL DEVELOPMENT COMMISSIONS:

Atlanta Regional Development Commission:
3715 Northside Pkwy, 200 North Creek, Suite 300, Atlanta, GA 30327; phone 404 364-2500.

Coosa Valley Regional Development Center:
No. 1 Jackson Hill Dr., Rome, GA 30163; phone 706 295-6485.

Georgia Mountains Regional Development Center:
1310 West Ridge Rd., Gainesville, GA 30501; phone 770 538-2626.

Limestone Valley Resource Conservation and Development Center:
650 North Main St., Suite A, Jasper, GA 30143; phone 706 692-5094.

North Georgia Regional Development Center:
503 W. Waugh St., Dalton, GA 30720; phone 706 272-2300.

COUNTY COMMISSION OFFICES:

Bartow County Commission:
135 West Cherokee Ave., Suite 251, Cartersville, GA 30120; phone 770 387-5030.

Cherokee County Commission
90 North St., Suite 310, Canton, GA 30114; phone 770 479-0501.

Cobb County Commission:
100 Cherokee St., Suite 300, Marietta, GA 30090; phone 770 528-3306.

Dawson County Commission:
P.O. Box 192, Dawsonville, GA 30534; phone 706 265-3164.

Floyd County Commission:
P.O. Box 946, Rome, GA 30162; phone 706 291-5110.

Forsyth County Commission:
110 E. Main St., Suite 210, Cumming, GA 30130; phone 770 781-2100.

Fulton County Commission:
141 Pryor St., Atlanta, GA 30303; phone 404 730-8206.

Lumpkin County Commission:
99 Courthouse Hill, Suite A, Dahlonega, GA 30533; phone 706 864-3742.

Paulding County Commission:
120 East Memorial Dr., Dallas, GA 30132; phone 770 443-7514.

Pickens County Commission:
52 North Main St., Suite 201, Jasper, GA 30143; phone 706 692-3556.

Polk County Commission:
P.O. Box 268, Cedartown, GA 30125; phone 706 749-2101.

ENVIRONMENTAL ORGANIZATIONS:

Coosa River Basin Initiative:
2887 Alabama Hwy., Rome, GA 30165; phone 706 235-1043.

Georgia Wildlife Federation:
1930 Iris Dr., Conyers, GA 30207; phone 770 929-3350.

Appendix 1. Continued.

The Georgia Conservancy:
   1776 Peachtree St. NW, Suite 400 South, Atlanta, GA 30309; phone 404 876-2900.
The Nature Conservancy:
   1330 W. Peachtree St., Suite 410, Atlanta, GA 30309; phone 404 873-6946.

FOUNDATIONS:

AT & T Foundation:
   1301 Sixth Ave., 31st Floor, New York, NY 10019; phone 212 841-4747.
Beldon Fund:
   2000 P St. NW, Suite 410, Washington, DC 20036; phone 202 293-1928.
Georgia Power Foundation, Inc.:
   333 Piedmont Ave., Bin No. 10230, Atlanta, GA 30308; phone 404 526-6784.
Jessie Smith Noyes Foundation, Inc.:
   16 East 34th St., New York, NY 10016; phone 212 684-6577.
Joseph B. Whitehead Foundation:
   50 Hurt Plaza, Suite 1200, Atlanta, GA 30303; phone 404 522-6755.
Lyndhurst Foundation:
   Tallan Building, Suite 701, 100 West Martin Luther King Blvd., Chattanooga, TN
   37402-2561; phone 423 756-0767.
Mary Reynolds Babcock Foundation, Inc.:
   102 Reynolda Village, Winston-Salem, NC 27106-5123; phone 910 748-9222.
Metropolitan Atlanta Community Foundation, Inc.:
   The Hurt Building, Suite 449, Atlanta, GA 30303; phone 404 688-5525.
National Fish and Wildlife Foundation:
   1120 Connecticut Ave. NW, Bender Building, Suite 900, Washington, DC 20036;
   phone 202 857-0166.
Robert W. Woodruff Foundation, Inc.:
   50 Hurt Plaza, Suite 1200, Atlanta, GA 30303; phone 404 522-6755.
Rockefeller Family Fund, Inc.:
   1290 Ave. of the Americas, New York, NY 10104; phone 212 373-4252.
The Pew Charitable Trusts:
   One Commerce Sq., 2005 Market St., Suite 1700, Philadelphia, PA 19103-7017;
   phone 215 575-9050.
The Sapelo Foundation:
   308 Mallory St., Suite C, St. Simons Island, GA 31522; phone 912 638-6265.
The Moriah Fund, Inc.:
   35 Wisconsin Circle, Suite 520, Chevy Chase, Maryland 20815; phone 202 783-8488.
Turner Foundation, Inc.:
   One CNN Center, Suite 1090-South Tower, Atlanta, GA 30303; phone 404 681-9900.
W. Alton Jones Foundation, Inc.:
   232 East High St., Charlottesville, VA 22902-5178; phone 804 295-2134.

CHAPTER 17

Management and Conservation of Rare Aquatic Resources: A Historical Perspective and Recommendations for Incorporating Ecosystem Management

Peggy W. Shute, Richard G. Biggins, and Robert S. Butler

R ivers of the southeastern United States contain some of the world's most diverse aquatic communities. The Southeast contains about 90 percent of the nearly 600 taxa of mussels and crayfishes (about 300 of each), approximately 73 percent of the aquatic snails, and about 50 percent of the freshwater fishes known from the continental United States (Burch, 1982; Hobbs, 1989; Williams et al., 1989; Warren and Burr, 1994; Neves, 1993; Lydeard and Mayden, 1995). Much of this diversity is found in the Tennessee and Cumberland rivers of the Mississippi Basin, and rivers entering Mobile

Aquatic Fauna in Peril: The Southeastern Perspective, edited by George W. Benz, and David E. Collins. 1997. Special Publication 1, Southeast Aquatic Research Institute, Lenz Design & Communications, Decatur, GA, 554 p.

Bay. Because of the Southeast's high diversity and endemism and the widespread modification of its aquatic ecosystems, this region also contains a significant portion of our country's endangered aquatic fauna.

Prior to settlement by Europeans, about 5.2 million km (about 3.23 million miles) of free-flowing rivers existed in the contiguous United States. However, only 42 free-flowing rivers longer than 200 km (124 miles) remain (Benke, 1990), and few of the Southeast's major rivers have escaped impoundment. For example, over 3,680 river km (2,287 miles) or about 20 percent of the Tennessee River and its major tributaries have been impounded (Tennessee Valley Authority, 1971). The effects of these impoundments extend well beyond the actual reservoirs, including alteration of river habitats downstream of dams, loss of connectivity between upstream and downstream reaches, and isolation of tributaries by reservoir pools.

Impoundments coupled with decades of chronic environmental degradation have altered stream hydrology, destabilized benthic stream habitat, and resulted in other physical, chemical, and biological changes to aquatic communities (Karr and Dudley, 1981; Allendorf, 1988; Neves, 1993) in the southeast. Due to environmental abuse, some species have been lost, many other species that were once widely distributed now survive in a few isolated populations at a fraction of their former abundance. Some of these now isolated species are threatened with extinction. In addition to extinctions and extirpations, there has also been a collapse of the complex interactions between the diverse organisms that co-evolved in southeastern riverine ecosystems (Allendorf, 1988; Sheldon, 1988; Bruton, 1995).

Riverine ecosystems and their rare aquatic species are especially difficult to conserve, manage, and restore because of the linear, flowing characteristic of streams. Many competing and often conflicting demands are placed on watersheds and the rivers that flow through them. Threats often arise from relatively minor, but cumulative, factors that do not respond to a single corrective action. Many users of watershed resources are generally unaware or apathetic about conserving lower vertebrates and invertebrates that are essential to the ecological integrity of these systems (Allendorf, 1988; Master, 1991). Lack of public support has translated into a low priority for conservation and recovery of aquatic ecosystems. In spite of assaults on southeastern aquatic ecosystems, however, much of the region's diverse aquatic fauna still survives in isolated stream reaches. Concerted and coordinated efforts among federal, state, and local government agencies, conservation organizations, and interested citizens are helping to insure that much of this rich natural heritage will be passed on to future generations.

In this paper, we will briefly describe the historic roles of natural resource agencies in managing our aquatic systems, outline steps to implement ecosystem management programs, provide examples of new initiatives that focus on ecosystem management as a means of protecting rare species and ecosystems, and discuss the role that science can play in management and protection.

HISTORICAL STRATEGIES FOR MANAGING AQUATIC RESOURCES

Historically, aquatic conservation and management initiatives were primarily driven by the economic, recreational, and subsistence values offered by fisheries resources (Williams and Finnley, 1977). Thus, although about 90 percent of the fishes in the United States are nongame species (Warren and Burr, 1994), conservation and management activities have been historically directed primarily toward maintaining and enhancing a few recreationally or commercially valuable fish stocks. This type of management was generally accomplished through: stocking hatchery reared species; creating impoundments and providing cold water releases to create artificial downstream trout fisheries; regulating harvest through bag limits, size limits, and open and closed seasons; stocking nonindigenous species for game and forage; and by enforcing laws to prevent overharvest. Some habitat improvement work was carried out, but most efforts centered on enhancing stocks of particular game species. Only minimal effort was directed toward maintaining native, nongame components of aquatic communities. Attention was sometimes given to preserving habitat and water quality by setting and regulating toxic discharge limits and reviewing construction projects to provide guidance to minimize environmental impacts.

Although the historic role of natural resource agencies was and remains, in large part, targeted towards sport and commercial species, in the early 1970s, roles of these agencies began to expand when two significant environmental laws were passed by the federal government: the 1973 Endangered Species Act (ESA) and the 1977 Clean Water Act (CWA). Both acts focused attention on the plight and value (e.g., aesthetic, ecological, educational, historical, recreational, and scientific) of all species and their habitats. These acts mandated that biodiversity and the habitat that supports it be maintained. The ESA requires federal agencies to consider the effects of their projects on endangered and threatened species. The CWA, through its National Pollution Discharge Elimination System permit provision, regulates the discharge of pollutants into waters of the United States and aims to maintain the biological integrity of the receiving waters. Biological components of many streams have benefited through the implementation of these acts. Passage of other federal regulations (e.g., Fish and Wildlife Coordination Act, surface mining regulations, National Forest Management Act, National Environmental Policy Act) have also benefited aquatic organisms, their habitats, and water quality. However, agencies directed to implement remedial actions are often underfunded and understaffed (Hughes and Noss, 1992), and in some cases, the protection afforded has come too late to conserve the region's sensitive aquatic resources.

In addition to federal legislation, many states have recognized the plight of their natural heritage during the last 20 years and have passed legislation to protect nongame species. State Natural Heritage Programs, aided by The Nature Conservancy and their Central Biological Conservation Data System, now track the occurrences of rare species. These heritage programs are established in all 50 states and within several additional agencies and organizations (Warner, 1993). Also, several states have recently sponsored symposia or publications that, address management and conservation of rare aquatic species along with other groups of organisms (e.g., Terwilliger, 1991; Georgia Department of Natural Resources, 1992).

Over the past two decades, new environmental groups have formed, and existing groups have expanded their advocacy roles to insure conservation of aquatic ecosystems. Environmental education has become part of the curriculum in many schools, and numerous books and television shows have described the plight of our national and global biodiversity.

Although the ESA and CWA stress the need for ecosystem protection, some rare aquatic organisms are so geographically restricted that a single-species approach should continue to be a conservation option (Sheldon, 1988; Eisner et al., 1995). Some single-species efforts have been successful in the Southeast. For example, an extirpated population of the rare spring pygmy sunfish (*Elassoma alabamae*) was successfully restored by reintroducing adults from another location (Jandebeur, 1982; Mayden, 1993); the snail darter (*Percina tanasi*) was successfully translocated into several rivers in the Tennessee River system, (Williams and Finnley, 1977; Etnier and Starnes, 1993); watercress darters (*Etheostoma nuchale*) were successfully translocated in a spring in Alabama (U.S. Fish and Wildlife Service, 1993); and the rare spiny riversnail (*Io fluvialis*) has been successfully reintroduced into a Tennessee River tributary (Ahlstedt, 1991; and R. Neves, National Biological Service, pers. comm.).

However, in spite of these limited single species successes, aquatic ecosystems continue to degrade, and the list of aquatic endangered and threatened species steadily increases (Williams et al., 1989; Williams et al., 1993; U.S. Fish and Wildlife Service, 1994a, 1994b; Warren and Burr, 1994). Furthermore, although the status of some rare species has been stabilized or is increasing, few have been recovered to the point where they no longer need ESA protection.

HOW WATERSHED PROTECTION SHOULD BE IMPLEMENTED

It is now widely recognized that the future of rare aquatic species is best secured by protecting and restoring biological integrity of entire watersheds (Karr, 1990; Moyle and Sato, 1991; Williams, 1991; Williams and Williams, 1992). Land acquisition would appear to be the most obvious means of affecting watershed protection. Through ownership, management of aquatic ecosystems would become much less complicated, eliminating the need to coordinate restoration activities with numerous landowners of varied interests. Except under unusual circumstances, acquisition of entire watersheds is not feasible. Therefore, land acquisition cannot be used as a method of reasonably conserving more than a fraction of the Southeast's aquatic fauna.

Ecosystem management is the most effective method of protecting the greatest number of species. Ecosystem management considers not just individual species or select groups of species, but takes a holistic approach to managing all communities that comprise the ecosystem by factoring in ecological relationships, land-use patterns, and threats to water and habitat quality. However, the complex nature of aquatic ecosystems and the watershed scale necessary for aquatic ecosystem protection is problematic. Ecosystem management is expensive, time consuming, and requires considerable coordination with and commitment from various agencies, organizations, and private individuals.

The following is a recommended series of steps for developing and implementing a watershed management program that follow an Ecosystem Management approach. These steps include prioritizing aquatic ecosystems in need of management; identifying all potential agencies and organizations with an interest in watershed management; prioritizing ecosystem threats; identifying strategies to minimize or eliminate threats; and most importantly, educating the ecosystem's inhabitants and other stakeholders. Without a sound and comprehensive education program that reaches all potential stakeholders in the watershed, management efforts will be difficult and slow.

Prioritizing Aquatic Ecosystems Needing Protection

Carroll and Meffe (1994) recommended several criteria to help prioritize conservation and management efforts. These include identifying areas with the following: 1) relatively high numbers of endemic, rare, and declining species or keystone species or ecological processes; 2) small, fragmented habitats; and 3) systems exhibiting low resilience to perturbations. More specifically, Angermeier et al. (1993) described a protocol to help prioritize Virginia streams to enhance cost-effectiveness of preservation, enhancement, management, recovery, and restoration efforts. This protocol may be modified for use in other parts of the Southeast.

Because financial and time constraints are universal, it is important to prioritize watershed management efforts based primarily on faunal diversity and the likelihood of successful restoration. Some watersheds have much greater natural diversity than others, and under normal circumstances these should receive high priority for conservation efforts. However, some of the most diverse ecosystems may have been so altered that it is unlikely they can be conserved or restored with the level of resources currently available. It is also important to consider size of the target watershed. If the area of interest is too large, management and restoration problems may be overwhelming.

Still other criteria may be important to consider when selecting target watersheds. Ownership complexity should be a critical consideration. For instance, the Conasauga and Etowah rivers are large, diverse tributaries in the headwaters of the Mobile Basin, Georgia and Tennessee. The Conasauga River has its headwaters in two national forests (Cherokee and Chattahoochee) and is otherwise primarily agricultural in watershed land use. In comparison, although it is a larger system, the Etowah River has virtually no federal lands in its watershed, but has a much more diverse land-use pattern comprised of various mining, agricultural, and metropolitan Atlanta developmental activities that are rapidly changing current land-use patterns. Based solely on these criteria, a watershed project would seem simpler to initiate in the Conasauga watershed.

Another important factor that may help assess or rank communities in need of conservation efforts is biogeographic history of rare species in the system under consideration. A factor which may help in the prioritization process is whether the rare species evolved in the area or dispersed into it. For example, when faced with a decision between conserving a watershed containing a once widespread, ancestral species or one containing a species whose historical distribution was more local, the potentials of each to future generations may offer critical information to the selection process (Mayden, 1992). Preserving formerly widespread species may preserve genomes that produce more adaptable organisms, and organisms more suitable for dispersal into former ranges, should habitat conditions improve.

Although watershed projects will generally concentrate on larger ecosystems that have relatively high levels of biodiversity and endemism, small, relatively depauperate aquatic ecosystems such as springs and caves should not be categorically dismissed from management considerations. In fact, these systems may represent high priorities for protection or management for several reasons: they contain uniquely adapted endemic faunas, exhibit extreme vulnerability and low resilience to relatively minor alterations, and show slow recovery from perturbations (Etnier and Starnes, 1991). These systems can often be protected with minimal effort and expense. Furthermore, projects focusing on said sites may be easier to coordinate than those encompassing larger watersheds because of the relatively fewer numbers of landowners and stakeholders involved and other factors associated with the small size of the area under consideration.

Some species inhabiting karst systems may be sensitive indicators of changes that occur in quality and quantity of groundwater for a region. For example, the Barrens topminnow (*Fundulus julisia*) has a small geographic range and is mainly restricted to a few spring-influenced areas in the Barrens Plateau region of central Tennessee. This species is highly susceptible to changes in habitat, water quantity, and possibly water quality. With increased demand on groundwater supplies in this region, many cool, heavily vegetated spring habitats, required by Barrens topminnows, have been impacted. Rakes (P. Rakes, Conservation Fisheries, Inc., pers. comm.) hypothesized that Barrens topminnows may be at a competitive disadvantage in other types of habitats. Regular monitoring of populations of this rare fish, and conservation, restoration, and management efforts aimed at helping the species are relatively inexpensive and require minimal effort (Rakes, 1994). However, Rakes (P. Rakes, Conservation Fisheries, Inc., pers. comm.) demonstrated how rapidly the topminnow population can change, thus indicating the need for management.

Identifying All Potential Agencies and Organizations With Watershed Interests

Other federal, state, and local agencies (e.g., U.S. Natural Resources Conservation Service, U.S. Environmental Protection Agency, U.S. Geological Survey, U.S. Bureau of Reclamation, state departments of natural resources, local planning commissions, and local and regional conservation organizations) may have active conservation-oriented programs in the watershed. The extent of agency and organization involvement in common watershed issues should be determined. Objectives of watershed projects should be made well-known, and wide support for these objectives should be nurtured. Many agencies actively seek partnerships to help reach conservation objectives. When one set of project objectives complements those of other groups, additional resource protection and recovery may be achieved without further expenditures.

Projects in river systems large enough to be used for water supply or transportation will require federal and possibly other permits. Any agencies and organizations responsible for planning and permitting in the project watershed should be notified of a project's intentions. Once appropriate contacts have been made, natural resources of the watershed can be considered early in the planning and permitting process, and negative effects of any proposed actions may be avoided or mitigated. As Montgomery et al. (1995) suggested, resource use and conservation are not necessarily incompatible; the best available scientific information should be incorporated into the ecosystem management planning process so that informed decisions can be founded solidly on science.

Prioritizing Ecosystem Threats

Most current and proposed land uses or activities have similar effects on aquatic ecosystems, especially in the same geographic region. Conversely, there may be other threats specific to the project watershed. An analysis identifying stressors and stress points that affect aquatic species and their habitats, should not be restricted to the immediate stream corridor. The entire watershed should ultimately be examined for potential land uses or other activities that could negatively impact aquatic habitat quality. For example, small headwater streams, even though they are often less biologically diverse than other streams within a watershed, can greatly influence chemical and physical properties further downstream, and should not be considered unimportant or ignored (Rabeni, 1992). Comprehensive basin-wide environmental threat assessments that consider physical and biological characteristics should be carried out when feasible (Rabeni, 1992).

When threats are identified during the analysis, each should be evaluated for magnitude, imminence, and cost of reduction. The magnitude of a threat constitutes an estimate of the level of adverse effects it will cause to the system. It is important to determine whether the threat will have widespread and long-lasting effects, or if it will be localized, short-term, and of little overall consequence to the ecosystem. When short-term threats are identified and associated with a proposed project, it should be determined whether timing of the proposed project can be altered so that it interferes as little as possible with survival and reproduction of native animals. Imminence of a threat is an estimate of how soon it will affect the aquatic environment, and the limited time frame in which addressing the threat can be postponed until irrevocable damage to habitat is done. Imminent versus non-imminent threats should be identified and categorized as follows: immediacy of threat; scale of impacts; species, communities, or habitats affected; and time and financial expenditures necessary to negate the threat. Instream effects from some proposed projects or activities may not be readily apparent and thus can only be predicted or anticipated. Beyond this, impacts of some projects can be cumulative, slow-acting, not easy to observe or measure, and may show up on a temporal scale that is not often considered (Rabeni, 1992). Of course some threats, no matter how serious, may be too socially and economically costly to eliminate or mitigate.

Currently it is not possible to identify all factors threatening some ecosystems. The faunas in some watersheds are in decline for as yet unknown and possibly non-anthropogenic reasons. Further research may be needed to determine specific causes of faunal decline.

Identifying Strategies to Minimize or Eliminate Threats

Once ecosystem threats have been identified and prioritized, strategies for their elimination or reduction should be developed. Usually there are a number of ways to address a problem, and alternatives should be evaluated in terms of time, cost, and probable effectiveness.

Agencies that have ultimate responsibility for regulating water releases from impoundments and zoning river basins for various uses must be reminded to consider ecological processes when considering holistic watershed management (Bruton, 1995). A cooperative approach with agencies, organizations, private landowners, and other individuals and stakeholders involved in the management project works best in the long-term. Various factors must be considered, including social, legal, and political issues, scientific and technical goals, and economic values (Gresswell and Liss, 1995).

Montgomery et al. (1995) described ecosystem management as a proactive planning process that may involve mitigation of adverse environmental impacts of human activities. Moyle and Moyle (1995) recommended that potential resource users determine cost-benefits of proposed use of this resource and "pay" for its degradation or alteration if appropriate. Although economic values of natural resources may be difficult to quantify, a comparison of the values associated with a healthy, functioning aquatic ecosystem and a degraded or altered ecosystem resulting from previous, poorly planned projects may be insightful — especially when considering the long-term viability of co-evolved aquatic resources versus the short-term economic gains of a proposed project.

Dunn (1993) described an example where this approach was used to help conserve freshwater mussels. As mitigation for a project impacting a significant mussel bed in the Ohio River, 5,000 mussels were removed from the project area and relocated within the system (Dunn, 1993). A trust fund also was established to fund monitoring of relocated mussels and future research on Ohio River Basin mollusks. Appalachian Power Company, once responsible for spills that affected aquatic fauna in the Clinch River, has funded studies on life history and reproduction of native mussels in this portion of the Tennessee River system.

Educating Stakeholders

Education is critical to the success of any restoration or conservation program. Informing various participants in the ecosystem project, other stakeholders, and the general public about project objectives and methods should begin early and be a continuing process as the project proceeds. Therefore, the education effort should strive to reach all levels within the community including young school children, community leaders, civic groups, and federal and state agency personnel.

Examples of grass roots programs with strong education components that address river conservation needs include Adopt-a-Watershed, a natural resource education program in which young students adopt a local watershed and follow it as a focal point in their science curriculum through grade 12. Incentives for public school projects like Adopt-a-Watershed, the Better Education Starts Today projects in Alabama, and the Harpeth River Project in Tennessee (see below) will greatly further educational efforts. Numerous nationwide grass roots watershed protection and management groups have also been organized to address various aspects of the ecosystem approach to watershed management outlined herein.

Many private organizations have hosted workshops or developed and distributed literature and other educational materials to agencies, organizations, businesses, and the general public on better management of riverine resources. For example, The Georgia Conservancy recently devoted an entire annual conference to protection of Georgia's waterways which included presentations by House Speaker Newt Gingrich, U.S. Department of the Interior Secretary Bruce Babbitt, and various conservation leaders. The Georgia Conservancy also recently produced an award-winning video called "Stream of Conscience," and the U.S. Fish and Wildlife Service funded companion literature on conservation and protection of riverine ecosystems in that state.

There is a growing body of literature that addresses various aspects of restoring, recovering, and managing aquatic ecosystems. Articles appear regularly in many scientific journals (e.g., *Aquatic Ecosystem Health, Bioscience, Conservation Biology, Environmental Management, Restoration Ecology*). Entire journal issues have been devoted to freshwater ecosystem conservation, restoration, and management (e.g., *Freshwater Biology* Volume 29, Number 2, 1993; *Journal of the North American Benthological Society* Volume 12, Number 2, 1993; *Restoration Ecology* Volume 3, Number 3, 1995). Numerous books on riverine ecosystem management are also available (e.g., Doppelt et al., 1993). While some of this information may be too technical for the general public, it is invaluable to scientists and other resource managers actively involved in riverine ecosystem management and restoration.

Several publications of various governmental and other organizations also focus on riparian and watershed management. These include "Riparian Forest Buffers: Function and Design for Protection and Enhancement of Water Resources," jointly produced by the U.S. Forest Service with various state and private forestry organizations. *NPS News-Note* is a monthly U.S. Environmental Protection Agency periodical with information on the control of nonpoint-source water pollution and the management and ecological restoration of watersheds. Much of this educational information can be obtained free of charge from these agencies or organizations.

Tear et al. (1995) suggested that general indifference to garnering public support and establishing a sound educational program has been a key reason for poor performance of recovery efforts for listed species. It is important for professionals responsible for the recovery of these species to participate in this public education effort (Bruton, 1995). It is also important for these professionals to persuasively communicate to policy makers, resource managers, the business community, other professionals, and the news media why aquatic species and ecosystems are important. Through such mechanisms, public policy may be influenced to achieve financial support for conservation education and management of aquatic systems.

CURRENT STRATEGIES FOR AQUATIC RESOURCE MANAGEMENT

Following are examples of ways that many federal and state natural resource management agencies and conservation organizations have positively responded to this new, more holistic approach, and how they are now emphasizing ecosystem management in addition to individual species management.

U.S. Fish and Wildlife Service

Ms. Mollie Beattie, the late director of the U.S. Fish and Wildlife Service (USFWS) realized that the old, piecemeal approach to conservation problems was not working well. Because of this, she emphasized that her organization would advocate and demonstrate for the management of ecosystems in their entirety. This philosophy has led the USFWS's reorganization according to ecosystem boundaries and development of plans for these ecosystem units. The ecosystem approach has led to better coordination among USFWS programs by focusing activities on common goals. It has helped to concentrate outreach and education efforts on ecosystem problems, and it has encouraged USFWS employees to become more active in establishing and funding partnerships with other agencies and groups. Many of the projects described below have received financial support from the USFWS.

U.S. Forest Service and Bureau of Land Management

The U.S. Forest Service (USFS) and the Bureau of Land Management, in conjunction with the National Fish and Wildlife Foundation, have embarked on a new program, Bring Back the Natives, that stresses the concept of ecosystem management (Williams and Williams, 1992). The Bring Back the Natives program encourages the formation of partnerships between federal and state agencies, private landowners, and other stakeholders to protect and restore watersheds so that populations of native species can be recovered. To date, this program has involved modification of livestock and timber management practices, restoration of riparian habitat, and reintroduction of extirpated populations of native fish species.

Although most of the projects thus far have involved streams in the western United States, the USFS is cooperating with the Tennessee and North Carolina wildlife resources agencies, the USFWS, and the National Park Service in a project to restore extirpated populations of four federally listed species (smoky madtom, *Noturus baileyi*; yellowfin madtom, *N. flavipinnis*; duskytail darter, *Etheostoma percnurum*; and spotfin chub, *Cyprinella monacha*) on a Little Tennessee River tributary (Shute et al., manuscript in preparation).

National Park Service

The National Park Service (NPS) is currently working in conjunction with the Office of Surface Mining to reclaim abandoned mine lands in the Big South Fork National River and Recreation Area (BSFNRRA) (S. Bakaletz, BSFNRRA, pers. comm.). This program will benefit several federally listed mussel species and one listed fish species. The water quality improvement associated with this initiative will also benefit sport fisheries and other recreational uses in the BSFNRRA.

As part of the fish restoration project on the Little Tennessee River tributary (see above), Great Smoky Mountains National Park has restricted stream access to livestock, and park officials have initiated restoration of degraded riparian zones in the project watershed. The NPS also has implemented fish and benthic invertebrate sampling in the Park to monitor success of this restoration.

U.S. Geological Survey

The U.S. Geological Survey (USGS) National Water Quality Assessment has identified 60 major hydrologic systems in the United States for assessing and monitoring our nation's water quality (U.S. Geological Survey, 1995). Long-term monitoring of aquatic macroinvertebrates and fishes is an integral part of these projects. A comparison of the historical and current biota of the watershed of concern and an analysis of possible reasons for extirpation of aquatic species is one of the initial steps in assessment of target watersheds. These assessments are intended for use by policy makers and managers to prioritize water quality issues and to coordinate projects within watersheds (U.S. Geological Survey, 1995).

The USGS is also assisting the National Biological Service (NBS) in a USFWS-funded study on the North Fork of the Holston River, an upper Tennessee River tributary.[1] The project's goal is to reintroduce components of the historic mussel fauna into this river. Much native fauna was eliminated by mercury contamination from a chemical plant in Saltville, Virginia. Through efforts of the states of Virginia and Tennessee, U.S. Environmental Protection Agency, Tennessee Valley Authority, and other organizations, the lower North Fork Holston River now appears suitable for reintroduction of a mussel community (S. Ahlstedt, USGS and R. Neves, USGS, both pers. comm.).

Tennessee Valley Authority

The Clean Water Initiative of the Tennessee Valley Authority (TVA) has established a watershed protection and restoration program within the Tennessee River system. TVA has formed multidisciplinary River Action Teams composed of biologists and water resource specialists that work within specific sub-watersheds in the Tennessee River drainage (Tennessee Valley Authority, 1995). Teams document valuable resources within their respective watersheds and identify pollution sources and other stressors that impact those resources. Once specific problems are pinpointed and solutions are identified, teams work to bring together appropriate people and organizations needed to improve the health of the watershed (Tennessee Valley Authority, 1995).

Recently, TVA has also structurally modified several of its dams. These modifications are designed to improve water quality, dissolved oxygen concentrations, and flow regimes to ben-

---

[1] Editors' footnote: since this chapter was finalized the National Biological Service has become the Biological Resources Division of the USGS.

efit aquatic organisms in tailwaters (Anonymous, 1995). In 1994, 386 river km (240 miles) in the Tennessee River Valley showed water quality improvements (Tennessee Valley Authority, 1995).

U.S. Environmental Protection Agency

The U.S. Environmental Protection Agency (EPA) is known for its assessments of factors that affect public health. However, in 1988 as a result of citizen concern for ecological issues (e.g., global climate change, habitat loss, declines in biodiversity, effects of pesticides and toxic chemicals), EPA began to focus more on ecosystem integrity. The result was an initiative to develop guidelines for conducting risk assessment for ecosystems (U.S. Environmental Protection Agency, 1992). EPA is currently developing Ecological Risk Assessment Guidelines (ERAG), using a series of test watersheds that include the Clinch and Powell rivers, headwater tributaries of the Tennessee River. ERAG will provide methodology to evaluate ecological effects of environmental stressors (e.g., chemical, physical, biological) that adversely impact ecosystems, communities, populations, or individual species. Once developed, this protocol should prove valuable for identifying environmental stressors and ascertaining the degree of threat for each. This in turn will facilitate prioritization of actions needed to address these stressors.

Southern Rivers Council

The Southern Rivers Council (SRC) is a newly formed group of professional aquatic biologists in the Southeast, interested in conserving biodiversity of southeastern streams. The SRC's mission is to facilitate funding for and to coordinate projects that restore the region's important aquatic habitats. The SRC also seeks ways to take an active role in aquatic resource education. Although SRC is just two years old, several ecosystem-oriented projects have already received funding from private sources with matching funding from the National Fish and Wildlife Foundation. Two of SRC's first projects focused on streams in the Tennessee River drainage. These include streambank restoration and erosion control on Shuler Creek, and water quality improvements in North Chickamauga Creek (Southern Rivers Council, 1995). Sediment in Shuler Creek from an adjacent road and eroding stream banks has altered a biologically significant portion of the Hiwassee River. The water quality of North Chickamauga Creek has been seriously impacted by acid mine drainage and urban pollution.

State Natural Resource Agencies

Various state natural resource agencies are also focusing on watershed conservation. For example, the Virginia Department of Game and Inland Fisheries (VDGIF) has undertaken a watershed protection and enhancement project on Copper Creek, a major tributary of the Clinch River in southwest Virginia (S. Bruenderman, VDGIF, pers. comm.). A number of rare mussels, fishes, amphibians, reptiles, and bats depend on Copper Creek and its riparian corridor for their existence. Recent surveys have documented a decline in the creek's mussel and fish communities, and nonpoint-source pollution appears to be the primary problem (S. Bruenderman, VDGIF, pers. comm.).

Biologists with VDGIF have undertaken a four-pronged approach to address problems in Copper Creek: 1) interagency participation — other natural resource agencies working in the basin were contacted to increase their awareness of the problems and to help determine the best way to coordinate efforts to address these threats; 2) identification of critical areas — the basin was intensively surveyed to identify areas critical to survival of rare species; 3) identification of threats — areas where physical habitat and water quality have been degraded were identified; and 4) public outreach — public education efforts were begun to encourage cooperation between landowners and natural resource organizations. As part of this education effort, a citizen's guide to the ecology of Copper Creek was produced (Flynn et al., 1994).

The Nature Conservancy

For over 40 years, The Nature Conservancy (TNC) has been successful in conserving biological diversity (Master, 1993). Historically, TNC's conservation efforts have been accomplished by acquiring and managing individual tracts of land. However, TNC recently began to emphasize protection of rare species through a larger, ecosystem approach referred to as "Bioreserve" protection (L. Master, TNC, pers. comm.). Because it is impractical and undesirable to create bioreserves entirely through land purchases, TNC seeks to protect and enhance biodiversity in these areas by minimizing or eliminating threats to the ecosystem and by developing partnerships with local residents, landowners, business and industry, government, and other private organizations to develop means that promote ecologically compatible human uses.

The Horse Lick Creek Bioreserve lies within a relatively unpopulated watershed in Kentucky which is partially owned by the USFS. This bioreserve project, a cooperative effort primarily between TNC, USFS, and the Kentucky State Nature Preserves Commission, has concentrated its efforts on public education, purchase of key properties, and control of nonpoint-source pollution.

The Clinch River Bioreserve is located within a much larger watershed which includes the Clinch River and its major tributary, the Powell River. The valley is primarily rural with some small communities. Coal mining is extensive in the Powell River sub-basin. This bioreserve contains over 400 rare plants and animals, 13 federally endangered freshwater mussels, and a labyrinth of caves and underground streams that support two endangered bats and more than 50 globally rare cave organisms. The Nature Conservancy has established two field offices in the valley and has become involved in numerous conservation programs, including the following: 1) a cooperative program utilizing funds and assistance from the USFWS, TVA, other federal agencies, Tennessee Department of Agriculture, and Tennessee Wildlife Resources Agency, and local landowners to restore riparian habitat to help control nonpoint-source pollution; 2) a cooperative project with the Cave Conservancy of Virginia, the Virginia Cave Board, and the Virginia Department of Conservation and Recreation to develop cave management agreements with private landowners; 3) scientific research involving several universities to determine habitat needs of the valley's rare species; and 4) coordination efforts with local planners, government agencies, and private industry to explore environmentally sound methods for treating sewage, harvesting timber, and mining coal.

Public School Projects

In a community near Nashville, Tennessee, four local high schools have "adopted" the Harpeth River of the Cumberland River drainage as their environmental laboratory. In addition to performing field and laboratory analyses, they also use the river as the focus for a multicultural education curriculum. For example, students in public relations classes and visual and performing arts have become involved in relating the importance of the area's resources, as well as problems and possible solutions, to the "real world." This project began with one teacher and has received funding from several local businesses and from the Tennessee Arts Commission. To date, over 1,000 students have participated in this project. The goal is to educate the entire community to the values of the Harpeth River and its aquatic community (Raines, 1994).

The state of Alabama has also encouraged environmental projects in public school systems with their Better Education Starts Today (BEST) Environmental Projects. The subjects of these projects are often local aquatic species that have state or federal protected status. Depending on the age group of the class undertaking a project, field and/or laboratory work on a species or its habitat may be included. Some examples are Everett's (Everett, 1994) elementary school project on the federally endangered shiny pigtoe pearly mussel (*Fusconaia cor*) in the Paint Rock River and Slade's high school projects to determine habitat and water chemistry requirements of the rare spring pygmy sunfish (*Elassoma alabamae*) (Pine, 1993; Elam and Burge, 1995).

Grass Roots Organizations

In addition to the programs and projects described above, there are numerous, active local conservation and restoration groups throughout the Southeast. Some of these groups have been in existence for over a decade and are well supported, financially and otherwise. A few examples of these types of organizations with watershed emphasis are the Cahaba River Society (Alabama); Friends of the Clinch and Powell Rivers (Tennessee); the Little Tennessee River Watershed Association (North Carolina); and the Broad River Watershed Association (Georgia). These grass roots groups should be applauded and supported for their efforts, as they are critical to the success of aquatic biodiversity conservation.

ROLE OF SCIENCE IN ECOSYSTEM MANAGEMENT

Meffe and Carroll (1994) suggested that the role of the conservation scientist is to collect information suitable for preservation of biodiversity and long-term viability of ecosystems. Conserving important aquatic habitats as we confront the continued development that is inevitable, will require good ecological research that supports the development of management recommendations. Montgomery et al. (1995) also emphasized that the new perspective in ecosystem management necessitates scientific investigations that precede land-use planning for a particular watershed. These scientific investigations will ensure that emphasis is placed on resource conservation and that all proposed activities in the watershed are compatible with this primary goal. This important information should be communicated quickly by informal methods (e.g., talks at conferences, internet interest groups) so that it may be used to help manage crises that may arise. However, political and legal constraints are frequently encountered when attempting to protect rare species or ecosystems, and detailed documentation is often necessary to prioritize conservation or recovery efforts. Therefore, in addition to the information methods mentioned above, ecological information should be objectively collected and published in peer-reviewed journals.

Scientific investigations will be needed to focus at several scales and in a wide variety of areas so that resource managers will have the information required to assess the status and specific needs of riverine communities and sensitive species. Landscape-level processes and pathways that influence water quality, flow regime, physical habitat, energy flow, and biotic interactions are of utmost importance in managing riverine systems for biotic integrity. However, detailed information on the scale necessary to recover or conserve populations of imperiled species is also important.

As Raven (1992) and Noss (1994) recommended, field biologists and taxonomists will be needed, but the current trend at universities is to de-emphasize field research in favor of more empirical laboratory research. If field research is needed to support conservation programs, new avenues of funding need to be developed to attract professionals and students, or perhaps the current method of funding allocations should be carefully considered. Lydeard and Mayden (1995) suggested that conservation funding be proportionally divided among federal agencies in various regions according to relative biodiversity and potential threats.

Following is a list of specific research areas which scientists interested in furthering the cause of ecosystem management in the Southeast may become involved. These activities include research at both scales (landscape-level and species- or population- level) described above. Recommendations are also included that will help government agencies to incorporate this information in management plans for southeastern aquatic ecosystems.

Factors Affecting Habitat and Water Quality

Management regimes that support community function will affect long-term ecosystem management. Therefore, processes and pathways critical to the functioning of riverine communities need to be described. For example, identifying corridors necessary for movement to spawning habitats, movement between juvenile and adult habitats, and access to refugia during stressful periods is critical. Further, we must quantify the suitability of habitats in terms of the system's capacity to support these critical processes. This may also involve an analysis of spatial heterogeneity and connectivity among habitats and the amount of temporal variability or stability present.

To understand how alternative management regimes affect the important pathways and processes discussed above, detailed information will be needed to describe the instream impacts resulting from changes in land use, riparian development, and water resource development. Siltation resulting from activities on land is often assumed to cause the degradation of aquatic habitats and resultant extinctions and extirpations (see Rabeni, 1992; Neves, 1993; Williams et al., 1993). Currently, however, there is little evidence specific to the Southeast that conclusively documents and correlates land-use activities outside and within the riparian corridor with the status of aquatic organisms or their habitats. Additional research is needed to determine whether recommendations for widths and vegetation types for riparian buffers are appropriate for various stream sizes, taxonomic groups, and physiographic provinces present in the Southeast.

In addition to land-use activities, water-use activities also affect stream habitats. As mentioned above, and illustrated by Dynesius and Nilsson (1994), few southeastern streams are spared from impoundment. Reservoirs act as settling basins for sediments, and water releases from them can drastically alter sediment transport. More research is needed to make recommendations for minimizing the impacts of these regulated systems on native riverine fauna. For example, Milhous (1994) briefly described research that resulted in recommendations for flows appropriate to flush sediment from streams where important tailwater trout fisheries existed. Milhous (1994) suggested additional research was needed to determine flow recommendations that would prevent silt from settling on stream bottoms in the first place.

Discharge of chemicals into streams is permitted by federal and state regulations. However, the test organisms used to set the limits on water quality parameters may not tell us how more sensitive species will be affected. Little information is currently available on the toxicity of many compounds to sensitive fish and freshwater mussels.

If environmental limits are set for the most sensitive species in an ecosystem, other species will also be protected. Research is needed to determine the environmental tolerance limits of sensitive species regarding various water quality parameters (e.g., dissolved oxygen, pH, turbidity, temperature).

Neves (1993) recommended customizing testing to set water quality parameters for various pollutants, according to watershed. This could be done by using surrogate mussel or fish species most closely related to the rare species within those watersheds as the test organisms; phylogenetic data, as discussed below will support the proper choice of surrogates. Neves (1993) further recommended using the larval (glochidia) stages of these mussels as test organisms to make the tests better reflect effects on the most sensitive life stages of these benthic organisms. Neves (1993) suggested that because sediments can be involved in the long-term storage of toxics, current surface water quality standards may not be sufficient to protect benthic species. More research is needed to describe the relationship between water quality, sediment toxicity, and abundance and diversity of benthic organisms.

Population Dynamics

Research that allows analysis of dispersal and recolonization abilities of species is important in the context of landscape-level processes. This information may provide insight on the importance of connectivity between watersheds in maintaining communities, and may also provide guidance on managing fragmented populations. At another scale, data on population dynamics also provide information critical to conserving or recovering imperiled species.

Little is known concerning the levels of population structure and geographic fluctuations that normally exist in local populations of aquatic species, how local populations interact with each other, or in the larger scale, metapopulations. If baseline data for long-term population and metapopulation fluctuations are available, positive changes related to restoration efforts or negative changes related to degrading influences may be more accurately assessed.

Some local populations may be more important for the long-term viability of a species; they may serve as sources of individuals for dispersal and recolonization when other more ephemeral local populations become extirpated. For example, Freeman and Freeman (1994) and Strange and Burr (1995) implied important dispersal and recolonization mechanisms in the long-term maintenance of the federally endangered amber darter, *Percina antesella* and the threatened blackside dace, *Phoxinus cumberlandensis*, respectively. As Tear et al. (1995) noted, this important information is usually lacking in recovery plans for listed species.

On the scale of conserving individual imperiled species, Strange and Burr (1995) provided information necessary for managing blackside dace. They performed genetic surveys to determine the metapopulation structure of the species and described significant genetic divergence among populations. In providing specific recommendations for recovery actions for this species, they emphasized that reintroductions must be carefully planned to conserve the genetic structure of the various populations. This species inhabits small streams in the upper Cumberland River Drainage. Many of these streams have been degraded by coal mining activities, and captive propagation and reintroduction has been suggested as the means to restore extirpated populations. Therefore, the genetic information reported by Strange and Burr (1995) is critical to conservation efforts for blackside dace, in that they allow for the proper choice of parental breeding stock for reintroduction efforts.

Propagation and Reintroduction Technologies

Even in restored watersheds, the abundance of some species may be so low that successful reproduction is unlikely or species no longer have access to portions of their former range because of habitat barriers. Propagation and reintroduction technologies may be needed to restore extirpated populations in recovered watersheds, to augment small existing populations, or to restore extirpated populations.

"Emergency" measures may also need to be developed to ensure preservation of as many aquatic organisms as possible under disaster conditions. For example, cryopreservation techniques are being developed to store sperm and eggs or larvae of freshwater mussels (R. Neves, USGS, pers. comm.). Because of the advent of the zebra mussel invasion in the Southeast, techniques for temporarily holding freshwater mussels are also being investigated (R. Neves and J. Layzer, both USGS, both pers. comm.).

Monitoring

Monitoring should be an important component of ecosystem management. Montgomery et al. (1995) and Kondolf (1995) suggested various factors important in stream ecosystem management and restoration projects. Monitoring was an important component of both sets of recommendations. Because watershed projects may be overwhelming in scope, relatively unimpacted reference sites in a watershed that focus on the entire community at that site, or sampling that regularly monitors the status of sensitive species throughout the watershed can efficiently supply important data needed in a large project. Although totally undisturbed aquatic communities are rare, systems that are relatively undisturbed should be monitored to serve as references for recovering ecosystems. Data obtained through monitoring are also needed to evaluate and document the success or failure of projects that aim to preserve or restore ecosystem biodiversity. Management activities can then be revised accordingly (Kondolf, 1995; Montgomery et al., 1995). Baseline (i.e., pre-project) and long-term monitoring data are needed to assess how various land uses influence water quantity, quality, sediment action, and temperature throughout watersheds as well as how they impact specific sites within watersheds (Rabeni, 1992). On the scale of individual species, and as described above, Inouge (1988) recommended regular monitoring to develop long-term data sets on population variability.

Adams and Alderman (1993) recommended that state resource agencies, in cooperation with biologists from other organizations, develop a checklist including historical distribution and an evaluation of the current status of all aquatic species occurring in various states. Regular monitoring that would allow for periodic re-evaluation of the status of sensitive species was also recommended by these authors. If these aforementioned recommendations were followed, sensitive or geographically restricted species would be monitored and possibly considered for protection or management before populations dwindle below a threshold of sustainability.

Genetic Information

In the future, many ecosystem projects may focus on remnants of larger systems. At the larger scale, genetic data will help identify sources of diversity among populations. This information may be useful in prioritizing activities or in revising management schemes. On a smaller scale, genetic data collection will allow an assessment of the rate of genetic change in remnant populations, especially for short-lived animals.

Genetic data provides information essential for developing phylogenies that describe relationships among and between species. These phylogenies may then be used to predict life history strategies and resource requirements of sensitive or rare species in a watershed. Studying a species directly is often difficult or may not be advisable or authorized because of its rarity. By using phylogenetic methods, species can be selected as surrogates for rare or sensitive species. For example, as suggested by Neves (1993), these surrogates can then be used for testing and setting water quality limits that would protect the rare species in a particular watershed.

Within a watershed, phylogenetic methods can also help to identify attributes of species that may be most vulnerable to degradation (Mayden, 1992). For example, laboratory experiments with the relatively common bloodfin darter, *Etheostoma sanguifluum*, were performed before initiating a captive propagation attempt for the very rare, federally endangered boulder darter, *E. wapiti* (Shute and Rakes, 1994).

These investigations indicated that boulder darter larvae, unlike many other darter larvae, may drift with the current for several days before settling to the benthic existence typical of adults. Therefore, while managing or restoring habitat in the immediate vicinity of existing boulder darter populations may conserve these populations, actions far downstream may be even more important in the long-term maintenance of the species. By ensuring that there are areas with appropriate boulder darter habitat downstream, the dispersing larvae may enable the population to expand.

Life History Requirements

Ecosystem management does not mean that the needs of individual species are forgotten. At an ecosystem level, declines in the abundance of sensitive species can be a warning signal of stressful conditions and degradation of habitat or water quality that otherwise might not be easily quantifiable or noticed until conditions are severe or irreversible. Therefore, monitoring the status of individual species may be one relatively simple way to evaluate the success of ecosystem management activities.

Tear et al. (1995) summarized recovery plans for listed species and noted little or no biological information in many of the plans. Life history requirements of many rare or sensitive species are virtually unknown. For example, as described above for boulder darters, snail darters, and amber darters (Freeman and Freeman, 1994) may be rare because larvae drift in the current for several days before settling to the benthic existence typical of adult darters. Therefore, habitat appropriate for juveniles may be the factor restricting these rare fishes to limited stream reaches. Life history information specific only to the adult portion of the life cycle of these fishes may not provide all of the information needed for long-term protection.

Specific information on spawning habitat and breeding season are still to be determined for many rare fishes, and fish hosts necessary for mussel reproduction are poorly known. Neves (1993) reported that the fish hosts have been identified for less than 20 percent of freshwater mussels.

CONCLUSION

Many disciplines have a role to play in managing and conserving rare aquatic resources. Herein we have made recommendations for expanding historical management methods and focusing scientific research to support conservation of our highly diverse southeastern ecosystems. To be successful in this venture, however, communication between various types of researchers, policy makers, and those responsible for management is imperative, and may result in strong partnerships linking many different stakeholder groups. In addition to scientific input, public opinion must also be considered. An educated public is critical to this process.

Gresswell and Liss (1995) described management responsibilities as extending beyond the immediate constituencies to future consumptive and nonconsumptive users and to the aquatic resource itself. Aldo Leopold (Leopold, 1949; pages 224-225) over 40 years ago anticipated ecosystem management when he stated, "A thing is right when it tends to preserve the integrity, stability, and beauty of the biotic community. It is wrong when it tends otherwise." Proper ecosystem management will preserve entire native biotic communities. Protecting threatened and restoring extirpated components of aquatic ecosystems are critical activities that support this reasonable management.

ACKNOWLEDGEMENTS

We thank George Benz, Mary Freeman, Carol Johnston, Richard Neves, Charles Nicholson, and Phil Pister for their suggestions which greatly improved this manuscript.

REFERENCES

Adams, W. F., and J. M. Alderman. 1993. Reviewing the status of your state's molluscan fauna: The case for a systematic approach. In *Conservation and Management of Freshwater Mussels.* K. S. Cummings, A. C. Buchanan, and L. M. Koch (eds.). Proceedings of a UMRCC Symposium, St. Louis, MO. Upper Mississippi River Conservation Committee, Rock Island, IL, p. 83-88.

Ahlstedt, S. A. 1991. Reintroduction of the spiny riversnail *Io fluvialis* (Say, 1825) (Gastropoda: Pleuroceridae) into the North Fork Holston River, southwestern Virginia and northeastern Tennessee. *American Malacological Bulletin* 8:139-142.

Allendorf, F. W. 1988. Conservation biology of fishes. *Conservation Biology* 2:145-148.

Angermeier, P. L., R. J. Neves, and J. W. Kaufmann. 1993. Protocol to rank value of biotic resources in Virginia streams. *Rivers* 4:20-29.

Anonymous. 1995. Bubbling on the Elk River. *Compressed Air Magazine* 100:40-43.

Benke, A. C. 1990. A perspective on America's vanishing streams. *Journal of the North American Benthological Society* 9:77-88.

Bruton, M. N. 1995. Have fishes had their chips? The dilemma of threatened fishes. *Environmental Biology of Fishes* **43**:1-27.

Burch, J. B. 1982. Freshwater snails (Mollusca: Gastropoda) of North America. Publication 600/3-82-026, U.S. Environmental Protection Agency, Cincinnati, OH, 294 p.

Carroll, C. R., and G. K. Meffe. 1994. Management to meet conservation goals: General principles. In *Principles of Conservation Biology.* G. K. Meffe, and C. R. Carroll (eds.). Sinauer Associates, Inc., Sunderland, MA, p. 307-337.

Doppelt, B., M. Scurlock, C. Frissel, and J. Karr. 1993. *Entering the Watershed: A New Approach to Save America's River Ecosystems.* Island Press, Washington, D.C.

Dunn, H. L. 1993. Survival of unionids four years after relocation. In *Conservation and Management of Freshwater Mussels.* K. S. Cummings, A. C. Buchanan, and L. M. Koch (eds.). Proceedings of a UMRCC Symposium, St. Louis, MO. Upper Mississippi River Conservation Committee, Rock Island, IL, p. 93-99.

Dynesius, M., and C. Nilsson. 1994. Fragmentation and flow regulation of river systems in the northern third of the world. *Science* **266**:753-762.

Eisner, T., J. Lubchenco, E. O. Wilson, D. S. Wilcove, and M. J. Bean. 1995. Building a scientifically sound policy for protecting endangered species. *Science* **268**:1231-1232.

Elam, J. E., and L. Burge. 1995. A comparison of the habits and populations of the spring pygmy sunfish. Unpublished report for 1995 BEST Environmental Project (Grade 10-12), Environmental Studies Class (Marsha Slate, Instructor), Huntsville High School, Huntsville, AL, 8 p. + figures.

Etnier, D. A., and W. C. Starnes. 1991. An analysis of Tennessee's jeopardized fish taxa. *Journal of the Tennessee Academy of Science* **66**:129-133.

Etnier, D. A., and W. C. Starnes. 1993. *The Fishes of Tennessee.* The University of Tennessee Press, Knoxville, TN.

Everett, R. 1994. The comeback of the shiny pigtoe pearly mussel. Unpublished report by Third Grade Class (Rahonda Everett, Instructor), Central School, Huntsville, AL, 9 p.

Flynn, J., D. L. Weigmann, and S. Bruenderman. 1994. Copper Creek a valuable resource. Virginia Water Resources Research Center, Virginia Polytechnic Institute and Virginia Department of Game and Inland Fishes, Blacksburg, VA, 13 p.

Freeman, B. J., and M. C. Freeman. 1994. Habitat use by an endangered riverine fish and implications for species protection. *Ecology of Freshwater Fishes* **3**:49-58.

Georgia Department of Natural Resources. 1992. Rules of Georgia Department of Natural Resources Game and Fish Division, Chapter 391-4-10, Protection of endangered, threatened, rare, or unusual species. Memorandum, Game and Fish Division, Georgia Department of Natural Resources, Atlanta, GA, 50 p.

Gresswell, R. E., and W. J. Liss. 1995. Values associated with management of Yellowstone cutthroat trout in Yellowstone National Park. *Conservation Biology* **9**:159-165.

Hobbs, H. H., Jr. 1989. An illustrated checklist of American crayfishes (Decapoda: Astacidae, Cambaridae and Parastacidae). *Smithsonian Contributions to Zoology* **480**:1-236.

Hughes, R. M., and R. F. Noss. 1992. Biological diversity and biological integrity: Current concerns for lakes and streams. *Fisheries* **17**(3):11-19.

Inouge, D. W. 1988. Variation in undisturbed plant and animal populations and its applications for studies of recovering ecosystems. In *Rehabilitating Damaged Ecosystems, Volume II.* J. Cairns, Jr. (ed.). CRR Press, Inc., Boca Raton, FL, p. 40-50.

Jandebeur, T. S. 1982. A status report on the spring pygmy sunfish, *Elassoma* sp., in northcentral Alabama. *Association of Southeastern Biologists Bulletin* **29**:66.

Karr, J. R. 1990. Viable populations, reserve size, and federal land management: A critique. *Conservation Biology* **4**:127-134.

Karr, J. R., and D. R. Dudley. 1981. Ecological perspective on water quality goals. *Environmental Management* **5**:55-68.

Kondolf, G. M. 1995. Five elements for effective evaluation of stream restoration. *Restoration Ecology* **3**:133-136.

Leopold, A. 1949. *A Sand County Almanac.* Oxford University Press, Oxford, MS.

Lydeard, C., and R. L. Mayden. 1995. A diverse and endangered aquatic ecosystem of the southeastern United States. *Conservation Biology* **9**:800-805.

Master, L. 1991. Aquatic animals: Endangerment alert. *Nature Conservancy* **41**:26-27.

Master, L. 1993. Information networking and the conservation of freshwater mussels. In *Conservation and Management of Freshwater Mussels.* K. S. Cummings, A. C. Buchanan, and L. M. Koch (eds.). Proceedings of a UMRCC Symposium, St. Louis, MO. Upper Mississippi River Conservation Committee, Rock Island, IL, p. 126-130.

Mayden, R. L. 1992. An emerging revolution in comparative biology and the evolution of North American freshwater fishes. In *Systematics, Historical Ecology, and North American Freshwater Fishes.* R. L. Mayden (ed.). Stanford University Press, Stanford, CA, p. 864-890.

Mayden, R. L. 1993. *Elassoma alabamae*, a new species of pygmy sunfish endemic to the Tennessee River Drainage of Alabama (Teleostei: Elassomatidae). *Bulletin of the Alabama Museum of Natural History* **16**:1-14.

Meffe, G. K., and C. R. Carroll. 1994. What is conservation biology? In *Principles of Conservation Biology.* G. K. Meffe, and C. R. Carroll (eds.). Sinauer Associates, Inc., Sunderland, MA, p. 3-23.

Milhous, R. T. 1994. Flushing flows for the water manager. In *Water Policy and Management: Solving the Problems.* D. G. Fontane, and H. N. Tuvel (eds.). Proceedings of the 21st Annual Conference of the American Society of Civil Engineers, Denver, CO, p. 226-229.

Montgomery, D. R., G. E. Grant, and K. Sullivan. 1995. Watershed analysis as a framework for implementing ecosystem management. *Water Resources Bulletin* **31**:369-386.

Moyle, P. B., and P. R. Moyle. 1995. Endangered fishes and economics: Intergenerational obligations. *Environmental Biology of Fishes* **43**:29-37.

Moyle, P. B., and G. M. Sato. 1991. On the design of preserves to protect native fishes. In *Battle Against Extinction: Native Fish Management in the American West.* W. L. Minckley, and J. E. Deacon (eds.). University of Arizona Press, Tucson, AZ, p. 155-169.

Neves, R. J. 1993. A state-of-the-unionids address. In *Conservation and Management of Freshwater Mussels.* K. S. Cummings, A. C. Buchanan, and L. M. Koch (eds.). Proceedings of a UMRCC Symposium, St. Louis, MO. Upper Mississippi River Conservation Committee, Rock Island, IL, p. 1-10.

Noss, R. F. 1994. Hierarchical indicators for monitoring changes in biodiversity: Various spatial and temporal scales. In *Principles of Conservation Biology.* G. K. Meffe, and C. R. Carroll (eds.). Sinauer Associates, Inc., Sunderland, MA, p. 79-80.

Pine, B. 1993. A study on the habitat of the spring pygmy sunfish of the genus *Elassoma*. Unpublished report for 1993 BEST Environmental Project (Grade 10-12), Environmental Studies Class (Marsha Slate, Instructor), Huntsville High School, Huntsville, AL, 5 p. + figures.

Rabeni, C. F. 1992. Habitat evaluation in a watershed context. In *Fisheries Management and Watershed Development.* R. H. Stroud (ed.). Symposium 13, American Fisheries Society, Bethesda, MD, p. 57-67.

Raines, W. 1994. Harpeth River: The great educator. *The Tennessee Conservationist* 60:30-32.

Rakes, P. L. 1994. Status survey for the Barrens topminnow, *Fundulus julisia*. Unpublished Final Report for Contract C06242 submitted to the National Biological Survey, Cooperative Fisheries Unit, Tennessee Technological University, Cookeville, TN, 12 p. + appendices.

Raven, P. H. 1992. A 50-year plan for biodiversity surveys. *Science* 258:1099-1110.

Sheldon, A. L. 1988. Conservation of stream fishes: Patterns of diversity, rarity and risk. *Conservation Biology* 2:149-156.

Shute, J. R., and P. L. Rakes. 1994. Captive propagation and population monitoring of rare southeastern fishes by Conservation Fisheries, Inc. Fiscal Year 1994 Third and Fourth Quarterly Reports for Contract FA-4-1072-4-00 submitted to the Tennessee Wildlife Resources Agency, Nashville, TN, 12 p.

Shute, P. W., J. R. Shute, and P. L. Rakes. manuscript in preparation. Status and recovery efforts for two rare catfishes, smoky and yellowfin madtoms (*Noturus bailey* and *N. flavipinnis*) in Citico Creek, and Abrams Creek, TN.

Southern Rivers Council. 1995. Restore our southern rivers: November 1994 project update, North Chickamauga Creek water quality restoration project, and Shuler Creek erosion control project. Unpublished Report submitted to the National Fish and Wildlife Foundation, Washington, D.C., 12 p.

Strange, R. M., and B. M. Burr. 1995. Genetic variability and metapopulation dynamics in the federally threatened blackside dace *Phoxinus cumberlandensis* (Pisces: Cyprinidae). Unpublished Final Report submitted to the Kentucky Department of Fish and Wildlife Resources, Frankfort, KY, 21 p. + tables and figures.

Tear, T. H., J. M. Scott, P. H. Haywood, and B. Griffith. 1995. Recovery plans and the Endangered Species Act: Are criticisms supported by data? *Conservation Biology* 9:182-195.

Tennessee Valley Authority. 1971. Stream length in the Tennessee River Basin. Tennessee River Authority, Knoxville, TN, 25 p.

Tennessee Valley Authority. 1995. Riverpulse: A report on the condition of the Tennessee River and tributaries in 1994. Tennessee Valley Authority, Knoxville, TN, 32 p.

Terwilliger, K. (coordinator). 1991. *Virginia's Endangered Species.* Proceedings of a symposium sponsored by Virginia Division of Game and Fish. McDonald and Woodward Publishing Company, Blacksburg, VA.

U.S. Environmental Protection Agency. 1992. Framework for ecological risk assessment. Publication 630/R-92/001, U.S. Environmental Protection Agency, Washington, D.C., 41 p.

U.S. Fish and Wildlife Service. 1993. Watercress darter (*Etheostoma nuchale*) recovery plan (second revision). U.S. Fish and Wildlife Service, Jackson, MS, 14 p.

U.S. Fish and Wildlife Service. 1994a. Endangered and threatened wildlife and plants. *U.S. Federal Register* **50** CFR (17.11 and 17.12):1-42.

U.S. Fish and Wildlife Service. 1994b. Endangered and threatened wildlife and plants, animal candidate review for listing as endangered or threatened species, proposed rule. *U.S. Federal Register* **59**:58982-59028.

U.S. Geological Survey. 1995. National Water-Quality Assessment Program - the upper Tennessee River basin study unit. Fact Sheet FS-150-95, Knoxville, TN, 2 p.

Warner, R. 1993. Operating as a network. *Biodiversity Network News* **6**:1-3,7.

Warren, M. L., Jr., and B. M. Burr. 1994. Status of freshwater fishes of the United States: Overview of an imperiled fauna. *Fisheries* **19**(1):6-18.

Williams, C. D., and J. E. Williams. 1992. Bring back the natives: A new strategy for restoring aquatic biodiversity on public lands. In *Transactions of the 57th North American Wildlife and Natural Resources Conference*. Wildlife Management Institute, Washington, D.C., p. 416-423.

Williams, J. D., and D. K. Finnley. 1977. Our vanishing fishes: Can they be saved? *Frontiers* 1977(Summer):1-9.

Williams, J. D., M. L. Warren, Jr., K. S. Cummings, J. L. Harris, and R. J. Neves. 1993. Conservation status of freshwater mussels of the United States and Canada. *Fisheries* **18**(9):6-22.

Williams, J. E. 1991. Preserves and refuges for native western fishes: History and management. In *Battle Against Extinction: Native Fish Management in the American West*. W. L. Minckley, and J. E. Deacon (eds.). University of Arizona Press, Tucson, AZ, p. 109-121.

Williams, J. E., J. E. Johnson, D. A. Hendrickson, W. Contreras-Balderas, J. D. Williams, M. Navarro-Mendoza, D. E. McAllister, and J. E. Deacon. 1989. Fishes of North America endangered, threatened, or of special concern: 1989. *Fisheries* **14**(6):2-20.

General Appendices

Threatened and endangered species list for southeastern states. Below we provide a list of species residing in the southeastern United States (Alabama, Arkansas, Florida, Georgia, Kentucky, Louisiana, Maryland, Mississippi, Missouri, North Carolina, South Carolina, Tennessee, Virginia, West Virginia) that are federally listed as Threatened or Endangered (as of July 31, 1997) by the U.S. Fish and Wildlife Service (USFWS). Taxon status: E = endangered, T = threatened. Basic habitat requirements are: A = aquatic, T = terrestrial. Taxa were designated aquatic if they rely primarily on aquatic or semiaquatic habitats. Summary data for each state detail the total number of species listed, number of aquatic species listed, number of terrestrial species listed, and percent of total listed species which are aquatic. This list was constructed using information provided on the web page of the USFWS. The USFWS periodically updates the web page listing of threatened and endangered species as new information becomes available. To consult this list use the web address: http://www.fws.gov

State (summary data): Taxon	Common Name	Taxon Status	Habitat
Alabama			
86 listed species: 69 aquatic, 17 terrestrial (80% of listed species are aquatic)			
Plants (19 species)			
Amphianthus pusillus	Little amphianthus	T	A
Apios priceana	Price's potato-bean	T	T
Arabis perstellata	Rock cress	E	T
Asplenium scolopendrium var. *americanum*	American hart's-tongue fern	T	T
Clematis morefieldii	Morefield's leather-flower	E	T
Clematis socialis	Alabama leather-flower	E	T
Dalea foliosa	Leafy prairie-clover	E	T
Helianthus eggertii	Eggert's sunflower	T	T
Lesquerella lyrata	Lyrate bladderpod	T	T
Lindera melissifolia	Pondberry	E	A
Marshallia mohrii	Mohr's Barbara's buttons	T	T
Ptilimnium nodosum	Harperella	E	A
Sagittaria secundifolia	Kral's water-plantain	T	A
Sarracenia orephila	Green pitcher-plant	E	A
Sarracenia rubra alabamensis	Alabama canebrake pitcher-plant	E	A
Spigelia gentianoides	Gentian pinkroot	E	T
Thelypteris pilosa var. *alabamaensis*	Alabama streak-sorus fern	T	T
Trillium reliquum	Relict trillium	E	T
Xyris tennesseensis	Tennessee yellow-eyed grass	E	A
Mollusks (38 species)			
Athearnia anthonyi	Anthony's riversnail	E	A
Cyprogenia stegaria	Fanshell	E	A
Dromus dromas	Dromedary pearlymussel	E	A
Epioblasma brevidens	Cumberlandian combshell	E	A
Epioblasma capsaeformis	Oyster mussel	E	A
Epioblasma florentina florentina	Yellow-blossom pearlymussel	E	A
Epioblasma metastriata	Upland combshell	E	A
Epioblasma obliquata obliquata	Purple cat's paw pearlymussel	E	A
Epioblasma othcaloogensis	Southern acornshell	E	A
Epioblasma penita	Southern combshell	E	A
Epioblasma turgidula	Turgid-blossom pearlymussel	E	A
Fusconia cor	Shiny pigtoe	E	A
Fusconaia cuneolus	Fine-rayed pigtoe	E	A

Threatened and endangered species list. Continued.

State (summary data): Taxon	Common Name	Taxon Status	Habitat
Hemistena lata	Cracking pearlymussel	E	A
Lampsilis abrupta	Pink mucket pearlymussel	E	A
Lampsilis altilis	Fine-lined pocketbook	T	A
Lampsilis perovalis	Orange-nacre mucket	T	A
Lampsilis virescens	Alabama lampmusssel	E	A
Medionidus acutissimus	Alabama moccasinshell	T	A
Medionidus parvulus	Coosa moccasinshell	E	A
Obovaria retusa	Ring pink mussel	E	A
Pegias fabula	Little-wing pearlymussel	E	A
Plethobasis cicatricosus	White wartyback pearlymussel	E	A
Plethobasus cooperianus	Orange-foot pimple back pearlymussel	E	A
Pleurobema curtum	Black clubshell	E	A
Pleurobema decisum	Southern clubshell	E	A
Pleurobema furvum	Dark pigtoe	E	A
Pleurobema georgianum	Southern pigtoe	E	A
Pleurobema marshalli	Flat pigtoe	E	A
Pleurobema perovatum	Ovate clubshell	E	A
Pleurobema plenum	Rough pigtoe	E	A
Pleurobema taitianum	Heavy pigtoe	E	A
Potamilus inflatus	Inflated heelsplitter	T	A
Ptychobranchus greeni	Triangular kidneyshell	E	A
Quadrula intermedia	Cumberland monkeyface pearlymussel	E	A
Quadrula stapes	Stirrupshell	E	A
Toxolasma cylindrellus	Pale lilliput pearlymussel	E	A
Tulotoma magnifica	Tulotoma snail	E	A
Crustaceans (1 species)			
Palaemonias alabamae	Alabama cave shrimp	E	A
Fishes (12 species)			
Acipenser oxyrhynchus desotoi	Gulf sturgeon	T	A
Cottus pygmaeus	Pygmy sculpin	T	A
Cyprinella caerulea	Blue shiner	T	A
Cyprinella monacha	Spotfin chub	T	A
Etheostoma boschungi	Slackwater darter	T	A
Etheostoma nuchale	Watercress darter	E	A
Etheostoma wapiti	Boulder darter	E	A
Notropis albizonatus	Palezone shiner	E	A
Notropis cahabae	Cahaba shiner	E	A
Percina aurolineata	Goldline darter	T	A
Percina tanasi	Snail darter	T	A
Speoplatyrhinus poulsoni	Alabama cavefish	E	A
Amphibians (1 species)			
Phaeognathus hubrichti	Red Hills salamander	T	A
Reptiles (5 speices)			
Caretta caretta	Loggerhead sea turtle	T	A
Drymarchon corais couperi	Eastern indigo snake	T	T
Gopherus polyphemus	Gopher tortoise	T	T
Pseudemys alabamensis	Alabama redbelly turtle	E	A
Sternnotherus depressus	Flattened musk turtle	T	A

Threatened and endangered species list. Continued.

State (summary data): Taxon	Common Name	Taxon Status	Habitat
Birds (5 species)			
Charadrius melodus	Piping plover	T	A
Falco peregrinus anatum	American peregrine falcon	E	T
Haliaeetus leucocephalus	Bald eagle	T	A
Mycteria americana	Wood stork	E	A
Picoides borealis	Red-cockaded woodpecker	E	T
Mammals (5 species)			
Myotis grisescens	Gray bat	E	A
Myotis sodalis	Indiana bat	E	T
Peromyscus polionotus ammobates	Alabama beach mouse	E	A
Peromyscus polionotus trissyllepsis	Perdido Key beach mouse	E	A
Trichechus manatus	West Indian manatee	E	A

Arkansas

25 listed species: 16 aquatic, 9 terrestrial (64% of listed species are aquatic)

Plants (5 species)			
Geocarpon minimum	(no common name)	T	T
Lindera melissifolia	Pondberry	E	A
Platanthera leucophaea	Eastern prairie fringed orchid	T	T
Ptilimnium nodosum	Harperella	E	A
Trifolium stoloniferum	Running buffalo clover	E	T
Mollusks (7 species)			
Arkansia wheeleri	Ouachita rock-pocketbook	E	A
Epioblasma florentina curtisi	Curtis' pearlymussel	E	A
Lampsilis abrupta	Pink mucket pearlymussel	E	A
Lampsilis powelli	Arkansas fatmucket	T	A
Lampsilis streckeri	Speckled pocketbook	E	A
Mesodon magazinensis	Magazine Mountain shagreen	T	T
Potamilus capax	Fat pocketbook	E	A
Crustaceans (2 species)			
Cambarus aculabrum	(no common name)	E	A
Cambarus zophonastes	(no common name)	E	A
Insects (1 species)			
Nicrophorus americanus	American burying beetle	E	T
Fishes (3 species)			
Amblyopsis rosae	Ozark cavefish	T	A
Percina pantherina	Leopard darter	T	A
Scaphirhynchus albus	Pallid sturgeon	E	A
Birds (4 species)			
Falco peregrinus anatum	American peregrine falcon	E	T
Haliaeetus leucocephalus	Bald eagle	T	A
Picoides borealis	Red-cockaded woodpecker	E	T
Sterna antillarum	Least tern	E	A
Mammals (3 species)			
Myotis grisescens	Gray bat	E	A
Myotis sodalis	Indiana bat	E	T
Plecotus townsendii ingens	Ozark big-eared bat	E	T

Threatened and endangered species list. Continued.

State (summary data): Taxon	Common Name	Taxon Status	Habitat
Florida			
92 listed species: 32 aquatic, 60 terrestrial (36% of listed species are aquatic)			
Plants (54 species)			
Amorpha crenulata	Crenulate lead-plant	E	T
Asimina tetramera	Four-petal pawpaw	E	T
Bonamia grandiflora	Florida bonamia	T	T
Campanula robinsiae	Brooksville bellflower	E	T
Cereus eriophorus var. *fragrans*	Fragrant prickly-apple	E	T
Chamaesyce deltoidea deltoidea	Deltoid spurge	E	T
Chamaesyce garberi	Garber's spurge	T	T
Chionanthus pygmaeus	Pygmy fringe-tree	E	T
Chrysopsis floridana	Florida golden aster	E	T
Cladonia perforata	Florida perforate cladonia	E	T
Clitoria fragrans	Pigeon wings	T	T
Conradina brevifolia	Short-leaved rosemary	E	T
Conradina etonia	Etonia rosemary	E	T
Conradina glabra	Apalachicola rosemary	E	T
Crotalaria avonensis	Avon Park harebells	E	T
Cucurbita okeechobeensis okeechobeensis	Okeechobee gourd	E	T
Deeringothamnus pulchellus	Beautiful pawpaw	E	T
Deeringothamnus rugelii	Rugel's pawpaw	E	T
Dicerandra christmanii	Garrett's mint	E	T
Dicerandra cornutissima	Longspurred mint	E	T
Dicerandra frutescens	Scrub mint	E	T
Dicerandra immaculata	Lakela's mint	E	T
Eriogonum longifolium gaphalifolium	Scrub buckwheat	T	T
Eryngium cuneifolium	Snakeroot	E	A
Euphorbia telephioides	Telephus spurge	T	T
Galactia smallii	Small's milkpea	E	T
Harperocallis flava	Harper's beauty	E	T
Hypericum cumulicola	Highlands scrub hypericum	E	T
Jacquemontia reclinata	Beach jacquemontia	E	A
Justicia cooleyi	Cooley's water-willow	E	A
Liatris ohlingerae	Scrub blazingstar	E	T
Lindera melissifolia	Pondberry	E	A
Lupinus aridorum	Scrub lupine	E	T
Macbridea alba	White birds-in-a-nest	T	T
Nolina brittoniana	Britton's beargrass	E	T
Paronychia chartacea	Papery whitlow-wort	T	T
Pilosocereus robinii	Key tree-cactus	E	T
Pinguicula ionantha	Godfrey's butterwort	T	T
Polygala lewtonii	Lewton's polygala	E	T
Polygala smallii	Tiny polygala	E	T
Polygonella basiramia	Wireweed	E	T
Polygonella myriophylla	Sandlace	E	T

Threatened and endangered species list. Continued.

State (summary data): Taxon	Common Name	Taxon Status	Habitat
Prunus geniculata	Scrub plum	E	T
Rhododendron chapmanii	Chapman rhododendron	E	T
Ribes echinellum	Miccosukee gooseberry	T	T
Schwalbea americana	American chaffseed	E	T
Scutellaria floridana	Florida skullcap	T	A
Silene polypetala	Fringed campion	E	T
Spigelia gentianoides	Gentian pinkroot	E	T
Thalictrum cooleyi	Cooley's meadowrue	E	A
Torreya taxifolia	Florida torreya	E	T
Warea amplexifolia	Wide-leaf warea	E	T
Warea carteri	Carter's mustard	E	T
Ziziphus celata	Florida ziziphus	E	T
Mollusks (1 species)			
Orthalicus reses	Stock Island tree snail	T	T
Crustaceans (1 species)			
Palaemonetes cummingi	Squirrel Chimney Cave shrimp	T	A
Insects (1 species)			
Heraclides aristodemus ponceanus	Schaus swallowtail butterfly	E	T
Fishes (2 species)			
Acipenser oxyrhynchus desotoi	Gulf sturgeon	T	A
Etheostoma okaloosae	Okaloosa darter	E	A
Reptiles (9 species)			
Caretta caretta	Loggerhead sea turtle	T	A
Chelonia mydas	Green sea turtle	E	A
Crocodylus acutus	American crocodile	E	A
Dermochelys coriacea	Leatherback sea turtle	E	A
Drymarchon corais couperi	Eastern indigo snake	T	T
Eretmochelys imbricata	Hawksbill sea turtle	E	A
Eumeces egregius lividus	Bluetail mole skink	T	T
Neoseps reynoldsi	Sand skink	T	T
Nerodia clarkii taeniata	Atlantic salt marsh snake	T	A
Birds (11 species)			
Ammodramus maritimus mirabilis	Cape Sable seaside sparrow	E	A
Ammodramus savannarum floridanus	Florida grasshopper sparrow	E	T
Aphelocoma coerulescens	Florida scrub jay	T	T
Charadrius melodus	Piping plover	T	A
Falco peregrinus anatum	American peregrine falcon	E	T
Haliaeetus leucocephalus	Bald eagle	T	A
Mycteria americana	Wood stork	E	A
Picoides borealis	Red-cockaded woodpecker	E	T
Polyborus plancus audubonii	Audubon's crested caracara	T	T
Rostrhamus sociabilis plumbeus	Everglade snail kite	E	A
Sterna dougallii dougallii	Roseate tern	T	A
Mammals (13 species)			
Felis concolor coryi	Florida panther	E	T
Microtus pennsylvanicus dukecampbelli	Florida salt marsh vole	E	A

Threatened and endangered species list. Continued.

State (summary data): Taxon	Common Name	Taxon Status	Habitat
Myotis grisescens	Gray bat	E	A
Neotoma floridana smalli	Key Largo woodrat	E	A
Odocoileus virginianus clavium	Key deer	E	T
Oryzomys palustris natator	Rice rat	E	A
Peromyscus gossypinus allapaticola	Key Largo cotton mouse	E	A
Peromyscus polionotus allophrys	Choctawahatchee beach mouse	E	A
Peromyscus polionotus niveiventris	Southeastern beach mouse	T	A
Peromyscus polionotus phasma	Anastasia Island beach mouse	E	A
Peromyscus polionotus trissyllepsis	Perdido Key beach mouse	E	A
Sylvilagus palustris hefneri	Lower Keys rabbit	E	A
Trichechus manatus	West Indian manatee	E	A

Georgia
48 listed species: 33 aquatic, 15 terrestrial (69% of listed species are aquatic)

Plant (22 species)

Amphianthus pusillus	Little amphianthus	T	A
Baptisia arachnifera	Hairy rattleweed	E	T
Echinacea laevigata	Smooth coneflower	E	T
Helonias bullata	Swamp pink	T	A
Isoetes melanospora	Black-spored quillwort	E	A
Isoetes tegetiformans	Mat-forming quillwort	E	A
Isotria medeoloides	Small whorled pogonia	T	T
Lindera melissifolia	Pondberry	E	A
Marshallia mohrii	Mohr's Barbara's buttons	T	T
Oxypolis canbyi	Canby's dropwort	E	A
Ptilimnium nodosum	Harperella	E	A
Rhus michauxii	Michaux's sumac	E	T
Sagittaria secundifolia	Kral's water-plantain	T	A
Sarracenia oreophila	Green pitcher-plant	E	A
Schwalbea americana	American chaffseed	E	T
Scutellaria montana	Large-flowered skullcap	E	T
Silene polypetala	Fringed campion	E	T
Spiraea virginiana	Virginia spiraea	T	A
Torreya taxifolia	Florida torreya	E	T
Trillium persistens	Persistent trillium	E	T
Trillium reliquum	Relict trillium	E	T
Xyris tennesseensis	Tennessee yellow-eyed grass	E	A

Mollusks (9 species)

Epioblasma metastriata	Upland combshell	E	A
Epioblasma othcaloogensis	Southern acornshell	E	A
Lampsilis altilis	Fine-lined pocketbook	T	A
Medionidus acutissimus	Alabama moccasinshell	T	A
Medionidus parvulus	Coosa moccasinshell	E	A
Pleurobema decisum	Southern clubshell	E	A
Pleurobema georgianum	Southern pigtoe	E	A
Pleurobema perovatum	Ovate clubshell	E	A
Ptychobranchus greeni	Triangular kidneyshell	E	A

Threatened and endangered species list. Continued.

State (summary data): Taxon	Common Name	Taxon Status	Habitat
Fishes (7 species)			
Cyprinella caerulea	Blue shiner	T	A
Etheostoma etowahae	Etowah darter	E	A
Etheostoma scotti	Cherokee darter	T	A
Percina antesella	Amber darter	E	A
Percina aurolineata	Goldline darter	T	A
Percina jenkinsi	Conasauga logperch	E	A
Percina tanasi	Snail darter	T	A
Reptiles (2 species)			
Drymarchon corais couperi	Eastern indigo snake	T	T
Caretta caretta	Loggerhead sea turtle	T	A
Birds (5 species)			
Charadrius melodus	Piping plover	T	A
Falco peregrinus anatum	American peregrine falcon	E	T
Haliaeetus leucocephalus	Bald eagle	T	A
Mycteria americana	Stork wood	E	A
Picoides borealis	Red-cockaded woodpecker	E	T
Mammals (3 species)			
Myotis grisescens	Gray bat	E	A
Myotis sodalis	Indiana bat	E	T
Trichechus manatus	West Indian manatee	E	A
Kentucky			
43 listed species: 31 aquatic, 12 terrestrial (72% of listed species are aquatic)			
Plants (9 species)			
Apios priceana	Price's potato-bean	T	T
Arabis perstellata	Rock cress	E	T
Arenaria cumberlandensis	Cumberland sandwort	E	T
Conradina verticillata	Cumberland rosemary	T	T
Helianthus eggertii	Eggert's sunflower	T	T
Solidago albopilosa	White-haired goldenrod	T	T
Solidago shortii	Short's goldenrod	E	T
Spiraea virginiana	Virginia spiraea	T	A
Trifolium stoloniferum	Running buffalo clover	E	T
Mollusks (21 species)			
Alasmidonta atropurpurea	Cumberland elktoe	E	A
Cyprogenia stegaria	Fanshell	E	A
Dromus dromas	Dromedary pearlymussel	E	A
Epioblasma brevidens	Cumberlandian combshell	E	A
Epioblasma capsaeformis	Oyster mussel	E	A
Epioblasma obliquata obliquata	Purple cat's paw pearlymussel	E	A
Epioblasma torulosa rangiana	Northern riffleshell	E	A
Epioblasma torulosa torulosa	Tubercled-blossom pearlymussel	E	A
Epioblasma walkeri	Tan riffleshell	E	A
Hemistena lata	Cracking pearlymussel	E	A
Lampsilis abrupta	Pink mucket pearlymussel	E	A
Obovaria retusa	Ring pink mussel	E	A
Pegias fabula	Little-wing pearlymussel	E	A

Threatened and endangered species list. Continued.

State (summary data): Taxon	Common Name	Taxon Status	Habitat
Plethobasus cicatricosus	White wartyback pearlymussel	E	A
Plethobasus cooperianus	Orange-foot pimple back pearlymussel	E	A
Pleurobema clava	Clubshell	E	A
Pleurobema plenum	Rough pigtoe	E	A
Potamilus capax	Fat pocketbook	E	A
Quadrula cylindrica strigillata	Rough rabbitsfoot	E	A
Quadrula fragosa	Winged mapleleaf mussel	E	A
Villosa trabalis	Cumberland bean pearlymussel	E	A
Crustaceans (1 species)			
Palaemonias ganteri	Kentucky cave shrimp	E	A
Fishes (4 species)			
Etheostoma chienense	Relict darter	E	A
Notropis albizonatus	Palezone shiner	E	A
Phoxinus cumberlandensis	Blackside dace	T	A
Scaphirhynchus albus	Pallid sturgeon	E	A
Birds (5 speices)			
Charadrius melodus	Piping plover	T	A
Falco peregrinus anatum	American peregrine falcon	E	T
Haliaeetus leucocephalus	Bald eagle	T	A
Picoides borealis	Red-cockaded woodpecker	E	T
Sterna antillarum	Least tern	E	A
Mammals (3 species)			
Myotis grisescens	Gray bat	E	A
Myotis sodalis	Indiana bat	E	T
Plecotus townsendii virginianus	Virginia big-eared bat	E	T

Louisiana
21 listed species: 14 aquatic, 7 terrestrial (67% of listed species are aquatic)

Plants (4 species)			
Geocarpon minimum	(no common name)	T	T
Isoetes louisianensis	Louisiana quillwort	E	A
Lindera melissifolia	Pondberry	E	A
Schwalbea americana	American chaffseed	E	T
Mollusks (3 species)			
Lampsilis abrupta	Pink mucket pearlymussel	E	A
Margaritifera hembeli	Louisiana pearlshell	T	A
Potamilus inflatus	Inflated heelsplitter	T	A
Fishes (2 species)			
Acipenser oxyrhynchus desotoi	Gulf sturgeon	T	A
Scaphirhynchus albus	Pallid sturgeon	E	A
Reptiles (3 species)			
Caretta caretta	Loggerhead sea turtle	T	A
Gopherus polyphemus	Gopher tortoise	T	T
Graptemys oculifera	Ringed map turtle	T	A
Birds (7 species)			
Charadrius melodus	Piping plover	T	A
Falco peregrinus anatum	American peregrine falcon	E	T
Haliaeetus leucocephalus	Bald eagle	T	A

Threatened and endangered species list. Continued.

State (summary data): Taxon	Common Name	Taxon Status	Habitat
Pelecanus occidentalis	Brown pelican	E	A
Picoides borealis	Red-cockaded woodpecker	E	T
Sterna antillarum	Least tern	E	A
Vireo atricapillus	Black-capped vireo	E	T
Mammals (2 species)			
Ursus americanus luteolus	Louisiana black bear	T	T
Trichechus manatus	West Indian manatee	E	A

Maryland
15 listed species: 10 aquatic, 5 terrestrial (67% of listed species are aquatic)

Plants (6 species)			
Aeschynomene virginica	Sensitive joint-vetch	T	A
Agalinis acuta	Sandplain gerardia	E	T
Helonias bullata	Swamp pink	T	A
Oxypolis canbyi	Canby's dropwort	E	A
Ptilimnium nodosum	Harperella	E	A
Scirpus ancistrochaetus	Northeastern bulrush	E	A
Mollusks (1 species)			
Alasmidonta heterodon	Dwarf wedge mussel	E	A
Insects (2 species)			
Cicindela puritana	Puritan tiger beetle	T	T
Cicindela dorsalis dorsalis	Northeastern beach tiger beetle	T	A
Fishes (1 species)			
Etheostoma sellare	Maryland darter	E	A
Birds (3 species)			
Charadrius melodus	Piping plover	T	A
Falco peregrinus anatum	American peregrine falcon	E	T
Haliaeetus leucocephalus	Bald eagle	T	A
Mammals (2 species)			
Myotis sodalis	Indiana bat	E	T
Sciurus niger cinereus	Delmarva Peninsula fox squirrel	E	T

Mississippi
32 listed species: 24 aquatic, 8 terrestrial (75% of listed species are aquatic)

Plants (3 species)			
Apios priceana	Price's potato-bean	T	T
Lindera melissifolia	Pondberry	E	A
Schwalbea americana	American chaffseed	E	T
Mollusks (11 species)			
Epioblasma penita	Southern combshell	E	A
Lampsilis perovalis	Orange-nacre mucket	T	A
Medionidus acutissimus	Alabama moccasinshell	T	A
Pleurobema curtum	Black clubshell	E	A
Pleurobema decisum	Southern clubshell	E	A
Pleurobema marshalli	Flat pigtoe	E	A
Pleurobema perovatum	Ovate clubshell	E	A
Pleurobema taitianum	Heavy pigtoe	E	A
Potamilus capax	Fat pocketbook	E	A

Threatened and endangered species list. Continued.

State (summary data): Taxon	Common Name	Taxon Status	Habitat
Potamilus inflatus	Inflated heelsplitter	T	A
Quadrula stapes	Stirrupshell	E	A
Fishes (3 species)			
Acipenser oxyrhynchus desotoi	Gulf sturgeon	T	A
Etheostoma rubrum	Bayou darter	T	A
Scaphirhynchus albus	Pallid sturgeon	E	A
Reptiles (5 species)			
Caretta caretta	Loggerhead sea turtle	T	A
Drymarchon corais couperi	Eastern indigo snake	T	T
Gopherus polyphemus	Gopher tortoise	T	T
Graptemys flavimaculata	Yellow-blotched map turtle	T	A
Graptemys oculifera	Ringed map turtle	T	A
Birds (7 species)			
Charadrius melodus	Piping plover	T	A
Falco peregrinus anatum	American peregrine falcon	E	T
Grus canadensis pulla	Mississippi sandhill crane	E	A
Haliaeetus leucocephalus	Bald eagle	T	A
Pelecanus occidentalis	Brown pelican	E	A
Picoides borealis	Red-cockaded woodpecker	E	T
Sterna antillarum	Least tern	E	A
Mammals (3 species)			
Myotis sodalis	Indiana bat	E	T
Trichechus manatus	West Indian manatee	E	A
Ursus americanus luteolus	Louisiana black bear	T	T

Missouri
22 listed species: 13 aquatic, 9 terrestrial (59% of listed species are aquatic)

	Common Name	Taxon Status	Habitat
Plants (7 species)			
Asclepias meadii	Mead's milkweed	T	T
Boltonia decurrens	Decurrent false aster	T	T
Geocarpon minimum	(no common name)	T	T
Lesquerella filiformis	Missouri bladderpod	E	T
Lindera melissifolia	Pondberry	E	A
Platanthera praeclara	Western prairie fringed orchid	T	T
Trifolium stoloniferum	Running buffalo clover	E	T
Mollusks (4 species)			
Epioblasma florentina curtisi	Curtis' pearlmussel	E	A
Lampsilis abrupta	Pink mucket pearlmussel	E	A
Lampsilis higginsi	Higgins'eye pearlmussel	E	A
Potamilus capax	Fat pocketbook	E	A
Fishes (4 species)			
Amblyopsis rosae	Ozark cavefish	T	A
Etheostoma nianguae	Niangua darter	T	A
Noturus placidus	Neosho madtom	T	A
Scaphirhynchus albus	Pallid sturgeon	E	A
Birds (4 species)			
Charadrius melodus	Piping plover	T	A
Falco peregrinus anatum	American peregrine falcon	E	T

Threatened and endangered species list. Continued.

State (summary data): Taxon	Common Name	Taxon Status	Habitat
Haliaeetus leucocephalus	Bald eagle	T	A
Sterna antillarum	Least tern	E	A
Mammals (3 species)			
Myotis grisescens	Gray bat	E	A
Myotis sodalis	Indiana bat	E	T
Plecotus townsendii ingens	Ozark big-eared bat	E	T

North Carolina
49 listed species: 26 aquatic, 23 terrestrial (53% of listed species are aquatic)

Taxon	Common Name	Taxon Status	Habitat
Lichens (1 species)			
Gymnoderma lineare	Rock gnome lichen	E	T
Plants (25 species)			
Aeschynomene virginica	Sensitive joint-vetch	T	A
Amaranthus pumilus	Seabeach amaranth	T	A
Cardamine micranthera	Small-anthered bittercress	E	A
Echinacea laevigata	Smooth coneflower	E	T
Geum radiatum	Spreading avens	E	T
Hedyotis purpurea var. *montana*	Roan Mountain bluet	E	T
Helianthus schweinitzii	Schweinitz's sunflower	E	T
Helonias bullata	Swamp pink	T	A
Hexastylis naniflora	Dwarf-flowered heartleaf	T	T
Hudsonia montana	Mountain golden heather	T	T
Isotria medeoloides	Small whorled pogonia	T	T
Liatris helleri	Heller's blazingstar	T	T
Lindera melissifolia	Pondberry	E	A
Lysimachia asperulaefolia	Rough-leaved loosestrife	E	A
Oxypolis canbyi	Canby's dropwort	E	A
Ptilimnium nodosum	Harperella	E	A
Rhus michauxii	Michaux's sumac	E	T
Sagittaria fasciculata	Bunched arrowhead	E	A
Sarracenia oreophila	Green pitcher-plant	E	A
Sarracenia rubra jonesii	Mountain sweet pitcher-plant	E	A
Schwalbea americana	American chaffseed	E	T
Sisyrinchium dichotomum	White irisette	E	T
Solidago spithamaea	Blue Ridge goldenrod	T	T
Spiraea virginiana	Virginia spiraea	T	T
Thalictrum cooleyi	Cooley's meadowrue	E	A
Mollusks (6 species)			
Alasmidonta heterodon	Dwarf wedge mussel	E	A
Alasmidonta raveneliana	Appalachian elktoe	E	A
Elliptio steinstansana	Tar river spinymussel	E	A
Lasmigona decorata	Carolina heelsplitter	E	A
Mesodon clarki nantahala	Noonday snail	T	T
Pegias fabula	Little-wing pearlymussel	E	A
Insects (1 species)			
Neonympha mitchellii francisci	Saint Francis' satyr butterfly	E	T
Arachnids (1 species)			
Microhexura montivaga	Spruce-fir moss spider	E	T

Threatened and endangered species list. Continued.

State (summary data): Taxon	Common Name	Taxon Status	Habitat
Fishes (3 species)			
Cyprinella monacha	Spotfin chub	T	A
Menidia extensa	Waccamaw silverside	T	A
Notropis mekistocholas	Cape Fear shiner	E	A
Reptiles (1 species)			
Caretta caretta	Loggerhead sea turtle	T	A
Birds (5 species)			
Charadrius melodus	Piping plover	T	A
Falco peregrinus anatum	American peregrine falcon	E	T
Haliaeetus leucocephalus	Bald eagle	T	A
Picoides borealis	Red-cockaded woodpecker	E	T
Sterna dougallii dougallii	Tern roseate	T	A
Mammals (6 species)			
Canis rufus	Red wolf	E	T
Glaucomys sabrinus coloratus	Carolina northern flying squirrel	E	T
Myotis sodalis	Indiana bat	E	T
Plecotus townsendii virginianus	Virginia big-eared bat	E	T
Sorex longirostris fisheri	Dismal Swamp southeastern shrew	T	A
Trichechus manatus	West Indian manatee	E	A

South Carolina
30 listed species: 16 aquatic, 14 terrestrial (53% of listed species are aquatic)

	Common Name	Taxon Status	Habitat
Plants (19 species)			
Amaranthus pumilus	Seabeach amaranth	T	T
Amphianthus pusillus	Little amphianthus	T	A
Echinacea laevigata	Smooth coneflower	E	T
Helianthus schweinitzii	Schweinitz's sunflower	E	T
Helonias bullata	Swamp pink	T	A
Hexastylis naniflora	Dwarf-flowered heartleaf	T	T
Isoetes melanospora	Black-spored quillwort	E	A
Isotria medeoloides	Small whorled pogonia	T	T
Lindera melissifolia	Pondberry	E	A
Lysimachia asperulaefolia	Rough-leaved loosestrife	E	A
Oxypolis canbyi	Canby's dropwort	E	A
Ptilimnium nodosum	Harperella	E	A
Rhus michauxii	Michaux's sumac	E	T
Ribes echinellum	Miccosukee gooseberry	T	T
Sagittaria fasciculata	Bunched arrowhead	E	A
Sarracenia rubra jonesii	Mountain sweet pitcher-plant	E	A
Schwalbea americana	American chaffseed	E	T
Trillium persistens	Persistent trillium	E	T
Trillium reliquum	Relict trillium	E	T
Mollusks (1 species)			
Lasmigona decorata	Carolina heelsplitter	E	A
Reptiles (2 species)			
Caretta caretta	Loggerhead sea turtle	T	A
Drymarchon corais couperi	Eastern indigo snake	T	T

Threatened and endangered species list. Continued.

State (summary data): Taxon	Common Name	Taxon Status	Habitat
Birds (6 species)			
Charadrius melodus	Piping plover	T	A
Falco peregrinus anatum	American peregrine falcon	E	T
Haliaeetus leucocephalus	Bald eagle	T	A
Mycteria americana	Wood stork	E	A
Picoides borealis	Red-cockaded woodpecker	E	T
Sterna dougallii dougallii	Roseate tern	T	A
Mammals (2 species)			
Myotis sodalis	Indiana bat	E	T
Trichechus manatus	West Indian manatee	E	A

Tennessee

87 listed species: 66 aquatic, 21 terrestrial (76% of listed species are aquatic)

Plants (19 species)			
Apios priceana	Price's potato-bean	T	T
Arabis perstellata	Rock cress	E	T
Arenaria cumberlandensis	Cumberland sandwort	E	T
Astragalus bibullatus	Pyne's ground-plum	E	T
Conradina verticillata	Cumberland rosemary	T	T
Dalea foliosa	Leafy prairie-clover	E	T
Echinacea tennesseensis	Tennessee purple coneflower	E	T
Geum radiatum	Spreading avens	E	T
Gymnoderma lineare	Rock gnome lichen	E	T
Hedyotis purpurea var. *montana*	Roan Mountain bluet	E	T
Helianthus eggertii	Eggert's sunflower	T	T
Isotria medeoloides	Small whorled pogonia	T	T
Lesquerella perforata	Spring Creek bladderpod	E	T
Pityopsis ruthii	Ruth's golden aster	E	T
Sarracenia oreophila	Green pitcher-plant	E	A
Scutellaria montana	Large-flowered skullcap	E	A
Solidago spithamaea	Blue Ridge goldenrod	T	T
Spiraea virginiana	Virginia spiraea	T	A
Xyris tennesseensis	Tennessee yellow-eyed grass	E	A
Mollusks (43 species)			
Alasmidonta atropurpurea	Cumberland elktoe	E	A
Alasmidonta raveneliana	Appalachian elktoe	E	A
Anguispira picta	Painted snake coiled forest snail	T	A
Athearnia anthonyi	Anthony's riversnail	E	A
Conradilla caelata	Birdwing pearlymussel	E	A
Cyprogenia stegaria	Fanshell	E	A
Dromus dromas	Dromedary pearlymussel	E	A
Epioblasma brevidens	Cumberlandian combshell	E	A
Epioblasma capsaeformis	Oyster mussel	E	A
Epioblasma florentina florentina	Yellow-blossom pearlymussel	E	A
Epioblasma metastriata	Upland combshell	E	A
Epioblasma obliquata obliquata	Purple cat's paw pearlymussel	E	A
Epioblasma othcaloogensis *gubernaculum*	Southern acornshell	E	A

Threatened and endangered species list. Continued.

State (summary data): Taxon	Common Name	Taxon Status	Habitat
Epioblasma torulosa	Green-blossom pearlymussel	E	A
Epioblasma torulosa torulosa	Tubercled-blossom pearlymussel	E	A
Epioblasma turgidula	Turgid-blossom pearlymussel	E	A
Epioblasma walkeri	Tan riffleshell	E	A
Fusconaia cor	Shiney pigtoe	E	A
Fusconaia cuneolus	Fine-rayed pigtoe	E	A
Hemistena lata	Cracking pearlymussel	E	A
Lampsilis abrupta	Pink mucket pearlymussel	E	A
Lampsilis altilis	Fine-lined pocketbook	T	A
Lampsilis virescens	Alabama lampshell	E	A
Medionidus acutissimus	Alabama moccasinshell	T	A
Medionidus parvulus	Coosa moccasinshell	E	A
Obovaria retusa	Ring pink mussel	E	A
Pegias fabula	Little-wing pearlymussel	E	A
Plethobasus cicatricosus	White-wartyback pearlymussel	E	A
Plethobasus cooperianus	Orange-foot pimple back pearlymussel	E	A
Pleurobema decisum	Southern clubshell	E	A
Pleurobema georgianum	Southern pigtoe	E	A
Pleurobema gibberum	Cumberland pigtoe	E	A
Pleurobema perovatum	Ovate clubshell	E	A
Pleurobema plenum	Rough pigtoe	E	A
Ptychobranchus greeni	Triangular kidneyshell	E	A
Pyrgulopsis ogmoraphe	Marstonia royal snail	E	A
Quadrula cylindrica strigillata	Rough rabbitsfoot	E	A
Quadrula fragosa	Winged mapleleaf mussel	E	A
Quadrula intermedia	Cumberland monkeyface pearlymussel	E	A
Quadrula sparsa	Appalachian monkeyface pearlymussel	E	A
Toxolasma cylindrellus	Pale lilliput pearlymussel	E	A
Villosa perpurpurea	Purple bean	E	A
Villosa trabalis	Cumberland bean pearlymussel	E	A
Crustaceans (1 species)			
Orconectes shoupi	Nashville crayfish	E	A
Arachnids (1 species)			
Microhexura montivaga	Spruce-fir moss spider	E	T
Fishes (15 species)			
Cyprinella monacha	Spotfin chub	T	A
Cyprinella caerulea	Blue shiner	T	A
Erimystax cahni	Slender chub	T	A
Etheostoma sp.	Bluemask darter	E	A
Etheostoma boschungi	Slackwater darter	T	A
Etheostoma percnurum	Duskytail darter	E	A
Etheostoma wapiti	Boulder darter	E	A
Noturus baileyi	Smoky madtom	E	A
Noturus flavipinnis	Yellowfin madtom	T	A
Noturus stanauli	Pygmy madtom	E	A
Percina antesella	Amber darter	E	A
Percina jenkinsi	Conasauga logperch	E	A
Percina tanasi	Snail darter	T	A

Threatened and endangered species list. Continued.

State (summary data): Taxon	Common Name	Taxon Status	Habitat
Phoxinus cumberlandensis	Blackside dace	T	A
Scaphirhynchus albus	Pallid sturgeon	E	A
Birds (4 species)			
Falco peregrinus anatum	American peregrine falcon	E	T
Haliaeetus leucocephalus	Bald eagle	T	A
Picoides borealis	Red-cockaded woodpecker	E	T
Sterna antillarum	Least tern	E	A
Mammals (4 species)			
Canis rufus	Red wolf	E	T
Glaucomys sabrinus coloratus	Carolina northern flying squirrel	E	T
Myotis grisescens	Gray bat	E	A
Myotis sodalis	Indiana bat	E	T

Virginia
49 listed species: 37 aquatic, 12 terrestrial (76% of listed species are aquatic)

Plants (10 species)			
Aeschynomene virginica	Sensitive joint-vetch	T	T
Arabis serotina	Shale barren rock-cress	E	T
Betula uber	Virginia round-leaf birch	T	A
Echinacea laevigata	Smooth coneflower	E	T
Helonias bullata	Swamp pink	T	A
Iliamna corei	Peter's mountain mallow	E	T
Isotria medeoloides	Small whorled pogonia	T	T
Platanthera leucophaea	Eastern prairie fringed orchid	T	T
Scirpus ancistrochaetus	Northwestern bulrush	E	A
Spiraea virginiana	Virginia spiraea	T	A
Mollusks (20 species)			
Alasmidonta heterodon	Dwarf wedge mussel	E	A
Condradilla caelata	Birdwing pearlymussel	E	A
Cyprogenia stegaria	Fanshell	E	A
Dromus dromas	Dromedary pearlymussel	E	A
Epioblasma brevidens	Cumberlandian combshell	E	A
Epioblasma capsaeformis	Oyster mussel	E	A
Epioblasma torulosa gubernaculum	Green-blossom pearlymussel	E	A
Epioblasma walkeri	Tan riffleshell	E	A
Fusconaia cor	Shiny pigtoe	E	A
Fusconaia cuneolus	Fine-rayed pigtoe	E	A
Hemistena lata	Cracking pearlymussel	E	A
Lampsilis abrupta	Pink mucket pearlmussel	E	A
Pegias fabula	Little-wing pearlymussel	E	A
Pleurobema collina	James River spinymussel	E	A
Pleurobema plenum	Rough pigtoe	E	A
Polygyriscus virginianus	Virginia fringed mountain snail	E	A
Quadrula cylindrica strigillata	Rough rabbitsfoot	E	A
Quadrula intermedia	Cumberland monkeyface pearlymussel	E	A
Quadrula sparsa	Appalachian monkeyface pearlymussel	E	A
Villosa perpurpurea	Purple bean	E	A

Threatened and endangered species list. Continued.

State (summary data): Taxon	Common Name	Taxon Status	Habitat
Crustaceans (2 species)			
Antrolana lira	Madison Cave isopod	T	A
Lirceus usdagalun	Lee County cave isopod	E	A
Insects (1 species)			
Cicindela dorsalis dorsalis	Northeastern beach tiger beetle	T	A
Fishes (5 species)			
Cyprinella monacha	Spotfin chub	T	A
Erimystax cahni	Slender chub	T	A
Etheostoma percnurum	Duskytail darter	E	A
Noturus flavipinnis	Yellowfin madtom	T	A
Percina rex	Roanoke logperch	E	A
Amphibians (1 species)			
Plethodon shenandoah	Shenandoah salamander	E	A
Birds (4 species)			
Charadrius melodus	Piping plover	T	A
Falco peregrinus anatum	American peregrine falcon	E	T
Haliaeetus leucocephalus	Bald eagle	T	A
Picoides borealis	Red-cockaded woodpecker	E	T
Mammals (6 species)			
Glaucomys sabrinus fuscus	Virginia northern flying squirrel	E	T
Myotis grisescens	Gray bat	E	A
Myotis sodalis	Indiana bat	E	T
Plecotus townsendii virginianus	Virginia big-eared bat	E	T
Sciurus niger cinereus	Delmarva Peninsula fox squirrel	E	T
Sorex longirostris fisheri	Dismal Swamp southeastern shrew	E	A

West Virginia
19 listed species: 12 aquatic, 7 terrestrial (63% of listed species are aquatic)

	Common Name	Taxon Status	Habitat
Plants (5 species)			
Arabis serotina	Shale barren rock-cress	E	T
Ptilimnium nodosum	Harperella	E	A
Scirpus ancistrochaetus	Northeastern bulrush	E	A
Spiraea virginiana	Virginia spiraea	T	A
Trifolium stoloniferum	Running buffalo clover	E	T
Mollusks (8 species)			
Cyprogenia stegaria	Fanshell	E	A
Epioblasma torulosa rangiana	Northern riffleshell	E	A
Epioblasma torulosa torulosa	Tuberculed-blossom pearlymussel	E	A
Lampsilis abrupta	Pink mucket pearlymussel	E	A
Obovaria retusa	Ring pink mussel	E	A
Pleurobema clava	Clubshell	E	A
Pleurobema collina	James River spinymussel	E	A
Triodopsis platysayoides	Flat-spired three-toothed snail	T	T
Amphibians (1 species)			
Plethodon nettingi	Cheat Mountain salamander	T	A
Birds (2 species)			
Falco peregrinus anatum	American peregrine falcon	E	T
Haliaeetus leucocephalus	Bald eagle	T	A

Threatened and endangered species list. Continued.

State (summary data): Taxon	Common Name	Taxon Status	Habitat
Mammals (3 species)			
Glaucomys sabrinus fuscus	Virginia northern flying squirrel	E	T
Myotis sodalis	Indiana bat	E	T
Plecotus townsendii virginianus	Virginia big-eared bat	E	T

TEAMING WITH WILDLIFE INITIATIVE

It's an unquestionable fact that the aquatic fauna of the Southeast is in peril. Yet through scientific research, education, and restoration and conservation efforts, as well as through sound individual, family, business, and community decisions truly made with *environmental* sustainability as a priority, this perilous trend can be curbed if not reversed. Luckily for all of us, more and more people are realizing the value of our natural surroundings and are willing to make the important decisions needed to eliminate environmental degradation.

Obtaining funds to drive programs aimed at maintaining and bettering our environment has often been difficult. And, as the information in this volume demonstrates, most of the aquatic species that are in peril within the Southeast (and elsewhere) are non-game species. As such, funds available to assist their preservation are relatively scarce. Just how scarce? A recent pamphlet distributed by B. Hatcher (Tennessee Wildlife Resources Agency) stated that since the 1930s, nationwide federal aid funds have totaled $3.4 million per game species, $42,000 per endangered species, and $11 per non-game species. The present methods of funding wildlife preservation efforts have been mentioned throughout this book as a major stumbling block which threatens to allow the continued dwindling of our precious natural heritage.

Working with other concerned stakeholders, the International Association of Fish and Wildlife Agencies (IAFWA) has drafted a proposal which would raise the dedicated funds required to fund the research, conservation and restoration, and education projects needed to assist non-game wildlife. Patterned after the highly successful Pittman-Robertson and Wallop-Breaux programs which provide funding for projects working with game species of wildlife and sport fish restoration, the IAFWA's proposal, called *Teaming With Wildlife*, would raise program dollars via a very modest "user fee" which would be linked to outdoor recreation equipment not already tied to either the Pittman-Robertson or Wallop-Breaux programs. The exact amount of the fee would be based on a percentage of the manufacturer's price of the product (ranging from a low of 0.25% to a maximum of 5%), and would be reflected in an increased retail price paid by the consumer. While this fee is modest, the volume of annual sales linked to the program is very significant and will yield the funds necessary to assist our imperiled and non-imperiled wildlife. For example, as reported by B. Hatcher (Tennessee Wildlife Resources Agency), if the Teaming With Wildlife program had been in effect in 1996, the average cost per Tennessee participant would have been only about $6.00. However, this minimal cost per user would have resulted in a national fund of $350 million. This fund would have contributed about $6.3 million for Tennessee, and with Tennessee's 25% match would have resulted in about $8.4 million for Tennessee's non-game wildlife. Similar benefits throughout the nation would go far to help resolve funding problems associated with programs focusing on non-game species.

Teaming With Wildlife funds would be allocated to each state using a formula based on the population (2/3) and land area (1/3) of each state. No state or territory would receive less than 0.5% or more than 5% of the total funds. States and territories will need to match these funds with non-federal dollars on a 25% state to 75% federal basis. Matching funds can be cash or in-kind donations, and states will have the flexibility to tailor particular programs to meet the unique and varying needs found across the country. A grants program will also be created for projects with regional or national significance. No new bureaucracy will be created through the proposed legislation, and program administrative costs will be capped at 6%.

A notable coalition has formed in support of the Teaming With Wildlife initiative, and the Teaming With Wildlife proposal has been endorsed by over 2,000 conservation and recreation organizations and related businesses. However, now is the time for all of us who care about our native wildlife to rally in support of Teaming With Wildlife.

How can you help? Well for one, you can learn more about the Teaming With Wildlife initiative by contacting your state fish and wildlife agency or the International Association of Fish and Wildlife Agencies (444 North Capital Street, NW, Suite 544, Washington, DC 20001; phone (202) 624-7890; FAX (202) 624-7891; Web Site: http//www.gorp.com/teamww/twwindex.htm).

Once you are familiar with the easy to understand proposal we encourage you to help make a difference:

1) by encouraging your organization or business to endorse the initiative in writing.
2) by writing letters to outdoor magazine, newsletter, and newspaper editors to promote public awareness of Teaming With Wildlife.
3) by writing letters of endorsement to outdoor-related suppliers regarding Teaming With Wildlife.
4) by encouraging your outdoor-related retailers to endorse Teaming With Wildlife.
5) by encouraging your outdoor-related retailers to advise their suppliers of their support for Teaming With Wildlife.
6) by advising your Congressman and Senator of your support for Teaming With Wildlife.

Legislation will be required to set the Teaming With Wildlife initiative in place. Working together we can express the wide-felt concern about our native wildlife which will drive this important legislation. Please act today.

Sincerely yours;
The Editors

ABOUT THE EDITORS

George Benz is Chief Research Scientist at the Tennessee Aquarium in Chattanooga, Tennessee, Director of the Southeast Aquatic Research Institute, and an adjunct faculty member at the University of Tennessee at Chattanooga. A native of New England, Benz received a B.Sc. and M.Sc. from The University of Connecticut and was employed for five years as a freshwater fisheries biologist with the State of Connecticut Bureau of Fisheries. He subsequently received a Ph.D. from The University of British Columbia, where he studied parasites of fishes. His research on the parasites of fishes has taken him from the Arctic to the tropics, and he has authored numerous research papers and review articles. His current research activities include a study of the parasites of freshwater mussels, an investigation of turtle population dynamics, and investigations of the parasites of cartilaginous fishes of the Sea of Cortez and the Arctic.

David Collins is Curator of Forests at the Tennessee Aquarium in Chattanooga, Tennessee. He holds a B.A. in Biology from the State University of New York at Albany. Collins' special passion is the ecology of freshwater turtles, and he has conducted field studies in New York, Ohio, and Tennessee. He is co-chair of the American Zoo and Aquarium Association Chelonian Advisory Group and a working member of the IUCN/SSC Tortoise and Freshwater Turtle Specialist Group.

CONTRIBUTORS

Steven A. Ahlstedt
U.S. Geological Survey
1820 Midpark Drive
Knoxville, Tennessee 37921

Paul L. Angermeier
U.S. Geological Survey
Biological Resources Division
Virginia Cooperative Fish and
Wildlife Research Unit
Department of Fisheries and
Wildlife Sciences
Virginia Tech
Backsburg, Virginia 24061-0321

Richard G. Biggins
U.S. Fish and Wildlife Service
160 Zillicoa Street
Asheville, North Carolina 28801

Arthur E. Bogan
North Carolina State Museum of
Natural Sciences
P.O. Box 29555
Raleigh, North Carolina 27626

Kurt A. Buhlmann
University of Georgia
Savannah River Ecology Laboratory
P.O. Drawer E
Aiken, South Carolina 29802

Noel M. Burkhead
U.S. Geological Survey
Biological Resources Division
Florida Caribbean Science Center
7920 NW 71st Street
Gainesville, Florida 32653

Brooks M. Burr
Department of Zoology
Southern Illinois University
Carbondale, Illinois 62901-6501

Robert S. Butler
U.S. Fish and Wildlife Service
160 Zillicoa Street
Asheville, North Carolina 28801

John E. Cely
South Carolina Wildlife and
Marine Resources Department
P.O. Box 167
Columbia, South Carolina 29202

Joseph D. Clark
Southern Appalachian Field
Laboratory
Biological Resources Division
U.S. Geological Survey
274 Ellington Plant Sciences
Building
University of Tennessee
Knoxville, Tennessee 37901-1071

Robert J. Cooper
University of Memphis
Biology Department
Memphis, Tennessee 38152

James G. Dickson
Wildlife Habitat Laboratory
Southern Research Station
U.S. Forest Service
Nacogdoches, Texas 75962

C. Kenneth Dodd, Jr.
U.S. Geological Survey
Biological Resources Division
Florida Caribbean Science Center
7920 NW 71st Street
Gainesville, Florida 32653

David A. Etnier
Department of Ecology and
Evolutionary Biology
University of Tennessee
Knoxville, Tennessee 37996-1610

George W. Folkerts
Department of Zoology and
Wildlife Science
331 Funchess Hall
Auburn University
Auburn, Alabama 36844

Robert P. Ford
Tennessee Conservation League
300 Orlando Avenue
Nashville, Tennessee 37209

Byron J. Freeman
Institute of Ecology
University of Georgia
Athens, Georgia 30602

J. Whitfield Gibbons
University of Georgia
Savannah River Ecology Laboratory
P.O. Drawer E
Aiken, South Carolina 29802

Wendell R. Haag
USDA Forest Service
Southern Research Station
Forest Hydrology Laboratory
1000 Front Street
Oxford, Mississippi 38655

Paul W. Hartfield
U.S. Fish and Wildlife Service
6578 Dogwood View Parkway
Suite A
Jackson, Mississippi 39213

Michael J. Harvey
Department of Biology
Tennessee Technological University
Cookeville, Tennessee 38505

Robert M. Hatcher
Tennessee Wildlife Resources Agency
P.O. Box 40747
Nashville, Tennessee 37204

Douglas L. Helmers
U.S. Department of Agriculture
Natural Resource Conservation
  Service
Parkdale Plaza
Suite 250
Business Loop 70 West
Columbia, Missouri 65203

John J. Jenkinson
Tennessee Valley Authority
Water Management
1101 Market Street
Chattanooga, Tennessee 37402

Linda V. LaClaire
U.S. Fish and Wildlife Service
6578 Dogwood View Parkway
Suite A
Jackson, Mississippi 39213

W. Patrick McCafferty
Purdue University
Department of Entomology
Entomology Hall
West Lafayette, Indiana 47907

John C. Morse
Department of Entomology
Clemson University
Long Hall
Box 340365
Clemson, South Carolina 29634

Richard J. Neves
U.S. Geological Survey
Biological Resources Division
Virginia Cooperative Fish and
  Wildlife Research Unit
Department of Fisheries and
  Wildlife Sciences
Virginia Tech
Blacksburg, Viginia 24061-0321

Don H. Orr
U.S. Fish and Wildlife Service
University of Memphis
South Campus
Memphis, Tennessee 38152

Guenter A. Schuster
Department of Biological Sciences
Eastern Kentucky University
Richmond, Kentucky 40475

Peggy W. Shute
Tennessee Valley Authority
Regional Natural Heritage Project
17 Ridgeway Road
Box 920
Norris, Tennessee 37828-0920

Bill P. Stark
Mississippi College
Department of Biology
P.O. Box 4186
Clinton, Mississippi 39058

Kenneth J. Tennessen
Tennessee Valley Authority
Water Management, CTR-2P
Muscle Shoals, Alabama 35660

Robert M. Todd
Tennessee Wildlife Resources
    Agency
P.O. Box 40747
Nashville, Tennessee 37204

Stephen J. Walsh
U.S. Geological Survey
Biological Resources Division
Florida Caribbean Resources Center
7920 NW 71st Street
Gainesville, Florida 32653

Melvin L. Warren, Jr.
USDA Forest Service
Southern Research Station
Forest Hydrology Laboratory
1000 Front Street
Oxford, Mississippi 38655

James D. Williams
U.S. Geological Survey
Biological Resources Division
Florida Caribbean Resources Center
7920 NW 71st Street
Gainesville, Florida 32653

Mark S. Woodrey
Mississippi Museum of Natural
    Science
Mississippi Department of Wildlife,
    Fisheries, and Parks
111 N Jefferson Street
Jackson, Mississippi 39202

REVIEWERS

Fred J. Alsop, III, Department of Biological Sciences, East Tennessee State University, Johnson City, Tennessee.

Steve Bennett, South Carolina Nongame and Heritage Trust Program, South Carolina Department of Natural Resources, Columbia, South Carolina.

Troy L. Best, Department of Zoology, Auburn University, Auburn, Alabama.

Richard G. Biggins, U.S. Fish and Wildlife Service, Asheville, North Carolina.

Alvin L. Braswell, North Carolina State Museum of Natural History, Raleigh, North Carolina.

Richard C. Bruce, Highlands Biological Station, Highlands, North Carolina.

Byron J. Freeman, Institute of Ecology, University of Georgia, Athens, Georgia.

Mary C. Freeman, U.S. Geological Survey, Biological Resources Division, Patuxent Wildlife Science Center, Institute of Ecology, University of Georgia Athens, Georgia.

Sidney A. Gauthreaux, Jr., Department of Biological Sciences, Clemson University, Clemson, South Carolina.

Paul B. Hamel, U.S. Forest Service, Southern Research Station, Southern Hardwoods Laboratory, Stoneville, Mississippi.

Julian R. Harrison, Department of Biology, College of Charleston, Charleston, South Carolina.

Paul Hartfield, U.S. Fish and Wildlife Service, Jackson, Mississippi.

Gary A. Heidt, Department of Biology, University of Arkansas, Little Rock, Arkansas.

Robert E. Jenkins, Department of Biology, Roanoke College, Salem, Virginia.

John J. Jenkinson, Water Management, Tennessee Valley Authority, Chattanooga, Tennessee.

Leroy Koch, U.S. Fish and Wildlife Service, Abingdon, Virginia.

Joshua Laerm, Institute of Ecology, University of Georgia, Athens, Georgia.

Richard L. Mayden, Department of Biology, The University of Alabama, Tuscaloosa, Alabama.

Robert H. Mount, Department of Zoology, Auburn University, Auburn, Alabama.

Charles P. Nicholson, Environmental Management, Tennessee Valley Authority, Knoxville, Tennessee.

Paul W. Parmalee, Frank H. McClung Museum, University of Tennessee, Knoxville, Tennessee.

Michael V. Plummer, Department of Biology, Harding University, Searcy, Arkansas.

William H. Redmond, Tennessee Valley Authority, Regional Natural Heritage Project, Norris, Tennessee.

Richard E. Sparks, River Research Laboratory, Illinois Natural History Survey, Havana, Illinois.

Bill P. Stark, Department of Biology, Mississippi College, Clinton, Mississippi.

Stephen J. Walsh, U.S. Geological Survey, Biological Resources Division, Florida Caribbean Resources Center, Gainesville, Florida.

G. Thomas Watters, Ohio Division of Wildlife, Aquatic Ecology Laboratory, Ohio State University, Columbus, Ohio.

Located along the Tennessee River in Chattanooga, the Tennessee Aquarium is home to more than 500 species of aquatic animals. Since its opening in May of 1992, over 6 million visitors have toured the aquarium and have marveled at its many exhibits which display native freshwater animals in simulated natural settings.

Under the supervision of scientists affiliated with the Southeast Aquatic Research Institute students participate in research projects aimed at gathering information needed to help ensure the health and long-term sustainability of natural resources.

TENNESSEE AQUARIUM

With its mission to foster the understanding, conservation, and celebration of aquatic environments of the world, the Tennessee Aquarium is the world's first major aquarium dedicated to freshwater ecosystems. Located along the Tennessee River in downtown Chattanooga, Tennessee, the $45 million, not-for-profit facility allows its visitors to take a journey from the Tennessee River's source in the Appalachian high country, through the Tennessee Valley, and down to the Mississippi Delta and beyond. Visitors also experience some of the mysteries of other great rivers of the world; including the Amazon, the Zaire, and the St. Lawrence. In addition to being home to over 500 species of animals and almost 300 species of plants, the Tennessee Aquarium also holds two simulated forests, as well as one of the world's largest freshwater tanks.

Since its opening in 1992, more than 6 million people have visited the educational facility, including numerous school children on organized field trips. Further expanding its influence, in 1996 the Tennessee Aquarium opened its IMAX® Center, consisting of an IMAX® 3-D theater which regularly features unparalleled nature films, and a state-of-the-art Environmental Learning Lab dedicated to environmental education aimed at students, teachers, and the general public.

The Tennessee Aquarium and its IMAX® Center are open every day except Thanksgiving and Christmas, and both are fully accessible to the physically challenged. Visit us on the world-wide-web at: www.tennis.org

SOUTHEAST AQUATIC RESEARCH INSTITUTE

Formed in 1996, the Southeast Aquatic Research Institute (SARI) is a not-for-profit organization created through collaboration of the Tennessee Aquarium, Inc., the University of Tennessee at Chattanooga, and the Tennessee River Gorge Trust, Inc. SARI's mission is to carry out environmental research needed to help ensure the health and long-term sustainability of regional natural resources. Toward achieving its mission, SARI seeks to open new opportunities for environmental research through creative partnerships.

Because of the importance of aquatic ecosystems, much of SARI's research focuses on wet environments. The Institute has completed and is currently involved in a number of projects, including research designed to inventory the region's natural resources, assess potential disease causing organisms within aquatic populations, monitor the progress of a significant ecosystem restoration project, and assess the sustainability of aquatic wildlife populations. Through its activity SARI has facilitated hands-on student internships which have played key roles in the professional development of some talented young scientists. SARI is currently headquartered in a modern, well-equipped laboratory facility located in Chattanooga, Tennessee. Visit us on the world-wide-web at: www.sari.org

Indices

SUBJECT INDEX

COMMON NAME INDEX

TAXON INDEX

A

Ampullaria luzonica 9
Anas crecca 240
Anas platyrhynchos 347
Anas strepera 240
Andrias spp. 166
Andropogon sp. 204
Aneides 169, 171
Aneides aeneus 310, 321
Anepeorus simplex 33
Anguilla rostrata 93, 140, 390
Anodonta spp. 63
Anodontoides denigrata 50
Anodontoides radiatus 400
Antrorbis breweri 57
Antroselates spiralis 275
Apeltes quadracus 154
Aphaostracon asthenes 57
Aphaostracon monas 57
Aphaostracon pycuum 57
Aphaostracon xynoelictus 57
Aphredoderus sayanus 99, 152
Aplodinotus grunniens 104, 163, 392
Apobaetis etowah 33
Ardea herodias 241
Arigomphus maxwelli 35
Aristida stricta 204
Arkansia wheeleri 48
Arundinaria gigantea 234
Ascaphus truei 7
Astronotus ocellatus 163
Athearnia anthonyi 49, 55, 58
Athya collaris 241
Atractosteus spatula 89, 93, 139
Aythya valisineria 241
Azolla filliculoides 10

B

Baetis ochris 33
Barbaetis benfieldi 26
Barbicambarus 269
Basilichthys bonairiensis 8
Belonesox belizanus 153
Beloneuria georgiana 25, 28
Beloneuria jamesae 36
Beloneuria stewarti 28

Biomphalaria glabrata 74
Boleichthys elegans 389
Bouchardina 269
Brachycentrus etowahensis 30
Branta canadensis 347
Bucephala albeola 241
Bufo 169
Bufo boreas 3, 184, 185
Bufo houstonensis 174, 183
Bufo marinus 166, 183
Bufo quercicus 174
Bufo spp. 182, 183
Bufo terrestris 170, 183
Bufo valliceps 174
Burhinus bistriatus 348
Buteo lineatus 236
Bythotrephes cederstroemii 8

C

Calidris minutilla 241, 348
Callibaetis pretiosus 26
Cambarus 269, 272,
Cambarus aculabrum 271
Cambarus zophonastes 271
Campeloma decampi 57
Campephilus principalis 236
Campostoma anomalum 94, 141
Campostoma oligolepis 94, 141, 390
Campostoma pauciradii 94, 141, 390
Carassius auratus 141
Cardinalis cardinalis 236, 237
Carex lacustris 263
Carpiodes carpio 97, 148
Carpiodes cyprinus 97, 148
Carpiodes velifer 97, 148
Carya aquatica 234
Casmerodius albus 241
Castanea dentata 23
Castor canadensis 357
Castor fiber 10
Catharus guttatus 237
Catostomus commersoni 97, 148
Celtis 234
Centrarchus macropterus 100, 155
Ceraclea alabamae 31

A plain pocketbook mussel, *Lampsilis cardium* (Rafinesque), extends its minnow-like mantle flap to lure a fish which will serve as a nursery for its young. Unfortunately, a recent paper published the American Fisheries Society considered over 71 percent of our native North American freshwater mussel fauna as endangered, threatened. or of special concern (see Williams et al. 1993. *Fisheries* 18(9):6-22). (photograph by Alan C. Buchanan)